French
Grammar
and Usage

Long trusted as the most comprehensive, up-to-date, and user-friendly grammar book available, *French Grammar and Usage* is a complete guide to French as it is written and spoken today. It includes clear descriptions of all the main grammatical phenomena of French and their uses, illustrated by numerous examples taken from contemporary French, and distinguishes the most common forms of usage, both formal and informal.

This book's key features are as follows:

- comprehensive content, covering all the major structures of contemporary French
- user-friendly organisation offering easy-to-find sections with cross-referencing and indexes of English words, French words, and grammatical terms
- clear and illuminating examples to help students at all stages of their degree
- useful indications of what cannot be written or said as well as what can.

Revised and updated throughout, this new edition offers updated examples to reflect current usage, headers to include chapter number and section parts, as well as cross-referencing for easier reference, and explanations of notoriously difficult points of grammar. This edition includes references to changes in French spelling now being introduced across French education and to social change towards inclusive writing.

The combination of reference grammar and manual of current usage is an invaluable resource for students and teachers of French at the intermediate and advanced levels.

This *Grammar* is accompanied by *Practising French Grammar: A Workbook* (available to purchase separately ISBN 978-1-032-44140-5) which features related exercises and activities. An Instructor and Student Resource site also accompanies this book and offers additional resources at https:// routledgelearning.com/frenchgrammarandusage.

Richard Towell is Emeritus Professor of French Applied Linguistics at the University of Salford, UK.

Marie-Noëlle Lamy is Emeritus Professor of Distance Language Learning at the Open University, UK.

Roger Hawkins is Emeritus Professor of Language and Linguistics at the University of Essex, UK.

ROUTLEDGE REFERENCE GRAMMARS

A Reference Grammar of Modern Italian, Second Edition
Edited by Martin Maiden and Cecilia Robustelli

French Grammar and Usage, Fifth Edition
Richard Towell, Marie-Noëlle Lamy and Roger Hawkins

A New Reference Grammar of Modern Spanish, Sixth Edition
John B. Butt, Carmen Benjamin and Antonia Moreira-Rodríguez

Hammer's German Grammar and Usage, Seventh Edition
Martin Durrell

For more information about the Routledge Reference Grammars series, please visithttps://www.routledge.com/Routledge-Reference-Grammars/book-series/RRG

Routledge Reference Grammars can be used alone or with companion workbooks from the Practising Grammar Workbooks series:

Practising Italian Grammar
A Workbook
Alessia Bianchi, Clelia Boscolo and Stephen Harrison

Practising Spanish Grammar, Fourth Edition
Angela Howkins, Christopher Pountain, and Teresa de Carlos

Practising French Grammar, Fifth Edition
A Workbook
Marie-Noëlle Lamy, Richard Towell and Roger Hawkins

Practising German Grammar, Fourth Edition
Martin Durrell, Katrin Kohl and Claudia Kaiser

For more information about the Practising Grammar Workbooks series, please visit https://www.routledge.com/Practising-Grammar-Workbooks/book-series/PGW

French
Grammar
and Usage

Fifth Edition

Richard Towell,
Marie-Noëlle Lamy,
and Roger Hawkins

Instructor Manual designed by Christophe Gagne
Instructor and Student Resource exercises designed by
Miriam Burton Pinchot

Routledge
Taylor & Francis Group

LONDON AND NEW YORK

Designed cover image: Yamac Beyter via Getty Images

Fifth edition published 2025
by Routledge
4 Park Square, Milton Park, Abingdon, Oxon, OX14 4RN

and by Routledge
605 Third Avenue, New York, NY 10158

Routledge is an imprint of the Taylor & Francis Group, an informa business

First edition published by Hodder Education 1997
Fourth edition published by Routledge 2009

British Library Cataloguing-in-Publication Data
A catalogue record for this book is available from the British Library

Library of Congress Cataloging-in-Publication Data
Names: Towell, Richard, author. | Lamy, Marie-Noëlle, 1949– author. |
Hawkins, Roger (Roger D.), author.
Title: French grammar and usage / Richard Towell, Marie-Noëlle Lamy, and
Roger Hawkins.
Description: Fifth edition. | Abingdon, Oxon; New York, NY: Routledge, 2025. |
Series: Routledge reference grammars | Includes bibliographical references
and index.
Identifiers: LCCN 2024032251 (print) | LCCN 2024032252 (ebook) |
Subjects: LCSH: French language—Textbooks for foreign speakers—English. |
French language—Grammar. | French language—Usage. | LCGFT: Textbooks.
Classification: LCC PC2129.E5 H39 2025 (print) | LCC PC2129.E5 (ebook) |
DDC 448.2/421—dc23/eng/20240807
LC record available at https://lccn.loc.gov/2024032251
LC ebook record available at https://lccn.loc.gov/2024032252

ISBN: 978-1-032-44791-9 (hbk)
ISBN: 978-1-032-44463-5 (pbk)
ISBN: 978-1-003-37392-6 (ebk)

DOI: 10.4324/9781003373926

Typeset in Palatino
by codeMantra

Access the Instructor and Student Resources: https://routledgelearning.com/frenchgrammarandusage

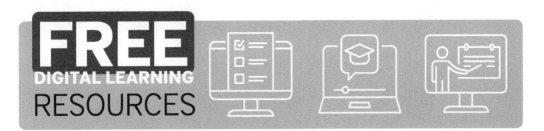

French Grammar and Usage

Long trusted as the most comprehensive, up-to-date and user-friendly grammar book available, this is a complete guide to French as it is written and spoken today. Revised and updated throughout, this new edition offers updated examples and references to reflect current usage. This is accompanied by *Practising French Grammar: A Workbook* featuring exercises and activities.

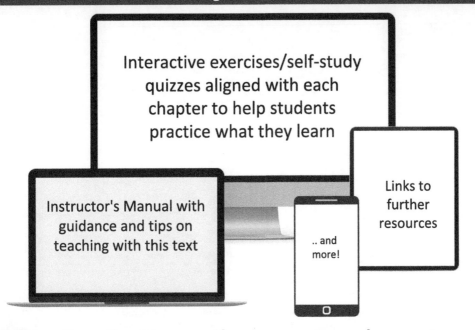

Interactive exercises/self-study quizzes aligned with each chapter to help students practice what they learn

Instructor's Manual with guidance and tips on teaching with this text

.. and more!

Links to further resources

FREE

INSTRUCTOR & STUDENT RESOURCES

Go online to access these resources and more at:
routledgelearning.com/frenchgrammarandusage

Routledge
Taylor & Francis Group

Contents

Guide for the user

This reference grammar of French has been written specifically to cater for the needs of English speakers. Such grammars are seldom read like novels. Usually, readers either want information on a specific grammatical point ('In what order do the pronouns *me* and *le* occur in imperatives?'; 'How do I translate "should" into French?'), or they want information about the behaviour of a class of grammatical phenomena such as 'pronouns', 'modal verbs', 'negation', etc.

For this reason, and in common with most other grammars, *French Grammar and Usage* is divided into chapters which deal with broad classes of grammatical phenomena; there are 17 chapters in all. Within each chapter, there are two further subdivisions: the first into particular phenomena, and the second into specific grammatical points concerning those phenomena. This gives rise to three kinds of heading in the text. For example:

Chapter 2	Determiners
Chapter 2.6	Omission of the article
Chapter 2.6.6	Omission of the article with nouns in apposition
Chapter 8	Verb constructions
Chapter 8.2	Intransitive constructions
Chapter 8.2.2	Intransitive verbs and auxiliary *être*

The chapters and their major subdivisions are listed in the *Contents* at the beginning of this book. If you want information about a broad class of grammatical phenomena, you will probably find it most quickly by looking there. At the end of this book, we have provided a more detailed *Index* where key French and English words and expressions are listed, along with grammatical points. The items listed there will direct you to a specific section of the grammar dealing with the property you want to know about.

If you are not familiar with grammatical terms, try the *Glossary of key grammatical terms*, which comes just after this *Guide for the user*. We briefly define common terms such as subject, object, transitive verb, intransitive verb, phrase, clause, etc., illustrating them from French.

The variety of French described in *French Grammar and Usage*

This book aims to describe one variety of French: standard European French. This is the variety used by educated speakers throughout metropolitan France and recognised worldwide. However, within this variety, there is a degree of variation. The differences are often described as being related to Medium (i.e. is the language displayed on paper or screen or is it spoken?) and/or Register (i.e. how do the speakers/writers relate to each other when they choose to use a certain turn of phrase?).

Medium: written and spoken forms

The most obvious differentiation is between the two media: written and spoken forms of French. There have always been some forms and constructions which are more appropriate for one of these media and rarely found in the other, unless a special effect is intended. For example, the simple past tense of verbs – *je partis* 'I left', *elle mangea* 'She ate' – is normally restricted to literary (therefore written) French. Questions formed by putting a question word at the front of a sentence without subject–verb inversion – *Où elle est, la patronne?* 'Where's the boss? ' – are normally restricted to spoken French.

However, usage in social media, messaging, email, and in some contemporary literature has now blurred these differences: these written forms of language frequently use the constructions of spoken French. Thus, on WhatsApp: *Te fais pas de bile pour le restau, je t'en parlais pour le cas où tu aurais pu nous rejoindre: Don't fret yourself about the restaurant, I only mentioned it in case you could join us there.* The first clause uses slang (*se faire de (la) bile, restau*) and leaves out the *ne*, but the second clause is fully grammatical. It is also possible to hear forms normally associated with the written language in official speeches. For these reasons, we will frequently discuss language in terms of its context of use rather than, as was more traditionally the case, in terms of written and spoken forms. What we mean by context of use is explained in the next section.

Register: context of use

All languages contain forms and constructions which are appropriate to specific contexts of use. In English, 'Would you care for a cup of tea?' is a formal way of expressing the same meaning as the informal 'Fancy a cuppa?'. Each construction would be appropriate in its context. A formal relationship between the speakers demands the use of formal language, whereas a more relaxed relationship requires informal language. These can be referred to as the formal and informal registers. French has the same nuances, and speakers and writers are generally very aware of them.

Some forms and constructions are mainly used in formal situations, while others are mainly used in informal situations. A formal situation is where native speakers are careful in what they say and write, often making use of forms and structures which have been learnt as part of their education.

An informal situation is where speakers are engaged in relaxed, spontaneous communication and are paying less attention to the form of the language or are purposefully choosing language that creates an atmosphere of familiarity/friendliness. While speaking face to face or in online communication, language users usually employ informal language.

How we use formal and informal in this edition

Whereas in past editions we have marked certain forms as more appropriate to written or spoken French, given the blurring between the media and the evolution of contexts of use mentioned above, we have decided to refer mainly to informal or formal French in this book, rather than signal the form as appropriate only to the spoken or the written medium.

Examples from both of these media and from different registers and some examples of the fusion between them in some literature, social media, and messaging can be found in the accompanying workbook.

Prescriptive and descriptive approaches to French grammar

In French, as in other languages, although there is plenty of evidence that change is resisted by, for example, grammarians, legislators, educators, dictionary editors, or newspaper columnists, usage is continually evolving in certain areas of the language, especially vocabulary. This makes it very difficult to describe categorically which forms are currently part of acceptable usage and therefore prescribe which forms learners should use. We have tried to steer a middle path in this respect. Where a grammatical phenomenon is clearly widespread and normal in the French of educated speakers and writers but in conflict with prescriptive norms, we have described the usage. An example is the widespread omission of *ne* in *ne….pas* 'not', frowned upon by some but in widespread use in informal French (see Section 16.4 and the WhatsApp example mentioned above).

Where there is a variability or hesitation in the use of a grammatical structure by speakers or writers, or where there is a change in progress in the language which has not yet been fully accepted, and there is an established prescriptive norm, we have presented the prescriptive norm. For example, agreement of the past participle with preceding direct objects, as in *La lettre que j'ai écrite* 'The letter I wrote', is subject to considerable variability in some contexts. Some speakers make the agreement, while others do not. In this case, we have followed the prescriptive norm.

Inclusive writing

There are two areas where social change is currently impacting aspects of the French language and usage: the role of women in society and the questioning of gender defined roles. As a result, there is a movement towards 'inclusive writing' which we can see reflected in three aspects: (a) vocabulary developments due to women's role in the world of work; (b) proposed changes to noun and adjective endings to counteract the built-in masculine bias in the language; and (c) the needs of LGBTQ+ people to use pronouns adapted to gender non-conformity.

The vocabulary developments are represented mainly in Chapter 1 in the section dealing with the feminisation of job titles, functions, and roles. This usage has largely been normalised, although there will still be hesitation over the choice of specific forms (see Section 1.2.2).

Changes intended to reflect greater equality between males and females through new forms of language use can be seen in the writing of noun and adjective endings. In traditional French, a group made up of, for example, 'registered male and female students' would be described as *des étudiants inscrits* (masculine plural, regardless of the presence of women in the group). New 'inclusive writing' proposes to write this as *des étudiant.e.s inscrit.e.s*, that is using a full stop (or sometimes a hyphen or a 'point médian') to separate masculine from feminine endings, followed by the mark of the plural. These developments are dealt with in Chapters 1, 3, and 4. Although evidenced in some quarters, this writing style is currently subject to intense debate and acceptance is uncertain.

More recently still, we are seeing further change as society realises that gender norms are not as fixed as once thought. The LGBTQ+ community would like to see specific changes in the usage of pronouns, for example, to allow the expression of different identities. These changes are not yet widespread in current usage, but we have tried to indicate in, for example, Section 3.1 where new forms have been proposed. Only time will tell whether these forms are adopted more widely.

Overall, while it can be confusing to assess current acceptability of masculine–feminine endings and of new pronouns, there is also a desire to ensure that when language is used, it is done in a non-discriminatory way and some guides have been produced on how to write in a non-sexist style: see introduction to Chapter 3 and further reading.

Officially accepted alternatives in French spelling

In 1990, the following officially accepted alternatives to French spelling were recommended by the *Conseil Supérieur de la langue française*. They are slowly making their way into usage, and from 2016, these are being presented in French school manuals and accepted in examination answers. However, they are only recommendations, and there is no presumption that everyone will change their usage overnight. It is hoped that these forms will percolate into usage over time. For many years to come, therefore, it is to be expected that in these areas, there will be competing forms, both of which are accepted. In this book, we maintain the use of the traditional orthography, but in this edition, we have shown where the new recommendations apply by introducing specific sections and subsections with a heading *nouvelle orthographe* where it is indicated that there is now more than one acceptable spelling.

The officially accepted alternatives apply to:

The use of hyphens in complex numbers (Section 6.1)
The singular and plural of compound nouns with a hyphen (Section 1.3.9)
The use of the grave accent on verbs of the type '*céder*' (Section 7.4 and Table 7H)
The use of the grave accent on certain words, mainly nouns (see examples in Section 1.4)
The use of the grave accent in interrogative inversions (Section 14.2.5)
The doubling of consonants in verbs in -*eler* and -*eter* (Table 7H)
The doubling of consonants in certain words (e.g. *boursouffler* to go alongside *souffler*)
The agreement of the past participle with *laisser* (Section 9.3.3)
The singular and plural of words borrowed into French, again mainly nouns (see examples in Section 1.4).

These alternative spellings also recommend that a circumflex may be left off those words where its presence does not relate to a difference in meaning. A verb such as *s'entraîner* or a noun such as *maître* can now be correctly written without a circumflex. But where there is a difference in meaning, such as *jeune* 'young' vs *jeûne* 'fast' or *mur* 'wall' *vs* *mûr* 'ripe' and in proper nouns, such as *Jérôme*, the circumflex is retained. Given that the two spellings are likely to be in operation for many years yet, we have not attempted to remove all the circumflexes where it would be possible to do so. We have, however, provided a short summary of the main recommendations as an appendix.

Conventions

In many places in this grammar book, we have presented examples not only of what native speakers do say and write but also of what they do NOT say and write. Such ungrammatical sentences are preceded by an asterisk *. For example:

Les cinq personnes (NOT *gens) qui ont mangé avec nous
The five people who ate with us (see Section 1.1.3)

Round brackets placed around a French or English word or part of a word in an example mean that it is optional, and its presence or absence has little or no effect on the meaning. For example:

par instant(s) at odd moments
(You can use either par instant or par instants)

par milliers in (their) thousands
(par milliers can be translated either by 'in thousands' or 'in their thousands')

Glossary of key grammatical terms

Adjective
A class of words which describe somebody or something and thereby modify nouns. Adjectives appear adjacent to nouns or separated from them by verbs like *être, devenir, rester:* e.g. *un* PETIT *problème* 'a small problem'; *une boîte* CARRÈE 'a square box'; *cette robe est* CHÈRE 'This dress is expensive'. Adjectives are commonly inflected to agree with nouns.

Adverb
A class of words which give extra meaning to or modify verbs, adjectives, another adverb, phrases, and whole sentences: e.g. *Je cours* VITE 'I can run quickly'; *Tout est* SI *clair* 'Everything is so clear'; *Le train roulait* TELLEMENT *vite qu'elle n'a pas pu en descendre.* 'The train was going so fast she couldn't get off'; JUSTE *avant le départ du train* 'Just before the train leaves' SOUDAIN; *j'ai entendu un bruit* 'Suddenly I heard a noise'.

Adverbial
A word, phrase, or clause that functions as an adverb, e.g. *parler* BAS 'to talk quietly' (*bas* – an adjective); *Je lui rends visite* DE TEMPS EN TEMPS 'I visit her from time to time' (*de temps en temps* – a prepositional phrase); *Elle travaille* LE MATIN 'She works in the mornings' (*le matin* – a noun phrase); *Le concert m'a beacoup plu* PARCE QUE J'AIME CE TYPE DE MUSIQUE (*parce que j'aime ce type de musique* – a subordinate clause).

Affirmative sentence
A sentence which is not a negative: e.g. *Elle parle* 'She is speaking'; *Parle-t-elle?* 'Is she speaking?' *Parle!* 'Speak' (as opposed to the negative sentences *Elle ne parle pas, Ne parle-t-elle pas? Ne parle pas!*).

Agreement
The way the form of a word changes to align with other words to which it is related. Thus, the verb must change its form to be compatible with a given subject: e.g. *Nous mange*ONS 'We're eating'/*vous man*GEZ 'You're eating'. A determiner and an adjective must change their form to be compatible with a given noun: e.g. UN BON *repas* 'A good meal'/UNE BONNE *bière* 'A good beer'. A past participle must change its form to be compatible with a preceding direct object: e.g. *Le coffre? Je l'ai* OUVERT 'The car boot? I've opened it'; *La porte? Je l'ai* OUVERTE 'The door? I've opened it'; etc.

Article, definite
Definite articles (*le, la, les*) indicate that the entity/concept referred to by the noun is uniquely identifiable by both speaker and hearer. If you say *Passe-moi* LA *fourchette* 'Pass me the fork', both speaker and hearer know that there is a unique, identifiable 'fork' in the context in which the conversation is taking place.

Article, indefinite
Indefinite articles (*un, une, des*) are used with count nouns (*bouteille* 'bottle', *billet* 'ticket') and indicate that the entity/concept referred to by the noun is not sufficiently 'known about' or 'specified' to justify the definite article. If you say *Passe-moi* UNE *fourchette* 'Pass me a fork', this implies that there is no uniquely identifiable 'fork' in the context of the conversation (perhaps because there are several of them).

Article, partitive
Partitive articles (*du, de la, des*) serve the same function as indefinite articles but are used with mass and abstract nouns: *J'ai acheté* DU *lait* 'I bought (some) milk', *Il faut avoir* DE LA *patience* 'You must have (some) patience'. The plural partitive article *des* is used with nouns that are

mass or abstract by virtue of their meaning, but happen to be grammatically plural: *des tripes* (f.pl.) 'tripe'; *des cheveux* (m.pl.) 'hair'; *des renseignements* (m.pl.) 'information'.

Auxiliary verb	The verbs *avoir* or *être* which accompany a past participle in compound tenses or the passive, e.g. *Elle A mangé* 'She has eaten'; *Le vélo A été réparé* 'The bike has been repaired'.
Clause	A string of words which contains just one verb phrase and a subject (whether overt or implied): e.g. *Elle part* 'She's leaving' – one clause: *Depuis janvier les prix ont augmenté* 'Since January, prices have gone up' – one clause; *Il est heureux/parce qu'il va se marier* 'He is happy because he getting married' – two clauses; *Elle est prête/à partir* 'She is ready to leave' – two clauses (in *à partir* the subject is implied: She is ready, and she will leave); *Les circonstances aidant/le parti gagnera les élections* 'If the conditions are right, the party will win this election' – two clauses; *Il dit/qu'on croit/qu'elle va partir* 'He says that they think that she will leave' – three clauses. Also see coordinate clause, main clause, relative clause, and subordinate clause.
Comparative	A way of modifying adjectives and adverbs to draw a comparison between one entity and another: *Il veut acheter UNE PLUS GRANDE/UNE MOINS GRANDE/UNE AUSSI GRANDE voiture* 'He wants to buy a bigger car/a car which is not so big/a car which is just as big'; *Cette voiture roule PLUS VITE/MOINS VITE/AUSSI VITE que l'autre* 'This car goes faster/slower/as quickly as the other one'.
Complement	Any phrase which follows a noun, verb, adjective, or adverb to form an expression with a cohesive meaning: e.g. *un appartement À LOUER* 'a flat to let'; *Ils se réunissent LE DIMANCHE AU STADE* 'They meet on Sundays at the stadium'; *Alice est devenue PROFESSEUR(E)* 'Alice has become a teacher'; *Pierre est difficile À VIVRE* 'Pierre is difficult to live with'.
Coordinate clause	A clause linked to another by *et, ou, mais*: e.g. *Il viendra demain ET il nous apportera des gâteaux.* 'He'll come tomorrow and he'll bring us some cakes'. These clauses are both main clauses.
Declarative sentence	A sentence which makes a statement (as opposed to a question or an imperative).
Demonstrative	Demonstratives 'point to' items in a way which is more specific than the definite articles. Demonstrative determiner *ce, cette, ces*, e.g. *ce bus, cette chatte, ces oignons* 'this bus, this female cat, these onions'. Demonstrative pronoun = *celui, celle, ceux, celles.* 'this one' (m. and f.) and 'those ones' (m. and f.).
Determiner	Words which modify nouns in specific ways to indicate definiteness and possession. Articles (*un, une/le, la, les/des*, etc.), demonstrative determiners (*ce, cette*, etc.), or possessive determiners (*mon, ma/ton, ta*, etc.) which modify a noun. All determiners have singular and plural forms, and in the singular have different forms depending on whether the noun is masculine or feminine.
Determiner, demonstrative	Demonstrative determiners are the forms *ce/cet, cette, ces* 'this/these, that/those'. They indicate that the noun is seen as 'known about' or 'specified' largely in contrast to another noun: *Passe-moi CETTE fourchette* 'Pass me that fork' (and not some other fork that might also be visible).
Determiner, possessive	Possessive determiners are forms like *mon, son, votre* 'my, his/her, your' that indicate that the noun is seen as belonging to someone.

Direct object	See Object
Directly transitive verb	See Verb
Ditransitive verb	See Verb
Finite verb	See Verb
Formal French	In this grammar book, 'formal French' refers to a style used by speakers of standard and educated French when they are paying particular attention to the form of what they are saying or writing. It is a style usually appropriate when someone is speaking in an official capacity (lectures, sermons, speeches, etc.) or writing in learned, academic, or literary style. Features of formal French which are absent from informal French include the use of the simple past tense (*Il sortit* 'He went out'), the use of the past anterior tense (*Aussitôt qu'il fut sorti* 'As soon as he had gone out'), and retention of *ne* in *ne....pas*.
Gender	A division of nouns into two classes: masculine and feminine: The distinction shows up mainly in determiners (*le* versus *la*, *ce* versus *cette*, *mon* versus *ma*, etc.) in pronouns (*il* versus *elle*) and in the agreement of adjectives with nouns (*beau* versus *belle*). Gender distinctions are grammatical and need not correspond to biological gender distinctions (although they mostly do): e.g. *médecin* 'doctor' is masculine, but can refer to men or women: *personne* 'person' is feminine but can refer to men or women.
Gerund	See participle
Imperative	A form of the verb used to give orders, express encouragement or give advice: e.g. *Asseyez-vous* 'Sit down'; *Allez!* 'Come on!'; *Fais attention!* 'Watch out!'.
Impersonal	Refers to a pronoun (usually a subject pronoun) which does not refer to any person, place, thing, idea, etc. *il, ce, cela, ça* can be impersonal pronouns in French: e.g. IL *est temps de partir* 'It's time to leave'; ÇA *me fait peur d'y aller la nuit* 'It scares me to go there at night'.
Indicative	The set of forms of the verb which are not subjunctive, imperative, infinitive, or participial.
Indirect object	See Object
Indirectly transitive verb	See Verb
Infinitive	A 'base' form of the verb which ends in *-er, -ir, -re*, or *-oir* and corresponds to English 'to': *aimer* 'to like', *finir* 'to finish', *vendre* 'to sell', *recevoir* 'to receive'.
Informal French	In this grammar book, 'informal French' refers to the language used when speakers are engaged in relaxed, spontaneous communication and are paying less attention to the form of the language or are purposefully choosing language that creates an atmosphere of familiarity/friendliness. While speaking face to face or in online communication, language users usually employ informal language. An example would be when speakers omit the *ne* of *ne...pas*.
Intransitive verb	See Verb
Main clause	A main clause is complete on its own and can form a complete sentence, e.g. *Il pleuvait hier vers trois heures* 'It was raining yesterday around three o'clock'.
Modify, to	To add to the meaning of a noun, verb, adjective, etc. by adding another word or phrase to it: e.g. *manteau*, UN *manteau*, *un manteau* GRIS; *oiseau*, UN *oiseau*, UN *oiseau* QUI CHANTE; *parle*, IL *parle*, IL *parle* LENTEMENT; *grand*, SI *grand*, PAS SI *grand*.

Negator	One of the elements *aucun, jamais, ni, nul, pas, personne, plus, rien* which can make expressions negative (see Chapter 16).
Noun	A class of words which refer to people, places, things, ideas, etc.; a noun is usually preceded by a determiner, e.g. *UN ami, LA France, UNE bière, LE bonheur*. Sub-classes of nouns are abstract: *le bonheur;* concrete: *un livre;* collective: *la foule;* count: *un ami;* mass: *du beurre;* proper: *la France, Coralie*.
Noun phrase	The phrase consisting of a noun alone, or a noun and the elements which modify it. Each of the following is a noun phrase: *Pierre, Le soleil, un cher ami* 'a dear friend', *une bière bien fraîche* 'a really cold beer', *chacun de mes amis les plus chers* 'each of my dearest friends'.
Number	A grammatical distinction between nouns or pronouns which are singular and those which are plural. Number distinctions need not correspond to real singular and plural distinctions in the world and can differ between English and French (although mostly the grammatical and real-world distinctions coincide): e.g. 'hair' (singular) versus *cheveux* (plural); trousers (plural) versus *pantalon* (singular).
Number, cardinal	A number in the series *un* (1), *deux* (2), *trois* (3), etc.
Number, ordinal	A number in the series *premier* (1er), *deuxième* (2e), *troisième* (3e), etc.
Object	A direct object is the noun phrase or pronoun whose referent is affected directly by the action described by the verb: e.g. *Il a pris LE TRAIN* 'He took the train' *Il L'a pris* 'He took it'; *Je crois CE QU'IL A DIT* 'I believe what he said'. An indirect object is the noun phrase or pronoun whose referent benefits in some way from the action described by the verb. In French, the indirect object noun phrases are most frequently introduced by *à*: e.g. *il a envoyé un cadeau À SA MÈRE* 'He sent a present to his mother'. The indirect object can also be introduced by *de*: e.g. *elle a hérité D'UNE FORTUNE* and less frequently by *sur, en,* etc. *je compte SUR VOUS, je crois EN Dieu*. Care is needed when deciding whether a prepositional phrase is an indirect object or an adverbial. An object of a preposition is any noun phrase which follows a preposition: e.g. *dans LE HALL* 'In the hall'; *à côté DU RESTAURANT* 'beside the restaurant'. See also Preceding direct object.
Ordinal number	See Number
Parenthetical expression	An aside made by a speaker to indicate a reservation about what is being said. It is the equivalent of putting something in brackets ('parentheses'): e.g. *Joris, SEMBLE-T-IL, a gagné le prix* 'Joris, it seems, won the prize. Parentheticals are kinds of adverbial.
Participle	Past participles are forms of the verb which occur with *avoir* or *être*, e.g. *J'ai mangé* 'I've eaten'; *Elle est partie* 'She has left'. Present participles end in *-ant* and correspond to English verbs ending in -ing: e.g. *disparaissant* 'disappearing', *attendant* 'waiting'. Gerunds are present participles preceded by *en: en disparaissant* 'while disappearing'; by disappearing', *en attendant* 'while waiting; by waiting'.
Passive	A form of a normally transitive verb where the direct object becomes the subject and the verb is turned into an *être* + past participle construction: e.g. *Elle a réparé le vélo* 'She repaired the bike'/*Le vélo a été réparé* 'The bike has been repaired'.
Past participle	See Participle
Person	The three categories into which noun phrases or pronouns can be divided depending on whether they refer to the person(s) speaking (*je,*

me, moi, nous – first person), the person(s) being spoken to (*tu, te, toi, vous* – second person), or the person(s) or thing(s) being talked about (*il, elle, lui, ils*, etc. – third person). Pronouns take different forms in the first, second, and third person, and finite verbs change their form to agree with the person of the subject (e.g. *je parle, nous parlons, vous parlez*, etc.).

Personal pronoun   A first person, second person, or third person pronoun which stands for a noun phrase mentioned or implied elsewhere in a text or discourse. Personal pronouns contrast with impersonal pronouns which do not refer to other noun phrases. Personal pronouns are pronouns like *je, me, moi, nous; tu, te, toi, vous; il, elle, lui, les*, etc. They take their name from the fact that they can be classified as first, second, or third person and do not necessarily refer to people; e.g. *elle* is a personal pronoun, but it refers to the inanimate *émission* in ELLE *est intéressante, cette émission* 'That programme's interesting'.

Phrase   Any string of words which gives rise to an expression with a cohesive meaning, e.g. *mon oncle Florent* 'my uncle Florent' (noun phrase); *Leila* MARCHE LENTEMENT 'Leila walks slowly' (verb phrase); etc.

Preceding direct object   When a verb is conjugated with *avoir*, the past participle agrees with the preceding direct object. This is usually a preceding unstressed pronoun: *Je* LES *ai vus;* the head of a relative clause: LA LETTRE *que j'ai écrit*E or, in questions, the interrogative form at the beginning of the question: QUELLE LETTRE *a-t-il écrit*E?

Preposition   Words like *à, de, dans, en, sur*, etc. which are followed by noun phrases and indicate the direction, location, orientation, etc. of an entity.

Prepositional phrase   A phrase consisting of a preposition and its complement. The following are all prepositional phrases: *à midi* 'at noon'; *à chaque virage* 'at every bend'; *au chevet de ma mère* 'at my mother's bedside'.

Present participle   See Participle

Pronoun   A form which is used in place of a noun phrase when that phrase is already known from the context: e.g. *je, tu, nous, le, la, leur*, etc. Pronouns have different forms depending on whether they are subjects, direct objects, indirect objects, or objects of a preposition. *Y* and *En* – these pronouns are often called adverbial pronouns because they often stand in for adverbial prepositional phrases. *Y* phrases are most often introduced by *à* but can also be introduced by *dans, sur*, etc. *Je vais à Nantes – J'y vais; Je pose le livre sur la table – Je l'y pose.* En phrases are introduced by *de: Je reviens de Nantes – J'en reviens.* However, *y* and *en* play a number of roles which are not adverbial, such as direct object when a partitive article is present: *Je vends du lait – J'en vends* or an indirect object when this is introduced by *de: Je parle souvent de mon avenir – J'en parle souvent.*

Proper noun   Names such as *Solène, le Canada*, are proper nouns.

Quantifier   A determiner-like expression which measures or quantifies a noun or noun phrase: e.g. BEAUCOUP *d'argent* 'a lot of money'; LA PLUPART *des spectateurs* 'most of the spectators'; TOUS *les jours* 'every day'.

Question   A direct question is addressed directly to the hearer or reader: e.g. *Viens-*
(direct versus indirect)   *tu?* 'Are you coming?'. An indirect question reports the asking of the question: e.g. *Il a demandé si tu venais* 'He asked if you were coming'.

Reciprocal   A type of sentence where either the direct object, the indirect object, or the object of a preposition refers to the same thing, idea, etc. as a plural subject, and the sentence is interpreted so that the subjects are doing things to each other: e.g. *Les boxeurs SE sont blessés* 'The boxers injured each other'; *Les participants SE sont posé des questions* 'The participants asked each other questions'; *Les manifestants ont lutté LES UNS CONTRE LES AUTRES* 'The demonstrators fought with each other'.

Reflexive
A type of sentence where either the direct object, the indirect object, or the object of a preposition refers to the same person, thing, or idea as the subject: e.g. *Je ME lave* 'I am washing (myself)'; *Elle SE cache la vérité* 'She is hiding the truth from herself'; *Elle parle CONTRE ELLE-MÊME* 'She is speaking against herself'.

Relative clause
A clause which modifies a noun phrase or a pronoun: e.g. *Il y avait deux hommes QUI SORTAIENT DU BAR* 'There were two men who were coming out of the bar'; *C'est lui QUI ME L'A DONNÉ* 'He is the one who gave it to me'.

Subject
The noun phrase or pronoun in a clause about which the verb and its complement say something. (For clauses as subjects, see Subordinate Clause.) Subjects usually appear in front of the verb: e.g. LE DÎNER *est servi* 'Dinner is served'; SA FEMME *parle lentement* 'His wife speaks slowly'; DELPHINE *a été battue'* Delphine was beaten'. It can appear after the verb in some constructions. See Subject–Verb Inversion.

Subject-verb inversion
Subjects normally precede finite verbs in French. But in questions, and after certain adverbs, the subject and the finite verb may change places: e.g. AIME-T-IL *le Roquefort?* 'Does he like Roquefort cheese?'; *à peine S'EST-IL ASSIS qu'on lui a demandé de se déplacer.* 'Hardly had he sat down when someone asked him to move'.

Subjunctive
See Chapter 11 for discussion

Subordinate clause
A clause which is part of a larger sentence and whose meaning is secondary to that of the main clause. It is useful to distinguish between two kinds of subordinate clauses: Those which serve as adverbials: PARCE QU'IL VA SE MARIER, *Camille est heureux* 'Because he is getting married, Camille is happy' – *parce qu'il va se marier* is subordinate to *Camille est heureux* and serves as an adverbial. Those which serve as subjects and objects; CE QU'ELLE A FAIT *ce jour-là me restera toujours dans l'esprit* 'What she did that day will stay in my mind for ever' – *Ce qu'elle a fait ce jour-là* is subordinate to *me restera dans l'esprit* and functions as the subject of the sentence. *Je ne vois pas CE QUE JE PEUX FAIRE* 'I don't see what I can do' *Ce que je peux faire* is subordinate to *Je ne vois pas* and functions as the object of the sentence. For relative clauses, see above.

Superlative
A way of modifying adjectives and adverbs to single out an entity as the best or the worst of its kind: e.g. *C'est la route la plus dangereuse/la moins dangereuse de la région* 'It's the most dangerous road/least dangerous road in the region'; *Cette voiture-là roule la plus vite/la moins vite* 'That car goes fastest/the least fast'.

Tense
A form of the verb which indicates the time at which an event took place relative to other events being talked about: e.g. *je prends* [present tense] *la route par où nous sommes venus* [compound past tense] 'I'm taking the road along which we came'. Tenses have names like present, future, simple past, compound past, etc. – See Chapter 7 for the forms of verbs in different tenses and Chapter 10 for their uses.

Transitive verb
See Verb

Verb	A class of words which refers to actions, states, events, accomplishments, etc. and has different forms to indicate tense and agreement, e.g. *Elle parle* 'She is speaking'; *L'eau scintillait* 'The water was sparkling'.
Verb, ditransitive	A verb which has two complements consisting of a direct object and a prepositional object: e.g. *J'ai envoyé L'EMAIL À MON FRÈRE* 'I sent the email to my brother'.
Verb, finite	A verb which is marked for tense and agreement, as opposed to non-finite forms such as the infinitive, imperative, participles: e.g. *Je PARLE* 'I'm speaking; *J'AI parlé* 'I spoke'; *Je SAIS parler arabe* 'I can speak Arabic'.
Verb, indirectly transitive	A verb which has a prepositional complement: e.g. *Il parle DE SES PARENTS* 'He is talking of his parents'.
Verb, intransitive	A verb which has no direct object: e.g. *La neige tombait* 'Snow was falling'.
Verb, pronominal	Pronominal verbs are accompanied by an unstressed pronoun which agrees with the subject and is one of *me, te, se, nous,* and *vous*. The unstressed pronoun may be a direct object, e.g. *je ME lave* or an indirect object: e.g. *je ME lave le visage*.
Verb, transitive	A verb which has a direct object: e.g. *Elle mange UNE POMME* 'She is eating an apple'.
Verb phrase	The phrase consisting of a verb alone or a verb and the elements which modify it (but excluding the subject). Each of the following is a verb phrase: *marchait* 'was walking'; *marchait lentement* 'was walking slowly'; *a envoyé un cadeau d'anniversaire à sa tante* 'sent a birthday present to his/her aunt'.

Acknowledgements

The influence of others is apparent in all forms of writing, but it is particularly pervasive in the writing of a grammar of French. So much has been said and written about French grammar over the centuries. The influence of the work of those who have gone before and the views of our colleagues and contemporaries who teach French or are interested in the structure of French have shaped the presentation of nearly every item we discuss.

It would therefore be impossible for us to cite all the sources of ideas and examples on which we have drawn in writing *French Grammar and Usage*. Nevertheless, we would like to single out some sources, and some friends and colleagues, for making a direct and significant contribution. The following friends and colleagues have taken time to comment on drafts of various chapters: Marie-Anne Hintze, Tony Lodge, Chris Lyons, Jean-Pierre Mailhac, Annie Rouxeville, Raphael Salkie, and Carol Sanders. John Butt, co-author of *A New Reference Grammar of Modern Spanish* (London, Arnold, 1988), provided us with valuable feedback on an early draft, as did several anonymous readers. Elaine Murphy, supported by the secretarial staff in the Department of Modern Languages at the University of Salford, skilfully typed and copied countless drafts of the book. We would like to thank all of these for their interest and their help and also Lesley Riddle at Arnold for waiting patiently for the final version while we juggled writing with the demands of running large university departments during difficult times.

We have discovered in undertaking this work that there are as many views about how a point of grammar should be presented and exemplified as there are people who are consulted. Those who have given us the benefit of their advice may not agree with the way we have finally decided to present the grammar of French. But we are certain that the end product is far better than it would have been without their advice.

Roger Hawkins and Richard Towell
Colchester and Salford
January 1996

Acknowledgements for the second edition

This second edition of *French Grammar and Usage* has benefitted considerably from the comments of friends, colleagues, and students who used the first edition and found areas where it could be improved. We would particularly like to thank the following for their significant help: Aidan Coveney, Jim Dolamore, Annick Leyssen, Matthew McNamara, and Jonathan Mallinson. We would also like to thank George Stephenson for his comments on the text prior to the reprinting of the second edition. We alone are responsible for any errors or weaknesses of presentation which remain.

Roger Hawkins and Richard Towell
Colchester and Salford
September 2000

Acknowledgements for the third edition

For the third edition of *French Grammar and Usage*, we have made some of the explanations more reader-friendly, added some new examples, and modified certain points in the light of comments received from our readers. We would particularly like to thank Penny Eley, Odile Cyrille-Thomas, and Agnès Gower for their comments, and Seth Whidden's website (http://www86.homepage. villanova.edu/seth.whidden.html) for directing us to Jean Girodet's (1996) discussion of adjective agreement with *gens*. To maintain consistency in the tone of entries, we have not always taken up suggestions made by our readers, and we hope they will forgive us where we appear to have ignored their advice. For weaknesses in presentation that still remain, and for errors that were not noticed before the book went to print, we alone are to blame.

Roger Hawkins and Richard Towell
Colchester and Salford
January 2010

Acknowledgements for the fourth edition

Perhaps it is in the nature of a reference grammar that there continue to be errors that were not spotted in the preparation of earlier editions and better ways of describing things than before. At any rate, we have made a number of changes in this fourth edition that we believe render it more accurate and reader-friendly. A number of the changes are in response to the comments of reviewers or users of the grammar. We would particularly like to thank Guillaume Fleury for his observations about *gens* and *personnes* that have led us to revise the entry for these words. As in previous editions, to maintain consistency in the tone of the entries, we have not always taken up suggestions made by our readers. We beg their forgiveness and hope that they will nevertheless find the new edition a useful source of information about the contemporary French language.

Roger Hawkins and Richard Towell
Colchester and Salford
August 2014

Acknowledgements for the fifth edition

The fifth edition has benefitted from feedback from reviewers and users of the previous editions, as has been the case throughout the evolution of this book. It perhaps differs from those editions in so far as it has been influenced by two significant changes in the way French is currently being used. These are the official introduction of certain modifications to the spelling of certain words and the way in which usage is becoming sensitive to society's response to both the desire to use language in a non-sexist way and to greater fluidity in gender roles. We have attempted to reflect what is happening in certain sections of the book and we hope that we have done so in a way which will inform users of these changes whilst at the same time not overstating the extent to which they are, as yet, present in everyday usage. As before, we hope that the new edition will prove a useful resource for those undertaking the adventure of discovering a new language.

Richard Towell and Marie-Noëlle Lamy
Salford and London
May 2024

1 Nouns

1.1 Types of noun

A noun is a word that typically refers to an entity or concept of some kind, e.g. *livre* 'book', *ami* 'friend', *bière* 'beer', *bonheur* 'happiness', and is the main constituent of the subject of a clause, the object of a verb, or the object of a preposition. French nouns may co-occur with articles (*le livre* 'the book', *un ami* 'a friend') and modifying adjectives (*un roman français* 'a French novel', *mon cher ami* 'my dear friend', *une connexion sécurisée* 'a secure connection'). Nouns generally change form when made plural and some, especially those derived from adjectives or past participles, may change form when there is a masculine and a feminine version: *l'élu* – elected person, male; *l'élue* – elected person, female; *les élus* for a male group, or traditionally, a mixed group and *les élues* for a female group. If ensuring that a text is non-sexist, the plural for a mixed group might be *les élus et les élue*s and proponents of inclusive writing would argue in favour of *les élu.e.s* (see Section 1.2.2).

There are different subclasses of noun, typically determined by meaning, that have different distributional properties which are described in this chapter: **abstract** (*bonheur* 'happiness', *beauté* 'beauty'), **concrete** (*bière* 'beer', *roman* 'novel'), **mass** (*eau* 'water', *beurre* 'butter'), **count** (*bouteille* 'bottle', *billet* 'ticket'), **collective** (*comité* 'committee', *gouvernement* 'government'), and **proper** (names) (*Jérémie, France*). French nouns belong to one of two gender classes – masculine or feminine (*le bâtiment* 'the building', but *la maison* 'the house') – and they may vary in form when they are singular or plural (*cheval* 'horse', but *chevaux* 'horses'). Nouns can be **simple** (*une cour* 'a yard', *un marteau* 'a hammer', *un boîtier* 'a box') or **compound** (*une basse-cour* 'a farmyard', *un marteau-piqueur* 'a pneumatic drill', *un boîtier de charge* 'a charger unit'). Compound nouns have their own rules for gender and number assignment (see Sections 1.2.11, 1.3.9, and 1.4 for proposed changes).

1.1.1 Abstract versus concrete nouns

Concrete nouns refer to entities with physical attributes which can be seen, heard, touched, etc. Abstract nouns refer to entities without such physical attributes:

Typical concrete nouns		Typical abstract nouns	
bière (f)	*beer*	beauté (f)	*beauty*
bonbon (m)	*sweet*	bonheur (m)	*happiness*
cadeau (m)	*present*	bonté (f)	*goodness*
carte (f)	*card*	patience (f)	*patience*
chargeur (m)	*charger*	mœurs (f pl)	*customs, morals*
église (f)	*church*	savoir (m)	*knowledge*
livre (m)	*book*	silence (m)	*silence*
mannequin (m)	*(fashion) model*	soif (f)	*thirst*

DOI: 10.4324/9781003373926-1

Abstract nouns in French are usually accompanied by a definite article, whereas English has no article:

La patience est une qualité qui se fait rare
Patience is a quality which is becoming rare

Je cherche **le** bonheur
I'm looking for happiness

But when abstract nouns refer to a particular example of 'patience', 'happiness', 'knowledge', etc. (e.g. when they are modified by an adjective), they occur with an indefinite article:

Il a fait preuve cette fois d'**une** patience appréciable
The patience he showed on this occasion was considerable

Il s'est alors produit **un** silence absolu
Absolute silence ensued

Tu m'as rendu **un** grand service
You did me a great favour

(See Chapter 2 for definite and indefinite articles.)

1.1.2 Mass versus count nouns

Count nouns identify individual entities and usually have both singular and plural forms. Mass nouns treat the entity or entities they refer to as a single unit and typically have only a singular form (although some mass nouns only have a plural form):

Typical count nouns		**Typical mass nouns**	
une bouteille	*a bottle*	de l'air	*air*
des bouteilles	*bottles*	du beurre	*butter*
un chien	*a dog*	du courant	*(electrical) power*
des chiens	*dogs*	de l'eau	*water*
une personne	*a person*	du gâteau	*cake*
des personnes	*people*	des cheveux	*hair*
		du sable	*sand*

Mass nouns in French are usually accompanied by the partitive article (see Section 2.4) – *du, de l', de la*, or *des* – in those cases where English has 'some' or no article at all:

Je voudrais **du** lait, s'il vous plaît
I would like some milk, please

Il y a **du** sucre dans le placard
There's sugar in the cupboard

Mass nouns used countably

Some mass nouns can be used countably to refer to specific examples of the substance in question:

les vins de France	*the wines of France*
les fromages de Normandie	*the cheeses of Normandy*
un pain	*a loaf of bread*
un petit pain	*a bun*

Some count nouns can also be used as mass nouns:

Prenez du poulet	*Have some chicken*
Il met du citron dans tout	*He puts lemon in everything*

1.1.3 **Collective nouns**

Collective nouns refer to a collection of people or things.

Typical collective nouns

assistance (f)	*audience*
comité (m)	*committee*
équipe (f)	*team*
foule (f)	*crowd*
gouvernement (m)	*government*
linge (m) de maison	*household linen*
main-d'œuvre (f)	*workforce*
personnel (m)	*staff*
vaisselle (f)	*dishes, crockery*

When a collective noun is the subject of a clause, the verb is usually singular. This contrasts with English, where the verb can be either singular or plural:

Le gouvernement se réunit tous les mercredis
The government meet or *meets every Wednesday*

L'équipe s'entraîne le jeudi soir
The team trains/train on Thursday evenings

(For more on subject-verb agreement, see Section 9.1.)

Personnes **and** *gens*

personnes and *gens*, both of which mean 'people', differ in their uses because *personnes* is a count noun and *gens*, which is only found in the plural form, behaves like a collective noun. Only *personnes* can be preceded directly by a number (e.g. *cinq*) or the quantifiers *plusieurs* 'several' and *quelques* 'a few':

Les cinq personnes (NOT *gens) qui ont mangé avec nous
The five people who ate with us

Plusieurs personnes (NOT *gens) sont restées tout l'après-midi
Several people stayed for the whole afternoon

By the same token, *gens* tends to be used in contexts where 'people' refers to people in general:

Les gens n'aiment pas rester à table trop longtemps
People don't like to spend too long over a meal

However, *gens* can be preceded by *beaucoup de* 'many', *peu de* 'few', *un nombre de* 'a number of', *tous les* 'all the', and *la plupart des* 'most', and when an adjective precedes *gens*, the adjective can be preceded by a number:

Nous avons vu les six jeunes gens devant la banque hier
We saw the six young people in front of the bank yesterday

1.1.4 **Proper nouns**

Proper nouns are names like *Chloé, Paris, Toulouse, Le Havre, la Seine, la France, le Canada.*

With persons there is usually no article:

Chloé viendra demain
Chloé will come tomorrow

In some cases, an article is inserted in informal speech:

Dis donc, elle était pas fière, la Chloé!
So Chloé must have felt a bit of a fool!

T'aurais vu la tête qu'il faisait, le Jérôme!
You should have seen Jérôme's face!

This conveys a familiar, affectionate attitude towards the individual concerned.

When reference is made to a family, as in 'the Jones family', a plural article is used, but the name itself is not pluralised:

J'ai invité les Oget à venir déjeuner dimanche
I have invited the Ogets for Sunday lunch

When a person's title is used, it is normally accompanied by the definite article:

Je vous présente **la** Professeure Bodin
May I introduce Professor Bodin

chez **le** Docteur Gleizes
c/o Dr Gleizes (on an envelope or package)

When proper nouns are modified by preceding adjectives, they require a definite article:

le petit Jules　　　　　　　　　*little Jules*
le vieux Raoul　　　　　　　　　*old Raoul*

Unlike in English, regions and countries are normally used with a definite article:

J'ai visité **la** Normandie　　　　　　*I visited Normandy*
la France d'aujourd'hui　　　　　　*today's France*
Nous survolons **la** Belgique　　　　　*We are flying over Belgium*

(See Section 2.2.2 for the use of articles with regions and countries.)

1.1.5 **Use of** *an/année, jour/journée, matin/matinée, soir/soirée*

English has only one word for each of 'morning', 'evening', 'day', and 'year'. French has two, but each is used under different circumstances. It is often said that the *-ée* forms are used when the activity which takes place during the morning, evening, etc. is highlighted. Compare:

Je travaille chaque **matin/soir/jour**
I work every morning/evening/day
(where the frequency rather than the activity is highlighted)

J'ai travaillé toute la **matinée/la soirée/la journée**
I worked all morning/evening/day
(where the length of work is highlighted)

But there are other cases where the forms have distinct uses which appear to be the result simply of convention:

au début de la matinée/la soirée/la journée
at the start of the morning/the evening/the day

en fin de matinée/soirée/journée
at the end of the morning/the evening/the day

par une belle matinée	*on a beautiful morning*
tôt le matin	*early in the morning*
un beau matin il est parti	*one fine morning he up and left*
tous les jours/matins/ans	*every day/morning/year*
l'an 2028	*the year 2028*
le jour de l'an	*New Year's Day*
le nouvel an	*the New Year*
souhaiter la bonne année à qn	*to wish someone a Happy New Year*
les années 90	*the 90s*
l'année précédente/suivante	*the previous/following year*

With preceding numbers the forms without *-ée* are normally used:

Il a cinq ans	*He is five*
trois fois par jour	*three times a day*

But if an adjective modifies the noun as well this seems to highlight the activity:

trois bonnes années pour la récolte	*three good years for the harvest*
six longues journées	*six long days*

1.2 **Gender**

Nouns in French are either masculine or feminine. Unfortunately, there are no simple rules which non-native speakers can use to predict with complete accuracy the gender of a given noun. However, there are some patterns, either in the form or meaning of nouns, which can normally be used to predict the correct gender with greater than chance accuracy. The reader should remember, however, that these patterns are not comprehensive, and that there are many exceptions.

1.2.1 **Gender signalled by the final letters of the written forms of nouns**

Masculine

Many nouns whose singular written form ends in a **consonant** are masculine:

-c   un tic *a twitch* (un lac *a lake*, le public *the public*, etc.)

-d   le bord *the edge* (le fond *the bottom*, le pied *the foot*, etc.)

-g   un camping *a camp site* (un parking *a car park*, un shampooing *a shampoo*, etc.)

-l   un détail *a detail* (le travail *work*, le soleil *the sun*, etc.)

-r   le fer *iron* (l'hiver *winter*, un couloir *a corridor*, etc.)

-t   le chocolat *chocolate* (le climat *the climate*, un jouet *a toy*, un poulet *a chicken*, le ciment *cement*, un jugement *a judgement*, etc.)

Exceptions are typically found with nouns which end in *-n*, *-r*, *-s*, *-t*, and *-x*:

une maison	*a house*
une cuiller (or cuillère)	*a spoon*
la mer	*the sea*
une tour	*a tower*
une fois	*one time*
une dent	*a tooth*
une nuit	*a night*
une jument	*a mare*
une croix	*a cross*

Nouns ending in *-on* are usually masculine (*un poisson* 'a fish', *un sillon* 'a furrow', etc., although *une chanson* 'a song' is an exception). But nouns ending in *-aison*, *-(s)sion*, *-tion*, or *-xion* are usually feminine:

une comparaison	*a comparison*
une liaison	*a liaison*
une maison	*a house*
une raison	*a reason*
une saison	*a season*
une décision	*a decision*
la tension	*tension, blood pressure*
une vision	*a vision*
une émission	*a broadcast*
une connexion	*a connection*

Exception: un bastion *a bastion*

Nouns ending in *-eur* are usually masculine (*un ordinateur* a computer, *un écouteur* a headphone, an earbud or an earpiece, *le bonheur* happiness, etc.), but the following frequently used nouns are feminine:

la chaleur	*the heat*
une couleur	*a colour*
une erreur	*a mistake*
une fleur	*a flower*

la largeur	*the width*
la longueur	*the length*
la peur	*fear*
la profondeur	*the depth*

Many nouns whose singular written form ends in a vowel (but excluding *-e* without an acute accent) are masculine, although there are a significant number of exceptions:

-ai, -oi
un délai	*a time limit*
un essai	*an attempt (a 'try' in rugby)*
un emploi	*a job*
un roi	*a king*

Exceptions: la foi *faith*, une loi *a law*, une paroi *a wall*

-é
le café	*the café* or *coffee*
un fossé	*a ditch*
le marché	*the market*
le thé	*tea*
un copié-collé	*a copy and paste*
le chassé-croisé (des automobilistes)	*the flow of leaving and returning holiday makers on the roads*

Exception: une clé *a key*

-eau
un couteau	*a knife*
un marteau	*a hammer*
le niveau	*the level*
le réseau	*the network*
un tableau	*a picture*

Exceptions: l'eau *water*, la peau *skin*

-i
l'abri	*shelter*
un ampli	*a (loud)speaker*
un cri	*a shout*
un pari	*a bet*
un pli	*a fold*
un raccourci	*a short-cut*

Exception: une appli, *an app*

-ou
un bijou	*a jewel*
un caillou	*a pebble*
un clou	*a nail*
un genou	*a knee*
le hibou	*the owl*

Feminine

Many nouns whose singular written form ends in *-e* without an acute accent are feminine:

l'audace *daring*, la façade *the front, the outside*, une salade *a salad*
une baie *a bay*, la haie *the hedge*
une douzaine *a dozen*, une fontaine *a fountain*
une ambulance *an ambulance*, une flèche *an arrow*
une thèse *a thesis*, une grève *a strike*
une araignée *a spider*, une bougie *a candle*, etc.

But there are a large number of exceptions to this rule:

-isme

Nouns ending in *-isme* are masculine: *le romantisme* 'romanticism', *le tourisme* 'tourism', *un idiotisme* 'an idiom (linguistic)', etc.

-ède, -ège, -ème

Nouns with these endings are usually masculine:

un intermède	an interlude
un cortège	a procession
un piège	a trap
un stratège	a strategist
un poème	a poem
le système	the system
le thème	the theme or translation into a foreign language

la crème *cream* is an exception (but see Section 1.2.4).

-age

Nouns ending in *-age* are usually masculine, but there are some notable exceptions:

le courage	courage
un garage	a garage
un message	a message
un stage	a work placement
un voyage	a journey
le covoiturage	car-sharing

Exceptions: une cage *a cage*, une image *a picture*, une page *a page*, une plage *a beach*, la rage *rabies*.

Other common exceptions:

un grade	a rank
un stade	a stadium
un groupe	a group
le monde	the world
le domaine	the area
le silence	silence
un musée	a museum
un lycée	a (sixth-form) college
un trophée	a trophy

un génie	*a genius*
un incendie	*a fire*
un cimetière	*a cemetery*
le derrière	*the backside*
un magazine	*a magazine*
le platine	*platinum*
un pare-brise	*a windscreen*
un intervalle	*an interval*
le rebelle	*the rebel*
le chèvrefeuille	*honeysuckle*
un chêne	*an oak tree*
un hêtre	*a beech tree*
un gorille	*a gorilla*
un portefeuille	*a wallet*
un carosse	*a carriage*
un squelette	*a skeleton*
un renne	*a reindeer*
le mercure	*mercury*
un murmure	*a murmur*
un gramme	*a gram*
un kilogramme	*a kilogram*
un mètre	*a metre*
un kilomètre	*a kilometre*
un litre	*a litre*
un parapluie	*an umbrella*

N.B.: Most words with the prefix *para-* are masculine: *un parachute* 'a parachute', *un paratonnerre* 'a lightning conductor', *le parapente* 'paragliding', *un paravent* 'wind-shield, screen'.

1.2.2 Nouns which refer both to males and to females without changing form: the feminisation of titles, professions, grades, and function

In the past, a number of nouns referring to professions, trades, or titles associated predominantly with men had only a masculine form. However, with women present in all spheres of society in the modern world, a French government commission of the 1980s (*la commission générale de terminologie et de néologie*) made a set of proposals for the *féminisation … des noms de métier, grade, fonction ou titre*. This was followed up by a report *Femme, j'écris ton nom. Guide d'aide à la féminisation des noms de métiers, professions, titres, grades et fonctions* by INALF in 1999 which includes some 2,000 examples and the *Académie française* produced a report in 2019. Some of the proposed feminine forms of nouns have been slow to enter general usage, others have been welcomed. They have strong political backing in France. It is not easy to know which forms are preferred by individuals or groups and, in practice, where feasible, it is probably best to ask the woman in question what the appropriate form of address is.

Some nouns can refer either to males or to females simply by changing the determiner from masculine to feminine:

un/une adulte	*an adult*
un/une adversaire	*an adversary*
un/une architecte	*an architect*
un/une artiste	*an artist*

un/une bibliothécaire	*a librarian*
un/une camarade	*a comrade*
un/une capitaine	*a captain*
un/une célibataire	*a bachelor/spinster (an unmarried person)*
un chef, une chef/cheffe	*a chef (kitchen) boss (in many organisations)*
un/une chimiste	*a chemist (scientist)*
un/une collègue	*a colleague*
un/une coloc	*a co-tenant, male or female but* une coloc *can also mean an apartment*
un/une compatriote	*a compatriot*
un/une complice	*an accomplice*
un/une concierge	*a caretaker*
un/une convive	*a guest*
un/une dentiste	*a dentist*
un/une élève	*a (school) pupil*
un/une enfant	*a child*
un/une esclave	*a slave*
un/une fonctionnaire	*a civil servant*
un/une gosse	*a kid (a word for a child in informal French)*
un/une intérimaire	*an intern, a temporary member of staff*
un/une interne	*a junior doctor (in a hospital); a boarder (in a school)*
un/une interprète	*an interpreter*
un/une journaliste	*a journalist*
un/une juge	*a judge*
un/une libraire	*a bookseller*
un/une locataire	*a tenant*
un/une maire	*a mayor*
un/une malade	*a person who is ill*
un/une ministre	*a minister*
un/une notaire	*a solicitor*
un/une partenaire	*a partner*
un/une patriote	*a patriot*
un/une peintre	*a painter*
un/une pensionnaire	*a boarder (as in boarding school)*
un/une philosophe	*a philosopher*
un/une photographe	*a photographer*
un/une pianiste	*a pianist*
un/une pique-assiette	*a sponger*
un/une secrétaire	*a secretary*
un/une touriste	*a tourist*

N.B.: *pupille* meaning 'pupil of the eye' is feminine only. In set expressions such as *pupille de la Nation, pupille de l'Etat* the noun refers to a child whose education is paid for by the state. With this meaning *pupille* may be masculine or feminine according to the sex of the child.

The words *témoin* and *vampire* are masculine even when they refer to females but female vampires are likely to be *des femmes-vampires*.

N.B.: *une cheffe* 'a leader/manager' as in *une cheffe de projets* 'a project manager' now seems to be the more used form.

Addressing female postholders versus referring to them

Female political personnel such as mayors and ministers can be referred to as *la Maire, la Mairesse* (see Section 1.2.3) or *le Maire*, while ministers can be *la Ministre* or *le Ministre, la Première Ministre,* or *le Premier Ministre*. When addressing them, *Madame la Maire* and *Madame la Ministre* are preferred. Other postholders such as a female chef can be referred to as *la chef* or *la cheffe* or *le chef*, while when addressing her the staff would use '*Chef*': '*Oui, Chef!*'

1.2.3 Nouns which change form when they refer to males or to females

Regular patterns

For words ending in *-i, -é, -u,* and *–l,* an *-e* is added in the written form and the pronunciation remains the same:

un ami	une amie	*a friend*
un employé	une employée	*an employee (worker)*
un rival	une rivale	*a rival*
un consul	une consule	*a consul*

For words ending in *-d, -t, -ois, -ais, -er,* and *-ier* an *-e* is added and the final consonant, previously not pronounced, is pronounced:

un marchand	une marchande	*a trader*
un adjoint	une adjointe	*a deputy, assistant*
un avocat	une avocate	*a lawyer*
un candidat	une candidate	*a candidate*
un magistrat	une magistrate	*a magistrate*
un préfet	une préfète	*a prefect*
un président	une présidente	*a president*
un bourgeois	une bourgeoise	*a bourgeois(e)*
un boulanger	une boulangère	*a baker*
un berger	une bergère	*a shepherd*
un fermier	une fermière	*a farmer*
un caissier	une caissière	*a checkout operator*
un menuisier	une menuisière	*a carpenter*
un pompier	une pompière	*a fireman, a firewoman*
un romancier	une romancière	*a novelist*

For words ending in *-ien, -on, -an, -in,* and *-ain* in written form, *-(n)e* is added and the final vowel, previously pronounced as a nasal vowel, is pronounced as an oral vowel plus *-n*:

un chien	une chienne	*a dog/a bitch*
un chirurgien	une chirurgienne	*a surgeon*
un électricien	une électricienne	*an electrician*
un informaticien	une informaticienne	*a computer scientist, an information technologist*
un lion	une lionne	*a lion/a lioness*
un artisan	une artisane	*a craftsman/craftswoman*
un gitan	une gitane	*a gypsy (pejorative)*
un paysan	une paysanne	*a farmer*
un voisin	une voisine	*a neighbour*
un Africain	une Africaine	*an African*
un écrivain	une écrivaine	*a writer*

Some nouns add *-esse*:

un âne	une ânesse	*a donkey*
un chanoine	une chanoinesse	*a canon/canoness*
un comte	une comtesse	*a count/countess*
un diable	une diablesse	*a devil/she-devil*
un drôle	une drôlesse	*a rascal*
un hôte	une hôtesse	*a host/hostess*
un ivrogne	une ivrognesse	*a drunkard*
un maître	une maîtresse	*a master/mistress*
un ogre	une ogresse	*an ogre*
un pauvre	une pauvresse	*a poor person*
un prêtre	une prêtresse	*a priest/priestess*
un prince	une princesse	*a prince/princess*
un Suisse	une Suissesse	*a Swiss person*
un tigre	une tigresse	*a tiger/tigress*

Although the nouns listed above are in common use, the *-esse* ending is no longer used productively to create feminine forms and is felt as somewhat pejorative.

With nouns that end in *-eur*, some simply add *-e*, others change to *-rice*, and yet others change to *-euse*:

un auteur	une auteure (possible, but currently favoured: autrice)	*an author*
un docteur	une docteure	*a doctor*
un ingénieur	une ingénieure	*an engineer*
un pasteur	une pasteure	*a (religious) minister*
un professeur	une professeure	*a teacher*
un proviseur	une proviseure	*a headteacher*
un sculpteur	une sculpteure (*also* une sculptrice)	*a sculptor*
un compositeur	une compositrice	*a composer*
un agriculteur	une agricultrice	*a farmer*
un animateur	une animatrice	*a course/youth leader, a (radio/TV) presenter*
un auditeur	une auditrice	*a listener*
un éditeur	une éditrice	*a publisher*
un instituteur	une institutrice	*a (primary school) teacher*
un rédacteur	une rédactrice	*an editor*
un conducteur de poids lourds	une conductrice de poids lourds	*a truck driver*
un chanteur	une chanteuse	*a singer*
un chercheur	une chercheuse	*a researcher*
un footballeur	une footballeuse	*a footballer*
un influenceur	une influenceuse	*an influencer (on social media)*
un menteur	une menteuse	*a liar*
un voleur	une voleuse	*a thief*
un youtubeur	une youtubeuse	*a youtuber*

Addressing female postholders versus referring to them

A female doctor can be referred to as *une docteure* or *un docteur*. The first of these terms is gradually overtaking *une doctoresse*. When addressing her, normal usage is *Docteur(e) + her surname*.

This also applies to academic doctors, except for *doctoresse* which was only ever used for medical doctors. A female professor is *une professeure* or *une professeur*, and in formal contexts she is addressed as *Professeur(e) + her surname*. Finally, the term *un médecin* to refer to a medical doctor has no feminine variant because *la médecine* has a different meaning (medicine, as a speciality). But a woman can be referred to as *une femme médecin*.

Irregular patterns

In addition to these regular patterns, there are a number of masculine/feminine forms where the words are quite different:

un confrère	une consœur	*a colleague*
un époux	une épouse	*a husband/wife*
un fils	une fille	*a son/daughter*
un garçon	une fille	*a boy/girl*
un héros	une héroïne	*a hero/heroine*
un homme	une femme	*a man/woman*
un neveu	une nièce	*a nephew/niece*

1.2.4 Nouns which can be masculine or feminine

Nouns which change meaning when they change gender

Some nouns have different meanings when they are masculine and when they are feminine:

un aide	*a helper*	l'aide (f)	*help*
un chèvre	*a goat's cheese*	une chèvre	*a goat*
un crème	*a white coffee*	la crème	*cream*
le crêpe	*crêpe (cloth)*	une crêpe	*a pancake*
un critique	*a critic/a reviewer*	une critique	*a criticism/a review*
un espace	*a space*	une espace	*a space (in printing)*
un laque	*artwork*	une laque	*a hair lacquer or gloss paint*
un livre	*a book*	une livre	*a pound (money or weight)*
un manche	*a handle*	une manche	*a sleeve*
		La Manche	*the English Channel*
un manœuvre	*an unskilled worker*	une manœuvre	*a manoeuvre*
un mémoire	*a dissertation*	la mémoire	*memory (faculty of)*
un merci	*a thank you*	la merci	*mercy*
un mode	*a way of*	une mode	*a fashion*
(un mode de vie)	*(a way of life)*		
un moule	*a mould*	une moule	*a mussel*
un pendule	*a pendulum*	une pendule	*a clock*
le physique	*appearance*	la physique	*physics*
un poêle	*a stove*	une poêle	*a frying pan*
un poste	*a job*	la poste	*the Post Office*
un poste de travail	*a work station*		
le solde	*balance (in an account)*	la solde	*pay (usually with reference to soldier's pay)*
un somme	*a nap*	une somme	*a sum (of money)*
un tour	*a turn, trick*	une tour	*a tower*
le Tour de France	*the Tour de France*	la Tour Eiffel	*the Eiffel Tower*
un vase	*a vase*	la vase	*mud*
un voile	*a veil*	une voile	*a sail*

Nouns which have variable gender depending on how they are being used

Chose is normally feminine when it means 'thing': *la/une chose*. But the expressions *quelque chose* 'something', *autre chose* 'something else', *peu de chose* 'nothing much', and *pas grand-chose* 'not a great deal' are masculine:

Quelque chose est **arrivé**   Versus   Cette chose est **arrivée**
Something happened   *This thing happened*

Gens 'people' or 'folk' requires immediately preceding adjectives or quantifiers to be feminine, but following adjectives/participles to be masculine. Where a preceding quantifier, adjective, or participle is separated from *gens*, it is also masculine:

C'est une tradition chez les **vieilles** gens de la campagne
It's a tradition among old country folk

certaines gens   *some people*
tous les gens   *everyone*

Rassurés, les gens qui manifestaient se sont **dispersés**
Having been reassured, those demonstrating dispersed

This can produce sentences with contradictory indications of gender as in:

Les **vieilles** gens sont **attachés** à leurs racines
Old people are close to their roots

N.B.: *jeunes gens* (mpl) can refer either to 'young men', or 'young people' if the group is composed of both boys and girls; *jeunes filles* (fpl) is used where the group consists solely of 'young women'.

Amour 'love' is normally masculine singular. It is sometimes, however, feminine plural: *les amours*. When feminine plural it can mean 'amorous adventures' or it can be a more poetic way of referring to love. *Délice* and *orgue* are also masculine in the singular but feminine in the plural.

Œuvre meaning 'a single artistic or literary work' or 'a collection of individual works' is feminine:

Une grande œuvre de Picasso est **exposée** dans ce musée
A large work by Picasso is on display in this museum

Les œuvres **complètes** de Goscinny et Uderzo
Goscinny and Uderzo's complete works

But when it refers to the totality of work envisaged as a single unit, it is masculine:

L'œuvre **peint** de Matisse
Matisse's paintings

And when it is used to refer to building work it is also masculine, usually in the set phrase *le gros œuvre*:

Le gros œuvre sera **terminé** dans une semaine
The main building work will be finished in a week

Pâques 'Easter', when conceived of as an event, is masculine:

Il a promis de me rembourser avant Pâques **prochain**
He promised to pay me back before next Easter

But in Easter greetings *Pâques* is feminine:

Joyeuses Pâques   *Happy Easter*
Bonnes Pâques   *Happy Easter*

Noël 'Christmas' is normally masculine and agreeing participles are masculine. However, it is possible to hear *la Noël*, which is a contraction of *la fête de Noël*:

Pour **la** Noël j'irai voir ma sœur en Lorraine
I will go to see my sister in Lorraine for the Christmas period

Noël est **tombé** le jeudi cette année-là
Christmas fell on a Thursday that year

1.2.5 Nouns which have the same spoken form but two different written forms, with different genders and different meanings

There are some words which, in spoken French, are pronounced in the same way but which have different meanings and different genders:

un cal	*callus*	un rai	*a ray of light*
une cale	*a wedge*	une raie	*a parting* (in hair) or *a skate* (fish)
un faîte	*a summit*	le sel	*salt*
une fête	*a party*	une selle	*a saddle*
le foie	*the liver*	le sol	*earth*
la foi	*faith*	une sole	*a sole* (fish)
le maire	*the mayor*	un tic	*a tic* (nervous)
la mer	*the sea*	une tique	*a tick* (insect)
une mère	*a mother*		
un pet	*a fart*	le vice	*vice* (crime)
la paie	*the pay*	une vis	*a screw*
la paix	*peace*		
le poids	*the weight*		
un pois	*a pea*		
la poix	*pitch*		

1.2.6 Gender of countries, towns, islands, rivers, regions, and states

Countries

Some countries are masculine, some are feminine. The best generalisation is that they are masculine unless they end in *-e*, in which case they are feminine:

le Canada	*Canada*	la Chine	*China*
le Danemark	*Denmark*	la Finlande	*Finland*
le Japon	*Japan*	la Libye	*Libya*
le Koweït	*Kuwait*	la Norvège	*Norway*
le Liban	*Lebanon*	la Mauritanie	*Mauritania*
le Maroc	*Morocco*	la Roumanie	*Romania*
le Nigéria	*Nigeria*	la Suisse	*Switzerland*
le Portugal	*Portugal*	la Syrie	*Syria*

N.B.: Les Etats-Unis (m pl).

Exceptions: *le Cambodge* 'Cambodia', *le Mexique* 'Mexico', *le Mozambique* 'Mozambique', and *le Zimbabwe* 'Zimbabwe'.

'To' or 'in' a country is either *en* or *au(x)*. *en* is used with countries of feminine gender, and countries of masculine gender beginning with a vowel. *au* is used with countries of masculine gender beginning with a consonant, and *aux* with those countries whose names are plural, whether masculine or feminine (see Sections 13.2.3 and 13.26.1):

en Chine	au Canada
en Norvège	au Japon
en Suisse	aux Etats-Unis
en Iran (m)	
en Israël	

Towns

Towns, in normal usage, are masculine. In formal French they are sometimes feminine, particularly those which end in *-e*:

Cambridge est plein(e) de touristes toute l'année
Cambridge is full of tourists all year long

Where the name of a town includes a definite article, adjectives and participles must agree with the gender of the article:

La Baule est situé**e** sur le littoral atlantique
La Baule is on the Atlantic coast

Le Touquet est moins fréquenté l'hiver
Le Touquet has fewer visitors in winter

Islands

Islands are usually feminine:

la Sardaigne	*Sardinia*
la Crète	*Crete*
la Nouvelle-Zélande	*New Zealand*

But *le Groenland* 'Greenland' is an exception.

Rivers, regions, and states

For rivers, French *départements*, French regions, for states and regions in other countries, the best generalisation is that if they end in *-e* they are feminine:

Rivers

le Rhin	*the Rhine*	la Sâone	*the Sâone*
le Tarn	*the Tarn*	la Seine	*the Seine*
le Cher	*the Cher*	la Tamise	*the Thames*

Exception: *le Rhône* 'the Rhône'.

Départements

le Calvados	la Haute-Garonne
le Gers	la Marne
le Jura	la Vendée

Exception: *le Finistère.*

French regions (geographical):

le Berry	la Vendée
le Limousin	la Drôme
le Périgord	la Savoie

French regions (administrative):

les Hauts de France	la Nouvelle Aquitaine
la Bourgogne Franche-Comté	le Grand Est
l'Auvergne Rhône-Alpes	les Pays-de-Loire
l'Occitanie	la Normandie
la Provence-Alpes-Côte-d'Azur	le Centre Val-de-Loire
la Corse	l'Ile-de-France
la Bretagne	

States and regions in other countries

For example, American states:

le Massachusetts	la Louisiane
le Nevada	la Californie
le Texas	la Floride

Exception: British counties appear mostly to be treated as masculine, even those ending in '-shire' because *comté* is masculine.

le Kent
le Perthshire
le Yorkshire

1.2.7 Gender of makes of vehicle and machines

Usually, the gender of makes of vehicle or makes of machines, such as cars, lorries, planes, lawnmowers, dishwashers, etc., is the same as the gender of the general name for the vehicle or machine.

voiture 'car' is feminine, so makes of car are feminine. The same applies to *moto* 'motorbike':

une Renault
une Citroën

    une Volkswagen
    une Peugeot hybride
    une Harley-Davidson

camion 'lorry, truck' is masculine, so makes of truck are masculine:

    un Berliet
    un Scania

avion 'plane' is masculine, so types of plane are masculine:

    un Boeing 787
    un Airbus 380
    un Canadair (planes which throw water on fires in the summer)

cuisinière 'cooker' is feminine, so makes of cooker are feminine:

    une Faure
    une Electrolux

1.2.8 **Names of ships and restaurants**

The names of ships are usually masculine because *navire* is masculine, e.g. *Le Normandie*, as is *trimaran*, e.g. *le Flo* (even though it is named after a woman navigator, Florence Arthaud). However, smaller vessels may be feminine, e.g. *La Marie-Joseph* because *la corvette* and *la frégate* are feminine. However, vessels now often take their name from their shape (single or multi-hulled) and their sponsors, e.g. *le monocoque Banque Populaire* or *le maxi Edmond de Rothschild*.

Traditionally, restaurant names were masculine because *restaurant* itself is masculine, However, restaurant names can be unconventional with plays on words, e.g. *L'âge de raisin*, *Parapluie* with no article, but some will keep to the tradition such as *Le France* or *Le Normandie*

The names of restaurants are now so varied that it is difficult to predict whether *le* or *la* is required when talking about them. Generally, it is safe to choose *le* if the first word of their title is masculine and *la* if it is feminine.

1.2.9 **Nouns which are only feminine, but can refer both to men and women**

There are a small number of nouns which are only feminine in gender, but which may refer both to men and women:

personne	*person*
recrue	*recruit*
sentinelle	*sentry*
star/vedette	*star (in the entertainment business)*
victime	*victim*

personne meaning 'person' is feminine: *la/une personne*. But *personne* in *ne … personne*, meaning 'nobody' (see Section 16.13) is masculine:

Personne n'est **venu**	versus	Cette personne est venue
Nobody came		*That person came*

1.2.10 **Nouns with genders which English speakers often get wrong**

The following nouns are masculine:

le caractère	*character/temperament*
un choix	*a choice*
le crime	*crime*
un légume	*a vegetable*
le manque	*lack, lacuna*
le mérite	*merit*
l'espace	*space*
l'exode	*exodus*
un groupe	*a group*
un parachute	*a parachute*
un parapluie	*an umbrella*
le silence	*silence*

N.B.: *espace* is feminine when it means 'a space in printing' (see Section 1.2.4).

The following nouns are **feminine**:

une croix	*a cross*
une espèce	*a type, kind*
la fin	*the end*
une forêt	*a forest*
une noix	*a nut*
une vis	*a screw*

1.2.11 **Gender of compound nouns**

Compound nouns fall into six main types in French, and it is possible to determine broadly the gender of a compound on the basis of the type it belongs to (although with some exceptions).

N.B.: In the majority of cases compound nouns are written with a hyphen: *basse-cour* 'farmyard', *auto-école* 'driving school'. However, compound nouns formed with *de* or *à* are not typically hyphenated: *chef d'œuvre* 'masterpiece', *brosse à dents* 'toothbrush'. See Section 1.4 for proposed amendments in Nouvelle Orthographe.

Adjective + noun compounds

Adjective + noun compounds normally take their gender from the noun. The noun part of the compound is highlighted in the following examples:

un **arc**-boutant	*a buttress*
un bas-**côté**	*a verge (of a road, motorway)*
une basse-**cour**	*a farmyard*
une belle-**fille**	*a daughter-in-law or a step-daughter*
un **cerf**-volant	*a kite*
un **coffre**-fort	*a safe*
un grand-**parent**	*a grandparent*
un libre-**service**	*self service*
un **mot**-dièse	*a hashtag*
un rond-**point**	*a roundabout*

Exception: un *rouge-gorge* 'a robin'.

Noun + noun compounds

In noun + noun compounds, the gender is determined by the more important noun. *un camion-citerne* 'a tanker (lorry)' is a type of *camion* 'lorry', so *camion* is the more important noun, and the compound is masculine. *un homme-grenouille* 'a frogman' is a type of *homme* 'man' (not a type of frog!), so *homme* is the more important noun, and the compound is masculine. The important nouns are highlighted in the following examples:

une auto-**école**	*a driving school*
un **bateau**-mouche	*a Parisian tourist boat*
un **bateau**-citerne	*a tanker (ship)*
un **bateau**-usine	*a factory ship*
un **camion**-citerne	*a tanker (lorry)*
un **chou**-fleur	*a cauliflower*
un **code**-barres	*a barcode*
les **gestes**-barrière (masc.)	*safety measures, such as hand washing, to prevent the spread of a disease, e.g. Covid-19*
un **homme**-grenouille	*a frogman*
un **hôtel**-Dieu	*a hospital*
une **idée**-force	*a central idea*
un **mot**-clé	*a keyword*
un **oiseau**-mouche	*a humming-bird*
du **papier**-toilette	*toilet paper*
une **pause**-café	*a coffee break*
une **porte**-fenêtre	*a French window*
un **timbre**-poste	*a stamp*
une **voiture**-restaurant	*a restaurant car*
un **wagon**-lit	*a sleeping car*

Adverb or prefix + noun compounds

In adverb + noun compounds, the compound is usually the same gender as the noun, but there are exceptions:

un sans-**abri**	*a homeless person*
l'éco-**anxiété (f)**	*eco-anxiety*
une cyber-**attaque**	*a cyber attack*
un hors-**bord**	*a speedboat*
une demi-**bouteille**	*a half bottle*
une sans-**contact** (carte bancaire)	*a contactless (card)*
un anti-**corps**	*an anti-body*
un sans-**fil**	*a wireless appliance*
une mini-**jupe**	*a miniskirt*
une contre-**offensive**	*a counter-offensive*
un haut-**parleur**	*a loudspeaker*
l'arrière-**plan** (m)	*the background*
une exo-**planète**	*an exoplanet*
une arrière-**pensée**	*an ulterior motive*
le point de non-**retour**	*the point of no return*
un exo-**squelette**	*an exo-skeleton*
un demi-**tarif**	*a half-price ticket or fee*
un anti-**vax**, une anti-**vax**	*an anti-vaxxer (m and f)*

Exceptions: *l'après-guerre* (m) 'the post-war period', *l'entre-deux-guerres* (m) 'the period between the 2 world wars', *un en-tête* 'a letterhead', *le sans-gêne* 'the lack of embarrassment'.

Noun + prepositional phrase compounds

The gender of noun + prepositional phrase compounds is usually that of the first noun:

un **aide**-de-camp	*an aide-de-camp*
un **arc**-en-ciel	*a rainbow*
un **chef** d'œuvre	*a masterpiece*
un **coup** d'œil	*a glance*
un **coup** de pied	*a kick*
un **croc**-en-jambe	*a trip*
une **langue**-de-chat	*a langue-de-chat (a long, flat, finger biscuit)*
la **main** d'œuvre	*the workforce*
un **mont**-de-piété	*a pawnshop*
une **pomme** de terre	*a potato*
un **pot**-de-vin	*a bribe*

Exceptions to this generalisation are: *un tête-à-queue* 'a spin' (head to tail in a car), *un tête-à-tête* 'a tête-à-tête conversation'.

Verb + noun compounds

Verb + noun compounds are usually masculine:

un abat-jour	*a lampshade*
un accroche-cœur	*a (kiss) curl*
un appui-tête	*a headrest*
des casse-noisettes	*nutcrackers*
un cache-nez	*a scarf*
un coupe-papier	*a paper-knife*
un couvre-lit	*a bedspread*
un cure-dents	*a toothpick*
un essuie-mains	*a hand towel*
un gratte-ciel	*a skyscraper*
un ouvre-boîte	*a tin-opener*
un pare-brise	*a windscreen*
un pare-chocs	*a bumper*
un porte-avions	*an aircraft carrier*
un porte-bagages	*a luggage rack*
un porte-monnaie	*a wallet*
un soutien-gorge	*a bra*
un taille-crayon	*a pencil sharpener*
un tire-bouchon	*a corkscrew*
un trompe-l'œil	*a 'trompe l'œil' (art)*

Verbal phrase compounds

Compounds constructed from verbal phrases are masculine:

le manque-à-gagner	*lost revenue*
le on-dit	*rumour, gossip*
le ouï-dire	*hearsay*
un m'as-tu-vu	*a show-off*
le qu'en dira-t-on	*the 'what might people say'*
un faire-part	*an announcement card (weddings, births, funerals)*
un laisser-passer	*a pass (document)*
du (grand) n'importe quoi	*(complete and) utter nonsense*

le reste-à-charge	*that part of the payment for a prescription etc which is not reimbursed by the Sécurité sociale*
le quoi qu'il en coûte	*the 'whatever it costs'*
le savoir-faire	*know-how*

N.B.: *un monsieur-je-sais-tout* and *une madame-je sais-tout*: 'a know-all' takes the gender from the main noun.

Acronyms

Acronyms usually take their gender from the main noun. If borrowed from English, they tend to be masculine.

l'ADN	*(the) DNA*
la BD (bande dessinée)	*the comic book or graphic novel industry*
une BD (bande dessinée)	*a comic book, a comic strip, a graphic novel*
un BTS (brevet de technicien supérieur)	*advanced technical qualification*
un CDI (contrat à durée indéterminée)	*a permanent job*
un CDD (contrat à durée déterminée)	*a temporary job*
un/une DRH (directeur/-trice des ressources humaines)	*a head of HR*
un GPS	*a satnav*
la 4 G, la 5 G	*4 G, 5 G*
une IRM	*an MRI test*
le JT	*the TV news*
un PC	*a PC*
un PCR	*a PCR test*
un QR code	*a QR code*
un/une SDF (sans domicile fixe)	*a homeless person (of no fixed abode)*
un SMS	*a text message*
le (or la) WiFi	*WiFi*

1.3 **Number**

All nouns must be either singular or plural. Although many nouns are marked for plural in written French, few differ in singular and plural form in spoken French. Usually, number is marked in the determiner in spoken French (*le/la* versus *les*, *ce/cette* versus *ces*, *mon/ma* versus *mes*, etc.).

1.3.1 **Regular plurals**

Regular plurals add -*s*, which is not pronounced, to the singular noun in written French:

une loi	des lois	*law(s)*
un drap	des draps	*sheet(s)*
une voiture	des voitures	*car(s)*
une remarque	des remarques	*remark(s)*
un chat	des chats	*cat(s)*
un enfant	des enfants	*child(ren)*
une maison	des maisons	*house(s)*
un chandail	des chandails	*cardigan(s)*
un éventail	des éventails	*fan(s)*

(For words ending in -*ail* which have an irregular plural, see Section 1.3.6.)

1.3.2 **Plurals of nouns ending in *-s, -x, -z***

With these words, there is no change between singular and plural:

un pois	des pois	*spot(s)*
une croix	des croix	*cross(es)*
un nez	des nez	*nose(s)*
un as	des as	*ace(s)*
un prix	des prix	*price(s)*
un corps	des corps	*body(ies)*
un bras	des bras	*arm(s)*

N.B.:

(a) *un os* 'bone': In the singular, the final 's' is pronounced. In the plural it is not pronounced: *des os* 'bones'.
(b) *un as* 'ace': The 's' is pronounced in both the singular and the plural.

1.3.3 **Plurals of nouns ending in *-eu, -au, -eau***

These nouns form their plural by adding *-x*:

un cheveu	des cheveux	*hair(s)*
un tuyau	des tuyaux	*pipe(s)*
un manteau	des manteaux	*coat(s)*
l'eau	des eaux	*water(s)*

Exceptions:

un bleu	des bleus	*bruise(s)*
un pneu	des pneus	*tyre(s)*
un landau	des landaus	*pram(s)*

1.3.4 **Plurals of nouns ending in *-ou***

Nouns ending in *-ou* form their plural with *-s*:

| un fou | des fous | *madman/men or jester(s)* |
| un trou | des trous | *hole(s)* |

But there are seven words which form their plural with *-x*:

un bijou	des bijoux	*jewel(s)*
un caillou	des cailloux	*stone(s)*
un chou	des choux	*cabbage(s)*
un genou	des genoux	*knee(s)*
un hibou	des hiboux	*owl(s)*
un joujou	des joujoux	*toy(s)*
un pou	des poux	*louse (lice)*

1.3.5 **Plurals of nouns ending in *-al***

Most nouns ending in *-al* form their plural as *-aux*:

un bocal	des bocaux	*jam jar(s)*
un cheval	des chevaux	*horse(s)*
un idéal	des idéaux	*ideal(s)*
un journal	des journaux	*newspaper(s)*
un mal	des maux	*evil(s)*
un terminal	des terminaux	*terminal(s)*
un val	des vaux (limited to poetic language)	*valley(s)*

There are, however, a number of exceptions which form their plural with -*s*:

un bal	des bals	*dance(s)*
un cal	des cals	*callus(es)*
un carnaval	des carnavals	*carnival(s)*
un cérémonial	des cérémonials	*ceremony(ies)*
un chacal	des chacals	*jackal(s)*
un festival	des festivals	*festival(s)*
un récital	des récitals	*recital(s)*
un régal	des régals	*feast(s)*

1.3.6 Irregular plurals for nouns ending in -*ail*

Many nouns ending in -*ail* have a regular plural, e.g. *des details, des chandails, des éventails*, as indicated in Section 1.3.1, but a number of -*ail* nouns also make their plural with -*aux*:

un bail	des baux	*lease(s)*
un corail	des coraux	*coral(s)*
un émail	des émaux	*enamel(s)*
un soupirail	des soupiraux	*(cellar) window(s)*
le travail	les travaux	*work(s)*
un vitrail	des vitraux	*stained glass window(s)*

1.3.7 Nouns which exist only in plural form

des affres (f)	*agonies*
aux alentours (m)	*around/surroundings*
des annales (f)	*annals*
des archives (f)	*archives*
des armoiries (f)	*(coat of) arms*
des arrérages (m)	*arrears*
des arrhes (f)	*a deposit*
des bestiaux (m)	*animals*
des condoléances (f)	*condolences*
des ébats (m)	*frolicking*
des entrailles (f)	*entrails*
des environs (m)	*surroundings*
des fiançailles (f)	*engagement*
des fringues (f) (informal)	*clothes*
des frusques (f) (informal)	*clothes*

des funérailles (f)	*funeral*
des gens	*people (for gender, see Section 1.2.4)*
des honoraires (m)	*fees*
des intempéries (f)	*bad weather*
des mœurs (f)	*customs*
des obsèques (f)	*funeral*
des vêpres (f)	*vespers*
des victuailles (f)	*victuals*

1.3.8 Nouns with irregular plurals

These are most notably:

un os	des os (pronounced as 'eau')	*bone(s)*
un œil	des yeux	*eye(s)*
un ciel	des cieux	*sky(ies)*
un œuf	des œufs (pronounced as 'œu')	*egg(s)*
un bœuf	des bœufs (pronounced as 'bœu')	*bullock(s)*
Monsieur	Messieurs	*Mr; sir(s); gentleman/gentlemen*
Madame	Mesdames	*Mrs; madam; lady/ladies*
Mademoiselle	Mesdemoiselles	*Miss; (young) lady/(young) ladies*
Monseigneur	Messeigneurs	*Your Highness(es); Your Lordship(s); Your Grace(s); Your Eminence(s)*

N.B.: The use of Mademoiselle is now banned from administrative forms, but in addressing a young woman, Mademoiselle continues to be used. However, Madame is an increasingly popular form of address for any young woman.

1.3.9 The plural of compound nouns

Adjective + noun compounds

In adjective + noun compounds (see Section 1.2.11 for the meanings of these compounds), both elements become plural:

un arc-boutant	des arcs-boutants
un bas-côté	des bas-côtés
une basse-cour	des basses-cours
une belle-fille	des belles-filles
un cerf-volant	des cerfs-volants
un coffre-fort	des coffres-forts
un grand-parent	des grands-parents
un rond-point	des ronds-points

N.B.	un grand-père	des grands-pères		
	un grand-oncle	des grands-oncles		
	une grand-mère	des grands-mères	or	des grand-mères
	une grand-tante	des grands-tantes	or	des grand-tantes
	un bonhomme	des bonshommes		
BUT	un bonjour	des bonjours		

Noun + noun compounds

In noun + noun compounds (see Section 1.2.11), the norm is for both nouns to become plural:

un bateau-citerne	des bateaux-citernes
un bateau-mouche	des bateaux-mouches
un camion-citerne	des camions-citernes
un chou-fleur	des choux-fleurs
un homme-grenouille	des hommes-grenouilles
une idée-force	des idées-forces
un mot-clé	des mots-clés
un oiseau-mouche	des oiseaux-mouches
une pause-café	des pauses-cafés
une porte-fenêtre	des portes-fenêtres
une voiture-restaurant	des voitures-restaurants
un wagon-lit	des wagons-lits

Exceptions:

une auto-école	des auto-écoles
un bain-marie	des bains-marie
un hôtel-Dieu	des hôtels-Dieu
un timbre-poste	des timbres-poste

N.B.: Not all noun + noun combinations are hyphenated. If there is no hyphen, the first noun alone will normally be marked for the plural:

empreinte carbone	empreintes carbone	*carbon footprint*
noeud papillon	noeuds papillon	*bow-tie*
maison mère	maisons mère	*headquarters, main branch*
compte épargne	comptes épargne	*savings account*

Adverb + noun compounds

In adverb + noun compounds (see Section 1.2.11), the noun alone becomes plural (although some remain invariable):

une arrière-boutique	des arrière-boutiques
une arrière-pensée	des arrière-pensées
un arrière-plan	des arrière-plans
une contre-offensive	des contre-offensives
une contre-offre	des contre-offres
une demi-bouteille	des demi-bouteilles
un demi-tarif	des demi-tarifs
un haut-parleur	des haut-parleurs
un hors-bord	des hors-bords
une mini-jupe	des mini-jupes
un non-lieu	des non-lieux
un non-paiement	des non-paiements
un sans-abri	des sans-abri

Noun + prepositional phrase compounds

In noun + prepositional phrase compounds (see Section 1.2.11), only the first noun becomes plural:

un aide-de-camp	des aides-de-camp
un arc-en-ciel	des arcs-en-ciel
un chef d'œuvre	des chefs d'œuvre
un coup d'œil	des coups d'œil
un coup de pied	des coups de pied
un croc-en-jambe	des crocs-en-jambe
une langue-de-chat	des langues-de-chat
la main d'œuvre	des mains d'œuvre
un mont-de-piété	des monts-de-piété
une pomme de terre	des pommes de terre
un pot-de-vin	des pots-de-vin

But not all change:

un pot-au-feu	des pot-au-feu
un tête-à-queue	des tête-à-queue
un tête-à-tête	des tête-à-tête

Verb + noun compounds

In verb + noun compounds (see Section 1.2.11), there are three possibilities:

(i) The form remains invariable whether its singular form contains a noun in the singular or plural. This is the usual pattern:

des abat-jour
des essuie-mains
des gratte-ciel
des ouvre-boîtes
des porte-monnaie

(ii) The second word becomes plural, normally -s or -x. This is the case with:

des accroche-cœurs
des tire-bouchons
des couvre-lits

These would appear to have been assimilated to the one-word versions such as

le(s) portemanteau(x)	*coat peg(s)*
le(s) portefeuille(s)	*wallet(s)*

(iii) The first word becomes plural (which is an indication that it is no longer related to any verbal form). This is the case with:

des appuis-tête
des soutiens-gorge

It has to be said that in the area of compound nouns not all 'authorities' agree on the rules and previous attempts to introduce 'logical' rules appear to have added further confusion to an already confused situation. The spelling amendments of 1990 have tried to simplify these rules:

Plural of compound nouns: Nouvelle Orthographe

The amendments to French spelling have recommended that when compound nouns linked with a hyphen are made plural there should be a single rule which is that the second element of the compound noun should alone be marked as plural, usually with an 's'.

Thus:

un pèse-lettre – des pèse-lettres
un cure-dent – des cure-dents
un perce-neige – des perce-neiges
un garde-meuble – des garde-meubles
un abat-jour – des abat-jours
un après-midi – des après-midis
un après-ski – des après-skis

There would be a few exceptions: when the noun element in the compound noun has a capital letter as in *un prie-Dieu*, 'a prie Dieu'; when the noun element has a singular article as in *un trompe-l'oeil* 'a trompe l'oeil painting' and *un trompe-la-mort*, 'death cheater' then there would be no 's' added: *des Prie-Dieu, des trompe-l'oeil* and *des trompe-la-mort*.

These recommendations would apply to almost all the examples 12.3.9. regardless of their internal structure. It remains to be seen to what extent this recommendation is widely adopted.

Clearly, all the compound nouns listed in Section 1.4. (*Nouvelle Orthographe*) as single words would now take a plural 's'.

Verbal phrase compounds

These do not generally have a different plural form:

des manque-à-gagner
des on-dit
des ouï-dire
des m'as-tu-vu
des qu'en dira-t-on
des laisser-passer
des reste-à-charge
des savoir-faire

1.3.10 **Number differences between French and English nouns**

Some nouns which are singular in English are plural in French, while others are plural in English and singular in French. The following are examples which sometimes cause difficulty for English speakers:

English singular	French plural
applause	les applaudissements
darkness	les ténèbres
feedback	des retours
sb's funeral	les funérailles de qn
hair	les cheveux

information	des informations, des renseignements
knowledge	les connaissances
to make progress	faire des progrès
to do research/my research	faire des recherches/mes recherches

English plural	**French singular**
boxers (underwear)	un caleçon
economics	l'économie
grapes (grape = un grain de raisin)	du raisin
linguistics	la linguistique
knickers	une culotte
physics	la physique
pyjamas	un pyjama
shorts	un short
stairs	l'escalier
tights	un collant
trousers	un pantalon
underpants	un slip

Although family names are not pluralised in French (see Section 1.1.4), plurals are normal with dynasties:

Les Rivière nous ont accompagnés tout au long du voyage
The Rivières came with us all the way on our trip

But:

Les Stuarts étaient des héritiers dans la succession au trône
The Stuarts were next in line of succession to the throne

Les Capétiens sont arrivés à la fin de leur lignée
The Capetians came to the end of their line of descent

N.B.: Some mass nouns in French can also be used as count nouns more freely than their English equivalents:

un fruit	*a piece of fruit*
un pain	*a loaf of bread (NOT *a bread)*
un raisin	*a type of grape*

1.4 Nouvelle Orthographe: hyphens, anomalies, and borrowings

Hyphens in compound nouns

As noted above, in most cases, in traditional spelling, compound nouns are written with a hyphen: *basse-cour* 'farmyard', *auto-école* 'driving school'. Compound nouns formed with *de* or *à* are not typically hyphenated: *chef d'oeuvre* 'masterpiece', *brosse à dents* 'toothbrush'.

In many cases, the hyphen indicates a difference in meaning so *une belle-fille* is *a* 'daughter-in-law' or 'stepdaughter' and *une belle fille* is 'a beautiful girl'.

The amendments recommended in 1990 allow a certain number of words to be written as one word with no hyphen. The recommendations apply to two classes of compound nouns (see examples below) but the number is limited and only time will tell whether the usage will spread to other words.

For a fuller explanation and a fuller list of the words affected, consult the original document: *Journal Officiel de la République française Édition des* Documents Administratifs 1990 *No. 100* 6 December 1990 by the *Conseil Supérieur de la langue française* (see Appendix 2).

Compound words with verb + noun or verb + tout

arrachepied (d') as in travailler d'arrachepied	*to work flat out*
boutentrain	*live wire or life and soul (of the party)*
brisetout	*butter-fingers*
clochepied (à)	*as in 'sauter à clochepied' to hop*
couvrepied	*small quilt*
croquemadame	*toasted ham and cheese sandwich with egg*
croquemonsieur	*toasted ham and cheese sandwich*
croquemort	*undertaker*
faitout	*stockpot*
fourretout	*holdall*
mangetout	*mangetout (bean)*
passepartout	*catch-all*
(tour de) passepasse	*sleight of hand*
piquenique	*picnic*
porteclé	*key-ring*
portecrayon	*pencil case*
portemine	*propelling pencil*
portemonnaie	*purse, wallet*
portevoix	*megaphone*
poussepousse	*rickshaw*
risquetout	*daredevil*
tapecul	*boneshaker*
tirebouchon	*corkscrew*
tournedos	*tournedos*
vanupied	*tramp, ragamuffin*

Compound words composed of nouns, prefixes, and adjectives

arcboutant	*buttress*
autostop	*hitch-hiking*
autostoppeur, euse	*hitchiker*
bassecour	*farmyard*
bassetaille	*low-waist*
branlebas	*commotion*
chauvesouris	*bat*
hautparleur	*loudspeaker*
jeanfoutre	*good-for-nothing*
lieudit	*place, locality*
millefeuille	*millefeuille*

millepatte	*centipede*
platebande	*flower-bed*
potpourri	*potpourri*
sagefemme	*midwife*
saufconduit	*safe-passage*
telefilm	*television film*
terreplein	*platform*
vélopousse	*bike rickshaw*
véloski	*skibob*
vélotaxi	*taxi bike*

Anomalies and borrowings

Further spelling amendments are proposed for nouns which have a spelling which is considered anomalous either because the pronunciation has changed or because it wasn't picked up and changed by the Academy in the 18th and 19th centuries, and/or which have been borrowed into French without changes which would make them conform to French rules of orthography. Here are some examples:

An acute accent becomes a grave accent:

céleri	*celery*	becomes	cèleri
crémerie	*cheese shop*	becomes	crèmerie
événement	*event*	becomes	évènement
sécheresse	*drought*	becomes	sècheresse

An acute accent is added to words borrowed into French:

artefact	*artefact*	becomes	artéfact
memorandum	*memorandum*	becomes	mémorandum
diesel	*diesel*	becomes	diésel
revolver	*revolver*	becomes	révolver

A word ending in *-er* borrowed from English may change according to current usage:

If the *-er* ending of the word pronounced like *mer*, then the French word should be written with *-er*:

docker	*docker*	remains	docker
revolver	*revolver*	remains	révolver (note the *é*)
starter	*starter*	remains	starter

But where the *-er* ending is pronounced as if it were *-eur* (*leader, speaker*) or if the *-er* is derived from a verb of the same form (*squat – squatter, kidnap – kidnapper*), then it should be written – *eur*: *leadeur, speakeur, squatteur, kidnappeur*.

Changes are recommended for some words deemed anomalous in their spelling:

oignon	*onion*	becomes	ognon
nénuphar	*water lily*	becomes	nénufar
saccharine	*saccarine*	becomes	saccarine
punch	*punch(drink)*	becomes	ponch

For more resources to practice your French grammar, including practice activities/quizzes for students, further resource links, and an instructor guide, please visit https://routledgelearning.com/frenchgrammarandusage.

2 Determiners

For the purposes of this grammar, the term 'determiner' refers to three classes of items that modify nouns:

Articles: definite, indefinite, and partitive
Demonstrative determiners
Possessive determiners

Each class functions in different (but sometimes overlapping) ways with the others to specify the status of the entity or concept referred to by the noun in the discourse.

Definite articles indicate that the entity/concept referred to by the noun is uniquely identifiable by both speaker and hearer. If you say *Passe-moi la fourchette* 'Pass me the fork', both speaker and hearer know that there is a unique, identifiable 'fork' in the context in which the conversation is taking place.

Indefinite articles are used with count nouns (*bouteille* 'bottle', *billet* 'ticket') and indicate that the entity/concept referred to by the noun is not sufficiently 'known about' or 'specified' to justify the definite article. If you say *Passe-moi une fourchette* 'Pass me a fork', this implies there is no uniquely identifiable 'fork' in the context of the conversation (perhaps because there are several of them).

Partitive articles (*du, de la, des*) serve the same function as indefinite articles, but are used with mass and abstract nouns: *J'ai acheté du lait* 'I bought (some) milk', *Il faut avoir de la patience* 'You must have (some) patience'. The plural partitive article *des* is used with nouns that are mass or abstract by virtue of their meaning, but happen to be grammatically plural: *des tripes* (fpl) 'tripe', *des cheveux* (mpl) 'hair', *des renseignements* (mpl) 'information'.

Demonstratives are the forms *ce/cet, cette, ces* 'this/these, that/those'. They indicate that the noun is seen as 'known about' or 'specified' largely in contrast to another noun: *Passe-moi cette fourchette* 'Pass me that fork (and not some other fork that might also be visible)'.

Possessives are forms like *mon, son, votre* 'my, his/her, your' that indicate that the noun is seen as belonging to someone.

All determiners have singular and plural forms, and in the singular have different forms depending on whether the noun is masculine or feminine.

2.1 Articles

TABLE 2.A Summary table of articles

	Definite	Indefinite	Partitive
masc	le, l' *the*	un *a*	du, de l' *some/no article*
fem	la, l' *the*	une *a*	de la, de l' *some/no article*
plur	les *the*	des	*some/no article*

DOI: 10.4324/9781003373926-2

2.1.1 **Form and pronunciation of the article with adjectives and nouns beginning with a vowel or an *h***

le and *la* are shortened to *l'*, and *du* and *de la* become *de l'* if they immediately precede an adjective or noun beginning with a vowel:

l'univers (m)	*the universe*
l'électricité (f)	*electricity*
de l'acier (m)	*steel*
de l'eau (f)	*water*
l'ancien régime (m)	*the Ancien Regime*

They also behave in the same way when they immediately precede an adjective or noun beginning with a so-called 'silent h' or *h muet*. This is a written *h* which has no counterpart in the spoken language:

l'hiver (m)	*winter*
l'histoire (f)	*history*
de l'héroïsme (m)	*heroism*
de l'herbe (f)	*grass*
l'horrible silence (m)	*the terrible silence*

There is also another set of adjectives and nouns beginning with a written *h* which do have a counterpart in the spoken language. This is misleadingly called an 'aspirate h' or *h aspiré*. It is misleading because there is no 'h' sound in spoken French. Rather, words which begin with an 'aspirate h' in written French also happen to block reduction of the article to *l'* or *de l'* in spoken French:

le hibou (m)	*the owl*
la haine (f)	*hate*
du hachis (m)	*minced beef*
de la honte	*shame*
la haute montagne	*high up in the mountains*

There is no easy way to distinguish adjectives and nouns which begin with a silent *h* from those which begin with an aspirate *h*. Some cases are idiosyncratic. For example, *héros* 'hero' does not allow contraction of the article: *le héros*; but *héroïne* 'heroine or heroin' and *héroïsme* 'heroism' do: *l'héroïne, l'héroïsme*. Many dictionaries indicate an aspirate *h* by putting ['] at the beginning of the phonetic transcription of the word. For example:

hibou ['ibu] (m)	*owl*
histoire [istwar] (f)	*story, history*

The final consonant of *les* and *des* is pronounced [z] when they immediately precede an adjective or a noun beginning with a vowel or a silent *h*:

les [z] enfants	*children*	BUT	les hérissons	*hedgehogs*
des [z] amis	*friends*	BUT	des haricots	*beans*
des [z] héroïnes	*heroines*	BUT	des héros	*heroes*

The final *n* of *un* is pronounced when *un* immediately precedes an adjective or noun beginning with a vowel or silent *h*, but not otherwise:

un [n] hôtel	*a hotel*	BUT	un homard	*a lobster*
un [n] honnête homme	*a decent man*	BUT	un haut fonctionnaire	*a senior civil servant*

N.B.: Verbs beginning with an *h* in the written language also divide into those which require contraction of *je, me, le, la, ne*, etc., and those which do not:

J'habite Londres
I live in London
Je l'héberge
I am letting her (or *him*) *stay with me*

Je hais Londres
I hate London
Je la heurte dans son orgueil
I hurt her pride

2.2 **Typical uses of the definite article**

(a) One use of the definite article indicates that the entity or concept referred to by the noun it accompanies is already known from the context:

Choisissez un fond de teint Veralorel. **Le** fond de teint Veralorel pour une base de maquillage parfaite!
Choose a Veralorel foundation. Veralorel foundation for a flawless base!

Tu as laissé sur la table **le** chargeur que je t'ai prêté hier
You left the charger which I lent you yesterday on the table

Since French and English are similar in this use of definite articles, a fairly reliable guide is: if English uses a definite article, use one in French.

(b) A second 'generic' use is to indicate that the noun refers to a general class of phenomena, a unique phenomenon or an abstract quality:

Les filles et **les** garçons ne fréquentaient pas les mêmes établissements
Girls and boys used not to go to the same schools

Les chercheurs disent que **la** tuberculose réapparaît
Scientists say that tuberculosis is coming back

Le lait est meilleur quand il se boit froid
Milk is better when drunk cold

Elle a toujours lutté contre **la** bêtise
She has always fought stupidity

La peur de prendre l'avion le retient en Grande Bretagne
Fear of flying keeps him in Britain

The generic use of definite articles with count plural nouns (*les filles* 'girls', *les médecins* 'doctors') or with singular mass or abstract nouns (*le lait* 'milk', *la peur* 'fear') contrasts with English, which more often than not uses no article when a general class or an abstract quality are indicated:

Girls and **boys** used not to go to the same schools
Milk is better when drunk cold

The definite article is obligatory in French in these cases.

2.2.1 **Fused forms of the definite article**

Masculine singular and plural definite articles fuse with preceding *de* or *à*:

du (= de + le) pain	au (= à + le) cinéma
de l'effort	à l'école
des (= de + les) épices	aux (= à + les) animaux

Where place names include a masculine singular or plural definite article (*Le Caire* 'Cairo', *Le Havre*, *Les Caraïbes* 'The West Indies') these also fuse with a preceding *de* or *à*:

Il vient **du** Caire
He comes from Cairo

La mer **des** Caraïbes
The Caribbean

Elle travaillera **au** Havre l'année prochaine
She will work in Le Havre next year

Such contraction is only possible with articles, however. It is not possible when *le, la, les* are pronouns (see Section 3.2): *J'ai essayé de le comprendre* 'I tried to understand it' (NOT **J'ai essayé du comprendre*).

An archaic contraction of *en les* to *ès* is still found in the set phrase: *licencié ès lettres* 'Bachelor of Arts'.

2.2.2 Use of the definite article with names of countries, regions, *départements*, and towns

In French the definite article is normally used with the names of countries, regions, and *départements*, whereas in English it is not:

La France est un très beau pays
France is a very beautiful country

Progressivement, **la** Champagne est devenue terre de rencontre et de conflits
Over time, Champagne (a French region) became a land of meetings and confrontations

Le lavage de voitures est interdit dans **le** Calvados en période de sécheresse
Washing your car is forbidden in Calvados (a French département) during a drought

When *en* 'to/in' or *de* 'from' are used with feminine countries or regions (or with masculine countries beginning with a vowel: *en Irak*), the definite article is omitted:

Nous irons en France l'année prochaine
We shall go to France next year

des pommes de Normandie
apples from Normandy

des vacances en Ille-et-Vilaine
holidays in Ille-et-Vilaine

But with masculine countries, regions, and *départements*, the definite article is retained with *à* 'to/in', *dans* 'in', and *de* 'from':

Les hôtels **au** Mexique sont d'un très bon niveau
The hotels in Mexico are of a very high standard

J'ai acheté une maison **dans le** Finistère
I have bought a house in Finistère

des pommes **du** Calvados
apples from Calvados

Towns whose names do not include a definite article (*Lille, Bordeaux, Metz*) require one when
modified:

Visitez Lille!   Visitez **le** vieux Lille!
Visit Lille!   *Visit old Lille!*

Bordeaux est une ville remarquable
Bordeaux is a remarkable city

Le Bordeaux d'aujourd'hui est une ville remarquable
Today's Bordeaux is a remarkable city

The names of large islands are usually accompanied by definite articles: *La Corse* 'Corsica', *La
Sardaigne* 'Sardinia', *La Nouvelle-Zélande* 'New Zealand'. But some small European islands, and
some large islands elsewhere in the world do not have an article *Chypre* 'Cyprus', *Malte* 'Malta',
Jersey, Taiwan, Cuba, Haiti, Java.

(For the gender of countries see Section 1.2.6, and for the use of *en, à, dans* see Section 13.26.1.)

2.2.3 **Use of the definite article with names of languages**

The names of languages in English start with a capital letter and have no article. The names of
languages in French start with a small letter, normally have a definite article, and are masculine
in gender:

C'est une école où les enfants apprennent **le** français, l'anglais et l'arabe
It's a school where the children learn French, English and Arabic

Le grec possède un alphabet tout à fait différent du nôtre
Greek has an alphabet which is quite different from our own

In the expressions *parler français, parler allemand*, etc., the name of the language functions more
like an adverbial than a noun, so no article is used. But note the following contrast:

Je parle français/Je parle souvent **le** français/Je parle bien **le** français
I speak French/I often speak French/I speak French well

When adverbs such as *souvent, bien* are present, *français* becomes a noun again, requiring the
definite article.

2.2.4 **Use of the definite article with seasons**

Seasons in French are usually accompanied by a definite article, except when they are preceded by *en*:

L'hiver est une saison de repos pour nous
Winter is a restful season for us

L'été s'accompagne maintenant de graves sécheresses, que l'automne ne réussit pas à compenser
Summer now comes with serious droughts, which autumn cannot make up for

Tout se réveille **au** printemps
Everything awakes in spring

BUT

en hiver	*in winter*
en été	*in summer*
en automne	*in autumn*

N.B.: 'in spring' is *'au printemps'*

(See also Section 13.26.1.)

2.2.5 Use of the definite article with titles

Titles in French prefaced by *Monsieur* or *Madame* include the definite article:

Monsieur **le** Maire	*Mr Mayor*
Madame **le/la** Maire	*Madam Mayor*
Monsieur **le** Président-Directeur-Général	*Mr Chairman*

Where women are the holders of the post in question, the feminine article is also used: *Madame la Maire, Madame la Ministre, Madame la Président-Directeur-Général* (see Section 1.2.2). Where women are the holders of the post in question, the feminine article can be used even if the post title is masculine, but, reflecting societal change, it is increasingly feminised: *Madame la Maire, Madame la Ministre, Madame la Présidente-Directrice-Générale*.

Such forms of address as: *Monsieur le Directeur des Achats* 'Mr Purchasing Director', *Madame le Directeur du Personnel* 'Madam Personnel Director' used to be frequent in French in writing (e.g. letters) or in very formal speeches, and can still be found today, but are almost unheard of in English.

The definite article is similarly present in French in greetings or expressions of encouragement like:

Salut **les** mecs!	*Hi, guys!*
Allez **les** bleus!	*Come on, you blues!*
Au lit, **les** enfants!	*Off to bed, kids!*

With kings and queens, however, French leaves out an article with numbers where English puts one in:

François I (François premier)	*François **the** first*
Henri III (Henri trois)	*Henry **the** third*
Elizabeth I (Elizabeth première)	*Elizabeth **the** first*
Elizabeth II (Elizabeth deux)	*Elizabeth **the** second*
Charles III (Charles trois)	*Charles **the** third*

(See also Section 6.4.2.)

2.2.6 Use of the definite article with superlatives

In superlatives involving adjectives which follow the noun (see Section 4.12.2), it is compulsory to repeat the definite article, which then agrees with the noun:

Le moment **le** plus intense de ma vie
The most exciting moment of my life

Les virages **les** plus dangereux de la région
The most dangerous bends in the region

2.2.7 Use of the definite article with quantities

Where English uses 'so much **a** pound', French refers to *tant* **la** *livre* / **le** *kilo*, etc.:

Avant, ils les vendaient à 5,50 € **le** kilo
Before they used to sell them for 5.50 euros a kilo

Vous en voulez combien, si je vous les propose à 1,30 € **les** 100 grammes?
How many would you like if I suggest 1.30 euros for 100 grammes?

Ce sont des verres antiques vendus 500 € **la** pièce (*or* 500 € pièce)
These are antique glasses which sell for 500 euros each

2.2.8 Use of the definite article with parts of the body

(a) In simple descriptions of body parts, French uses a definite article where English uses a possessive determiner (e.g. *his, my, their*):

Il a **les** yeux bleus	*His eyes are blue*
Elle a **les** cheveux coupés court	*She has her hair cut short*

(b) When people activate parts of their own bodies, French also uses a definite article with the body part:

Il a plissé **les** yeux	*He screwed up his eyes*
Elle a agité **le** bras	*She waved*
J'ai baissé **la** tête en y entrant	*I lowered my head as I went in*
Elle a hoché / secoué **la** tête	*She nodded/shook her head*

(c) When people do things which affect their own bodies, or those of others, the usual construction is a definite article in front of the body part, and a reflexive or indirect object pronoun:

Je **me** suis fracturé **la** jambe	*I broke my leg*
Elle **s**'est fait couper **les** cheveux	*She had her hair cut*
Je **lui** serre **la** main	*I shake his hand*
On **lui** a coupé la tête	*They cut his head off*
Elle **lui** essuie **les** yeux avec un mouchoir	*She wipes his eyes with a handkerchief*

These constructions are also possible with a possessive determiner, as in English, however:

Je prends **sa** main	*I take her hand*
Elle caresse **mes** cheveux	*She strokes my hair*
J'appuie **mes** deux mains sur sa poitrine	*I press with both my hands on his chest*

(d) When body parts are the subject of a sentence, they usually have a possessive determiner, as in English, rather than a definite article:

Mon cœur s'est arrêté une fraction de seconde	*My heart stopped for an instant*
Ma tête me fait mal	*My head hurts*
Ses paupières se sont abaissées	*His eyelids lowered*
Leurs regards se sont croisés	*Their eyes met*

(e) When descriptions of parts of the body or items of clothing are used adverbially, they are accompanied by the definite article:

l'homme **au** nez retroussé	*the man with the turned-up nose*
le comédien **au** chapeau de paille	*the actor in the straw hat*
Il parlait, **le** sourire aux lèvres	*He spoke, with a smile*
Elle est partie, **les** mains dans **les** poches	*She left with her hands in her pockets*
Il s'est agenouillé, **le** chapeau à la main	*He knelt down with his hat in his hands*
Il a avoué son crime, **les** yeux baissés	*He confessed his crime, looking down*

2.2.9 Singular or plural when a number of individuals have one item each

When reference is made to one body part, one item of clothing, or one more general personal attribute, but two or more people are involved, the entity is usually referred to in the singular:

Nous nous sommes tous **les** deux cassés **le bras**
We both broke our arms

Ils ont levé **la main droite**
They raised their right hands

Les postulants sont priés d'inscrire **leur nom de famille** à l'endroit prévu
Candidates are requested to write their surnames in the space provided

Ils ont tous accroché **leur manteau** dans l'entrée
They all hung their coats up in the entrance hall

Les jumeaux ont vécu **leur vie** d'une manière indépendante
The twins lived their lives independently

2.2.10 Use of the definite article to indicate a habitual action

Where English uses 'on + … day(s)' to indicate a habitual action e.g. 'On Monday(s) I go to the market', French uses the definite article: *Je vais faire mon marché le lundi:*

Nous allons au cinéma **le** vendredi soir
We go to the cinema on Friday evenings

Le cours d'histoire a lieu **le** mercredi
The history lecture is on Wednesdays

Ils viennent ramasser les poubelles **le** lundi et **le** jeudi
They come to empty the dustbins on Mondays and Thursdays

2.2.11 Repetition of the definite article

In French the article usually has to be repeated with each noun, whereas in English one use at the beginning of a 'list' is enough:

Tu me rapporteras **le** panier, **la** bouteille et **les** caramels
Bring back to me the basket, bottle and toffees

2.3 **Typical uses of the indefinite article**

(a) One use of the indefinite article is to introduce a new, countable, concrete noun (*maison, tableau, livre, voiture*, etc.) into the discourse where the entity referred to is not 'known about' or 'specified' sufficiently to justify the use of the definite article:

Je me suis trouvé **une** belle maison en Ecosse
I have found myself a lovely house in Scotland

Voulez-vous voir **un** Picasso?
Do you want to see a Picasso?

(b) Another is to indicate that the noun describes a general class of countable, concrete entities ('generic' reference):

Normalement **une** voiture a quatre roues et **une** moto en a deux
Normally a car has four wheels and a motorbike two

C'est une erreur caractéristique d'**un** enfant en première année de violon
That's an example of a typical error made by a child in his or her first year of playing the violin

In this 'generic' use, the indefinite article overlaps with and is usually interchangeable with a plural definite article (see Section 2.2(b)):

Normalement **les** voitures ont quatre roues et **les** motos en ont deux
Il s'agit là d'une erreur caractéristique **des** enfants en première année de violon (*de* + definite article *les*)

(c) The third use is with abstract nouns (*courage, beauté, réalisme, importance*, etc.). Abstract nouns are normally accompanied by the definite article (see Section 1.1.1). But when they are modified by an adjective they take an indefinite article. Compare:

Il admire **le** courage
He admires courage

Il a fait preuve d'**un** courage peu ordinaire
He showed extraordinary courage

La beauté du paysage nous éblouissait
The beauty of the countryside dazzled us

Le paysage était d'**une** beauté éblouissante
The countryside was astonishingly beautiful

2.3.1 **The plural indefinite article** *des*

The plural indefinite article *des* refers to an unspecified quantity of entities described by a plural count noun. In English the article is most frequently omitted:

Je lui ai offert **des** roses
I gave her roses

Les places avaient déjà été réservées par **des** Américains
The seats had already been reserved by Americans

Vous me posez **des** questions impossibles
You ask me impossible questions

N.B.: An error often made by English speakers is to omit the article; plural indefinite *des* cannot be omitted in French: NOT **Je lui ai offert roses*.

2.3.2 Omission of plural indefinite *des* after the preposition *de*

When the plural indefinite article is preceded by the preposition *de*, it is omitted in French. Compare:

Elle a été accusée **d'un** meurtre particulièrement horrible
She was accused of a particularly nasty murder

Elle a été accusée **de** meurtres particulièrement horribles
(être accusé de + des meurtres horribles)
She was accused of particularly nasty murders

Avec l'aide **d'une** amie, elle a fini son projet
With the help of a friend, she finished her project

Avec l'aide **d'amies**, elle a fini son projet
(avec l'aide de + des amies)
With the help of friends, she finished her project

Omission of plural indefinite article *des* only occurs after the preposition *de*. With other prepositions, it is not omitted:

Elle est sortie **avec des** amies
She went out with friends

Des attaques violentes **contre des** policiers
Violent attacks on policemen

Because plural indefinite *des* is omitted after the preposition *de*, this means that it is omitted when it is the complement of a number of verbs which are always followed by the preposition *de* (see Section 8.4):

Il a déjeuné **de** fruits
His lunch consisted of fruit
(*versus* Il a mangé **des** fruits)

Elle parlait **de** choses oubliées depuis longtemps
She spoke of things long since forgotten
(*versus* Elle décrivait **des** choses oubliées depuis longtemps)

Plural indefinite *des* is also omitted after many quantifiers (see Section 6.9) or quantifier-like expressions which incorporate the preposition *de*:

Il y a un bon nombre **de** participants au tournoi
There are a good many participants at the tournament

Un kilo **de** cerises, s'il vous plaît
A kilo of cherries, please

Beaucoup **de** personnes ont déjà remarqué ton absence
Many people have already noticed your absence

J'ai déjà entendu assez **d'excuses** de ta part; je n'en accepterai plus
I have heard enough excuses from you; I won't accept any more

Où as-tu mis la boîte **de** sardines?
Where did you put the tin of sardines?

Exception: *bien des* 'many':

Bien **des** personnes ont déjà remarqué ton absence
Many people have already noticed your absence

2.3.3 Comparing the use of plural indefinite article *des* with preposition *de* + definite article *les*

Compare the use of the plural indefinite article and the plural definite article in similar contexts:

Elle mangeait **des coquillages**
She was eating shellfish

Elle mangeait **les coquillages qu'elle avait achetés au marché**
She was eating the shellfish she had bought in the market

When the highlighted expressions follow the preposition *de*, *des* is deleted (Section 2.3.2), but *de* + *les* becomes *des* (Section 2.2.1):

Elle dînait souvent *de* coquillages
She often dined on shellfish

Elle dînait *des* coquillages qu'elle avait achetés au marché
She dined on the shellfish which she had bought in the market

Thus *des* can be either a plural indefinite article corresponding to English 'some' or no article or a plural definite article fused with the preposition *de*.

Note the following contrasts with quantifiers:

Beaucoup **de** personnes (indefinite) trouvent cela difficile
Many people find that difficult

Beaucoup **des** personnes (definite) à qui nous avons parlé (specification) trouvent cela difficile
Many of the people to whom we spoke find that difficult

Un kilo **de** cerises, s'il vous plaît
A kilo of cherries, please

Un kilo **des** (definite) cerises espagnoles (specification), s'il vous plaît
A kilo of the Spanish cherries, please

2.3.4 *d'autres* and *des autres*

A contrast which English speakers often find difficult is between *d'autres* and *des autres*. *d'autres* 'other(s)' is an indefinite expression which is not accompanied by the plural indefinite article *des*:

Dans son article, elle a présenté **d'autres** idées (normally NOT **des autres idées* although this may be heard in informal French)
In her article, she presented other ideas

D'autres auraient agi différemment (normally NOT *des autres* although this may be heard in informal French)
Others would have acted differently

Si tu n'aimes pas les bleus, on peut continuer à chercher. J'en ai vu **d'autres** (NOT *des autres*)
If you don't like the blue ones, we can keep looking. I saw some others

des autres is only used where *des* is the fused form of preposition *de* and the definite article *les* of *les autres* 'the others':

Elle parlait **des** autres projets qu'elle dirige
She spoke of the other projects she directs

Je ne me rappelle rien **des** autres jours de ce mois
I remember nothing of the other days of that month

2.3.5 **The use of *de* when an adjective precedes the noun**

When an adjective precedes the noun, it is customary, at least in formal French, to use *de* and not *des*:

Je lui ai offert **de** jolies roses
I gave her pretty roses

De gros miroirs comme ça, on n'en voit plus beaucoup
You don't see many large mirrors like that any more

N.B.: This does not apply when the adjective and the noun are joined in a compound noun or something which is seen as a single unit: *des jeunes gens, des jeunes filles, des petits pois, des petites annonces, des grands magasins, des grands jours.*

2.4 **The partitive article: *du, de l', de la, des***

The partitive article *du, de l', de la, des* is used with mass nouns in French where English uses 'some' or no article at all:

Il charriait **du** bois pour son voisin
He carted wood about for his neighbour

Vous auriez dû acheter **du** lait en même temps
You ought to have bought some milk at the same time

Avec **de** l'ail ça aurait encore meilleur goût!
It would taste even better with garlic!

Il me manque **de** l'argent
I'm lacking funds

The partitive article is also used with abstract nouns such as *courage, beauté, patience, silence* when these qualities are attributed to people or things:

Il faut avoir **de la** patience avec les enfants
You must be patient with children

Elle a **de l'**intelligence à revendre
She is really intelligent

Vos enfants ont **de la** malice
Your children are mischievous

When a partitive article follows the preposition *de* it is deleted, just as plural indefinite *des* is deleted (see Section 2.3.2):

beaucoup **de** bois	*a lot of wood*
une bouteille **de** lait	*a bottle of milk*
une tête **d'**ail	*a bulb of garlic*
J'ai besoin **d'**argent	*I need money*

2.4.1 Use of *faire* + partitive: *faire du/de la*

Many constructions exist with *faire* + noun, introduced by the partitive:

Faire du sport	*To take part in sport*
Faire du basket	*To play basketball*
Faire du piano	*To play the piano*
Faire de la politique	*To go in for politics*
Faire du bien (à quelqu'un)	*To do good (to somebody)*
Faire du mal (à quelqu'un)	*To do harm (to somebody)*

2.5 Use of indefinite and partitive articles after the negative forms *ne ... pas, ne ... jamais, ne ... plus,* and *ne... guère*

After *ne ... pas, ne ... jamais, ne ... plus,* and *ne ... guère,* any indefinite article (*un, une, des*) or partitive article (*du, de l', de la, des*) accompanying a direct object normally becomes *de*:

Elle n'a pas écrit **de** lettre
She didn't write a letter

Nous ne vendons pas **de** chaussettes
We don't sell socks

Elle ne porte jamais **de** casque
She never wears a helmet

Pourquoi ne peut-on jamais acheter **de** vêtements d'hiver au printemps?
Why can you never buy winter clothes in spring?

Je n'ai plus **de** crayon
I don't have a pencil any more

Il n'a plus **de** médicaments
He doesn't have any more medication

Il n'y a guère **de** visiteurs
There are hardly any visitors

There are three cases where this does not apply:

(a) when a contrast is made between a negative and a positive direct object:

Je ne veux pas **des** chaussettes mais **des** chaussures
I don't want socks, but shoes

Je ne cherche pas **un** cours de grammaire mais **un** cours d'histoire
I am not looking for a grammar class but a history class

(b) after the verb *être:*

Ce n'est pas **un** oiseau
It isn't a bird

(c) when the meaning is 'not a (single) one' rather than 'not a':

On n'entendait pas **un** bruit dehors
We couldn't hear a single noise outside

2.6 Omission of the article

There are a number of cases where no article is used in French.

2.6.1 Omission of the article in compound nouns linked by *à*

In compound nouns linked by *à*, there is usually no article in front of the second noun:

une brosse à dents	*a toothbrush*
un couteau à pain	*a bread knife*
une corbeille à papiers	*a waste-paper basket*
une cuiller à café	*a tea (coffee) spoon*
une planche à roulettes	*a skateboard*
une planche à voile	*a sailboard*
une tasse à café	*a coffee cup*
une tasse à thé	*a tea cup*
un verre à vin	*a wine glass*
un verre à pied	*a stemmed glass*

2.6.2 Omission of the article in noun constructions linked by *de*

The article is frequently omitted before the second noun in noun + noun constructions linked by *de,* where the second noun functions like an adjective (and is often translated into English as an adjective):

une ambassade de France	*a French embassy*
une carte de visite	*a visiting card*
une carte de France	*a map of France*
un billet de bus	*a bus ticket*
un arrêt de bus	*a bus stop*
un tableau d'affichage	*a notice board*
une question d'argent	*a question of money*
une affaire de cœur	*a matter of the heart*
un problème de liquidité	*a cash-flow problem*

une salle de classe	*a classroom*
une salle de bains	*a bathroom*
une agence de voyages	*a travel agent/agency*
un verre de vin	*a glass of wine*
une tasse de thé	*a cup of tea*
une tasse de café	*a cup of coffee*

But note that when the second noun is modified (e.g. by an adjective or a clause) it becomes definite, and a definite article appears (see Section 2.3.3):

une carte **de la** France métropolitaine
a map of mainland France

Il va être question **de** l'argent que je t'ai prêté
There'll be a discussion about the money I lent you

un arrêt **du** bus no 25
a stop for the number 25 bus

2.6.3 Omission of the article in participle + noun constructions linked by *de*

The article is omitted after *de* in participle + noun constructions where the participle functions as an adjective

couvert de boue	*covered with mud*
rempli d'eau	*full of water*
dépourvu de sens	*lacking any meaning*
comblé de bonheur	*overwhelmed with happiness*
entouré d'imbéciles	*surrounded by idiots*

2.6.4 Omission of the article after *sans, avec, en, sur, sous, par, ni… ni*

The article is frequently omitted when a noun alone follows *sans, avec, en, sur, sous, par,* or two nouns alone appear in the expression *ni … ni*:

sans arrêt	*continuously*
sans difficulté	*without difficulty*
sans délai	*without delay*
sans sucre	*without sugar*
sans manche	*with no handle*
avec patience	*with patience*
avec difficulté	*with difficulty*
en colère	*angry*
en guerre	*at war*
en réparation	*being repaired*
en théorie	*in theory*
en marbre	*in marble*
sur commande	*by order*
sous verre	*under glass*
sous pression	*under pressure*
deux fois par semaine	*twice a week*
par pitié	*out of pity*

| Il ne portait ni veste | *He was wearing neither a jacket* |
| ni cravate | *nor a tie* |

(For *ne … ni … ni* see Section 16.14.)

But if the noun is modified (e.g. by an adjective) the article is not omitted:

sans **la** moindre difficulté	*without the least difficulty*
sans même **le** plus petit retard	*without even the slightest delay*
avec **une** patience admirable	*with admirable patience*
sous **la** pression du gouvernement	*under pressure from the government*

N.B.: *en* cannot normally co-occur with an article. When an article is required, the preposition changes to *dans*:

en théorie	BUT	dans la théorie d'Einstein
in theory		*in Einstein's theory*
en pratique	BUT	dans la pratique
in practice		*in practice*

2.6.5 **Omission of the article in set phrases and verbal constructions**

avoir besoin (de)	*to need*
avoir envie (de)	*to desire*
avoir peur (de)	*to be afraid*
avoir raison	*to be right*
chercher noise (à)	*to try and pick a quarrel (with)*
demander pardon (à)	*to ask for forgiveness*
donner congé (à)	*to sack*
faire attention (à)	*to pay attention*
garder rancune (à)	*to bear a grudge (against)*
prendre fait et cause (pour)	*to defend*
rendre justice (à)	*to be fair (to)*
rendre service (à)	*to help*
tenir parole	*to keep one's word*

2.6.6 **Omission of the article with nouns in apposition**

When proper nouns are juxtaposed with common nouns which identify them, the common nouns are said to be in apposition. In such cases the article is usually omitted:

Versailles, palais de Louis XIV et son entourage
Versailles, the palace of Louis XIV and his court

Victor Lagrange, concierge, cherchait un nouveau poste
Victor Lagrange, caretaker, was looking for a new job

Léa, fille de dentiste, a annoncé son mariage avec Damien, fils de médecin
Léa, a dentist's daughter, has announced her marriage to Damien, a doctor's son

Le Bergerac, vin de qualité, est vendu dans toute l'Europe
Bergerac, a quality wine, is sold throughout Europe

But when the common noun is modified, for example by an adjective, the article is not omitted:

Léa, **la** fille **aînée** du dentiste, …
Versailles, **le célèbre** palais de Louis XIV …

2.6.7 **Omission of the article with nouns following the verbs *être*, *demeurer, devenir, élire, nommer, rester***

When a noun alone follows the verbs *être* be' *demeurer* 'stay', *devenir* 'become', *élire* 'elect', *nommer* 'appoint', *rester* 'stay', the article is omitted:

Sa mère est ingénieur(e)	*Her mother is an engineer*
Il est devenu architecte très tôt	*He became an architect early on*
Elle est restée maire de la commune	*She remained mayor of the village*
On l'a élu président	*He was elected president*
Pierre a été nommé Directeur Commercial	*Pierre was appointed Business Director*

But when the noun is modified, for example by an adjective, the article is not omitted:

Depuis, il est devenu un architecte innovateur
Since then, he has become an innovatory architect

Pierre a été nommé le premier Directeur Commercial
Pierre was appointed as the first Business Director

2.6.8 **Omission of the article in lists**

In lists of nouns the article is frequently omitted:

Hommes, femmes et enfants sont tous invités à la fête
Men, women and children are all invited to the party

J'ai acheté pommes de terre, tomates, courgettes, prunes et navets chez le même marchand de primeurs
I bought potatoes, tomatoes, courgettes, plums and turnips at the same greengrocer's

N.B.: Either all the articles are omitted (as in these examples) or they are all included (see Section 2.2.11).

2.6.9 **Omission of the article with days and months**

The nouns referring to days and months do not have an article when they are used without modification:

Venez mardi	Les derniers jours de décembre
Come on Tuesday	*The final days of December*

However, when modified, for example by a date or a relative clause, a definite article is required:

Venez **le** mardi 17
Come on Tuesday 17th

Les derniers jours **du** décembre qui vient de se terminer
The final days of last December

2.7 **Demonstrative determiners**

TABLE 2.B Summary table of demonstrative determiners

		Proximate	Non-proximate
masc	ce, cet *this, that*	ce, cet ... ci *this... (here)*	ce, cet ... là *that... (there)*
fem	cette *this, that*	cette ... ci *this... (here)*	cette ... là *that... (there)*
plur	ces *these, those*	ces ... ci *these... (here)*	ces ... là *those... (there)*

N.B.: Masculine *cet* appears only when the demonstrative determiner immediately precedes a noun or adjective beginning with a vowel or a 'silent h' (*h muet*) (see Section 2.1.1):

cet enfant	*this child*
cet ancien marin	*that ex-sailor*
cet héroïsme	*that heroism*

2.7.1 **Typical use of demonstrative determiners**

Demonstrative determiners imply a contrast between the entity referred to by the noun they accompany and other entities of a similar type:

Cette voiture a fait le tour du monde
This car has been around the world

(The car referred to is implicitly contrasted with other cars which haven't been around the world.)

A **cet** instant, la porte s'est brusquement refermée derrière eux
At that moment the door suddenly closed behind them

(The moment referred to is implicitly contrasted with other moments when the door didn't close.)

Note that *ce, cet/cette* translate both 'this' and 'that', *ces* translates both 'these' and 'those'. The form *-ci* can be added to the noun accompanied by *ce*, etc., to stress proximity in space or time. Proximity in English is part of the meaning of 'this', but it can also be emphasized by stressing 'this' or sometimes by adding 'here' after the noun:

Cette voiture-**ci** a fait le tour du monde
THIS car/This car here has been around the world

Ce mois-**ci** je ne peux pas vous payer
THIS month I can't pay you

The form *-là* can be added to the noun accompanied by *ce*, etc., to stress non-proximity in space or time. Non-proximity in English is part of the meaning of 'that', but it can also be emphasized by stressing 'that' or sometimes by adding 'there' after the noun:

Cette année-**là** nous ne sommes pas allés à la mer
THAT year we did not go to the sea

Ce matin-**là**, je m'étais réveillé très tard
THAT morning I had woken up very late

-ci and *-là* are necessary if a comparison is made between 'this X' and 'that X':

Est-ce que vous préférez **ce** pull-**ci** ou **ce** pull-**là**?
Do you prefer this pullover or that pullover?

2.8 **Possessive determiners**

TABLE 2.C Summary table of possessive determiners

First person	masc	mon	*my*	notre	*our*
	fem	ma	*my*		
	plur	mes	*my*	nos	*our*
Second person	masc	ton	*your*	votre	*your*
	fem	ta	*your*		
	plur	tes	*your*	vos	*your*
Third person	masc	son	*his, her, its*	leur	*their*
	fem	sa	*his, her, its*		
	plur	ses	*his, her, its*	leurs	*their*

Possessive determiners agree in gender and number with the nouns they precede:

Elle a levé **son** verre	*She raised her (or his) glass*
Il a rempli **sa** tasse	*He filled his (or her) cup*
Il a cassé **ses** lunettes	*He broke his (or her) glasses*

The feminine singular forms *ma, ta, sa* become *mon, ton, son* when they immediately precede a noun or adjective beginning with a vowel or 'silent h' (h *muet*) (see Section 2.1.1):

ma classe	*my class*	BUT	**mon** école	*my school*
sa permission	*her permission*	BUT	**son** approbation	*her approval*
ta hardiesse	*your audacity*	BUT	**ton** hésitation	*your hesitation*

The possessive determiners *votre* and *vos* can be used to indicate possession in the second person plural:

Pour rejoindre la visioconférence, il faut connaître **votre** identifiant et **votre** mot de passe
To access the videoconference you need to know your login and password

They can be used to refer to more than one possessor:

Mesdames, messieurs **votre** table est prête
Ladies and gentlemen, your table is ready

and as a polite form:

Suivez-moi, Madame, **votre** table est prête
Follow me, Madam, your table is ready

(For the use of the definite article rather than possessive determiners with parts of the body, see Section 2.2.8.)

(For the use of a singular determiner when a single item is possessed by more than one person, see Section 2.2.9.)

FREE

INSTRUCTOR & STUDENT RESOURCES

For more resources to practice your French grammar, including practice activities/quizzes for students, further resource links, and an instructor guide, please visit https://routledgelearning.com/frenchgrammarandusage.

3 Pronouns

Personal pronouns are forms that are used in place of a noun phrase when that phrase is already known from the situation, linguistic, or contextual. Personal pronouns have different (but overlapping) forms depending on whether they are subjects, direct objects, indirect objects, or objects of a preposition. They agree in person and number with the noun phrase for which they stand.

Personal pronouns take their name from the fact that they can be classified as first person (*je, me, moi, nous*), second person (*tu, te, toi, vous*), or third person (*il, elle, lui, les; ils, leur, eux, elles*). They do not necessarily refer to people; e.g. *elle* is a personal pronoun, but it refers to the inanimate *émission* in: *elle est intéressante, cette émission* 'That programme's interesting'.

Personal pronouns contrast with impersonal pronouns, which do not refer to other noun phrases. An impersonal pronoun (usually in subject position) does not stand for any person, place, thing, idea, etc. *il, ce, cela, ça* can be impersonal pronouns in French: e.g. *Il pleut* 'It's raining'; *Il est tard* 'It's late'; *Ça me fait peur d'y aller la nuit* 'It scares me to go there at night'.

Neutral pronouns (*ce, cela, ça*) normally refer to events, actions, states, or general classes of people or things, e.g. *Vous viendrez dîner ce soir. C'est prévu.* 'Come to dinner this evening. It's all taken care of' (C' refers to the event 'Come to dinner').

Stressed pronouns (*moi, toi, lui, elle, soi, nous, vous, eux, elles*) are used for emphasis and also appear after prepositions.

Demonstrative pronouns (*celui, celle, ceux*, and *celles*, which can have the suffix *-ci* or *-là*) are used where English uses 'the one', i.e. to specify noun phrases in a way which distinguishes one from another. They can refer to people or things.

Possessive pronouns (*le(s)mien(s) le(s) tien(s), le(s) sien(s), le(s) nôtre(s), le(s) vôtre(s)*, and *le(s) leur(s)*) are used where English uses 'mine', 'hers', 'yours', etc.

Y and *En*: These pronouns stand in for prepositional phrases which usually contain a noun phrase introduced, respectively, by *à* (also *dans, sur*, etc.) and *de*: *Il va à Paris-Il y va* and *Il vient de Paris-Il en vient*. However, these prepositional phrases can play a variety of roles: adverbial as in these examples (leading to the name adverbial pronouns often used for these pronouns), indirect object as in *Il parle de ses amis-Il en parle* or direct object with a partitive article *Il achète du pain-Il en achète*.

Over the last 20 years there has been growing interest in finding a way to write French which eliminates gender differences. This is problematic in a language which recognises grammatical gender in nouns and pronouns, and requires agreements with articles, adjective, and verbal forms. The proponents of what is now known as inclusive writing have suggested the use of gender neutral pronouns, notably *'iel'* as a third-person singular pronoun and the use of what is variously called a *'point médian'* or *'point milieu'* to allow more than one agreement to be signalled as in *acteur.rice.s* or *intellectuel.le.s*. *Ceux-elles* has also been proposed, although usage seems to prefer *celles et ceux*.

In 2021 the dictionary makers at Le Robert included the *'iel'* pronoun in the online version of their dictionary as a form which was now being used in some contexts. However, in a Bulletin Officiel of May 2021 the Ministère de l'Éducation Nationale forbade the use of such forms in administration

DOI: 10.4324/9781003373926-3

and in education and the Académie française produced a *Lettre Ouverte* condemning their use. Members of LGBTQ+ communities have nevertheless adopted *iel*, while others may use the pronoun out of solidarity.

Whilst these specific forms have not gained widespread use, there have been moves to recommend uses of language which avoid gender stereotyping. Part of this is the feminisation of job titles (see Section 1.2.2) which is now widely accepted and another part is learning to use language in a way which avoids sexist bias. See, for example, the *Guide pratique pour une communication publique sans stéréotype de sexe* published by the *Haut Conseil à l'égalité entre les femmes et les hommes* in 2015 or the *Guide Egalité-femmes-hommes-Mon entreprise s'engage* pdf Gouv.fr 2017 and the *Usage d'un langage neutre du point de vue du genre* pdf European Parliament 2018.

3.1 **Subject pronouns**

TABLE 3.A Summary table of subject pronouns

Person	Singular		Plural	
First person	je	*I*	nous	*we*
Second person	tu	*you*	vous	*you* (plural, polite)
Third person				
Masculine	il	*he, it*	ils	*they*
Feminine	elle	*she, it*	elles	*they*
Non-specific	on	*one, we, people, they*		
Neutral	ce, cela, ça	*it, that*		
Impersonal	il, ce, cela, ça	*it, that, there*		

Those who wish to see inclusive writing have proposed the gender neutral third-person singular subject pronoun '*iel*' which could be used instead of '*il*' and '*elle*'. The third-person plural would be '*iels*' to be used instead of '*ils*' and '*elles*' (see Section 3.1.7).

3.1.1 Position of subject pronouns

In declarative sentences, subject pronouns normally appear immediately before the verb which carries the tense:

Nous voulons voir la responsable
We want to see the woman in charge

Tu comprends vite
You catch on quickly

Elle a servi le vin chambré
She served the wine at room temperature

Maintenant, **elle** fait des visioconférences plusieurs fois par mois
Now she has conference calls several times a month

They can only be separated from this verb by the *ne* of negation and by other pre-verbal pronouns:

Elle **ne** prend pas de café
She's not having any coffee or she doesn't drink coffee

Elle **ne** prend plus de café
She no longer drinks coffee

Tu **l'**as mangé
You ate it

Vous **ne le** ferez pas
You won't do it

Unlike in English, subject pronouns cannot normally be separated from the verb by adverbials or parenthetical expressions:

NOT	*Je souvent dîne avec Laura *I often dine with Laura*
NOT	*Il, paraît-il, ne prend plus de café *He, it seems, no longer drinks coffee*

versus the grammatical *Je dîne souvent avec Laura, Il ne prend plus de café, paraît-il*.

In yes/no questions involving inversion (see Section 14.2.3), subject pronouns appear immediately after the verb which carries the tense:

Sait-**il** nager?	*Can he swim?*
Est-**elle** arrivée?	*Has she arrived?*
Ont-**ils** mangé?	*Have they eaten?*

(For the formation of yes/no questions, see Section 14.2.)

When subject pronouns follow the verb in this way nothing else can intervene:

Ne le croyez-**vous** pas?	*Don't you believe it?*
Ne le lui avez-**vous** pas donné?	*Didn't you give it to him?*
Dînent-**ils** souvent ensemble?	*Do they often dine together?*

3.1.2 The use of *vous* and *tu*

vous can have two functions: to address more than one person, and as a polite form of address to one person when there is a certain 'social distance' between the speaker and the addressee. *tu* is used only to address one person when there is no social distance between speaker and addressee.

In its plural use, *vous* refers simply to more than one addressee, whether social intimates or not:

Vous voulez aller au match dimanche?
Do you want to go to the match this Sunday?
(e.g. several friends discussing where to go)

Vous devez scanner le code-barres
You must scan the barcode
(e.g. a trainer talking to trainees)

When one person is being addressed it is difficult to give hard and fast rules about when to use *tu* and when to use the polite *vous*. Generally, one can say that the non-native speaker would be well advised to use *vous* from the outset and to allow the native speaker to take the initiative about any change to *tu*. Table 3B illustrates some uses of *tu* and polite *vous*, but it is not possible to give an exhaustive list of such usage. Individual speakers may vary in their own preferences, and usage may vary regionally.

TABLE 3.B Examples of the use of *tu* and polite *vous*

Context	Typical usage by two speakers
Adult strangers meeting for the first time in formal contexts: e.g. business meetings, interviews, dealing with state administration and services.	Both use *vous*.
Adults meeting in informal contexts: e.g. neighbours, socializing, shopping.	Initially both use *vous*, but with continued contact it is likely that they will change to *tu*, especially with young adults (under 40).
Professional superior and inferior	Generally both use *vous*, but in some organizations the inferior may use *vous* and the superior *tu*.
Professional equals	Both use *tu*, but older speakers (50-ish or over) may use *vous*.
Immediate family	Both use *tu*.
Distant relatives: e.g. second cousins, great aunts/uncles, etc.	Both use *tu*, it is possible to use *vous* when older family members are involved.
Friends	Typically *tu* but older speakers (50-ish or over) may use *vous*. This does not necessarily indicate less warmth in the friendship.
Adults to young children	Adults use *tu* to young children up to early adolescence. When very young they will respond with *tu*, but as they grow older they are expected to learn when and where *vous* is required of them.
Teachers and pupils	Teachers typically use *tu* to children under 14 and *vous* to older pupils, but some teachers continue to use *tu*, either to express power over their pupils or solidarity with them. The younger the teacher, the greater the likelihood that *tu* will be used. Pupils typically use *vous* to teachers, occasionally *tu*. Under tens are rarely expected to say *vous* to their teacher.
Students	Both use *tu* from the first meeting.

It is often said that *tu* is used more liberally on first acquaintance the younger the speaker. Where social media or advertisements are aimed at young audiences, *tu* is more prevalent than *vous*. In some parts of the French-speaking world (e.g. in Québec) the use of *tu* has long been accepted in many contexts where Metropolitan French would prefer *vous*.

3.1.3 'Marked' use of *tu*

Certain social sub-groups have their own internal norms for the use of *tu* and polite *vous*. For example, in sports teams, in left-wing political parties, and in trade unions, *tu* is the generalized form of address.

There are also a number of contexts where the expected use of polite *vous* between speakers is not met, and the actual pronoun form used is *tu*. For example, a stranger approaching you in the street and using the *tu* form, where normally *vous* is expected, may create the impression of an unwanted degree of intimacy; or it may indicate arrogance or contempt. Other examples of such 'marked' use are:

In street altercations, e.g. between motorists. The effect produced is one of insult.

Police interrogating suspects use the *tu* form in some parts of an interview if they feel a suspect is being difficult, but suspects are expected to reciprocate with the *vous* form. The effect produced is one of domination.

As a special case of the use of *tu*, Protestants have always addressed God with the *tu* form, but Catholics have only done so since 1967; before that God was addressed with the *vous* form.

3.1.4 Use of *il/ils* and *elle/elles*

The third person pronouns *il/ils* and *elle/elles* normally refer to people and things (both concrete and abstract) and the choice of which one to use is usually determined by the grammatical person, gender and number of the noun referred to:

Qu'est-ce qu'il fait, le facteur? **Il** est en retard
What's the postman up to? He's late

Il est intéressant, ce film
That movie's interesting

Où est la directrice? **Elle** est en réunion
Where's the headmistress? She's in a meeting

Elle est intéressante, cette émission
That programme's interesting

Il n'y a plus d'abricots. **Ils** sont finis
There are no more apricots. They're finished

Elles sont dangereuses, ces falaises
These cliffs are dangerous

3.1.5 Grammatical and real gender

With a handful of nouns, the real gender (biological sex) of the person referred to may determine the choice of third-person pronouns *il/ils* or *elle/elles*. For example, *victime, recrue*, and *sentinelle* are grammatically feminine nouns, but not all 'victims', 'recruits', or 'sentries' are necessarily female: *mannequin, témoin* are grammatically masculine nouns, but not all 'models' or 'witnesses' are necessarily male. In such cases the **real** gender of the person referred to normally determines the choice of *il/ils* or *elle/elles*:

Nous accueillons une nouvelle recrue. **Il** va se joindre à nous ce soir
We're welcoming a new recruit. He will join us this evening

C'est à toi que je viens de donner la clé. Justine est témoin! **Elle** m'a vu le faire
I gave the key to you. Justine is a witness. She saw me do it.

3.1.6 Grammatical and real number

With grammatically singular nouns that refer to more than one person or thing, the choice of pronoun is normally singular *il* or *elle*:

Quant au gouvernement, **il** ne prendra jamais les mesures qui s'imposent
As for the government, they will never take the necessary steps

Le covid, **il** nous a fait perdre au moins deux ans
Covid ruined at least two years for us

En ce qui concerne l'équipe française, on peut dire qu'**elle** est en grande forme en ce moment
As for the French team, they are currently on top form

For collective nouns, see Section 1.1.3.

3.1.7 **Pronouns referring to groups of mixed gender**

When a group (of people or things) of mixed gender is referred to, *ils* is the pronoun used. Compare:

Le directeur, son frère et son neveu? **Ils** sont tous les trois démissionnaires
The director, his brother and his nephew? All three are resigning

Louise, sa fille et sa petite-fille partagent des fichiers pour le travail. **Elles** doivent les sauvegarder fréquemment.
Louise, her daughter and her granddaughter share files for work. They have to save them frequently

with:

Louise, sa fille et son petit-fils partagent des fichiers pour le travail. **Ils** doivent les sauvegarder fréquemment.
Louise, her daughter and her grandson share files for work. They have to save them frequently

In cases of mixed gender groups, the pronoun '*iels*' (plural of '*iel*' proposed by LGTBQ+ communities to mainly reflect a person identifying as non-binary) may also be found. However, usage has not broadly integrated this.

3.1.8 *ils* **with arbitrary reference**

Plural *ils* may be used to refer to an indefinite or arbitrary group of people:

Ils vont tester la bande passante
They are going to test the bandwidth

Ils disent qu'il va y avoir de l'orage
They say that there will be a storm

Comment votent-**ils** par ici?
How do they vote around here?

3.1.9 **Coordination of subject pronouns**

When clauses containing unstressed subject pronouns are coordinated by *et, ou,* or *ne ... ni,* the second pronoun may be deleted:

Elle se réveille et (elle) regarde l'horloge
She wakes up and looks at the clock

Je ne lis ni (je) n'écris à présent
I am neither reading nor writing at the moment

When the verb is accompanied by auxiliary *avoir* or *être,* if the subject pronoun is deleted, the auxiliary must be too:

Il a chanté et (il a) dansé
(NOT *Il a chanté et a dansé)
He sang and danced

3.1.10 **Use of *on***

on can refer to a person or people whose identity is not really known:

On dit que la première année de mariage est la plus difficile
People say that the first year of marriage is the most difficult

C'est une région où l'**on** continue de mourir davantage de maladies de cœur que du cancer
It is an area where more people continue to die from heart disease than from cancer

On n'en fabrique plus
They don't make them any more

On m'a volé tout mon argent
Someone stole all my money

3.1.11 *on* **as an alternative to the English passive**

A construction with *on* can often be used where a passive is used in English:

On croyait la crise du logement définitivement réglée
The housing shortage was thought to be definitely over

On ne soupçonne guère le véritable rôle économique joué par les enfants
The real economic role that children play is thoroughly underestimated

On sait qu'il a eu des démêlés avec la police, mais **on** ne sait pas pourquoi
It is well known that he was once in trouble with the police, but it is not known why

(For the passive, see Section 8.6.)

3.1.12 *on* **as an equivalent for English 'you'**

on can sometimes be used where English uses 'you' and French could use *vous* or *tu*:

Est-il vrai qu'**on** distingue un Américain d'un Français à cent mètres?
Is it true you can tell an American from a Frenchman at a hundred metres?

Avec le moteur devant, **on** est au moins protégé
With the engine at the front you are at least protected

Comment savoir si **on** est doué pour la musique si l'**on** n'a jamais essayé?
How do you know whether you have a talent for music if you've never tried it?

3.1.13 *on* **as an equivalent for *nous***

on can often be used as a synonym for *nous*:

On avait d'abord tenté l'opération inverse
We had at first taken the opposite tack

On sait à quelles extrémités peuvent arriver certaines personnes
We know to what extremes some people can go

On s'y est habitué depuis longtemps
We have been used to it for a long time

The use of *on* instead of *nous* is very frequent in informal French:

Pourquoi **on** rentre pas à la maison?
Why don't we go home?

On avait chanté la Marseillaise, tu te souviens pas?
We sang the Marseillaise, don't you remember?

On y va?
Shall we go?

N.B.: When *on* refers to more than one person, many writers make any adjective or past participle which should indicate agreement show plural agreement. Not all native speakers agree with this. Teachers, for instance, require the masculine singular agreement to be observed.

On est tous très fatigués
We are all very tired

Après on est tous sortis en boîte
Afterwards we all went to a club

A frequent use of *on* in informal French combines it with a phrase introduced by *avec* to express the meaning 'Somebody and I did something' or 'We, together with somebody else, did something':

Avec Flora, **on** est allé en ville pour déjeuner
Flora and I went into town to have lunch OR *We went with Flora to have lunch in town*

Avec ton frère, **on** a acheté 2 casques bluetooth
Your brother and I bought 2 bluetooth headsets OR *We bought 2 bluetooth headsets with your brother*

While the meaning of *on* in this use is unspecified for number, the verb is always third-person singular. This usage is slightly more colloquial than the same structure used with *nous* (see Section 3.3.5(b)).

3.1.14 Use of *l'on*

l'on is sometimes used in French for *on* when it follows a word ending in a vowel (like *et, ou, qui, que,* and *si*). This is a feature of formal, rather than informal, French:

Comment savoir si **l'on** ne demande pas?
How can you know if you don't ask?

Il faut savoir choisir la personne avec qui **l'on** s'engage pour la vie
You have to be careful choosing the person to whom you will commit your life

The use of *l'* is not obligatory, however.

3.1.15 Use of *ce, cela, ça* as neutral pronouns

When *ce, cela,* and *ça* are used as neutral pronouns they normally refer to events, actions, states, or general classes of people or things:

Vous viendrez dîner ce soir. **C'**est prévu.
Come to dinner this evening. It's all taken care of
(*c* referring to 'coming to dinner')

L'élection d'un nouveau président aura lieu en mars. **Ce** sera l'occasion pour le pays de s'exprimer
The election of a new president takes place in March. The country will be able to have its say
(*ce* referring to 'the election of a president')

L'extérieur, **ce** n'est rien. Il faudrait voir l'intérieur
The outside is nothing. You should see the inside
(*ce* referring to the 'state of the outside')

N.B.: *il* cannot usually be used to refer to events, actions, states, or general classes.

While *ce* is normally used with *être* (see also Section 3.1.23), *cela*, and *ça* are used with other verbs:

Partez à l'étranger. **Cela** vous fera du bien
Travel abroad. It will do you good
(*cela* referring to 'travelling abroad')

Ils y sont allés un peu fort. **Cela** risque de faire du bruit
They went a bit far. It is likely to cause a stir
(*cela* referring to 'having gone a bit far')

J'essayais pas d'être premier. **Ça** m'intéressait pas.
I wasn't trying to come first. It didn't interest me.
(*ça* referring to coming first)

cela tends to be used in formal French, or for emphasizing the subject in informal French; *ça* is widely used as the unstressed subject in more informal styles.

Formal French:

Le marché de la bicyclette est en plein essor mais dans Paris trop peu de rues sont adaptées aux vélos. **Cela** montre bien le décalage entre l'évolution sociale et les budgets municipaux.
Bike sales are going up all the time but in Paris too few of the streets are designed for cycles. That clearly shows the gap between social change and council budgets.

2.5 millions de Français ne savent pas lire. **Cela** incite à poser des questions sur l'efficacité du système éducatif
2.5 million French people cannot read. This raises questions about the effectiveness of the educational system

Informal French:

Elle est heureuse. **Ça** se voit
She's happy. You can tell just from looking at her

Ça lui servira de leçon
That'll teach him

3.1.16 Comparing neutral *ce, cela, ça* with personal *il/elle, ils/elles*

il/ils and *elle/elles* refer to people and things (both concrete and abstract). *ce, cela*, and *ça* refer to events, actions, states, or general classes of phenomena. Compare:

C'est bon, le fromage
Cheese is good
(refers to cheese in general)

Il est bon, le fromage
The cheese is good
(refers to a specific example of cheese)

C'est lourd, cette valise
This suitcase is heavy
(implies that it is heavy to carry)

Elle est lourde, cette valise
This suitcase is heavy
(refers to the object itself)

J'adore m'occuper des enfants. **C'est** si câlin à cet âge-là
I love looking after children. They're so cuddly when they're that age
(c' referring to small children in general)

J'adore m'occuper de tes enfants. **Ils** sont si câlins
I love looking after your children. They're so cuddly
(referring to specific small children)

In informal French many speakers use *ça* where *il/ils, elle/elles* are used in more formal French:

J'ai astiqué mes casseroles. Regardez comme **ça** brille!
I gave my pans a scrub. Look how shiny they are!

Les pintades, **ça** couche souvent dehors
Guinea-fowl often sleep outside

Tu sais, ces gens-là, **ça** boit
You know, those people, they like their drink

N.B.: Because this usage is regarded as a feature of informal French, the foreign learner should avoid using it in formal language, particularly in writing.

3.1.17 Use of *il, ce, cela*, and *ça* as impersonal pronouns

The clearest use of impersonal subject pronouns is with verbs where *il, ce, cela*, and *ça* simply mark the subject position without referring to someone or something elsewhere in the conversation or text:

Il pleut	*It's raining*
Il neige	*It's snowing*
Il fait du vent	*It's windy*

C'est difficile de le joindre au téléphone
It's difficult to reach him by phone

C'est dommage qu'elle ne soit pas venue
It's a pity that she didn't come

Cela inquiète ma mère de les savoir dehors par ce temps
It worries my mother to know that they are out in this weather

Ça m'étonne qu'elle n'ait rien dit
It amazes me that she said nothing

In these cases *il, ce, cela,* and *ça* express very little meaning (indeed, in some languages impersonal constructions are characterized by the absence of a subject, for example, Spanish *Llueve* '(it) is raining'). This impersonal use of *il, ce, cela,* and *ça* in French corresponds to the impersonal use of 'it', and sometimes 'there' in English.

3.1.18 **Impersonal subject restricted to *il***

Some impersonal verbs and verbal expressions always take impersonal subject *il* (and NOT *ce, cela,* or *ça*):

Expressions of clock time do:

Quelle heure est-**il**?
What time is it?

Il est 6 heures
It's 6 o'clock

Il est midi
It's noon

As do the related time expressions:

Il est temps de, que …
It's time to, that …

Il est tard
It's late

Certain frequently occurring constructions also take impersonal *il*:

Il y a (quelqu'un, deux hommes à la porte)
There is/are (somebody, two men at the door)

Il est question de (lui interdire l'accès aux enfants)
There's talk of (stopping her seeing the children)

Il s'agit de (refaire les fondations)
It's a question of (rebuilding the foundations)

Il faut (se lever tôt le matin)
You've got to (get up early in the morning)

Il reste (des phénomènes qu'il est difficile de catégoriser)
There remain (phenomena which it is difficult to classify)

Il convient (de faire le point)
It is advisable (to take stock)

Il vaut mieux (rester chez vous)
It's better (for you to stay at home)

N.B.: *Il s'agit de* is a frequently used impersonal construction which learners often misuse because one way of translating it into English is as 'X is about Y', e.g. *Il s'agit dans ce roman d'une jeune fille* 'This novel is about a girl'. *Il s'agit de* can never have a personal subject, however:

NOT **Ce roman s'agit d'une jeune fille*

By contrast, the verb *agir* 'to act' must have a personal subject:

Fabien agit de façon bizarre
Fabien is acting in a strange way

Il agit en ami
He is acting as a friend

(For impersonal verbs see also Section 8.8.)

3.1.19 *il* or *ça* with impersonal verbs

Some impersonal verbs and verbal expressions have *il* as subject in formal French, but *il* or *ça* may occur in informal French. *Ça* is reserved for informal styles.

Some weather verbs behave in this way:

Il pleut, ça pleut	*It's raining*
Il neige, ça neige	*It's snowing*
Il gèle, ça gèle	*It's freezing*
Il bruine, ça bruine	*It's drizzling*

Constructions not listed under Section 3.1.18 also behave in this way:

Il/ça se peut que la carte soit démagnétisée
Perhaps the card has lost its magnetism

Il/ça n'empêche pas qu'elle ait raison
That doesn't stop her from being right

Il/ça suffit de voir ce qui se passe
You only have to see what's happening

3.1.20 *il/ça* alternating with clauses or infinitives as subjects

Some impersonal verbs allow both *il* (or *ça* in informal French) and a clause or infinitive as a subject:

Il plaît beaucoup à mes parents que les Nguyen habitent à côté *or*
Que les Nguyen habitent à côté plaît beaucoup à mes parents
It appeals to my parents to have the Nguyens living next door

Ça me fait peur d'y aller la nuit *or*
D'y aller la nuit me fait peur
I am afraid to go there at night

Others:

Il/ça déplaît à Olivier de/que …
It displeases Oliver to/that …

Il/ça fait mal à Arnaud de/que …
It hurts Arnaud to/that …

Il/ça fait plaisir à Céline de/que …
It gives Céline pleasure to/that …

Il/ça va à Romain de/que …
It suits Romain to/that …

Il/ça arrive à Béatrice de/que …
It sometimes happens to Béatrice that …

Verbs of this type which have **direct objects**, as opposed to indirect objects introduced by *à*, always take the impersonal subject *cela* (or *ça* in informal French) and NOT *il*:

Cela/ça impressionne Yann qu'elle fasse de la planche à voile *or*
Qu'elle fasse de la planche à voile impressionne Yann
It impresses Yann that she goes wind-surfing

Cela/ça ennuie Georgia de devoir recommencer *or*
De devoir recommencer ennuie Georgia
Georgia finds it annoying to have to start again

Cela/ça attriste Antoine de/que …	… *saddens* …
Cela/ça effraye Véronique de/que …	… *frightens* …
Cela/ça énerve Joël de/que …	… *annoys* …
Cela/ça épuise Fabien de/que …	… *exhausts* …
Cela/ça étonne Jérôme de/que …	… *astonishes* …
Cela/ça fatigue Charlotte de/que …	… *tires* …
Cela/ça gêne Violette de/que …	… *embarrasses* …
Cela/ça inquiète Maud de/que …	… *worries* …
Cela/ça intéresse Rachel de/que …	… *interests* …
Cela/ça irrite Sophie de/que …	… *irritates* …

3.1.21 *il/ça* alternating with noun phrase subjects

A handful of common verbs alternate between an impersonal construction with *il* (or *ça* in informal French) and a personal construction with a noun phrase subject:

Il semble que Nordine soit passé lundi *or*
Nordine semble être passé lundi
It seems that Nordine came round on Monday

Il apparaît que vous êtes le dindon de la farce *or*
Vous apparaissez comme étant le dindon de la farce
It seems that you have been made a fool of

Il s'est avéré que Sophie était consciencieuse *or*
Sophie s'est avérée consciencieuse
It turned out that Sophie was conscientious

3.1.22 Choosing between *il est* and *c'est*

il est **versus** *c'est* **with reference to professions, nationality, or social status**

There are two ways of indicating a person's profession, nationality, or social status: *il/ils* and *elle/elles* are used with the verbs *être, devenir, rester* and a noun **without** an article:

Il est médecin	*He is a doctor*
Elle est devenue réalisatrice de cinéma	*She became a film-maker*
Elles sont avocates	*They are lawyers*
Elle n'a pas voulu être femme au foyer	*She didn't want to be a housewife*

Ils restent hollandais, bien qu'ils aient quitté les Pays-Bas il y a 20 ans
They remain Dutch, although they left the Netherlands 20 years ago

ce is used when the noun is preceded by a determiner (*un, une, le, la*, etc.):

C'est un Russe	*He's a Russian*
C'est un avocat	*He's a lawyer*

When the noun is modified, a determiner is required and therefore *ce* (not *il/elle*) must be used:

C'est un médecin connu	*He's a famous doctor*
C'est un boxeur professionnel	*He's a professional boxer*
C'est une avocate qui connaît le droit anglais	*She's a lawyer who knows English law*
C'est une ingénieure toulousaine	*She's an engineer from Toulouse*

il est versus *c'est* in more general contexts

When *être* is followed by anything other than an adjective, *ce* is the pronoun to use, NOT *il*:

C'est un plaisir	(NOT *il est un plaisir)
It's a pleasure	
C'est Lulu	(NOT *il, *elle est Lulu)
It's Lulu	
C'était en été	(NOT *il était en été)
It was in summer	
Ce sera pour elle	
It'll be for her	

il est versus *c'est* when *être* is followed by an adjective alone

When *être* is followed by an adjective alone, both *il* and *ce* are possible but there is a difference in meaning. In these examples, *il* is personal but *ce* is impersonal or neutral:

Il est stupide	will normally mean	*He is stupid*
C'est stupide	will normally mean	*That's silly*
Il est curieux	will normally mean	*He's inquisitive*
C'est curieux	will normally mean	*That's odd*
Il est incroyable	will normally mean	*He's amazing*
C'est incroyable	will normally mean	*That's unbelievable*

il est versus *c'est* when *être* is followed by adjective + clause or infinitive

When *être* is followed by an adjective which is itself followed by a clause or infinitive, both *il* and *ce* are possible and both are then used in an impersonal sense:

Il/c'est difficile de formuler une politique
It's difficult to formulate a policy

Il/c'est intéressant d'observer les passants
It's interesting to watch the passers-by

Il/c'est impossible d'ouvrir cette boîte
It's impossible to open that box

Some grammars will sometimes claim that *il est* is the only form to use in these constructions, but *c'est* is widely used in all informal styles of French and is often also found in these constructions in more formal language.

Other common adjectives which behave in this way are:

agréable	*fun*	intéressant	*interesting*
bon	*good*	inutile	*useless*
commode	*convenient*	mauvais	*bad*
dangereux	*dangerous*	nécessaire	*necessary*
difficile	*difficult*	pénible	*tiresome*
étrange	*odd*	périlleux	*perilous*
évident	*obvious*	possible	*possible*
facile	*easy*	peu probable	*unlikely*
important	*important*	utile	*useful*
impossible	*impossible*	vrai	*true*
insupportable	*intolerable*		

N.B.: In the impersonal constructions illustrated above, the preposition which links the adjective to the following infinitive is always *de*.

(For discussion of adjective + infinitive constructions, see Section 12.7.)

_il_ versus _ce_ used with _être_ + adjective + _à_

In the examples immediately above, *il* and *ce* are impersonal. They are used like 'it' and 'there' in English without reference to anything else in the conversation or text: in these cases the adjective is linked to the infinitive by the preposition *de*. But *il* can also be used as a personal pronoun and *ce* as a neutral pronoun in similar constructions when the preposition linking the adjective and the infinitive is *à*:

Leur politique est difficile **à** accepter
(Leur politique), elle est difficile **à** accepter
(Leur politique), c'est difficile **à** accepter

Ce document est intéressant **à** analyser
(Ce document), il est intéressant **à** analyser
(Ce document), c'est intéressant **à** analyser

Here *il*, *elle*, and *ce* refer to something mentioned elsewhere in the conversation or text (in this case to *leur politique, ce document*).

(For more on these constructions, see Section 12.7.)

3.1.23 *ce* and compound forms of *être*

ce can be used with various compound forms of *être*, such as *ce doit être, ce peut être*, and *ç'a été*:

Ce pourrait être un facteur important
It could be an important factor

Ce doit être Marianne
It must be Marianne

Ç'aurait été trop
It would have been too much

When the phrase following *être* in this construction is plural, some grammars suggest that the verb should be in the third-person plural form:

Ce sont mes amis
It's my friends

Ce devraient être eux/elles
It should be them

But many speakers use *c'est*, etc. in these cases:

C'est mes amis

Ce doit être eux/elles

When first- or second-person plural pronouns *nous* or *vous* follow *être* in these constructions, the verb is always singular:

C'est vous, c'est nous
It's you, it's us

3.2 **Object pronouns**

Correctly identifying the direct and indirect objects in English and French

Many of the problems which learners have with pronouns are not caused by a failure to know what the pronouns are, but by a failure to recognise which pronoun French requires in a particular structure. This is especially true of indirect object pronouns. The structure of English and French verbs, even when they have similar meanings, is not necessarily the same: in a given sentence it is **essential** to know whether the object is direct or indirect in relation to the **French** verb and NOT the English verb.

Thus, in the English sentence 'They advised Stéphane to leave', 'Stéphane' is the **direct object** of 'advised', and with a pronoun the sentence becomes 'They advised **him** to leave'. But in the French equivalent – *Ils ont conseillé à Stéphane de partir* – *Stéphane* is the **indirect object** of *conseiller*. With a pronoun the French sentence becomes:

Ils **lui** ont conseillé de partir

For a full list of verbs which behave differently with respect to objects in English and French, see Chapter 8.

TABLE 3.C Summary table of object pronouns

Person	Singular		Plural	
First person				
Direct and indirect	me	*(to) me*	nous	*(to) us*
Second person				*(to) you plural or*
Direct and indirect	te	*(to) you*	vous	*polite*
Third person				
Direct				
Masculine	le	*him, it*	les	*them*
Feminine	la	*her, it*	les	*them*
Neutral	le	*it*	—	
Indirect				
Masculine	lui	*to him, to it*	leur	*to them*
Feminine	lui	*to her, to it*	leur	*to them*
Direct and indirect				
Reflexive, reciprocal, benefactive	se	*(to) oneself*	se	*(to) themselves*

There appears to be less agreement about the form of object pronouns in inclusive writing and the following forms have been proposed: *li, lia, lo,* and *lu.*

TABLE 3.D *y* and *en*

Pronoun	Stands in the place of
y	a phrase introduced by *à, en, dans, sur*
	e.g. à Paris, en ville, dans sa chambre
en	a phrase which begins with *de*
	e.g. *de son idée*

3.2.1 Direct object and indirect object pronouns: differences between English and French

The following common French verbs take **indirect object pronouns**; learners often treat them as if they required direct object pronouns, perhaps because their English equivalents take direct objects:

Sa sœur **lui** a appris à parler espagnol
His sister taught him to speak Spanish
(apprendre **à** qn à faire qc)

Mehdi **leur** a conseillé de se taire
Mehdi advised them to be quiet
(conseiller **à** qn de faire qc)

Sa mère **lui** défendait de fumer à la maison
Her mother used to forbid her to smoke at home
(défendre **à** qn de faire qc)

Le film **lui** a (dé)plu
He (dis)liked the film
((dé)plaire **à** qn)

Elle **lui** manque
He misses her
(manquer **à** qn)

There are several verb constructions which tend to give rise to this problem, each slightly different.

Verbs followed by: ... *à quelqu'un:*

... lui a téléphoné	... *phoned him*
... lui a survécu	... *outlived her*
... lui a (dés)obéi	... *(dis)obeyed her*
... lui a nui	... *disadvantaged him*
... lui ressemble	... *looks like him*

Verbs followed by: ... *quelque chose à quelqu'un:*

... lui a passé le sel	... *passed her the salt*
... lui a permis du repos	... *allowed him some rest*
... lui a promis une lettre	... *promised her a letter*
... lui a reproché son attitude	... *criticized her attitude*
... lui a enseigné le chant	... *taught him to sing*
... lui a donné un cadeau	... *gave her a present*
... lui a envoyé un email	... *sent her an email*
... lui a offert une clarinette	... *offered her a clarinet*

Verbs followed by: ... *à quelqu'un de faire quelque chose:*

... lui a ordonné de signer	... *ordered him to sign*
... lui a dit de se taire	... *told him to shut up*
... lui a demandé de partir	... *asked him to leave*
... lui a permis de l'acheter	... *allowed her to buy it*

The following common French verbs take **direct objects**; learners often treat them as if they required indirect objects, perhaps because of a confusion over the status of *à* (or sometimes *de*) which these verbs require when they are followed by an infinitive:

Je **l'**ai aidé à changer la roue
I helped him to change the wheel

L'animatrice du stage **l'**avait encouragé à participer
The course leader had encouraged him to take part

Je **les** ai persuadés de venir
I persuaded them to come

Others:

... l'a contraint à rester	... *forced him to stay*
... l'a dissuadée	... *dissuaded her*

... l'a empêché de courir	*... stopped him from running*
... l'a forcée à rester	*... forced her to stay*
... l'a invité à dîner	*... invited him to dinner*
... l'a menacée	*... threatened her*
... l'a obligé à parler	*... forced him to talk*
... l'a remerciée	*... thanked her*

3.2.2 **Position of direct and indirect object pronouns**

Direct and indirect object pronouns are closely linked with the verb to which they are most closely related in declarative, negative and interrogative sentences.

When the verb is a **main verb**, they appear immediately before it:

L'Etat **me** paie	*The state pays me*
Les gens ne **me** remarquent pas	*People don't notice me*
Elle **le** croit	*She believes it*
A son âge, vous ne **la** referez pas	*You won't change her, at her age*
Il **lui** a soufflé quelques mots	*He whispered a few words to her*
Tu **me** donnes une idée	*You've given me an idea*
Ça **leur** apprendra à mentir	*That will teach them to lie*

When the verb is accompanied by the **auxiliary** verbs *avoir* or *être*, direct and indirect object pronouns appear immediately before the auxiliary:

Il **m'**a vu	*He saw me*
M'a-t-il vu?	*Did he see me?*
Vous ne **les** avez pas goûtés?	*Didn't you taste them?*
Elle **lui** avait proposé un voyage	*She had suggested a trip to her (or to him)*
Je **vous** suis très reconnaissant	*I am very grateful to you*

Il **leur** a raconté beaucoup d'histoires passionnantes
He told them a lot of fascinating stories

Nous **l'**avons déjà traduite, cette lettre
We have already translated this letter

N.B.: The past participle agrees with a preceding direct object in these cases, but not with the indirect object.

(For the agreement of the past participle, see Sections 9.2 and 9.3.)

Note also that pronouns ending in *-e* (*me, te, se, le*) and *-a* (*la*) are shortened to the consonant alone before verbs beginning with a vowel: *elle m'aide, je t'ai déjà remercié, je te l'ai dit*, etc.

3.2.3 **Position of object pronouns with infinitives**

When the verb governing a direct or indirect object pronoun is an infinitive (including a compound infinitive made up of an auxiliary verb and a past participle), direct and indirect objects usually come in front of the infinitive:

On peut toujours **lui** téléphoner
He or *she can always be reached by phone*

Il pourra **te** voir demain
He will be able to see you tomorrow

Nous irons **leur** raconter l'histoire demain
We will go and tell them what happened tomorrow

Il pourrait bien **l'**avoir dit
He may well have said that

N.B.: When *à* or *de* followed by *le* or *les* come before the infinitive, these forms do NOT combine to form *au, du, aux, des: Je suis obligé de les aider.*

3.2.4 **Position of object pronouns with *faire, laisser,* and *envoyer* or verbs of perception + infinitive**

Where the infinitive has *faire, laisser, envoyer,* or perception verbs like *voir, regarder, entendre,* and *sentir* in front of it, object pronouns appear before this other verb. There are two different constructions in play:

a)   The pronoun is the object of *faire, voir,* etc. and is the subject of the infinitive:

Je **la** voyais venir
I saw her coming

(who did I see? – 'her' (object of *voir*), who is coming? 'she' subject of *venir*)

Sa mère **lui** a fait manger du potage
Her mother made her eat some soup

(Who did her mother make do something? – 'her' (object of *faire*) Who ate the soup? –'she' (subject of *manger*))

In the second example, **lui** is an indirect object pronoun because the verb *manger* has a direct object – *du potage*: Compare *Sa mère a fait manger du potage à elle.* If there is no direct object for the infinitive, then the pronoun 'her' would be realised as a direct object:

Sa mère **l'**a fait manger
Her mother made her eat

(Who did her mother make do something? 'her' (object of *faire*) Who ate? 'she' (Subject of *manger*.)

b)   The pronoun is the object of the infinitive and there is usually an 'understood' or non-expressed 'someone' as the subject of the infinitive:

Il fait construire une nouvelle maison/Il **la** fait construire
He is having a new house built/He is having it built (Someone is building the house but this is not expressed)

J'ai envoyé chercher l'architecte/Je **l'**ai envoyé chercher
I sent for the architect/I sent for him (I sent someone to get the architect but this is not expressed)

J'ai entendu dire qu'il viendra demain/Je **l'**ai entendu dire
I have heard that he will come tomorrow/I have heard it said (someone, not expressed, said it/he would come)

On occasions, these two constructions can overlap so that a given sentence with a pronoun in front of *faire,* etc. can be interpreted in different ways according to the context, especially when *faire* is the verb as there is no agreement (for agreement with the past participle in these constructions, see Section 9.3.3):

> *J'ai fait venir mes frères* and *J'ai fait venir les bagages* with a pronoun will both produce:
> *Je **les** ai fait venir.*

> I made my brothers/them come or I made (someone) bring it (bring it/bring the luggage).

In the first example, *mes frères/les* are the object of *faire* as in 'I made them do something' and the subject of *venir* as in 'They came'. In the second example *les bagages/les* are the direct object of *venir* as in 'Someone brought it/brought the luggage'. The meaning will usually be made clear by the context.

(For the position of two pronouns with *faire etc.* + infinitive, see Section 3.2.32.)

3.2.5 **Position of object pronouns with imperatives**

In affirmative imperatives direct and indirect object pronouns come immediately after the verb which governs them, and the pronouns *me, te* become the stressed forms *moi, toi*:

Prends-**les**!	*Take them!*
Suivez-**nous**!	*Follow us!*
Arrêtez-**les**!	*Stop them!*
Ecoutez-**moi**!	*Listen to me!*
Tais-**toi**!	*Shut up!*

BUT in negative imperatives, direct and indirect object pronouns precede the verb:

Ne **les** suivez pas!	*Don't follow them!*
Ne **la** mange pas!	*Don't eat it!*
Ne **me** fais pas rire!	*Don't make me laugh!*

(See also Section 11.5 on imperatives.)

3.2.6 **Position of object pronouns with *voici* and *voilà***

Direct object pronouns may appear before *voici* and *voilà*:

Nous voici	*Here we are*
Les voilà	*There they are*

3.2.7 **Ambiguity of reference of *lui* and *leur***

Because the indirect object pronouns *lui, leur* can refer both to masculine and to feminine nouns they are inherently ambiguous:

> Je **lui** ai indiqué le chemin
> *I showed him* or *her the way*

> Romain **leur** a parlé
> *Romain spoke to them* (either male or female or mixed)

This ambiguity can be resolved if one wishes, however, by copying the pronoun with a stressed pronoun and a preposition:

Je lui ai indiqué le chemin à **elle**/Je lui ai indiqué le chemin à **lui**
Jules leur a parlé à **elles**/Jules leur a parlé à **eux**

3.2.8 **Use of the neutral pronoun *le***

le, in addition to its function as a third-person singular pronoun referring to masculine nouns, may also have a 'neutral' function when it refers to states, general ideas, or whole propositions:

Pour que nous vous remboursions vos frais de déplacement, il faut présenter des justificatifs, si vous **le** pouvez (*le* refers to 'justifying the expenditure')
For us to be able to pay your travelling expenses, you must prove you have spent the money, if you can

Vous n'êtes plus président, je **le** sais (*le* refers to 'no longer being the president')
You are no longer the president, I know

Je **le** répète: tu ne travailles pas assez (*le* refers to 'you're not doing enough work')
I'll say it again: you're not doing enough work

In this usage, neutral *le* is the object counterpart of the neutral subjects *ce, cela, ça* (see Section 3.1.15).

3.2.9 **Use of neutral *le* where no equivalent exists in English**

Sometimes neutral *le* is required in French where English normally has no object pronoun at all, typically where the verb *être* + adjective/identifying expression are involved:

J'étais en colère, mais je ne **le** suis plus
(*le* refers to 'being angry')
I was angry, but I'm not any more

Est-ce qu'elle est prête? Elle **le** sera dans un instant
(*le* refers to 'being ready')
Is she ready? She will be in a moment

Moi, je n'étais pas étonné, mais Myriam **l**'a été
(*le* refers to 'being surprised')
I wasn't surprised, but Myriam was

3.2.10 **Wrong use of neutral *le* in phrases where 'it' occurs in English**

The English constructions 'find it difficult to', 'consider it easy to', 'reckon it possible that', and similar cases have French counterparts in which *le* must not appear. The verbs usually involved are *croire, penser, trouver, juger, estimer*, and *considérer*:

Je trouve difficile de me faire des amis
I find it difficult to make friends

NOT *Je le trouve difficile de me faire des amis

Il considère important que tous ses amis soient prévenus
He considers it important that all his friends be notified

NOT *Il le considère important que tous ses amis soient prévenus

The *le* is absent in these cases because the construction is impersonal, and, while English requires 'it', French requires an absence of pronoun. Where the construction is personal (i.e. where a person or thing is referred to), *le*, *la*, or *les* are required:

Je trouve cette série difficile à comprendre
I find this series difficult to understand

Je la trouve difficile à comprendre
(*la* refers to 'the series')

J'ai trouvé le guitariste impossible à écouter
I found I couldn't bear to listen to the guitarist

Je l'ai trouvé impossible à écouter
(*le* refers to 'the guitarist')

(For more on this construction, see Section 12.7.)

3.2.11 **Optional use of neutral *le***

Neutral *le* is optional in the following environments:

(a) With the verbs *croire, penser, dire, vouloir,* and *savoir* when these are used as stock conversational responses to questions or statements by other people:

Ils sont heureux? Oui, je (**le**) pense
Are they happy? Yes, I think so

Est-ce que vous viendrez ce soir? Non, je ne (**le**) crois pas
Will you come this evening? No, I don't think so

Elle revient directement de Londres. Oui, je (**le**) sais
She has come straight back from London. Yes, I know

(b) In the second clause of a comparison (where the particle *ne* is also optional). The use of **ne** and **le** is typical of formal French:

Il est autre que je (**ne**) (**le**) croyais
He is different from what I expected

Un abonnement est moins cher que vous (**ne**) (**le**) pensez
A subscription costs less than you think

A son âge, il faut admettre que Maurice est plus naïf qu'il (**ne**) devrait (**l'**)être
When you realize how old he is, you have to admit that Maurice is more naïve than he should be

3.2.12 **Reflexive use of *me, te, se, nous,* and *vous***

Where *me, te, se, nous,* and *vous* refer to the subject of the verb to which they are attached, they are being used reflexively. This use can correspond to English 'my-, your-, him-, her-, it-, oneself; our-, your-, themselves':

Arnaud adore **se** regarder dans les vitrines
Arnaud loves looking at himself in shop windows

Je **me** connais
I know myself

Vous **vous** critiquez trop
You are too critical of yourselves

(See also Section 8.7.1.)

3.2.13 **Reciprocal *se* and cases of potential ambiguity**

When the subject is third-person plural, *se* may also be interpreted as a 'reciprocal' pronoun, corresponding to English 'each other'. In some cases *se* is therefore ambiguous, having a 'reflexive' or 'reciprocal' interpretation, and the meaning may depend on the context:

Les deux scientifiques s'admirent depuis 20 ans

is most likely to be:

The two scientists have admired each other for 20 years

but could possibly be:

The two scientists have (each) admired themselves for 20 years

Les deux amis **se** connaissent bien
The two friends know themselves or *each other well*

(See also Section 8.7.5.)

3.2.14 **Benefactive *me*, *te*, *se*, *nous*, and *vous***

me, te, se, nous, and *vous* may also be used to indicate that the subject 'benefits' from some action. This use, known as the 'benefactive', can often be paraphrased in English by 'for him-, her-, it-, oneself/themselves, etc.':

Josée **s'**est acheté un nouvel ordinateur
Josée bought herself a new computer

Marwann **s'**est commandé un café
Marwann ordered himself a coffee

J'ai hâte de rentrer et de **me** faire couler un bain
I can't wait to get home and run myself a bath

Etienne et Rime **se** sont offert un baptême de l'air
Etienne and Rime treated themselves to a first flight

3.2.15 ***se* as an alternative to an English passive**

se may be used with a verb as an alternative to an English passive:

Ces verres peuvent-ils **se** laver en machine?
Can these glasses be put in the dishwasher?

Le Gamay **se** boit frais
Gamay (light red wine) is best drunk chilled

L'uni **se** vend bien cet hiver
Plain colours are selling well this winter

This usage is restricted to special circumstances. The sentence must describe a state of affairs and not an action and the verb must not suggest through its tense that the action takes place in a limited time span (See also Section 8.7.6.)

3.2.16 *me, te, se, nous,* and *vous* as part of certain verbs but with no specific meaning

me, te, se, nous, and *vous* also normally accompany some verbs without any detectable reflexive, reciprocal, or benefactive meaning:

Raphaël **s'**est évanoui
Raphaël fainted

Elle **se** souvient de son arrière-grand-père
She remembers her great-grandfather

La foule **s'**est éloignée
The crowd moved away

(For a list of common pronominal verbs in which *se* has no detectable reflexive, reciprocal, or benefactive meaning, see Section 8.7.3.)

3.2.17 Emphasizing *me, te, se, nous,* and *vous* by adding a pronoun + *même*

The reflexive and benefactive interpretations of *me, te, se, nous,* and *vous* can be emphasized by the addition of one of the expressions *moi-même, toi-même, lui-même, elle-même, soi-même, eux-mêmes, elles-mêmes,* etc.:

Connais-toi, toi-même
Know thyself

Elle est grande maintenant: elle s'habille elle-même
She's a big girl now, she dresses herself

Puisque personne d'autre ne le fait, Eric s'admire lui-même!
Since no-one else does so, Eric admires himself!

De nos jours, malheureusement, il faut se soigner soi-même
Nowadays, unfortunately, you have to be your own doctor

3.2.18 Emphasizing the reciprocal use of *se* by adding *l'un l'autre*

The reciprocal interpretation of *se* can be made explicit by the addition of one of the phrases *l'un(e) l'autre, l'un(e) à l'autre, les un(e)s les autres,* and *les un(e)s aux autres,* all with the meaning 'each other' or 'one another'.

l'un(e) l'autre or *l'un(e) à l'autre* are used when the subject refers to just two people or things:

Les deux boxeurs se regardaient fixement **l'un l'autre**
The two boxers were staring at each other

Mes deux sœurs se copient **l'une l'autre**
My two sisters copy one another

les un(e)s les autres and *les un(e)s aux autres* are used when the subject refers to more than two people or things:

Les équipiers se connaissent depuis longtemps **les uns les autres**
The team members have known each other for a long time

Les enfants se sont donné des petits cadeaux **les uns aux autres**
The children gave each other small presents

3.2.19 **Constructions which do not allow indirect object pronouns**

A small set of verbs and adjectives in French look as if they take indirect objects because they are followed by the preposition *à*, but in fact they do not allow preceding *me, te, se, nous, vous, lui*, and *leur* and require stressed pronouns to follow à:

Il pense **à** Gaëtan	Il pense **à lui** (NOT *Il lui pense)
He is thinking of Gaëtan	*He is thinking of him*
Il fait allusion **à** Sonia	Il fait allusion **à elle** (NOT *Il lui fait allusion)
He is referring to Sonia	*He is referring to her*
Elle aura affaire **à** Zac	Elle aura affaire **à lui** (NOT *Elle lui aura affaire)
She will have to deal with Zac	*She will have to deal with him*
Ce sac est **à** Julien	Ce sac est **à lui** (NOT *Ce sac lui est)
This bag is Julien's	*This bag is his*

The explanation for this behaviour seems to be that *à* has two functions: as a marker of indirect objects and as an ordinary preposition. In the above examples it is a preposition and can only be followed by stressed pronouns (see Section 3.3).

Other common verbs followed by *à* which behave similarly are:

en appeler à	*appeal to*
faire appel à	*appeal to*
avoir recours à	*have recourse to*
recourir à	*have recourse to*
faire attention à	*pay attention to*
faire allusion à	*allude to*
s'habituer à	*get used to*
revenir à	*come back to*
rêver à	*dream of*
songer à	*think of*
tenir à	*be fond of*
venir à	*come to*

The set of verbs which behave in this way is quite small. We have listed most of them here.

When the phrase introduced by *à* in these cases refers to things, rather than people, pre-verbal *y* may replace it (see Sections 3.2.21 and 3.2.23).

Verbs like these can be made reflexive or reciprocal by adding the appropriate forms *lui(-même)*, *elle(-même)*, etc., or *l'un l'autre*, etc.:

Il pense à lui(-même)
He is thinking of himself

Elles auront affaire les unes aux autres
They will have to deal with each other

3.2.20 **Indirect object pronouns used in possessive constructions with body parts**

The indirect object pronouns are used in a possessive construction in French with 'body parts' where English would use possessive determiners (like 'my', 'your', 'his', and 'her'):

On **lui** a cassé **le** bras
They broke his arm

Elle **s'**était coupé **le** doigt
She had cut her finger

La sueur **me** coulait dans **le** dos
Sweat was running down my back

However, the indirect object construction is not possible with verbs which do not describe actions:

Elle **lui** lave le visage
She is washing his face

BUT NOT:
*Elle **lui** aime le visage
She likes his face

RATHER:
Elle aime *son* visage

This construction is also normally impossible with non-body-parts. However, it can be found in some regional varieties of French:

Elle **lui** a cassé l'écran de portable
She broke his laptop screen (or his phone screen)

(See also Sections 2.2.8 and 8.7.2.)

3.2.21 **Use of *y***

y usually plays the same role in sentences as phrases which follow the verb and are introduced by prepositions like *à, en, dans, sur, sous*:

Je vais à Paris demain
I am going to Paris tomorrow

J'**y** vais demain
I'm going there tomorrow

Elle vit dans une grande maison
She lives in a large house

Elle **y** vit
She lives there

Il a écrit son nom sur le cahier
He wrote his name on the book

Il **y** a écrit son nom
He wrote his name there

Although *y* can generally replace any phrase of this type, both concrete and abstract (as in the examples below), it is usually restricted to non-animate entities:

Je pense souvent au jardin de mon enfance
I often think about the garden of my childhood
J'**y** pense souvent

Elle est fidèle à ses principes
She is faithful to her principles
Elle **y** est fidèle

Nous sommes entrés dans le débat
We joined in the debate
Nous **y** sommes entrés

3.2.22 **Non-specific use of *y***

In a number of common constructions, *y* is used without a very specific meaning being attached to it:

Pensez-**y**!	*Think about it!*
Je n'**y** suis pour rien	*It's nothing to do with me*
J'**y** suis, j'**y** reste	*Here I am and here I stay*
Il **y** a …	*There is … there are …*

3.2.23 **Use of *y* in constructions where *à* does not introduce an indirect object**

y is normally used to refer to non-human objects which occur with verbs like *penser à* where *à* does not introduce an indirect object (see Section 3.2.19):

Je pense à la guerre	*I'm thinking of the war*
J'**y** pense	*I'm thinking of it*
Je tiens à mes valeurs	*I cherish my values*
J'**y** tiens	*I cherish them*
Je ferai très attention à vos affaires	*I'll look after your belongings very carefully*
J'**y** ferai très attention	*I'll look after them carefully*

y can also be found on rare occasions referring to people with such verbs: *J'y pense* 'I'm thinking of him'.

3.2.24 **Use of *en***

en is the pronoun used to replace phrases introduced by *de* which follow the verb. Where these include a noun, *en* can refer to both human and non-human nouns:

Il a déjà parlé de son idée	Il **en** a déjà parlé
He has already spoken about his idea	*He has already spoken about it*
Il a empêché Yannis de travailler	Il l'**en** a empêché
He stopped Yannis working	*He stopped him doing it*
Inès s'occupe des enfants	Inès s'**en** occupe
Inès is looking after the children	*Inès is looking after them*

Céleste est fière de son frère
Céleste is proud of her brother

Céleste **en** est fière
Céleste is proud of him

In informal French, where people are referred to, it is quite likely that a stressed pronoun following *de* will be used instead (see Section 3.3.3):

Inès s'occupe d'eux
Céleste est fière de lui

N.B.: An exception to the generalization that *en* can replace phrases introduced by *de* is those verbs, such as *permettre, défendre* and *interdire*, with a construction using *… à quelqu'un de faire quelque chose*. The infinitive clause is treated as a direct object:

Elle a permis à Gauthier d'emprunter sa voiture
She allowed Gauthier to borrow her car

Elle **le** lui a permis (*le* means 'to borrow the car')
She allowed him to do it

Il a défendu aux jumeaux de sortir ce soir
He forbade the twins to go out this evening

Il **le** leur a défendu (*le* means 'to go out this evening')
He forbade them to do it

3.2.25 Use of *en* with numerals and quantifiers

It is important to use *en* when numerals (*deux, trois, une dizaine, une douzaine*, etc.) and quantifiers (*beaucoup, trop, la plupart*, etc.) are on their own after a verb. In English a pronoun is normally absent in these cases, but in French *en* is obligatory:

J'ai acheté dix roses
I bought ten roses

J'**en** ai acheté dix
I bought ten

Il a commandé une douzaine d'huîtres
He ordered a dozen oysters

Il **en** a commandé une douzaine
He ordered a dozen

Elle produit beaucoup de documents
She produces a lot of papers

Elle **en** produit beaucoup
She produces a lot

Elle a cueilli plusieurs tomates
She picked several tomatoes

Elle **en** a cueilli plusieurs
She picked several

Le comité avait demandé certains manuscrits
Le comité **en** avait demandé certains

The committee had asked for selected manuscripts
The committee had asked for selected ones

Note that *quelques* 'some, a few' belongs to this group, but when *en* is present *quelques* becomes *quelques-un(e)s*:

On voyait quelques voiles au loin
We could see some sails in the distance

On **en** voyait quelques-unes au loin

(See also Section 6.9.2.)

3.2.26 *y* and *en* as an integral part of the verb structure

There is a small set of verbs in French which involve *y* or *en* as an integral part of their structure without any detectable specific meaning. Common examples are:

il **y** a …	*there is/are …*	Il **y** avait trois hommes
s'**en** aller	*go away*	Samira s'**en** va
en imposer	*impress*	Elle **en** impose
s'**en** prendre à	*lay into*	Il s'**en** est pris à Régis
en revenir	*get over*	Je n'**en** reviens pas
s'**en** tenir à	*stick to*	Tenez-vous-**en** aux faits
en vouloir à	*hold a grudge*	Je lui **en** veux
en voilà un	*there's someone*	**En** voilà un qui m'énerve
c'**en** est fait	*that's the end of*	C'**en** est fait de nos espoirs
en découdre	*to get into a fight*	Il est toujours prêt à **en** découdre
en être à	*to be at, get to*	Où **en**-sommes-nous?

3.2.27 **Position of *y* and *en* with negative infinitives**

When *y* and *en* appear with negative infinitives, they normally appear directly adjacent to the infinitive, just as all other object pronouns do:

Il vaudrait mieux ne pas en parler
It would be better not to speak of it

Elle avait décidé de ne plus y penser
She had decided not to think about it any more

Cases where *y* and *en* 'split' the negative are regarded as archaic:

Il vaudrait mieux n'en pas parler
Elle avait décidé de n'y plus penser

3.2.28 *y* and *en* in French where the English translation has no preposition

The foreign learner of French should remember that the use of *y* and *en* is determined by the presence of *à* or *de* in the **French** verb phrase and should not be misled by an English equivalent which does not have a preposition, e.g.:

to use something BUT se servir **de** qch
I often use it = Je m'**en** sers souvent

to need something BUT avoir besoin **de** qch
I need it = J'**en** ai besoin

to give something up BUT renoncer **à** qch
I will give it up = J'**y** renoncerai

to enter/join BUT entrer **dans** qch
I joined the firm when I was twenty
Je suis entré **dans** l'entreprise quand j'avais vingt ans
J'**y** suis entré quand j'avais vingt ans

to doubt something BUT douter **de** qch
I doubt it = J'**en** doute

But see the N.B. in Section 3.2.24.

3.2.29 **Order of unstressed object pronouns when more than one is present**

When two (and more rarely three) unstressed object pronouns appear before a verb, their order usually follows the pattern indicated in Table 3.E (known by generations of British schoolchildren as the 'soccer team' of pronouns with a ball (*en*), a goalkeeper (*y*), two full-backs (*lui, leur*), three midfield players (*le, la, les*) and five strikers (*me, te, se, nous, vous*):

TABLE 3.E The order of unstressed object pronouns

Position				
First	**Second**	**Third**	**Fourth**	**Fifth**
me				
te	le			
se	la	lui	y	en
nous	les	leur		
vous				

Examples:

Il **me l'a** dit
He told me about it

Elle **le lui** a dit
She told him about it

Elle **nous les** a donnés
She gave them to us

Nous **le leur** avons dit
We told them about it

Soisic **m'en** a parlé
Soisic spoke to me about it

Nous **nous y** sommes beaucoup attachés
We have become very fond of it

Nous **y en** avons beaucoup trouvé
We found a lot of it there

Elle **les y** a souvent vus
She has often seen them there

Nous **leur en** avons promis beaucoup
We have promised a lot of those to them

Ne **me le** donne pas
Don't give it to me

Lui en auras-tu parlé avant demain?
Will you have spoken to him about it before tomorrow?

En voudriez-vous s'il **y en** avait?
Would you want some if there were any?

M'y accompagnerez-vous?
Will you come there with me?

Il **y en** a beaucoup
There are a lot of them

Nous **y en** avons trouvé plusieurs
We found several of them there

More rarely three pronouns may occur in combination where the first is a benefactive (i.e. indicates that the action described by the verb is 'for the benefit' of the person in question), although this benefactive use is regarded as colloquial:

Tu vas **me le lui** écrire, et plus vite que ça!
You will write it to her for me, and be quick about it!

In formal French the benefactive interpretation would be expressed through other means:

Tu vas me le lui écrire = Tu vas me faire le plaisir de le lui écrire

3.2.30 **Restrictions on possible combinations**

Although Table 3.E describes in general the possible sequences of unstressed object pronouns, there are some restrictions on possible combinations. No pronoun from the first column (*me, te, se, nous, vous*) can normally appear in combination with a pronoun from the third column (*lui, leur*):

Whilst:	Je vous présenterai Eva *I will introduce Eva to you*
can, with two pronouns, become:	Je vous la présenterai *I will introduce her to you*
the sentence	Je vous présenterai à Eva *I will introduce you to Eva*
cannot become	*Je vous lui présenterai *I will introduce you to her*
Instead, you would use:	Je vous présenterai à elle
Whilst:	Je vous recommande Damien *I recommend Damien to you*
can, with two pronouns, become:	Je vous le recommande *I recommend him to you*
the sentence	Je vous recommande à Damien *I recommend you to Damien*
cannot become	*Je vous lui recommande *I will recommend you to him*
Instead, you would use:	Je vous recommande à lui

Nor can any pronouns from within the same column appear together:

Fabrice s'est joint à notre petit groupe
Fabrice joined our little group

cannot become:

*Il se nous est joint
NOR *Il nous s'est joint

BUT ONLY:

Fabrice s'est joint à **nous**
Fabrice joined us

3.2.31 Order of multiple pronouns with imperatives

When two pronouns follow the verb in affirmative imperatives the ordering of pronouns is slightly different in that pronouns from the first column (*me, te, se, nous, vous*) follow pronouns from the second column (*le, la, les*). The other orders remain the same. Pronouns after imperatives are linked to the verb that governs them by hyphens:

Donne-le-moi	(NOT *Donne-moi-le)
Give it to me	
Passez-les-nous	(NOT *Passez-nous-les)
Pass them over to us	
Nettoyez-la-moi	(NOT *Nettoyez-moi-la)
Clean it for me	

N.B.: *Donne-moi-le, Passez-nous-les*, etc., are often heard in informal French. The foreign learner should avoid them, however.

BUT:

Donne-le-lui
Give it to him

Passez-les-leur
Pass them over to them

Parlez-lui-en
Talk to him about it

The pronouns *me, te* become *moi, toi* in affirmative imperatives when they are the last pronoun in the sequence, but become *m', t'* before *y* or *en*:

Donne-le-moi	*Give it to me*
Donne-m'en	*Give me some*

In these cases in informal French, it is not unusual to hear *moi, toi* retained with a linking -z-, but the learner should avoid this usage:

Parlez-moi-z-en	*Talk to me about it*
Accroche-toi-z-y	*Hang on to it*

In negative imperatives pronouns precede the verb and the order of multiple pronouns is as indicated in the table:

Ne me le donne pas	*Don't give it to me*
Ne me les nettoyez jamais!	*Don't you ever clean them for me!* (i.e. I forbid you to …)

3.2.32 **Position of more than one object pronoun with *faire* etc. + infinitive**

When the verbs *faire*, *laisser*, *envoyer* and perception verbs like *voir*, *entendre*, *regarder*, *sentir* are followed by an infinitive, there are different ways of placing two pronouns depending on which verb is being used.

If the verb is *faire*, both the pronouns come before *faire* (or *avoir* if *faire* is in a compound tense):

Je **les lui** ferai dessiner	Je **les lui** ai fait dessiner
I shall make him draw them	*I made him draw them*

If the verb is *laisser, envoyer,* or one of the perception verbs, there are two possibilities illustrated below:

Tu **les lui** laisses lire?	Tu **la** laisses **les** lire?
Will you let her read them?	*Will you let her read them?*
Je **le leur** ai entendu dire	Je **les** ai entendus **le** dire
I heard them say so	*I heard them say so*

(For the structure of sentences involving *faire, laisser, envoyer* and perception verbs, see Sections 12.3.8 and 12.3.9.)

3.2.33 **Position of object pronouns with *devoir, pouvoir* + infinitives**

After *devoir, pouvoir* (modal verbs) followed by an infinitive, object pronouns come before the infinitive:

Je dois **vous l'**avouer tout de suite
I must admit it to you immediately

Ils peuvent **nous le** signaler dès son arrivée
They can tell us about it as soon as he arrives

3.2.34 **Object pronouns in coordinated clauses**

When clauses containing unstressed object pronouns are coordinated by *et* or *ou*, it is normally necessary to repeat the pronoun in the second clause:

Cela **m'**agace et **m'**ennuie
That irritates and bores me

Je **les** ai préconisés et **les** ai proposés
I advocated and proposed them

Elle **l'**a aidé et **lui** a donné de l'argent
She helped him and gave him money

However, where the two pronouns are identical in form and attached to an auxiliary (*avoir* or *être*), the second pronoun and auxiliary may be deleted together:

Je les ai préconisés et proposés

The pronouns must be identical, however, and both the pronoun and the auxiliary must be deleted together. Hence the following are impossible:

NOT	*Je les ai préconisés et ai proposés
NOT	*Cela m'agace et ennuie
NOT	*Elle l'a aidé et donné de l'argent

In this last example it is not so much that the pronouns have different functions (*le* being a direct object and *lui* an indirect object), as that they differ in their surface forms. In the following example, the first *me* is a direct object and the second *me* an indirect object, but the second *me* can be deleted with the auxiliary because the two *me*'s are identical in surface form:

Elle **m'**a aidé et **m'**a donné de l'argent
Elle m'a aidé et donné de l'argent

3.3 **Stressed pronouns**

TABLE 3.F Summary table of stressed pronouns

Person	Singular		Plural	
First person	moi	*me*	nous	*us*
Second person	toi	*you*	vous	*you* (plural or polite)
Third person				
Masculine	lui	*him*	eux	*them*
Feminine	elle	*her*	elles	*them*
Neutral	cela, ça	*that*		
Non-specific	soi	*oneself*		

In inclusive writing it has been suggested that the forms *ellui* and *elleux* may be used to replace the first-person singular and the third-person plural-stressed pronouns.

3.3.1 **Use of stressed pronouns for emphasis**

To highlight or emphasize a pronoun a common strategy is to 'double up' by the addition of a stressed pronoun. This can be done with:

Subject pronouns

Toi, tu le crois peut-être mais **lui, il** ne le croit pas
YOU might believe that, but HE doesn't

Moi, je veux travailler ce soir, mais **lui** pas
I want to work this evening, but HE doesn't

The stressed subject pronoun copy may equally appear at the end of the clause with the same effect:

Tu le crois peut-être, **toi**, mais **il** ne le croit pas, **lui**
Je veux travailler ce soir, **moi**, mais pas **lui**

When third-person subject pronouns are highlighted or emphasized, the stressed pronoun alone may, on occasions, be used:

Lui pourrait le faire
HE could do it

Eux sauraient quoi dire
THEY would know what to say

This is not possible with first and second person pronouns:

NOT *Moi pourrais le faire (but Moi, je pourrais le faire)
NOT *Toi saurais quoi dire (but Toi, tu saurais quoi dire)

Only stressed pronouns and not unstressed subject pronouns can be separated from the tense-marked verb by adverbs or parenthetical expressions:

Lui, souvent, critique nos décisions
(NOT *Il souvent critique nos décisions)
He often criticizes our decisions

Eux, par exemple, connaissent l'arabe
(NOT *Ils, par exemple, connaissent l'arabe)
They, for example, know Arabic

(For stressed pronouns introduced by *c'est/ce sont*, sometimes followed by relative clauses, see Section 9.1.6.)

Object pronouns

A common strategy is to add a second, stressed pronoun at either the beginning or the end of the clause:

Lui, on **le** sait innocent
HE is known to be innocent

On l'a souvent vu au café du coin, **lui**
We often saw HIM at the local café

Il **me** parle à **moi** (et pas à toi)
He confides in ME (and not in you)

Eux, on va **leur** demander de participer aux frais
We'll be asking THEM for a financial contribution

When the unstressed pronoun is an **indirect object**, the stressed pronoun being used to highlight it is preceded by *à* only when it is at the end of the clause:

Nous, elle nous a souvent écrit or
Elle nous a souvent écrit, **à nous**
She has often written to US

Moi, cela me ferait plaisir *or*

Cela me ferait plaisir, **à moi**
That would give ME pleasure

This 'doubling' of an unstressed pronoun by a stressed pronoun is also used to disambiguate ambiguous pronouns. In the following sentence *leur* is ambiguous between a masculine and a feminine interpretation:

Sébastien **leur** a dit de partir
Sébastien told them to leave

But it can be disambiguated by the addition of stressed pronouns:

Sébastien leur a dit à **eux** de partir
*Sébastien leur a dit à **elles** de partir*

3.3.2 **Stressed pronouns standing alone**

Stressed pronouns are normally used where the pronoun stands alone or is in a phrase without a verb:

Qui est là?   **Moi** (NOT *je)
Qui tu as vu?   **Lui** (NOT *il)
C'est elle qui t'aidera, pas **moi**
(NOT *pas je)

3.3.3 **Stressed pronouns used as the object of a preposition**

Stressed pronouns are the forms to use after all prepositions other than *à* (but see Section 3.2.19):

Je suis venu malgré **lui**   *I came in spite of him*
J'ai agi comme **elle**   *I acted as she did*
Ne le dites pas devant **eux**   *Don't say it in front of them*
Elle s'est assise à côté de **moi**   *She sat down next to me*
Je n'ai rien contre **elles**   *I have nothing against them*

Phrases introduced by *de* are normally pronominalized using *en*, but, when humans are referred to, *de* followed by a stressed pronoun is more usual:

Ma mère avait parlé de **lui**
My mother had spoken of him

3.3.4 **Stressed pronouns with *même, aussi, seul, autres, tous,* and numerals**

Stressed pronouns are used in conjunction with the forms: *même, aussi, seul, autres, tous,* and numerals (*deux, trois,* etc.):

Les enfants avaient préparé la salade **eux-mêmes**
The children had prepared the salad themselves

Lui aussi aura des problèmes
He too will have problems

Eux seuls pourraient la convaincre
They alone could persuade her

Nous autres Européens, on se comprend
We Europeans understand one another

Vous tous irez prendre une douche
You will all go and have a shower

N.B.: Some adjectives, such as *fier* 'proud', *fidèle* 'faithful', *sûr* 'sure' are followed by a stressed pronoun alone, and not by *moi-même, lui-même, elles-mêmes*, etc., when used reflexively:

Elle est très fière d'**elle**
She is very proud of herself

Je ne suis plus sûr de **moi**
I am not sure of myself any more

3.3.5 **Coordination of stressed pronouns**

Only stressed pronouns can be coordinated with each other or with other nouns by *et, ou*:

Maud et **moi** (NOT *je) en avons discuté à fond
Maud and I have discussed it in depth

Lui (NOT *il) et vous devrez vous mettre d'accord
You and he ought to come to an agreement

J'ai dit la même chose à vous et à **lui** (NOT *il)
I said the same thing to you and him

N.B.: The form the verb takes with coordinated subjects involving stressed pronouns is determined in the following way:

(a) If one of the pronouns is first person, the verb will be first person:

Lui et moi connaissons la famille
He and I know the family

Vous et moi connaissons la famille
You and I know the family

(b) In the absence of a first-person pronoun, if one of the pronouns is second person, the verb will be second person:

Vous et lui connaissez la famille
You and he know the family

(See also Section 9.1.1.)

A frequent way of expressing the notion 'somebody and I did X' is:

Avec quelqu'un nous avons fait X

Avec Christine nous avons ouvert les colis
Christine and I opened the parcels

3.3.6 **Stressed pronouns with *ne ... que* and *ni ... ni ... ne***

Stressed pronouns are used with the expressions *ne ... que* and *ni ... ni ... ne:*

Ce n'est que **lui**
It's only him

Gaële ne connaît qu'**eux**
Gaële only knows them

Pour moi, il n'y a qu'**elle** qui compte
For me, she's the only one who matters

Ni **moi** ni **lui** ne saurons quoi faire
Neither I nor he will know what to do

3.3.7 **Use of *soi***

soi is a non-specific stressed pronoun which is normally used either when it refers to non-specific persons or things or indefinite phrases like *on, chacun, nul, aucun, personne,* and *tout le monde*. It tends to be used after prepositions, with *-même*, and after *ne ... que:*

On pense à soi
People think of themselves

Pour une fois, personne ne songeait à soi
For once, no-one was thinking of themselves

On doit prendre la décision soi-même
One must take the decision oneself

3.4 **Demonstrative pronouns**

TABLE 3.G Summary table of demonstrative pronouns

		Proximate	Non-proximate
masc	celui	celui-ci	celui-là
sing	*the one*	*this one; the latter*	*that one; the former*
fem	celle	celle-ci	celle-là
sing	*the one*	*this one; the latter*	*that one; the former*
masc	ceux	ceux-ci	ceux-là
plur	*the ones*	*these ones; the latter*	*those ones; the former*
fem	celles	celles-ci	celles-là
plur	*the ones*	*these ones; the latter*	*those ones; the former*

Demonstrative pronouns are used where English uses 'the one'. They agree in gender with the noun they refer to

Sur ce mur nous voyons deux **portraits. Celui** qui est à droite représente Robespierre
On this wall we see two portraits. The one on the right is of Robespierre

On a expérimenté trois **AirBnBs** en Dordogne. **Celui** qui est près de Bergerac est le moins cher.
We tested three AirBnBs in the Dordogne. The one near Bergerac is the cheapest.

Demonstrative pronouns are used particularly frequently to 'head' relative clauses (see Section 15.1):

Ceux qui m'écoutent ce soir sauront que je n'ai rien à cacher
Those who are listening to me tonight will know that I have nothing to hide

Je ne peux rien faire pour vous : il faut vous adresser à **celui** qui est responsable de l'administration
I can do nothing for you: you must talk to the person who is responsible for administration

(For *ce qui, ce que, ce dont*, etc., see Section 15.9.)

3.4.1 Demonstrative pronouns with *-ci* and *-là*

The forms *celui-ci/celle-ci/ceux-ci/celles-ci* and *celui-là/celle-là/ceux-là/celles-là* translate English 'this one/these ones' and 'that one/those ones', respectively. These distinctions are mainly used in formal French:

Des deux tissus qui sont sur le comptoir, là-bas, il est évident que **celui-ci** est plus cher que **celui-là**
Of the two pieces of material on the counter over there, it's obvious that this one is dearer than that one

Pour moi tous les diamants se ressemblent. Mais **ceux-ci** coûtent deux fois plus cher que **ceux-là**
To me diamonds all look the same. But these ones here cost twice as much as those over there

N.B.: The pronouns with *-ci* can also mean 'the latter', and those with *-là* 'the former':

J'ai rencontré Yvon et Jordan au café. **Celui-là** arrivait à l'instant d'un entretien avec le percepteur
I met Yvon and Jordan at the café. The former had just come from a meeting with the tax inspector

Est-ce que vous désirez le flan ou la tarte aux pommes? **Celle- ci** sort directement du four
Do you want the custard pie or the apple tart? The latter has just come out of the oven

3.5 Possessive pronouns

TABLE 3.H Summary table of possessive pronouns

First person	**msg**	le mien	*mine*	le nôtre	*ours*
	fsg	la mienne		la nôtre	
	mpl	les miens		les nôtres	
	fpl	les miennes			
Second person	**msg**	le tien	*yours*	le vôtre	*yours*
	fsg	la tienne		la vôtre	
	mpl	les tiens		les vôtres	
	fpl	les tiennes			
Third person	**msg**	le sien	*his* *hers*	le leur	*theirs*
	fsg	la sienne		la leur	
	mpl	les siens		les leurs	
	fpl	les siennes			

Possessive pronouns agree in gender and number with a noun mentioned or implied elsewhere in the discourse:

Voici ta clef. Rends-moi **la mienne**
Here is your key. Give me back mine

Il avait une casquette qui n'était pas **la sienne**
He was wearing a cap which wasn't his

Ils ont emporté mes notes, mais j'ai gardé **les leurs**
They took away my notes, but I kept theirs

Tu ne peux pas prendre ceux-là, ils ne sont pas à nous. Ce sont **les leurs**
You can't take those, they don't belong to us. They are theirs.

Vos idées ne sont pas toujours **les nôtres**
Your ideas aren't always the same as ours

N.B.: *les siens* also has the special meaning of 'one's family': *On travaille pour les siens* 'People work for their families'.
les nôtres can mean 'with us', as in: *Elle n'était pas des nôtres* 'She wasn't with us'.

FREE

INSTRUCTOR & STUDENT RESOURCES

For more resources to practice your French grammar, including practice activities/quizzes for students, further resource links and an instructor guide, please visit https://routledgelearning.com/frenchgrammarandusage.

4 Adjectives

An adjective is a word that modifies a noun. It normally agrees with the noun it modifies. Adjectives may occur next to the noun (before or after) or separated from the noun in the second part of a sentence, e.g. after a verb such as *être, devenir, rester*. Adjectives may sometimes have complements:

un **petit** problème (preceding adjective, agreeing with a masculine noun)
a small problem

une boîte **carrée** (following adjective agreeing with a feminine noun)
a square box

Cette moto est **chère** (following a verb, agreeing with a feminine noun)
This motorbike is expensive

Ce problème est **facile à résoudre** (adjective with a complement)
This problem is easy to solve

4.1 Adjectives modifying the noun

Most French adjectives follow the noun. But there is a small set which normally precede, and another set which regularly appear before and after the noun, often with a change of meaning.

4.1.1 Adjectives which normally follow the noun

Since the majority of French adjectives normally follow the noun, English speakers really only need to learn those which can precede. However, here are some typical classes of adjectives which almost always follow the noun:

Colour adjectives

bleu, gris, vert, blanc, noir, violet, etc.:

un manteau gris
a grey coat

une souris grise
a grey mouse

un gazon vert
a green lawn

une veste verte
a green jacket

un nuage noir
a black cloud

une robe noire
a black dress

Adjectives of nationality

français 'French', *britannique* 'British', *grec* 'Greek', *tunisien* 'Tunisian', etc.:

un livre français
a French book

de la bière française
French beer

DOI: 10.4324/9781003373926-4

du vin algérien	une ville algérienne
Algerian wine	*an Algerian town*
du fromage grec	une antiquité grecque
Greek cheese	*a Greek antique*

N.B.: Adjectives of nationality in French begin with a small letter, unlike English. When *français, britannique*, etc., are used as nouns, however, they begin with a capital letter. Compare: *Elle est française* 'She is French' with *C'est une Française* 'She is a Frenchwoman' (see also Sections 4.5 and 3.1.22).

Adjectives of shape or form:

rond 'round', *carré* 'square', *rectangulaire* 'rectangular', *oval* 'oval', etc.:

un bureau carré	une boîte carrée
a square desk	*a square box*
un plateau rond	une table ronde
a round tray	*a round table*
un cadre rectangulaire	une cour rectangulaire
a rectangular frame	*a rectangular courtyard*

Adjectives describing religious affiliation

anglican 'Anglican', *catholique* 'Catholic', *musulman* 'Muslim', *protestant* 'Protestant', *orthodoxe* 'Orthodox';

un prêtre catholique	une jeune fille catholique
a Catholic priest	*a Catholic girl*
un père juif pratiquant	une mère juive pratiquante
a Jewish father	*a Jewish mother*
un garçon musulman	une jeune fille musulmane
a Muslim boy	*a Muslim girl*
un auteur athée	une auteure or une autrice athée
an atheistic author	*an atheistic woman author*

Adjectives which relate to a time or place of origin

une église médiévale	*a medieval church*
une ambiance citadine	*an urban atmosphere*
un paysage rural	*a rural landscape*
un accent campagnard	*a rustic accent*

Past and present participles

un mariage arrangé	une grille rouillée
an arranged marriage	*a rusty gate*
un élève brillant	une étoile brillante
a brilliant pupil	*a brilliant star*
un voyage fatigant	une voiture puissante
a tiring journey	*a powerful car*

N.B.: Present participles, which are formed by adding -*ant* to the first-person plural stem of a verb (e.g. *amus-ons/amusant, ralentiss-ons/ralentissant, dev-ons/devant*), can function both as a verb in a subordinate clause and as an adjective. As verbs in subordinate clauses present participles are invariable (see Section 17.9.2):

En **enfilant** son manteau, elle a dit au revoir
Putting her coat on, she said goodbye

J'ai rencontré des touristes **prenant** l'air sur l'esplanade
I met some tourists taking a stroll along the promenade

As adjectives they agree in gender and number with the noun they modify, as in the examples above: *une étoile brillante* (see Section 17.9.1).

A number of present participles are also spelled differently when they function as verbs in subordinate clauses and when they are adjectives. Some common cases are:

Verb in subordinate clause

convainquant	*convincing*
différant	*differing*
équivalant	*being equivalent to*
fatiguant	*tiring*
négligeant	*neglecting*
précédant	*preceding*

Adjective

convaincant	*convincing*
différent	*different*
équivalent	*equivalent*
fatigant	*tiring*
négligent	*negligent*
précédent	*previous*

4.1.2 Adjectives which normally occur before the noun

autre	une autre histoire	*another story*
beau/bel/belle	un bel homme	*a good-looking man*
bon/bonne	un bon professeur	*a good teacher*
bref/brève	un bref épisode	*a brief episode*
double	un double whisky	*a double whisky*
haut/e	de hautes montagnes	*high mountains*
joli/e	une jolie vue	*a pretty view*
mauvais/e	une mauvaise odeur	*a bad smell*
nouveau/nouvel/ nouvelle	une nouvelle maison	*a new house*
petit/e	un petit problème	*a small problem*
vaste	une vaste enceinte	*a vast arena*
vieux/vieil/vieille	un vieux château	*an old castle*

4.1.3 Adjectives which regularly occur before and after the noun, but with a change of meaning

The meaning given to a certain number of adjectives when they occur after a noun and when they occur after the verb *être* is the same:

Cette maison est ancienne *It's an old house*

But when these adjectives occur before the noun the meaning is different. Compare:

La rue est bordée de maisons anciennes
The street is lined with old(-style) houses
Son ancienne maison a été détruite
His former house was destroyed

When adjectives occur before the noun they tend to contribute to the meaning of the noun itself. So, *un ancien soldat* is an 'ex-soldier' rather than a soldier who is old; *un gros fumeur* is not 'a fat smoker', but 'a heavy smoker' (*un fumeur gros* is 'a fat smoker').

Common adjectives which have different meanings when they precede or follow nouns are:

ancien	un ancien élève	*an old boy/girl i.e. (ex-)pupil*
	une maison ancienne	*an old house*
brave	un brave type	*a nice guy*
	un homme brave	*a courageous man*
certain	d'un certain âge	*middle-aged*
	une vérité certaine	*a certain truth*
cher	mon cher ami	*my dear friend*
	une robe chère	*an expensive dress*
chic	un chic type (*rather old-fashioned now*)	*a nice guy*
	une robe chic	*a smart dress*
curieux	une curieuse histoire	*an odd story*
	une personne curieuse	*an inquisitive person*
dernier	son dernier livre	*his last book (latest)*
	la semaine dernière	*last week*
drôle	une drôle d'histoire	*an odd story*
	une histoire drôle	*a funny story*
fameux	ton fameux problème	*the problem you keep on going on about*
	un vin fameux	*a delicious wine (now rather old fashioned in this meaning)*
franc	une franche idiote	*a real idiot*
	une personne franche	*a frank person*
grand	un grand homme	*a great man*
	un homme grand	*a tall man*
gros	un gros effort	*a big effort*
	un homme gros	*a big man, a fat man*
jeune	une jeune femme	*a young woman*
	une femme jeune	*a woman who is not old*
Méchant	une méchante histoire	*a nasty business*
	une fille méchante	*an unpleasant girl*

même	toujours les mêmes histoires	*always the same stories/problems*
	le jour même	*that very day*
pauvre	un pauvre homme	*a man you feel sorry for*
	un homme pauvre	*a man who isn't rich*
propre	ma propre chambre	*my own bedroom*
	une serviette propre	*a clean towel*
pure	une pure illusion	*a complete illusion*
	de race pure	*pure bred*
rare	un rare moment de paix	*a precious moment of peace*
	un moment rare de l'histoire	*an exceptional moment in history*
sale	une sale histoire	*a nasty business*
	une nappe sale	*a dirty tablecloth*
seul	le seul inconvénient …	*the only disadvantage …*
	un homme seul	*a lonely man*
simple	une simple question de …	*simply a matter of …*
	une question simple	*an easy question*
triste	une triste histoire	*a sorry story*
	une histoire triste	*a sad story*
véritable	un véritable problème	*a real problem (serious)*
	un problème véritable	*a genuine problem (not invented)*
vert	une verte réprimande	*a real dressing-down*
	une voiture verte	*a green car*
vilain	une vilaine action	*a bad deed*
	un enfant vilain	*an ugly (or naughty) child*

N.B.: *neuf* and *nouveau*. *Ma voiture neuve* is likely to be 'my brand new car' (not second-hand), while *ma nouvelle voiture* is a car which is different from the one I had before (it may or may not be 'brand new'). *feu* 'late, deceased' can be used in two ways: *feu la reine/la feue reine*. Both mean 'the late queen', but note that in the first case *feu* does not agree with *reine*. Usually limited to legal papers.

4.1.4 Adjectives which normally follow the noun but can also precede, without significant changes in meaning

Most adjectives which normally follow the noun can occur before it as well, without a significant change in the meaning of the adjective. Such pre-positioning is usually for stylistic effect: to vary sentence structure or avoid having two or more adjectives following the same noun. The position before the noun is favoured where the adjective in some way measures or quantifies the meaning of the noun:

un léger rhume	*a slight cold*
une charmante soirée	*a delightful evening*
une forte odeur	*a strong smell*
un misérable repas	*a measly meal*
une importante augmentation	*a large increase*

4.1.5 **Combinations of adjectives**

Multiple adjectives before the noun

Cardinal numbers are usually the first in any combination of adjectives preceding a noun, but after that the order of adjectives is the same as it is in English:

les **deux** premières semaines	*the first two weeks*
les **quatre** dernières jolies phrases	*the last four pretty sentences*
au bon vieux temps	*in the good old days*
une autre nouvelle maison	*another new house*
un vrai beau grand château	*a really beautiful large castle*
ce pauvre cher homme	*that poor dear man*

The exception to cardinal numbers occurring first is when a complex number is involved:

Il m'a versé les derniers **sept cents** euros qu'il me devait
He paid me the last seven hundred euros he owed me

To avoid having a long string of adjectives before the noun, one or more may be combined with *et*, and/or moved after the noun. To illustrate, 'a young pretty little cat' could be

un jeune et joli petit chat *or*
un petit chat jeune et joli

Multiple adjectives after the noun

The order of adjectives after the noun is the mirror image of English. For example, 'the Spanish Civil War' becomes 'the War Civil Spanish': *la guerre civile espagnole*

des lignes parallèles invisibles	*invisible parallel lines*
des milieux politiques américains	*American political circles*
des feuilles mortes humides	*damp dead leaves*
un agent commercial français	*a French business agent*
une fibre optique dédiée d'un très haut débit	*a dedicated high-speed fibre optic*

4.1.6 **Adjectives modified by adverbs and prepositional phrases**

When adjectives, which normally precede the noun, are modified by adverbs or prepositional phrases, they may appear after the noun. The longer the modifying expression, the more likely this is:

un bel homme	*a handsome man*
un très bel homme	*a very handsome man*
un homme vraiment beau	*a really handsome man*
un gros effort	*a great effort*
un effort démesurément gros	*an inordinately large effort*
une jolie figure	*a pretty face*
une figure un peu trop jolie	*a face which is a bit too pretty*
un grand jardin	*a large garden*
un jardin grand comme un mouchoir de poche	*a garden the size of your hand*

This also applies to superlatives (see Section 4.12.2):

un bref aperçu	*a brief outline*
le plus bref aperçu	*the briefest outline*
un aperçu des plus brefs	*the briefest of outlines*

4.1.7 **Adjectives preceded by** *de*

When nouns are quantified by numbers, following adjectives may directly follow the noun or they may be preceded by *de*. The use with *de* is found in informal French. For a number of speakers there is a difference in meaning between the two. When *de* is present, the implication is that there were more of the things described by the noun than the number indicates:

Il y avait dix voyageurs de blessés
There were ten travellers injured
(implies that there were more than ten involved, but the rest weren't injured)

Il y avait dix voyageurs blessés
There were ten injured travellers
(has no implication about whether there were other, non-injured travellers)

J'ai une heure de libre aujourd'hui
I have an hour free today
(implies that all the other hours in my day are busy)

J'ai une heure libre aujourd'hui
I have a free hour today
(has no implication about whether my other hours are busy or not)

Note that the contrast in English is captured by whether the adjective precedes or follows the noun.

4.2 **Adjectives which follow verbs or verbal expressions**

Some verbs and verbal expressions can be followed by adjectives. With the following verbs/ verbal expressions, adjectives must agree in number and gender with the subject:

avoir l'air	*to seem, appear*
être	*to be*
être considéré comme	*to be thought of as*
devenir	*to become*
se montrer	*to show oneself to be*
paraître	*to appear*
passer pour	*to be considered to be*
sembler	*to seem*

Il est aussi **beau** que son frère
He's as handsome as his brother

Les enfants semblent **énervés** par ce temps
The children seem over-excited by this weather

Tous les membres de la famille passent pour **pauvres**
All the members of the family are thought to be poor

With the following verbs, mainly those which express an opinion, adjectives must agree in number and gender with the direct object:

croire	*to believe*
considérer	*to consider*
deviner	*to guess*
imaginer	*to imagine*
s'imaginer	*to imagine oneself*
traiter qn de	*to call sb sth*
trouver	*to find*
voir	*to see*
se voir	*to see oneself*

Je croyais la bataille **perdue** d'avance
I thought the battle was already lost

Je les devine un peu **fâchés** par cette histoire
I guess they are a little bit annoyed by this affair

Vous les voyez toujours **petits**; mais ils ont grandi
You see them as if they were still little; but they've grown up

Les enfants traitaient les petits voisins de **lâches**
The children were calling the little neighbours cowards

4.3   Adjectives with complements

Some adjectives can be followed by nouns, pronouns or infinitives, with a linking *de* or *à*:

Ils étaient **blancs de** colère
They were white with anger

Ces jeunes femmes sont très **sûres d'**elles
These young women are very self-confident

Je suis très **heureux de** faire votre connaissance
I am very pleased to meet you

Ce problème est **facile à** résoudre
This problem is easy to solve

(For the use of *de* with adjectives followed by nouns, see Section 13.15.2; and followed by infinitives, see Section 12.7.)

4.4 Indefinite and negative noun phrases with adjective complements

Indefinite noun phrases such as *quelque chose* 'something', *quelqu'un* 'someone', *ceci* 'this', *cela* 'that', *quoi?* 'what?', and negative expressions such as *rien* 'nothing', *personne* 'no-one', can be followed by adjectives linked by *de*. The adjective is invariable in this construction:

quelque chose de **bon**	*something good*
quelqu'un d'**intéressant**	*someone interesting*

rien de plus **facile**	*nothing easier*
Quoi de **neuf**?	*What's new?*

4.5 **Adjectives used as nouns**

In French it is almost always possible to convert an adjective into a noun simply by placing an article in front of it:

Je ne veux que **les mûrs**	*I only want the ripe ones*
Nous prendrons **les grands**	*We'll take the big ones*
Les petits sont déjà partis	*The small ones have already gone*
Les gentils gagnent à la fin	*The goodies win in the end*
Les méchants sont punis	*The baddies are punished*
J'adore **le rustique**	*I love rural styles*
Elle aurait préféré **du contemporain**	*She would have preferred something up-to-date*
Le plus énervant, c'est sa voix	*It's her voice that is the most annoying thing*
Le rouge te va bien	*Red suits you*
L'important c'est de partir tôt	*The important thing is to leave early*

As can be seen, because English does not permit the creation of nouns with such freedom, translations either have to use vague terms like 'ones', 'thing(s)', or it is necessary to rephrase the sentence.

N.B.: Compare the post-verbal use of adjectives as nouns with the post-verbal use of numbers and quantifiers as nouns:

Nous prendrons **les grands**	*We'll take the big ones*
Nous **en** prendrons deux	*We'll take two*
Nous avons acheté **les ovales**	*We bought the oval ones*
Nous **en** avons acheté plusieurs	*We bought several*

With numbers and quantifiers *en* must be inserted in front of the verb (see Sections 3.2.25 and 6.1.7).

Adjectives of nationality and nouns of nationality are usually identical in form when used as adjectives or nouns EXCEPT that the nouns are written with capital letters:

Elle est **américaine**	*She is American*
C'est une **Américaine**	*She is an American*
Tout Français qui se respecte aime	*Every true French person loves*
le fromage	*cheese*
Elle est de nationalité française	*She is of French nationality*

4.6 **Adjectives used as adverbs and adverbs used as adjectives**

A limited number of adjectives can also be used as adverbs. In this case they are invariable (see also Section 5.3):

bas	Ils parlent bas	*They're talking very quietly*
bon	Le café sent bon	*The coffee smells good*
cher	Cela coûte trop cher	*That's too expensive*
clair	Je n'arrive pas à y voir clair dans son raisonnement	*I can't make much sense of his argument*

droit	Ils marchent droit	*They are walking straight*
dur	Ils travaillent dur	*They work hard*
faux	Elles chantent faux	*They sing out of tune*
fin	Il faut couper le jambon très fin	*You must slice the ham very thinly*
fort	Ils parlent trop fort	*They're talking too loudly*
grand	Ils ont vu trop grand	*They attempted too much*
jeune	Ils s'habillent jeune	*They dress in a youthful manner*
juste	Tu as vu juste dès le début	*You understood from the beginning*
lourd	Cet acte pèse lourd sur ma conscience	*That act weighs heavily on my conscience*
menu	de la viande hachée menu	*meat cut up finely*
vieux	Ils font vieux	*They look old*

A few adverbs are used as adjectives as in:

Il y a un problème avec les roues **arrière**
There is something wrong with the back wheels

J'ai dû nettoyer les sièges **avant**
I had to clean the front seats

J'ai toujours pensé que c'était une femme **bien**
I always thought she was a woman of integrity

Il ne reste que des places **debout**
There is only standing room left

In these cases the adverb/adjective is always invariable.

4.7 **Masculine and feminine forms of adjectives**

The general rule is that an -*e* is added to the masculine written form of adjectives to produce the feminine form. (See Section 4.15 for how inclusive writing proposes to deal with this.)

4.7.1 **A change in written, but not spoken, French**

In cases where the masculine form ends in one of the following vowels or consonants, there is a change in the written form but not in the spoken form:

	Masculine	**Feminine**	
-*u*	absolu	absolue	*absolute*
	aigu	aiguë	*high (sound)*
	ambigu	ambiguë	*ambiguous*
	contigu	contiguë	*contiguous*

N.B.: In the case of *aigu, ambigu,* and *contigu*, a diaresis (ë) is added to the feminine -*e* in written French to indicate that the -*u* sound is maintained in spoken French (*aigue** would be pronounced rather like English 'egg' otherwise; compare *long/longue*). (See Appendix 2 for possible changes in the position of the diaresis in *Novuvelle Orthographe*.)

-*é*	fermé	fermée	*closed*
-*er*	fier	fière	*proud*
	cher	chère	*expensive*
	amer	amère	*bitter*

N.B.: In these cases, where the final *r* is pronounced in the masculine, a grave accent is added to the first written *e*.

-i	hardi	hardie	*bold*

N.B.: Exception:	favori	favorite	*favourite*

-c	public	publique	*public*
	turc	turque	*Turkish*

N.B.: c is maintained in:	grec	grecque	*Greek*

-ct	direct	directe	*direct*

-r	sûr	sûre	*certain*
	pur	pure	*pure*

-al	national	nationale	*national*
	général	générale	*general*
	hivernal	hivernale	*winter*
	final	finale	*final*

-el	personnel	personnelle	*personal*
	professionnel	professionnelle	*professional*
	passionnel	passionnelle	*emotive*
	cruel	cruelle	*cruel*

-ul	nul	nulle	*no-good*

N.B.: In these cases, it is *-le* which is added and not just *-e*.

-ol	espagnol	espagnole	*Spanish*

-il	puéril	puérile	*childish*
	civil	civile	*civil*

N.B.: In these cases, the *l* is pronounced in the masculine.

By contrast in the following adjectives the final *-il* is pronounced as indicated:

gentil [-i]	gentille [-ij]	*kind*
pareil [-ej]	pareille [-ej]	*similar*
vermeil [-ej]	vermeille [-ej]	*bright red*

4.7.2 A change in written and spoken French

In the following cases, addition of feminine *-e* to the written masculine form also corresponds to the pronunciation of a final consonant in spoken French:

Addition of -e without further changes:

-t	petit	petite	*small*
	cuit	cuite	*cooked*
-s	gris	grise	*grey*
	mauvais	mauvaise	*bad*
-d	grand	grande	*tall, big*

Addition of -*e* and doubling of the final consonant

-as	bas	basse	*low*
	gras	grasse	*fatty*
	épais	épaisse	*thick*
	las	lasse	*tired*
-et	muet	muette	*mute*
	coquet	coquette	*cute*
-ot	sot	sotte	*stupid*

Addition of -*e* and a grave accent

-et	complet	complète	*complete*
	inquiet	inquiète	*worried*
	secret	secrète	*secret*
	discret	discrète	*discreet*
	concret	concrète	*concrete*
	replet	replète	*plump*

4.7.3 A change from a nasal vowel to an oral vowel

In the following cases, addition of -*e*, and sometimes the doubling of the final consonant, corresponds to a change from a nasal vowel to an oral vowel + consonant in spoken French:

paysan	paysanne	*peasant/farming*
partisan	partisane	*biased*
ancien	ancienne	*old*
enfantin	enfantine	*childlike*
européen	européenne	*European*
féminin	féminine	*feminine*
fin	fine	*fine*
mignon	mignonne	*pretty*
bon	bonne	*good*
brun	brune	*brown*
opportun	opportune	*opportune*

N.B.: In some cases -*ne* is added and not just -*e*.

4.7.4 A change in the final consonant or syllable

In the following cases, addition of final -*e* is accompanied by a change in the final consonant or the whole of the final syllable:

-ais/aîche	frais	fraîche	*fresh*
-aux/ausse	faux	fausse	*false*
-er/ère	premier	première	*first*
	dernier	dernière	*last*
	étranger	étrangère	*foreign*

-eux/euse	heureux	heureuse	*happy*
	amoureux	amoureuse	*in love*
	nerveux	nerveuse	*nervous*
	affreux	affreuse	*frightful*
	peureux	peureuse	*frightened*

-eux/-eille	vieux	vieille	*old*
-eur/euse	voleur	voleuse	*thieving, dishonest*
	flatteur	flatteuse	*flattering*
	trompeur	trompeuse	*misleading*
	moqueur	moqueuse	*likes to make fun of others*
	joueur	joueuse	*playful*

-eur/eresse	vengeur	vengeresse	*vengeful*

-eur/rice	consolateur	consolatrice	*consoling*
	observateur	observatrice	*observant*
	créateur	créatrice	*creative*
	conservateur	conservatrice	*conservative*

-eau/elle	nouveau	nouvelle	*new*
	beau	belle	*beautiful*
	jumeau	jumelle	*twin*

-c/che	sec	sèche	*dry*
	blanc	blanche	*white*
	franc	franche	*frank*

-f/ve	neuf	neuve	*new*
	actif	active	*active*
	bref	brève	*brief*
	créatif	créative	*creative*
	vif	vive	*lively*

-in/igne	bénin	bénigne	*benign*
	malin	maligne	*sharp, clever*

-ong/ongue	long	longue	*long*
-ou/olle	mou	molle	*soft*
	fou	folle	*mad*

-oux/ouce/	doux	douce	*gentle*
ousse	roux	rousse	*red-haired*

N.B.: *beau, fou, mou, nouveau,* and *vieux* also have a special masculine form – *bel, fol, mol, nouvel,* and *vieil* – which appears when a following noun begins with a vowel or a so-called 'silent h':

un bel effet	*a fine effect*
un fol espoir	*a vain hope*
un nouvel homme	*a new, a changed man*
un mol effort	*a weak effort*
un vieil hélicoptère	*an old helicopter*

4.7.5 **No change in written or spoken French**

In cases where the adjective already ends in -*e*, there is no change:

manifeste	masculine and feminine	*obvious*
sale	masculine and feminine	*dirty*
tranquille	masculine and feminine	*calm*
utile	masculine and feminine	*useful*

4.8 **Plural forms of adjectives**

4.8.1 **The normal case**

In most cases -*s* is added to the singular form of the adjective and there is no change in the pronunciation:

Elle est contente
She is happy

Elles sont contentes
They (f) are happy

Il est content
He is happy

Ils sont contents
They (m) are happy

La veste est rouge
The jacket is red

Les vestes sont rouges
The jackets are red

Le sac est rouge
The bag is red

Les sacs sont rouges
The bags are red

If the word ends in -*s* or -*x*, it will be invariable:

Notre fils est heureux
Our son is happy

Nos fils sont heureux
Our sons are happy

Le cahier est gris
The exercise book is grey

Les cahiers sont gris
The exercise books are grey

4.8.2 **Adjectives which end in -*eau* add *x* rather than *s***

Un nouveau portable
A new laptop (or mobile phone)

De nouveaux portables
New laptops (or mobile phones)

Un beau cadre
A beautiful setting

De beaux cadres
Beautiful settings

4.8.3 **Adjectives which end in -*al* generally change to -*aux***

L'acteur principal
Main actor

Des acteurs princip**aux**
Main actors

Le principe général
The general principle

Des principes génér**aux**
General principles

Un homme marginal	Des hommes margin**aux**
A man on the margins (of society)	*Men on the margins (of society)*

Un point de vue normal	Des points de vue norm**aux**
A normal point of view	*Normal points of view*

Exceptions: *banal, bancal, fatal, glacial, naval, natal*

Un discours banal	Des discours banal**s**
A banal speech	*Banal speeches*

Un buffet bancal	Des buffets bancal**s**
A sideboard with a damaged leg	*Sideboards with damaged legs*

Un revirement fatal	Des revirements fatal**s**
A fatal change of heart	*Fatal changes of heart*

Un vent glacial	Des vents glacial**s**
A very cold wind	*Very cold winds*

Un chantier naval	Des chantiers naval**s**
A naval dockyard	*Naval dockyards*

Mon pays natal	Des pays natal**s**
My home country	*Home countries*

Adjectives which alternate:

idéal	idéals	*and*	idéaux	*ideal*
matinal	matinals	*and*	matinaux	*early morning*
pascal	pascals	*and*	pascaux	*related to Easter*
astral	astrals	*and*	astraux	*related to stars*

With these adjectives the plural in *-aux* is tending to dominate.

4.9 Adjective agreement with nouns

4.9.1 Adjectives agreeing with just one noun

Adjectives agree in gender and number with the noun whose meaning they modify. This is usually straightforward when there is just one noun:

d'une voix hésitant**e**	*in a faltering voice*
ce fameu**x** dimanche	*that famous Sunday*
L'eau était froid**e**	*The water was cold*

Il lançait aux passants	*He shot rapid and*
des regards rapide**s** et insistants	*insistent glances at the passers-by*

N.B.: A plural noun might be modified by a string of singular adjectives, depending on the meaning: *Les économies **russe**, **bulgare** et **roumaine** rencontraient de graves difficultés* 'The Russian, Bulgarian and Romanian economies were (each) encountering serious difficulties'.

4.9.2 **An adjective agreeing with nouns linked by *et, ou*, or *ni***

The adjective may agree with the closest noun only:

une table et une chaise bleue	*a table and a blue chair*

The adjective may agree with all the nouns, in which case it will be plural and will be feminine only if all the nouns are feminine. Otherwise it will be masculine:

une table et une chaise bleues	*a blue table and chair*
Il ne portait ni veste ni pantalon bleus	*He was wearing neither a blue jacket nor a blue pair of trousers*
un stylo ou un cahier bleus	*a blue pen or exercise book*

4.9.3 **An adjective agreeing with nouns linked by *de***

The adjective may agree with the first or the second noun, depending on the meaning:

un groupe de **chanteuses** talentueuses	*a group of talented female singers*
une **bande** de voyous agressive	*an aggressive gang of layabouts*
des **bains** de mer fréquents	*frequent dips in the sea*
un geste de **générosité** déplacée	*an act of misplaced generosity*

N.B.: *un/une drôle de* can be used adjectivally meaning 'weird', 'strange'. Its gender is determined by the following noun: *une drôle d'idée* 'a strange idea', *un drôle de type* 'a weird bloke'.

4.9.4 **Adjective agreement with *gens***

Gens 'people' is usually said in dictionaries to be feminine plural. When an adjective precedes *gens* it takes a feminine plural form, as in *de **bonnes** gens* 'good people', *de **vieilles** gens* 'old people'. BUT when the adjective follows *gens* it is masculine plural, as in *des gens **bons** et honnêtes* 'good, honest people'.

When the adjective follows a verb, e.g. *être*, it is also masculine plural as in *Ces bonnes gens sont bien **naïfs*** 'Those good people are rather naïve'. *Les vieilles gens sont **attachés** à leurs racines* 'Old people are close to their roots'.

Jeunes gens is always masculine, as in *de beaux jeunes gens* 'fine young people/men', and *des jeunes gens* 'young men' is often opposed to the set phrase *des jeunes filles* 'young women'. (See also Section 1.2.4.)

4.10 **Invariable adjectives**

A number of adjectives do not change either in relation to gender or to number. It is sometimes argued that these are nouns being used adjectivally.

un pull **marron**	une jupe **marron**	des chaussures **marron**
a brown pullover	*a brown skirt*	*brown shoes*
un carton **orange**	une voiture **orange**	des rideaux **orange**
an orange box	*an orange car*	*orange curtains*

un haut **crème**	une jupe **crème**	des sous-vêtements **crème**
a cream top	*a cream skirt*	*cream underwear*

un portable **bon marché**	*a cheap laptop* (or *mobile phone*)
une planche à roulettes **bon marché**	*a cheap skateboard*
des fruits **bon marché**	*cheap fruit*

un pull **cerise**	*a cherry pullover*
une tapisserie **cerise**	*cherry-coloured wallpaper*
des uniformes **cerise**	*cherry-coloured uniforms*

Other invariable adjectives:

angora	*angora*
baba	*flabbergasted (informal)*
bath	*great*
cucu (*or* cucul)	*naff (informal)*
gaga	*nuts (informal)*
gnangnan	*gormless, dopey (informal)*
kaki	*khaki*
pop	*pop*
porno	*porn (used as an adjective; informal)*
riquiqui	*inadequate (too small, informal)*
rococo	*rococo*
snob	*snobbish*
sympa	*friendly (informal)*

The adjective *grand* appears in invariable form in certain fixed combinations, notably:

grand-mère	*grandmother*
grand-tante	*great aunt*
grand-route	*main road, highway*
pas grand-chose	*not much*
grand-rue	*high street*
grand-messe	*High Mass*
à grand-peine	*with great difficulty*
avoir grand-faim	*to be starving (formal)*

In these cases *grand* and the following noun should be linked with a hyphen. They alternate with the uses of *grand* in 'non-fixed' and non-hyphenated expressions such as *On n'oublie jamais les grandes peines de cœur de sa jeunesse* 'You can't forget the big heartbreaks of your youth', *ils ont suivi une grande rue le long du marché* 'They followed a long, wide street by the market'.

N.B.: *chic* is invariable for gender but agrees for number:

un manteau **chic**	une robe **chic**	des vêtements **chics**
a smart coat	*a smart dress*	*smart clothes*

4.11 Compound adjectives

Like compound nouns (see Section 1.2.11), compound adjectives can be made up in a variety of ways. Their internal structure determines the way in which they agree with the noun they modify.

4.11.1 **Adjective–adjective compounds**

Where adjectives are coordinated, both agree with the noun:

sourd-muet *deaf-mute*	Nous luttons pour sensibiliser le public contre l'usage de l'expression 'enfants sourds-muets' *We are campaigning to encourage people not to use the term 'deaf-mute children'.*
aigre-doux *sweet and sour*	J'adore les sauces aigres-douces *I adore sweet and sour sauces*
nouveau-né *new-born*	Les bébés nouveaux-nés sont très fatigants pour leurs parents *New-born babies are very exhausting for their parents*
dernier-né *last-born*	Les filles dernières-nées profitent de la présence de leurs frères et sœurs *Last-born girls take advantage of the presence of their brothers and sisters*
grand-ouvert *wide open*	Ils dorment la bouche grande-ouverte *They sleep with their mouths wide open*

Exception: where the first adjective ends in -*i*, -*o*, only the second part agrees:

tragi-comique *tragi-comedy*	Toutes ses pièces étaient tragi-comiques *All her plays were tragi-comedies*
franco-allemand *Franco-German*	Dans le cadre de l'union européenne, les accords franco-allemands ont duré près d'un demi-siècle *Within the European framework, the Franco-German agreements have lasted for almost half a century*

4.11.2 **Adverb-adjective compounds**

Where an adverb and an adjective are combined, the adverb (always the first element) remains invariable and the adjective agrees:

haut placé *highly placed*	Je connais des fonctionnaires haut placés qui pourraient nous aider *I know some highly placed civil servants who could help us*
bien intentionné *well-intentioned*	Ce sont toujours les personnes bien intentionnées qui créent le plus de problèmes *It's always the well-intentioned people who cause the most problems*
avant-coureur *early-warning*	Voilà les signes avant-coureurs d'une maladie grave *There are the early-warning signs of a serious illness*

4.11.3 **Colour adjective compounds**

Combinations of colour adjectives remain invariable:

des cheveux **châtain clair**	*light-brown hair*
une veste **bleu foncé**	*a dark-blue jacket*
une mer **vert-bouteille**	*a bottle-green sea*
une couverture **gris-rouge**	*a red-grey cover*

4.11.4 **Compounds involving *demi-*, *nu-*, and *mi-***

In combinations involving *demi-*, *nu-* and *mi-*, *demi-*, and *nu-* are invariable before the noun, but agree when they follow it:

une **demi**-heure	but	une heure et **demie**
a half-hour		*an hour and a half*
une **demi**-page		une page et **demie**
a half-page		*a page and a half*
nu-tête		sortir tête **nue**
bareheaded		*to go out without a hat*
nu-pieds		sortir pieds **nus**
barefoot		*to go out bare footed*

mi- can only occur before the noun and is invariable:

à **mi**-temps	*part-time (e.g. work)*
la **mi**-juin	*halfway through June*
la **mi**-saison	*middle season (Spring, Autumn)*
la **mi**-journée	*the middle of the day*
mi-américain	*half-American*
mi-clos	*half-open, half-closed*
mi-cuisse	*mid-thigh*

4.12 **Comparative and superlative forms of adjectives**

4.12.1 **Comparatives**

In English, adjectives can be used to compare one entity with another by adding '-er', or putting 'more' or 'less' in front: 'bigger', 'lighter', 'more dangerous', 'less interesting'. In French, the comparative forms of adjectives are created by putting *plus* 'more' or *moins* 'less' in front of them. The adjective stays in the position it would normally occupy, before or after the noun, and agrees with the noun as usual (see Section 4.9):

Il désire avoir une **plus petite** voiture
He wants to have a smaller car

Je n'ai jamais fait de traversée **plus dangereuse**
I have never made a more dangerous crossing

Ce film est **moins intéressant** pour les enfants
This film is less interesting for children

Elle semble **moins malade** aujourd'hui
She seems less ill today

plus and *moins* make unequal comparisons between entities. A related construction is *aussi* 'as' (which often changes to *si* after a negation), which makes a comparison of equality between entities:

Il désire avoir une **aussi grande** voiture
He wants to have as big a car

Le courant n'est pas **si dangereux** par ici
The current isn't as dangerous here

N.B.: Adding *aussi* to a preceding adjective does not alter its position. This contrasts with English. Compare: *une* **aussi grande** *voiture* with 'as big a car'.

In clauses dependent on nouns modified by comparative adjectives with *plus* and *moins*, writers often insert *ne, le*, or *ne le* in formal French:

Le télétravail est plus difficile qu'on **(ne) (le)** pense
Working from home is more difficult than one thinks

Le film est moins intéressant qu'on **(ne) (l')**espérait
The film is less interesting than we hoped

In clauses dependent on nouns modified by comparative adjectives with *aussi*, only *le* may be inserted in formal French:

La charge de travail est aussi lourde que je le croyais
The workload is as demanding as I thought

There are two irregular comparative forms of adjectives which are used productively in French:

meilleur/-e	*better* (comparative of *bon* 'good')
pire	*worse* (comparative of *mauvais* 'bad')

meilleur is used everywhere that *bon* could be and agrees with the noun it modifies:

Elle désire avoir une **meilleure** place
She wants to have a better seat

Ces marchandises sont **meilleures**
These goods are better

Le texte est **meilleur** maintenant que tu l'as raccourci
The text is better now you have shortened it

(For the distinction between *meilleur* and *mieux*, see Section 5.6.6.)

pire and *plus mauvais* both exist. *plus mauvais* is the most commonly used form, but *pire* will be used where the comparison is between two things which are already both bad:

Le remède est **pire** que le mal
The cure is worse than the illness

or to refer to abstract nouns:

La vérité est cruelle, mais le mensonge est **pire**
The truth is cruel, but lying is worse

4.12.2 **Superlatives**

In English, adjectives can be used to describe the best or worst of something by adding '-est' or putting 'most' or 'least' in front of them: 'biggest', 'lightest', 'most dangerous', 'least interesting'. These are superlative forms of adjectives.

In French the superlative forms of adjectives are created by putting the definite article – *le, la, les* – in front of the comparative forms: *la plus grande voiture* 'the biggest car', *la plus forte odeur* 'the strongest smell'. When adjectives follow the noun, this means that there are two definite articles, one before the noun and one before the comparative form of the adjective: *la voiture la plus puissante* 'the most powerful car', *les virages les plus dangereux* 'the most dangerous bends'. Note that the article agrees in gender and number with the noun:

C'était **le plus grand** joueur de tous.
He was the greatest player of all

Elle est **la moins ambitieuse** de sa fratrie
She is the least ambitious of all her siblings

C'est la route **la plus dangereuse** de la région
It's the most dangerous road in the region

N.B.: 'in' after superlative adjectives is usually *de: la route la plus dangereuse de la région, la moins malade de sa famille.* (See Section 13.15.3.)

There are three irregular superlative forms of adjectives which are used productively in French:

le/la/les meilleur(e)(s)	*the best* (superlative of *bon* 'good')
le/la/les pire(s)	*the worst* (superlative of *mauvais* 'bad')
le/la/les moindre(s)	*the least* (superlative of *petit* 'small')

The conditions under which *meilleur* and *pire* are used are the same as those described in Section 4.12.1:

Notre chef de cuisine est **le meilleur** de la ville
Our chef is the best in town

Elle s'entoure **des meilleurs** musiciens
She surrounds herself with the best musicians

Cette solution est **la pire** des trois proposées
This solution is the worst of the three proposed

Le pire, c'était qu'elle voulait revenir
The worst thing was that she wanted to come back

le/la/les moindre(s) is used in semi-fixed expressions, and with abstract nouns:

le principe du moindre effort
the principle of least effort

Ils ont essayé de suivre la politique du moindre mal
They tried to follow the policy which would do the least harm

Where concrete nouns are involved, however, *le/la/les plus petit(e)(s)* is used:

Il a choisi **le plus petit** diamant
He chose the smallest diamond

When adjectives, which normally precede nouns, are used in a superlative form, they may follow the noun they modify on the grounds that they are 'too long' to appear in front of the noun (see Section 4.1.6):

un bref aperçu	**le plus bref** aperçu *or* l'aperçu **le plus bref**
a brief outline	*the briefest outline*
un jeune homme	**le plus jeune** homme *or* l'homme **le plus jeune**
a young man	*the youngest man*

4.13 **Subjunctive versus indicative in clauses dependent on a superlative adjective**

Clauses dependent on nouns modified by a superlative adjective have a verb in the subjunctive if the construction claims a unique status for the noun. For example:

Ils ont acheté le plus grand sapin de Noël qu'ils **aient** pu trouver
They bought the biggest Christmas tree that they could find
(They couldn't find a bigger tree, so it is unique)

But where the construction does not claim a unique status for the noun, the verb in the dependent clause is in the indicative:

Ils ont acheté le plus grand sapin de Noël qu'ils **ont** pu transporter dans leur voiture
They bought the biggest Christmas tree that they could take in their car
(there is no claim that it is the biggest Christmas tree available)

(For more on this construction, see Sections 11.1.8 and 15.11.3.)

4.14 **Absolute use of the superlative**

One way of translating into French expressions like 'the simplest of all', 'the most interesting imaginable' (known as 'absolute superlatives') is to put the expression *des plus* in front of the adjective: *des plus simple(s)*, *des plus intéressant(s)*. In this construction the adjective must agree in gender with the noun it modifies, but if the noun is singular the adjective may be either singular or plural:

C'était une journée des plus intéressante(s)
It was the most interesting of days

C'était un voyage des plus intéressant(s)
It was the most interesting trip imaginable

In modern French the plural form is probably the more frequent of the two.

Other ways of expressing an absolute superlative are:

Ce raisonnement est tout ce qu'il y a de plus simple
This line of argument is of the simplest kind

Un raisonnement on ne peut plus simple
The simplest line of argument of all

Il préfère des solutions les plus simples possible (*possible* is invariable in this construction)
He prefers the simplest possible solutions

4.15 **Adjective agreement in inclusive writing**

In many cases adjective agreement in inclusive writing would be the same as in traditional writing. However, where more than one noun is involved and the gender of the nouns is different, proponents of *l'écriture inclusive* would seek to give equal value to each of the nouns.

If we take the following sentence:

Les acteurs et les actrices renvoyés par la direction ont manifesté devant le théâtre.
The actors and actresses sacked by the management demonstrated in front of the theatre

Following the rules given in this chapter, *renvoyés* would be taken to include both male and female actors on the grounds that the masculine includes the feminine. However, in order to give full and equal value to both sexes, those who endorse inclusive writing might propose:

Les act.eur.rice.s renvoyé.e.s par la direction ont manifesté devant le théâtre.

This approach will work more or less well depending on the combinations of nouns and adjectives and on how the word endings are divided, which may vary as practice is not currently finalised. As shown in this chapter, these combinations can be varied and producing sentences like this one with some of the examples in this chapter would be complex.

In the introduction to Chapter 3 (Pronouns) we have introduced some of the issues surrounding inclusive writing and provided some references. However, this is a subject in current and constant evolution: many blogs, websites, and chats can be found which promote *l'écriture inclusive*. If you are curious to see how they propose to deal with adjective agreement, try exploring some of those.

FREE

**INSTRUCTOR
& STUDENT
RESOURCES**

For more resources to practice your French grammar, including practice activities/quizzes for students, further resource links, and an instructor guide, please visit https://routledgelearning.com/frenchgrammarandusage.

5 Adverbs

5.1 Function of adverbs

Adverbs are words or phrases of invariable form which modify the meaning of words, phrases, or whole sentences:

Il est entré dans un monde **étrangement** silencieux
He entered a strangely silent world

(*étrangement* modifies just *silencieux*; it is the silence which is strange, not the person or the world he enters)

J'ai entendu un bruit **dehors**
I heard a noise outside

(*dehors* modifies just *entendre un bruit*; it indicates where the noise was, not where the person hearing it was)

Soudain j'ai entendu un bruit
Suddenly I heard a noise

(*soudain* modifies the sentence and expresses the suddenness of the whole event)

5.2 Formation of adverbs with the ending *-ment*

5.2.1 Adverbs ending in *-ment* derived from the feminine form of an adjective

Most adverbs ending in *-ment* are formed from the **feminine** form of a corresponding adjective:

Adjective		Feminine		Adverb	
affreux	*awful*	affreuse	*awful*	affreusement	*awfully*
clair	*clear*	claire	*clear*	clairement	*clearly*
distinct	*distinct*	distincte	*distinct*	distinctement	*distinctly*
doux	*gentle*	douce	*gentle*	doucement	*gently*
mou	*soft*	molle	*soft*	mollement	*softly*
naturel	*natural*	naturelle	*natural*	naturellement	*naturally*
public	*public*	publique	*public*	publiquement	*publicly*
professionnel	*professional*	professionnelle	*professional*	professionnellement	*professionally*
sec	*dry*	sèche	*dry*	sèchement	*drily*
sûr	*sure*	sûre	*sure*	sûrement	*surely*
vif	*alive*	vive	*alive*	vivement	*lively*

Exception:

gentil	*kind*	gentille	*kind*	gentiment	*kindly*

Although *-ment* corresponds broadly to English '-ly', French is much less productive than English. Often English '-ly' adverbs must be translated by phrases (see Section 5.5).

DOI: 10.4324/9781003373926-5

5.2.2 **Adverbs ending in *-ment* derived from the masculine form of an adjective**

Where an adjective ends in *-i* (not *-oi*), *-é*, or *-u* (not *-eau* or *-ou*), the adverb is formed from the masculine form:

Adjective		Feminine		Adverb	
absolu	*absolute*	absolue	*absolute*	absolument	*absolutely*
ambigu	*ambiguous*	ambiguë	*ambiguous*	ambigument	*ambiguously*
aisé	*easy*	aisée	*easy*	aisément	*easily*
joli	*pretty*	jolie	*pretty*	joliment	*prettily*
vrai	*true*	vraie	*true*	vraiment	*truly*

Exception:

gai	*cheerful*	gaie	*cheerful*	gaiement	*cheerfully*

Seven adjectives which end in *-u* but add a circumflex accent in the adverbial form are:

assidu	*assiduous*	assidue	*assiduous*	assidûment	*assiduously*
continu	*continuous*	continue	*continuous*	continûment	*continuously*
cru	*crude*	crue	*crude*	crûment	*crudely*
dû	*owed*	due	*owed*	dûment	*duly*
goulu	*greedy*	goulue	*greedy*	goulûment	*greedily*
incongru	*incongruous*	incongrue	*incongruous*	incongrûment	*incongruously*
indu	*inappropriate*	indue	*inappropriate*	indûment	*inappropriately*

(See Appendix 2 for possible changes with regard to the use of circumflexes in *Nouvelle Orthographe.*)

5.2.3 **Adverbs ending in *-amment* and *-emment* derived from adjectives ending in *-ant* or *-ent***

Adjectives ending in *-ant* and *-ent* form the adverb with *-amment* and *-emment*, respectively:

Adjective		Adverb	
abondant	*abundant*	abondamment	*abundantly*
apparent	*apparent*	apparemment	*apparently*
brillant	*brilliant*	brillamment	*brilliantly*
constant	*constant*	constamment	*constantly*
courant	*current*	couramment	*fluently*
précédent	*preceding*	précédemment	*beforehand*
prudent	*prudent*	prudemment	*prudently*
violent	*violent*	violemment	*violently*
vaillant	*valorous*	vaillamment	*with valour*

There are three forms which do not follow this pattern exactly:

lent	*slow*	lentement	*slowly*
présent	*present*	présentement	currently
véhément	*vehement*	véhémentement	*vehemently*

N.B.: *véhémentement* is quite rare, and *avec véhémence* is usually preferred.

Three forms follow the pattern, but the present participles from which they derive no longer exist in modern French:

précipiter *to precipitate* (précipitant – old French)	précipitamment *precipitately*
noter to *note* (notant – old French)	notamment *notably*
(scire – old French/Latin)	sciemment *knowingly*

5.2.4 **Adverbs ending in -(é)*ment* derived from past participles**

Adverbs can also be formed in a similar way from the masculine form of past participles:

Verb		Past participle	Adverb	
aveugler	*to blind*	aveuglé	aveuglément	*blindly*
conformer	*to conform*	conformé	conformément	*in order*
forcer	*to force*	forcé	forcément	*necessarily*
préciser	*to specify*	précisé	précisément	*precisely*

In a similar, but irregular, vein we find:

impuni	*unpunished*	impunément	*with impunity*

5.2.5 **Adverbs ending in -*ément* derived from adjectives ending in -*e***

A small number of adverbs ending in -*ément* have been created from adjectives ending in -*e*: some always end in -*e*, others are the feminine form of adjectives:

Adjectives which always end in -*e*

Adjective		Adverb	
énorme	*enormous*	énormément	*enormously*
immense	*immense*	immensément	*immensely*
intense	*intense*	intensément	*intensely*
uniforme	*uniform*	uniformément	*uniformly*
commode	*useful*	commodément	*usefully*

Exceptions

probable	*probable*	probablement	*probably*
véritable	*real*	véritablement	*really*

Feminine forms

Adjective		Feminine	Adverb	
commun	*common*	commune	communément	*commonly*
confus	*embarrassed*	confuse	confusément	*indistinctly, vaguely*
importun	*disagreeable*	importune	importunément	*disagreeably*
obscur	*obscure*	obscure	obscurément	*obscurely*
opportun	*appropriate*	opportune	opportunément	*appropriately*
profond	*deep*	profonde	profondément	*deeply*
profus	*profuse*	profuse	profusément	*profusely* (literary)

5.2.6 Adverbs ending in *-ment* derived from words no longer in the language

Some adverbs ending in *-ment* are derived from words which no longer exist in the language:

Adjective	Feminine	Adverb	
bref *brief* (brief – old French)	brève	brièvement	*briefly*
grave *serious* (grief – old French)	grave	grièvement	*seriously*
traître *treacherous* (traîtreux – old French)	traîtresse	traîtreusement	*treacherously*
(journel – old French)		journellement	*daily*
(nuitantre – old French)		nuitamment	*nightly*

N.B.: *grief* is still used in certain set expressions: *faire grief à quelqu'un de quelque chose* 'to hold something against somebody', *formuler des griefs* 'to express grievances'.

5.2.7 Adverbs ending in *-ment* derived from nouns

There are a few adverbs ending in *-ment* which are derived from nouns and function like degree adverbs (see Section 5.6.2). These would be used only in spoken French: *vachement* in particular is used in very informal spoken French:

bougrement	C'est **bougrement** difficile	*It's bloody difficult*
diablement	Cette voiture est **diablement** lourde	*This car is hellishly heavy*
vachement	Elles sont **vachement** jolies, tes bottes	*Those are great boots!*

5.3 Adjectives used as adverbs without addition of *-ment*

Not all adverbs derived from adjectives end in *-ment*. The masculine forms of several adjectives can be used as adverbs in combination with a particular set of verbs. They do not change in gender or in number when used in this way:

Adjective	Used in expressions such as	
bas	parler bas	*to talk quietly*
	voler bas	*to fly low*
bon	sentir bon	*to smell nice*
	tenir bon	*to hold on*
chaud	servir chaud	*to serve hot*
cher	coûter cher	*to cost a lot*
	payer cher	*to pay a lot (for sth)*
clair	voir clair	*to see clearly*
court	tourner court	*to come to an abrupt end*
	couper court à qch	*to cut sth short*
	s'habiller court	*to wear one's skirts/dresses short*
creux	sonner creux	*to ring hollow*
doux	filer doux	*to keep a low profile*

droit	aller droit	*to go straight on*
dru	tomber dru	*to fall in stair-rods (rain), falling heavily (snow)*
dur	travailler dur	*to work hard*
faux	chanter faux	*to sing out of tune*
ferme	tenir ferme	*to hold out*
fort	parler fort	*to talk loudly*
frais	servir frais	*to serve chilled*
franc	parler franc	*to say what you think*
gras	manger gras	*to eat rich food*
gros	parier gros	*to bet heavily*
	risquer gros	*to take big risks*
haut	être haut placé	*to be in a position of authority*
juste	viser juste	*to aim correctly*
	deviner juste	*to guess right*
lourd	peser lourd	*to weigh heavily*
mauvais	sentir mauvais	*to smell bad*
net	s'arrêter net	*to stop dead*
	casser net	*to make a clean break*
pareil	penser pareil (informal)	*to think the same*
profond	creuser profond	*to dig deep*
serré	jouer serré	*to play a close game*

The fact that some of these adjectives are used as adverbs has allowed the creation of related forms ending in *-ment* with different meanings:

bon	bonnement

bonnement is used almost always with *tout* to give *tout bonnement*: 'quite simply'

cher	chèrement

chèrement is used with the verb *vendre* in the set phrase: *vendre chèrement sa peau* 'to sell one's life dearly'.

bas	bassement

bassement has taken the meaning: 'in a mean or despicable way' and is used in the set phrase *agir bassement*: 'to act in a mean or despicable way'.

5.4 **Phrases used as adverbs**

A number of adverbs are composed of invariable phrases. The following are a sample:

au maximum	*to the utmost*
à bon escient	*advisedly*
au fur et à mesure	*as we go along*
à brûle-pourpoint	*point blank*
à côté	*beside*
à l'heure	*on time*
à tire-larigot (informal)	*non-stop*
à tue-tête	*at the top of one's voice*
à plat ventre	*on one's belly*

à qui mieux mieux	*each one more than the next*
à peu près	*nearly*
à la fois	*at the same time*
à part	*separately*
d'ores et déjà	*from this time onwards*
d'habitude	*usually*
d'emblée	*straightaway*
de plus belle	*with renewed vigour*
d'arrache-pied	*flat out (to work)*
de bonne heure	*early*
de temps en temps	*from time to time*
en haut	*up(stairs)*
en bas	*down(stairs)*
en arrière	*behind*
en avant	*in front*
en retard	*late*
en avance	*early*
en amont	*upstream*
en aval	*downstream*
en dehors	*outside*
en vain	*in vain*
en catimini	*in secret*
en général	*in general*
en particulier	*in particular*
en définitive	*finally*
n'importe où	*anywhere*
n'importe quand	*anytime*
n'importe qui	*anybody*
par hasard	*by chance*
par monts et par vaux	*over hill and dale*
par ailleurs	*in addition*
par devant	*in the front*
par dessus	*over and above*
par contre	*on the other hand*
dans la suite	*in what followed*
et ainsi de suite	*and so on*
de suite	*immediately*
par la suite	*in what followed*
sans cesse	*continuously*
sans détour	*straight, to the point*
sur ces entrefaites	*just then*
tout à fait	*completely*
tout de suite	*immediately*
tout à l'heure	*in a moment, later*
tout d'un coup	*suddenly*
tout de go	*straight out*

côte à côte	*side by side*
ça et là	*here and there*
petit à petit	*little by little*
sur-le-champ	*immediately*
vaille que vaille	*somehow or other*

Borrowings from Latin, frequently heard, are:

grosso modo	*more or less*
a fortiori	*even more so*
a priori	*a priori*
a posteriori	*a posteriori*
vice versa	*vice versa*
in extremis	*at the last moment*

5.5 English and French adverb formation

'-ly' is a more productive form in English than -*ment* is in French. Therefore, not every English form in '-ly' will find a ready translation in -*ment* in French. The most frequent solution is an adverbial phrase introduced by a preposition such as *avec, d'une manière…, d'une façon…, sur un ton …*:

avec colère, sur le ton de la colère	*angrily*
d'une manière concise, avec concision	*concisely*
avec charme, d'une manière charmante	*charmingly*
avec beaucoup de talent/d'imagination	*creatively*
sur le ton de la plaisanterie	*jokingly*
de façon possessive	*possessively*
de façon réfléchie	*reflectively*
avec tristesse	*sadly*
avec entêtement	*stubbornly*
de façon surprenante, à ma/ta grande surprise	*surprisingly*
sur un ton vengeur	*vengefully*

When colours are used as adverbs they are preceded by *en:*

| le colorier en bleu | *to colour it blue* |
| le peindre en rouge | *to paint it red* |

When shapes are used as adverbs, they have to be turned into an expression involving a noun in French:

| lui donner une forme ronde | *to make it round* |
| le couper au carré | *to cut it square* |

5.6 Types of adverbs

There are five main types of adverbs: manner adverbs, degree adverbs, time adverbs, place adverbs, and sentence-modifying adverbs. Some forms fall into more than one of these categories. Typical examples of each are given in Tables 5.A–5.E (but the lists are not exhaustive).

5.6.1 **Manner adverbs**

Adverbs which describe the manner in which something is done are manner adverbs:

Je dors **bien**	*I sleep well*
Les choses tournent **mal**	*Things are turning out badly*

TABLE 5.A Typical manner adverbs

Typical manner adverbs		Ending in -ment	
ainsi	*like this/that, so, thus*	affectueusement	*affectionately*
(can also be a sentence-modifying adverb – see Section 5.6.17)			
bien	*well*	autrement	*differently*
(can also be a degree adverb – see Section 5.6.2)		(can also be a degree adverb – see 5.6.2)	
debout	*standing*	clairement	*clearly*
ensemble	*together*	confusément	*in a confused manner*
exprès	*purposely, on purpose*	correctement	*correctly*
mal	*badly*	facilement	*easily*
mieux	*better*	lentement	*slowly*
(for a comparison with *meilleur*, see Section 5.6.6)			
vite	*quickly*	précautionneusement	*cautiously*
		soigneusement	*carefully*
		vaguement	*vaguely*
		Invariable phrases	
		à dessein	*purposely*
		à genoux	*on one's knees*
		à pied	*on foot*
		à la fois	*at the same time*
		à tort	*wrongly*
		de travers	*crookedly*

Representative examples:

Il s'est toujours comporté **ainsi**	*He always behaved like that*
Tu chantes **bien**	*You sing well*
Mets-toi **debout**	*Stand up*
Il a **mal** lu l'étiquette	*He misread the label*

Hier soir ça n'allait guère **mieux**
It was hardly any better yesterday evening

Je l'oublierai très **facilement**
I'll forget it very easily

Elle étendait **soigneusement** les housses de couette
She carefully laid out the duvet covers

5.6.2 **Degree adverbs**

Adverbs which indicate the extent to which something is the case are degree adverbs. As a class they can modify every kind of sentence element: verbs, adjectives, nouns, prepositions, and other adverbs. But individually some of them may be restricted to modifying particular categories of item (e.g. *très* can modify adjectives, prepositions, and adverbs – *très heureux* 'very happy', *très à la mode* 'very fashionable', *très bien* 'very well' – but not verbs **Je fume très* 'I smoke very'):

Je bois du vin **modérément**
I drink wine moderately

Tout est **si** clair maintenant
Everything is so clear now

Ce ne sera pas **tout à fait** la vérité
That won't be entirely the truth

Je tends ma main jusqu'à **presque** toucher son visage
I stretch out my hand almost to touch his face

Elle a dressé **trop** brusquement la tête
She lifted her head up too quickly

TABLE 5.B Typical degree adverbs

Typical degree adverbs		Ending in -ment	
assez	*sufficiently*	autrement	*much more*
		(can also be a manner adverb – see Section 5.6.1)	
aussi	*as*	complètement	*completely*
(modifies adjectives and adverbs)			
autant	*as much* (modifies verbs)	démesurément	*inordinately*
beaucoup	*much*	modérément	*moderately*
bien	*really*	particulièrement	*particularly*
(can also be a manner adverb – see Section 5.6.1)			
davantage	*more*	tellement	*so; so much*
encore	*again; still; another*	terriblement	*terribly*
juste	*just*	vraiment	*truly*
même	*even*		
(when it follows a noun it may correspond to English 'very')			
moins	*less* (see Section 5.6.5)	**Invariable phrases**	
peu	*little*	au moins	*at least*
		(expresses a concrete estimate of a quantity: *au moins dix personnes blessées; du moins* expresses the speaker's view of an event: *du moins, il n'est pas blessé* – see Section 5.6.17)	
plus	*more*	à peine	*hardly*
(can modify verbs, adjectives, adverbs and prepositions – see Section 5.6.5)			

TABLE 5.B (continued)

Typical degree adverbs		Ending in -ment	
plutôt	*rather*	à peu près	*nearly*
presque	*almost*	de loin	*by far*
(does NOT contract to *presqu'* in front of a vowel: *presque à la fin*)			
si	*so*	par trop	*by far*
tant	*so much*	tout à fait	*completely*
tout	*completely; quite* (see Section 5.6.7)	un peu	*a little*
très	*very*		
trop	*too*		

Representative examples

C'est un acteur **assez** connu — *He is quite a well-known actor*

Les sans-abri meurent à la rue **autant** l'été que l'hiver — *Homeless people die on the street in summer just as much as in winter*

Elle est **autrement** intelligente que son frère — *She is much more intelligent than her brother*

Ils ont **beaucoup** discuté pendant le weekend — *They spent a lot of time discussing over the weekend*

C'est **bien** bête — *That's really stupid*

Il y en a **davantage** qu'on ne le pense — *There are more than you think*

Elle a acheté un billet **juste** avant de prendre le train — *She bought a ticket just before catching the train*

On ramène **même** des souvenirs — *They even bring back souvenirs*
Voici le vélo **même** dont il s'est servi — *This is the very bike he used*
un monde **si** étrangement silencieux — *such a strangely silent world*
Elle est **tellement** plus sympathique — *She is so much nicer*
J'ai répondu **tout** de travers — *I replied in a quite confused way*
Je suis ici depuis **très** longtemps — *I have been here for a very long time*
Il parle **trop** — *He talks too much*

A number of degree adverbs also function as quantifiers modifying nouns (see Section 6.9):

assez d'excuses — *enough excuses*
autant d'argent — *as much money*
beaucoup de clients — *many customers*
bien des problèmes — *many problems*
tellement de travail — *so much work*

Translating sentences such as 'She was **so** beautiful', 'He drives **so** fast that he will have an accident', 'They cried **so much**', '**So many** people came', '**(Very) many more** are expected', 'The clothes are **much prettier**', 'They work **a lot faster**' can be difficult for English speakers because of the complex correspondences between English 'so', '(so) much', '(so) many', 'more', on the one hand and French *si, tellement, tant, beaucoup, bien, davantage*, and the exclamative construction *Qu'elle était jolie!* 'She was so pretty', *Qu'il conduit vite!* 'He drives so fast' on the other. Here are some rules of thumb, followed by examples of ways of translating such constructions.

si meaning 'so' can modify an adjective, or an adverb: *Il est si grand!* (adjective) 'He is so tall!', *Tu chantes si bien!* (adverb) 'You sing so well!', *Il conduit si vite* (adverb) *qu'il risque d'avoir un accident!* 'He drives so fast that he will have an accident!'

tellement meaning 'so' can modify an adjective, an adverb, or a verb: *Il est tellement grand!* (adjective) 'He is so tall!', *Tu chantes tellement bien!* (adverb) 'You sing so well!', *Il conduit tellement vite qu'il risque d'avoir un accident!* (adverb) 'He drives so fast that he will have an accident!', *Ils ont tellement crié!* (verb) 'They shouted so much!'

tant and *tellement* meaning 'so much' can modify a verb: *Ils ont tant/tellement crié!* 'They shouted so much'.

tant and *tellement* meaning 'so much, so many' can modify nouns: *Tant de personnes sont venues, Tellement de personnes sont venues* 'So many people came', *Tant de travail a été accompli, Tellement de travail a été accompli* 'So much work has been done'.

davantage meaning 'more' can modify nouns: *Les PMEs emploient davantage de personnes* 'Small and medium-sized businesses are employing more people'.

Here are some examples of these uses. Often, word for word translations are impossible and other ways of rendering the same idea may need to be considered:

She was so beautiful!
Elle était si jolie! *or* Elle était tellement jolie! *or* Qu'elle était jolie!

The requiem was sung so beautifully that I nearly cried
Le requiem était si bien chanté que j'ai failli pleurer *or*
Le requiem était tellement bien chanté que j'ai failli pleurer

He drives so fast!
Il conduit si vite! *or* Il conduit tellement vite! *or* Qu'il conduit vite!

He drives so fast that he is sure to cause an accident one of these days
Il conduit tellement vite qu'il va sûrement provoquer un accident un de ces jours *or*
Il conduit si vite qu'il va sûrement provoquer un accident un de ces jours

She cried so much her mother was quite desperate
Elle a tant pleuré que sa mère était au désespoir *or*
Elle a tellement pleuré que sa mère était au désespoir

So many people came that I was overwhelmed
Tant de personnes sont venues que j'ai été un peu dépassé *or*
Tellement de personnes sont venues que j'ai été un peu dépassé

(*beaucoup de* and *bien de* are not possible in this *tant/tellement de personnes … que* construction, and nor is *si*; **si beaucoup* is an impossible combination under any circumstances)

The clothes this season are (so) much prettier
Les vêtements cette saison sont beaucoup plus jolis *or*
Les vêtements cette saison sont bien plus jolis *or*
Les vêtements cette saison sont tellement plus jolis

The crowds are (so) much more difficult to control in narrow streets
Les foules sont beaucoup plus difficiles à contrôler dans des rues étroites *or*
Les foules sont bien plus difficiles à contrôler dans des rues étroites *or*
Les foules sont tellement plus difficiles à contrôler dans des rues étroites

Very many more can be expected tomorrow
On doit s'attendre à beaucoup plus demain *or*
On doit s'attendre à bien plus demain
(it is not possible to use *très* in this kind of sentence: *très* and *beaucoup* never combine)

The designers have produced (so) much better models
Les couturiers ont produit de bien meilleurs modèles *or*
Les couturiers ont produit de tellement meilleurs modèles
(*beaucoup* is not possible in this sentence before *meilleurs*)

This year more people want to see the fashion shows
Cette année davantage de personnes souhaitent voir les défilés *or*
Cette année plus de personnes souhaitent voir les défilés

Many more people want to see the fashion shows
Beaucoup plus de personnes veulent assister aux défilés *or*
Bien plus de personnes veulent assister aux défilés *or*
Bien davantage de personnes veulent assister aux défilés
('many more' can NOT be rendered by *beaucoup davantage*)

The models will have to work a lot more often
Les mannequins devront travailler beaucoup plus souvent *or*
Les mannequins devront travailler bien plus souvent

5.6.3 **Comparative and superlative forms of adverbs**

In English, the majority of adverbs can be made into comparative forms by putting 'more', 'less', or 'as' in front of them and into superlative forms by putting 'the most' or 'the least' in front of them:

These days I can remember it	easily
	more easily (than I used to)
	less easily (than I used to)
	as easily (as I used to)

| This window opens | the most easily (of all of them) |
| | the least easily (of all of them) |

A small set of English adverbs, however, have special comparative and superlative forms:

She finishes	fast
	faster
	the fastest

She sings	well
	better
	the best

He behaves

| badly
| worse
| the worst

A similar pattern exists in French where the majority of adverbs can be made into comparative forms by putting the degree adverbs *plus, moins,* or *aussi* in front of the adverb and into superlative forms by putting *le plus* or *le moins* in front of the adverb. In the latter case *le plus* and *le moins* do not change in gender and number:

Après mon opération je me suis rendu compte que je marchais

| facilement
| plus facilement (qu'auparavant)
| moins facilement (qu'auparavant)
| aussi facilement (qu'auparavant)

Cette fenêtre-ci ouvre

| le plus facilement (de toutes)
| le moins facilement (de toutes)

5.6.4 *bien* 'well', *mieux* 'better', *mal* 'badly', *pis* 'worse'

One adverb in French has special comparative and superlative forms:

bien	mieux	le mieux
well	*better*	*the best*
	moins bien	le moins bien
	less well	*the least well*

Elle chante

| bien
| mieux
{ moins bien
| le mieux
| le moins bien

She sings

| well
| better
{ less well
| the best
| the least well

The adverb *mal* 'badly' has two sets of comparative and superlative forms, one regular and one irregular:

Regular			
mal *badly*	plus mal	*worse*	le plus mal	*the worst*
	moins mal	*less badly*	le moins mal	*the least badly*

Irregular		
pis	*worse*	le pis	*the worst*

pis and *le pis* only occur these days in fixed expressions like:

tant pis	*too bad*
au pis aller	*at worst*
un pis aller	*a lesser evil, second choice*
les choses vont de mal en pis	*things are going from bad to worse*

| qui pis est | *what's worse* |
| en mettant tous au pis | *at the worst* |

The last two examples are now rather old-fashioned.

5.6.5 *beaucoup* 'much', *plus* 'more', *peu* 'little', *moins* 'less'

The comparative and superlative forms of the degree adverb *beaucoup* are *plus* and *le plus* (the final s is pronounced except in front of words beginning with a consonant); the comparative and superlative forms of the degree adverb *peu* are *moins* and *le moins*:

Elle mange	beaucoup	*She eats*	*a lot*
	plus [s]		*more*
	le plus [s] (de toutes)		*the most (of all)*
	autant (que moi)		*as much (as me)*

Elle mange	peu	*She eats*	*little*
	moins		*less*
	le moins (de toutes)		*the least (of all)*
	aussi peu (que moi)		*as little (as me)*

plus and *moins* are also used in expressions such as:

De plus en plus de couples veulent connaître le sexe de leur bébé
More and more couples want to know what sex their baby is

De moins en moins de voitures émettent du CO_2
Fewer and fewer cars emit CO_2

Plus on est âgé **plus** on a de difficultés à s'adapter au changement
The older one is, the more difficulty one has adapting to change

Moins on a de revenus **moins** on a de choix dans la vie
The less wealthy one is, the fewer choices one has in life

Elle est **encore plus** talentueuse que je n'avais pensé
She is even more talented than I had thought

Le public aujourd'hui est **encore moins** favorable à la réforme
The general public today supports the reform even less

5.6.6 Difference between *meilleur(e)(s)* and *mieux*, and *le/la/les meilleur(e)(s)* and *le mieux*

meilleur(e)(s) and *le/la/les meilleur(e)(s)* are the comparative and superlative forms, respectively, of the adjective *bon* 'good'. *mieux* and *le mieux* are the comparative and superlative forms, respectively, of the adverb *bien* 'well':

Adjective	bon	*good*	meilleur(s) meilleure(s)	*better*	le meilleur la meilleure les meilleur(e)s	*the best*
Adverb	bien	*well*	mieux	*better*	le mieux	*the best*

Il désire avoir une **meilleure** place
He wants to have a better seat

Ces marchandises sont **meilleures**
These goods are better

Elle travaille **mieux** que les autres
She works better than the others

Elle travaille **le mieux** de toutes
She works the best of all

Since the adverb *bien* 'well' can also sometimes function as an adjective close in meaning to *bon*, particularly with *être*, there are contexts where *meilleur* and *mieux* are both possible:

Tout est **bien**/Tout est **mieux**
Everything is fine/Everything is better

Tout est **bon**/Tout est **meilleur**
Everything is good/Everything is better

Elle est **bien** comme directrice/Elle est **mieux** comme directrice
She is fine as a director/She is better as a director

Elle est **bonne** comme directrice/Elle est **meilleure** comme directrice
She is good as a director/She is better as a director

On est **bien** ici/On est **mieux** ici
We're fine here/We're better here

C'est **bon** ici/C'est **meilleur** ici
It's good here/It's better here

5.6.7 **Form and uses of *tout***

tout can function as a determiner, a quantifier, a pronoun, and an adverb. It behaves differently with respect to agreement in each of these roles, so it is important to distinguish them.

tout **as a determiner**

tout is a determiner in constructions such as the following. Here there is no article and *tout* agrees with the noun which it determines:

Tout parent veut le bien de son enfant
Every parent wants what is best for his or her child

Toutes taxes comprises
All taxes included

Les repas sont servis à **toute** heure
Meals are served at any time

Une sortie familiale qui convient à **tous** âges
A family outing which is suitable for all ages

Voici une tenue qui convient à **toute** occasion
Here is an outfit that is suitable for any occasion

Prenez de la farine **tous** usages
Use all-purpose flour

tout as a quantifier

tout is a quantifier (see Section 6.9) in the following examples. Its translation equivalent in English is usually 'all'. It agrees with the noun which it modifies:

Tous les garçons sont arrivés
All the boys have arrived

Toutes les chansons de son début de carrière ont eu du succès
All the songs in his early career were hits

Il s'en est plaint **toute** la journée
He complained about it all day

tout as a pronoun

tout is a pronoun when it is used as a subject, direct object, indirect object or follows a preposition.

When it has the indefinite meaning 'everything, all' it is invariable:

Tout bien considéré, j'ai décidé de ne pas signer
All things considered, I've decided not to sign

Tu m'avais dit que **tout** serait réglé avant ce soir
You told me that everything would be sorted out by this evening

When it refers to people or things mentioned or implied elsewhere in the discourse, it agrees in gender and number with those entities and takes one of the forms *tout, toute, tous, toutes*. In this use, the final *-s* of *tous* is pronounced:

Nous sommes infiniment redevables à **tous** (final *-s* pronounced)
We are eternally grateful to everyone

Nous allons chanter **tous** ensemble (final *-s* pronounced)
We'll all sing together

Je revends les affaires de ma fille. **Toutes** sont trop petites
I'm selling my daughter's clothes. They are all too small

tout as an adverb

tout is an adverb when it modifies another adverb, a preposition, or an adjective. It has the meaning of 'completely, very'.

In front of an adverb, preposition, and most adjectives it is invariable:

Elle chante **tout** bas
She is singing very quietly

Son succès était **tout** bonnement la meilleure surprise de l'année
His success was quite simply the best surprise of the year

L'hôtel se trouve **tout** près de la gare
The hotel is really near the station

Tu sais bien que ta sœur serait **tout** heureuse de te revoir
You know full well that your sister would be delighted to see you again

Mes deux siamoises étaient **tout** excitées par les sauts de la bobine de fil
My two Siamese cats were thoroughly excited by the movement of the cotton reel

There is one exception: *tout* agrees when it is followed by a feminine adjective which begins with a consonant or an 'aspirated h':

Les adolescentes étaient **toutes** désemparées par l'annonce de la directrice
The teenage girls were completely taken aback by the headmistress's announcement

Tes sœurs sont **toutes** prêtes à venir te rejoindre
Your sisters are quite ready to come out and join you

Mes petites King Charles avaient l'air **toutes** honteuses d'avoir mâchonné le canapé
My King Charles puppies looked as though they were very ashamed of having chewed the sofa.

5.6.8 **Time adverbs**

Adverbs which indicate the time at which something takes place, or the duration or frequency of an event, are time adverbs (as shown in Table 5.C):

L'image est nette **à présent**
The picture is clear now

Il y est **toujours**
He is still there

Soudain il y a eu comme un déplacement d'air
Suddenly there was a kind of movement of air

TABLE 5.C Typical time adverbs

Typical time adverbs			
alors	*then, at that time*	soudain	*suddenly*
(can also be a sentence-modifying adverb – see Section 5.6.17)			
aujourd'hui	*today*	souvent	*often*
auparavant	*beforehand*	tantôt	*this afternoon*
		tantôt … tantôt	*one minute… the next…*
aussitôt	*immediately*	tard	*late*
autrefois	*in the past*	tôt	*early*
bientôt	*soon*	toujours	*always; still*
déjà	*already*		
demain	*tomorrow*	**Ending in -ment**	
depuis	*since then*	actuellement	*currently*
désormais	*henceforth*	dernièrement	*recently*
dorénavant	*henceforth*	fréquemment	*frequently*
encore	*again; still; yet*	précédemment	*previously*
(can also be a sentence-modifying adverb – see Section 5.6.17)			
enfin	*finally*	prochainement	*soon*
ensuite	*afterwards*	récemment	*recently*

TABLE 5.C (continued)

Typical time adverbs			
entre-temps	*meanwhile*		
hier	*yesterday*	**Invariable phrases**	
		à présent	*at present*
jadis	*in the (distant) past*	dès lors	*from then on*
(the final -s is always pronounced)			
jamais	*ever*	d'un instant à l'autre	*at any moment*
longtemps	*a long time*	en ce moment	*at the moment*
maintenant	*now*	par la suite	*subsequently*
naguère	*in the recent past*	tout à coup	*suddenly*
parfois	*sometimes*	tout à l'heure	*just now; presently*
quelquefois	*sometimes*	tout de suite	*immediately*

Representative examples:

Actuellement il sort avec ma sœur — *Currently, he's going out with my sister*

Il l'avait rencontrée deux ans **auparavant** — *He had met her two years before*

Dès lors il voulait passer sa vie avec elle — *From then on he wanted to spend his life with her*

Elle s'en est rendu compte **aussitôt** — *She realized immediately*
Ensuite il ne s'est rien passé — *Afterwards nothing happened*

Entre-temps elle avait rencontré quelqu'un d'autre — *Meanwhile she had met someone else*

Son sourire n'a plus été le même **par la suite** — *His smile was never the same afterwards*

Nous avons parlé **longtemps** — *We spoke for a long time*

Le bureau occupe deux étages, **naguère** habités — *The office occupies two floors, formerly living accommodation*

Quelquefois on me conduisait à Roubaix — *Sometimes they took me to Roubaix*
J'ai **souvent** voulu le faire — *I've often wanted to do it*
Sors **tout de suite** — *Get out of here immediately*

5.6.9 *alors*

alors has two distinct adverbial uses. One as a time adverb meaning 'then, at that time':

Elle était **alors** directrice d'une petite agence immobilière en province
At that time she was the manager of a small provincial estate agency

In this use it can appear in the middle of a clause, as in the above example (for the position of adverbs see Section 5.7).

Its other use is as a sentence-modifying adverb meaning 'so', which occurs at the beginning of a clause. This use is as frequent in spoken French as 'so' is in spoken English:

Alors, quoi de neuf?   *So, what's new?*
Alors, qu'est-ce que tu en penses?   *So, what do you think about it?*

5.6.10 *encore* and *toujours*

encore and *toujours* have several meanings and overlap in one of those meanings, which makes them difficult for the learner. Both *encore* and *toujours* can mean 'still' in clauses which express an ongoing state of affairs:

Est-il **encore/toujours** là?   *Is he still here?*
(His being here is an ongoing state of affairs)

Elle se plaint **encore/toujours**   *She is still complaining*
(Her complaining is an ongoing state of affairs)

In clauses which describe a completed action, or the potential for the completion of an action, however, *encore* means 'again':

Il a **encore** perdu sa clef   *He has lost his key again*
(His losing of the key is a completed action)

J'ai peur de m'évanouir **encore**   *I am afraid of fainting again*
(Although I haven't done so yet, fainting has
the potential for being a completed action)

Note that if *encore* modifies the first clause, which expresses a state of affairs, it could mean either 'still' or 'again': *J'ai encore peur de m'évanouir* 'I'm still afraid of fainting' or 'Once again I am afraid of fainting'.

Where *encore* modifies noun phrases or other adverbs it means 'still more, further':

Encore du pain, s'il vous plaît
More bread, please

Ils ont roulé **encore** dix ou vingt kilomètres
They travelled a further ten or twenty kilometres

Elle est **encore** plus douée que sa sœur
She is even more gifted than her sister

J'aime **encore** mieux votre idée que la mienne
I like your idea even more than mine

toujours, in addition to meaning 'still', can also mean 'always':

Elles ont **toujours** refusé de me parler
They have always refused to talk to me

On s'efforçait depuis **toujours** de me le cacher
They had always tried to hide it from me

In sentences negated by *pas*, if *toujours* precedes the *pas* it means 'still', if it follows it means 'always':

Il n'est **toujours** pas arrivé	*He still hasn't arrived*
Il n'est pas **toujours** arrivé	*He didn't always arrive/turn up*

encore can only follow *pas* and means 'yet':

Il n'est pas **encore** arrivé   *He hasn't yet arrived*

5.6.11 *ensuite* and *puis*

ensuite and *puis* both mean 'afterwards, then', but *ensuite* is a time adverb which can occur in the middle of a clause (for the position of adverbs see Section 5.7), while *puis* is a coordinating conjunction which can occur only at the beginning of a clause (see Section 17.2):

Il a payé l'addition, et il est **ensuite** parti
He paid the bill, and afterwards left

Il a payé l'addition, **puis** il est parti
He paid the bill, then he left

5.6.12 *jamais*

jamais is mostly used with *ne* to mean 'never' (see Section 16.9). It can, however, also mean 'ever' in questions, in *si-* clauses or when it is a complement to *sans*:

As-tu **jamais** vu une chose pareille?
Have you ever seen anything like it?

Si **jamais** tu rencontres Jules, tu lui diras bonjour de ma part
If you ever meet Jules, say hello to him from me

Il a fait cet exercice cent fois sans **jamais** se tromper
He's done that exercise a hundred times without ever making a mistake

5.6.13 *tard* versus *en retard*

Both of these terms translate as 'late' into English. However, *en retard* is restricted in meaning to the idea of 'not on time':

Tu es de nouveau **en retard**. Tu feras signer ce mot par tes parents s'il te plaît !
You are late again. Please have your parents sign this note!

tard has a wider range of meaning:

Il est déjà **tard**, nous devons rentrer
It's already late, we must go home

Pour toi, il est trop **tard**. Tu aurais dû commencer à cotiser il y a plusieurs années
For you it's too late. You should have started contributing several years ago

Il n'est jamais trop **tard**
It's never too late

5.6.14 *tout à l'heure*

The meaning of *tout à l'heure* is determined by the tense of the verb in the clause which contains it. If the verb is in a past tense it means 'just now'; if the verb is in a present or future tense it means 'presently':

Je suis arrivé **tout à l'heure**
I arrived just now

Elle va arriver **tout à l'heure**
She will arrive presently

5.6.15 **Choice of some time adverbs relative to the moment of speaking**

The meaning of some time adverbs is determined by their relation to the time of speaking. If someone says:

Je suis arrivé **hier**
I arrived yesterday

hier refers to the day before the day on which the person is speaking. Similarly, if someone says:

J'arriverai **demain**
I'll arrive tomorrow

demain refers to the day after the day on which the person is speaking. By contrast, if someone says:

Je suis arrivé **la veille**
I arrived the day before

they are referring to a day before some point prior to the time when they are speaking. Similarly in:

Je suis arrivé **le lendemain**
I arrived the day after

le lendemain refers to the day after some point prior to the moment of speaking.

Different series of adverbs must be used depending on whether they refer to before or after the actual moment of speaking, or whether they refer to before or after some point prior to the moment of speaking. Examples are presented in Tables 5.D and 5.E.

TABLE 5.D Adverbs and time reference 1

More distant past	Recent past	Concurrent with the time of speaking	Near future	More distant future
avant-hier *the day before yesterday*	hier *yesterday*	aujourd'hui *today*	demain *tomorrow*	après-demain *the day after tomorrow*
	alors *then*	maintenant *now*	bientôt *soon*	

TABLE 5.D (continued)

More distant past	Recent past	Concurrent with the time of speaking	Near future	More distant future
	hier matin hier midi hier après-midi hier soir *yesterday morning, midday, etc.*	ce matin ce midi cet après-midi/ tantôt, ce soir *this morning, midday, this afternoon, this evening*	demain matin demain midi demain après-midi demain soir *tomorrow morning, midday, etc.*	
autrefois jadis (literary) *formerly*	tout à l'heure *just now* récemment dernièrement naguère *recently*	actuellement *currently*	tout à l'heure ('tantôt' in parts of France, in Belgium and Quebec) *presently*	à l'avenir *in the future*

TABLE 5.E Adverbs and time reference 2

More distant past	Recent past	Prior to the time of speaking	Near future	More distant future
l'avant-veille *the day before the day before*	la veille *the day before*	ce jour-là *that day*	le lendemain *the day after*	le surlendemain *the day after the day after*
	la veille au matin *the morning of the day before*	ce matin-là *that morning*	le lendemain matin *the morning of the day after*	
	la veille à midi *midday of the day before*	ce midi-là *that midday*	le lendemain midi *midday of the day after*	
	dans l'après-midi de la veille *the afternoon of the day before*	cet après-midi-là *that afternoon*	dans l'après-midi du lendemain *the afternoon of the day after*	
	la veille au soir *the evening of the day before*	ce soir-là *that evening*	le lendemain soir *the evening of the day after*	

5.6.16 **Place adverbs**

Adverbs which describe the place where an event occurs are place adverbs:

J'entendis des pas précipités **dehors**
I heard hurried steps outside

On m'a tiré **en arrière**
I was pulled backwards

TABLE 5.F Typical place adverbs

Typical place adverbs			
ailleurs	*elsewhere*	en amont en aval	*upstream* *downstream*
dedans en dedans au-dedans là-dedans	*inside* *inwardly; facing inwards* *on the inside* *in there*	en avant en arrière	*in/at the front* *in/at the back*
Dehors en dehors au-dehors	*outside* *outwardly; facing outwards* *on the outside*	ici	*here*
derrière par derrière	*behind* *from behind*	là	*there* (used a lot to mean here: 'I'm here' *Je suis là*)
dessous en dessous	*underneath, on the bottom* *underneath, on the back*	loin	*far away*
au-dessous par-dessous	*below* *underneath* (implying motion: *passer par-dessous* 'to go underneath')		
dessus en dessus au-dessus par-dessus	*over, on the top* *on the top, on the front* *above* *across* (*sauter par-dessus* 'to jump across')	partout	*everywhere*
ci-contre ci-dessous	*opposite* (on a page) *below* (in a piece of writing: *voir ci-dessous* 'see below')	près	*nearby*
ci-dessus ci-après ci-devant	*above* (*voir ci-dessus* 'see above') *later* *earlier*		
en bas en haut	(*down*) *below* (*up*) *above*		

Representative examples:

Nous voulons habiter **ailleurs**	*We want to live elsewhere*
Vous entrez **dedans**	*You go inside*
Quelqu'un, **dehors**, s'est inquiété	*Someone, outside, got nervous*
Derrière il y a un champ de betteraves	*Behind there is a beet field*
Vous trouverez l'étiquette **dessous**	*You'll find the label on the bottom*
L'adresse est marquée **dessus**	*The address is written on the top*
bras **dessus** bras **dessous**	*arm in arm*
On a laissé des papiers un peu **partout**	*Papers were left almost everywhere*

5.6.17 **Sentence-modifying adverbs**

Sentence-modifying adverbs fall into two types. Those which establish a link between what has been said already and what is being said now:

La porte de la cuisine est fermée. Je l'ai **pourtant** laissée ouverte derrière moi
The door to the kitchen is closed. Yet I left it open behind me (*pourtant* highlights the contrast between a previous state of affairs and the current state of affairs)

Les arguments en faveur de cette ligne politique sont clairs. Nous devons **donc** la suivre de près
The arguments in favour of this policy are clear. Therefore we should follow it closely (*donc* signals a causal link between the first sentence and the second)

The second group of sentence-modifying adverbs express the speaker's assessment of the probability or desirability of the event described by the sentence being true:

Elle était vexée, **probablement** *She was probably offended*
(*probablement* is the speaker's judgement of the likelihood of her being offended)

Je n'ai **malheureusement** pas pu venir *Unfortunately I wasn't able to come*
(*malheureusement* is an expression of the speaker's regret at not being able to come)

See Table 5.G for typical cases.

Examples:

J'ai beaucoup travaillé pour terminer à temps. **Cependant**, ils n'ont pas voulu me payer mes heures supplémentaires
I worked very hard to finish in time. Yet they refused to pay me for extra time

Aurélien a expliqué la situation très clairement. **En effet**, nous devrons prendre une décision aujourd'hui même
Aurélien explained the situation very clearly. Indeed, we must take a decision this very day

Le ski est un excellent sport pour ceux qui sont en pleine santé. **En revanche**, il n'est pas recommandé pour les gens qui ont les articulations fragiles
Skiing is an excellent sport for those in good health. On the other hand, it is not recommended for those with weak joints

Le bateau a coulé au mois de juin. **Néanmoins**, la compagnie d'assurance en était toujours à établir toujours les faits en décembre
The boat sank in June. Nonetheless, the insurance company was still trying to establish the facts in December

Mon fils ne m'écrit jamais. Sa sœur, **par contre**, me tient au courant de tout ce qu'elle fait
My son never writes to me. His sister, on the other hand, keeps me informed of everything she is doing

Alors, que préférait-elle?
So, what did she prefer?

Ils me répondraient, **bien sûr**, que j'aurais pu le faire depuis longtemps
They would reply, of course, that I could have done it long before

Je n'aurais **certainement** pas pu le comprendre
I certainly couldn't have understood it

Elle ne s'en doutait **certes** pas
She certainly didn't suspect it

Le prof a **du moins** cette qualité qu'il articule bien
The teacher has at least this quality, that he speaks very clearly

C'est **sans doute** un ami
He's probably a friend

Il a entrepris cette démarche avec de très bonnes intentions. **Seulement**, il ne possédait pas les connaissances requises
He took these steps with the very best of intentions. Only he didn't have the knowledge required

TABLE 5.G Typical sentence-linking and speaker-oriented adverbs

Typical sentence-linking adverbs		Typical speaker-oriented adverbs	
ainsi	*so, in the same way*	alors	*so*
(can also be a manner adverb – see Section 5.6.1)		(can also be a time adverb – see Section 5.6.8)	
au contraire	*conversely*	assurément	*surely*
aussi	*so, thus*	bien sûr	*of course*
(can also be a degree adverb – see Section 5.6.2)			
cependant	*yet*	certainement	*certainly*
d'ailleurs	*moreover, what's more*	certes	*certainly*
encore	*for all that*	du moins	*at least*
(can also be a time adverb – see Section 5.6.8)		(expresses the speaker's reservation – *au moins* is a degree adverb (see Section 5.6.2) used when 'at least' is concrete: *au moins dix fois* 'at least ten times')	
en effet	*indeed*	en général	*in general*
en revanche	*on the contrary*	évidemment	*evidently*
en somme	*in sum, briefly*	heureusement	*fortunately*
néanmoins	*nonetheless*	peut-être	*perhaps*
par conséquent en conséquence	*consequently*	probablement	*probably*
par contre	*on the other hand*	sans doute	*doubtlessly, no doubt*
plutôt	*rather*	seulement	*only*
pourtant	*yet*	soit	*so be it*
quand même	*all the same*	sûrement	*surely*
toutefois	*nevertheless*	vraisemblablement	*in all likelihood*

5.7 Location of adverbs

5.7.1 Location of adverbs modifying adjectives, prepositions, noun phrases, and other adverbs

Adverbs which modify adjectives, prepositions, noun phrases, and other adverbs appear immediately in front of those items:

Je ne suis pas **vraiment** mauvais (modifying an adjective)
I'm not really bad

Nous irons **loin** au-delà de la frontière (modifying a preposition)
We'll go far beyond the frontier

Il y a **au moins** dix ans (modifying a noun phrase)
At least ten years ago

Je suis ici depuis **très** longtemps (modifying an adverb)
I have been here for a very long time

5.7.2 **Location of adverbs modifying verb phrases**

Adverbs which modify the verb phrase (manner, degree, some time and place adverbs) and adverbs which modify the sentence may have several possible locations.

Manner, degree, and time adverbs which consist of just one word usually immediately follow the tense-marked verb:

Elle a **soigneusement** étendu son tailleur-pantalon sur le lit
She carefully laid out her trouser suit on the bed

On ramène **parfois** des souvenirs
We sometimes bring back souvenirs

J'ai **souvent** voulu le faire
I have often wanted to do it

Ils ont **beaucoup** discuté pendant le weekend
They discussed a lot during the weekend

Il a **mal** lu l'étiquette
He misread the label

Elles ont **toujours** refusé de me parler
They have always refused to talk to me

N.B.: With verbs in simple tenses it is normal in French for these adverbs to occur between the verb and its complement, but not between the subject and the verb: the reverse is the case in English:

On ramène **parfois** des souvenirs	NOT	*On parfois ramène des souvenirs
Je veux **souvent** le faire	NOT	*Je souvent veux le faire
Elles refusent **toujours** de me parler	NOT	*Elles toujours refusent de me parler

Usually manner, degree, and time adverbs consisting of just one word and modifying the verb phrase can also appear at the end of the clause:

Elle a étendu son tailleur-pantalon **soigneusement**
On ramène des souvenirs **parfois**

But some appear most naturally in a clause-internal position after the verb. This tends to be the case for short monosyllabic adverbs: *bien, mal, vite, trop, tant*. An exception, though, is time adverbs which designate specific moments in the past or future: *hier* 'yesterday', *demain* 'tomorrow', *la veille* 'the day before', etc.. These usually appear at the beginning or the end of a clause, not in the middle:

J'ai ramassé les clefs **hier**   *or*   **Hier** j'ai ramassé les clefs
I picked up the keys yesterday

La veille elle avait vendu sa maison   *or*   Elle avait vendu sa maison **la veille**
She had sold her house the day before

Adverbs of manner, degree, and time which consist of more than a single word, together with place adverbs as a class, usually come at the beginning or end of a clause, not in the middle:

Il a emporté le dossier **à dessein**	*He took the file away on purpose*
Ici tout le monde fait la vaisselle	*Everybody does the washing-up here*
Nous voulons habiter **ailleurs**	*We want to live elsewhere*
Derrière il y a un champ de betteraves	*Behind there is a beet field*
Vous trouverez l'étiquette **dessous**	*You'll find the label on the bottom*
On a laissé des papiers un peu **partout**	*Papers were left almost everywhere*

It is always possible, however, for such adverbs to occur clause-internally with heavy pausing on either side (indicated by commas in written French). This has the effect of stressing the adverb:

J'ai ramassé, **hier**, les clefs
Quelqu'un, **dehors**, s'est inquiété
Il y a, **derrière**, un champ de betteraves

5.7.3 **Location of adverbs modifying sentences**

Sentence-modifying adverbs can usually appear at the beginning, in the middle, or at the end of clauses:

La porte de la cuisine est fermée. Je l'ai **pourtant** laissée ouverte derrière moi/**Pourtant** je l'ai laissée ouverte derrière moi/Je l'ai laissée ouverte derrière moi **pourtant**
The door to the kitchen is closed. Yet I left it open behind me

Il s'ensuit **donc** que nous devons la suivre de près/**Donc** il s'ensuit que nous devons la suivre de près/Il s'ensuit que nous devons la suivre de près **donc**
It follows, therefore, that we should follow it closely

Malheureusement, je n'ai pas pu venir/Je n'ai **malheureusement** pas pu venir/Je n'ai pas pu venir **malheureusement**
Unfortunately, I wasn't able to come

There is a tendency in French not to put short constituents at the end of a sentence where a long constituent precedes. This can sometimes determine a preferred location for adverbs. For example, it is less natural to say:

Il s'ensuit que nous devons la suivre de près **donc**

where the short *donc* is in sentence-final position and is preceded by the long constituent *que nous devons la suivre de près*, than:

Il s'ensuit **donc** que nous devons la suivre de près

In a sentence such as

On a laissé des papiers **partout**

the place adverb *partout* would normally appear at the end of the clause rather than in the middle. But if the direct object is made longer, it becomes more natural to put it at the end, leaving *partout* in the middle:

On a laissé **partout** des papiers couverts de gribouillis
They left papers covered in doodles lying about everywhere

5.7.4 **Inversion of subject and verb after some sentence-initial adverbs**

In formal French, a small set of adverbs (drawn from several of the classes described in this chapter) may provoke subject–verb inversion when they occur in sentence-initial position. Inversion is likely with the following adverbs:

A peine Renaud s'est-il assis qu'on lui a demandé de se déplacer
Hardly had Renaud sat down when he was asked to move

Peut-être Alice arrivera-t-elle demain
Perhaps Alice will arrive tomorrow

Sans doute vous a-t-elle écrit
Doubtless she has written to you

Toujours est-il que je ne peux pas vous payer
The fact remains that I cannot pay you

(For the properties of subject–verb inversion see Section 14.2.3.)

An alternative in the case of *peut-être* and *sans doute* is the use of a following *que* without inversion:

Peut-être qu'Alice arrivera demain
Sans doute qu'elle vous a écrit

In informal French *peut-être que* and *sans doute que* are frequent, but inversion is not, speakers locating the adverbs in a different position, or simply not inverting after the adverb.

Other adverbs after which inversion is possible (but less likely) in formal French are:

Ainsi a-t-elle gagné le prix
In that way she won the prize

Il n'a plus d'argent; **aussi** doit-il rentrer
He has no more money; so he must go home

Du moins ont-ils gardé leur calme
At least they kept their cool

Encore ne suis-je là que pour prendre des notes
For all that, I'm here just to take notes

En vain a-t-il cherché
In vain he searched

Rarement a-t-on vu des citoyens aussi remontés contre le gouvernement
Rarely have the citizens been seen to be so angry with the government

FREE

**INSTRUCTOR
& STUDENT
RESOURCES**

For more resources to practice your French grammar, including practice activities/quizzes for students, further resource links, and an instructor guide, please visit https://routledgelearning.com/frenchgrammarandusage.

6 Numbers, measurements, time, and quantifiers

6.1 Cardinal numbers

Numbers like *un, deux, trois*, are called cardinal numbers:

0	zéro	
1	un	*un* (masculine) is used in contexts like the following: *il porte le numéro 'un'*, 'He is wearing the number "one"'; *à la page un*, 'on page one'; *la partie un*, 'part one'. It is also used as a masculine pronoun: *As-tu un stylo? Pierre en a un* 'Have you got a pen? Pierre has one'. *une* (feminine) is used as a feminine pronoun: *Il ne m'en reste qu'une (carte postale)*, 'I've only got one left (postcard)'. N.B.: *à la une* 'on the front page'.
2	deux	
3	trois	
4	quatre	*quatre* is invariable and never takes a plural *-s: les quatre chats* 'the four cats'.
5	cinq	The final *q* of *cinq* is always pronounced [k], except when it precedes *cent*, where it is not pronounced: *cinq cents*.
6	six	*six* is pronounced with a final [s] when it is at the end of a phrase: *j'en ai vu six* 'I saw six'; it is pronounced with a final [z] when it precedes a noun beginning with a vowel: *six hommes* 'six men'. When it precedes a noun beginning with a consonant the *x* is not pronounced: *six joueurs* 'six players'.
7	sept	
8	huit	*huit* is pronounced with a final [t] when it is at the end of a phrase: *j'en ai vu huit* 'I saw eight', and when it precedes a noun beginning with a vowel: *huit entreprises ont fermé* 'eight firms have closed'. When it precedes a noun beginning with a consonant the *t* is not pronounced: *huit semaines plus tard* 'eight weeks later'.
9	neuf	The final *f* of *neuf* is always pronounced [f], except in *neuf ans* 'nine years' and *neuf heures* 'nine hours, nine o'clock' where it is pronounced [v].
10	dix	The pronunciation of *dix* is the same as for *six*.

DOI: 10.4324/9781003373926-6

11	onze	Forms of *le* and *de* do not shorten before *onze*: *le onze janvier* 'the eleventh of January', (NOT *l'onze janvier*), *le train de onze heures* 'the eleven o'clock train'. In plural expressions like *les onze membres d'une équipe de football* 'the eleven members of a football team', the final *s* of *les* or *des* is not pronounced.
12	douze	*douze* is invariable and never takes a plural *-s*: *douze hommes* 'twelve men'.
13	treize	
14	quatorze	
15	quinze	
16	seize	
17	dix-sept	
18	dix-huit	The pronunciation of *dix-huit* is the same as for *huit*.
19	dix-neuf	The pronunciation of *dix-neuf* is the same as for *neuf*.
20	vingt	*vingt* is pronounced like *vin*, with the following exceptions: it is pronounced with a final [t] when it precedes a noun beginning with a vowel: *vingt exercices* 'twenty exercises', and also in the numbers *21–29* inclusive.
21	vingt et un	*vingt et un(e)*, *trente et un(e)*, *quarante et un(e)*, etc. are used in similar ways to *un(e)*; *un(e)* agrees with the gender of a following noun: *vingt et un joueurs* 'twenty-one players', *vingt et une voitures* 'twenty-one cars'.
22	vingt-deux	
23	vingt-trois	
…		
29	vingt-neuf	
30	trente	
31	trente et un	
32	trente-deux	
…		
39	trente-neuf	
40	quarante	
41	quarante et un	
42	quarante-deux	
…		
49	quarante-neuf	
50	cinquante	
51	cinquante et un	
52	cinquante-deux	
…		
59	cinquante-neuf	
60	soixante	
61	soixante et un	
62	soixante-deux	
…		
69	soixante-neuf	

70	soixante-dix	In Belgian and Swiss French the word *septante* is used instead of *soixante-dix: septante et un, septante-deux*, etc.
71	soixante et onze	
72	soixante-douze	
73	soixante-treize	
...		
79	soixante-dix-neuf	
80	quatre-vingts	
81	quatre-vingt-un	The [t] of *vingt* is NOT pronounced.
82	quatre-vingt-deux	
...		
89	quatre-vingt-neuf	
90	quatre-vingt-dix	In Belgian and Swiss French the word *nonante* is used instead of *quatre-vingt-dix: nonante-un, nonante-deux*, etc.
91	quatre-vingt-onze	The [t] of *vingt* is NOT pronounced.
92	quatre-vingt-douze	
93	quatre-vingt-treize	
...		
99	quatre-vingt-dix-neuf	
100	cent	'**one** hundred, **a** hundred' is simply *cent*: 'a hundred times' *cent fois*
101	cent un	*cent une réponses* 'a hundred and one answers'. The [t] of *cent* is NOT pronounced.
102	cent deux	
...		
111	cent onze	The [t] of cent is NOT pronounced in *cent un, cent huit, cent onze*, but it is pronounced when followed by a non-numeral noun beginning with a vowel: *cent ans* 'a hundred years'.
200	deux cents	
201	deux cent un	
202	deux cent deux	
...		
1 000	mille	'**one** thousand, **a** thousand' is simply *mille*: 'a thousand times' *mille fois*
1 001	mille un	You will hear the idiom (*j'ai*) *mille et une choses à faire* '(I've) a thousand and one things to do'. This is not meant as a precise figure.
...		
1 100	onze cents *or* mille cent	There are two ways of describing numbers between 1 100 and 1 999: *onze cents* or *mille cent* (1 100); *dix huit cent soixante* or *mille huit cent soixante* (1 860); *dix-neuf cent quatre-vingt-dix-neuf* or *mille neuf cent quatre-vingt-dix-neuf* (1 999), etc.
1 101	onze cent un *or* mille cent un	
...		

1 200	douze cents *or* mille deux cents
1 201	douze cent un *or* mille deux cent un
…	
1 500	quinze cents *or* mille cinq cents
…	
2 000	deux mille mille is invariable, never plural
2 001	deux mille un
2 101	deux mille cent un
1 000 000	un million
1 201 101	un million deux cent un mille cent un
1 000 000 000	un milliard

6.1.1 *et* in cardinal numbers

et is used for cardinal numbers ending in –1 between 21 and 71 inclusive (note the absence of hyphens but see *Nouvelle Orthographe* below):

21	vingt et un
31	trente et un
41	quarante et un
51	cinquante et un
61	soixante et un
71	soixante et onze

et is NOT used in numbers ending in –1 between 81 and 101 inclusive (note the use of hyphens in the case of 81 and 91), nor in 1 001, 1 000 001 and 1 000 000 001:

81	quatre-vingt-un
91	quatre-vingt-onze
101	cent un
1 001	mille un
1 000 001	un million un
1 000 000 001	un milliard un

6.1.2 Hyphens in written cardinal numbers

Compound cardinal numbers less than 100 are linked by hyphen (other than those ending in –1 between 21 and 71 inclusive):

17	dix-sept
18	dix-huit
19	dix-neuf
22	vingt-deux
23	vingt-trois
…	
32	trente-deux
33	trente-trois
…	
72	soixante-douze

80	quatre-vingts
81	quatre-vingt-un

But cardinal numbers of 100 and above are not linked to other numbers by hyphen, in compound numbers:

101	cent un
102	cent deux
…	
192	cent quatre-vingt-douze
…	
10,340	dix mille trois cent quarante
…	
520	cinq cent vingt
…	
522	cinq cent vingt-deux
…	

Nouvelle Orthographe

As indicated above, in traditional spelling numbers the use of hyphens varied according to the specific numbers e.g. whether or not they were above 100. However, the spelling recommendations allow all compound numbers to be linked by hyphens, including numbers under and above 100 and numbers linked by *et*:

Vingt-et-un
Trente-et-un
Cent-un
Cent-onze
Cent-quatre-vingt-deux
Douze-cents or mille-deux-cents
Dix-mille-trois-cent-quarante

6.1.3 **Plurals in cardinal numbers**

The numbers *quatre-vingts* and *deux cents, trois cents, quatre cents*, etc., take a plural *-s* in the written language when they are used in isolation or phrase-final position:

J'en ai vu **quatre-vingts**	*I saw eighty*
La capacité de la salle est de **huit cents**	*The room can hold eight hundred*

and when they precede non-numeral nouns:

trois cents visiteurs	*three hundred visitors*
quatre-vingts candidats	*eighty applicants*

However, when these numbers precede other numerals, there is generally no plural *-s*:

quatre-vingt-deux
quatre-vingt-trois
…
deux cent deux
deux cent trois
trois cent mille
…

unless those numerals are *millions* or *milliards*:

deux cents millions d'habitants	*two hundred million inhabitants*
cinq cents milliards d'euros	*five hundred billion euros*

mille never takes a plural *-s*:

mille personnes	*a thousand people*
dix mille gagnants	*ten thousand winners*
deux mille vingt lecteurs	*two thousand and twenty readers*

When *quatre-vingt* or *cent* are used in phrases such as *à la page quatre-vingt* 'on page 80', *à la page trois cent* 'on page 300', *les années quatre-vingt*, they are generally written without a final *-s*.

6.1.4 **When to use figures and when to use words**

Numbers are usually written in words, except in the following cases:

in scientific or academic texts
in dates: *Elle est arrivée le **25** mars **2019*** 'She arrived on the 25th of March 2019'
in prices: *Cela coûte **32** euros* 'That costs 32 euros'
in weights and measures: *Il mesure **1** mètre **50*** 'He is 1 metre 50 tall'
describing kings and queens: *Henri **IV*** 'Henry the Fourth'
in percentages: ***12** pour cent* '12 per cent'

6.1.5 **Conventions for writing cardinal numbers in figures**

Where English uses a comma to separate hundreds from thousands, and thousands from millions, French normally uses spaces; and where English uses a full stop to separate whole numbers from decimals, French normally uses a comma:

English	**French**
1,200	1 200
63,321	63 321
412,633,221	412 633 221
4.25	4,25
0.25	0,25
€4.50	4,50 EUR/4,50€

In speech, the English 'four point five' is *quatre virgule cinq*.

(For money, see Section 6.8.)

6.1.6 *nombre, chiffre*, and *numéro*

nombre refers to a number as a concept:

Choisissez un **nombre** (dans votre tête)	*think of a number*
nombres entiers	*whole numbers*
un **nombre** cardinal	*a cardinal number*

Le **nombre** de femmes qui fument a augmenté
The number of women who smoke has increased

chiffre refers to the figures or digits which make up a number; it can also be used to mean 'statistics':

Ecrire un nombre en **chiffres** et en lettres
To write a number in figures and words

Ces **chiffres** ne reflètent pas la situation exacte
These figures do not reflect the real situation

numéro refers to a numbered entity:

mon **numéro** de portable	*my mobile number*
le **numéro** d'une maison	*a house number*
Il porte le **numéro** un	*he's wearing the number one*
un **numéro** d'immatriculation	*a car number plate*

6.1.7 **Necessity to use *en* when numbers are direct objects**

The pronoun *en* must be inserted before the verb when a number on its own (or followed by an adjective, e.g. *deux grands*) is a direct object:

J'**en** prends **deux (grands)**, s'il vous plaît
I'll take two (big ones), please

Elle lui **en** a offert **une douzaine**
She offered him a dozen

This is not the case, however, when a number alone (or followed by an adjective) is a subject:

Deux (grands) ont disparu	*Two (big ones) have disappeared*
Une douzaine me suffira	*A dozen will be enough for me*

en must be similarly inserted before the verb when quantifiers like *quelques-uns, plusieurs* and *certains* stand alone as direct objects:

J'**en** ai encore **quelques-uns**	*I still have a few*
J'**en** ai encore **plusieurs**	*I still have several*
J'**en** ai encore **certains**	*I still have some*

(For quantifiers, see Section 6.9.)

6.1.8 **Non-agreement of direct object numerals with *coûter*, *peser* and *mesurer***

Although past participles normally agree with preceding direct objects (see Section 9.3.1), including direct objects involving numerals:

Les cinq cents euros que j'ai **gagnés**
The five hundred euros I won

with the verbs *coûter* 'cost', *peser* 'weigh', *mesurer* 'measure', and other measure verbs, numerals are normally adverbs rather than direct objects, so there is no agreement when the numeral precedes the past participle:

> Les cinq cents euros que cela m'a **coûté**
> *The five hundred euros which that cost me*

(See Section 9.3.5.)

6.1.9 **Simple arithmetic (*le calcul*)**

trois et quatre font sept (trois plus quatre égale sept)	$3 + 4 = 7$
trois moins un égale deux (trois ôtez un reste deux)	$3 - 1 = 2$
deux fois cinq font dix (cinq multiplié par deux égale dix)	$2 \times 5 = 10$
dix divisé par deux égale cinq	$10 \div 2 = 5$

N.B.: As in English, the verbs can vary between singular and plural: *trois et quatre fait/font sept* 'three plus four makes/make seven'.

6.2 **Ordinal numbers**

Numbers like *premier, deuxième, troisième* are called ordinal numbers:

English	French	
1st	1er/1ère	premier, première
2nd	2e	deuxième *or* second, seconde (*deuxième* and *second* are interchangeable except in *en seconde* 'in the fifth form'/Year 11' (UK)) When there were second-class seats on trains or planes that also would have been '*en seconde*').
3rd	3e	troisième
4th	4e	quatrième
5th	5e	cinquième
6th	6e	sixième
7th	7e	septième
8th	8e	huitième
9th	9e	neuvième
10th	10e	dixième
11th	11e	onzième
12th	12e	douzième
13th	13e	treizième
14th	14e	quatorzième
15th	15e	quinzième
16th	16e	seizième
17th	17e	dix-septième
18th	18e	dix-huitième
19th	19e	dix-neuvième
20th	20e	vingtième
21st	21e	vingt et unième
22nd	22e	vingt-deuxième
...		
40th	40e	quarantième
41st	41e	quarante et unième
...		

70th	70e	soixante-dixième
71st	71e	soixante et onzième
...		
80th	80e	quatre-vingtième
81st	81e	quatre-vingt-unième
...		
90th	90e	quatre-vingt-dixième
91th	91e	quatre-vingt-onzième
...		
100th	100e	centième
...		
1000th	1000e	millième

6.3 Fractions

6.3.1 Ordinal numbers as fractions

The majority of fractions can be constructed from the ordinal numbers and are masculine in gender. They are usually introduced by the definite article (as opposed to the indefinite article or absence of article in English):

Le cinquième des élèves ont été recalés
A fifth of the pupils have failed

Les cinq dixièmes de la population du monde ont été directement affectés
Five-tenths of the world's population were directly affected

Another way of expressing these figures is: *Un sur cinq des élèves a échoué* 'One in five pupils has failed'; *Cinq sur dix personnes de la population du monde sont directement affectés* 'Five out of ten people in the world are directly affected'.

6.3.2 'half', 'third', and 'quarter'

'Half', 'third', and 'quarter' have their own names. 'Half' is translated by *la moitié* (*de*) when it is a noun (i.e. is followed by *de* or stands alone):

La moitié des conducteurs ont dépassé la limite de vitesse
Half of all drivers have broken the speed limit

La moitié seront recyclés
Half will be recycled

However, 'half' is translated by *demi* when it is part of a hyphenated compound noun (and is invariable):

un **demi-verre** d'eau	*half a glass of water*
une **demi-heure**	*a half an hour*
la **demi-finale**	*the semi-final*

It is also translated by *demi* in compounds involving *et*, but here it agrees with the preceding noun in gender:

deux heures et **demie**	*two and a half hours/ half past two*
un litre et **demi**	*one and a half litres*
deux kilos et **demi**	*two and a half kilos*

Some compounds are constructed with invariable *mi-*:

la **mi-trimestre**	*half-term*
à **mi-chemin**	*half-way*
mi-clos	*half-closed*

'Third' is translated by *tiers*:

Un tiers des étudiants se déclarent stressés
A third of students say they feel stressed

Les deux tiers des blessés ont été évacués
Two-thirds of the injured were evacuated

N.B.: *le tiers monde* 'the Third World'.

'Quarter' is translated by *quart*:

Un quart seulement des accidents ont lieu sur les autoroutes
Only a quarter of accidents happen on motorways

Les trois quarts étaient des hommes
Three-quarters were men

N.B.:   Il est deux heures et **quart**   *or*   Il est deux heures **un quart**
              It's quarter past two
              Il est deux heures moins **le quart**
              It's quarter to two
              cinq kilos **et quart**   *or*   cinq kilos **un quart**
              five and a quarter kilos

(See Section 6.7 for time.)

6.3.3 **Verb agreement with fractions**

Verbs are usually plural when fractions are subjects and refer to plural entities:

Le cinquième (des élèves) **ont** été recalés
A fifth (of the pupils) have failed

La moitié (des conducteurs) **ont** dépassé la limite de vitesse
Half (of all drivers) have broken the speed limit

Un tiers (des étudiants) **se déclarent** stressés
A third (of students) say they feel stressed

Verbs are singular when fractions are subjects and refer to singular entities:

La moitié (de l'année) **est** déjà passée
Half (of the year) has already passed

Un tiers (de l'album) **reste** à enregistrer
A third (of the album) is still to be recorded

6.4 Some differences in the use of cardinal and ordinal numbers in French and English

6.4.1 Dates

While English uses ordinal numbers in dates French uses cardinal numbers, with the exception of 'first', which is *premier*:

le **premier** janvier	*the first of January*
le **deux** février	*the second of February*
le **trois** mars	*the third of March*

In letter headings, the normal way of writing dates is

le 1er janvier 2025
le 2 février 2025
le 3 mars 2025

or where the day is included:

le lundi 1er janvier 2025	*or*	lundi, le 1er janvier 2025
le vendredi 2 février 2025	*or*	vendredi, le 2 février 2025

N.B.: Months and days are written with a lower-case initial letter in French, but with a capital letter in English.

6.4.2 Kings, queens, and popes

As with dates, where English uses ordinal numbers, French uses cardinal numbers, with the exception of 'first' *premier*:

François I	François **premier**	*Francis the First*
Elizabeth I	Elizabeth **première**	*Elizabeth the First*
Henri II	Henri **deux**	*Henry the Second*
Louis XIV	Louis **quatorze**	*Louis the Fourteenth*
Jean XXIII	Jean **vingt-trois**	*(Pope) John the Twenty-third*
Charles III	Charles **trois**	*Charles the Third*

6.4.3 Ordinal number abbreviations

The abbreviated forms of *premier, première* are:

1er, 1ère	*1st*

where ^{er} and ^{ère} are superscripts. The abbreviation for all other ordinal numbers is an *e* which can either be a superscript or a simple lower-case letter:

2^{e}	2e	*2nd*
3^{e}	3e	*3rd*
4^{e}	4e	*4th etc.*

6.4.4 **Order of cardinal numbers and adjectives**

In English, cardinal numbers follow adjectives:

the **last nine** chapters
the **other four** guests
the **first three** winners

In French, they precede adjectives:

les **neuf derniers** chapitres
les **quatre autres** invités
les **trois premiers** gagnants

(See also Section 4.1.5.)

6.4.5 **Page numbers, bus numbers, etc.**

As in English, French page numbers, bus numbers, etc. are cardinal numbers which follow the noun; *un* is invariable in this usage. *Quatre-vingt* and *cent* are written without an -s. A definite article always accompanies the noun in French:

à **la** page un	*on page one*
Prenez **le** trente-deux	*Catch the number 32*
Suivez **le** quatre-vingt	*Follow the number 80*
Il habite dans **le** quatre vingt douze	*He lives in the département 92 (Hauts-de-Seine)*
Le train part **du** quai vingt	*The train leaves from platform twenty*

6.4.6 **Addresses**

Like English, address numbers are cardinal numbers in French. But the French for 'a', 'b', 'c' is *bis, ter, quater*:

12, rue Lamarck
12bis, rue Lamarck
12ter, rue Lamarck

N.B.: In addresses, *rue, avenue, boulevard*, etc., usually begin with lower-case letters.

6.4.7 **'hundreds', 'thousands', 'millions', and 'billions'**

The numeral nouns *centaine, millier, million*, and *milliard* are always followed by *de* when they are followed by other nouns:

des centaines **de** personnes	*hundreds of people*
des milliers **de** personnes	*thousands of people*
un million **de** dollars	*a million dollars*
des millions **de** personnes	*millions of people*
cinq milliards **de** dollars	*five billion dollars*
des milliards **de** personnes	*billions of people*
des centaines **de** milliers **de** personnes	*hundreds of thousands of people*
des centaines **de** millions **de** personnes	*hundreds of millions of people*

6.4.8 *mille, milliers, milliards*

These numbers are often confused by English speakers:

mille 'thousand' is directly followed by a noun: *mille euros* 'a thousand euros'
des milliers 'thousands' is followed by *de* when followed by another noun:
des milliers d'euros 'thousands of euros'
des milliards 'billions' is also followed by *de* when followed by another noun:
des milliards d'euros 'billions of euros'

6.4.9 'once', 'twice', 'three times', etc.; 'both', 'all three', 'all four', etc.

Whereas English has the forms 'once', 'twice', then a regular pattern from 'three' onwards: 'three times', 'four times' etc., French has a fully regular pattern from 'one' on:

une fois	*once*
deux fois	*twice*
trois fois	*three times*
quatre fois	*four times*
…	

French has alternative forms for 'both', 'all three', 'all four', one with a definite article and one without (found only in formal French); but from 'all five' onwards the definite article must be used:

tous/toutes les deux	tous/toutes deux	*both*
tous/toutes les trois	tous/toutes trois	*all three*
tous/toutes les quatre	tous/toutes quatre	*all four*
tous/toutes les cinq	NOT *tous/toutes cinq	*all five*
tous/toutes les six	NOT *tous/toutes six	*all six*
…		

Tous les deux sont arrivés	*Both have arrived*
Je les ai invitées **toutes les six**	*I invited all six*

N.B.: These expressions cannot precede a noun directly. To translate phrases like 'both players', 'all six singers', either use the definite article and a numeral alone: *les deux joueurs, les six chanteuses*:

Les deux joueurs sont arrivés
J'ai invité **les six chanteuses**

or, when the phrase is in subject position, move the *tous/toutes* (*les*) X to a position after the verb marked for tense:

Les joueurs sont **tous deux** arrivés

(See also Section 6.9.5.)

6.5 **Measurements and comparisons**

6.5.1 **Numbers with length, height, depth, etc.**

With the verb *être*, numbers specifying length, height, depth, width, distance, thickness, etc., are preceded by *de*:

La piscine est longue **de** 50 mètres
La longueur de la piscine est **de** 50 mètres
The swimming pool is 50 metres long

Cette tour est haute **de** 20 mètres
La hauteur de cette tour est **de** 20 mètres
This tower is 20 metres high

Le lac est profond **de** 300 mètres
La profondeur du lac est **de** 300 mètres
The lake is 300 metres deep

Le fleuve est large **de** 2 kilomètres à cet endroit
La largeur du fleuve à cet endroit est **de** 2 kilomètres
The river is 2 kilometres wide at this point

Le mur est épais **de** 89 centimètres
L'épaisseur du mur est **de** 89 centimètres
The wall is 89 centimetres thick

La distance de Londres à Paris est **de** 500 kilomètres
The distance from London to Paris is 500 kilometres

For *long, haut, large* there is another way of expressing the same idea using the verbs *faire* and *avoir*; in this case *de* precedes *long, haut, large*, which remain invariable in form:

La piscine fait/a 50 mètres **de long**
Cette tour fait/a 20 mètres **de haut**
Le fleuve fait/a 2 kilomètres **de large**

However, this structure can NOT be used with *profond* or *épais*.

With *faire* and *avoir* it is also possible to say *La piscine fait* (or *a*) *50 mètres de longueur, Cette tour fait* (or *a*) *20 mètres de hauteur, Le fleuve fait* (or *a*) *2 kilomètres de largeur*, although the construction with the adjectives *long, haut, large* is probably more natural.

Profondeur and *épaisseur* are also possible in this construction: *La piscine fait* (or *a*) *2 mètres de profondeur, Le mur fait* (or *a*) *89 centimètres d'épaisseur*.

In talking about how tall people are, the verbs *mesurer, faire* are usually used:

Je mesure 1,97 mètres   *I am 1.97 metres tall*
Elle fait 1,80 mètres   *She is 1.80 metres tall*

The verbs *mesurer, faire* are the equivalent of English 'is' in describing dimensions:

La table **mesure** (or **fait**) trois mètres sur deux
The table is three metres by two

6.5.2 **Numbers in comparisons**

When numbers figure in comparisons with the verb *être*, they are often preceded by *de:*

Elle est mon aînée **de** six ans
She is six years older than me

La fenêtre est trop grande **de** cinq centimètres
The window is five centimetres too big

La remorque est plus lourde **de** huit kilos
The trailer is eight kilograms heavier

In some of these cases, alternative expressions with *avoir* are possible:

Elle a six ans **de** plus que moi
J'ai six ans **de** moins qu'elle

Translating 'more than' and 'less than' into French often causes English speakers some difficulty, because there are two possibilities:

plus de   plus que
moins de   moins que

plus de, moins de imply that there is a specific benchmark against which something is measured as being 'more than' or 'less than', and this is often a number:

Elle gagne **plus de** 3 000 euros par mois
She earns more than 3,000 euros a month
(*3 000 euros* is the benchmark – she earns more than this)

Il travaille **moins de** deux heures par jour
He works less than two hours a day
(*deux heures* is the benchmark – he works less than this)

Interdit aux **moins de** 15 ans
Not suitable for children under fifteen
(*15 ans* is the benchmark – below this age, children are not allowed)

plus que, moins que imply a comparison between one person or thing and another, without a specific benchmark being mentioned:

Elle gagne **plus que** moi
She earns more than me
(how much I earn isn't specified – but she earns more)

Il travaille **moins que** son frère
He works less than his brother
(how much his brother works isn't specified – but he works less)

The difference between the two can be illustrated in the following pair of sentences:

Elle a réuni **plus de** cinquante de ses collègues pour son pot de départ
She got more than fifty of her colleagues together for her leaving do
(*cinquante de ses collègues* is the benchmark – she managed to persuade more colleagues than this to come)

Elle a gagné **plus que** l'ensemble de ses collègues pendant l'année
She earned more than all her colleagues during the year
(her colleagues earned an unspecified amount during the year – however much it was, she earned more than this)

N.B.: The following expressions compare one measurement with another:

quatre mètres **sur** trois	*four metres by three*
un Français **sur** sept	*one French person in seven*
une chose **à la** fois	*one thing at a time*
20% **par** an	*20% a year*
deux heures **par** jour	*two hours a day*

'miles per gallon' is measured in French by the number of litres consumed per hundred kilometres: *dix litres aux cent (kilomètres)* (roughly 30 miles per gallon).

6.5.3 **Numeral nouns and approximations**

The following numeral nouns describe approximate, rather than specific, numbers:

une dizaine	*ten or so*
une quinzaine	*fifteen or so*
une vingtaine	*twenty or so*
une trentaine	*thirty or so*
une quarantaine	*forty or so*
une cinquantaine	*fifty or so*
une soixantaine	*sixty or so*
une centaine	*a hundred or so*

Je reviendrai dans une quinzaine (une huitaine) de jours
I'll come back in about a fortnight (a week) or so

Il a environ la trentaine
He is thirty something

Elle a une quarantaine d'années
She is in her forties

J'approche de la cinquantaine
I'm approaching my fifties

une douzaine (une demi-douzaine), however, means 'a dozen (a half-dozen)' exactly: *une douzaine d'œufs* 'a dozen eggs'.

A variety of other expressions, when used with numbers, also express approximations:

Ça coûte environ 300€/à peu près 300€/dans les 300€/près de 300€
That costs around/about/nearly 300 euros

Il a cinquante ans **et quelques**	*He is over fifty*
Il a **autour de** cinquante ans	*He is around fifty*
Elle **va sur ses** vingt-six ans	*She is going on twenty-six*
Je l'ai rencontrée il y a **quelque** trente ans	*I met her about thirty years ago*

Le train arrive vers 11h/aux alentours de 11h/aux environs de 11 heures
The train arrives around 11 a.m.

N.B.: *ans* is always present when describing a person's age.

6.6 **Dates, days, years**

6.6.1 **Dates**

Dates always begin with *le* (which does not contract to *l'* even before numbers beginning with a vowel: *le huit mars, le onze septembre*):

le 1er janvier
le 2 mai
le 8 mars
lundi **le** 11 juin
Quelle est la date d'aujourd'hui? C'est **le** 2 janvier
On est le combien? On est **le** 2 janvier

N.B.: When writing dates, months always begin with lower case letters. When referring to events in a particular month use either *au mois de janvier, février,* etc., or *en janvier, février*, etc. (See also Section 6.4.1 for dates.)

Significant national dates in the French calendar include:

Le jour de l'an	*New Year's Day*
L'Épiphanie	*Twelfth Night*
Le vendredi saint	*Good Friday*
Le premier mai	*Labour Day*
Le quatorze juillet	*Bastille Day*
La Toussaint	*All Saints Day*
Le onze novembre	*Armistice Day*
Noël	*Christmas Day*

6.6.2 **Days**

When days of the week are used without a determiner, they usually refer to a specific day:

Je viendrai vous voir **lundi**   *I'll come and see you on Monday*

(But in dates, days of the week are preceded by *le: le lundi 8 août*.)

When days of the week are preceded by a definite article they usually describe what habitually happens:

Le magasin est fermé **le** lundi (*or* tous les lundis)
The shop is closed on Mondays

le matin, l'après-midi, le soir, la nuit are used in the same way:

Elle se lève tôt **le** matin
She gets up early in the mornings

(versus *Elle s'est levée tôt lundi matin* 'She got up early on Monday morning'.)

Seasons can be used in a similar way:

faire du ski l'hiver (also en hiver)	*to go skiing in winter*
jouer au tennis l'été (also en été)	*to play tennis in summer*

But the definite article may be used to stress that an event occurred on a particular day:

Le concours s'est déroulé **le** lundi
The competition took place on the Monday

Note the following expressions:

dimanche en huit	*a week on Sunday*
vendredi en quinze	*a fortnight on Friday*
tous les deux jours	*every other day*

6.6.3 Years

In referring to years in a date, *cent* is obligatory (while 'hundred' is often omitted in English):

1945	dix-neuf *or* mille neuf cent quarante-cinq
	nineteen (hundred and) forty-five
le 2 mai 1993	le deux mai dix-neuf cent quatre-vingt-treize
	the second of May nineteen (hundred and) ninety-three

'BC' is *av. J-C* (*avant Jésus-Christ*) and 'AD' is *ap. J-C* (*après Jésus-Christ*):

50 av. J-C	50 BC
500 ap. J-C	500 AD

If *mille* is used in AD dates, it can be written optionally *mille* or (very rarely) *mil:*

en **mille** neuf cent quinze *or* en **mil** neuf cent quinze
in nineteen fifteen

an is used in *l'an 2000* (*l'an deux mille*) 'the year 2000', *en l'an 2010* (*en l'an deux mille dix*) 'in the year 2010', etc.; but *année* is used in *les années 60* (*les années soixante*) 'the 60s', *les années 30* (*les années trente*) 'the 30s', etc. (see Section 1.1.5 for *an/année*).

6.7 Clock time

In telling time, 'it is' is always *il est*, never * *c'est:*

Quelle heure est-il? (*Or* Quelle heure avez-vous?)
What time is it?

heures is obligatory:

Il est deux **heures** vingt; il est trois **heures** moins vingt
It's two twenty; it's twenty to three

et links *quart* and *demi* to the hour in times past the hour – *demi* agrees in gender with the noun:

onze heures et quart	*a quarter past eleven*
midi et quart	*a quarter past midday*

minuit et quart	*a quarter past midnight*
onze heures et demie	*half past eleven*
midi et demi	*half past midday*
minuit et demi	*half past midnight*

'a quarter to' the hour is *moins le quart* (or *moins un quart*):

| onze heures moins le quart | *a quarter to eleven* |

As in English, one can equally say *onze heures quinze* 'eleven fifteen', *midi trente* 'thirty minutes past midday', etc.

In French timetables, times are usually written as *21 h 35* or *21:35*.

N.B.:	à l'heure	*on time*	
	à temps	*in time*	
	à deux heures	précises	*at two o'clock precisely* (official report)
		justes	*exactly two o'clock* (looking at watch)
		sonnantes	*bang on two o'clock* (for effect)
		tapantes	*spot on two* (for effect, more informal)

vers deux heures/vers les deux heures/	*about two*
autour de deux heures/	
à deux heures environ/dans les environs	*o'clock*
de deux heures	

| Je peux faire mes comptes dans une heure | *I can do my accounts in an hour's time* |
| Je peux faire mes comptes en une heure | *I can do my accounts within an hour* |

(See Sections 13.14.4 and 13.26.3.)

6.8 **Money**

euro is always present in quoting prices, but *centime* is optional:

huit euros cinquante (centimes)
eight euros fifty (*centimes*)

deux cents euros quatre-vingts (centimes)
two hundred euros eighty (*centimes*)

Foreign currencies are described in the same way:

deux livres cinquante
two pounds fifty

trois dollars cinquante
three dollars fifty

Prices can be written in different ways:

8,50EUR
8,50€
€8,50

Ça va chercher dans les quatre cents euros
That'll fetch around four hundred euros
(informal spoken style)

Paying for things in French does not involve a preposition equivalent to 'for':

J'ai payé ce fauteuil 500 euros
I paid 500 euros for this armchair

6.9 Quantifiers

6.9.1 Common quantifiers

Quantifiers, like numbers, determine 'how much' there is of something, but are less specific than numbers:

assez de		*enough*	
autant de		*as many*	
beaucoup de		*many*	
bien des		*many*	
certains	client(s)	*some, specific ones*	*customer(s)*
chaque		*every*	
chacun des		*each one of the*	
une majorité de		*a majority of*	
une minorité de		*a minority of*	

moins de		*fewer*	
nombre de		*a lot of*	
une partie des		*a portion of*	
peu de		*few*	
pas mal de (informal French)		*quite a lot of*	
la plupart des	client(s)	*most*	*customer(s)*
plus de		*more*	
plusieurs		*several*	
quantité de		*a lot of*	
quelques		*some, a few*	
le reste des		*the rest of the*	
tous les		*all the*	

6.9.2 **Direct object quantifiers and *en***

When a quantifier on its own is a direct object, *en* must be inserted in front of the verb, as in the case of numbers (see Section 6.1.7):

J'**en** ai encore certains	*I still have some*
Ils n'**en** consomment qu'une partie	*They only consume a portion*
Il **en** a vendu la plupart	*He has sold most of it*

N.B.: When *quelques* 'some, a few' stands alone, it becomes *quelques-un(e)s*:

Il y avait **quelques** clients dans le magasin	*There were a few customers in the shop*
Il y en avait **quelques-uns** dans le magasin	*There were a few in the shop*

6.9.3 ***de* or *du, de la, des* after quantifiers**

The indefinite article *des* and the partitive articles *du, de la, des* (see Sections 2.3.1 and 2.4) are omitted when a noun phrase follows one of the quantifiers listed with *de* in Section 6.9.1:

assez **de**	+	**des** clients	→	assez **de** clients
enough		*customers*	→	*enough customers*
autant **de**	+	**de** l'argent	→	autant **d**'argent
as much		*money*	→	*as much money*
peu **de**	+	**du** travail	→	peu **de** travail
not much		*work*	→	*not much work*

Quantifiers listed in Section 6.9.1 with *des*, however, are those which are followed by *des, du*, or *de la*:

bien **des** clients
many customers

la plupart **de** l'argent
most of the money

une partie **du** travail
part of the work

When the quantifiers listed with *de* in Section 6.9.1 are followed by a noun with a definite article, this is not omitted. Compare:

Beaucoup **d**'étudiants (indefinite) dorment moins qu'ils ne le souhaitent
Many students sleep less than they would wish

Beaucoup **des** étudiants interviewés (definite) dorment moins qu'ils ne le souhaitent
Many of the students interviewed sleep less than they would wish

(See also Sections 2.3.2 and 2.4.)

6.9.4 **Quantifiers and personal pronouns**

certains			some		them
beaucoup		eux	many		them
peu	d'entre	elles	few	of	them
plusieurs		nous	several		us
la plupart		vous	most		you
chacun			each		

The preposition *d'entre* is used with quantifiers which precede stressed pronouns (for stressed pronouns, see Section 3.3):

One can also find *certains parmi eux* 'some of them', *chacun de nous* 'each of us'.

6.9.5 *tout* and *chaque*

tous/toutes, like other quantifiers, can appear with the nouns they quantify or on their own:

Toutes les assiettes sont sales/**Toutes** sont sales
All the plates are dirty/All are dirty

J'ai cassé **toutes les assiettes**/Je les ai **toutes** cassées
I broke all the plates/I broke them all

When *tous/toutes* quantifies a subject, it can be optionally moved to a position after the verb:

Tous les invités sont maintenant arrivés *or* Les invités sont maintenant **tous** arrivés
All the guests have arrived now/The guests have all arrived now

When *tous/toutes* is used alone as a direct object, it can be optionally moved to a position after the verb marked for tense:

Je les ai **tous** vus   Je les ai vus **tous**   *I saw them all*

chaque means 'each, every':

Chaque passager est prié de se présenter à la porte 12
Every passenger is requested to go to gate 12

chaque cannot stand alone: it becomes *chacun(e)*:

Chaque assiette est peinte à la main/**Chacune** est peinte à la main
Every plate is hand painted/Every one is hand painted

(For adverbial use of *tout*, as in *toute blanche, tout blanc*, see Section 5.6.7.)

6.9.6 **Subject–verb agreement when subject quantifiers are present**

With some quantifiers, the verb agrees not with the quantifier but with the noun:

Beaucoup d'infirmières **sont** surmenées
Many nurses are overworked

Similar quantifiers are:

bien des, nombre de, pas mal de, peu de, la plupart de, quantité de, trop de

With other quantifiers, however, the verb may agree with the noun or with the quantifier:

La majorité de nos étudiants **ont/a** moins de quarante ans
The majority of our students are under forty

Une bonne partie de ses clients **viennent/vient** de l'étranger
A good portion of his customers come from abroad

Similar quantifiers are: *une minorité de, le reste de, la moitié de, un tiers de,* and numeral nouns such as *une dizaine de, une vingtaine,* etc. (see Section 9.1.5).

FREE

INSTRUCTOR & STUDENT RESOURCES

For more resources to practice your French grammar, including practice activities/quizzes for students, further resource links, and an instructor guide, please visit https://routledgelearning.com/frenchgrammarandusage.

7 Verb forms

7.1 Introduction

As in many languages, verbs in French have different forms for the different functions they perform in sentences. It is traditional (and easiest for reference) to present verb forms in **paradigms** (i.e. lists), and this is what we do in this chapter. We follow earlier scholars in dividing the paradigms into **simple forms**, **compound forms** and **double compound forms**. Simple forms are made up of stems to which endings are attached (see Section 7.3 for stems and endings). Compound forms are made up of forms of the auxiliary verbs *avoir* and *être* plus a past participle. Double compound forms are made up of forms of the compound auxiliary verbs *avoir eu* or *avoir été* plus a past participle. The set of verb forms that this produces is illustrated below, using the third-person singular form of the verb *donner* 'to give' (stems are in normal type, endings are in bold).

Not all books and teachers use the terminology we employ here, so we have added other terms in common use in brackets:

Simple tenses	**Example**
Present	Il donn-**e**
Imperfect	Il donn-**ait**
Simple past (past historic)	Il donn-**a**
Future	Il donn-**era**
Conditional	Il donn-**erait**
Present subjunctive	Qu'il donn-**e**
Imperfect subjunctive	Qu'il donn-**ât**

Simple non-finite forms

Simple infinitive	donn-**er**
Present participle	donn-**ant**
Past participle	donn-**é**
Imperative	donn-**e**
	donn-**ez**
	donn-**ons**

Compound tenses

Compound past (perfect)	Il **a** donné
Pluperfect	Il **avait** donné
Past anterior	Il **eut** donné
Compound future (future perfect)	Il **aura** donné
Compound conditional (conditional perfect)	Il **aurait** donné
Compound past subjunctive	Qu'il **ait** donné
Pluperfect subjunctive	Qu'il **eût** donné

DOI: 10.4324/9781003373926-7

Compound non-finite forms

Compound infinitive	**avoir** donné
Compound present participle	**ayant** donné
Compound past participle	**eu** donné
Compound imperative	**aie** donné
	ayez donné
	ayons donné

Double compound tenses

Double compound past	Il **a eu** donné
Compound pluperfect	Il **avait eu** donné
Double compound future	Il **aura eu** donné
Double compound conditional	Il **aurait eu** donné
Double compound past subjunctive	Qu'il **eût eu** donné

Double compound non-finite forms

Double compound infinitive	**avoir eu** donné
Double compound participle	**ayant eu** donné

7.2 **Conjugations**

For the purposes of systematic presentation, French verbs are best grouped into four **conjugations**. These are:

(1) Verbs whose infinitive ends in *-er* (e.g. *donner, chanter, parler*). This is by far the largest group.

(2) Verbs whose infinitive ends in *-ir*. Within this group there are two subgroups:

    (a) verbs whose stems sometimes end in -iss- (e.g. finir: fin-iss-ons, fin-iss-ant, and fin-iss-aient);

    (b) verbs whose stems do not add -iss- (e.g. dormir, mentir).

(3) Verbs whose infinitive ends in *-re* (e.g. *vendre, rendre*).

(4) Verbs whose infinitive ends in *-oir* (e.g. *recevoir*).

Verbs which differ from this pattern are included in the list of irregular verbs under Section 7.6.8.

7.2.1 **Organization of the paradigms**

The paradigms which follow in this chapter are divided into eight sections:

Sections 7.6.1 and 7.6.2 describe the forms of *avoir* and *être* because these two verbs are essential to all the compound forms.

Section 7.6.3 describes the forms of regular verbs belonging to the *-er* conjugation (e.g. *donner, chanter, parler*).

Sections 7.6.4 and 7.6.5 describe the forms of regular verbs belonging to the *-ir* conjugation. These subdivide into those whose stem sometimes ends in *-iss-* (such as *finir: fin-iss-ons, fin-iss -ant, fin-iss-aient* – these are the majority of verbs in the *-ir* conjugation), and those whose stem does not add *-iss-* (such as *dormir*: *dor-mons, dorm-ant, dorm-aient*). There are only about 30 of these verbs.

Section 7.6.6 describes the forms of regular verbs belonging to the *-re* conjugation (e.g. *vendre, rendre*).

Section 7.6.7 describes the forms of regular verbs belonging to the *-oir* conjugation (e.g. *recevoir, décevoir, concevoir*).

Section 7.6.8 lists the forms of irregular verbs (i.e. those whose stems change idiosyncratically at various points in the paradigm).

7.3 Easy ways of generating some parts of the paradigms

A number of the parts of the verb paradigms can be productively generated using a few simple rules. It is sometimes easier to learn these rules than learning every verb form individually. However, be aware that these only work with regular verbs – irregular verbs have idiosyncratic forms which have to be learned.

7.3.1 An easy way of generating the present tense

For regular verbs ending in *-er* (like *donner*), *-ir* (the *finir* kind whose stems sometimes end in *-iss-*: *fin-iss-ons, fin-iss-ant, fin-iss-aient*, etc., but NOT the *dormir* kind – see Sections 7.6.4 and 7.6.5) or *-re* (such as *vendre*), take the infinitive form of the verb, omit the ending *-er, -ir,* or *-re* (this creates a stem: *donn-, fin-, vend-*) and add the following endings:

	je	tu	il/elle	nous	vous	ils/elles
-er verbs	-e	-es	-e	-ons	-ez	-ent
-ir verbs (most verbs – see Section 7.6.4)	-is	-is	-it	-issons	-issez	-issent
-re verbs	-s	-s	–	-ons	-ez	-ent

For example:

Infinitive	Stem	Present tense
donner	Donn	je donn- e, etc.
finir	Fin	je fin- is, etc.
vendre	Vend	je vend- s, etc.

7.3.2 An easy way of generating the imperfect tense

For all regular verb conjugations, take the first-person plural *nous* form of the present tense, omit *-ons*, and add the following endings:

je	tu	il/elle	nous	vous	ils/elles
-ais	-ais	-ait	-ions	-iez	-aient

For example:

Infinitive	First-person plural	Stem	Imperfect tense
donner	donnons	donn	je donn- ais, etc.
commencer	commençons	commenç	je commenç- ais, etc.
partager	partageons	partage	je partage- ais, etc.
finir	finissons	finiss	je finiss- ais, etc.
dormir	dormons	dorm	je dorm- ais, etc.
vendre	vendons	vend	je vend- ais, etc.
recevoir	recevons	recev	je recev- ais, etc.

7.3.3 An easy way of generating the simple past (past historic)

For -er verbs, take the first-person plural *nous* form of the present tense, omit -ons, and add the following endings: -ai, -as, -a, -âmes, -âtes, and -èrent.

For -ir (both *finir* and *dormir* types – see Sections 7.6.4 and 7.6.5) and -re verbs, take the past participle, omit the final vowel and add the following endings: -is, -is, it, -îmes, -îtes, and -irent.

For -oir verbs, take the past participle, omit the final vowel and add the following endings: -us, -us, -ut, -ûmes, -ûtes, and -urent.

	je	tu	il/elle	nous	vous	ils/elles
-er verbs (most verbs – see Section 7.6.3)	-ai	-as	-a	-âmes	-âtes	-èrent
-ir verbs -re verbs	-is	-is	-it	-îmes	-îtes	-irent
-oir verbs	-us	-us	-ut	-ûmes	-ûtes	-urent

For example:

Infinitive	First-person plural	Stem	Simple past tense
donner	donnons	donn	je donn- ai, etc.
commencer	commençons	commenç	je commenç- ai, etc.
partager	partageons	partage	je partage- ai, etc.
	Past participle		
finir	fini	fin	je fin- is, etc.
dormir	dormi	dorm	je dorm- is, etc.
vendre	vendu	vend	je vend- is, etc.
recevoir	reçu	reç	je reç- us, etc.

7.3.4 **An easy way of generating the future and conditional**

Take the infinitive form of *-er, -ir,* and *-re* verbs (deleting the final *e* in the latter case) and add the following endings:

For example:

	je	tu	il/elle	nous	vous	ils/elles
Future	-ai	-as	-a	-ons	-ez	-ont
Conditional	-ais	-ais	-ait	-ions	-iez	-aient

Infinitive	Stem	Future/conditional
donner	donner	je donner- ai, etc. je donner- ais, etc.
finir	finir	je finir- ai, etc. je finir- ais, etc.
dormir	dormir	je dormir- ai, etc. je dormir- ais, etc.
vendre	vendr	je vendr- ai, etc. je vendr- ais, etc.

(For the doubling of consonants in verbs like *je jetterai, j'appellerai,* the change from *e* to *è* in verbs like *j'achèterai, il gèlera,* and the change from *é* to *è* in verbs like *j'espèrerai, je compléterai,* see Sections 7.4 and 7.6.9 and Appendix 2 for *Nouvelle Orthographe* proposals.)

7.3.5 **An easy way of generating the present subjunctive**

For all regular verb conjugations, take the third-person plural *ils/elles* form of the present tense, omit *-ent,* and add the endings:

je	tu	il/elle	nous	vous	ils/elles
-e	-es	-e	-ions	-iez	-ent

For example:

Infinitive	Third-person plural	Stem	Present subjunctive
donner	donnent	donn	je donn- e, etc.
finir	finissent	finiss	je finiss- e, etc.
dormir	dorment	dorm	je dorm- e, etc.
vendre	vendent	vend	je vend- e, etc.
recevoir	reçoivent	reçoiv	je reçoiv- e, etc.

N.B.: The stem *reçoiv-* changes when the ending does not begin with *-e: reçoive,* but *recevions, receviez.*

7.3.6 **An easy way of generating the imperfect subjunctive**

For all regular verb conjugations, take the first-person singular *je* form of the simple past tense, omit the last letter and add the endings:

je	tu	il/elle	nous	vous	ils/elles
-sse	-sses	-^t	-ssions	-ssiez	-ssent

For example:

Infinitive	First-person simple past	Stem	Imperfect subjunctive
donner	donnai	donna	je donna- sse, etc.
commencer	commençai	commença	je commença- sse, etc.
partager	partageai	partagea	je partagea- sse, etc.
finir	finis	fini	je fini- sse, etc.
dormir	dormis	dormi	je dormi- sse, etc.
vendre	vendis	vendi	je vendi- sse, etc.
recevoir	reçus	reçu	je reçu- sse, etc.

7.3.7 **An easy way of generating the imperative**

For all verbs (with four exceptions – see below) take the second-person singular *tu* form, the second-person plural *vous* form, and the first-person plural *nous* form of the present tense, delete the subject and the final -*s* of any verb which ends in -*es* or -*as*. For example:

Infinitive	Present tense	Imperative
donner	tu donnes	donne!
	vous donnez	donnez!
	nous donnons	donnons!
aller	tu vas	va!
	vous allez	allez!
	nous allons	allons!
finir	tu finis	finis!
	vous finissez	finissez!
	nous finissons	finissons!
dormir	tu dors	dors!
	vous dormez	dormez!
	nous dormons	dormons!
vendre	tu vends	vends!
	vous vendez	vendez!
	nous vendons	vendons!
recevoir	tu reçois	reçois!
	vous recevez	recevez!
	nous recevons	recevons!

N.B.: The final -*s* which disappears from second-person singular verbs ending in -*es* or -*as* reappears where the pronouns *y* or *en* follow the imperative:

aller	Va!	Vas-y!
parler	Parle!	Parles-en!

Four exceptions:

Infinitive	Present tense	Imperative
être	tu es	sois!
	vous êtes	soyez!
	nous sommes	soyons!
avoir	tu as	aie!
	vous avez	ayez!
	nous avons	ayons!
savoir	tu sais	sache!
	vous savez	sachez!
	nous savons	sachons!
vouloir	tu veux	veuille
	vous voulez	veuillez
	nous voulons	not used

(Both *veuille* and *veuillez* mean 'please'.)

N.B.: Although *vouloir* has irregular imperative forms, the related verb *en vouloir à qn* 'to hold a grudge against sb' has regular forms:

Tu ne lui en veux pas	Ne lui en veux pas!
Vous ne lui en voulez pas	Ne lui en voulez pas!
Nous ne lui en voulons pas	Ne lui en voulons pas!

7.4 Changes in the stem form of some *-er* conjugation verbs

The stems of a number of verbs of the *-er* conjugation change their form when they are followed by an *e*. (See also listings under irregular verbs, Table 7.H.)

The majority of verbs ending in *-eler* or *-eter* double the final consonant of the stem when it is followed by *-e* in the present, future, conditional, and present subjunctive:

appeler	
Present	j'appelle, tu appelles, il/elle appelle, ils/elles appellent
Future	J'appellerai, …, nous appellerons, etc.
Conditional	j'appellerais, …, nous appellerions, etc.
Present subjunctive	que j'appelle, que tu appelles, qu'il/elle appelle, qu'ils/elles appellent
jeter	
Present	je jette, … etc.
Future	je jetterai, … etc.
Conditional	je jetterais, … etc.
Present subjunctive	que je jette, … etc.

The following verbs, however, do not double the final stem consonant, but change the first *e* to *è*: *acheter, celer, ciseler, corseter, crocheter, démanteler, écarteler, fureter, geler, haleter, marteler, modeler, peler* (together with verbs derived from these like *congeler, dégeler*, etc.):

acheter
Present   j'achète, ... etc.
Future   j'achèterai, ... etc.

Other verbs which have an unstressed *e* in the syllable before the final *-er* also change that vowel to *è* in the same circumstances, for example *mener, semer*:

mener
Present   je mène, ... etc.
Future   je mènerai, ... etc.

Verbs of the *-er* conjugation whose stem ends in -y, for example, *employer, nettoyer, essayer*, change the *y* to *i* in the same circumstances:

employer
Present   j'emploie, ... etc.
Future   j'emploierai, ... etc.

Verbs which have an *é* in the syllable before the final *-er*, for example, *céder, espérer, révéler*, change the vowel to *è* when the stem is followed by *-e* only in the present tense and the present subjunctive:

espérer
Present   j'espère, tu espères, il/elle espère, ils/elles espèrent.
Present subjective   que j'espère, que tu espères, qu'il/elle espère, qu'ils/elles espèrent.
BUT
Future   j'espérerai, tu espéreras, il/elle espérera, etc.
Conditional   j'espérerais, tu espérerais, il/elle espérerait, etc.

See Section 7.6.9 and Appendix 2 for proposed changes in *Nouvelle Orthographe*.

7.4.1 The forms of *créer, nier, scier, rire*, etc.

Verbs whose stems end in *-é* or *-i* behave just like any other verb: the final vowel does not change, for example:

je cr**ée** (present tense)
j'ai cr**éé** (compound past)
l'entreprise que j'ai cr**éée** (past participle agreement with a preceding feminine direct object – see Section 9.3).
nous r**ions** (present tense)
nous r**iions** (imperfect tense or present subjunctive)
etc.

7.5 Verbs whose stems end in *c-* or *g-*

Verbs whose stems end in *c-*(pronounced [s]) change to *ç-*before an ending beginning with *-a, -o*, or *-u*, e.g. *commenc-er, rec-evoir*:

commenc-er   nous commenç- ons (present)
                        je commenç- ais (imperfect)
                        nous commenç- âmes (simple past) etc.
rec-evoir   je reç- ois (present)
                        nous reç- ûmes (simple past) etc.

Verbs whose stems end in a g- (pronounced like 'je') change to ge- before an ending beginning with -a or -o, e.g. *partag-er*, *protég-er*:

partag-er	nous partage- ons (present)
	je partage- ais (imperfect)
	nous partage- âmes (simple past) etc.

7.6 **Verb paradigms**

7.6.1 **The irregular verb** *avoir*

TABLE 7.A

Infinitive:	avoir	Compound infinitive:	avoir eu
Past participle:	eu	Compound present	
Present participle:	ayant	participle:	ayant eu
Simple forms		**Compound forms**	
Present:		Compound past:	
j'ai	nous avons	j'ai eu	nous avons eu
tu as	vous avez	tu as eu	vous avez eu
il a	ils ont	il a eu	ils ont eu
Imperfect:		Pluperfect:	
j'avais	nous avions	j'avais eu	nous avions eu
tu avais	vous aviez	tu avais eu	vous aviez eu
il avait	ils avaient	il avait eu	ils avaient eu
Simple past (past historic):		Past anterior:	
j'eus	nous eûmes	j'eus eu	nous eûmes eu
tu eus	vous eûtes	tu eus eu	vous eûtes eu
il eut	ils eurent	il eut eu	ils eurent eu
Future:		Compound future:	
j'aurai	nous aurons	j'aurai eu	nous aurons eu
tu auras	vous aurez	tu auras eu	vous aurez eu
il aura	ils auront	il aura eu	ils auront eu
Conditional:		Compound conditional:	
j'aurais	nous aurions	j'aurais eu	nous aurions eu
tu aurais	vous auriez	tu aurais eu	vous auriez eu
il aurait	ils auraient	il aurait eu	ils auraient eu
Present subjunctive:		Compound past subjunctive:	
que j'aie	que nous ayons	que j'aie eu	que nous ayons eu
que tu aies	que vous ayez	que tu aies eu	que vous ayez eu
qu'il ait	qu'ils aient	qu'il ait eu	qu'ils aient eu

TABLE 7.A (*Continued*)

Imperfect subjunctive:		Pluperfect subjunctive:	
que j'eusse	que nous eussions	que j'eusse eu	que nous eussions eu
que tu eusses	que vous eussiez	que tu eusses eu	que vous eussiez eu
qu'il eût	qu'ils eussent	qu'il eût eu	qu'ils eussent eu
Imperative:		Compound imperative:	
aie		not used	
ayons			
ayez			

7.6.2 **The irregular verb** *être*

TABLE 7.B

Infinitive:	être	Compound infinitive:	avoir été
Past participle:	été	Compound past participle:	eu été
Present participle:	étant	Compound present participle:	ayant été
Simple forms		**Compound forms**	
Present:		Compound past:	
je suis	nous sommes	j'ai été	nous avons été
tu es	vous êtes	tu as été	vous avez été
il est	ils sont	il a été	ils ont été
Imperfect:		Pluperfect:	
j'étais	nous étions	j'avais été	nous avions été
tu étais	vous étiez	tu avais été	vous aviez été
il était	ils étaient	il avait été	ils avaient été
Simple past (past historic):		Past anterior:	
je fus	nous fûmes	j'eus été	nous eûmes été
tu fus	vous fûtes	tu eus été	vous eûtes été
il fut	ils furent	il eut été	ils eurent été
Future:		Compound future:	
je serai	nous serons	j'aurai été	nous aurons été
tu seras	vous serez	tu auras été	vous aurez été
il sera	ils seront	il aura été	ils auront été
Conditional:		Compound conditional:	
je serais	nous serions	j'aurais été	nous aurions été
tu serais	vous seriez	tu aurais été	vous auriez été
il serait	ils seraient	il aurait été	ils auraient été

TABLE 7.B (*Continued*)

Present subjunctive:		Compound past subjunctive:	
que je sois	que nous soyons	que j'aie été	que nous ayons été
que tu sois	que vous soyez	que tu aies été	que vous ayez été
qu'il soit	qu'ils soient	qu'il ait été	qu'ils aient été
Imperfect subjunctive:		Pluperfect subjunctive:	
que je fusse	que nous fussions	que j'eusse été	que nous eussions été
que tu fusses	que vous fussiez	que tu eusses été	que vous eussiez été
qu'il fût	qu'ils fussent	qu'il eût été	qu'ils eussent été
Imperative:		Compound imperative:	
sois		not used	
soyons			
soyez			

7.6.3 Conjugation 1: verbs whose infinitive ends in -*er*

TABLE 7.C

Infinitive:	Parler	Compound infinitive:	avoir parlé
Past participle:	Parlé	Compound past participle:	eu parlé
Present participle:	parlant	Compound present participle:	ayant parlé
Simple forms		**Compound forms**	
Present:		Compound past:	
je parle	nous parlons	j'ai parlé	nous avons parlé
tu parles	vous parlez	tu as parlé	vous avez parlé
il parle	ils parlent	il a parlé	ils ont parlé
Imperfect:		Pluperfect:	
je parlais	nous parlions	j'avais parlé	nous avions parlé
tu parlais	vous parliez	tu avais parlé	vous aviez parlé
il parlait	ils parlaient	il avait parlé	ils avaient parlé
Simple past (past historic):		Past anterior:	
je parlai	nous parlâmes	j'eus parlé	nous eûmes parlé
tu parlas	vous parlâtes	tu eus parlé	vous eûtes parlé
il parla	ils parlèrent	il eut parlé	ils eurent parlé
Future:		Compound future:	
je parlerai	nous parlerons	j'aurai parlé	nous aurons parlé
tu parleras	vous parlerez	tu auras parlé	vous aurez parlé
il parlera	ils parleront	il aura parlé	ils auront parlé

TABLE 7.C *(Continued)*

Conditional:		Compound conditional:	
je parlerais	nous parlerions	j'aurais parlé	nous aurions parlé
tu parlerais	vous parleriez	tu aurais parlé	vous auriez parlé
il parlerait	ils parleraient	il aurait parlé	ils auraient parlé
Present subjunctive:		Compound past subjunctive:	
que je parle	que nous parlions	que j'aie parlé	que nous ayons parlé
que tu parles	que vous parliez	que tu aies parlé	que vous ayez parlé
qu'il parle	qu'ils parlent	qu'il ait parlé	qu'ils aient parlé
Imperfect subjunctive:		Pluperfect subjunctive:	
que je parlasse	que nous parlassions	que j'eusse parlé	que nous eussions parlé
que tu parlasses	que vous parlassiez	que tu eusses parlé	que vous eussiez parlé
qu'il parlât	qu'ils parlassent	qu'il eût parlé	qu'ils eussent parlé
Imperative:		Compound imperative:	
parle (but parles-en)		aie parlé	
parlons		ayons parlé	
parlez		ayez parlé	

N.B.: Verbs whose stem ends in *c* or *g* are written *ç* and *ge*, respectively, before endings which begin with *a* or *o*: e.g. *nous commençons* and *je mangeais* – see Section 7.5.

N.B.: Verbs of the *-er* conjugation whose stem changes, like *compléter*, *espérer* (and other verbs ending in *-éter*, *-érer*), *appeler*, *mener*, *jeter*, *employer*, *nettoyer* (and other verbs ending in *-oyer* – see Section 7.4), are individually listed under irregular verbs.

7.6.4 Conjugation 2 (a): verbs whose infinitives end in *-ir* and whose stems end in *-iss-* in certain paradigms

N.B.: Verbs which approximate to this pattern but which have significant differences are *fleurir* and *haïr*. These are listed as irregular verbs.

TABLE 7.D

Infinitive:	finir	Compound infinitive:	avoir fini
Past participle:	fini	Compound past participle:	eu fini
Present participle:	finissant	Compound present participle:	ayant fini
Simple forms		**Compound forms**	
Present:		Compound past:	
je finis	nous finissons	j'ai fini	nous avons fini
tu finis	vous finissez	tu as fini	vous avez fini
il finit	ils finissent	il a fini	ils ont fini

TABLE 7.D (*Continued*)

Imperfect:		Pluperfect:	
je finissais	nous finissions	j'avais fini	nous avions fini
tu finissais	vous finissiez	tu avais fini	vous aviez fini
il finissait	ils finissaient	il avait fini	ils avaient fini
Simple past (past historic):		Past anterior:	
je finis	nous finîmes	j'eus fini	nous eûmes fini
tu finis	vous finîtes	tu eus fini	vous eûtes fini
il finit	ils finirent	il eut fini	ils eurent fini
Future:		Compound future:	
je finirai	Nous finirons	j'aurai fini	nous aurons fini
Tu finiras	Vous finirez	tu auras fini	vous aurez fini
Il finira	Ils finiront	il aura fini	ils auront fini
Conditional:		Compound conditional:	
je finirais	Nous finirions	j'aurais fini	nous aurions fini
Tu finirais	Vous finiriez	tu aurais fini	vous auriez fini
Il finirait	Ils finiraient	il aurait fini	ils auraient fini
Present subjunctive:		Compound past subjunctive:	
que je finisse	que nous finissions	que j'aie fini	que nous ayons fini
que tu finisses	que vous finissiez	que tu aies fini	que vous ayez fini
qu'il finisse	qu'ils finissent	qu'il ait fini	qu'ils aient fini
Imperfect subjunctive:		Pluperfect subjunctive:	
que je finisse	que nous finissions	que j'eusse fini	que nous eussions fini
que tu finisses	que vous finissiez	que tu eusses fini	que vous eussiez fini
qu'il finît	qu'ils finissent	qu'il eût fini	qu'ils eussent fini
Imperative:		Compound imperative:	
finis		aie fini	
finissons		ayons fini	
finissez		ayez fini	

7.6.5 Conjugation 2 (b): verbs whose infinitives end in *-ir* and whose stems do not end in *-iss-* (e.g. *dormir*)

N.B.: *S'endormir, servir, desservir, mentir, démentir, partir, repartir, se repentir, sentir, consentir, ressentir, sortir,* and *ressortir* conjugate like *dormir* BUT *asservir, impartir, répartir, assortir,* conjugate like *finir*.

Verbs which are similar to one or other of these *-ir* conjugations are: *cueillir, accueillir, recueillir, assaillir, tressaillir, couvrir, découvrir, recouvrir, offrir, ouvrir, rouvrir,* and *souffrir,* but they have special characteristics. They are listed individually as irregular verbs.

TABLE 7.E

Infinitive:	dormir	Compound infinitive:	avoir dormi
Past participle:	dormi	Compound past participle:	eu dormi
Present participle:	dormant	Compound present participle:	ayant dormi

Simple forms		**Compound forms**	
Present:		Compound past:	
je dors	nous dormons	j'ai dormi	nous avons dormi
tu dors	vous dormez	tu as dormi	vous avez dormi
il dort	ils dorment	il a dormi	ils ont dormi
Imperfect:		Pluperfect:	
je dormais	nous dormions	j'avais dormi	nous avions dormi
tu dormais	vous dormiez	tu avais dormi	vous aviez dormi
il dormait	ils dormaient	il avait dormi	ils avaient dormi
Simple past (past historic):		Past anterior:	
je dormis	nous dormîmes	j'eus dormi	nous eûmes dormi
tu dormis	vous dormîtes	tu eus dormi	vous eûtes dormi
il dormit	ils dormirent	il eut dormi	ils eurent dormi
Future:		Compound future:	
je dormirai	nous dormirons	j'aurai dormi	nous aurons dormi
tu dormiras	vous dormirez	tu auras dormi	vous aurez dormi
il dormira	ils dormiront	il aura dormi	ils auront dormi
Conditional:		Compound conditional:	
je dormirais	nous dormirions	j'aurais dormi	nous aurions dormi
tu dormirais	vous dormiriez	tu aurais dormi	vous auriez dormi
il dormirait	ils dormiraient	il aurait dormi	ils auraient dormi
Present subjunctive:		Compound past subjunctive:	
que je dorme	que nous dormions	que j'aie dormi	que nous ayons dormi
que tu dormes	que vous dormiez	que tu aies dormi	que vous ayez dormi
qu'il dorme	qu'ils dorment	qu'il ait dormi	qu'ils aient dormi
Imperfect subjunctive:		Pluperfect subjunctive:	
que je dormisse	que nous dormissions	que j'eusse dormi	que nous eussions dormi
que tu dormisses	que vous dormissiez	que tu eusses dormi	que vous eussiez dormi
qu'il dormît	qu'ils dormissent	qu'il eût dormi	qu'ils eussent dormi
Imperative:		Compound imperative:	
dors		aie dormi	
dormons		ayons dormi	
dormez		ayez dormi	

7.6.6 Conjugation 3: verbs with infinitives which end in *-re* (e.g. *vendre*)

TABLE 7.F

Infinitive:	vendre		Compound infinitive:	avoir vendu
Past participle:	vendu		Compound past participle:	eu vendu
Present participle:	vendant		Compound present participle:	ayant vendu
Simple forms			**Compound forms**	
Present:			Compound past:	
je vends	nous vendons		j'ai vendu	nous avons vendu
tu vends	vous vendez		tu as vendu	vous avez vendu
il vend	ils vendent		il a vendu	ils ont vendu
Imperfect:			Pluperfect:	
je vendais	nous vendions		j'avais vendu	nous avions vendu
tu vendais	vous vendiez		tu avais vendu	vous aviez vendu
il vendait	ils vendaient		il avait vendu	ils avaient vendu
Simple past (past historic):			Past anterior:	
je vendis	nous vendîmes		j'eus vendu	nous eûmes vendu
tu vendis	vous vendîtes		tu eus vendu	vous eûtes vendu
il vendit	ils vendirent		il eut vendu	ils eurent vendu
Future:			Compound future:	
je vendrai	nous vendrons		j'aurai vendu	nous aurons vendu
tu vendras	vous vendrez		tu auras vendu	vous aurez vendu
il vendra	ils vendront		il aura vendu	ils auront vendu
Conditional:			Compound conditional:	
je vendrais	nous vendrions		j'aurais vendu	nous aurions vendu
tu vendrais	vous vendriez		tu aurais vendu	vous auriez vendu
il vendrait	ils vendraient		il aurait vendu	ils auraient vendu
Present subjunctive:			Compound past subjunctive:	
que je vende	que nous vendions		que j'aie vendu	que nous ayons vendu
que tu vendes	que vous vendiez		que tu aies vendu	que vous ayez vendu
qu'il vende	qu'ils vendent		qu'il ait vendu	qu'ils aient vendu
Imperfect subjunctive:			Pluperfect subjunctive:	
que je vendisse	que nous vendissions		que j'eusse vendu	que nous eussions vendu
que tu vendisses	que vous vendissiez		que tu eusses vendu	que vous eussiez vendu
qu'il vendît	qu'ils vendissent		qu'il eût vendu	qu'ils eussent vendu
Imperative:			Compound imperative:	
vends			aie vendu	
vendons			ayons vendu	
vendez			ayez vendu	

A few verbs follow this pattern in its entirety, especially those ending in *-andre, -endre, -ondre, -erdre*, and *-ordre*, e.g. *épandre, répandre, attendre, défendre, descendre, détendre, entendre, étendre, fendre, prétendre, rendre, tendre, vendre, confondre, correspondre, fondre, pondre, répondre, tondre, mordre, perdre, tordre*.

Other verbs which have sufficient differences to be listed individually as irregular verbs are: *prendre* (and compounds of *prendre*), *rompre* (and compounds of *rompre*), *battre* (and compounds of *battre*), *vaincre* (and compounds of *vaincre*), verbs ending in *-a/e/oindre: contraindre, craindre, plaindre, enfreindre, éteindre, étreindre, astreindre, atteindre, ceindre, dépeindre, déteindre, enceindre, feindre, geindre, peindre, restreindre, teindre,* and *joindre,* and verbs ending in *-aître: apparaître, connaître, disparaître, méconnaître, paraître, reconnaître, repaître, accroître, décroître,* and *croître.*

A distinct group of verbs end in *-uire*, e.g. *conduire, construire, cuire, déduire, détruire, enduire, introduire, produire, séduire,* and *traduire.* These all follow the same pattern which is illustrated by *construire* in the table of irregular verbs.

7.6.7 Conjugation 4: verbs with infinitives which end in *-oir* (e.g. *recevoir*)

N.B.: A number of verbs, e.g. *voir* and derivatives, do not follow this pattern. They are listed individually as irregular verbs.

TABLE 7.G

Infinitive:	recevoir	Compound infinitive:	avoir reçu
Past participle:	reçu	Compound past participle:	eu reçu
Present participle:	recevant	Compound present participle:	ayant reçu
Simple forms		**Compound forms**	
Present:		Compound past:	
je reçois	nous recevons	j'ai reçu	nous avons reçu
tu reçois	vous recevez	tu as reçu	vous avez reçu
il reçoit	ils reçoivent	il a reçu	ils ont reçu
Imperfect:		Pluperfect:	
je recevais	nous recevions	j'avais reçu	nous avions reçu
tu recevais	vous receviez	tu avais reçu	vous aviez reçu
il recevait	ils recevaient	il avait reçu	ils avaient reçu
Simple past (past historic):		Past anterior:	
je reçus	nous reçûmes	j'eus reçu	nous eûmes reçu
tu reçus	vous reçûtes	tu eus reçu	vous eûtes reçu
il reçut	ils reçurent	il eut reçu	ils eurent reçu
Future:		Compound future:	
je recevrai	nous recevrons	j'aurai reçu	nous aurons reçu
tu recevras	vous recevrez	tu auras reçu	vous aurez reçu
il recevra	ils recevront	il aura reçu	ils auront reçu

TABLE 7.G (*Continued*)

Conditional:		Compound conditional:	
je recevrais	vous recevrions	j'aurais reçu	nous aurions reçu
tu recevrais	vous recevriez	tu aurais reçu	vous auriez reçu
il recevrait	ils recevraient	il aurait reçu	ils auraient reçu
Present subjunctive:		Compound past subjunctive:	
que je reçoive	que nous recevions	que j'aie reçu	que nous ayons reçu
que tu reçoives	que vous receviez	que tu aies reçu	que vous ayez reçu
qu'il reçoive	qu'ils reçoivent	qu'il ait reçu	qu'ils aient reçu
Imperfect subjunctive:		Pluperfect subjunctive:	
que je reçusse	que nous reçussions	que j'eusse reçu	que nous eussions reçu
que tu reçusses	que vous reçussiez	que tu eusses reçu	que vous eussiez reçu
qu'il reçût	qu'ils reçussent	qu'il eût reçu	qu'ils eussent reçu
Imperative:		Compound imperative:	
reçois		aie reçu	
recevons		ayons reçu	
recevez		ayez reçu	

7.6.8 Irregular verbs

TABLE 7.H

Infinitive:	Simple present:		Participles:	abattant	abattu
abattre	j'abats	nous abattons	**Future:**	j'abattrai	
to knock down	tu abats	vous abattez	**Simple past:**	j'abattis	
	il abat	ils abattent	**Imperfect:**	j'abattais	
			Subj (pres):	que j'abatte	
			Subj (imp):	que j'abattisse	
Infinitive:	**Simple present:**		**Participles:**	absolvant	absous/ absoute (f)
absoudre	j'absous	nous absolvons	**Future:**	j'absoudrai	
to absolve	tu absous	vous absolvez	**Simple past:**	-	
	il absout	ils absolvent	**Imperfect:**	j'absolvais	
			Subj (pres):	que j'absolve	
			Subj (imp):	-	
Infinitive: s'abstenir de *to abstain from:* see tenir					

TABLE 7.H (*Continued*)

Infinitive:					
abstraire *to abstract:* see traire					

Infinitive:					
accourir *to run up:* see courir					

Infinitive:	Simple present:		Participles:	accroissant	accru
accroître	j'accrois	nous accroissons	**Future:**	j'accroîtrai	
to increase	tu accrois	vous accroissez	**Simple past:**	j'accrus	
	il accroît	ils accroissent	**Imperfect:**	j'accroissais	
			Subj (pres):	que j'accroisse	
			Subj (imp):	que j'accrusse	

Infinitive:					
accueillir *to welcome:* see cueillir					

Infinitive:	Simple present:		Participles:	achetant	acheté
acheter	j'achète	nous achetons	**Future:**	j'achèterai (è in all forms)	
to buy	tu achètes	vous achetez	**Simple past:**	j'achetai	
	il achète	ils achètent	**Imperfect:**	j'achetais	
			Subj (pres):	que j'achète	
				que nous achetions	
				que vous achetiez	
			Subj (imp):	que j'achetasse	

Infinitive:					
achever *to finish:* is like **acheter** in the distribution of *è*					

Infinitive:	Simple present:		Participles:	acquérant	acquis
acquérir	j'acquiers	nous acquérons	**Future:**	j'acquerrai	
to acquire	tu acquiers	vous acquérez	**Simple past:**	j'acquis	
	il acquiert	ils acquièrent	**Imperfect:**	j'acquérais	
			Subj (pres):	que j'acquière	
			Subj (imp):	que j'acquisse	

Infinitive:					
adjoindre *to join with:* see joindre					

Infinitive:					
admettre *to let in:* see mettre					

TABLE 7.H (*Continued*)

Infinitive:					
advenir *to occur*, see venir					

Infinitive:	**Simple present:**		**Participles:**	allant	allé
aller	je vais	nous allons	**Future:**	j'irai	
to go	tu vas	vous allez	**Simple past:**	j'allai	
	il va	ils vont	**Imperfect:**	j'allais	
			Subj (pres):	que j'aille	
			Subj (imp):	que j'allasse	

Infinitive:					
amener *to bring*, is like *mener* in the distribution of *è* in certain forms					

Infinitive:	**Simple present:**		**Participles:**	apparaissant	apparu
apparaître	j'apparais	nous apparaissons	**Future:**	j'apparaîtrai	
to appear	tu apparais	vous apparaissez	**Simple past:**	j'apparus	
	il apparaît	ils apparaissent	**Imperfect:**	j'apparaissais	
			Subj (pres):	que j'apparaisse	
			Subj (imp):	que j'apparusse	

Infinitive:					
appartenir *to belong:* see tenir					

Infinitive:	**Simple present:**		**Participles:**	appelant	appelé
appeler	j'appelle	nous appelons	**Future:**	j'appellerai (ll in all forms)	
to call	tu appelles	vous appelez	**Simple past:**	j'appelai	
	il appelle	ils appellent	**Imperfect:**	j'appelais	
			Subj (pres):	que j'appelle	
				que vous appeliez	
			Subj (imp):	que j'appelasse	

Infinitive:					
apprendre *to learn, to teach:* see prendre					

Infinitive:	**Simple present:**		**Participles:**	assaillant	assailli
Assaillir	j'assaille	nous assaillons	**Future:**	j'assaillirai	
to assail	tu assailles	vous assaillez	**Simple past:**	j'assaillis	
	il assaille	ils assaillent	**Imperfect:**	j'assaillais	
			Subj (pres):	que j'assaille	
			Subj (imp):	que j'assaillisse	
			Imperative:	assaille (assailles before *y* and en)	

TABLE 7.H (*Continued*)

Infinitive:	Simple present:		Participles:	s'asseyant	assis
s'asseoir	je m'assieds	nous nous	**Future:**	je m'assiérai (or je	
to sit down	tu t'assieds	asseyons		m'assoirai)	
	il s'assied	vous vous	**Simple past:**	je m'assis	
		asseyez	**Imperfect:**	je m'asseyais (or	
		ils s'asseyent		je m'assoyais)	
			Subj (pres):	que je m'asseye	
			Subj (imp):	que je m'assisse	
(Also possible					
are:					
	je m'assois	nous nous			
		assoyons			
	tu t'assois	vous vous			
		assoyez			
	il s'assoit	ils s'asseoient)			
Infinitive:	**Simple present:**		**Participles:**	astreignant	astreint
astreindre	j'astreins	nous astreignons	**Future:**	j'astreindrai	
to oblige	tu astreins	vous astreignez	**Simple past:**	j'astreignis	
	Il astreint	ils astreignent	**Imperfect:**	j'astreignais	
			Subj (pres):	que j'astreigne	
			Subj (imp):	que j'astreignisse	
Infinitive:	**Simple present:**		**Participles:**	atteignant	atteint
atteindre	j'atteins	nous atteignons	**Future:**	j'atteindrai	
to attain	tu atteins	vous atteignez	**Simple past:**	j'atteignis	
	il atteint	ils atteignent	**Imperfect:**	j'atteignais	
			Subj (pres):	que j'atteigne	
			Subj (imp):	que j'atteignisse	
Infinitive:	**Simple present:**		**Participles:**	avançant	avancé
avancer	j'avance	nous avançons	**Future:**	j'avancerai	
to advance	tu avances	vous avancez	**Simple past:**	j'avançai	
	il avance	ils avancent	**Imperfect:**	j'avançais	
			Subj (pres):	que j'avance	
			Subj (imp):	que j'avançasse	

N.B.: Always ç before an '*a*' or '*o*'

88

TABLE 7.H (*Continued*)

Infinitive:	Simple present:		Participles:	battant	battu
battre	je bats	nous battons	**Future:**	je battrai	
to beat	tu bats	vous battez	**Simple past:**	je battis	
	il bat	ils battent	**Imperfect:**	je battais	
			Subj (pres):	que je batte	
			Subj (imp):	que je battisse	

Infinitive:	Simple present:		Participles:	buvant	bu
boire	je bois	nous buvons	**Future:**	je boirai	
to drink	tu bois	vous buvez	**Simple past:**	je bus	
	il boit	ils boivent	**Imperfect:**	je buvais	
			Subj (pres):	que je boive	
			Subj (imp):	que je busse	

Infinitive:	Simple present:		participles:	bouillant	bouilli
bouillir	je bous	nous bouillons	**Future:**	je bouillirai	
to boil	tu bous	vous bouillez	**Simple past:**	je bouillis	
	il bout	ils bouillent	**Imperfect:**	je bouillais	
			Subj (pres):	que je bouille	
			Subj (imp):	que je bouillisse	

Infinitive:	Simple present:		participles:	brayant	-
braire	il brait	ils braient	**Future:**	il braira	
to bray			**Simple past:**	-	
			Imperfect:	il brayait	
			Subj (pres):	-	
			Subj (imp):	-	

Infinitive:	Simple present:		Participles:		-
bruire	il bruit	ils bruissent	**Future:**	il bruira	
to buzz			**Simple past:**	-	
(*of insects*)			**Imperfect:**	-	
			Subj (pres):	-	
			Subj (imp):	-	

Infinitive:
céder *to give up* is like *espérer and compléter* in the way é and è are distributed

Infinitive:	Simple present:		Participles:	ceignant	ceint
ceindre	je ceins	nous ceignons	**Future:**	je ceindrai	
to put sth	tu ceins	vous ceignez	**Simple past:**	je ceignis	
around sth	il ceint	ils ceignent	**Imperfect:**	je ceignais	
(rare)			**Subj (pres):**	que je ceigne	
			Subj (imp):	que je ceignisse	

TABLE 7.H (*Continued*)

Infinitive:	Simple present:		participles:	chu
choir	je chois	-	**Future:**	je choirai
to fall (rare)	tu chois	-	**Simple past:**	je chus
	il choit	ils choient	**Imperfect:**	-
			Subj (pres):	-
			Subj (imp):	-

Infinitive:
circonscrire *to circumscribe:* see écrire

Infinitive:
circonvenir *to circumvent*, see venir

Infinitive:	Simple present:		Participles:	
clore	je clos	-	**Future:**	je clorai
to conclude	tu clos	-	**Simple past:**	-
dose	il clôt	ils closent	**Imperfect:**	-
			Subj (pres):	que je close
			Subj (imp):	-

Infinitive:	Simple present:		Participles:	combattant	combattu
combattre	je combats	nous combattons	**Future:**	je combattrai	
to fight	tu combats	vous combattez	**Simple past:**	je combattis	
	il combat	ils combattent	**Imperfect:**	je combattais	
			Subj (pres):	que je combatte	
			Subj (imp):	que je combattisse	

Infinitive:
commettre *to commit*, see mettre

Infinitive:
comparaître *to appear before a court*, see paraître

Infinitive:
complaire à *to humour*, see plaire

Infinitive:	Simple present:		Participles:	complétant	complété
compléter	je complète	nous complétons	**Future:**	je compléterai	
to complete	tu complètes	vous complétez	**Simple past:**	je complétai	
	il complète	ils complètent	**Imperfect:**	je complétais	
			Subj (pres):	que je complète	
				que nous complétions	
				que vous complétiez	
			Subj (imp):	que je complétasse	

TABLE 7.H (*Continued*)

Infinitive:					
comprendre *to understand:* see prendre					

Infinitive:					
compromettre *to compromise:* see mettre					

Infinitive:	Simple present:		Participles:	concluant	conclu
conclure	je conclus	nous concluons	**Future:**	je conclurai	
to conclude	tu conclus	vous concluez	**Simple past:**	je conclus	
	il conclut	ils concluent	**Imperfect:**	je concluais	
			Subj (pres):	que je conclue	
			Subj (imp):	que je conclusse	

Infinitive:					
concourir *to converge, to compete:* see courir					

Infinitive:					
conduire *to drive:* see construire					

Infinitive:	Simple present:		Participles:	confisant	confit
confire	je confis	nous confisons	**Future:**	je confirai	
to preserve in	tu confis	vous confisez	**Simple past:**	je confis	
fat or sugar	il confit	ils confisent	**Imperfect:**	je confisais	
			Subj (pres):	que je confise	
			Subj (imp):	-	

Infinitive:	Simple present:		Participles:	connaissant	connu
connaître	je connais	nous connaissons	**Future:**	je connaîtrai	
to know	tu connais	vous connaissez	**Simple past:**	je connus	
	il connaît	ils connaissent	**Imperfect:**	je connaissais	
			Subj (pres):	que je connaisse	
			Subj (imp):	que je connusse	

Infinitive:					
conquérir *to conquer,* see acquérir					

Infinitive:	Simple present:		Participles:	construisant	construit
construire	je construis	nous construisons	**Future:**	je construirai	
to build	tu construis	vous construisez	**Simple past:**	je construisis	
	il construit	ils construisent	**Imperfect:**	je construisais	
			Subj (pres):	que je construise	
			Subj (imp):	que je construisisse	

Infinitive:					
contenir *to contain:* see tenir					

TABLE 7.H (*Continued*)

Infinitive:	Simple present:		Participles:	contraignant	constraint
contraindre	je contrains	nous contraignons	**Future:**	je contraindrai	
to constrain	tu contrains	vous contraignez	**Simple past:**	je contraignis	
	il contraint	ils contraignent	**Imperfect:**	je contraignais	
			Subj (pres):	que je contraigne	
			Subj (imp):	que je contraignisse	

Infinitive:
contredire *to contradict:* see interdire

Infinitive:
contrefaire *to imitate:* see faire

Infinitive:
contrevenir *to contravene:* see venir

Infinitive:
convaincre *to convince:* see vaincre

Infinitive:
convenir *to agree:* see venir

Infinitive:	Simple present:		Participles:	corrompant	corrompu
corrompre	je corromps	nous corrompons	**Future:**	je corromprai	
to corrupt	tu corromps	vous corrompez	**Simple past:**	je corrompis	
	il corrompt	ils corrompent	**Imperfect:**	je corrompais	
			Subj (pres):	que je corrompe	
			Subj (imp):	que je corrompisse	

Infinitive:	Simple present:		Participles:	cousant	cousu
coudre	je couds	nous cousons	**Future:**	je coudrai	
to sew	tu couds	vous cousez	**Simple past:**	je cousis	
	il coud	ils cousent	**Imperfect:**	je cousais	
			Subj (pres):	que je couse	
			Subj (imp):	que je cousisse	

Infinitive:	Simple present:		Participles:	courant	couru
courir	je cours	nous courons	**Future:**	je courrai	
to run	tu cours	vous courez	**Simple past:**	je courus	
	il court	ils courent	**Imperfect:**	je courais	
			Subj (pres):	que je coure	
			Subj (imp):	que je courusse	

TABLE 7.H (*Continued*)

Infinitive:	Simple present:		Participles:	couvrant	couvert
couvrir	je couvre	nous couvrons	**Future:**	je couvrirai	
to cover	tu couvres	vous couvrez	**Simple past:**	je couvris	
	il couvre	ils couvrent	**Imperfect:**	je couvrais	
			Subj (pres):	que je couvre	
			Subj (imp):	que je couvrisse	
			Imperative:	couvre (couvres before *y* and *en*)	

Infinitive:	Simple present:		Participles:	craignant	craint
craindre	je crains	nous craignons	**Future:**	je craindrai	
to fear	tu crains	vous craignez	**Simple past:**	je craignis	
	il craint	ils craignent	**Imperfect:**	je craignais	
			Subj (pres):	que je craigne	
			Subj (imp):	que je craignisse	

Infinitive:	Simple present:		Participles:	créant	créé
créer	je crée	nous créons	**Future:**	je créerai	
to create	tu crées	vous créez	**Simple past:**	je créai	
(regular verb)	il crée	ils créent	**Imperfect:**	je créais	
			Subj (pres):	que je crée	
			Subj (imp):	que je créasse	

Infinitive:	Simple present:		Participles:	croyant	cru
croire	je crois	nous croyons	**Future:**	je croirai	
to believe	tu crois	vous croyez	**Simple past:**	je crus	
	il croit	ils croient	**Imperfect:**	je croyais	
			Subj (pres):	que je croie	
			Subj (imp):	que je crusse	

Infinitive:	Simple present:		Participles:	croissant	crû (crue)
croître	je croîs	nous croissons	**Future:**	je croîtrai	
to increase	tu croîs	vous croissez	**Simple past:**	je crûs	
	il croît	ils croissent	**Imperfect:**	je croissais	
			Subj (pres):	que je croisse	
			Subj (imp):	que je crûsse	

Infinitive:	Simple present:		Participles:	cueillant	cueilli
cueillir	je cueille	nous cueillons	**Future:**	je cueillerai	
to pick	tu cueilles	vous cueillez	**Simple past:**	je cueillis	
	il cueille	ils cueillent	**Imperfect:**	je cueillais	
			Subj (pres):	que je cueille	
			Subj (imp):	que je cueillisse	
			Imperative:	cueille (cueilles before *y* and *en*)	

TABLE 7.H (*Continued*)

N.B.: The future and conditional have *cueiller* as a base and not *cueillir*. The same is true of *acceuillir* and *recueillir* (but not *assaillir*).				

Infinitive:	Simple present:		Participles:	débattant	débattu
débattre	je débats	nous débattons	**Future:**	je débattrai	
to discuss	tu débats	vous débattez	**Simple past:**	je débattis	
	il débat	ils débattent	**Imperfect:**	je débattais	
			Subj (pres):	que je debatte	
			Subj (imp):	que je débattisse	

Infinitive:	Simple present:		Participles:		déchu
déchoir	je déchois	nous déchoyons	**Future:**	je déchoirai	
to decline	tu déchois	vous déchoyez	**Simple past**	je déchus	
	il déchoit	ils déchoient	**Imperfect:**	-	
			Subj (pres):	que je déchoie	
				que nous déchoyions	
				que vous déchoyiez	
			Subj (imp):	que je déchusse	

Infinitive:
découdre *to unstitch*, see coudre

Infinitive:	Simple present:		Participles:	découvrant	découvert
découvrir	je découvre	nous découvrons	**Future:**	je découvrirai	
to discover	tu découvres	vous découvrez	**Simple past:**	je découvris	
	il découvre	ils découvrent	**Imperfect:**	je découvrais	
			Subj (pres):	que je découvre	
			Subj (imp):	que je découvrisse	
			Imperative:	découvre (découvres before y and en)	

Infinitive:
décrire *to describe:* see écrire

Infinitive:	Simple present:		Participles:	décroissant	décru
décroître	je décrois	nous décroissons	**Future:**	je décroîtrai	
to decrease	tu décrois	vous décroissez	**Simple past:**	je décrus	
	il décroît	ils décroissent	**Imperfect:**	je décroissais	
			Subj (pres):	que je décroisse	
			Subj (imp):	que je décrusse	

Infinitive:
se dédire de *to go back on:* see interdire

TABLE 7.H (*Continued*)

Infinitive:					
déduire *to deduce:* see construire					

Infinitive:					
défaillir *to become feeble:* see assaillir					

Infinitive:					
défaire *to undo:* see faire					

Infinitive:					
démettre *to dislocate,* see mettre					

Infinitive:	Simple present:		Participles:	dépeignant	dépeint
dépeindre	je dépeins	nous dépeignons	**Future:**	je dépeindrai	
to describe	tu dépeins	vous dépeignez	**Simple past:**	je dépeignis	
	il dépeint	ils dépeignent	**Imperfect:**	je dépeignais	
			Subj (pres):	que je dépeigne	
			Subj (imp):	que je dépeignisse	

Infinitive:					
déplaire à *to displease:* see plaire					

Infinitive:					
désapprendre *to unlearn:* see prendre					

Infinitive:	Simple present:		Participles:	déteignant	déteint
déteindre	je déteins	nous déteignons	**Future:**	je déteindrai	
to fade	tu déteins	vous déteignez	**Simple past:**	je déteignis	
	il déteint	ils déteignent	**Imperfect:**	je déteignais	
			Subj (pres):	que je déteigne	
			Subj (imp):	que je déteignisse	

Infinitive:					
détenir *to be in possession of:* see tenir					

Infinitive:					
détruire *to destroy:* see construire					

Infinitive:					
dévêtir *to undress:* see vêtir					

Infinitive:	Simple present:		Participles:	devant	dû (due)
devoir	je dois	nous devons	**Future:**	je devrai	
must	tu dois	vous devez	**Simple past:**	je dus	
	il doit	ils doivent	**Imperfect:**	je devais	
			Subj (pres):	que je doive	
			Subj (imp):	que je dusse	

TABLE 7.H (*Continued*)

Infinitive:	Simple present:		Participles:	disant	dit
dire	je dis	nous disons	**Future:**	je dirai	
to say	tu dis	vous dites	**Simple past:**	je dis	
	il dit	ils disent	**Imperfect:**	je disais	
			Subj (pres):	que je dise	
			Subj (imp):	que je disse	

Infinitive:
disconvenir à *to be unsuited to:* see venir

Infinitive:
discourir *to hold forth:* see courir

Infinitive:
disjoindre *to sever.* see joindre

Infinitive:	Simple present:		Participles:	disparaissant	disparu
disparaître	je disparais	nous disparaissons	**Future:**	je disparaîtrai	
to disappear	tu disparais	vous disparaissez	**Simple past:**	je disparus	
	il disparaît	ils disparaissent	**Imperfect:**	je disparaissais	
			Subj (pres):	que je disparaisse	
			Subj (imp):	que je disparusse	

Infinitive:
dissoudre *to dissolve:* see absoudre

Infinitive:
distraire *to distract:* see traire

Infinitive:
s'ébattre *to frolic:* see battre

Infinitive:	Simple present:		Participles:	échéant	échu
échoir	-	-	**Future:**	il échoira	
to fall due	-	-	**Simple past:**	il échut	
	il échoit	ils échoient			

Infinitive:
éclore *to blossom:* see clore

Infinitive:	Simple present:		Participles:	écrivant	écrit
écrire	j'écris	nous écrivons	**Future:**	j'écrirai	
to write	tu écris	vous écrivez	**Simple past:**	j'écrivis	
	il écrit	ils écrivent	**Imperfect:**	j'écrivais	
			Subj (pres):	que j'écrive	
			Subj (imp):	que j'écrivisse	

TABLE 7.H (*Continued*)

Infinitive:					
élire *to elect*, see lire					

Infinitive:					
émettre *to emit*, see mettre					

Infinitive:	Simple present:		Participles:	émouvant	ému
émouvoir	j'émeus	nous émouvons	Future:	j'émouvrai	
to excite	tu émeus	vous émouvez	Simple past:	j'émus	
	il émeut	ils émeuvent	Imperfect:	j'émouvais	
			Subj (pres):	que j'émeuve	
			Subj (imp):	que j'émusse	

Infinitive:	Simple present:		Participles:	employant	employé
employer	j'emploie	nous employons	Future:	j'emploierai	
to use	tu emploies	vous employez	Simple past:	j'employai	
	il emploie	ils emploient	Imperfect:	j'employais	
			Subj (pres):	que j'emploie	
			Subj (imp):	que j'employasse	

Infinitive:					
empreindre *to stamp:* see craindre					

Infinitive:					
s'en aller to *go away*, see aller					

Infinitive:					
enceindre *to surround'*, see ceindre					

Infinitive:					
enclore *to fence in:* see clore					

Infinitive:					
encourir *to incur*, see courir					

Infinitive:					
enduire *to coat, render*, see construire					

Infinitive:	Simple present:		Participles:	enfreignant	enfreint
enfreindre	j'enfreins	nous enfreignons	Future:	j'enfreindrai	
to infringe	tu enfreins	vous enfreignez	Simple past:	j'enfreignis	
	il enfreint	ils enfreignent	Imperfect:	j'enfreignais	
			Subj (pres):	que j'enfreigne	
			Subj (imp):	que j'enfreignisse	

Infinitive:					
s'enfuir *to flee:* see fuir					

Infinitive:					
enjoindre *to call upon:* see joindre					

TABLE 7.H (*Continued*)

Infinitive: enlever *to remove:* is like *mener* in the use of è in some forms of the verb					

Infinitive: s'enquérir *to make enquiries*, see acquérir					

Infinitive: s'ensuivre *to result, follow*, see suivre An impersonal verb used only in the infinitive and third singular form					

Infinitive: s'entremettre *to intervene:* see mettre					

Infinitive: entreprendre *to undertake:* see prendre					

Infinitive: entretenir *to maintain:* see tenir					

Infinitive: entrevoir *to make out, glimpse:* see voir					

Infinitive: entrouvrir *to half-open:* see ouvrir					

Infinitive:	**Simple present:**		**Participles:**	envoyant	envoyé
envoyer	j'envoie	nous envoyons	**Future:**	j'enverrai	
to send	tu envoies	vous envoyez	**Simple past:**	j'envoyai	
	il envoie	ils envoient	**Imperfect:**	j'envoyais	
			Subj (pres):	que j'envoie	
			Subj (imp):	que j'envoyasse	

Infinitive: épeler *to spell:* is like *appeler* in the distribution of single 'l' and double 'll'					

Infinitive: s'éprendre de *to fall in love with:* see prendre					

Infinitive: équivaloir à *to be equivalent to:* see valoir					

Infinitive:	**Simple present:**		**Participles:**	espérant	espéré
espérer	j'espère	nous espérons	**Future:**	j'espérerai	
to hope	tu espères	vous espérez	**Simple past:**	j'espérai	
	il espère	ils espèrent	**Imperfect:**	j'espérais	
			Subj (pres):	que j'espère	
			Subj (imp):	que j'espérasse	

TABLE 7.H *(Continued)*

Infinitive:	Simple present:		Participles:	éteignant	éteint
éteindre	j'éteins	nous éteignons	**Future:**	j'éteindrai	
to extinguish	tu éteins	vous éteignez	**Simple past:**	j'éteignis	
	il éteint	ils éteignent	**Imperfect:**	j'éteignais	
			Subj (pres):	que j'éteigne	
			Subj (imp):	que j'éteignisse	

Infinitive:	Simple present:		Participles:	étreignant	étreint
étreindre	j'étreins	nous étreignons	**Future:**	j'étreindrai	
to embrace	tu étreins	vous étreignez	**Simple past:**	j'étreignis	
	il étreint	ils étreignent	**Imperfect:**	j'étreignais	
			Subj (pres):	que j'étreigne	
			Subj (imp):	que j'étreignisse	

Infinitive:					
exclure *to exclude:* see conclure					

Infinitive:					
extraire *to extract,* see traire					

Infinitive:	Simple present:		Participles:	-	failli
faillir	-		**Future:**	je faillirai	
to almost do, nearly do			**Simple past:**	je faillis	
e.g.	j'ai failli/il a failli, etc., tomber		**Imperfect:**	je faillais	
	I/he nearly fell		**Subj (pres):**	-	
	Je ne faillirai pas à mon devoir		**Subj (imp):**	-	
	I won't fail in my duty				

Infinitive:	Simple present:		Participles:	faisant	fait
faire	je fais	nous faisons	**Future:**	je ferai	
to do	tu fais	vous faites	**Simple past:**	je fis	
	il fait	ils font	**Imperfect:**	je faisais	
			Subj (pres):	que je fasse	
			Subj (imp):	que je fisse	

Infinitive:	Simple present:		Participles:	-	fallu
falloir	il faut		**Future:**	il faudra	
to be necessary,			**Simple past:**	il fallut	
'must'			**Imperfect:**	il fallait	
			Subj (pres):	qu'il faille	
			Subj (imp):	qu'il fallût	

TABLE 7.H (*Continued*)

Infinitive:	Simple present:		Participles:	feignant	feint
feindre	je feins	nous feignons	**Future:**	je feindrai	
to feign	tu feins	vous feignez	**Simple past:**	je feignis	
	il feint	ils feignent	**Imperfect:**	je feignais	
			Subj (pres):	que je feigne	
			Subj (imp):	que je feignisse	

Infinitive:
fleurir: has two present participles depending on meaning: *fleurissant* for the meaning of 'coming into flower', but *florissant* for 'flourishing' as in 'a flourishing business'.

Infinitive:	Simple present:		Participles:		frit
frire	je fris		**Future:**	je frirai	
to fry	tu fris		**Simple past:**	-	
	il frit		**Imperfect:**	-	
			Subj (pres):	-	
			Subj (imp):	-	

Infinitive:	Simple present:		Participles:	fuyant	fui
fuir	je fuis	nous fuyons	**Future:**	je fuirai	
to flee	tu fuis	vous fuyez	**Simple past:**	je fuis	
	il fuit	ils fuient	**Imperfect:**	je fuyais	
			Subj (pres):	que je fuie	
			Subj (imp):	que je fuisse	

Infinitive:	Simple present:		Participles:	geignant	geint
geindre	je geins	nous geignons	**Future:**	je geindrai	
to groan	tu geins	vous geignez	**Simple past:**	je geignis	
	il geint	ils geignent	**Imperfect:**	je geignais	
			Subj (pres):	que je geigne	
			Subj (imp):	que je geignisse	

Infinitive:
geler *to freeze:* is like *mener* in the use of *è* in some forms

Infinitive:	Simple present:		Participles:	gisant	-
gésir	je gis	nous gisons	**Future:**	-	
to be at rest	tu gis	vous gisez	**Simple past:**	-	
(as in grave), *lie*	il gît	ils gisent	**Imperfect:**	je gisais	
about (as clothes	N.B.: ci-gît ... *here lies...*		**Subj (pres):**	-	
on floor)			**Subj (imp):**	-	

TABLE 7.H (*Continued*)

Infinitive:	Simple present:		Participles:	haïssant	haï
haïr *to hate*	je hais tu hais	nous haïssons vous haïssez	**Future: Simple past:**	je haïrai je haïs	
	il hait	ils haïssent	**Imperfect:**	je haïssais	
			Subj (pres):	que je haïsse	
			Subj (imp):	que je haïsse	

N.B.: The *ï* (i with trema) indicates two syllables. The verb is regular apart from the use of the trema.

Infinitive:					
inscrire *to inscribe:* see écrire					

Infinitive:					
instruire *to instruct,* see construire					

Infinitive:	Simple present:		Participles:	interdisant	interdit
interdire	j'interdis	nous interdisons	**Future:**	j'interdirai	
to forbid	tu interdis	vous interdisez	**Simple past:**	j'interdis	
	il interdit	ils interdisent	**Imperfect:**	j'interdisais	
			Subj (pres):	que j'interdise	
			Subj (imp):	que j'interdisse	

Infinitive:					
intervenir *to intervene:* see venir					

Infinitive:					
introduire *to insert,* see construire					

Infinitive:	Simple present:		Participles:	jetant	jeté
jeter	je jette	nous jetons	**Future:**	je jetterai	
to throw	tu jettes	vous jetez	**Simple past:**	je jetai	
	il jette	ils jettent	**Imperfect:**	je jetais	
			Subj (pres):	que je jette que nous jetions	
			Subj (imp):	que vous jetiez que je jetasse	

Infinitive:	Simple present:		Participles:	joignant	joint
joindre	je joins	nous joignons	**Future:**	je joindrai	
to join	tu joins	vous joignez	**Simple past:**	je joignis	
	il joint	ils joignent	**Imperfect:**	je joignais	
			Subj (pres):	que je joigne	
			Subj (imp):	que je joignisse	

TABLE 7.H (*Continued*)

Infinitive:	Simple present:		Participles:	lisant	lu
lire	je lis	nous lisons	**Future:**	je lirai	
to read	tu lis	vous lisez	**Simple past:**	je lus	
	il lit	ils lisent	**Imperfect:**	je lisais	
			Subj (pres):	que je lise	
			Subj (imp):	que je lusse	

Infinitive:
luire *to shine:* is similar to *construire*, except that its past participle is '*lui*' and it normally does not have a simple past or an imperfect subjunctive.

Infinitive:
maintenir *to maintain:* see tenir

Infinitive:	Simple present:		Participles:	mangeant	mangé
manger	je mange	nous mangeons	**Future:**	je mangerai	
to eat	tu manges	vous mangez	**Simple past:**	je mangeai	
	il mange	ils mangent	**Imperfect:**	je mangeais	
			Subj (pres):	que je mange	
			Subj (imp):	que je mangeasse	

Infinitive:	Simple present:		Participles:	maudissant	maudit
maudire	je maudis	nous maudissons	**Future:**	je maudirai	
to curse	tu maudis	vous maudissez	**Simple past:**	je maudis	
	il maudit	ils maudissent	**Imperfect:**	je maudissais	
			Subj (pres):	que je maudisse	
			Subj (imp):	que je maudisse	

Infinitive:	Simple present:		Participles:	méconnaissant	méconnu
méconnaître	je méconnais	nous méconnaissons	**Future:**	je méconnaîtrai	
to misunderstand	tu méconnais	vous méconnaissez	**Simple past:**	je méconnus	
	il méconnaît	ils méconnaissent	**Imperfect:**	je méconnaissais	
			Subj (pres):	que je méconnaisse	
			Subj (imp):	que je méconnusse	

Infinitive:	Simple present:		Participles:	menant	mené
mener	je mène	nous menons	**Future:**	je mènerai	
to lead	tu mènes	vous menez	**Simple past:**	je menai	
	il mène	ils mènent	**Imperfect:**	je menais	
			Subj (pres):	que je mène	
			Subj (imp):	que nous menions	
				que vous meniez	
				que je menasse	

N.B.: *è* in cases where the following syllable contains a 'silent' 'e'.

TABLE 7.H (*Continued*)

Infinitive: se méprendre *to be mistaken:* see prendre					
Infinitive:	**Simple present:**		**Participles:**	mettant	mis
mettre	je mets	nous mettons	**Future:**	je mettrai	
to put	tu mets	vous mettez	**Simple past:**	je mis	
	il met	ils mettent	**Imperfect:**	je mettais	
			Subj (pres):	que je mette	
			Subj (imp):	que je misse	
Infinitive:	**Simple present:**		**Participles:**	moulant	moulu
moudre	je mouds	nous moulons	**Future:**	je moudrai	
to grind	tu mouds	vous moulez	**Simple past:**	je moulus	
	il moud	ils moulent	**Imperfect:**	je moulais	
			Subj (pres):	que je moule	
			Subj (imp):	que je moulusse	
Infinitive:	**Simple present:**		**Participles:**	mourant	mort
mourir	je meurs	nous mourons	**Future:**	je mourrai	
to die	tu meurs	vous mourez	**Simple past:**	je mourus	
	il meurt	ils meurent	**Imperfect:**	je mourais	
			Subj (pres):	que je meure	
			Subj (imp):	que je mourusse	
Infinitive:	**Simple present:**		**Participles:**	mouvant	mû (mue, mus)
mouvoir	je meus	nous mouvons	**Future:**	je mouvrai	
to move	tu meus	vous mouvez	**Simple past:**	je mus	
	il meut	ils meuvent	**Imperfect:**	je mouvais	
			Subj (pres):	que je meuve	
			Subj (imp):	que je musse	
Infinitive:	**Simple present:**		**Participles:**	naissant	né
naître	je nais	nous naissons	**Future:**	je naîtrai	
to be born	tu nais	vous naissez	**Simple past:**	je naquis	
	il naît	ils naissent	**Imperfect:**	je naissais	
			Subj (pres):	que je naisse	
			Subj (imp):	que je naquisse	
Infinitive:	**Simple present:**		**Participles:**	nettoyant	nettoyé
nettoyer	je nettoie	nous nettoyons	**Future:**	je nettoierai	
to clean	tu nettoies	vous nettoyez	**Simple past:**	je nettoyai	
	il nettoie	ils nettoient	**Imperfect:**	je nettoyais	
			Subj (pres):	que je nettoie	
			Subj (imp):	que je nettoyasse	

TABLE 7.H (*Continued*)

Infinitive: nuire *to harm:* is similar to *construire*, except that its past participle is *'nui'* and it normally does not have a simple past or an imperfect subjunctive.					

Infinitive: obtenir *to obtain:* see tenir					

Infinitive:	**Simple present:**		**Participles:**	offrant	offert
offrir	j'offre	nous offrons	**Future:**	j'offrirai	
to give	tu offres	vous offrez	**Simple past:**	j'offris	
	il offre	ils offrent	**Imperfect:**	j'offrais	
			Subj (pres):	que j'offre	
			Subj (imp):	que j'offrisse	
			Imperative:	offre (offres before *y* and *en*)	

Infinitive: omettre *to omit,* see *mettre*					

Infinitive:	**Simple present:**		**Participles:**	ouvrant	ouvert
ouvrir	j'ouvre	nous ouvrons	**Future:**	j'ouvrirai	
to open	tu ouvres	vous ouvrez	**Simple past:**	j'ouvris	
	il ouvre	ils ouvrent	**Imperfect:**	j'ouvrais	
			Subj (pres):	que j'ouvre	
			Subj (imp):	que j'ouvrisse	
			Imperative:	ouvre (ouvres before *y* and *en*)	

Infinitive:	**Simple present:**		**Participles:**	paraissant	paru
paraître	je parais	nous paraissons	**Future:**	je paraîtrai	
to seem	tu parais	vous paraissez	**Simple past:**	je parus	
	il paraît	ils paraissent	**Imperfect:**	je paraissais	
			Subj (pres):	que je paraisse	
			Subj (imp):	que je parusse	

Infinitive: parcourir *to travel through,* see courir					

Infinitive: parfaire *to perfect,* see faire					

Infinitive: parvenir *to reach:* see venir					

Infinitive:	**Simple present:**		**Participles:**	peignant	peint
peindre	je peins	nous peignons	**Future:**	je peindrai	
to paint	tu peins	vous peignez	**Simple past:**	je peignis	
	il peint	ils peignent	**Imperfect:**	je peignais	
			Subj (pres):	que je peigne	
			Subj (imp):	que je peignisse	

Infinitive: permettre *to allow,* see *mettre*					

TABLE 7.H (*Continued*)

Infinitive: peser *to weigh:* is like *mener* in the use of *è* in some forms					
Infinitive:	**Simple present:**		**Participles:**	se plaignant	plaint
se plaindre	je me plains	nous nous	**Future:**	je me plaindrai	
to complain	tu te plains	plaignons	**Simple past:**	je me plaignis	
	il se plaint	vous vous	**Imperfect:**	je me plaignais	
		plaignez	**Subj (pres):**	que je me plaigne	
		ils se plaignent	**Subj (imp):**	que je me plaignisse	
Infinitive:	**Simple present:**		**Participles:**	plaisant	plu
plaire	je plais	nous plaisons	**Future:**	je plairai	
to please	tu plais	vous plaisez	**Simple past:**	je plus	
	il plaît	ils plaisent	**Imperfect:**	je plaisais	
			Subj (pres):	que je plaise	
			Subj (imp):	que je plusse	
Infinitive:	**Simple present:**		**Participles:**	pleuvant	plu
pleuvoir	il pleut		**Future:**	il pleuvra	
to rain			**Simple past:**	il plut	
(impersonal)			**Imperfect:**	il pleuvait	
			Subj (pres):	qu'il pleuve	
			Subj (imp):	qu'il plût	
Infinitive: poursuivre *to pursue:* see *suivre*					
Infinitive:	**Simple present:**		**Participles:**	pourvoyant	pourvu
pourvoir	je pourvois	nous pourvoyons	**Future:**	je pourvoirai	
to provide	tu pourvois	vous pourvoyez	**Simple past:**	je pourvus	
	il pourvoit	ils pourvoient	**Imperfect:**	je pourvoyais	
			Subj (pres):	que je pourvoie	
			Subj (imp):	que je pourvusse	
Infinitive:	**Simple present:**		**Participles:**	pouvant	pu
pouvoir	je peux	nous pouvons	**Future:**	je pourrai	
to be able to	(alternative: je puis)				
	tu peux	vous pouvez	**Simple past:**	je pus	
	il peut	ils peuvent	**Imperfect:**	je pouvais	
			Subj (pres):	que je puisse	
			Subj (imp):	que je pusse	
Infinitive: prédire *to predict,* see *interdire*					

TABLE 7.H (*Continued*)

Infinitive:	Simple present:		Participles:	prenant	pris
prendre	je prends	nous prenons	**Future:**	je prendrai	
to take	tu prends	vous prenez	**Simple past:**	je pris	
	il prend	ils prennent	**Imperfect:**	je prenais	
			Subj (pres):	que je prenne	
				que nous prenions	
				que vous preniez	
			Subj (imp):	que je prisse	

N.B.: Two *ns* when *n* is followed by a 'silent' *e: prenne, prennes, prennent.*

Infinitive:
prescrire *to prescribe:* see écrire

Infinitive:
prévaloir *to prevail:* see valoir

Infinitive:
prévenir *to anticipate,* see venir

Infinitive:	Simple present:		Participles:	prévoyant	prévu
prévoir	je prévois	nous prévoyons	**Future:**	je prévoirai	
to foresee	tu prévois	vous prévoyez	**Simple past:**	je prévis	
	il prévoit	ils prévoient	**Imperfect:**	je prévoyais	
			Subj (pres):	que je prévoie	
			Subj (imp):	que je prévisse	

Infinitive:
produire *to produce:* see construire

Infinitive:
projeter *to plan:* is like jeter in the use of single *t* and double *tt.*

Infinitive:
promettre *to promise:* see mettre

Infinitive:
proscrire *to outlaw,* see écrire

Infinitive:
protéger *to protect,* is like *espérer, compléter in* the distribution of é and è

Infinitive:
provenir de *to arise from:* see venir

Infinitive:
r-, re-, ré-: for derived verbs with these prefixes, e.g. *rasseoir, reconstruire, réélire,* etc., see the entry for the non-prefixed counterpart, i.e. *s'asseoir, construire, lire,* etc.

TABLE 7.H (*Continued*)

Infinitive:	Simple present:		Participles:	rabattant	rabattu
rabattre	je rabats	nous rabattons	**Future:**	je rabattrai	
to pull down (e.g.	tu rabats	vous rabattez	**Simple past:**	je rabattis	
hat)	il rabat	ils rabattent	**Imperfect:**	je rabattais	
			Subj (pres):	que je rabatte	
			Subj (imp):	que je rabattisse	

Infinitive:					
(se) rappeler *to recall:* is like appeler in the distribution of single 'l' and double 'll'					

Infinitive:	Simple present:		Participles:	reconnaissant	reconnu
reconnaître	je reconnais	nous reconnaissons	**Future:**	je reconnaîtrai	
to recognize	tu reconnais	vous reconnaissez	**Simple past:**	je reconnus	
	il reconnaît	ils reconnaissent	**Imperfect:**	je reconnaissais	
			Subj (pres):	que je reconnaisse	
			Subj (imp):	que je reconnusse	

Infinitive:	Simple present:		Participles:	recouvrant	recouvert
recouvrir	je recouvre	nous recouvrons	**Future:**	je recouvrirai	
to cover	tu recouvres	vous recouvrez	**Simple past:**	je recouvris	
	il recouvre	ils recouvrent	**Imperfect:**	je recouvrais	
			Subj (pres):	que je recouvre	
			Subj (imp):	que je recouvrisse	

Infinitive:					
rejeter *to throw back*, is like *jeter* in the use of single *t* and double *tt*					

Infinitive:	Simple present:		Participles:	renvoyant	renvoyé
renvoyer	je renvoie	nous renvoyons	**Future:**	je renverrai	
to sack, send back	tu renvoies	vous renvoyez	**Simple past:**	je renvoyai	
	il renvoie	ils renvoient	**Imperfect:**	je renvoyais	
			Subj (pres):	que je renvoie	
			Subj (imp):	que je renvoyasse	

TABLE 7.H (*Continued*)

Infinitive:					
repéter *repeat* is like *espérer and compléter* in the distribution of é and è (second syllable)					

Infinitive:	Simple present:		Participles:	résolvant	résolu
résoudre	je résous	nous résolvons	**Future:**	je résoudrai	
to resolve	tu résous	vous résolvez	**Simple past:**	je résolus	
	il résout	ils résolvent	**Imperfect:**	je résolvais	
			Subj (pres):	que je résolve	
			Subj (imp):	que je résolusse	

Infinitive:	Simple present:		Participles:	restreignant	restreint
restreindre	je restreins	nous restreignons	**Future:**	je restreindrai	
to restrain	tu restreins	vous restreignez	**Simple past:**	je restreignis	
	il restreint	ils restreignent	**Imperfect:**	je restreignais	
			Subj (pres):	que je restreigne	
			Subj (imp):	que je restreignisse	

Infinitive:	Simple present:		Participles:	riant	ri
rire	je ris	nous rions	**Future:**	je rirai	
to laugh	tu ris	vous riez	**Simple past:**	je ris	
	il rit	ils rient	**Imperfect:**	je riais	
			Subj (pres):	que je rie	
			Subj (imp):	que je risse	

Infinitive:	Simple present:		Participles:	rompant	rompu
rompre	je romps	nous rompons	**Future:**	je romprai	
to break	tu romps	vous rompez	**Simple past:**	je rompis	
	il rompt	ils rompent	**Imperfect:**	je rompais	
			Subj (pres):	que je rompe	
			Subj (imp):	que je rompisse	

Infinitive:					
satisfaire *to satisfy*, see *faire*					

Infinitive:	Simple present:		Participles:	sachant	su
savoir	je sais	nous savons	**Future:**	je saurai	
to know	tu sais	vous savez	**Simple past:**	je sus	
	il sait	ils savent	**Imperfect:**	je savais	
			Subj (pres):	que je sache	
			Subj (imp):	que je susse	

Infinitive:					
secourir *to help:* see *courir*					

Infinitive:					
séduire *to seduce:* see *construire*					

Infinitive:					
semer *to sow* is like *mener* in the distribution of è in certain forms					

TABLE 7.H (*Continued*)

Infinitive:	Simple present:		Participles:	souffrant	souffert
souffrir	je souffre	nous souffrons	**Future:**	je souffrirai	
to suffer	tu souffres	vous souffrez	**Simple past:**	je souffris	
	il souffre	ils souffrent	**Imperfect:**	je souffrais	
			Subj (pres):	que je souffre	
			Subj (imp):	que je souffrisse	

Infinitive:
soumettre *to submit*, see mettre

Infinitive:
sourire *to smile:* see rire

Infinitive:
souscrire *to sign:* see écrire

Infinitive:
soustraire *to withdraw*, see traire

Infinitive:
soutenir *to support*, see tenir

Infinitive:
se souvenir de *to remember*, see venir

Infinitive:
subvenir *to subsidize:* see venir

Infinitive:	Simple present:		Participles:	suffisant	suffi
suffire	il suffit		**Future:**	il suffira	
to suffice			**Simple past:**	il suffit	
			Imperfect:	il suffisait	
			Subj (pres):	qu'il suffise	
			Subj (imp):	qu'il suffît	

Infinitive:	Simple present:		Participles:	suivant	suivi
suivre	je suis	nous suivons	**Future:**	je suivrai	
to follow	tu suis	vous suivez	**Simple past:**	je suivis	
	il suit	ils suivent	**Imperfect:**	je suivais	
			Subj (pres):	que je suive	
			Subj (imp):	que je suivisse	

Infinitive:
surprendre *to surprise:* see prendre

Infinitive:	Simple present:		Participles:	sursoyant	sursis
surseoir	je sursois	nous sursoyons	**Future:**	je surseoirai	
to postpone	tu sursois	vous sursoyez	**Simple past:**	je sursis	
	il sursoit	ils sursoient	**Imperfect:**	je sursoyais	
			Subj (pres):	que je sursoie	
			Subj (imp):	que je sursisse	

Infinitive:
survenir *to happen:* see venir

TABLE 7.H (*Continued*)

Infinitive:					
survivre à *to survive:* see vivre					

Infinitive:	Simple present:		Participles:	se taisant	tu
se taire	je me tais	nous nous taisons	Future:	je me tairai	
to be quiet	tu te tais	vous vous taisez	Simple past:	je me tus	
	il se tait	ils se taisent	Imperfect:	je me taisais	
			Subj (pres):	que je me taise	
			Subj (imp):	que je me tusse	

Infinitive:	Simple present:		Participles:	teignant	teint
teindre	je teins	nous teignons	Future:	je teindrai	
to dye	tu teins	vous teignez	Simple past:	je teignis	
	il teint	ils teignent	Imperfect:	je teignais	
			Subj (pres):	que je teigne	
			Subj (imp):	que je teignisse	

Infinitive:	Simple present:		Participles:	tenant	tenu
tenir	je tiens	nous tenons	Future:	je tiendrai	
to hold	tu tiens	vous tenez	Simple past:	je tins	
	il tient	ils tiennent	Imperfect:	je tenais	
			Subj (pres):	que je tienne	
			Subj (imp):	que je tinsse	

Infinitive:					
traduire *to translate*, see construire					

Infinitive:	Simple present:		Participles:	trayant	trait
traire	je trais	nous trayons	Future:	je trairai	
to milk	tu trais	vous trayez	Simple past:	-	
	il trait	ils traient	Imperfect:	je trayais	
			Subj (pres):	que je traie	
				que nous trayions	
				que vous trayiez-	
			Subj (imp):	-	

Infinitive:					
transcrire *to transcribe:* see écrire					

Infinitive:					
transmettre *to transmit*, see mettre					

Infinitive:					
transparaître *to show through:* see paraître					

TABLE 7.H (*Continued*)

Infinitive:	Simple present:		Participles:	vainquant	vaincu
vaincre	je vaincs	nous vainquons	**Future:**	je vaincrai	
to defeat	tu vaincs	vous vainquez	**Simple past:**	je vainquis	
	il vainc	ils vainquent	**Imperfect:**	je vainquais	
			Subj (pres):	que je vainque	
			Subj (imp):	que je vainquisse	
Infinitive:	**Simple present:**		**Participles:**	valant	valu
valoir	je vaux	nous valons	**Future:**	je vaudrai	
to be worth	tu vaux	vous valez	**Simple past:**	je valus	
	il vaut	ils valent	**Imperfect:**	je valais	
			Subj (pres):	que je vaille	
			Subj (imp):	que je valusse	
Infinitive:	**Simple present:**		**Participles:**	venant	venu
venir	je viens	nous venons	**Future:**	je viendrai	
to come	tu viens	vous venez	**Simple past:**	je vins	
	il vient	ils viennent	**Imperfect:**	je venais	
			Subj (pres):	que je vienne	
			Subj (imp):	que je vinsse	
Infinitive:	**Simple present:**		**Participles:**	vêtant	vêtu
vêtir	je vêts	nous vêtons	**Future:**	je vêtirai	
to clothe	tu vêts	vous vêtez	**Simple past:**	je vêtis	
	il vêt	ils vêtent	**Imperfect:**	je vêtais	
			Subj (pres):	que je vête	
			Subj (imp):	que je vêtisse	
Infinitive:	**Simple present:**		**Participles:**	vivant	vécu
vivre	je vis	nous vivons	**Future:**	je vivrai	
to live	tu vis	vous vivez	**Simple past:**	je vécus	
	il vit	ils vivent	**Imperfect:**	je vivais	
			Subj (pres):	que je vive	
			Subj (imp):	que je vécusse	
Infinitive:	**Simple present:**		**Participles:**	voyant	vu
voir	je vois	nous voyons	**Future:**	je verrai	
to see	tu vois	vous voyez	**Simple past:**	je vis	
	il voit	ils voient	**Imperfect:**	je voyais	
			Subj (pres):	que je voie	
			Subj (imp):	que je visse	

TABLE 7.H *(Continued)*

Infinitive:	Simple present:		Participles:	voulant	voulu
vouloir	je veux	nous voulons	**Future:**	je voudrai	
to want	tu veux	vous voulez	**Simple past:**	je voulus	
	il veut	ils veulent	**Imperfect:**	je voulais	
			Subj (pres):	que je veuille	
			Subj (imp):	que je voulusse	

7.6.9 **Nouvelle Orthographe**

The proposed changes in spelling mainly concern verbs in two categories (see Section 7.4): (a) verbs like *céder, espérer, révéler* with regard to the use of the acute and grave accents and (b) some verbs which end in *-eler* or *-eter.*

Verbs like *céder* can now be assimilated to verbs like *semer* or *mener*, so where they previously would have had an acute accent in *je céderai, j'espérerai*, and *je révélerai* it is proposed they can now have a grave accent: *je cèderai, j'espèrerai*, and *je révèlerai.*

Many verbs which end in *-eler* or *-eter* which traditionally pattern like *appeler* and *jeter* in the use of doubled consonants, *j'appelle, je jette* can now be assimilated to verbs like *peler* or *acheter* and therefore do not double the consonants but instead have a grave accent on the syllable before the consonant and the following unstressed vowel: épousseter to dust – *j'époussète, j'époussèterai; ruisseler* to drip, to be running with – *cela ruissèle, cela ruissèlera;* étiqueter to label – *j'étiquète, j'étiquèterai.*

However, the above does **NOT** apply to *appeler, rappeler* or *jeter* or the verbs which are related to them.

It is also proposed that the past participles of *absoudre* and *dissoudre* can be changed to become: *absout (absoute)* and *dissout (dissoute)* (see Section 7.6.8, Table 7.H).

These proposed changes are in no way obligatory and it remains to be seen to what extent they are adopted in the coming years.

FREE

INSTRUCTOR & STUDENT RESOURCES

For more resources to practice your French grammar, including practice activities/quizzes for students, further resource links, and an instructor guide, please visit https://routledgelearning.com/frenchgrammarandusage.

8 Verb constructions

8.1 Relations between verbs and their complements

Verbs can be classified by the kinds of complement they take. Table 8.A outlines the main types dealt within this chapter.

TABLE 8.A Classification of verbs by the complements they take

Verb type	Complement type	
	Direct object	**Prepositional object**
Intransitive (Section 8.2)	No	No
e.g. *partir*		
Jeanne partira	–	–
Directly Transitive (Section 8.3)	Yes	No
e.g. *fermer*		
Il ferme	*les yeux*	–
Indirectly Transitive (Section 8.4)	No	Yes
e.g. *hériter*		
Yvon hérite	–	*d'une fortune*
Ditransitive (Section 8.5)	Yes	Yes
e.g. *planter*		
Hervé a planté	*ie jardin*	*de roses*
Pronominal (Section 8.7)		
(a) *se* is a direct object		
e.g. *s'évanouir*	(a) *Perrine s'est évanouie*	–
(b) *se* is an indirect object		
e.g. *se faire mal*	–	(b) *Elle s'est fait mal* (à elle-*même*)

8.2 Intransitive constructions

Intransitive verbs have no object:

Depuis janvier les prix ont augmenté	*Since January prices have gone up*
Il a acquiescé	*He agreed*
L'eau scintillait	*The water sparkled*
La neige tombe	*Snow is falling*
La fête continue	*The party is going on*
Elle avait disparu	*She had disappeared*
Vous descendez?	*Are you going down?*
Il ne souffrira pas	*He won't suffer*

DOI: 10.4324/9781003373926-8

They may be accompanied (usually optionally, but sometimes obligatorily) by adverbs (see Chapter 5). Examples shown in brackets indicate that the adverb is optional:

Elle part (**en vacances**)	*She is going (on holiday)*
Un léger brouillard montait (**de la mer**)	*A mist rose (from the sea)*
Il a respiré **fortement**	*He breathed deeply*
Mourad serait tombé (**du haut de la falaise**)	*Mourad apparently fell (from the cliff)*
Elle est descendue (**péniblement**)	*She went down (gingerly)*
Cet homme avait vécu **plus de 90 ans**	*That man had lived into his nineties*
Louis tremblait (**de tous ses membres**)	*Louis was trembling (all over)*
Les minutes passaient (**lentement**)	*The minutes passed (slowly)*

8.2.1 **Intransitive verbs and auxiliary** *avoir*

Most intransitive verbs employ the auxiliary *avoir* in compound tenses:

Depuis janvier les prix **ont** augmenté	*Since January prices have gone up*
Il **aurait** acquiescé	*He agreed, apparently*
La fête **avait** continué	*The party had gone on*
Elle **avait** disparu	*She had disappeared*
Il n'**a** pas souffert	*He didn't suffer*
La situation **aura** probablement empiré	*The situation will probably have got worse*

A small set of verbs, including *commencer, changer, disparaître*, and *vieillir*, normally appear with the auxiliary *avoir* in compound tenses, but their past participles may be used with *être* to describe a state of affairs. In this case the past participle is used in very much the same way as an adjective (for adjectives, see Chapter 4). Compare the following sentences:

Il **a** commencé à lire des mangas	*He began to read mangas*
La pièce **est** commencée	*The play has begun*
Il **a** changé les pneus de sa voiture	*He changed the tyres on his car*
Elle est devenue veuve et maintenant elle **est** vraiment changée	*She was widowed, and now she is a changed person*

N.B.: With *être* and a state of affairs, there will be agreement between the past participle and the subject. With *avoir* and an action there will not (see Sections 9.2 and 9.3).

8.2.2 **Intransitive verbs and auxiliary** *être*

Intransitive verbs with *être*

A small set of intransitive verbs, some very frequently used, appear with the auxiliary *être* in compound tenses:

Un léger brouillard **est** monté de la mer	*A mist rose from the sea*
Maxence **est** tombé du haut de la falaise	*Maxence fell from the cliff*
Elle **était** descendue	*She had gone down*
Pauline **est** née en 1968	*Pauline was born in 1968*

The verbs which take *être* in this way are:

aller	*to go*	naître	*to be born*
arriver	*to arrive*	partir	*to leave*
décéder	*to die*	rentrer	*to go home*
demeurer	*to remain*	rester	*to stay*
descendre	*to go down*	retourner	*to return*
devenir	*to become*	revenir	*to come back*
entrer	*to enter*	sortir	*to go out*
monter	*to go up*	tomber	*to fall*
mourir	*to die*	venir	*to come*

and verbs derived from the above: *redescendre, remonter, renaître, repartir, retomber, parvenir* and *survenir*.

Intransitive verbs with *avoir* or *être*

A further set of intransitive verbs, e.g. *accourir, apparaître, passer,* can appear either with *avoir* or with *être* in compound tenses.

Quand il a appris la nouvelle il **est** accouru	*When he heard the news he came quickly*
Il nous **est** apparu que le gardien avait menti	*It became apparent to us that the porter had lied*
Il **est** / **a** passé de l'autre côté du fleuve	*He went over to the other side of the river*

(See Section 8.3.4 for intransitive verbs which can be used with *avoir* when used transitively.)

8.3 Directly transitive verbs

Directly transitive verbs have direct objects:

regarder **les infos** à la télévision	*to watch the news on television*
quitter **le Pays de Galles**	*to leave Wales*
composter **un billet**	*to punch a ticket*
fumer **une cigarette**	*to smoke a cigarette*
ouvrir **la portière**	*to open the (car, train) door*
prendre **le train**	*to take the train*
rencontrer **un ami**	*to meet a friend*
expliquer **les faits**	*to explain the facts*
étouffer **un juron**	*to stifle an oath*
lever **la tête**	*to raise one's head*

8.3.1 Directly transitive verbs without objects

Sometimes the objects of transitive verbs may be omitted. When this happens the object is still 'understood', but with a general or non-specific interpretation:

Clément boit	*Clément drinks* ('alcohol' understood)
La vitesse tue	*Speed kills* ('people' understood)
Gustave enseigne	*Gustave teaches* ('pupils' understood)
Il ne sait pas conduire	*He can't drive* ('cars' understood)
On attend	*We're waiting* ('for something to happen' understood)

8.3.2 **Directly transitive verbs take the auxiliary** *avoir*

All transitive verbs take the auxiliary *avoir* in compound tenses, whether the object is present or omitted:

Elle **a** quitté le Pays de Galles	*She has left Wales*
J'**ai** rencontré un ami	*I met a friend*
Dans la bousculade Laurent **avait** reçu des coups	*In the confusion Laurent had been hit*
On **a** attendu	*We waited*

8.3.3 **Verbs with intransitive and transitive uses**

Some verbs can be used intransitively (without an object) and transitively (with an object):

Les prix augmentent	*Prices are going up*
La chaîne augmente ses prix	*The store is increasing its prices*
Il rentre	*He is going home*
Il rentre la voiture au garage	*He is putting the car in the garage*
Elle sort	*She is going out*
Elle sort son appareil-photo	*She is getting her camera out*
Le moteur a calé	*The engine stalled*
Alain a calé le moteur	*Alain stalled the engine*

8.3.4 *être* **and** *avoir* **with verbs used intransitively and transitively**

Intransitive verbs which take the auxiliary *être* in compound tenses take *avoir* when they are used transitively:

Florian **est** descendu	*Florian went down*
BUT	
Florian **a** descendu les valises	*Florian has taken the suitcases down*
Cléo **est** montée prendre son maillot de bain	*Cléo has gone up to fetch her swimming costume*
BUT	
Cléo **avait** monté un gros colis	*Cléo had taken a big parcel up*
Mickey **est** sorti	*Mickey has gone out*
BUT	
Mickey **a** sorti une pièce d'identité	*Mickey got out some identification*
Olivia **sera** rentrée	*Olivia will have gone home*
BUT	
Olivia **avait** rentré la voiture au garage	*Olivia had put the car in the garage*
Manu **était** retourné à la banque	*Manu had gone back to the bank*
BUT	
Manu **a** retourné tout l'appartement	*Manu has turned the flat upside down*

The verbs *descendre* and *monter* also take the auxiliary *avoir* in compound tenses when they are used with adverbials of place like *l'escalier, la rue, la côte*:

Il **a** descendu l'escalier, la rue	*He went down the stairs/the street*
Elle **a** monté la côte	*She went up the hill*

Compare with:

Il **est** descendu vers la rue	*He went down towards the street*
Elle **est** monté à l'échelle	*She climbed up the ladder*

8.3.5 **Verbs which are directly transitive in French but whose translation equivalents involve the object of a preposition in English**

English speakers should pay special attention to the following verbs. Unlike their English counterparts, their objects are not preceded by a preposition:

approuver **un choix**	*to approve of a choice*
attendre **le train**	*to wait for the train*
chercher **une enveloppe**	*to look for an envelope*
demander **un verre d'eau**	*to ask for a glass of water*
descendre **la rue**	*to go down the street*
écouter **la radio**	*to listen to the radio*
espérer **une récompense**	*to hope for a reward*
habiter **une maison, une ville, une région**	*to live in a house, in a town, in a region*
longer **la falaise**	*to go along the cliff*
monter **la côte**	*to go up the hill*
payer **un tour de manège**	*to pay for a ride on a roundabout*
payer **une tournée**	*to pay for a round (of drinks)*
présider **une séance**	*to be the chairperson of a session*
regarder **le soleil**	*to look at the sun*
viser **la cible**	*to aim at the target*

habiter also appears in constructions such as *habiter à la campagne, habiter en ville,* and *habiter en France*. Here *à la campagne, en ville* and *en France* are not objects but adverbials; they can co-occur with direct objects: *habiter une petite maison à la campagne, habiter un bon quartier en ville,* etc.

Examples:

Il approuve mon choix	(NOT *Il approuve de mon choix)
J'attends le train	(NOT *J'attends pour le train)
Nous cherchons la gare	(NOT *Nous cherchons pour la gare)
Cette publicité vise les jeunes	(NOT *Cette publicité vise aux jeunes)

(See Section 3.2 to see how this influences the choice of object pronouns.)

8.4 **Indirectly transitive verbs**

Indirectly transitive verbs take an object introduced by a preposition:

Introduced by *à*

assister **à** une réunion	*to be present at a meeting*
compatir **à** la douleur de quelqu'un	*to feel for somebody in their sorrow*
croire **au** diable	*to believe in the devil*
en vouloir **à** son cousin	*to hold a grudge against one's cousin*
participer **aux** activités	*to take part in the activities*
penser **à** son avenir	*to think about one's future*
pourvoir **aux** besoins de quelqu'un	*to provide for somebody's needs*
réfléchir **à** son passé	*to reflect on one's past*
songer **à** un voyage en Italie	*to envisage a trip to Italy*
veiller **au** bon règlement d'une affaire	*to see to the proper handling of a matter*

N.B.: **(a)** *Croire à* is used to mean 'to believe in the existence of some phenomenon': *croire au Père Noël* 'to believe in Father Christmas', *croire au bonheur* 'to believe in (human) happiness'. *Croire* can also take direct objects: *Je crois cette histoire* 'I believe this story', *Elle le croit* 'She believes him'. *Croire en* means 'to believe in' in the sense of 'to have faith in': *croire en Dieu* 'to believe in God', *croire en ses co-équipiers* 'to believe in one's team-mates'.

(b) *Penser* can also take an object preceded by *de* with the meaning 'to have an opinion about something': *Qu'est-ce que vous pensez de son article?* 'What do you think of his article?'

(c) *veiller sur quelqu'un* means 'to watch over somebody'.

Introduced by *de*

déborder **d'**eau	*to overflow with water*
déjeuner **de** fruits	*to lunch on fruit*
dépendre **des** circonstances	*to depend on the circumstances*
dîner **de** moules et **de** frites	*to dine on mussels and French fries*
fourmiller **d'**abeilles	*to swarm with bees*
gémir **de** douleur	*to groan with pain*
grouiller **de** fourmis	*to swarm with ants*
parler **de** ses amis	*to speak of one's friends*
regorger **de** richesses	*to abound in wealth*
répondre **de** son ami	*to answer for one's friend*
rire **de** ses compagnons	*to laugh at one's friends*
rougir **de** honte	*to go red with shame*
tenir **de** sa mère	*to take after one's mother*
trembler **de** peur	*to tremble with fear*
triompher **de** son adversaire	*to overcome one's opponent*
vivre **de** l'air du temps	*to live on fresh air alone*
vivre **de** presque rien	*to live on next to nothing*

(For pronominal verbs which take prepositional objects (*s'habituer à, s'éloigner de*, etc.), see Section 8.7.3.)

8.4.1 **Verbs which are indirectly transitive in French but whose translation equivalents are directly transitive in English**

Special attention should be given to the following verbs because, while they are indirectly transitive in French, their English counterparts are directly transitive.

Objects introduced by *à*

contravenir **à** la réglementation	*to break the rule*
convenir **à** Julie	*to suit Julie*
(dé)plaire **à** son ex	*to (dis)please one's ex*
(dés)obéir **à** ses parents	*to (dis)obey one's parents*
échapper **à** la police	*to evade capture by the police*
échouer **à** un examen	*to fail an exam*
jouer **au** football, **au** rugby, **au** tennis	*to play football, rugby, tennis*
nuire **à** la réputation de quelqu'un	*to harm somebody's reputation*
parvenir **au** sommet	*to reach the summit*
plaire **à** quelqu'un	*to please somebody*
remédier **à** la situation	*to rectify the situation*
renoncer **à** l'alcool	*to give up alcohol*
résister **à** une force	*to resist a force*
ressembler **à** son chien	*to look like one's dog*
subvenir **aux** besoins de quelqu'un	*to look after somebody financially*
succéder **à** son père	*to succeed one's father*
survivre **à** un accident	*to survive an accident*
téléphoner **à** quelqu'un	*to telephone somebody*
toucher **aux** affaires de quelqu'un	*to mess about with somebody's things*

While *échapper à* means 'to evade capture', *s'échapper de* means 'to escape from': *s'échapper de la prison*.

Examples:

Elle joue **au** football	(NOT *Elle joue football)
Il a téléphoné **à** sa femme	(NOT *Il a téléphoné sa femme)
Elle ressemble beaucoup **à** son père	(NOT *Elle ressemble beaucoup son père)
Le nouveau poste plaisait **à** Antoine	(NOT *Le nouveau poste plaisait Antoine)

(See Section 3.2 for the relevance of this distinction to the choice of object pronoun.)

Objects introduced by *de*

abuser **de** son héritage	*to misuse one's inheritance*
douter **de** la vérité d'une histoire	*to doubt the truth of a story*
hériter **d'**une fortune	*to inherit a fortune*
jouer **du** piano/**du** violon/**de** la flûte	*to play the piano/violin/flute*
jouir **de** privilèges sans précédent	*to enjoy unprecedented privileges*
médire **de** son voisin	*to slander one's neighbour*
redoubler **d'**efforts	*to double one's efforts*

Note that *entrer* is usually followed by *dans: entrer dans la maison*. *Grimper* is usually followed either by *sur* or by *à: grimper sur un escabeau* 'to climb a stepladder', *grimper à l'échelle* 'to climb a ladder'.

Examples:

Elle espère hériter **d**'une fortune   (NOT *Elle espère hériter une fortune)
Elle jouait **du** piano   (NOT *Elle jouait le piano)

(For pronominal verbs which take prepositional objects – *s'apercevoir de, se servir de*, etc. – see Section 8.7.3.)

8.5 **Ditransitive verbs**

Ditransitive verbs take a direct object and an object introduced by a preposition.

Introduced by *à* and corresponding typically to English 'to'

accoutumer un apprenti **au** métier	*to get an apprentice used to a trade*
admettre un invité **à** la fête	*to admit a guest to the party*
appeler quelqu'un **au** téléphone	*to call somebody to the phone*
apprendre le français **à** des élèves	*to teach French to pupils*
avouer un crime **à** la police	*to confess to the police about a crime*
condamner un malfaiteur **à** une peine de prison	*to condemn a criminal to prison*
conduire les hôtes **à** leur chambre	*to take the guests to their room*
contraindre les rebelles **à** l'obéissance	*to force the rebels into obedience*
convier des amis **à** une fête	*to invite friends to a party*
dire ses quatre vérités **à** quelqu'un	*to tell someone the unadorned truth*
destiner son fils **à** une belle carrière	*to arrange a great career for one's son*
dire des mensonges **à** sa famille	*to tell lies to one's family*
emmener les invités **à** leur hôtel	*to take guests to their hotel*
exposer sa famille **à** des dangers	*to expose one's family to danger*
forcer les citoyens **à** la révolution	*to drive the citizens to revolution*
habituer les motocyclistes **au** port du casque	*to get motorcycle riders used to wearing a helmet*
inciter les ouvriers **à** la révolte	*to incite workers to revolt*
inviter les syndicalistes **à** une réunion	*to invite the trade union representatives to a meeting*
jurer amitié **à** quelqu'un	*pledge one's friendship to someone*
louer une voiture **à** un touriste	*to rent a car to a tourist*
obliger ses créanciers **au** remboursement	*to force one's debtors to pay up*
ordonner la retraite **à** ses troupes	*to order one's troops to retreat*
provoquer quelqu'un **à** une réaction trop vive	*to provoke somebody into a hasty reaction*
réduire quelqu'un **à** la mendicité	*to reduce somebody to beggary*
rendre la tondeuse **à** son voisin	*to return the lawn-mower to one's neighbour*
suggérer une idée **à** un collègue	*to suggest an idea to a colleague*

N.B.: *louer une voiture à un garagiste* is likely to mean: 'to hire a car from a garage owner'.

Introduced by *à* and corresponding typically to English 'from' or 'for'

acheter un camion **à** un garagiste	*to buy a lorry from a garage owner*
arracher de l'argent **à** un avare	*to prise money from a miser*
cacher la catastrophe **à** sa famille	*to hide the disaster from one's family*
dérober de l'argent **à** ses enfants	*to steal money from one's children*
emprunter cinq cents euros **à** un ami	*to borrow five hundred euros from a friend*
enlever le pistolet **à** l'agresseur	*to take the revolver away from the attacker*
ôter une écharde **à** quelqu'un	*to remove a splinter from somebody's flesh*

louer une camionette **au** garagiste	*to hire a van from the garage owner*
préparer la famille **à** de bien tristes nouvelles	*to prepare the family for very sad news*
reprocher une liaison **à** son mari	*to be angry with one's husband for having had an affair*
réserver des sièges **aux** invités	*to reserve some seats for the guests*
retirer son permis **au** conducteur	*to take the driver's licence away from him*
soustraire une grosse somme **à** quelqu'un	*to swindle someone out of a large sum*
voler une bague **à** sa cousine	*to steal a ring from one's cousin*

Introduced by *de* and corresponding typically to English 'with' or 'in' or, less frequently, 'from' or 'on'

accabler son amie **de** cadeaux	*to overwhelm one's girlfriend with presents*
accompagner ses commentaires **de** sarcasme	*to bring sarcasm into one's comments*
affranchir une population **de** l'esclavage	*to free a population from slavery*
armer ses soldats **de** mitrailleuses	*to arm one's soldiers with machine guns*
charger un voisin **d'**une commission	*to entrust an errand to a neighbour*
coiffer un enfant **d'**un chapeau de paille	*to put a straw hat on a child's head*
combler ses invités **de** gentillesses	*to cover one's guests in kindness*
couvrir sa petite amie **de** cadeaux	*to drown one's girlfriend in presents*
cribler un corps **de** balles	*to riddle a body with bullets*
éloigner sa fille **de** ses admirateurs	*to remove one's daughter from her admirers*
encombrer la voiture **d'**affaires de sport	*to clutter up the car with sports equipment*
entourer la famille **de** bons amis	*to surround the family with good friends*
envelopper le cadeau **d'**un papier de soie	*to wrap the present in tissue paper*
habiller son mari **de** vêtements sport	*to buy casual styles of clothes for one's husband*
menacer ses employés **d'**une réduction de salaire	*to threaten one's employees with a drop in salary*
munir les étudiants **du** savoir nécessaire	*to provide students with the necessary knowledge*
orner le parebrise **d'**autocollants	*to decorate the windscreen with stickers*
planter le jardin **de** roses	*to plant the garden with roses*
pourvoir un réfugié **d'**un faux passeport	*to provide a refugee with a false passport*
remplir une salle **de** spectateurs	*to fill a hall with spectators*
semer un champ **de** haricots	*to sow a field with beans*
souiller un drap **de** sang	*to soil a sheet with blood*
tacher un pantalon **de** graisse	*to stain trousers with grease*
tapisser la chambre **d'**un papier peint rose	*to paper the bedroom in pink*
vêtir un cardinal **d'**une robe de pourpre	*to dress a cardinal in a purple robe*

N.B.: A very small number of verbs, notably *parler* and *se confesser*, can have two indirect objects: *parler de ses amis à ses parents* and *se confesser de ses péchés au curé*. The indirect object introduced by *à* is sometimes referred to as a *complément d'objet second*.

8.5.1 In French, unlike English, double object constructions with no preposition are impossible

Some ditransitive verbs in English allow the preposition introducing the second object to be omitted and the order of the objects to be switched around. This is not possible in French:

to give a present to one's uncle		*to give one's uncle a present*
offrir un cadeau **à** son oncle	BUT NOT	*offrir son oncle un cadeau
to pass the salt to one's neighbour		*to pass one's neighbour the salt*
passer le sel **à** son voisin	BUT NOT	*passer son voisin le sel

(See Section 8.6.3 for the consequences of this in forming a passive.)

8.6 **The passive**

By use of the passive, emphasis may be placed on the receiver of an action (usually what would be the object in the equivalent active sentence) rather than on the agent of the action (usually the subject).

8.6.1 **Formation of the passive**

Passives are produced from directly transitive sentences by moving the object noun phrase into the position of the grammatical subject, introducing the verb *être* and, optionally, moving the erstwhile subject into a phrase introduced by *par* or *de*:

Nantes a battu Paris St Germain
Nantes beat Paris St Germain

becomes:

Paris St Germain a été battu (par Nantes)
Paris St Germain were beaten (by Nantes)

Quand elle est arrivée au commissariat, son mari l'accompagnait
When she got to the police station, her husband was with her

becomes:

Quand elle est arrivée au commissariat, elle était accompagnée de son mari
When she got to the police station, she was in the company of her husband

Note that the rules of agreement for the past participle are those of *être* (see Section 9.2.2): i.e. it agrees with the subject:

Delphine a été battue au tennis par Lola
Delphine was beaten at tennis by Lola

Arnaud a été battu au tennis par Blaise
Arnaud was beaten at tennis by Blaise

N.B.: The use of the preposition *par* to introduce the subject usually implies some degree of voluntary involvement; the use of *de* suggests more a state of affairs (see also Section 13.15.5).

8.6.2 **Problems in the formation of the passive arising from different kinds of direct objects**

Most verbs which have a direct object (directly transitive verbs – see Section 8.3) will convert into a passive, but there are limitations to whether the meaning is sensible or not. *Connaître* can be turned into a sensible passive:

Les milieux policiers connaissent cette organisation
The police know this organisation

Cette organisation est connue des milieux policiers
This organisation is known to the police

but *lire* produces a less natural sentence:

> Je lis ce livre
> *I am reading this book*

> Ce livre est lu par moi (???)
> *This book is being read by me (???)*

Usually passives which make an inanimate direct object a subject and put an animate subject in a *par* or *de* phrase are unnatural.

N.B.: The verb *avoir* is used in the passive only in the colloquial *J'ai été eu* 'I have been had' in the sense of 'swindled'.

8.6.3 Possible confusions between English and French over what is a direct object: English 'double object' verbs

English has a set of verbs which allow two structures for a similar meaning: one has a direct object and a prepositional object, the other has two non-prepositional objects and the word order is different:

> *John gave flowers to Naomi*
> *John gave Naomi flowers*

In both sentences 'Naomi' is the indirect object of the verb 'give' and 'flowers' is the direct object, but in the 'double object' construction 'Naomi' directly follows the verb, which gives the impression that it is the direct object.

English allows either object to become the subject in a passive sentence:

> *Flowers were given to Naomi by John*
> *Naomi was given flowers by John*

French, however, only allows the prepositional object construction *offrir quelque chose à quelqu'un*: *Jean a offert des fleurs à Naomi* (NOT **Jean a offert Naomi des fleurs*) Furthermore, French only allows **the direct object** to become the subject in a passive sentence. Thus:

> **Des fleurs** furent offertes à Naomi par Jean
> *Flowers were given to Naomi by Jean*

is an acceptable French sentence, but

> *Naomi fut offerte des fleurs par Jean

is entirely unacceptable.

Sentences constructed with similar verbs run into the same problems:

English	
To teach somebody something:	*I taught French to John*
	I taught John French
	French was taught to John by me
	John was taught French by me

French

Enseigner **quelque chose à quelqu'un**:		J'ai enseigné le français à Jean
	But	*J'ai enseigné Jean le français is **unacceptable**
	Therefore	Le français fut enseigné à Jean par moi is **acceptable**
	But	*Jean fut enseigné le français par moi is **unacceptable**

English

To tell somebody something:	I told a story to John
	I told John a story
	A story was told to John by me
	John was told a story by me

French

Raconter **quelque chose à quelqu'un**:		J'ai raconté une histoire à Jean
	But	*J'ai raconté Jean une histoire is **unacceptable**
	Therefore	Une histoire fut racontée à Jean par moi is **acceptable**
	But	*Jean fut raconté une histoire par moi is **unacceptable**

Common French verbs whose prepositional objects must keep the preposition and cannot be made the subject of a passive are listed below:

accorder qc à qn	*to grant sb sth*
apprendre qc à qn	*to teach sb sth*
commander qc à qn	*to order sb to do sth/to order sth from sb*
conseiller qc à qn	*to advise sb to do sth*
défendre qc à qn	*to forbid sb sth*
demander qc à qn	*to ask sb sth*
donner qc à qn	*to give sb sth*
écrire qc à qn	*to write sb sth*
enseigner qc à qn	*to teach sb sth*
laisser qc à qn	*to leave sb sth*
montrer qc à qn	*to show sb sth*
offrir qc à qn	*to offer sb sth, treat sb to sth*
pardonner qc à qn	*to forgive sb sth*
passer qc à qn	*to pass sb sth*
permettre qc à qn	*to allow sb sth*
prescrire qc à qn	*to prescribe sb sth*
prêter qc à qn	*to lend sb sth*
promettre qc à qn	*to promise sb sth*
refuser qc à qn	*to refuse sb sth*

8.6.4 **Use of the passive in English and French**

The passive is used much more frequently in English than in French. This is partly because there are fewer restrictions on which verbs can be made passive, and partly because there are many other ways in French of removing the agent from subject position or reducing the specificity of the subject.

Alternatives to the English passive which reduce the role of the subject as agent include:

(a) The use of *on* with the active form (see also Section 3.1.11):

On ne nous a pas facilité l'accès à l'Ambassade
Access to the Embassy has not been made easy for us

(b) The use of an impersonal verb and/or an impersonal pronoun:

Il est interdit de fumer à l'intérieur de l'établissement
Smoking is forbidden inside the building

Cela n'a certainement pas facilité notre travail
Our work certainly wasn't made any easier

(c) The use of a reflexive verb (see Section 8.7.6):

Les mirabelles ne **se** vendent plus le long de la route
Mirabelle plums are no longer sold on the roadside

Les faux ne **s'**emploient plus dans les champs
Scythes are no longer used in the fields

(d) The use of a noun to represent a process:

L'assemblage de ces alarmes par la société Sécurat-France a lieu en Chine
These alarms are assembled in China by Sécurat-France

To avoid using a passive, it is sometimes worth considering whether there is a verb with the opposite meaning that could be used in a non-passive transitive construction. For example, instead of:

Des pommes ont été vendues à Marianne
Some apples were sold to Marianne

Une guitare a été donnée à Paul
A guitar was given to Paul

the following transitive constructions might be used:

Marianne a acheté des pommes
Marianne bought some apples

Paul a reçu une guitare
Paul received a guitar

However, whether these alternatives are appropriate will depend on the context in which the sentence occurs.

8.7 **Pronominal verbs**

Pronominal verbs are accompanied by an unstressed pronoun which agrees with the subject and is one of *me, te, se, nous,* and *vous.* This can function as a direct object:

Direct object

se laver 'to wash (oneself)'

je **me** lave	nous **nous** lavons
tu **te** laves	vous **vous** lavez
Paul **se** lave	ils **se** lavent
Virginie **se** lave	elles **se** lavent

or as an indirect object:

Indirect object

se laver le visage 'to wash one's face' (literally: 'to wash the face to oneself')

je **me** lave le visage	nous **nous** lavons le visage
tu **te** laves le visage	vous **vous** lavez le visage
Paul **se** lave le visage	ils **se** lavent le visage
Virginie **se** lave le visage	elles **se** lavent le visage

Some verbs exist in both a pronominal and non-pronominal form, as *laver* does: *laver la voiture* 'to wash the car', *se laver le visage* 'to wash one's face'. Others are always pronominal, for example *s'évanouir* 'to faint', *s'enorgueillir de* 'to take pride in', *s'évertuer à* 'to try very hard to'.

All pronominal verbs are conjugated with *être* in compound tenses. (For the agreement of past participles with pronominal verbs, see Sections 8.7.7 and 9.4.)

8.7.1 **Pronominal verbs used reflexively**

When pronominal verbs are used to describe something which the subject does to herself, himself, themselves, etc., they are being used reflexively:

Je me vois dans la glace	*I can see myself in the mirror*
Je me déteste	*I hate myself*
Il s'est fait mal	*He hurt himself*
Elle s'était cassé la jambe	*She had broken her leg*

Note that English translations of pronominal verbs used reflexively do not always require a form of *-self.* In French, however, the reflexive pronoun is always required:

Je me lave	*I am washing (myself)*
Il se rase	*He is shaving (himself)*
Il s'est roulé par terre	*He rolled (himself) on the ground*

The pronoun itself may be the direct or indirect object of the verb. If the verb in its non-pronominal form is directly transitive, the pronoun will be a direct object. If the verb in its non-pronominal form is indirectly transitive, the pronoun will be an indirect object pronoun. For example, *laver* takes a direct object: *laver la voiture.* Therefore in *Je me lave* the pronoun is direct. But *parler (parler à qn)* takes an indirect object, e.g. *parler à une amie.* Therefore in *Je me parle* the pronoun is indirect.

The reflexive pronoun is the direct object

Je me lave à l'eau froide	*I wash in cold water*
Elle est maladroite et se blesse fréquemment	*She is clumsy and often injures herself*
Il se coiffe pendant des heures	*He spends hours doing his hair*
Tu te baignes tous les jours?	*Do you have a swim every day?*
Magalie s'habille élégamment	*Magalie dresses elegantly*
Lucas se nourrit très bien	*Lucas has a healthy diet*
Marianne se cache dans l'armoire	*Marianne is hiding in the cupboard*

The reflexive pronoun is the indirect object

Je me parle constamment en me promenant	*I constantly talk to myself when I go for a walk*
En répétant des confidences on ne peut que se nuire	*By repeating secrets you only succeed in doing yourself harm*
Tu t'achèteras un nouveau blouson pour la rentrée	*You'll buy yourself a new jacket to go back to school*
Je me reproche ces bêtises	*I feel bad about this foolishness*
Je me jure de continuer à travailler	*I promise myself that I will continue to work*
Il faut bien s'admettre la vérité	*We just have to accept the truth*
Marianne se cache la vérité	*Marianne is hiding the truth from herself*

The difference between direct object reflexives and indirect object reflexives is clear from the last example in each set:

Marianne se cache dans l'armoire
Marianne se cache la vérité

In the first example the *se* is the person who is hidden: *Marianne cache **Marianne** dans l'armoire*. In the second example it is *la vérité* which is hidden and the *se* is the indirect object: *Marianne cache la vérité **à Marianne***. These differences are significant when it comes to past participle agreement (see Sections 8.7.7 and 9.4).

Many ordinarily directly transitive, indirectly transitive and ditransitive verbs can be used pronominally as reflexives, for example:

Il critique **son patron**	Il **se** critique
He criticizes his boss	*He criticizes himself*
Elle regarde **son amie**	Elle **se** regarde
She is looking at her girl friend	*She is looking at herself*
Tu offres un cadeau **à Léo**	Tu **t'**offres un cadeau
You are giving a present to Leo	*You are giving a present to yourself*
Il parle **à sa mère**	Il **se** parle
He's talking to his mother	*He's talking to himself*
Elle cache la vérité **à son mari**	Elle **se** cache la vérité
She is hiding the truth from her husband	*She is hiding the truth from herself*

8.7.2 **Pronominal verbs and body parts**

The normal way of describing events in which subjects do things to their own bodies is to use a pronominal verb and the part of the body preceded by a definite or indefinite article and not by a possessive determiner as in English:

Je **me** lave toujours **les mains** avant de déjeuner
I always wash my hands before lunch

Elle va **se** couper **le doigt** si elle ne fait pas attention
She will cut her finger if she's not careful

Nathan **s'**est cassé **la jambe** en jouant au football
Nathan broke his leg playing football

Tu as encore oublié de **te** brosser **les dents!**
You forgot to brush your teeth again!

J'aime bien **me** brosser **les cheveux**
I like brushing my hair

Elle **s'**est cassé **une dent de devant**
She broke one of her front teeth

(See also Section 2.2.8 for the use of the definite article with parts of the body.)

8.7.3 **Pronominal verbs without a reflexive interpretation**

Some verbs include a pronoun but it is impossible to see in what way they can be assigned a reflexive interpretation, e.g. *s'abstenir, se douter, s'en aller, s'enfuir, s'évanouir, se repentir,* and *se taire*:

Je **m'abstiendrai** de tout commentaire
I will refrain from making any comment

Tu **t'es** toujours **douté** qu'il lui ferait faux bond
You always guessed he would let her down

Il reste encore aujourd'hui mais il **s'en va** demain
He's staying today but he is going tomorrow

A la vue de tout ce sang, ils **se sont évanouis**
At the sight of so much blood they fainted

Il **s'est** toujours **repenti** de ces paroles
He always regretted those words

Ils **se sont tus** pour protéger leur camarade
They kept quiet to protect their friend

Common pronominal verbs which do not have a reflexive interpretation:

s'abstenir de tout commentaire	*to refrain from making any comment*
s'accouder au parapet	*to lean on one's elbows on the parapet*
s'accoutumer à conduire la nuit	*to get used to driving at night*
s'accroupir derrière un arbre	*to crouch behind a tree*

s'affaiblir lentement	*to get slowly weaker*
s'affaisser/s'affaler/s'écrouler par terre	*to collapse on the ground*
s'agenouiller près de quelqu'un	*to kneel down next to somebody*
s'amuser en vacances	*to have fun on holiday*
s'apercevoir de qch	*to notice something*
s'appeler Drissi	*to be called Drissi*
s'approcher de qn	*to approach somebody*
s'appuyer au rebord de la fenêtre	*to lean on the windowsill*
s'arrêter aux feux	*to stop at the lights*
s'asseoir dans un fauteuil	*to sit down in an armchair*
s'assoupir au volant	*to doze off at the wheel*
s'avancer vers la montagne	*to advance towards the mountain*
se blottir contre sa mère	*to cuddle up to one's mother*
se briser/se casser en miettes	*to break into pieces*
se charger d'une tâche	*to take on a task*
se comporter mal	*to behave badly*
se contenter d'une carrière médiocre	*to make do with a mediocre career*
se coucher tôt	*to go to bed early*
se dépêcher de poser sa candidature	*to hurry to apply for the job*
se déshabiller dans le noir	*to get undressed in the dark*
se diriger vers la maison	*to go towards the house*
se distinguer par son intelligence	*to stand out by one's intelligence*
se douter de qc	*to suspect something*
se dresser contre une injustice	*to protest against an injustice*
s'écarter du chemin	*to stray from the track*
s'échapper/s'évader d'une prison	*to escape from a prison*
s'écouler vite	*to pass quickly (of time)*
s'écrier	*to shout, exclaim*
s'éloigner de la ville	*to move away from the town*
s'emparer de son adversaire	*to get hold of one's opponent*
s'en aller ailleurs	*to go away somewhere else*
s'endormir dans la voiture	*to go to sleep in the car*
s'enfuir dans les bois	*to flee into the woods*
s'ennuyer à la campagne	*to become bored in the country*
s'enquérir auprès de l'ambassade	*to enquire at the Embassy*
s'étonner de la vitesse de la voiture	*to be surprised at the speed of the car*
s'évanouir	*to faint*
se fâcher de quelque chose	*to get annoyed at something*
se fatiguer facilement	*to get easily tired*
se fermer doucement	*to close gently*
se fier à ses collègues	*to trust one's colleagues*
s'habiller en tenue de soirée	*to wear evening dress*
s'habituer à un nouvel emploi	*to get used to a new job*
s'intéresser au latin	*to be interested in Latin*
se lever tard	*to get up late*
se méfier de la police	*to distrust the police*
se mêler à la conversation	*to join in the conversation*
se mettre debout	*to stand up*
se moquer de qn	*to make fun of somebody*
se nourrir de pain	*to live on bread*
s'occuper de ses enfants	*to look after one's children*
se passer de cigarettes	*to go without cigarettes*
se plaindre du temps	*to complain about the weather*
se rappeler une amie	*to remember a friend*

se raviser brusquement	*to change one's mind suddenly*
se réfugier sous les arbres	*to take refuge under the trees*
se repentir de ses paroles	*to regret one's words*
se retourner	*to turn around*
se réunir le dimanche	*to meet on Sundays*
se réveiller	*to wake up*
se servir d'une scie	*to use a saw*
se soucier de la santé de qn	*to worry about somebody's health*
se souvenir d'une amie	*to remember a friend*
se taire	*to keep quiet*
se tenir droit	*to stand straight*
se tromper	*to be wrong*

8.7.4 *se faire* and *se laisser*

se faire and *se laisser* are used to convey the idea that the subject causes some event to befall himself or herself without necessarily intending that it should:

Julie **s'est fait écraser** par un camion	*Julie was run over by a lorry*
Romain **s'est fait sortir** du terrain	*Romain got (himself) sent off the field*
Lilian **s'est fait inscrire** par Olivia	*Lilian got Olivia to register him*
Elle **s'est laissé convaincre** par son père	*She let herself be persuaded by her father*
Il **se laissait guider**	*He let himself be led*
Guido **s'est laissé pousser** les moustaches	*Guido allowed his moustache to grow*

(See Section 9.4 for agreement of the past participle of *faire* and *laisser* in this construction.)

8.7.5 Pronominal verbs used reciprocally

When a pronominal verb is used in the plural and describes a situation where several subjects are doing things **to each other**, it is being used reciprocally:

D'ordinaire, les journalistes **se consultent** avant de publier un article de ce genre
Journalists usually consult each other before publishing this kind of article

Ils **se rencontreront** à Paris	*They will meet (each other) in Paris*
Nous **nous connaissons**	*We know each other*
Les enfants **se disputent**	*The children are arguing (with each other)*

The pronoun can be a direct object, as in the above examples, or an indirect object, as in the following examples:

Souvent les participants **s'écrivent** et restent en contact après la conférence
Participants often write to one another and keep in touch after the conference

Il a ensuite été demandé aux élèves de **se poser** des questions sans le secours du professeur
Pupils were then required to ask each other questions without the teacher's help

Nous **nous envoyons** des cadeaux à Noël chaque année
We send each other presents every year at Christmas

Sometimes there is a possible ambiguity between a reflexive interpretation of the pronoun and a reciprocal interpretation, for example:

Les boxeurs **se sont blessés**
The boxers hurt each other or *The boxers hurt themselves* (i.e. each hurt himself but not the other)

Les participants **se sont posé** des questions
The participants asked each other questions or *The participants asked questions of themselves*

One way to make the reciprocal interpretation entirely clear is to add the expression *l'un l'autre* 'each other' in its appropriate form. For example, where a direct object is involved:

Les boxeurs se sont blessés **l'un l'autre**
The boxers hurt each other

But where an indirect object is involved:

Les participants se sont posé des questions **l'un à l'autre**
The participants asked each other questions

l'un l'autre also varies for gender and number. If the subjects are feminine in gender *l'une l'autre* is required:

On s'aide **l'une l'autre** pour la garde des enfants
We help each other out with looking after the children

If more than just two subjects are involved a plural form of *l'un l'autre* is required:

Les musiciens du groupe peuvent se contacter **les uns les autres** avant chaque concert
The musicians in the band can contact each other before each concert
(For agreement of the past participle, see Sections 8.7.7 and 9.4.)

8.7.6 **Pronominal verbs used as passives**

Pronominal verbs are increasingly used with a meaning equivalent to an English passive:

Les jeux électroniques **se vendent** comme des petits pains
Computer games are selling like hot cakes

Ces verbes **se conjuguent** avec 'être'
These verbs are conjugated with 'être'

Le français **se parle** au Canada et en Afrique
French is spoken in Canada and in Africa

Les casques **s'achètent** dans les magasins de sport
Helmets can be bought in sports shops

Les valeurs **se maintiennent** à la Bourse
Stocks and shares are holding up on the Stock Exchange

Cela ne **se fait** pas	*That is just not done*
Ce vin **se boit** chambré	*This wine is drunk at room temperature*
La vengeance est un plat qui **se mange** froid	*Revenge is a meal to be eaten cold*
C'est un roman qui **se lit** facilement	*This novel is easy to read*

8.7.7 **Pronominal verbs, the auxiliary *être*, and the agreement of the past participle**

Pronominal verbs are always conjugated with *être* in their compound tenses, and the question arises as to when the past participle is marked for agreement. Whereas the past participle of non-pronominal verbs which take *être* always agrees with the subject (*elle est arrivée, nous sommes arrivés, elles sont arrivées* – see Section 9.2), the participle with pronominal verbs only agrees with a direct object pronoun. For example:

(a) Where the meaning of the pronoun is reflexive and it is a direct object:

Je (fem) **me** suis lav**ée** à l'eau froide
I washed in cold water

Elle était maladroite et **s'**était fréquemment bless**ée**
She was clumsy and often injured herself

Magalie **s'**est habill**ée** élégamment
Magalie dressed elegantly

Marianne **s'**est cach**ée** dans l'armoire
Marianne hid in the cupboard

(See also Section 8.7.1.)

(b) Where the meaning of the pronoun is reciprocal and it is a direct object:

Les deux équipes **se** sont rencontr**ées** à Paris
The two teams met (each other) in Paris

Nous **nous** sommes attend**us** les uns les autres avant de rentrer
We waited for each other before going home

Nordine et Jérémie **se** sont rencontr**és** à Lyon
Nordine and Jérémie met in Lyons

Marianne et sa mère **se** sont attend**ues** à la gare
Marianne and her mother waited for each other at the station

(c) Where the pronoun has no detectable reflexive or reciprocal meaning, but is an integral part of the verb, and is a direct object:

A la vue de tout ce sang, elles **se** sont évanou**ies**
At the sight of so much blood, they fainted

Ils **se** sont toujours repent**is** de ces paroles
They always regretted those words

Ils **se** sont t**us** dès qu'ils ont vu le patron
They kept quiet as soon as they saw the boss

This includes when the pronominal verb is used as a passive:

Les jeux vidéo **se** sont vend**us** comme des petits pains
Video games sold like hot cakes

BUT the past participle will not agree in any case where the pronoun is an indirect object (see Section 8.7.1). In particular, this will be the case:

(i) where the non-pronominal version of the verb has a prepositional indirect object e.g. *nuire à qn, cacher qch à qn, écrire à qn* and therefore the *se* is seen as an indirect object:

Elle **s'**est nui en faisant de telles demandes
She did herself harm by these requests

Marianne **s**'est caché la vérité
Marianne hid the truth from herself

Les participants **se** sont écrit
The participants wrote to each other

(ii) where the pronoun is indirect, given that the direct object is a body part (as in Section 8.7.2):

Je (fem) **me** suis lavé les mains avant de déjeuner
I washed my hands before lunch

Elle **s**'est coup**é** le doigt parce qu'elle ne faisait pas attention
She cut her finger because she was careless

Nathan **s**'est cass**é** la jambe en jouant au football
Nathan broke his leg playing football

N.B.: Where the pronoun is an indirect object (and hence the participle does not agree with it), the participle may nevertheless agree with a **preceding** direct object, as in:

Les deux **valises qu**'il s'est achet**ées** sont cassées
The two suitcases he bought are broken

Combien de valises s'est-il achet**ées**?
How many suitcases did he buy?

(See Chapter 9 for the general rules of past participle agreement.)

8.8 Impersonal verbs

A number of verbs only exist in an impersonal (and infinitive) form. They only take the pronoun *il* as their subject, which in this case does not refer to a person or thing: i.e. it is an impersonal use.

8.8.1 Weather verbs

The best-known group of impersonal verbs describe the weather:

Il pleut	*It's raining*
Il pleut des cordes	*It's raining cats and dogs*
Il neige	*It's snowing*
Il grêle	*It's sleeting*
Il tonne	*There's thunder about*
Il vente	*It's windy*
Il bruine	*It's drizzling*

More generally climatic conditions can be expressed by an impersonal use of *faire* followed by an adjective or a noun:

Il fait beau	*It's a nice day*
Il fait du soleil	*It's sunny*
Il fait mauvais	*It's not a nice day*
Il fait chaud	*It's hot*
Il fait lourd	*The weather is oppressive*
Il fait sec	*It's very dry*

Il fait humide   *It's very humid*
Il fait du brouillard   *It's foggy*
Il fait de l'orage   *It's stormy*
Il fait un froid de canard   *It's very cold*

8.8.2 *falloir*

falloir only exists in impersonal forms (see the list of irregular verbs in Chapter 7). It may be followed by a noun, by an infinitive, by a clause – with the verb in the subjunctive – and it may be preceded by a pronoun acting as indirect object:

Il faut du temps   *Time is needed*
Il faut partir   *It is time to leave*
Il faut que nous partions   *We must leave*
Il nous faut partir   *We must leave*
Il nous faudra revenir dans trois semaines   *We must come back in three weeks*
Il a fallu trois mois pour que nous nous   *It took us three months to make up our minds*
décidions
Il faudrait être certain que cela soit la bonne   *We need to be sure that this is the right decision*
décision

8.8.3 *il y a*

il y a ('there is' or 'there are') also exists only in the impersonal form. It is usually followed directly by a noun but may also be followed by an infinitive introduced by *à* or by *de quoi*. It is frequently used in spoken French in the construction: *il y a* + noun + relative clause. In spoken French the pronunciation often reduces to /ja/:

Il y a quelques problèmes au garage
There are a few problems at the garage

Il y a eu de bons gouvernements, autrefois
There have been good governments, in the past

Il y avait toujours quelque chose à faire
There was always something to be done

Il y a à faire dans la cuisine
There are things to do in the kitchen

Il y a à boire et à manger dans le frigo
There's something to eat and drink in the fridge

Il y a de quoi vous occuper ici
There's lots to do here

Il y avait de quoi vous faire peur la nuit
It was enough to make you afraid at night

Il y a des gens qui vous attendent dehors
There are people waiting for you outside

Il y a ceux qui prétendent tout savoir
There are those who think they know everything

Il y en a qui disent du mal des autres
Some people say bad things about others

8.8.4 *il s'agit de*

il s'agit de is only ever used impersonally. It may be followed by a noun, by an infinitive and, rarely, by a clause. English-speaking learners frequently attempt to use it with a personal subject, e.g. **ce livre s'agit de....* This is **impossible**.

Il s'agit de votre frère
It's about your brother

Il s'agit de faire ce qui vous intéresse
You have to do what interests you

Il s'agit de convaincre votre tante
It is a matter of convincing your aunt

Il s'agissait de vous faire changer d'avis
It was an attempt to make you change your mind

Tout au long de cette affaire il s'est agi de mon honnêteté
Throughout this matter it has been a question of my honesty

Il ne s'agit pas que vous preniez toute la responsabilité sur vous
There is no question of your taking on the whole responsibility

Il ne s'agit pas de prendre du retard
We'd better not get behind schedule

8.8.5 Verbs which take a personal subject can also on occasions be used impersonally

Il se passe ici des choses qui vous intéresseront sûrement
There are things going on here which will probably interest you

Il est arrivé hier soir un événement très curieux
A very unusual event took place yesterday evening

Il convient d'être très circonspect de nos jours
It is sensible to be very careful these days

Il nous arrive assez souvent de recevoir des personnalités importantes
We quite often have important people as guests

Il manque des couverts à cette table
This table has not been laid properly

Il y va de sa vie
His life is at stake

Il nous manque plusieurs de nos camarades ce soir
Several of our comrades are missing tonight

Il ne me souvient pas d'avoir été présenté à cette personne
I don't (seem to) remember having been introduced to this person (formal language)

être can also be used impersonally, either in set expressions or more formally as an alternative to *il y a:*

Il est grand temps que nous partions	*It is high time we went*
Il n'est absolument pas question d'attendre	*There can be no question of waiting*
Il est dommage d'avoir attendu si longtemps	*It is a pity to have waited so long*
Est-il besoin de vous le rappeler?	*Is there any need to remind you?* (formal style)
Il est des jours où l'on souhaiterait être ailleurs	*There are days when one would wish to be elsewhere*

There are two set phrases used to introduce fairy stories:

Il était une fois … and
Il y avait une fois …
Once upon a time there was …

8.9 Verbs which take noun + adjective or noun + noun complements

A small number of verbs allow an adjective or predicative noun (*président, directeur,* etc.) to follow the noun which is the direct object:

boire qc frais	*to drink sth chilled*
considérer qc peu probable	*to consider sth unlikely*
croire qn heureux	*to believe sb happy*
élire qn président	*to elect sb president*
estimer qn inapte	*to reckon sb unsuitable*
juger qn maladroit	*to judge sb clumsy*
laisser qn tranquille	*to leave sb alone*
manger qc chaud	*to eat sth hot*
nommer qn directeur	*to appoint sb director*
rendre qn malade	*to make sb ill*
trouver qc difficile	*to find sth difficult*

Note that 'to make somebody happy, sad, etc.' or 'to make something difficult, easy, etc.' is the verb *rendre*, and NOT * *faire*: *rendre qn heureux, rendre qn triste, rendre qc difficile, rendre qc facile.*

8.10 Subject–verb inversion

The most frequent order in French is subject–verb but on occasions the order is changed to verb–subject. For subject–verb order in questions, see Chapter 14, especially Section 14.2.3.

(i) When there is a preceding specific sentence-initial adverb (see Section 5.7.4)

A peine **étaient-ils arrivés** qu'ils ont dû repartir
They had hardly got here when they had to leave again

Sans doute **vous a-t-il prévenu** à temps
No doubt he told you in good time

(ii) In reporting direct speech:

> C'est plus fort en goût, **précise Vincent**
> C'est plus fort en goût, **précise-t-il**
> *It has a stronger taste, Vincent adds/he adds*

> Faux! **répondirent les autres** aussitôt.
> *Wrong! the others answered immediately*
> (for punctuation see Appendix One)

(iii) As a stylistic choice in relative clauses introduced by the relative *'que'* as the object of the verb (see Sections 15.1 and 15.3).

> Les Revel ont acheté la voiture que **recherchait la police**
> *The Revels bought the car the police were looking for*

> Les paysages qu'**envisagaient les artistes** ont été submergés par les nouveaux réservoirs
> *The landscapes which the artists saw in their minds have been submerged under new reservoirs*

(iv) In relative clasues beginning with *comme*

> J'ai appris à faire la confiture de coings comme **faisait ma grand-mère** (or) comme la faisait ma grand-mère
> *I learnt to make quince jelly like my grandmother used to*

> On s'informera auprès des résaux sociaux, comme **font tous les jeunes** (or) comme le font tous les jeunes)
> *We will learn about it from the social networks as all the young people do.*

8.11 **Verb constructions and inclusive writing**

In inclusive writing there is a rejection of the principle that the masculine form takes precedence. Therefore, in all the verb constructions mentioned in this chapter, where the referent of the past participle contains both masculine and feminine, the intention is to mark explicitly both genders.

Thus, where intransitive verbs are used with *être* (Section 8.2.2), the past participle will be marked
Marie et Jean sont monté.e.s dans la voiture

Passive sentences (Section 8.6) where the subject is masculine and feminine will be marked:
Bernard et Sylvie ont été battu.e.s au tennis par Suzanne et Asif

Where pronominal verbs are used reflexively (Section 8.7.1) and the reflexive pronoun is the direct object and contains masculine and feminine references, the past participle will be marked:

Yasmina et Pierre se sont lavé.e.s à l'eau froide

Where pronomal verbs are used reciprocally (Sections 8.7.5 and 8.7.7) and the reciprocal pronoun is the direct object, the past participle will be marked:

Tom et Aline se sont rencontré.e.s au pied de la tour Eiffel

Where the reflexive pronoun is an integral part of the verb but has no detectable reflexive or reciprocal meaning (Section 8.7.7), and the reflexive pronoun refers to masculine and feminine, the past participle will be marked:

Mon frère et ma soeur se sont évanoui.e.s à la vue de tant de sang

Finally, do remember that while the examples above are meant to help you understand the basic principles of *écriture inclusive* when you come across this style of writing, neither usage nor language policy has firmed up in this matter and you are not expected to produce these forms yourself. (For some history, see Introduction to Chapter 3.)

FREE

INSTRUCTOR & STUDENT RESOURCES

For more resources to practice your French grammar, including practice activities/quizzes for students, further resource links, and an instructor guide, please visit https://routledgelearning.com/frenchgrammarandusage.

9 Verb and participle agreement

9.1 Subject–verb agreement

As in English, French verbs agree with their subject in person and number:

Je ne voul**ais** pas jouer
I didn't want to play

Elle voul**ait** partir en vacances
She wanted to go on holiday

Les garçons voul**aient** tous participer au match
The boys all wanted to take part in the match

9.1.1 Agreement with more than one subject linked by *et*

If one of the subjects is a **first-person pronoun**, the verb will be in the first-person plural form:

Hubert et moi **sommes** allés vous chercher
Hubert and I went to look for you

Ma sœur et moi **serons** dans la même famille en Belgique
My sister and I are staying with the same family in Belgium

Toi/Vous et moi **sommes** toujours d'accord
You and I always agree

If one of the subjects is a **second-person pronoun** and there is no first-person pronoun, the verb will be in the second-person plural form:

Toi et ton copain **avez** intérêt à nettoyer cette pièce avant que tes parents ne rentrent.
You and your friend had better clean this room before your parents get back

Vous et vos amis **devrez** vous dépêcher si vous voulez prendre le train de 15 heures
You and your friends will have to hurry if you want to catch the 3 o'clock train

If all the subjects are **third person**, the verb will be in a third-person plural form:

Lila et Maud **sont** venues toutes les deux
Lila and Maud both came

Les deux grands groupes **sont** arrivés à un accord pour une réduction de leur consommation de gaz
The two large companies have reached agreement on a reduction of their gas consumption

(See also Section 3.3.5 for coordinated stressed pronouns.)

DOI: 10.4324/9781003373926-9

9.1.2 **Agreement with more than one subject linked by: *ni... ni*, 'neither ... nor', *soit... soit*, 'either ... or' *and ou*, 'or'**

French tends to make a distinction between the two kinds of meaning which may be conveyed by these methods of coordination. If the meaning emphasizes the individual and does not 'add them together', the verb may well be singular:

Ni Simon ni Steven n'**a** pu me dire où se trouvaient les autres
Neither Simon nor Steven was able to tell me where the others were

C'est soit lui soit sa sœur qui **doit** te téléphoner
Either he or his sister must be responsible for telephoning you

If, on the other hand, the intention is to consider the two elements as a group, the verb will be plural:

Ni la Syrie ni la Turquie n'**ont** été épargnées par le tremblement de terre de 2023
Neither Syria nor Turkey were spared by the 2023 earthquake

The same principle underlies agreement with *ni l'un ni l'autre*. Where they are 'additive' the verb is likely to be plural, where they act as 'alternative individuals' the verb is likely to be singular:

Ni Nadia ni Léa n'**avaient** pu rencontrer le peintre
Neither Nadia nor Léa managed to meet the painter

Ni l'une ni l'autre n'**ont** pu rencontrer le peintre
Neither the one nor the other was able to meet the painter

Ni Nadia ni Léa ne **viendra**
Neither Nadia nor Léa will come

Ni l'une ni l'autre ne **viendra**
Neither the one nor the other will come

9.1.3 **Verb agreement with collective noun subjects**

Normally collective nouns which are singular require the verb to be in a singular form, unlike English where speakers use either a singular or plural verb form:

Le gouvernement **a** décidé de modifier la loi sur la nationalité
The government has/have decided to change the nationality law

Le comité **a** proposé une réunion pour 16 heures
The committee has/have suggested a meeting at 4 o'clock

La famille **passe** les vacances de Noël en Bretagne
The family is/are spending the Christmas holidays in Brittany

N.B.: *Tout le monde* always agrees with a singular verb:

Tout le monde **vient** passer le weekend chez moi
Everybody's coming to my place for the weekend

This may change, however, when the collective noun is followed by a plural complement. The verb may then be in the singular or the plural (although some speakers still have a preference for the singular):

L'équipe de footballeurs anglais **a** (or **ont**) dû quitter la ville très rapidement
The team of English football players had to leave town in a hurry

La foule des supporters **ont** (or **a**) été rapidement dispersé(e)(s)
The crowd of supporters were rapidly dispersed

Note that in English there is a preference for a plural verb in these cases.

9.1.4 **Verb agreement with fractions**

When fractions (see Section 6.3) are subjects and have plural complements, whether they are present or implied, verbs normally agree with those complements:

La moitié (**des gens**) se **sont** exprimés
Half (of the people) made their views known

Un tiers (de **ceux** qui étaient présents) se **sont** exprimés
A third (of those present) made their views known

But when the fraction has a singular complement, whether present or implied, verbs agree with the fraction:

La moitié (de la population) s'**est** exprimée
Half (the population) made their view known

Un tiers (de la maison) **a** été détruit
A third (of the house) was destroyed

N.B.: *les deux tiers* and percentages usually agree with a plural verb:

Les deux tiers des électeurs **ont** voté pour la droite
Two-thirds of the electorate voted for the right

66% **ont** voté pour la droite
66% voted for the right

9.1.5 **Verb agreement with numeral nouns and quantifiers**

When numeral nouns like *une dizaine* 'ten or so', *une vingtaine* 'twenty or so', *une douzaine* 'a dozen', etc. (see Section 6.5.3) are subjects, the verb can agree with the numeral noun or its complement, depending on where the emphasis lies:

Nous sommes vingt ce midi à la maison: **une douzaine** d'œufs ne nous **suffira** pas
There are twenty of us having lunch at home today: a dozen eggs won't be enough

Une vingtaine de **policiers ont** été blessés
Twenty or so policemen were injured

When most quantifiers (like *la plupart de* 'most', *(un grand) nombre de* 'a large number of', *quantité de* 'a lot of', *beaucoup de* 'many') are subjects, the verb agrees with their complement, whether it is present or implied:

La plupart (des **résidents**) **partagent** mes sentiments
Most (of the residents) share my feelings

La plupart (d'entre **eux**) **sont** prêts à nous aider
Most (of them) are ready to help us

Un grand nombre (des **locataires**) **sont** déjà allés se plaindre
A large number (of the tenants) have already been to complain

Beaucoup (de **manifestants**) se **présenteront** à la mairie cet après-midi
A lot (of demonstrators) will go to the Town Hall this afternoon

With *la majorité de* 'the majority of', *une minorité de* 'a minority of', *le reste de* 'the rest of', the verb can agree either with the quantifier or its complement:

La majorité (des **fans**) **ont/a** moins de quarante ans
The majority (of fans) are under forty

Plus d'un tends to be singular:

Plus d'un ami m'**a** incité à me présenter au premier tour
More than one friend suggested I should stand in the first round

But *moins de* tends to be plural:

Moins de dix personnes m'**ont** indiqué leur désaccord
Fewer than ten people told me they disagreed

9.1.6 **Agreement with the verb** *être*

Where two nouns are linked by the verb *être*, the verb normally agrees with the preceding subject, although some speakers will make it agree with what follows:

Mon problème **était** mes enfants, car je n'avais personne pour les garder
My problem was my children, for I had no-one to look after them

When *ce* is the subject of *être*, there is a choice between using *c'est* or *ce sont*. Whereas most nouns and pronouns follow *c'est*, for example:

C'est moi/nous	*It's me/us*
C'est toi/vous/lui/elle	*It's you/him/her*
C'est le facteur	*It's the postman*

in formal French, plural nouns and third-person plural pronouns are supposed to follow *ce sont*:

Ce sont mes parents	*It's my parents*
Ce sont eux	*It's them*

However, most speakers (and even writers) of formal French use *c'est* in these cases these days:

C'est mes parents
C'est eux

Where numbers are involved, *c'est* is always used:

> C'est 1 000 euros que je vous dois
> *It's 1,000 euros that I owe you*

The *c'est/ce sont* construction is often used with relative clauses, and it is important to remember that the verb in the relative clause agrees in person and number with the complement of *c'est/ce sont*:

> C'est **moi** qui **suis** le plus âgé
> *It's me who's the oldest*

> C'est **nous** qui **sommes** les responsables
> *We are the ones responsible*

> C'est **vous** qui **avez** pris ma serviette de bain
> *It's you who has taken my towel*

> Ce sont **elles** qui **ont** fait cela
> *They are the ones who did that*

9.2 Agreement of the past participle with the subject of *être*

There are three cases where the past participle agrees with the subject of *être*: (a) with intransitive verbs which select the auxiliary *être* in compound tenses; (b) in passives; (c) where the past participle functions like an adjective.

9.2.1 Agreement of the past participle with the subject of intransitive verbs which select auxiliary *être* in compound tenses

The past participles of *aller* 'to go', *monter* 'to go up', *mourir* 'to die', *naître* 'to be born', *sortir* 'to go out', *tomber* 'to fall', etc. (see Section 8.2.2 for the full list) agree with the subject in gender and number in compound tenses:

Les **Hoarau** étaient allés à La Réunion	*The Hoaraus had gone to La Réunion*
Naïma est sortie	*Naïma went out*
Elles sont tombées	*They fell over*
Samira et Luc sont montés au troisième	*Samira and Luc went up to the third floor*

N.B.: Some intransitive verbs which select auxiliary *être* in compound tenses can also be used transitively (see Section 8.3.4). In this case, they select the auxiliary *avoir* in compound tenses, and there is no agreement between the subject and the past participle:

> **Samira et Luc** ont monté les valises au troisième
> *Samira and Luc took the cases up to the third floor*

9.2.2 Agreement of the past participle following *être* with the subject of a passive

Passives are constructed from transitive verbs by turning the direct object into the subject and making the verb an *être* + past participle construction (see Section 8.6). The past participle agrees with the subject in gender and number in these cases:

> **La guerre** a été déclenchée par un attentat à la bombe
> *The war was started by a bomb attack*

Tous les villageois ont été bouleversés par sa mort
All the people in the village were shocked by his death

Une nouvelle icône a été placée sur la barre d'outils
A new icon has been placed on the toolbar

9.2.3 Past participles used as adjectives with *être*

When past participles are used like adjectives and follow *être*, they agree with the subject:

La piscine est couverte   *The swimming pool is indoors*
Les guichets sont fermés   *The (ticket office) windows are closed*

9.3 Agreement of the past participle of verbs conjugated with *avoir* with a preceding direct object

There are three cases where past participles agree with preceding direct objects in the compound tenses of verbs conjugated with *avoir*: (a) when the preceding direct object is an unstressed pronoun like *le, la, les, me, te* etc., e.g. *Je les ai vus* 'I saw them'; (b) when the preceding direct object is the head of a relative clause: e.g. *La photo que j'ai postée* 'The photo which I posted'; (c) in questions, when the direct object has been moved to a position preceding the past participle, e.g. *Quelle photo a-t-elle postée?* 'Which photo did she post?'

9.3.1 Agreement of the past participle with preceding direct object pronouns

In compound tenses, the past participle of verbs conjugated with *avoir* normally agrees with preceding unstressed direct object pronouns:

J'ai vu Alizée: Je l'ai vue
I saw Alizée: I saw her

Les policiers avaient repéré les casseurs: Les policiers **les** avaient repérés
The police had spotted the troublemakers: The police had spotted them

Les voisins ont appelé ma sœur et moi (fem): Les voisins **nous** ont appelées
The neighbours called my sister and me: The neighbours called us

N.B.: *le* used to refer to a clause is invariably masculine (see Section 3.2.8), and so there is no agreement with the past participle:

Sa mère est malade; il l'a souvent dit
His mother is ill; he has often said so

Past participles do NOT agree with any other preceding pronouns, nor with indirect objects, nor with *en*:

J'ai parlé à Aurore: Je **lui** ai parlé (NOT *parlée)
I spoke to Aurore: I spoke to her

J'ai indiqué le chemin à Tristan et Sacha: Je **leur** ai indiqué (NOT *indiqués) le chemin
I told Tristan and Sacha how to get there: I told them how to get there

Ce matin il y a eu des vaches qui sont passées dans le champ du voisin. J'**en** ai vu (NOT * vues) hier aussi
This morning there were some cows which got into the neighbour's field. I saw some yesterday as well

9.3.2 **Recognizing when an unstressed pronoun is a direct object**

Whilst English speakers may learn to remember to make the agreement between a preceding direct object pronoun and the past participle without too much difficulty, they often still have problems in recognizing when a preceding pronoun is a direct object and when it is not. This is particularly the case where the pronouns are *me, te, nous,* and *vous* which can function either as direct object or indirect object pronouns, and when the verbs involved are directly transitive in English but have indirectly transitive counterparts in French (see Section 8.4.1). For example, there is no agreement in the following cases because the pronouns are all indirect objects:

convenir **à** qn	La situation nous a conven**u**	*The situation suited us*
désobéir **à** qn	Noah vous a désobé**i**	*Noah disobeyed you*
nuire **à** qn	Olivier m'a nu**i**	*Olivier did me (fem) some damage*
succéder **à** qn	Khadija m'a succéd**é**	*Khadija succeeded me (fem)*
téléphoner **à** qn	Les voisins vous ont téléphon**é**	*The neighbours phoned you*
résister **à** qn	Les syndicats nous ont résist**é**	*The unions opposed us*

9.3.3 **Agreement with a preceding direct object pronoun when the participle is followed by infinitives**

When a verb is preceded by a direct object pronoun and followed by an infinitive, it is usually said that the participle only agrees when the pronoun is **the subject of the infinitive and is the direct object of the verb containing the participle**. There will be **no agreement when it is the object of the infinitive**. This means that there will be agreement in cases like the following:

Nathalie a vu **une voiture** écraser son chien
Nathalie saw a car run her dog over
(*une voiture* is the subject of *écraser* and the object of *vu*)

Nathalie l'a v**ue** écraser son chien
Nathalie saw it run her dog over

Hisham a regardé **sa fille** gagner la course
Hisham watched his daughter win the race
(*sa fille* is the subject of *gagner* and the object of *regardé*)

Hisham l'a regard**ée** gagner la course
Hisham watched her win the race

On a entendu **les voix** résonner dans la caverne
We heard the voices echoing in the cave
(*les voix* is the subject of *résonner* and the object of *entendu*)

On **les** a entend**ues** résonner dans la caverne
We heard them echoing in the cave

But no agreement in cases like the following:

Nathalie a vu maltraiter **des animaux**
Nathalie saw some animals being mistreated
(*des animaux* is the object of *maltraiter*)

Nathalie **les** a v**u** maltraiter
Nathalie saw them being mistreated

Martial a regardé détruire **la forêt** par des bulldozers
Martial watched the forest being destroyed by bulldozers
(*la forêt* is the object of *détruire*)

Martial **l**'a regard**é** détruire par des bulldozers
Martial watched it being destroyed by bulldozers

Derrière la haie, j'ai entendu chanter **une vieille chanson**
Behind the hedge I heard (someone) singing an old song
(*une vielle chanson* is the object of *chanter*)

Derrière la haie, je **l**'ai entendu chanter
Behind the hedge I heard (someone) singing it

Verbs which are likely to be preceded by direct object pronouns and followed by infinitives are perception verbs like *écouter* 'to listen to', *entendre* 'to hear', *voir* 'to see', etc. (see Section 12.3.8).

Verbs of movement like *amener* 'to bring', *emmener* 'to take', *envoyer* 'to send' may also be followed by infinitives with subjects which give rise to agreement:

J'ai emmené **les invités** prendre le petit déjeuner à l'hôtel
I took the guests to have breakfast at the hotel
(*les invités* is the subject of *prendre* and the object of *emmené*)

Je **les** ai emmen**és** prendre le petit déjeuner à l'hôtel
I took them to have breakfast at the hotel

Mourad a envoyé les **coursiers** livrer tous les colis
Mourad sent the dispatch riders off to deliver all the parcels
(*les coursiers* is the subject of *livrer* and the object of *envoyer*)

Mourad **les** a envoy**és** livrer tous les colis
Mourad sent them off to deliver all the parcels

The verb *laisser* follows the same pattern:

Nous avons laissé **les enfants** partir en vacances tout seuls
We let the children go on holiday on their own
(*les enfants* is the subject of *partir* and the object of *laisser*)

Nous **les** avons laiss**és** partir en vacances tout seuls
We let them go on holiday on their own

Les voisins ont laissé **les chiens** jouer dans le jardin
The neighbours let the dogs play in the garden
(*les chiens* is the subject of *jouer* and the object of *laisser*)

Les voisins **les** ont laiss**és** jouer dans le jardin
The neighbours let them play in the garden

(But see Section 9.4 for agreement of *se laisser*. See Appendix 2 for the proposals regarding *laisser* in *Nouvelle Orthographe*.)

Faire, however, is an exception. When it is followed by an infinitive, its past participle never agrees with a preceding direct object:

Nous **les** avons fait (NOT *faits) partir en vacances tout seuls
We made them go on holiday on their own

Les voisins **les** ont fait (NOT *faits) jouer dans le jardin

(See also Section 12.3.9. For object pronouns in this construction, see Sections 3.2.32 and 9.4 for agreement of *se faire*.)

N.B.: Perception verbs and *laisser* may allow a following infinitive with either a preceding or following subject:

J'ai entendu **les voisins** parler *or*
J'ai entendu parler **les voisins**
I heard the neighbours talk(ing)

J'ai laissé **les enfants** partir *or*
J'ai laissé partir **les enfants**
I let the children leave

In either case, if the subject of the infinitive is turned into an unstressed pronoun, it will give rise to agreement with the past participle:

Je **les** ai entend**us** parler
I heard them talk(ing)

Je **les** ai laiss**és** partir
I let them go

(See Section 3.2.32 for position of pronouns. See Appendix 2 for the proposals regarding *laisser* in *Nouvelle Orthographe*.)

9.3.4 Agreement of past participles with preceding direct objects in relative clauses

When the head of a relative clause (see Section 15.1) is the implied direct object of that clause, and it precedes the verb, a past participle agrees with it in gender and number:

Voilà **l'homme** que j'ai rencontré à la gare hier
There's the man I met at the station yesterday

Voilà **la femme** que j'ai rencontrée à la gare hier
There's the woman I met at the station yesterday

Voilà **les enfants** que j'ai rencontrés à la gare hier
There are the children I met at the station yesterday

Voilà **les jeunes filles** que j'ai rencontr**ées** à la gare hier
There are the girls I met at the station yesterday

N.B.: The past participles of impersonal verbs (see Section 8.8), such as *il y a* 'there is/are', never agree with a preceding complement:

Il y a eu des problèmes
There were problems

Les problèmes qu'il y a **eu** (NOT *eus) ont été vite oubliés
The problems that there were were quickly forgotten

It is important to distinguish this **impersonal** use from the **personal** use where agreement would take place:

Les problèmes **qu'il a eus** ont été vite oubliés
The problems which he had have been quickly forgotten

9.3.5 Recognizing when the head of a relative clause is a direct object

Sometimes it is not easy to determine whether the head of a relative clause is a direct object or not. Verbs such as *courir* 'to run', *coûter* 'to cost', *dormir* 'to sleep', *marcher* 'to walk', *mesurer* 'to measure', *payer* 'to pay', *peser* 'to weigh', *valoir* 'to be worth', *vivre* 'to live' can take complements which look like direct objects, but are in fact measure adverbs:

La contravention m'a coûté **cent cinquante euros**
The fine cost me a hundred and fifty euros

La valise pèse **vingt kilos**
The suitcase weighs twenty kilos

Il a marché une **dizaine de kilomètres**
He walked ten kilometres or so

Elle a dormi **deux heures**
She slept for two hours

In each of these cases the phrase in bold is a measure adverb and not a direct object. One test you can use to find out if the complement of a verb is a direct object or not is to try to make it the subject of a passive sentence – most direct objects can be turned into passive subjects. None of the above examples can be: you cannot say *Cent cinquante euros ont été coûté par la contravention*, nor *Une dizaine de kilomètres ont été marché*, etc.

If the head of a relative clause is an adverb, there is no agreement between it and the past participle:

Les cent cinquante euros que la contravention m'a coûté …
The hundred and fifty euros that the fine cost me …

Les deux heures qu'elle a dormi …
The two hours she slept …

But to make matters more confusing, some of these verbs can also take direct objects. When direct objects are the heads of relative clauses there is agreement with the past participle:

J'ai pesé **la valise** (direct object)
I weighed the suitcase

La valise a pesé **vingt kilos** (adverb)
The suitcase weighed twenty kilos

La valise que j'ai pesée …
Les vingt kilos que la valise a pesé …

9.3.6 Agreement with a preceding direct object in a relative clause when the participle is followed by an infinitive

As in the case of preceding direct object pronouns (see Section 9.3.3), when a verb is preceded by a direct object which is the head of a relative clause and followed by an infinitive, the participle only agrees when that head is the implied direct object of the verb containing the participle and the subject of the infinitive. This means that there will be agreement in cases like the following:

Nathalie a vu **une énorme roche** écraser sa maison
Nathalie saw a huge rock crush her house

Voilà **l'énorme roche que** Nathalie a **vue** écraser sa maison
There's the huge rock which Nathalie saw crush her house

On a entendu **les voix** résonner dans la caverne
We heard the voices echoing in the cave

Ce sont **les voix qu'** on a enten**dues** résonner dans la caverne
Those are the voices we heard echoing in the cave

But no agreement in cases like the following:

Nathalie a vu écraser **sa maison** par une énorme roche
Nathalie saw her house crushed by a huge rock

C'est **sa maison que** Nathalie a **vu** écraser par une énorme roche
It's her house that Nathalie saw crushed by a huge rock

Lionel a regardé détruire **la forêt** par des bulldozers
Lionel watched the forest being destroyed by bulldozers

Voilà **la forêt que** Lionel a regardé détruire par des bulldozers
There's the forest that Lionel watched being destroyed by bulldozers

As in the case of preceding direct object pronouns, the types of verb which give rise to these contexts are perception verbs, movement verbs and *laisser* (but not *faire*) (see Section 9.3.3). (See Appendix 2 for proposals concerning *laisser* in *Nouvelle Orthographe*.)

9.3.7 **Agreement of past participles with preceding direct objects in questions**

Questions can be formed in various ways (see Chapter 14). When they are constructed in such a way that the direct object precedes the past participle in compound tenses, the past participle agrees with it in gender and number:

Quel livre as-tu acheté?
Which book did you buy?

Quelle voiture as-tu achetée?
Which car did you buy?

Laquelle a-t-il choisie?
Which one did he choose?

Lesquels ont-ils acceptés?
Which ones did they accept?

Combien de citrons as-tu achetés?
How many lemons did you buy?

Combien de bouteilles de vin as-tu achetées?
How many bottles of wine did you buy?

N.B.: The past participles of impersonal verbs (see Section 8.8), such as *il y a* 'there is/are', never agree with a preceding questioned complement:

Quels problèmes y a-t-il eu (NOT *eus)?
What problems were there?

This must be distinguished from the personal use where agreement would take place:

Quels problèmes a-t-il eus?
What problems did he have?'

9.3.8 **Recognizing when a questioned phrase is a direct object**

Sometimes it is not easy to determine whether a questioned phrase is a direct object or not. Verbs such as *courir* 'to run', *coûter* 'to cost', *dormir* 'to sleep', marcher 'to walk', *mesurer* 'to measure', payer 'to pay', *peser* 'to weigh', *valoir* 'to be worth', *vivre* 'to live' can take complements which look like direct objects, but are in fact measure adverbs. Where such phrases are questioned there is no agreement with a past participle (see also Section 9.3.5):

Elle a dormi deux heures
She slept for two hours

Combien d'heures a-t-elle dormi (NOT *dormies)?
How many hours did she sleep?

La contravention m'a coûté cent cinquante euros
The fine cost me a hundred and fifty euros

Combien d'euros la contravention a-t-elle coûté (NOT *coûtés)?
How many euros did the fine cost?

9.3.9 **Agreement with a preceding questioned direct object when the participle is followed by an infinitive**

As in the case of preceding direct object pronouns (see Section 9.3.3), when a verb is preceded by a questioned direct object and followed by an infinitive, the participle only agrees when the questioned phrase is the implied direct object of the verb containing the participle and is the subject of the infinitive. This means that there will be agreement in cases like the following:

Nathalie a vu **une voiture** écraser son chien
Nathalie saw a car run her dog over

Quelle voiture Nathalie a-t-elle vu**e** écraser son chien?
Which car did Nathalie see run her dog over?

On a entendu **les voix** résonner dans la caverne
We heard voices echoing in the cave

Quelles voix avez-vous entend**ues** résonner dans la caverne?
What voices did you hear echoing in the cave?

But no agreement in cases like the following:

Nathalie a vu écraser **sa maison** par une énorme roche
Nathalie saw her house crushed by a huge rock

Quelle maison Nathalie a-t-elle **vu** écraser par une énorme roche?
Which house did Nathalie see crushed by a huge rock?

Lionel a regardé détruire **la forêt** par des bulldozers
Lionel watched the forest being destroyed by bulldozers

Quelle forêt Lionel a-t-il regardé détruire par des bulldozers?
Which forest did Lionel see destroyed by bulldozers?

As in the case of preceding direct object pronouns, the types of verb which give rise to these contexts are perception verbs, movement verbs, and *laisser* (but not *faire*). (See Appendix 2 for proposals concerning *laisser* in *Nouvelle Orthographe*.)

9.4 **Agreement of the past participle of pronominal verbs in compound tenses**

Pronominal verbs (see Section 8.7) include an unstressed object pronoun which agrees with the subject:

Je me rase — *I'm shaving*
Elle se lève — *She's getting up*

In compound tenses the past participle agrees with this preceding object pronoun only if it is a direct object. The problem is determining when it is a direct object and when it is not.

With verbs where the pronoun is not understood as a reflexive (that is, where it does not mean anything, but is just a part of the verb – see Section 8.7.3), the participle always agrees, with one exception:

Elle **s'**est levée	*She got up*
Ils **se** sont tus	*They fell silent*
Nous **nous** sommes abstenus de tout commentaire	*We refrained from making any comment*

Exception: *se rire de* 'to make light of': *Ils se sont ri de vos menaces* 'They made light of your threats'.

Where a pronominal verb is used reflexively (see Section 8.7.1), it will have a non-reflexive counterpart. If the verb has a direct object in its non-reflexive counterpart, the reflexive pronoun is a direct object, and a past participle will agree with it in compound tenses:

Reflexive use	**Non-reflexive counterpart**
Je **me** rase	Le coiffeur rase **son client**
I am shaving	*The barber is shaving his client*
Elle **se** sert la première	Elle sert **sa fille** la première
She serves herself first	*She serves her daughter first*
Ils **se** sont rasés de bonne heure	
They shaved early	
Elle **s'**est servie la première	
She served herself first	

If the verb has an indirect object in its non-reflexive counterpart, the reflexive pronoun is an indirect object, and there will be no agreement with a past participle:

Reflexive use	**Non-reflexive use**
Elle **s'**offre un gâteau	Elle offre un gâteau **à son fils**
She treats herself to a cake	*She treats her son to a cake*
Nous **nous** cachons la vérité	Nous cachons la vérité **à nos amis**
We hide the truth from ourselves	*We hide the truth from our friends*
Elle **s'**est offert (NOT *offerte) un gâteau	
She treated herself to a cake	
Nous **nous** sommes caché (NOT *cachés) la vérité	
We hid the truth from ourselves	

The past participles of pronominal verbs used with parts of the body do not agree with the preceding pronoun where the body part is a direct object:

Elle **s'**est coupé (NOT *coupée) **le doigt** (= Elle a coupé le doigt à elle-même, although you cannot say this)
She cut her finger (can even mean *'Her finger was cut off'*)

But where the body part is an indirect object, the pronoun is a direct object and a past participle agrees with it:

Elle **s'**est coupée **au doigt** (= Elle a coupé sa main au doigt, although again you cannot say this)
She cut her finger (can only mean a surface cut)

There is no agreement between the past participle and the preceding pronoun with *se laisser* + infinitive, *se faire* + infinitive or *se voir* + infinitive:

Elle s'est laissé (NOT *laissée) convaincre
She let herself be persuaded

Julie s'est fait (NOT *faite) écraser par un camion
Julie got run over by a lorry

Yasmine s'est vu (NOT *vue) offrir des fleurs par Julien
Yasmine has been given flowers by Julien

9.5 Verb and past participle agreement and inclusive writing

In inclusive writing, the principle is that the presence of both masculine and feminine identities should be made clear and that the masculine should not dominate patterns of agreement.

9.5.1 Agreement of the past participle with the subject of intransitive verbs which use *être* (see Section 9.2.1)

Samira et Luc sont monté.e.s au troisième
Samira and Luc went up to the third floor

9.5.2 Agreement of the past participle following *être* with the subject of a passive (see Section 9.2.2)

Aline et Tom ont été choqué.e.s par sa mort
Aline and Tom were shaken by his death

9.5.3 Agreement of verbs conjugated with *avoir* when the past participle agrees with the preceding direct object which is an unstressed pronoun referring to masculine and feminine (see Section 9.3.1)

Aline et Tom? Je les ai vu.e.s hier après-midi.
Aline and Tom? I saw them yesterday afternoon

9.5.4 Agreement of verbs conjugated with *avoir* when the past participle agrees with the head of a relative clause which refers to masculine and feminine (see Section 9.3.4)

Les garçons et les filles que j'ai rencontré.e.s au parc sont parti.e.s en Angleterre la semaine dernière.
The boys and girls I met in the park left for England last week

9.5.5 Agreement of verbs conjugated with *avoir* when the past participle agrees with a direct object which has been moved to a position preceding the part participle, as in questions

Quels garçons et quelles filles as-tu rencontré.e.s au parc il y a deux semaines?
Which boys and girls did you meet in the park two weeks ago?

These usages are controversial and it remains to be seen to what extent French users adopt these forms.

FREE

**INSTRUCTOR
& STUDENT
RESOURCES**

For more resources to practice your French grammar, including practice activities/quizzes for students, further resource links, and an instructor guide, please visit https://routledgelearning.com/frenchgrammarandusage.

10 Tense

10.1 Introduction

One of the essential functions of verbs is to express distinctions in time. Tenses serve (a) to situate events as taking place in the present, past, or future and (b) to indicate the time at which events occur relative to other events. The verb forms for each of the tenses mentioned in this chapter are given in full in Chapter 7.

10.2 The present

(a) The present tense is used to refer to an action or a state of affairs which exists at the time of speaking:

Je ne **peux** pas lui parler parce que je **suis** dans mon bain
I can't speak to him because I'm in the bath

Il vous **appelle** pour demander votre aide
He's calling to ask for your help

(b) It is used to express timeless facts:

L'eau **se transforme** en vapeur quand elle bout
Water turns to steam when it boils

La Terre **tourne** autour du soleil
The earth goes round the sun

(c) It is used to refer to an action which is habitual:

Je **prends une douche** tous les matins à huit heures
I have a shower every morning at eight o'clock

Il **vient** me voir toutes les semaines pour s'assurer que tout va bien
He comes to see me every week to check that everything's OK

(d) In certain contexts, notably when the context provides a clear temporal reference to the future, it can refer to the future:

Je **viens** demain, c'est sûr
I'll come tomorrow for sure

Demain, il **part** pour Paris
Tomorrow he will be leaving for Paris

DOI: 10.4324/9781003373926-10

(e) Some writers use the present tense to refer to past events when they wish to render the past event more immediate. This can be found particularly in the writings of historians, journalists, etc.:

Grâce au vignoble, les villes **sont** prospères dès le 16e siècle
The vineyard enabled the towns to prosper from the 16th century

10.2.1 Differences between French and English in the use of the present tense

French simple present for the English progressive

English indicates that an event is in progress via a special form of the verb called the 'progressive': 'be + V-ing', e.g. 'I am thinking'. French does not have an equivalent special form for this. The English present progressive will normally be translated into French by the simple present:

Je réfléchis
I think or *I am thinking*

However, if it is important to stress the length of time, or the simultaneity of the event, French can use *en train de*:

Je **suis en train** de réfléchir
I am thinking

Thus, when French uses a present tense, this may correspond either to the simple present or the present progressive of English. The meaning will depend on the context. For example, *Je promène mon chien* will be 'I walk my dog' in the first example below, but 'I am walking my dog' in the second:

Je promène mon chien tous les matins sur le front de mer
I walk my dog on the seafront every morning
(Simple present in English because it expresses a habitual action)

Qu'est-ce que vous faites?
What are you doing?

Je promène mon chien
I am walking my dog
(Progressive form in English because it stresses the ongoing nature of the current action)

French simple present for English perfect

English has a form of the verb called the 'present perfect': 'have + V-ed / V-en', e.g. 'I have walked', 'He has spoken'. It is used for reference to an event which happened in the past, but whose consequences continue into the present. In some cases the English present perfect will be translated by the simple present in French:

J'**envisage** souvent de partir
I have often thought of leaving

Je vous **apporte** des fraises
I have brought you some strawberries

10.3 **The past**

Three forms are available to express PAST events:

The imperfect:	Je jouais du piano
The simple past (past historic):	Je jouai du piano
The compound past (perfect):	J'ai joué du piano

10.3.1 **The imperfect**

(a) This tense is used to describe ongoing past events without reference to a time of starting or finishing:

Stéphanie **lisait**	*Stéphanie was reading*
Il **était** tard	*It was late*
La ville **dormait**	*The town was sleeping*

In narratives, the imperfect typically provides a background of ongoing events against which particular completed events are acted out. If the narrative is written, these completed events will be in the compound past and/or simple past; if the narrative is spoken, they will be in the compound past (see Section 10.3.3):

Il **était** tard. Jules **arrêta** sa voiture devant un café
It was late. Jules pulled up in front of a café

Les voleurs **faisaient** beaucoup de bruit. Les gendarmes **se glissèrent** dans la pièce sans se faire remarquer
The thieves were making a great deal of noise. The policemen slipped into the room without being noticed

Je **somnolais** tranquillement quand quelqu'un **a sonné** à la porte
I was dozing quietly when someone rang the door bell

(b) It also typically refers to a habitual action in the past. This is generally described in English through the use of the forms 'used to' or 'would':

Raphaël **s'arrêtait** toujours au café quand il avait le temps
Raphaël always used to stop at the café when he had the time or
Raphaël would always stop at the café when he had the time

Since 'would' can also express the conditional in English, it is important for the English speaker to distinguish the 'would' which corresponds to the French imperfect from the 'would' which corresponds to the French conditional. If 'would' is imperfect, it should be possible to replace it with 'used to' and still have a grammatical sentence. If substitution of 'would' by 'used to' produces an ungrammatical sentence, it is a conditional:

Le dimanche, **j'allais** manger dans un restaurant au bord de l'Yonne
On Sundays, I would go to a restaurant along the Yonne ('used to' is possible here)

Si j'avais de l'argent, j'**irais** manger dans un grand restaurant à Paris tous les dimanches
If I had money, I would go to a top restaurant in Paris on Sunday ('used to' is not possible here, therefore a conditional)

(See Section 10.4.2 for the conditional tense. See Section 11.3.1 for the use of 'would'.)

(c) It can be used to describe completed past events where the speaker or writer wishes to make the past event more immediate by presenting it as if it were in progress:

Je **courais** jusqu'à la voiture. J'**attendais** un instant, puis je **faisais** marche arrière. Je **roulais** en me répétant: « Fais attention »
I ran to the car. I waited a moment, then I put it into reverse. I drove, repeating to myself: 'Be careful'

10.3.2 **The simple past (past historic)**

The simple past tense refers to completed events in the past which are not seen as having any particular relevance to the present from the point of view of the speaker. Nowadays, the simple past (past historic) is usually only used in writing (including literature aimed at small children) and in very formal spoken French (e.g. very formal speeches) or occasionally in jokey imitation of formal discourse.

Les Jeux Olympiques **eurent** lieu à Paris en 2024
The Olympic Games took place in Paris in 2024

Les dinosaures **vécurent** au jurassique
Dinosaurs lived in the Jurassic period

Le président **partit** à 22h pour New York
The president left at 10 p.m. for New York

10.3.3 **The compound past (perfect)**

The compound past tense refers to a completed event in the past. In contrast to the simple past (past historic), however, it may refer to an action in the past whose effect continues into the present. It is available both in spoken and written French:

Nous **sommes arrivés** hier de Dijon
We came in from Dijon yesterday

Ils **ont vendu** leur appartement et ils **sont partis** à l'étranger
They sold their flat and went abroad

Il a **acheté** six croissants pour le petit déjeuner
He bought six croissants for breakfast

In some texts the simple past and the compound past are used together. The simple past refers to completed events which do not give rise to consequences continuing into the present, from the perspective of the writer. The compound past, by contrast, refers to past events whose consequences do continue to have present relevance, from the perspective of the writer. For example, the following extract from a newspaper article marking the 50th anniversary of the death of the French airman and novelist Antoine de Saint-Exupéry, opens with the following passage:

Le 31 juillet 1944, quand un officier **porta** [*simple past*] officiellement disparu le Lightning P38 no. 223 piloté par Antoine de Saint-Exupéry, un colosse trop à l'étroit dans sa combinaison d'aviateur **est entré** [*compound past*] dans la légende
On 31 July 1944, when an officer officially reported as lost the Lightning P38 no. 223 piloted by Antoine de Saint-Exupéry, a giant of a man, too big for his aviator's suit, became a legend

The simple past *porta* describes an event which is seen as over and done with; the compound past *est entré* describes an event which is seen as having a continuing consequence for the present, from the perspective of the writer: Saint-Exupéry became **and still is** a legendary figure.

10.3.4 **An illustration of the working of the past tenses in context**

Compound past (perfect) and imperfect

Here is a literary example taken from the novel *L'Eté meurtrier* by Sébastien Japrisot, Editions Denoël, Paris, 1977. The completed events are in the compound past because, although written, this particular piece of narrative is told in the first person from the point of view of one of the characters, giving the effect of a spoken narrative. These events are set against a descriptive background defined by the imperfect:

> **J'ai connu** Gabriel [*compound past – completed event*] en avril 1945, quand nous **avons fui** Berlin [*compound past – completed event*], et que je **suivais** [*imperfect – background context*] avec ma mère et d'autres réfugiés, les colonnes des soldats qui **allaient** [*imperfect – background context*] vers le sud. C'**était** dans un village [*imperfect – background context*] un matin très tôt, près de Chemnitz. Nous **avions** déjà **perdu** ma cousine Herta [*pluperfect – see* Section 10.5.1 *– earlier completed event*] qui **avait** trois ans de plus que moi [*imperfect – background context*] entre Torgën et Leipzig, parce qu'elle **avait trouvé** un camion et nous un autre [*pluperfect – see* Section 10.5.1 *– earlier completed event*]. Et c'est ce matin-là que j'**ai perdu** ma mère [*compound past – completed event*]. Je crois qu'elle **a changé** de direction [*compound past – completed event*], qu'elle **est allée** vers Kassel [*compound past – completed event*], à l'ouest, où elle **avait** des amis [*imperfect – background context*] …

> *I met Gabriel in April 1945 when we fled from Berlin, and when I was following, with my mother and other refugees, the columns of soldiers going south. It was in a village very early one morning, near Chemnitz. We had lost my cousin Herta, who was three years older than me, between Torgën and Leipzig because she had found one lorry, and we another. And it was the same morning that I lost my mother. I believe she changed direction, and that she went towards Kassel, to the West, where she had friends …*

Simple past (past historic)

The simple past tense refers to completed events in the past which are not seen as having any particular relevance to the present from the point of view of the speaker. For example, consider the following narrative from another novel *La Dame dans l'auto avec des lunettes et un fusil* by Sébastien Japrisot, Editions Denoël, Paris 1966. Here a series of events are over and done with at some point prior to when the narrator is speaking:

> Elle **ramassa** ses vêtements épars [*simple past – completed event with no consequences continuing into the present from the perspective of the narrator*]. Elle les **rangea** soigneusement dans sa valise noire [*simple past – completed event with no continuing consequences*]. Elle ne **prit** pas la route déserte [*simple past – completed event with no continuing consequences*] par où ils **étaient venus** [*pluperfect – see Section 10.5.1 – earlier completed event*]. Elle **gravit** à nouveau la colline [*simple past – completed event with no continuing consequences*] et, sur la roche plate où ils **s'étaient assis** [*pluperfect – see Section 10.5.1 – earlier completed event*], elle **étala** [*simple past – completed event with no continuing consequences*], ouvert en deux, le sac en papier qui **avait enveloppé** [*pluperfect – see Section 10.5.1 – earlier completed event*] ses nu-pieds neufs. Elle **écrivit** dessus [*simple past – completed event with no continuing consequences*] …

She picked up her scattered clothes. She packed them carefully into her black suitcase. She didn't take the deserted road along which they had come. She climbed the hill again and, on the flat rock where they had sat, she spread the opened-out paper bag which had contained her new flip-flops. She wrote on it …

In modern French the simple past tense is mostly restricted to written French, either in formal contexts or in narratives. It is found in literary texts (novels, plays, poems) and in newspaper articles. It is used typically in passages of **impersonal third-person narration**, as in the above example.

As noted above, the simple past is not found in all contexts in written French, even in literary French. Where a narrative is told from a personal, first person perspective (and hence is more like spoken French than written) it is very likely that it will be told in the compound past. Japrisot, for example, in the novel quoted from above, has passages narrated in the third person and simple past tense, and passages narrated in the first person and compound past. The extract cited above would become the following if recounted from the point of view of the woman in question:

J'**ai ramassé** mes vêtements épars. Je les **ai rangés** dans ma valise noire. Je n'**ai** pas **pris** la route déserte par où nous **étions venus**. J'**ai gravi** à nouveau la colline et, sur la roche plate où nous nous **étions assis**, j'**ai étalé**, ouvert en deux, le sac en papier qui **avait enveloppé** mes nu-pieds neufs. J'**ai écrit** dessus …

10.3.5 Differences between French and English in the use of past tense forms

French compound past/simple past and imperfect for English simple past

The English simple past is used in a range of contexts where French distinguishes between the compound past/simple past on the one hand and the imperfect on the other. Take, for example, the English sentence 'He slept all afternoon'. This can describe a one-off, completed past event, in which case the French equivalent would be a compound past or a simple past form of the verb:

Une fois rentré, il **a dormi** tout l'après-midi
Une fois rentré, il **dormit** tout l'après-midi
(compound past or simple past (past historic) because it is a completed action in the past)
Once he was back home, he slept all afternoon

Or it can describe a habitual action, in which case the French equivalent would be an imperfect form of the verb:

Quand il était adolescent, il **dormait** tout l'après-midi
When he was a teenager, he slept all afternoon (= he used to sleep …)

Note that there is a distinction between viewing an action as habitual and viewing it as repeated. Repeated actions which are completed are described by verbs in the compound past/simple past in French:

Tous les jours de cette année-là elle **a travaillé** d'arrache-pied/elle **travailla** d'arrache-pied
(compound past or simple past because each of the repeated actions, i.e. the work carried out each day, is envisaged as a completed action in the past)
Every day that year she worked like mad

French imperfect for English past progressive

English indicates that an event was in progress in the past via a special form of the verb known as the 'progressive': 'was/were V-ing', e.g. 'He was sleeping'. French does not have an equivalent special form for this. The English past progressive will normally be translated into French by the imperfect tense:

Quand je l'ai trouvé, il **dormait** paisiblement sur la plage
When I found him he was sleeping peacefully on the beach

Nous **allions** vers l'Arc de Triomphe quand les avions sont passés/passèrent au-dessus de nous
We were going towards the Arc de Triomphe when the planes flew over us

If there is a need to emphasize the duration, *en train de* can be used:

Elle **était en train de** mettre la dernière touche à son dessin quand on a frappé/frappa à la porte
She was putting the finishing touches to her drawing when someone knocked at the door

10.4 **The future**

Two tenses are used to refer to future time: the future and the conditional, although the conditional also expresses meanings which are not simply related to future time.

10.4.1 **The future tense**

The future tense has three main functions:

(a) It is used to describe events which take place in the future:

Il **faudra** que tu épluches les annonces de travail à distance
You'll have to go through the teleworking adverts

(b) As in English, it can be used as a more polite alternative to the imperative to give orders:

Vous **fermerez** la porte, s'il vous plaît
Will you close the door, please

Je **prendrai** un kilo de vos prunes jaunes
I'll have a kilo of your yellow plums

Vous m'**excuserez**
Will you excuse me

(c) It is sometimes the equivalent of English 'may', when a speaker is speculating about possible causes or outcomes:

Il **aura** encore sa migraine
He may have his migraine again

Peut-être qu'elle **viendra**
She may perhaps come

(See Section 11.3.4 for more on 'may'.)

10.4 The future **261**

N.B.: The future can be replaced by a present tense form of the verb *aller* + an infinitive where a greater certainty about the likelihood of an event taking place is implied than is given by the future. In many contexts the future and *aller* + an infinitive can be interchanged, e.g.:

Tu **vas** y aller, je le sais bien *or* Tu **iras**, je le sais bien
I'm quite sure you will go

But in some contexts there is a clear difference in meaning between the two:

Elle **va avoir** un bébé
She will have a baby or She's having a baby (i.e. She's pregnant)

Compared with:

Elle **aura** un bébé (un jour, mais elle n'est pas pressée)
She will have a baby (one day, but she is in no hurry)

10.4.2 **The conditional tense**

The conditional has six main functions:

(a) It refers to events which **would** take place in the future if certain conditions were met:

Mon père **m'achèterait** un petit studio si je le laissais faire
My father would buy me a small studio if I let him

Je l'**accompagnerais** volontiers si je ne devais pas retourner à Dijon
I would love to go with him if I didn't have to go back to Dijon

(b) In reported speech (see Section 10.7), it is the equivalent of a future tense in direct speech:

Il a dit: 'Je viendrai' Il a dit qu'il **viendrait**
He said: 'I will come' He said he would come

Je lui ai demandé: 'Est-ce tu pourras venir?'
I asked him, 'Will you be able to come?'

Je lui ai demandé s'il **pourrait** venir
I asked him if he could come

This use of the 'future in the past' is not restricted to cases where the reported events are introduced by verbs like *dire que* 'say that', *demander si* 'ask whether', *écrire que* 'write that', etc. If a situation like the following:

Aurélien **habite** déjà le village, mais Charlotte ne **viendra** le rejoindre que dans deux ans
Aurélien is already living in the village, but Charlotte won't come to join him for another two years

is reported as having occurred in the past, the future form *viendra* can become a conditional:

Aurélien **habitait** déjà le village, mais Charlotte ne **viendrait** le rejoindre que deux ans plus tard
Aurélien was already living in the village, but Charlotte wouldn't come to join him for another two years

The conditional is not obligatory here, however, and past tense forms of the verb are also possible:

Aurélien **habitait** déjà le village, mais Charlotte n'**est venue** le rejoindre que deux ans plus tard
Aurélien was already living in the village, but Charlotte didn't come to join him for another two years

(c) The conditional is used, especially in journalistic language, to state something as an 'alleged' fact, i.e. one which the writer doesn't wish to state as definitely true and often one attributed to other sources:

Selon des sources proches du gouvernement, la Première Ministre **tiendrait** une conférence de presse demain.
According to government sources, the Prime Minister will be holding a press conference tomorrow.

D'après cette annonce, les participants **pourraient** gagner des milliers d'euros en cliquant simplement sur une image, mais attention, c'est une arnaque.
According to this advert, participants could win thousands of euros by simply clicking on an image, but careful, it's a scam.

(d) The conditional (and even the compound conditional – see Section 10.5.5) can be used in French as 'could' and 'would' are in English to make a request sound more polite:

Je **voudrais** réserver deux places, s'il vous plaît
I would like to book two seats, please

Je **voudrais** vous demander un renseignement
J'**aurais voulu** vous demander un renseignement
I was wondering if I could ask you for information

(e) Sometimes the conditional can be the equivalent of English 'might' when the speaker is speculating about possible causes or outcomes – it expresses greater uncertainty than the future tense used for the same purpose:

Il **aurait** encore sa migraine
He might be having one of his migraines again

Peut-être qu'elle **viendrait**
She might come, perhaps

(See Section 11.3.5 for more on 'might'.)

(f) In formal French, a clause with a conditional verb followed by a *que*-clause, also with a verb in the conditional tense, can be used as an alternative to a *si*-clause (see also Section 17.3.7). Compare the following:

Je n'**irais** pas même s'il me **proposait** la lune!
I wouldn't go even if he offered me the moon!

Il me **proposerait** la lune que je n'**irais** pas!
Even if he offered me the moon I still wouldn't go!

In (very) informal French two clauses with verbs in the conditional tense, but without the *que*, can also be used as an alternative to a construction involving *si*:

Il me **proposerait** la lune, je n'**irais** pas!
Even if he offered me the moon I still wouldn't go!

Ils **viendraient** demain, on le **saurait**
If they were coming tomorrow, we'd know about it

Ils **seraient venus**, on l'**aurait su** (*or* on le **saurait**)
If they'd come, we'd have known

(For tenses in *si* clauses, see Sections 10.8 and 17.3.6.)

10.4.3 Differences between French and English in the use of future and conditional tenses

In English, verbs in clauses introduced by conjunctions such as 'when', 'as soon as', 'as long as', 'after', once' are usually in a present or past tense verb form:

*When she **comes** I'll tell her*
*He will arrive as soon as **I have left***

Where such clauses refer to events which are yet to happen (as they mostly do), in French you must use a future, conditional, compound future, or compound conditional, as appropriate. These clauses are introduced by conjunctions such as *quand, lorsque, aussitôt que, dès que, sitôt que, dès lors que, tant que, après que, une fois que.*

Quand elle **viendra** (NOT *vient), je le lui dirai

Il arrivera **dès que** je **serai parti** (NOT *suis parti)

Une fois que nous **serons passés** à l'hôtel je pourrai enfin me débarrasser de ces valises
Once we've been to the hotel I will finally be able to get rid of these suitcases

A good indicator that the event has yet to happen is the verb in the other clause, which will be in a future tense, conditional tense, etc., in English: 'He *will* arrive as soon as I have left' (see also Section 17.3.2).

10.4.4 Use of tenses with *depuis, il y a, pendant,* and *pour*

depuis

In clauses containing the preposition *depuis* 'for' or 'since', the tense of the verb differs systematically between French and English.

(a) In the case of the present, there are two points in time, now and an event in the past. Where the consequences of the event in the past continue into the present, from the perspective of the speaker, French uses a present tense, while English uses the perfect:

Je **suis** ici depuis plus d'un an
*I **have been** here for more than a year*
(My being here continues at the time I am speaking)

Elle **habite** notre village depuis Pâques
*She **has been** living in our village since Easter*
(She is still living there at the time of speaking)

However, if the event does **not** have consequences which continue into the present, a past tense form of the verb will be used in French:

Il n'**est** pas **venu** ici depuis plus d'un an
He hasn't been here for more than a year
(The last time he was here was over a year ago, so the event does not continue at the time of speaking)

Il **a arrêté** de fumer depuis plus d'un an
He has stopped smoking for more than a year
(His giving up smoking was an event which was completed more than a year ago and so does not continue at the time of speaking)

Compare with:

Il **fume** depuis plus d'un an
He has been smoking for more than a year
(His smoking started more than a year ago and continues into the present)

(b) In the case of the past, there are also two points in time: one in the past and one further back in the past. If the consequences of the event further back in the past continue forwards to the event in the past, French uses the imperfect tense where English uses the pluperfect:

J'**étais** là depuis plus d'un an
*I **had been** there for more than a year*

But if the more distant event does not have continuing consequences, a pluperfect form of the verb will be used in French:

Il **avait arrêté** de fumer depuis plus d'un an quand il est tombé malade
He had stopped smoking for more than a year when he became ill

(For *depuis que*, see Section 17.3.4.)

il y a

By contrast *il y a* 'ago' focuses on the completion of an event in the past, and the tense used in French is a past tense, just as it is in English:

Je **suis arrivé** il y a un an
I arrived a year ago

Elle **a commencé** à habiter notre village il y a six mois
She began living in our village six months ago

Nous y **sommes allés** il y a plus de dix ans
We went there more than ten years ago

pendant

pendant 'for', enables the speaker to indicate the length of time associated with an event, whether it is in the present, future, or is a completed event in the past: It can sometimes be translated in English by 'during':

Nathan prétend qu'il **veut** maintenir son silence pendant trois semaines
Nathan says that he wants to keep quiet about it for three weeks

Ensuite nous **irons** passer des vacances en Irlande pendant quinze jours
After that we will spend a fortnight on holiday in Ireland

J'y **suis resté** pendant trois semaines l'année dernière
I stayed there for three weeks last year

(For *il y a un mois que* ... 'it's a month since ...', *voilà/voici plusieurs ans que* ... 'it's several years since ...', see Section 17.3.4.)

pour

Pour 'for' is generally used to indicate an intended length of time in the future and is most frequently associated with the verbs *aller, venir,* and *partir*. It does not normally occur with *rester*. It is preferred in such usage to *pendant*.

J'**irai** à Londres **pour** trois semaines à partir de demain
I'll be in London for three weeks from tomorrow

Je **viendrai** à Rome **pour** le week-end
I will come to Rome for the weekend

Je me suis inscrite dans un bureau partagé **pour** six mois
I took up memberhsip of a co-working space for six months

But:

Je suis resté trois semaines à Londres
I stayed in London for three weeks

(See section 13.47.)

10.5 Other tenses indicating the time at which events occur relative to other events

10.5.1 The pluperfect tense

Whereas the simple past and compound past tenses refer to events completed in the past from the perspective of the speaker or writer, the pluperfect describes events completed at some point even before these past events:

La police laissa une balise pour indiquer où l'accident **était arrivé**
The police left a marker to show where the accident happened/had happened
(Pluperfect – an event which occurred prior to the police marking the spot)

Je n'ai pas pris la route déserte par où nous **étions venus**
I didn't take the very quiet road along which we had come
(Pluperfect – an event which occurred prior to me taking a different road)

10.5.2 The past anterior tense

The past anterior is not used very frequently and can only occur in texts in which the simple past is used. It has two functions:

(a) It refers to a past event which **immediately** precedes another past event described by the simple past (as opposed to one past event preceding another without any specification of the length of the period between the two events – in this case a pluperfect would be used).

A typical context for the past anterior is a clause introduced by the conjunctions *quand, lorsque* 'when', *aussitôt que, dès que, sitôt que, dès lors que* 'as soon as', *tant que* 'as long as', *après que* 'after', *une fois que* 'once':

Après qu'elle **fut sortie**, il **enleva** la nappe
After she left, he removed the tablecloth
(Her leaving immediately preceded his removing the tablecloth)

Dès que j'**eus fini**, je **me rendis** chez moi
As soon as I had finished, I went home
(My finishing immediately preceded my going home)

(b) It is used with adverbs such as *vite* 'quickly', *bientôt* 'soon', where the idea of speed or urgency is expressed, and the verb would otherwise be in the pluperfect:

Elle **eut** bientôt écrit la lettre
She had soon written the letter

Il **fut** vite envoyé chercher un médecin
He had quickly been sent to fetch a doctor

(See also Section 17.3.3.)

10.5.3 The double compound past and compound pluperfect tenses

The double compound past tense and compound pluperfect tense can be used in spoken French where the past anterior is used in written French, to describe an event which immediately precedes another past event (typically in clauses introduced by *quand* and *lorsque* 'when', etc. – see Section 10.5.2), or to express speed or urgency. Where the verb describing the main past event is in a compound past tense form, the verb describing the preceding event is in a double compound past form:

Ils ont gardé le silence pendant tout mon discours, mais ils **ont applaudi** quand j'**ai eu fini**
They were quiet throughout my speech but they applauded when I had finished
(The main past event is their applauding, and the verb is in a compound past form; my finishing the speech immediately precedes their applauding, and is in a double compound past form)

Where the verb describing the main past event is in a pluperfect tense form, the verb describing the preceding event is in a compound pluperfect form:

Quand ils **avaient eu fini** de préparer leurs questions, ils les **avaient données** au Président de séance
When they had finished preparing their questions, they had given them to the Chair of the session
(The main past event is their having given the questions to the Chair, and the verb is in a pluperfect form; their finishing preparing the questions immediately precedes their giving the questions to the Chair and is in a compound pluperfect form)

In expressing speed or urgency, only the double compound past tense is possible:

J'**ai eu** vite fini le livre
I quickly finished the book

The use of the double compound past and compound pluperfect tenses is not obligatory and is in fact relatively rare. Ordinary compound past and pluperfect tenses are the normal forms to use in these contexts.

10.5.4 The compound future tense (future perfect)

Typically the compound future tense describes a future event from the perspective of its completion (as opposed to the future tense, which views an event simply from the perspective of its futurity). It usually corresponds to English 'will have':

J'**aurai** fini mon travail dès lundi
I will have finished my work from Monday
(versus: *Je finirai mon travail lundi* 'I will finish my work on Monday')

Given this perspective, a compound future can describe an event which takes place before another event in the future:

J'**aurai fini** mon travail avant de partir en vacances
I will have finished my work before going on holiday

The compound future can also be the equivalent of English 'may have', when a speaker is speculating about an event which may have occurred before another in the past

Elle **aura éteint** son portable avant l'arrivée de la gendarmerie vingt minutes plus tard.
She may have switched off her mobile before the police got there twenty minutes later.

10.5.5 **The compound conditional tense (conditional perfect)**

The compound conditional has four main functions:

(a) It refers to events which would have taken place if certain conditions had been met (but weren't):

Ç'**aurait été** la chute du gouvernement, s'il y avait eu des élections à ce moment-là
The government would have fallen if there had been elections at that time

Tu l'**aurais vu** partir si tu étais venu plus tôt
You would have seen him leave if you had come earlier

(b) In reported speech (see Section 10.7), it is the equivalent of a compound future in direct speech:

Direct speech:	Il a dit: 'J'aurai fini mon travail avant de partir en vacances' *He said: 'I will have finished my work before going on holiday'*
Reported speech:	Il a dit qu'il **aurait fini** son travail avant de partir en vacances *He said he would have finished his work before going on holiday*

(c) The compound conditional can be used to indicate that the speaker is stating something as a possible fact and not as a certainty, most often a fact asserted by others:

Le Président **serait** déjà **parti** pour l'Allemagne
(It is said that) the President may have already left for Germany
(i.e. I have been told he has but I am not repeating it as a fact)

Selon mes collègues, j'**aurais annoncé** que j'allais prendre ma retraite
According to my colleagues, I claimed that I was going to retire

This is widely used in the press to express unsubstantiated or alleged facts:

On ne sait donc toujours pas si l'assassin présumé, qui **aurait avoué** son crime, était bien le seul tireur ou s'il avait été aidé de plusieurs complices
*We therefore still do not know whether the suspected killer, who **has allegedly admitted** his crime, was indeed the only one who fired or whether he was helped by several accomplices*

(d) In formal French the compound conditional can be used as an alternative to a *si* clause containing a verb in the pluperfect (see also Section 17.3.7):

Il me l'**aurait dit** plus tôt, j'aurais pu m'y prendre autrement
S'il me l'**avait dit** plus tôt, j'aurais pu m'y prendre autrement
If he'd told me earlier, I could have done it another way

10.5.6 **The double compound future**

The double compound future can be used (but need not be) to describe an event completed in the future **immediately** before another future event. Typical contexts where it might be found are clauses introduced by *dès que, quand, lorsque, aussitôt que*, etc. (see Section 10.5.2 for the list):

Dès qu'ils **auront eu bu** leur café, il faudra qu'ils se dépêchent de partir
As soon as they have drunk their coffee, they will have to hurry up and leave

10.6 **Combining tenses**

When it is necessary to use tenses to indicate one moment in time relative to another, French is much more precise than English. In many sentences one clause establishes the main tense and another situates a second event in relation to it. When this is the case, it is essential to express the relative time relationship clearly in French by use of the appropriate tense as exemplified below.

10.6.1 **Time relative to the present**

(a) Assuming that one clause of a sentence relates to the present, events which precede the present will be in:

the **imperfect** if one wishes to stress the duration of the action;

the **compound past (perfect)** if one wishes to link the past action to the present or to leave that possibility open;

and in the **simple past (past historic)** if one wishes to indicate, in written French mainly, that the action is definitely completed.

The English sentence:

She often played the violin, now she no longer picks up her instrument

could be rendered into French in each of the following ways, depending on which of three possible meanings is intended:

(i) If 'played' refers to a habitual action in the past compared with the situation now, then the imperfect will be the appropriate tense:

Elle **jouait** souvent du violon, maintenant elle ne touche plus son instrument
(*jouait* indicates that she was in the habit of playing the violin: a meaning which could have been conveyed by the English 'used to' or 'would')

(ii) If 'played' refers to an event completed in the past but possibly still relevant to the present, then the compound past (perfect) will be the appropriate tense:

Elle **a souvent joué** du violon, maintenant elle ne touche plus son instrument
(*a joué* indicates that on several occasions in the past, she played the violin: it is neutral about whether she still plays it or not but leaves open that possibility)

(iii) If 'played' refers to an event (or a repeated set of events) seen as completed in the past and with no relevance to the present, the simple past (past historic) will be the appropriate tense in writing:

Elle **joua** souvent du violon, maintenant elle ne touche plus son instrument
(*joua* suggests that for a specified period in the past (e.g. up to the age of ten), she played the violin but that the event is sharply cut off from the present)

(b) Assuming that one clause of the sentence relates to the present, events which follow the present will be expressed through the future:

J'exige une excellente performance de mes employés aujourd'hui, et je l'**exigerai** encore demain
I demand a high-level of performance from my employees now and I will continue to do so in the future

Il pleut aujourd'hui et il **va** pleuvoir encore demain
It's raining today and it will rain again tomorrow

(c) An event which occurs immediately before an event which is in the present can be expressed by the present tense of *venir de*. The English translation usually involves 'just':

Mais non! Tu ne fais que répéter ce que je **viens de** te dire!
Not at all! You are simply repeating what I have just told you!

Nous **venons de** présenter nos idées aux clients
We have just presented our ideas to the clients

Nous reviendrons sur la question que nous **venons d'**évoquer
We will come back again to the topic we have just been discussing

10.6.2 **Time relative to the past**

(a) Assuming that one clause of a sentence indicates that an event has taken place in the past, the following forms are used to indicate events further in the past than the given past event. Where the past event is expressed by the compound past (perfect) or the simple past (past historic), an event further in the past will be expressed by the pluperfect (see Section 10.5.1), or, in certain styles, the past anterior (see Section 10.5.2). These differences are frequently not expressed in the equivalent English sentences where simple past forms are used:

Elle **a voulu** revendre le meuble dès qu'elle l'avait acheté
She wanted to sell the piece of furniture as soon as she bought it

Quand elle **eut fini** son dernier morceau, elle entama le bis
When (or as soon as) she finished playing her last piece, she started the encore

It is frequently possible for English to use the pluperfect 'had bought', 'had finished playing', etc. but most often users prefer the simpler forms and leave the interpretation to the reader: normally it is clear in context what is meant. However, despite the fact that English frequently does not mark these temporal distinctions, they cannot be left vague in French:

Papa veut savoir à quelle heure elle **est** rentrée hier soir
Dad wants to know at what time she came in last night

Papa a voulu savoir à quelle heure elle **était** rentrée hier soir
Dad wanted to know at what time she came in last night

On déposa des fleurs sur le trottoir pour indiquer où l'accident **était** arrivé
Flowers were left (or people left flowers) on the pavement to show where the accident happened

Quand je suis entré dans la pièce je me suis rendu compte que Nathan **était** arrivé avant moi
*When I went into the room I realized that Nathan **had got there** before me*

(b) The double compound past is used in cases where it is required that the event further in the past is marked as completed:

Ils ont gardé le silence pendant tout mon discours, mais ils ont applaudi quand j'ai **eu fini**
*They were quiet throughout my speech but they applauded when **I had finished***

(c) The compound conditional is used to refer to a hypothetical event related to an event in the past:

Nous **aurions fait** une offre pour votre appartement si nous en avions entendu parler à temps
We would have put in an offer for your flat if we had heard of it in time

Vous **auriez pu** l'acheter si vous aviez voulu
You could have bought it if you had wanted to

(d) The imperfect of *venir de* can be used when one event is indicated as just having been completed prior to another one already expressed in the past tense. Note that the French imperfect must be translated by an English pluperfect 'had told/presented etc.':

Il ne faisait que répéter ce que je **venais de** lui dire
He simply repeated what I had just told him

Nous **venions de** conclure notre présentation quand la panne d'électricité est survenue
We had just finished our presentation when there was a power cut

La question que nous **venions d'**évoquer avait soulevé beaucoup de controverse
The matter we had just discussed raised a great deal of controversy

10.6.3 **Time relative to the future**

(a) A sequential relationship between two events in the future can be expressed through the compound future:

Est-ce qu'elle **aura fini** ses devoirs **avant de partir** demain matin?
Will she have finished her homework before she leaves tomorrow morning?

marks a future action which **precedes** the indicated future point in time.

Est-ce qu'elle **finira** ses devoirs **après avoir pris** sa douche demain matin?
Will she finish her homework after having her shower tomorrow morning?

marks a future action which follows the indicated future point in time. (Note the preferred translation with '-ing'.)

Une fois que nous **serons passés** à l'hôtel je **pourrai** enfin me débarrasser de ces valises
Once we've been to the hotel I will finally be able to get rid of these suitcases

Lorsqu'il m'**aura fourni** des explications valables, nous **pourrons** nous mettre d'accord sur la solution à adopter
Once he has provided me with a satisfactory explanation, we shall be able to agree on the solution to be chosen

both mark a future action which **precedes** another future action. (Note the translation into English by a present perfect.)

(b) The double compound future is used to indicate the completed nature of the event preceding another event in the future:

Quand vous **aurez eu fini** de préparer vos questions, vous les **présenterez** au Président de séance
When you have finished preparing your questions, you (will) give them to the Chair of the session

10.7 **Tenses in direct and reported descriptions of events**

When descriptions of events (e.g. *Le prisonnier s'est évadé par la fenêtre* 'The prisoner escaped through the window') or the utterances of others ('direct speech' – e.g. *"Je viens demain"* 'I'm coming tomorrow') are **reported** to a third party, the tense of the verb in the original sentence can change in certain circumstances, and there may also be consequential changes in any associated time adverbs:

Direct description:	Le prisonnier **s'est évadé** par la fenêtre *The prisoner escaped through the window*
Reported description:	La police croyait que le prisonnier **s'était évadé** par la fenêtre *The police thought that the prisoner had escaped through the window*
Direct speech:	Je **viens demain** *I'm coming tomorrow*
Reported speech:	Il a dit qu'il **venait le lendemain** *He said that he was coming the following day*

(For the choice of appropriate time adverbs, see Section 5.6.15.)

Verbs which introduce reported descriptions or reported speech are those such as *dire que* 'to say that', *expliquer que* 'to explain that', *penser que, croire que* 'to think, believe that', *maintenir que* 'to maintain that', *prétendre que* 'to claim that', etc.

Mostly, the tense of the verb in the **reported** clause is the same as the tense of the verb in the original statement or utterance. But where the **reporting** verb is in a past tense – imperfect, compound past/simple past or pluperfect – the following systematic changes occur in the tense of the reported verb:

Original tense		Reported tense
present	→	imperfect
(compound) future	→	(compound) conditional
compound/simple past	→	pluperfect

Table 10.A illustrates the pattern.

TABLE 10.A Tenses following a reporting verb in a past tense

Direct description	Reporting verb (imperfect, compound or simple past, pluperfect)	Reported verb
Elle parle (present) *She is speaking*	Ils croyaient qu' Ils ont cru/crurent qu' *They thought that* Ils avaient cru qu' *They had thought that*	elle parlait (imperfect) *she was speaking/spoke*
Elle parlera (future) *She will speak*	Ils croyaient qu' Ils ont cru/crurent qu' *They thought that*	elle parlerait (conditional) *she would speak*
Elle aura parlé (compound future) *She will have spoken*	Ils avaient cru qu' *They thought that*	elle aurait parlé (compound conditional) *she would have spoken*
Elle a parlé (compound past) *She spoke/has spoken*	Ils croyaient qu' Ils ont cru/crurent qu' *They thought that*	elle avait parlé (pluperfect) *she had spoken*
Elle parla (simple past) *She spoke*	Ils avaient cru qu' *They had thought that*	

Other tenses of reported verbs remain the same as the original. To take some typical examples:

Direct description	Reported
Elle parlait	Ils avaient cru qu'elle parlait *They had thought that she was speaking*
Elle aurait parlé	Ils ont cru qu'elle aurait parlé *They thought that she would have spoken*
Elle avait parlé	Ils croyaient qu'elle avait parlé *They thought that she had spoken*

And where the **reporting** verb is in a non-past tense (i.e. present or any form of the (compound) future or (compound) conditional) the tense of the reported verb remains the same as the original:

Direct description	Reported
Elle parle	Ils croiraient qu'elle parle *They would think that she is speaking*

Elle parlera

Ils croient qu'elle parlera
They think that she will speak

Elle a parlé

Ils auraient cru qu'elle a parlé
They would have thought that she spoke

10.8 **Tenses with** *si*

si has two distinct functions. One is to introduce indirect questions and corresponds to English 'if' when it can also mean 'whether': *Elle m'a demandé* **si** *je voulais y aller* 'She asked me **if/whether** I wanted to go there'. Tenses following indirect question *si* are determined in exactly the same way as for reported speech, as described in Section 10.7 (see also Section 17.3.6).

The other function of *si* is to introduce 'hypothetical clauses'. In this use, it corresponds to English 'if' when it cannot alternate with 'whether', e.g. 'I won't stay if (NOT *whether) he comes' *Je ne resterai pas s'il vient*. The tense of the verb in the hypothetical *si* clause can never be in the (compound) future or (compound) conditional tense. Rather, it will typically obey one of the following patterns:

A. The speaker's mind is made up and the hypothetical event is presented as close to a fact

C'est d'accord, je passe une tête à ton anniversaire ce soir mais je ne **reste** pas s'il **vient**
Ok, I will show up for your birthday party tonight but I'm not staying if he comes

C'est d'accord, je passe (or je passerai) une tête à ton anniversaire ce soir mais je ne **resterai** pas s'il **vient**
Ok, I will show up for your birthday party tonight but I won't stay if he comes

B. The speaker is more doubtful of the likelihood of the hypothetical event

C'est d'accord, je passe (or je passerai) une tête à ton anniversaire ce soir mais je ne **resterais** pas s'il **venait**
Ok, I will show up for your birthday party tonight but I wouldn't stay if he came

J'espère que tu ne l'as pas invité, parce que je ne **resterais** pas s'il **venait**
I hope you didn't invite him, because I wouldn't stay if he came

C. The event is now past and the speaker is going over what he or she intended to do at the time

Heureusement, il n'était pas invité : je ne **serais** pas **resté** s'il **venait/était venu**
Fortunately he wasn't invited : I wouldn't have stayed if he came/had come

Heureusement, il n'était pas invité : je ne **restais** pas s'il **venait**
Fortunately he wasn't invited : I wasn't staying if he was coming

FREE

INSTRUCTOR & STUDENT RESOURCES

For more resources to practice your French grammar, including practice activities/quizzes for students, further resource links, and an instructor guide, please visit https://routledgelearning.com/frenchgrammarandusage.

11 The subjunctive, modal verbs, exclamatives, and imperatives

11.1 The attitude of the subject to events: The subjunctive

The **subjunctive** is expressed by a particular set of forms which verbs can typically take only in subordinate clauses (but see Section 11.4.4 for an exception). Verb forms that are not those of the subjunctive (e.g. the simple present, imperfect, simple past, compound past) are traditionally called the **indicative**. This distinction is used in this chapter for expository purposes. The selection of the subjunctive in a subordinate clause (rather than the normal indicative) is always determined by the nature of the clause on which it is dependent.

> It should be noted that in many cases, **there is no choice** about whether to use the subjunctive or indicative: certain types of main clause ALWAYS select the subjunctive in a dependent subordinate clause; others ALWAYS select the indicative. However, some main clause constructions are ambiguous and allow the verb in a dependent subordinate clause to be either subjunctive or indicative: the choice of one or the other produces different meanings.

The majority of main clause constructions which select the subjunctive have a general property in common, and it is useful to consider the subjunctive from this perspective. The subjunctive is selected in a subordinate clause where the subject of the main clause views the event described in the subordinate clause **with a significant degree of personal interpretation**. This notion of 'personal interpretation' can be broken down into three types, which are illustrated below:

(a) The subject judges an event to be more towards the 'unlikely' end of a scale going from 'probable' to 'unlikely'.
(b) The subject projects his or her personal desires or feelings on to an event.
(c) The subject cannot present an event as probable from his or her point of view because it is in some way conditional on other events, is hypothetical, is unknowable or is simply vague.

Subjunctive: Dependent on the subject's belief that an event is unlikely to occur

Where the subject of the main clause expresses a belief in the relative probability of an event's occurring (whether in the past or the future), the indicative will be used. For example, expressions like the following give rise to the indicative in dependent subordinate clauses:

Alban affirme que		*Alban declares that*	
Alban pense que	Sofiane **est venu**	*Alban thinks that*	*Sofiane came*
Alban imagine que		*Alban reckons that*	

In the case of impersonal subjects – *il est certain que, il est probable que*, etc. – or with verbs where the subject is in the first person – *je crois que, j'imagine que*, etc. – it is the speaker of the sentence who expresses a belief in the **probability** of an event's occurring and this equally gives rise to the indicative:

DOI: 10.4324/9781003373926-11

| Je crois que
Je juge que
Je pense que
Je suppose que
Il est certain que
Il est probable que | } Sofiane **viendra** | *I believe that*
I reckon that
I think that
I suppose that
It's certain that
It's probable that | } *Sofiane will come* |

BUT where the main clause expresses the subject's belief that an event is **unlikely** to occur or to have occurred, the **subjunctive** is required. For example, where the above expressions are negated or questioned, or when other terms suggesting less certainty are used, the event becomes more 'unlikely' than 'probable'. This gives rise to the subjunctive in dependent subordinate clauses:

Alban ne pense pas que Alban n'imagine pas que, etc.	} Sofiane **soit venu**	*Alban doesn't think that* *Alban doesn't imagine* *that*, etc.	} *Sofiane came*
Je ne crois pas que Il n'est pas certain que Il est possible que, etc.	} Sofiane **vienne**	*I don't believe that* *It's not certain that* *It's possible that*, etc.	} *Sofiane will come*
Est-il certain que Crois-tu que, etc.	} Sofiane **vienne?**	*Is it certain that…* *Do you think that*, etc.	} *Sofiane will come?*
Est-ce que Alban pense que Est-ce que Alban imagine que, etc.	} Sofiane **soit venu?**	*Does Alban think that …* *Does Alban imagine that,* etc.	} *Sofiane came?*

Subjunctive: Dependent on the subject's attitude to an event

Where the construction which introduces the subordinate clause inherently presents the event as simply a matter of fact, the indicative will be used. For example, after the verb *savoir que* 'to know that' the indicative will always be used because *savoir que* states the subject's view of an event as a matter of fact, uncoloured by a significant degree of personal interpretation:

Il sait que Sofiane est venu
(*il sait que* states 'Sofiane's having come' as a factual reality)

BUT where the construction which introduces the subordinate clause inherently expresses the subject's personal desires or feelings, the subjunctive will be required. For example, after the verb *regretter que* 'to be sorry that', the subjunctive will always be used because *regretter* places the event in the context of an emotional, personal interpretation by the subject:

Il regrette que Sofiane **soit venu** ('Sofiane's having come' is not in doubt, but *il regrette que* expresses a personal attitude towards that event)

Thus, where a subject places a particular personal interpretation on an event described in a subordinate clause, the **subjunctive** is likely to be used – even if the factual reality of the event is not in doubt. It is the attitude towards the event, the way the subject wishes it to be seen, which is more important than the reality or otherwise of the event. For example, Josette Alia, writing in the Nouvel Observateur in 1990 about the beginning of the feminist movement wrote:

L'essentiel, pour nous, était que le scandale **fût** là
The most important thing for us was that there should have been a scandal

To have written the following, equally grammatical, sentence would have changed the meaning in an important way:

> L'essentiel, pour nous, était que le scandale **fut** là
> *The most important thing for us was that there **was** a scandal*

In using the subjunctive Josette Alia does not lay the stress on the concept that there actually was a scandal (although she certainly thinks that there was) because that, from her point of view, is not what is important: she wishes to stress that the important thing was for the early feminists (with whom she identifies herself) to have created one – hence the subjunctive.

Subjunctive: Dependent on the subject's view of an event as conditional, hypothetical, unknowable or vague

In cases where the idea of conditionality is expressed overtly through the conditional word *si*, the indicative is always used (for tenses with *si*, see Section 10.8):

> **Si tu finis** l'enregistrement demain, nous mettrons le morceau en ligne tout de suite.
> *If you finish recording the piece tomorrow, we will upload it immediately*

> S'ils **avaient répondu** à mon premier SMS, j'aurais arrêté de les relancer
> *If they had replied to my first text, I would have stopped bothering them*

BUT certain expressions introducing dependent clauses place a condition on an event; the subject can then only present it as something which, from his or her point of view, is possible in certain circumstances, but no more than that. Therefore, with expressions such as *à condition que* 'on the condition that' and *à moins que* 'unless', the subjunctive is obligatory:

> Je veux bien y aller, à condition qu'on **prenne** nos vélos
> *I'd be very pleased to go, as long as we use our bikes*

> Thibault devra changer d'avis à moins qu'il **veuille** qu'on le prenne pour un imbécile
> *Thibault will have to change his mind unless he wants people to think he is a complete idiot*

When time constraints make the outcome of events unknowable by the subject, references to events in an unknown time scale tend to be in the subjunctive: *avant que* 'before' and *jusqu'à ce que* 'until' must be followed by the subjunctive:

> Avant que tu (ne) me le **dises**, je te promets que je serai là à l'heure
> *Before you say anything to me, I promise that I will be there on time*

> Je serai inquiète jusqu'à ce qu'il **soit rentré** chez lui et qu'il m'**ait envoyé** un SMS
> *I will be worried until he has got home and sent me a text.*

When subjects are confronted with a degree of vagueness which means that they do not know enough about the situation to be certain of anything they say, the subjunctive is used: *quoi que, quel(le(s)) que* 'whichever, whatever' must be followed by the subjunctive:

> Quoi que je **fasse**, je n'arrive pas à valider mon inscription sur le site
> *Whatever I do, I can't manage to register on the site.*

> Quels que **soient** ses problèmes, je ne vois pas très bien comment je pourrais l'aider
> *Whatever her problems may be, I can't easily see how I could help her*

SUMMARY
Contexts which give rise to the subjunctive
(a) The subjunctive is used mainly in subordinate clauses (but see 11.4.4).
(b) The subordinate clause is dependent on constructions which express a significant degree of personal interpretation of events: these interpretations present events as more unlikely than probable, and/or in a way which is coloured by the desires or feelings of the subject, and/or as conditional, hypothetical or unknowable.

N.B.: **(i)** As noted earlier, in the great majority of cases where the subjunctive is used, there is no choice: it is required after the relevant expression. However, in some limited subordinate contexts there is a genuine choice between using the indicative and the subjunctive because the construction on which the subordinate clause is dependent can be used with more than one meaning. This is the case in the example from Josette Alia used above. It is also the case in the following examples:

A speaker trying to find a suitable taxi might say:

Je cherche un taxi qui **a** deux sièges bébé
I'm looking for a taxi which has two child seats

This would be used if the speaker is reasonably sure that there is such a taxi available (i.e. 'I know there are taxis around with child seats – I'm looking for one of them'). By contrast, if the speaker said:

Je cherche un taxi qui **ait** deux sièges bébé
I'm looking for a taxi which has two child seats

he or she would be expressing reservations about whether such a taxi is likely to be available (i.e. 'I'm looking for any taxi with child seats – I don't know if there are any').

An irate parent waiting for a teenager who is coming in late might say:

Je suppose que tu **vas** me dire que tu es allé au cinéma avec ta copine
I suppose you're going to tell me that you went to the cinema with your girl friend.

The indicative is used because the parent wants to express his or her certainty about what excuses are likely to be offered.

By contrast, an insurance agent wanting to sell holiday insurance to a client might say:

Supposez toujours que vous **soyez** aux Etats-Unis et que vous **tombiez** malade, qu'est-ce que vous allez faire sans assurance?
Just suppose that you are in the United States and you fall ill, how could you manage without health insurance?

Here the whole issue is hypothetical. Hence the subjunctive.

(ii) Although the subjunctive is typically marked in verbs in subordinate clauses introduced by *que*, **not every subordinate clause introduced by** *que* **requires the verb to be in the subjunctive** – in fact most of them don't! It is only when the subordinate clause is dependent on a construction which expresses a significant degree of subjective interpretation of the event along the lines described above, usually through the use of one of the specific ways of introducing the subordinate clause, that the subjunctive is used.

11.1.1 **Forms of the subjunctive**

The conjugation of verbs in the subjunctive is described fully in Chapter 7. Here is a brief summary of the way that regular verbs form the subjunctive in the various tenses (but see Chapter 7 for irregular verbs).

Present subjunctive

For many verbs, take the third-person plural, present tense form of the indicative, delete *-ent*: for example:

(ils)	parlent	→	parl-
	finissent	→	finiss-
	dorment	→	dorm-
	vendent	→	vend-
	reçoivent	→	reçoiv-

and add the endings:

-e
-es
-e
-ions
-iez
-ent

for example:

parl*e*, parl*es*, parl*e*, parl*ions*, parl*iez*, parl*ent*
finiss*e*, finiss*es*, finiss*e*, finiss*ions*, finiss*iez*, finiss*ent*, etc.

N.B.: The stem *reçoiv-* changes when the ending does not begin with *-e*: *reçoive, reçoives, reçoive,* ***recevions, receviez, reçoivent.***

Imperfect subjunctive

For many verbs, take the first-person singular, simple past tense form of the indicative, delete the last letter: for example:

(je)	parlai	→	parla-
	finis	→	fini-
	dormis	→	dormi-
	vendis	→	vendi-
	reçus	→	reçu-

and add the endings:

-sse
-sses
-^t
-ssions
-ssiez
-ssent

for example:

parla*sse*, parla*sses*, parl*ât*, parla*ssions*, parla*ssiez*, parla*ssent*
fini*sse*, fini*sses*, fin*ît*, fini*ssions*, fini*ssiez*, fini*ssent*
reçu*sse*, reçu*sses*, reç*ût*, reçu*ssions*, reçu*ssiez*, reçu*ssent*, etc.

Compound past and pluperfect subjunctive

The compound past subjunctive is formed from the present subjunctive forms of *avoir* or *être*, as appropriate, followed by the past participle. The pluperfect subjunctive is formed from the imperfect subjunctive of *avoir* or *être*, as appropriate, followed by the past participle. (See Chapter 7 for details.)

11.1.2 Which tense of the subjunctive should be used?

In formal French, it is still possible to use all of the tenses of the subjunctive: present, imperfect, compound past and pluperfect. In such cases the tense to use is determined in a broadly similar way to the choice of tenses with indicative forms of the verb (see Chapter 10). The only difference is that because there is no future or conditional subjunctive, the present tense form of the subjunctive is normally used in contexts where the future or conditional would be appropriate.

However, in less formal French, and generally in informal French, only the present tense and the compound past tense of the subjunctive are used. In this case, the present tense forms of the subjunctive typically cover all cases where present, imperfect, simple past, future or conditional tenses of the indicative would be used. For example:

Nous préférons qu'il **soit** au courant
We prefer him to know about it
(Compare: *Nous savons qu'il **est** au courant* – present tense)

Les enseignants se plaignaient que les élèves ne **sachent** pas distinguer les infos des infox.
Teachers used to complain that pupils didn't know how to differentiate between news and fake news.
(Compare: *Les enseignants disaient que les élèves ne **savaient** pas distinguer les infos des intox.* – imperfect tense)

Les visiteurs admiraient les fauves dans leur enclos jusqu'à ce que le léopard **saute** par-dessus la barrière.
The visitors were admiring the big cats in their enclosure until the leopard jumped over the fence.
(Compare: *Les visiteurs admiraient les fauves dans leur enclos. Mais alors le léopard **sauta** par-dessus la barrière.* – simple past tense)

Votre lettre de résiliation ne prendra pas effet à moins que vous ne la **renvoyiez** signée des quatre co-propriétaires
Your cancellation letter won't take effect unless you send it back signed by all four co-owners. (Compare: *Vous ne la **renverrez** pas signée des quatre co-propriétaires? Alors votre lettre de résiliation ne prendra pas effet* – future tense)

Il serait peu probable que des stagiaires **sachent** restaurer une commode Renaissance
It would be unlikely that trainees would know how to restore a Renaissance chest of drawers (Compare: *Il serait probable que des stagaires **sauraient** restaurer une commode Renaissance* – conditional tense)

The compound past tense forms of the subjunctive typically cover all cases where compound past, pluperfect, compound future or compound conditional tenses of the indicative would be used. For example:

Quoiqu'ils **aient fait** de gros efforts, l'entreprise reste en difficulté
Although they have made considerable efforts, the company is still in difficulty
(Compare: *Ils **ont fait** de gros efforts, mais l'entreprise reste en difficulté* – compound past tense)

Avez-vous douté même quelques instants que la photo **ait été** authentique?
Did you doubt even for a moment that the photo was authentic?
(Compare: *Il avait douté quelques instants: pour lui la photo **n'avait** peut-être pas **été** authentique* – pluperfect tense)

Je n'avais même pas imaginé que la photo **ait pu** être authentique!
I hadn't even imagined that the photo might have been authentic
(Compare: *La photo avait pu être authentique, mais ça, je ne l'**avais** même pas **imaginé**!* – pluperfect tense)

Quoi que mes parents **aient décidé**, je n'y consentirai pas
Whatever my parents have decided, I won't agree to it
(Compare: *Mes parents **auront décidé**, mais quoi que ce soit je n'y consentirai pas* – compound future tense)

Crois-tu que Crémieux **ait fini** les travaux en temps voulu s'il n'y avait pas eu la pandémie ?
Do you believe that Crémieux would have finished the job on time if the pandemic hadn't happened? (Compare: *Je crois que Crémieux **aurait fini** les travaux en temps voulu s'il n'y avait pas eu la pandémie* – compound conditional tense)

Where it would seem that it might be necessary to use imperfect subjunctive forms ending in –(*a*)*sse* (*i*)*sse* (*u*)*sse*, especially in any person other than the first or third – e.g. *il aurait fallu que tu reçusses les visiteurs plus tôt* – 'you should have received the visitors earlier' – it is sensible to see if there are other ways of expressing the same idea which would allow you to avoid these forms which may be considered ugly, comical or pretentious: e.g. *Est-ce que tu aurais pu recevoir les visiteurs plus tôt?* Or *Peut-être aurais-tu pu* (alternative – *peut-être que tu aurais pu*) *recevoir les visiteurs plus tôt*.

11.1.3 Subjunctive after verbs, adjectives and nouns which express the personal desires, orders, expectations, fears, regrets or other emotional states of the subject in relation to the event

Verbs and adjectives

Verbs and adjectives of wishing, ordering, expressing fears and other emotional states are normally followed by subjunctive subordinate clauses. The verb in subordinate clauses dependent on the following verbs is almost always in the subjunctive:

aimer que	*to wish that*
attendre que	*to wait for*
s'attendre à ce que	*to expect that*
avoir envie que	*to really want that*
commander que	*to order that*
consentir à ce que	*to agree or to accept that*
être content que	*to be pleased that*

craindre que	*to fear that*
demander que	*to ask that*
désirer que	*to wish that*
être désolé que	*to be sorry that*
être dommage que	*to be a pity or to be regretted that*
douter que	*to doubt that*
s'étonner que	*to be surprised that*
exiger que	*to require that*
être heureux que	*to be happy that*
insister pour que	*to insist that*
ordonner que	*to order that*
permettre que	*to allow that*
avoir peur que	*to be afraid that*
préférer que	*to prefer that*
être ravi que	*to be delighted that*
regretter que	*to regret that*
se réjouir que	*to rejoice that*
souhaiter que	*to wish that*
être surpris que	*to be surprised that*
tenir à ce que	*to be anxious that*
être triste que	*to be sad that*
veiller à ce que	*to be careful that*
vouloir que	*to want that*

J'aimerais que tous les invités **puissent** repartir avec de merveilleux souvenirs
I would like all the guests to be able to leave with wonderful memories

'Attendez que ma joie **revienne** et que **soit** mort le souvenir …' (chanson de Barbara)
'Wait until I can be happy again and for the memory to die …'

Je consens à ce que que tu **fasses** ce stage de photo mais n'oublie pas que tu devras quand-même aller à tes cours
I agree that you can go on this photography course, but don't forget that you will still have to go to your lectures

Je crains que cela (ne) **soit** une infox
I'm afraid that may be fake news

On regrette que la patinoire n'**ait** pas **prévenu** le public de sa fermeture exceptionnelle ce soir
It is a pity that the skating rink did not warn the public it was closing exceptionally tonight

Personnellement, je ne doute pas que sa version **soit** véridique mais il aura du mal à convaincre le jury
I don't doubt that his version is true but he will find it difficult to convince the jury

Je m'étonne que nous n'**ayons** pas encore **reçu** la marchandise
I'm surprised that we haven't yet received the goods

Il a exigé que nous l'**emmenions** jusqu'à Bordeaux
He demanded that we should take him all the way to Bordeaux

Elle était ravie que ses jumeaux **aient obtenu** l'autorisation de passer dans la classe supérieure
She was very happy that her twins had been allowed to move up to the next class

Imaginez que les deux logiciels **soient** incompatibles, comment ferons-nous alors?
Suppose that the two pieces of software are incompatible, how will we manage then?

J'ai peur que la vérité **soit** différente
I'm afraid that the truth might be different

Nous préférons qu'il **soit** au courant
We prefer him to know about it

Je suis ravi que tu **aies trouvé** l'âme sœur
I am delighted that you have found your partner for life

Je veux que tu **sois** là à la naissance
I want you to be present at the birth

(For the use of non-negative *ne* in subordinate clauses, see Section 16.16.)

Nouns

The subjunctive is normally required in clauses dependent on nouns which express similar meanings to the verbs listed above, i.e. wishing, ordering, being pleased, sad, surprised, etc.: *l'attente que, la crainte que, le désir que, l'ordre que, la peur que, le souhait que*:

La crainte qu'il **soit libéré** a provoqué une émeute devant la prison
The fear that he might be freed gave rise to a riot in front of the prison

Samira et Khaled ont exprimé le désir qu'elle **soit invitée**
Samira and Khaled have said that they want her to be invited

L'ordre que les citoyens **soient confinés** avait été donné au plus haut niveau
The order that citizens should go into lockdown was given at the highest level

N.B.: Where the subject of the main clause is unspecified, as in a passive, or is the same as the subject of the subordinate clause, the subjunctive can be avoided by the use of an infinitive with *la crainte de, le désir de, la peur de, l'ordre de*, etc.:

L'ordre que les citoyens **soient confinés** avait été donné au plus haut niveau
L'ordre **de confiner** les citoyens **avait été donné** au plus haut niveau

11.1.4 Subjunctive after verbs of saying, thinking and believing in negatives and questions

Verbs of saying, thinking and believing – *affirmer que* 'to state that', *croire que* 'to believe that', *déclarer que* 'to declare that', *imaginer que* 'to imagine that', *penser que* 'to think that', *trouver que* 'to find that', and so on – normally present an event simply as a fact and, where they are followed by a dependent subordinate clause, the verb in this clause is in the indicative:

Ils ont cru quelques instants que la photo **avait été** truquée
They thought for a moment that the photo had been falsified

But when such verbs are **negated** or **questioned**, this introduces uncertainty about the likelihood of the event occurring, and verbs in the dependent clause are in the subjunctive:

Ont-ils cru quelques instants que la photo **ait été** truquée?
Did they think for a moment that the photo was falsified?

Nous n'affirmons pas que l'accident **soit** de votre faute, mais les circonstances prêtent à croire que cela pourrait être le cas
We are not saying that the accident was your fault, but the circumstances lead us to believe that this might be the case

Croyez-vous que la guerre froide **soit** vraiment terminée?
Do you think the cold war is really over?

Peut-on dire que ce pochoir **soit** un bon exemple du style de Banksy?
Would you say that this stencil is a good example of Banksy's style?

Je ne pense pas que cela **soit** vrai
I don't think that is correct

Je ne trouve pas que votre plaisanterie **soit** de mauvais goût, mais simplement déplacée dans ce contexte
I don't think that your joke was in bad taste but merely out of place in this context

Similarly, when verbs of saying, thinking and believing are used to introduce hypothetical cases, verbs in clauses dependent on them will be in the subjunctive:

Imaginez quelle **ait été** sa surprise
Just imagine what her surprise must have been

Supposons que nous **ayons gagné** au Loto
Let's suppose that we won the national lottery

On imagine mal que ce film **ait été tourné** par Ozon
It's difficult to imagine that this film was made by Ozon

N.B.: Note that *espérer que* 'to hope that' does NOT give rise to the subjunctive in a dependent affirmative clause, but, when negated or questioned, the subjunctive might occur:

Je n'espère plus qu'elle viendra/vienne.
I've given up hope that she will/may come.

Espère-t-elle qu'il reviendra/qu'il revienne?
Is she hoping that he will/might come back?

11.1.5 **Subjunctive after impersonal verbs expressing the belief that an event is unlikely as opposed to probable**

Some impersonal verbs and expressions present the occurrence of events described in dependent subordinate clauses as probable: verbs in these clauses are in the indicative. Examples of such cases are: *il est certain que* 'it is certain that', *il s'ensuit que* 'it follows that', *il est évident que* 'it is obvious that', *il est probable que* 'it is probable that', *il me semble que* 'I think that', *il est vrai que* 'it is true that':

Il est probable que nous **arriverons** à Mandelieu après-demain
It is probable that we will arrive in Mandelieu the day after tomorrow

Il me semble que tout ce travail **valait** la peine
I think that all this work was worth it

But others present the events as less probable, only possible or even impossible; these require the subjunctive in dependent clauses: *il n'est pas certain que* 'it is not certain that'; *il est douteux que* 'it is doubtful that'; *il est impossible que* 'it is impossible that'; *il est invraisemblable que* 'it is unbelievable that'; *il se peut que, il est possible que* 'it is possible that'; *il est peu probable que* 'it is unlikely that'; *il n'est pas sûr que* 'it is not sure that'; *il n'est pas vrai que* 'it is not true that'.

Note particularly the following contrasts:

il est certain que + indicative	il n'est pas certain que + subjunctive
il est probable que + indicative	il est peu probable que + subjunctive
il est sûr que + indicative	il n'est pas sûr que + subjunctive
il est vrai que + indicative	il n'est pas vrai que + subjunctive

Il n'est pas certain que tes explications **soient acceptées** par tous
It is not certain that your explanations would be accepted by everyone

Il est douteux que le contrat **ait été** signé à temps
It is doubtful the contract will have been signed on time

Il est invraisemblable qu'ils **aient pu** s'enfuir sans être repérés
It is incredible that they should have been able to escape without anyone noticing

Il se peut qu'il **faille** scanner le QR code
It may be that the QR code needs to be scanned

Il est possible que nous **puissions** trouver une solution à votre problème
It is possible that we may be able to find a solution to your problem

Il est peu probable que vous **réussissiez** le permis la première fois
It is not very likely that you'll pass your driving test first time

Il n'est pas sûr que nous **ayons choisi** le meilleur site pour y implanter des éoliennes
We can't be sure that we have chosen the best site for setting up a windfarm

Il n'est pas vrai que Juliette nous **ait proposé** de participer au tournage
It is not true that Juliette proposed that we should be part of the filming

Some impersonal constructions express the subjective desires or feelings of the speaker of the sentence: *il faut que* 'it is necessary that' (often equivalent to 'must'); *il est important que* 'it is important that'; *il est nécessaire que* 'it is necessary that'; *il est regrettable que* 'it is regrettable that'; *il semble que* 'it seems that'; *il est temps que* 'it is time that'; *il vaut mieux que* 'it is better if'.

Il faut qu'ils **soient** prêts à partir tout de suite
They must be ready to leave immediately

Il est important que tous **comprennent** la nécessité d'améliorer la productivité
It is important that everyone understands the need to increase productivity

Il est nécessaire que vous **partiez** avec eux: il serait imprudent de les laisser voyager seuls
It is necessary for you to go with them: it would be reckless to let them travel on their own

Il est regrettable que nous n'**ayons** pas **pu** vous contacter en ligne
It is a pity that we were not able to reach you online

Il semble que l'ennemi **soit** mieux préparé
It seems that the enemy is better prepared

Il est temps que nous **admettions** l'importance des réseaux sociaux
It is time for us to accept the importance of social networks

Il vaut mieux que ce **soit** Yussuf qui fournisse les explications
It is better that it should be Yussuf who puts forward the explanations

N.B.: Note in particular the contrast:

il me semble que + indicative	Il me semble que leur génération **est** dépolitisée
	I think that their generation lacks interest in politics
il semble que + subjunctive	Il semble que leur génération **soit** dépolitisée
	It seems that their generation lacks interest in politics

11.1.6 Subjunctive after certain conjunctions

Some subordinating conjunctions introduce hypothetical situations or establish conditions: these are normally followed by verbs in the subjunctive in the subordinate clause:

afin que pour que	*in order that*
en attendant que	*whilst waiting for*
non que ce n'est pas que	*not that*
à moins que	*unless*
à supposer que supposé que en supposant que en admettant que	*supposing that*
bien que quoique encore que malgré que	*although*
de façon que de manière que de sorte que si bien que	*so that, in such a way that*
de peur que de crainte que	*for fear that*
pour peu que si peu que	*however little that*
pourvu que à condition que	*provided that*

sans que	*without*
soit que	*whether*
tel que	*such as*

On nous disait: "Couvrez vos cahiers **afin qu**'ils ne se **salissent** pas"
We used to be told: 'Cover your exercise books so that they won't get dirty'

Ils sont allés habiter à Paris **pour que** leur fils **puisse** suivre des cours à Henri IV
They moved to Paris so that their son could study at the 'lycée Henri IV'

En attendant que le beau temps **revienne**, on passait les soirées à lire au coin du feu
Waiting for the fine weather to return, we spent the evenings reading by the fireside

Je vais modifier le manuscrit; **non que** j'en **sois mécontente**, mais je voudrais qu'il y ait plus de dialogue
I will amend the manuscript; it's not that I am unhappy with it, but I would like there to be more dialogue

Je passe te prendre à six heures **à moins que** tu ne **m'appelles** avant
I'll call by to pick you up at six unless you call me beforehand

A supposer que la réponse **soit** favorable, qu'est-ce que vous allez faire?
Supposing that the reply is positive, what will you do?

Bien que ces influenceuses **soient** massivement suivies, elles ne sont pas nécessairement crédibles.
Although these influencers have a huge following, they aren't necessarily trustworthy

Quoique nous **ayons fourni** de gros efforts pour nous intégrer, la société nous rejetait à cette époque-là
Although we made considerable efforts to integrate, society rejected us in those days

J'ai mis mon portable en mode avion **de crainte qu**'il ne **sonne** pendant le concert
I've put my mobile in aeroplane mode for fear that it might ring during the concert

Ils débranchent leur fixe **de peur qu**'on ne les **dérange** chez eux
They unplug their landline for fear of being disturbed at home

Je te montrerai comment cela fonctionne **de façon que** tu **puisses** l'expliquer à Amina plus tard
I'll show you how it works so that you can explain it to Amina later

Je vais mettre les chaises au jardin **de manière que** tu **puisses** lire au soleil
I'll set out the garden chairs in such a way that you can read in the sun

Expliquez-moi ce que vous avez décidé **de sorte que** je **sois** en mesure de finir mon rapport
Let me know in detail what you have decided, so that I may finish my report

Je veux bien vous conduire jusqu'à Chambéry **à condition que** vous **payiez** mon billet de retour
I am quite willing to drive you to Chambéry as long as you buy me a ticket to come back

Nous nous offrirons des vacances cette année, **pourvu que** nos marges bénéficiaires nous le **permettent**
We will take some holidays this year, provided that we make sufficient profit

Elle aurait bien pu quitter le village **sans que** je **m'en aperçoive**
She could well have left the village without my noticing

Et s'il avait créé un scandale **tel que** vous **ayez** été obligé de céder, votre réputation en aurait souffert
And if he had created such a scandal that you had been obliged to give in, your reputation would have would been damaged

The conjunctions *de façon que, de manière que, de sorte que, si bien que* 'so that' have two distinct meanings. On the one hand, they express a wish that something which has not yet happened might happen. With this meaning they have the force of 'creating the conditions for another event to occur' and are followed by the subjunctive:

Je te montrerai comment cela fonctionne **de façon que** tu **puisses** l'expliquer à Georges
I'll show you how it works so that ('creating the conditions for you to') you can explain it to George

Dis-m'en un peu plus sur ce qui se passe au bureau, **de sorte que** je **puisse** te conseiller
Tell me a little more about what's happening at the office so that ('creating the conditions for me to') I can advise you

On the other hand, they can describe a causal effect of one event on another. With this meaning they have the force of 'with the result that' and are followed by the indicative:

Le mécanicien a réglé le dérailleur **de façon que** tu **peux** t'en servir de nouveau
The mechanic has adjusted the derailleur so that ('with the result that') you can use it again

Tu ne me racontes plus jamais ce qui se passe au bureau, **de sorte que** je **suis** incapable de te conseiller
You never tell me any more about what's happening at the office so ('with the result that') I cannot advise you

(See also Section 17.3.8.)

11.1.7 **Subjunctive after time conjunctions**

With the time conjunctions: *avant que* 'before' and *jusqu'à ce que* 'until' the subjunctive is always used:

Il faut réagir vite, **avant que** le problème ne **devienne** insurmontable
We must react quickly before the problem becomes impossible to deal with

Sébastien veut assurer son avenir **avant qu'**il ne **démissionne**
Sébastien intends to safeguard his future before he resigns

Il a persisté **jusqu'à ce qu'**elle se sente obligée de sortir avec lui
He kept on until she felt obliged to go out with him

avant que can be replaced by *avant de* when the subject of the verb in the subordinate clause is the same as that in the introducing clause:

Sébastien veut assurer son avenir avant qu'il ne démissionne
Sébastien veut assurer son avenir avant de démissionner

The conjunction *après que* 'after' is normally followed by the indicative and not the subjunctive:

Nous avons commencé après qu'ils **étaient arrivés**
We began after they arrived

However, presumably by analogy with *avant que*, you will often hear people using the subjunctive after *après que*. (See also Section 17.3.1.)

(For the use of non-negative *ne* in dependent clauses, see Section 16.16, and for non-negative *ne* in clauses dependent on conjunctions, see Section 17.3.8.)

11.1.8 Subjunctive in clauses dependent on expressions which claim a unique status for an entity

Verbs in clauses, which are dependent on superlatives, on nouns modified by one of the adjectives *dernier, premier, seul, unique* or on *personne* or *rien*, are in the subjunctive if the sentence makes the claim that the entity referred to is 'peerless' (i.e. is the biggest, best, worst, first, last and only one of its kind ever):

Ce chou-fleur est **le plus gros** que j'**aie** jamais **vu**
This cauliflower is the biggest I have ever seen

Aïsha est **la meilleure** spécialiste que j'**aie entendue** sur ce sujet
Aïsha is the best specialist I have heard on this subject

Appolline est **la seule** qui **soit** capable de lui dire ses quatre vérités
Appolline is the only woman who could tell him a few home truths

Mon frère est **l'unique** candidat qui **ait été selectionné**
My brother is the only candidate who has been selected

Je ne connais **personne** qui **soit** mieux qualifié que lui pour exprimer nos espoirs olympiques au fleuret
I don't know anyone better qualified than him to express our Olympic aspirations in foil fencing

En quelle année est sortie **la première** voiture qui **soit** équipée d'un moteur électrique?
In which year was the first car with an electric engine produced?

However, where there is no claim about the 'peerless' quality of the entity (e.g. when it is described as the biggest, best, worst, first, etc. of a particular set, but there may be other bigger, better, worse, etc., entities in the world) the verb is in the indicative:

C'est le premier film que j'**ai** vu
That's the first film I saw

There is nothing peerless about this. It is simply the assertion of a fact. Other people see their first film as well. But compare with:

C'était la première personne qui **ait fait** l'ascension du Matterhorn
He was the first person to scale the Matterhorn

This was a 'peerless' first, and so the subjunctive is used. Similarly, compare:

Je n'ai aucun étudiant qui **soit** plus doué pour le piano que lui
None of my studients is more gifted for the piano than him (peerless)

Je ne connais personne qui **sait** jouer du violon
I don't know anyone who plays the violin
(not peerless – there are plenty of people in the world who can play the violin; it's just that one of them is not in my set of acquaintances)

Other examples of non-peerless cases:

C'est la dernière fois que je **viens** vous voir
This is the last time I am coming to see you

La première fois que je t'**ai vu**, je t'ai trouvé un peu farfelu
The first time I saw you I thought you were a bit eccentric

Le livre de cuisine est le seul qui **est tombé** de l'étagère
The cook book is the only one which fell off the shelf

(See also Section 15.11.3.)

11.1.9 Use of the indicative in clauses introduced by an adverb

When an adverb, such as *peut-être que* 'perhaps', *heureusement que* 'luckily', *certainement que* 'of course', *apparemment que* 'apparently', is used in the first part of a clause, despite the fact that they often express the meanings which in other clauses give rise to the subjunctive, the subjunctive is NOT used:

Peut-être qu'il **viendra**, peut-être qu'il viendra pas
Maybe he'll make it, maybe not

Heureusement que tu **étais** là, sinon j'aurais eu peur
Lucky you were here otherwise I'd have been afraid

Certainement que ton copain **peut** dormir ici
Of course your friend can sleep here

N.B.: This construction is more frequent in informal than formal French – hence the absence of *ne* in the first example.

11.1.10 Use of the subjunctive in hypothetical clauses coordinated by *et que*

When a hypothetical clause introduced by *si* is extended by a coordinated clause, the second clause is introduced by *que* and the verb is usually in the subjunctive:

Si tu ré-essaies tout à l'heure et que tu ne **réussisses** toujours pas à te connecter, demande un nouveau mot de passe
If you try later and still fail to connect, ask for a new password

Si Hélène hérite de la maison et qu'elle la **vende**, tante Zoë sera furieuse
If Helen inherits the house and sells it, Aunt Zoë will be furious

Si le temps change et qu'il **se mette** à pleuvoir, on annulera la sortie
If the weather changes and it starts to rain, we'll cancel the outing

(See also Section 17.5.)

A related construction is an adverbial clause introduced by *que* which also requires the subjunctive and is translated by 'whether … or' in English:

Que Sandrine **vienne ou ne vienne pas**, il faudra inviter sa fille
Whether Sandrine comes or not, we will have to invite her daughter

Que tu **sois** présent **ou que** tu **sois absent**, cela m'indiffère totalement
Whether you are present or absent is all the same to me

11.1.11 Subjunctive in subject clauses

When a clause, rather than a noun phrase, is the subject of a sentence, the verb in that clause is in the subjunctive:

Que des Allemands **soient présents** à la cérémonie du souvenir ne peut que renforcer la solidarité européenne
European solidarity can only be reinforced by the fact that Germans are present at the commemoration

Que Jade et Adam **aient choisi** le mariage religieux a pu choquer certains de leurs amis
(The fact) That Jade and Adam chose a religious ceremony for their wedding may have shocked some of their friends

The subjunctive is also used when such subject clauses are introduced by *le fait que* 'the fact that' or *l'idée que* 'the idea that':

Le fait que Jade et Adam **aient accepté** de se marier … L'idée que tu **veuilles** assister à cette cérémonie …

Note that the subjunctive is required in subject clauses even with verbs and adjectives which normally require the indicative when subordinate clauses are not in subject position. Compare:

Il est probable que nous **arriverons** à Padoue après-demain (indicative)
It is likely that we will arrive in Padua the day after tomorrow

Que nous **arrivions** à Padoue après-demain est probable (subjunctive)
That we shall arrive in Padua the day after tomorrow is likely

Il me semble certain qu'il **est parti** (indicative)
I think it certain that he has left

Qu'il **soit parti** me semble certain (subjunctive)
That he has left seems certain

11.1.12 Use of the subjunctive in clauses dependent on indefinite expressions

Verbs in subordinate clauses following the indefinite expressions *qui que* 'whoever', *quoi que* 'whatever', *où que* 'wherever', *quelque* + [*noun*] *que* 'whichever, whatever [noun]', *quel que* 'whatever', *quelque/si/aussi/pour* + [*adjective*] *que* 'however [adjective]' are in the subjunctive:

Qui que vous **soyez**, vous n'avez pas à me parler sur ce ton
Whoever you are, you can't talk to me in that way

Quoi qu'en **disent** mes parents, j'ai décidé d'y aller
Whatever my parents say, I have decided to go there

Où qu'il **se cache**, je le trouverai
Wherever he is hiding, I will find him

Quelques bêtises que tu **aies faites**, on mettra ça sur le compte de l'inexpérience
Whatever stupid things you may have done, we will chalk it up to a lack of experience

Quelles que **soient** les raisons qui vous ont amené chez nous, je suis heureux de vous accueillir
Whatever might be the reasons which have brought you to us, I am happy to welcome you

Quelque rares que **soient** ces découvertes, elles font néanmoins avancer la connaissance scientifique
However rare these discoveries may be, they nevertheless contribute to advancing scientific knowledge

Note that in this last example *quelque* does not agree with *rares* or *découvertes*. (For more on these constructions, see Sections 15.10 and 15.11.1.)

More generally, where a subordinate clause is dependent on an indefinite expression which describes a hypothetical, rather than real, state of affairs, the verb in the subordinate clause is likely to be in the subjunctive:

S'il connaissait **un endroit** qui **convienne**, il le dirait
If he knew of a place which was suitable, he would say so

(There is no particular place that he knows of)

Elle veut trouver **un airbnb** qui **ait** une piscine
She wants to find an airbnb with a swimming pool

(She has no particular airbnb in mind)

Compare with:

S'il connaît **un endroit** qui **convient**, allons-y
If he knows of a suitable place, let's go there

Elle veut trouver un airbnb qui **a** une piscine
(Which suggests that there is a specific airbnb with a swimming pool which she knows about and wants to find)

(See also Sections 15.11.2 and 15.11.4.)

11.2 The use of *devoir, pouvoir, savoir,* and *falloir*

The modal verbs *devoir, pouvoir, savoir,* and *falloir* enable a speaker to express a number of attitudes about events and the participants in events: the likelihood of an event occurring; the ability of a participant to perform some action; how obligated a participant is in an event. Modal verbs are also used in granting permission and in formulas expressing politeness.

In this section we describe the various uses of these four verbs. Then in Section 11.3 we take a different perspective and describe how the English modals 'would', 'should', 'could', 'may', 'might', 'ought to', and 'must' are rendered in French.

11.2.1 *devoir*

devoir expresses four main meanings:

(a) something which the speaker sees as very probable, usually because it is logical;
(b) something which the speaker sees as a moral obligation;
(c) something which the speaker thinks of as planned or agreed;
(d) something which the speaker thinks of as an act, usually in the past, which was a necessary outcome of events.

Probability (logical necessity)

Les nouveaux joueurs sont les premiers sélectionnés du département, donc l'équipe **devrait** maintenant faire de meilleures performances
The new players are the best in the département, so the team should now produce some better performances

Ton portable **doit** avoir capté le réseau puisque je vois 4 barres sur l'icône
You mobile must be connected to the network since I can see 4 bars on the icon

Il **doit** être revenu puisqu'il recommence le travail demain
He must have come back because he starts work again tomorrow

Il pleut depuis trois semaines presque constamment. Nous **devrons** nous attendre à des inondations
It has been raining almost constantly for three weeks. We must expect floods

J'**ai dû** payer la facture puisque je n'ai reçu aucun courrier de relance
I must have paid the bill since I haven't had a reminder

Moral obligation

Il est impératif que je parle à Sylvain. Vous savez où il est et vous **devez** me le dire
It is crucial that I speak to Sylvain. You know where he is and you must tell me

Je **dois** recomencer les cours demain sinon je crains de rater mon contrôle continu
I must go back to lectures tomorrow or I'm scared I might fail my continuous assessment

Vous êtes allés dîner chez eux, maintenant vous **devrez** les inviter chez vous
You have been to dinner at their house, now you will have to invite them to yours

Ce toit est abîmé; vous **devriez** en parler au propriétaire
This roof is damaged; you should speak to the landlord about it

A planned event (usually which did not or will not happen)

Ils **devaient** annoncer le nom du gagnant à 18 heures mais une panne d'électricité est survenue
They were to reveal the name of the winner at 6pm when a power cut happened

Le jour de l'accident je **devais** accompagner mon père à Toulouse
The day of the accident I was to accompany my father to Toulouse

A necessary outcome of events

Plus tard, il **devait** souvent repenser à ces quelques instants
Later on he was often to reflect on these few moments

Raphaël avait déménagé toutes ses affaires. Nina **devait** en tirer les inévitables conclusions
Raphaël had moved out all his things. Nina had to accept the obvious conclusions

50 ans après la fin de la guerre, son héroïsme **devait** être reconnu par la nation
Fifty years after the end of the war her heroism was to be recognised by the nation

11.2.2 *pouvoir*

pouvoir expresses five main meanings:

(a) The granting or refusing of permission by the speaker;
(b) An indication that the speaker believes someone else is capable of doing something;
(c) An indication that the speaker feels that something is probable in the future;
(d) A general assertion by the speaker about what may happen;
(e) An expression of politeness by the speaker.

The granting or refusing of permission by the speaker

Vous **pouvez** disposer!
You are dismissed!

Non, tu ne **peux** pas aller chez ce garçon
No, you cannot go to this boy's house

Il **pourra** m'en parler quand il voudra
He may talk to me about it when he wishes

Vous **pourrez** partir dès que la réunion sera terminée mais pas avant
You may go as soon as the meeting is over but not before

An indication that the speaker believes someone is capable of doing something

Elle a déjà réparé l'imprimante: elle **peut** très bien s'occuper de reconnecter la box
She has already mended the printer: she is quite capable of reconnecting the router

Un grand garçon comme toi! Bien sûr que tu **pourras** porter ma valise jusqu'à ma chambre
A big boy like you! Of course you will be able to carry my case up to my room

Nous ne **pourrons** prendre notre décision que lorsque les experts nous auront remis leur rapport
We will only be able to make our decision once the experts have put in their report

An indication that the speaker feels that something is quite probable in the future

Votre colis **peut** très bien arriver lundi matin; il a sans doute été retardé à cause des fêtes de Noël
Your package may very well arrive on Monday morning; it has probably been delayed by the Christmas holidays

S'ils continuent à jouer comme ça, ils **pourraient** gagner le championnat
If they go on playing like that, they could well win the title

Tu passes trop de temps sur ta tablette: tu **peux** t'abîmer la vue
You spend too much time on your tablet: you could damage your eyesight

La gouttière fuit: si cela continue, l'eau **pourrait** abîmer le mur
The gutter's leaking: if it goes on, the water could ruin the wall

Il faut soigner cette égratignure, elle **pourrait** s'infecter
Treat this scratch, it could get infected

A general assertion by the speaker about what may happen

On **peut** toujours faire mieux
It is always possible to do better

Dans une pièce où il y a une cheminée, une étincelle **peut** toujours mettre le feu
In a room with an open hearth, a spark can always cause a fire

Il n'est pas trop tard; il **peut** encore venir
It is not too late; he may still come

Comme papa a trouvé du travail, on **va pouvoir** déménager
Since dad has got a job we'll be able to move house

An expression of politeness by the speaker

Puis-je vous demander de m'aider?
May I request your assistance?

Pourriez-vous m'indiquer le chemin de Douaumont?
Could you show me the way to Douaumont?

On **pourrait** voir les choses sous cet angle, mais personnellement je pense que l'important est ailleurs
It would be possible to see things in this way but I personally think that there is a much more important point

11.2.3 *savoir*

savoir expresses two main meanings:

(a) 'to know' in the sense of 'to possess knowledge about';
(b) 'to know' in the sense of 'to know how to do something'.

'to know' (possess knowledge)

Je **sais** mes répliques par cœur
I know my lines by heart

Manuel et Eliott **savent** où nous trouver
Manuel and Eliott know where to find us

Monet **savait** beaucoup de choses sur l'utilisation de la couleur en peinture
Monet knew a lot about the use of colour in painting

'to know' (know how to ...)

N'ayez pas peur. Je **sais** nager
Don't worry. I can swim

Elle n'a que quatre ans mais elle **sait** déjà lire
She is only four but already she can read

On peut les interviewer, ils **savent** parler français
We can interview them, they can speak French

Nous n'avons pas peur d'y aller. Nous **savons** nous défendre
We are not frightened to go there. We know how to look after ourselves

N.B.: There can be confusion between *pouvoir* and *savoir* in this area. *Savoir* is 'to know how to in principle' and *pouvoir* is 'to be able to do it in a particular situation':

Oui je **sais** réparer le moteur mais je ne **peux** pas le faire sans outils
Yes I can (= I know how to) repair the engine, but I can't do it (= I am unable to do so here and now) without tools

If people were feeling threatened in some way, they might say:

Nous **savons** nous défendre
We can look after ourselves

to indicate that they have necessary skills (karate, boxing, a willingness to fight, etc.). In a situation where they may have to make use of these skills, they would say:

Nous **pourrons** nous défendre contre leurs attaques
We can defend ourselves against their attacks

to indicate that they think they will be able to apply these skills in these circumstances.

11.2.4 *falloir*

falloir (impersonal) expresses one main meaning: it is equivalent to English: 'must' or 'ought to':

Il **faut** qu'ils viennent m'aider
They must come and help me

Il **aurait fallu** que j'intègre une école de journalisme dès la fin de ma licence
I should have gone to a school of journalism as soon as I finished my degree

11.3 The French equivalents of the English modal verbs: 'would', 'should', 'could', 'may', 'might', 'ought to', and 'must'

As can be seen from the translations in the preceding section, *devoir, pouvoir, savoir* and *falloir* can be translated in a number of ways depending on the context. The most frequent translations are 'would', 'should', 'can', 'could', 'may', 'might', 'ought to', and 'must'. The problems which arise in this area for English speakers are mainly to do with errors in establishing how these forms relate to the English modal verbs which express many of the same meanings.

The English modal verbs also, however, express a number of other meanings. For correct usage, it is essential that learners should be able to distinguish the meanings of the English modals in order to know which French forms to use. In some cases, one of the French modal verbs is appropriate; in other cases, a sentence with *si*, a conditional tense, an imperfect tense, a present or future tense or a subjunctive may be the appropriate form.

11.3.1 'would'

'would' has three main meanings:

(a) 'would' may be used in English to express possible future behaviour which is dependent on some condition. It will usually be rendered by the conditional form of the verb in French:

Je **viendrais** à ton anniversaire si seulement je pouvais obtenir mon après-midi
I would come to your birthday party if only I could get the afternoon off work
(the conditional form *viendrais* is used to denote a possible future action envisaged IF certain other events take place)

(b) 'would' may be used to indicate something which is desired or not desired. In this case it is often rendered by a form of the verb *vouloir*:

Elle n'a pas **voulu** me dire où le trouver
She wouldn't tell me where to find him
(the 'wouldn't' in English is quite close in meaning to 'did not want to': it is therefore rendered as *n'a pas voulu*)

(c) 'would' may also indicate a habitual action in the past. This is generally rendered by the imperfect form of the verb in French:

Ces événements **avaient** souvent lieu pendant les vacances d'été
These events would often take place during the summer holidays

(The imperfect tense is used to indicate a habitual action in the past – see Section 10.3.1.)

11.3.2 'should'

'should' has four main meanings:

(a) 'should' may indicate a moral obligation. This is usually rendered by the use of *devoir*:

Tu **devrais** faire des sauvegardes plus souvent
You should back up your files more often
(*devoir* in the conditional form to indicate the moral duty)

Note also that the English 'should have' is rendered by *aurait dû* plus an infinitive and not by a participle form of the main verb:

Tu **aurais dû** me dire (not *avoir dit) cela plus tôt
You should have told me that before
falloir is also possible here:
Il **aurait fallu** me le dire plus tôt

(b) 'should' may convey a conditional. This is usually rendered by a conditional form of the verb in French:

Si j'avais su cela, je ne **serais** pas venu
If I had known about that I should not have come

(c) 'should' may express a probable future action. Depending on the degree of probability, this may be rendered by a form of *devoir* or by a future tense:

La Saison 6 **devrait** sortir le mois prochain
La Saison 6 **devra** sortir le mois prochain
La Saison 6 **sortira** le mois prochain
*The sixth season **should** be coming out next month*

These three sentences indicate an increasing degree of probability going from top to bottom.

(d) 'should' can also indicate a chance event. This may be translated by some means of expression other than the verb:

Si **par hasard** vous entendez parler d'un appartement à louer, dites-le-moi
If you should hear of a flat to let, do let me know
(a present tense plus an adverb expressing the idea of chance conveys the meaning of 'should')

Sometimes a simple present tense will convey the meaning of 'should':

Si Mourad **téléphone**, dis-lui que je le rappellerai
If Mourad should telephone, tell him I'll call him back

Where one wants to stress the improbability of the chance event occurring, a form of *devoir* can be used:

Si Mourad **devait** téléphoner, il faudrait lui dire que je le rappellerai
In the unlikely event of Mourad telephoning, tell him I'll call him back

(For more on the use of tenses with *si*, see Sections 10.8 and 17.3.6.)

11.3.3 'could'

'could' has four main meanings:

(a) 'could' may be a simple past tense of the verb 'can', i.e. 'was able to'. This is particularly frequent in reported speech. There is little difficulty here in using *pouvoir*:

Malgré tout le mal qu'on s'est donné, il n'**a** quand même pas **pu** accepter notre version des faits
*After all the trouble we had taken he still **couldn't** accept our version of the facts*

Il a dit: 'Je **peux** venir'
He said: 'I can come'

and in reported speech:

Il a dit qu'il **pouvait** venir
He said he could come

(See Section 10.7.)

(b) 'could' may indicate a possibility. This will normally be a conditional or a form of the impersonal verb *il se peut que*:

Il faut que les skieurs fassent attention; le temps **pourrait** se dégrader dans l'après-midi
*Skiers need to be careful; the weather **could** worsen in the afternoon*

Cela fait plusieurs jours que je ne le vois plus: il **se peut qu**'il soit parti
*I haven't seen him for a few days: he **could** have left*

(c) 'could' may indicate that permission has been given. This may be rendered by the use of *pouvoir* or by another verb such as *permettre*:

Sa mère a dit qu'il **pouvait** venir
Sa mère lui **a permis** de venir
*Her mother said he **could** come*

(d) 'could' may imply that something should be done or should have been done: this can be rendered by a suitable tense of *pouvoir*:

Elle **aurait pu** me dire qu'elle ne serait pas libre le 15
She could have told me that she wouldn't be available on the 15th

11.3.4 'may'

'may' has four main meanings:

(a) 'may' indicates something which is simply envisaged. Sometimes, especially in informal speech, an adverb will suffice. Or the impersonal forms *cela se peut, il se peut que* + *subjunctive*:

Peut-être qu'elle viendra, ou **peut-être** qu'elle ne viendra pas
*She **may** come or she **may** not*

Cela **se peut** mais nous ne pouvons en être certains
*That **may** be the case but we can't be sure*

Il **se peut** que ce **soit** lui le coupable mais cela reste à prouver
*He **may** be the guilty party but it has yet to be proved*

The subjunctive on its own is used very often when possible consequences are feared:

Je scanne le certificat de peur que tu **ne le perdes**
I am scanning the certificate because I am worried you may lose it

(b) 'may' can indicate permission. This is most often rendered by the use of *pouvoir*:

Cendrillon **peut** aller au bal, dit à contre-coeur la méchante belle-mère
*'Cinderella **may** go to the ball', said the wicked stepmother reluctantly*

Vous **pouvez** rester jusqu'à onze heures
*You **may** stay till eleven*

(c) 'may' can be a kind of blessing. This will normally be rendered by a subjunctive in the main clause:

Que votre Dieu vous **bénisse**
***May** your God bless you*

Que la Force **soit** avec vous
***May** the Force be with you*

(d) 'may' can indicate an open-ended possibility. This is often rendered by a subjunctive:

Quoi qu'il en **soit**, je n'ai toujours pas récupéré mon acompte
*That's as **may** be, I still haven't got my deposit back*

Quoi qu'il **dise**, il a quand même maigri
*Whatever he **may** say, he has lost weight*

11.3.5 'might'

'might' has three main meanings:

(a) 'might' is sometimes simply a past 'may' as in giving permission in indirect speech. In this case, a form of *pouvoir* is to be expected:

Elle a dit: Vous **pouvez** y aller
*She said: You **may** go*

Elle a dit qu'on **pouvait** y aller si on finissait nos devoirs d'abord
*She said we **might** go if we finished our homework first*

(b) 'might' indicates something which is envisaged. The French equivalents are the same as for 'may' (see Section 11.3.4(a)). Sometimes, especially in informal speech, an adverb will suffice. Or the impersonal form *il se peut que + subjunctive* may be used. Or the subjunctive on its own may be used when possible consequences are feared:

Peut-être qu'elle viendra, ou peut-être pas
Il **se peut** qu'elle **vienne** (on ne sait pas)
*She **might** come or she might not*

Je surveillais les enfants de peur qu'ils ne **se fassent mal**
*I kept an eye on the children for fear that they **might** hurt themselves*

(c) 'might' can be a polite form. This usually corresponds to a form of *pouvoir* or a use of *permettre*:

Puis-je vous suggérer une autre explication?
***Might** I offer you an alternative explanation?*

Permettez-moi de vous demander pourquoi vous êtes venu?
***Might** I ask why you have come?*

11.3.6 'ought to'

'ought to' conveys one main meaning:

'ought to' expresses a moral obligation. It is usually rendered by *devoir*, often in a conditional form:

Vous **devriez** voir un peu plus de monde
*You **ought** to mix with more people*

Tu **devrais** rafraîchir la page
*You **ought** to refresh the page*

falloir is also possible:

> Il **faut que** tu voies un peu plus de monde
> Il **faut que** tu rafraîchisses la page

11.3.7 'must'

'must' has two main meanings:

(a) 'must' can express moral obligation. This usually requires *devoir* or *falloir*:

> Vous **devez** venir: nous ne pourrions pas prendre de décision sans vous
> Il **faut que** vous veniez: nous ne pourrions pas prendre de décision sans vous
> Il vous **faut** venir: nous ne pourrions pas prendre de décision sans vous
> *You **must** come: we couldn't decide without you*

(b) 'must' can indicate a logical possibility/certainty. This is usually rendered by *devoir*:

> Si elle le dit, c'est que ça **doit** être vrai …
> *If she says so, then it **must** be the case …*

> Vous **avez dû** sortir ma veste de la voiture parce qu'elle n'y est plus
> *You **must have** got my jacket out of the car because it isn't there now*

11.4 Exclamatives

Exclamatives are the direct expression of a speaker's surprise, disgust, anger, fervour and analogous emotions:

> Comme elle a grandi!   *How she's grown!*
> Que de monde!   *What a lot of people!*
> Que le diable l'emporte!   *The devil take him!*
> Vive la République, vive la France!   *Long live the Republic, long live France!*

There are four types of exclamative in French.

11.4.1 Exclamatives formed with *comme* or *que* + the indicative

Sentences can be turned into exclamations simply by putting *comme* or *que* in front of them and without changing word order. The verb remains in the indicative:

> Fabien a changé   **Comme** Fabien a changé!
> *Fabien has changed*   **Que** Fabien a changé!
>   *How Fabien has changed!*

> Il était beau   **Comme** il était beau!
> *He was handsome*   **Qu'**il était beau!
>   *How handsome he was!*

> C'est dégoûtant   **Comme** c'est dégoûtant!
> *It's disgusting*   **Que** c'est dégoûtant!
>   *How disgusting it is!*

Elle parle vite	**Comme** elle parle vite!
She speaks quickly	**Qu'**elle parle vite!
	How quickly she speaks!

N.B.: In informal French, *ce que* and *qu'est-ce que* are common alternatives to *comme* and *que*: *Ce que Fabien a changé! Qu'est-ce qu'il fait chaud!*, etc.

When exclamations are reported – that is when they follow verbs like *savoir, raconter, dire* and so on – *comme/que* are replaced by *combien*:

Elle sait **combien** Fabien a changé
She knows how Fabien has changed

Ils nous ont tous dit **combien** il faisait chaud
All of them told us how hot it was

11.4.2 **Exclamatives formed with** *quel*

Exclamations can bear specifically on nouns. French uses *quel* to perform this function. Where a sentence is involved, the *quel*-phrase is placed at the beginning of the sentence and *quel* agrees in gender and number with the noun:

Quel vent!	*What a wind!*
Quelle surprise!	*What a surprise!*
Quels progrès vos patients ont faits!	*What progress your patients have made!*
Avec **quelle** adresse il a résolu le problème!	*With what skill he solved the problem!*

N.B.: Note the set phrase "Quel temps!" which should not be rendered as *What a weather! but Look at the weather!

When the direct object is the focus of the exclamation, in formal French it is possible optionally to invert the subject and the verb (in an operation known as 'stylistic inversion' – see Section 14.3.7), providing that there is no other material following the verb:

Quels progrès vos patients ont faits!
Quels progrès ont faits vos patients!

11.4.3 *que de* + noun meaning 'what a lot of X!'

que de followed by a noun is used to create an exclamative of the form 'what a lot of X!' or 'so much/so many X!':

Que de monde!	*What a lot of people!*
Que de difficultés!	*So many difficulties!*
Que de problèmes on doit affronter!	*What a lot of problems we have before us!*

11.4.4 **The subjunctive used in two kinds of main clause exclamative**

Although the subjunctive normally only occurs in subordinate clauses, it can be used in main clause exclamations like:

Vive la Bretagne!	*Long live Brittany!*
Dieu **soit** loué!	*Praise God!*
Sauve qui peut!	*Every man for himself!*
Puissiez-vous réussir!	*May you succeed!*

and also those headed by *que*:

> Que la Sainte Vierge vous **bénisse**!
> *May the Holy Virgin bless you!*

> Que votre Dieu vous **protège**!
> *May your God help you!*

> Qu'il **aille** au diable!
> *The devil take him!*

> Qu'il **aille** se faire voir ailleurs!
> *May he get lost!*

Both of these types of exclamation are remnants from an earlier period in the history of French and are rather formal and archaic. Only *Vive X!* and *Qu'il/elle/ils/elles V!* are used productively in modern French (*Vive les vacances!* 'Long live the holidays!', *Vive la révolution!* 'Long live the revolution!'; *Qu'il m'attende!* 'Let him wait for me!', *Qu'elle cherche ailleurs!* 'Let her look elsewhere!', etc.).

11.5 **Imperatives**

Imperatives in French are used very much as they are in English to give orders, express encouragement, give advice and so on:

Asseyez-vous	*Sit down*
Allez la France!	*Come on, France!*
Allons-y	*Let's go*
Fais attention!	*Watch out!*

11.5.1 **Form of imperatives**

Imperatives are formed from the second person, singular and plural, and the first-person plural of the present tense forms of verbs. Delete the subject and the final *s* of any verb that ends in *es* or *as*:

tu parles	→	parle	*speak*
vous parlez		parlez	*speak*
nous parlons		parlons	*let's speak*

tu vas	→	va	*go*
vous allez		allez	*go*
nous allons		allons	*let's go*

tu ouvres	→	ouvre	*open*
vous ouvrez		ouvrez	*open*
nous ouvrons		ouvrons	*let's open*

tu finis	→	finis	*finish*
vous finissez		finissez	*finish*
nous finissons		finissons	*let's finish*

tu dors	→	dors	*sleep*
vous dormez		dormez	*sleep*
nous dormons		dormons	*let's sleep*
tu reçois	→	reçois	*receive*
vous recevez		recevez	*receive*
nous recevons		recevons	*let's receive*

There are four verbs with irregular imperative forms:

être		**avoir**	
sois	*be*	aie	*have*
soyez	*be*	ayez	*have*
soyons	*let's be*	ayons	*let's have*

savoir		**vouloir**	
sache	*know*	veuille	(used almost
sachez	*know*	veuillez	exclusively to
sachons	*let's know*	—	mean *please* – see Section 11.5.5)

Verbs which double a consonant in their present tense singular forms (like *appeler* – *tu appelles*, *jeter* – *tu jettes*) or change a vowel (like *acheter* – *tu achètes*, *espérer* – *tu espères*, *nettoyer* – *tu nettoies*) carry this change over to the imperative: *appelle!*, *jette!*, *nettoie!*, etc. (See Section 7.4 for these changes.) (See Appendix 2 for proposals in Nouvelle Orthographe concerning verbs which double consonants.)

The final *s* which disappears from the second-person singular of verbs ending in *es* or *as* reappears when the verb is followed by *y* or *en*:

parle	*speak*	parles-en	*speak about it*
va	*go*	vas-y	*go on*

The equivalent of English contrastive imperatives like 'you go (instead of me)', 'you shut up (instead of me)' are the forms *vous-même, toi-même*: *Allez-y vous-même, Tais-toi toi-même*.

11.5.2 **Pronominal verbs in imperatives**

Pronominal verbs like *se lever* 'to get up', *se réveiller* 'to wake up', *se servir* 'to help (serve) oneself', *se taire* 'to shut up', etc., drop their subjects in the imperative, but keep their object pronouns:

tu te lèves	→	lève-**toi**	*get up*
vous vous levez		levez-**vous**	*get up*
nous nous levons		levons-**nous**	*let's get up*
tu te sers	→	sers-**toi**	*help yourself*
vous vous servez		servez-**vous**	*help yourself*
nous nous servons		servons-**nous**	*let's help ourselves*

11.5.3 **Location and order of pronouns with imperatives**

In affirmative imperatives, direct and indirect object pronouns, and the pronouns *y* and *en*, come immediately after the verb which governs them. The pronouns *me* and *te* become the stressed forms *moi* and *toi*. Pronouns are linked to their governing verb in written French by hyphens (see also Section 3.2.5):

Prends-**les**	*Take them*
Suivez-**nous**	*Follow us*
Ecoutez-**moi**	*Listen to me*
Tais-**toi**	*Shut up*

N.B.: Pronouns governed by an infinitive following an imperative are NOT linked to the imperative by a hyphen:

Monte **les** chercher	*Go up and look for them* (*les* is the object of *chercher*)
Courez **lui** téléphoner	*Run and phone him* (*lui* is the indirect object of *téléphoner*)

When more than one pronoun is present the order is

verb – direct object – indirect object – *y/en*

moi and *toi* become *m', t'* if they are followed by *y* or en:

Donne-**le-moi**	*Give it to me*
Donnez-**le-lui**	*Give it to him*
Donne-**m'en**	*Give me some of it*
Approche-**t'en** avec précaution	*Be careful as you come closer to it*

N.B.: But in some cases you will hear the use of *moi* or *toi* with an extra 'z' inserted, especially with *toi*, as in:

Accroche **toi-z-y!** *Hang on to it!*

(See also Section 3.2.31.)

In negative imperatives pronouns precede the verb and the order is the same as in simple non-imperative sentences (see Sections 3.2.5 and 3.2.31):

Ne **me le** donne pas	*Don't give it to me*
Ne **le lui** donnez pas	*Don't give it to him*
Ne **m'en** donne pas	*Don't give me any*
Ne **t'en** approche pas	*Don't come any closer to it*

11.5.4 Compound imperatives

Compound imperatives are formed from the imperative of *avoir* or *être*, as appropriate, and a past participle. They are used to express orders to be fulfilled in the future:

Ayez nettoyé ces tables avant le deuxième service!
Get those tables cleaned before the second sitting!

11.5.5 Toning down imperatives

Orders can be toned down by the use of *veuillez*, which is an equivalent of *s'il vous plaît*:

Asseyez-vous	*Sit down*
Veuillez vous asseoir	*Please sit down*
Asseyez-vous, s'il vous plaît	*Sit down, please*

or by the use of a non-imperative declarative sentence with a future tense:

Vous **fermerez** la porte, s'il vous plaît
Close the door, please

Vous me **donnerez** deux baguettes
Give me two baguettes, please

11.5.6 **Infinitives used as imperatives**

Infinitives can be used in French as imperatives when the addressee is non-specific (e.g. in road signs addressed to all road users or in instructions addressed to the purchasers of a food product):

Ralentir	*Slow down*
Ouvrir doucement	*Open carefully*
Enregistrer	*Save (on a computer)*

(See also Section 12.10.)

11.5.7 **Third-person imperatives**

Third-person imperatives which are formed in English by the use of 'let' are formed in French by the use of *que* + a verb in the subjunctive (see Section 11.4.4):

Qu'elle **s'asseye**	*Let her sit down*
Qu'il **descende** me chercher un café	*Let him go downstairs and get me a coffee*
Qu'ils te le **donnent**, on le copiera après	*Let them give it to you, we'll copy it later*

FREE

**INSTRUCTOR
& STUDENT
RESOURCES**

For more resources to practice your French grammar, including practice activities/quizzes for students, further resource links, and an instructor guide, please visit https://routledgelearning.com/frenchgrammarandusage.

12 The infinitive

12.1 Introduction: what are infinitives?

'Infinitive' means 'not expressing tense, person or number'. The infinitive forms of the verb are those such as *aller* 'to go', *finir* 'to finish', *descendre* 'to go down', *recevoir* 'to receive'. Whereas in English the infinitive form of the verb is signalled by the presence of 'to': '**to** go', in French the infinitive is signalled by an infinitive ending: all**er**. There are four infinitive endings, and all French verbs take one of these endings in their infinitive form:

-er	e.g. *aimer, placer, arriver, étudier, télécharger*
-ir	e.g. *finir, courir, venir, dormir*
-re	e.g. *vendre, rire, être, paraître*
-oir(e)	e.g. *s'asseoir, recevoir, avoir, boire, croire*

Most dictionaries, by convention, use the infinitive form of the verb as the headword for the entry for all parts of the verb.

A past infinitive is made up of the appropriate auxiliary verb (*être* or *avoir*) and the past participle: *être allé, s'être promené, avoir vendu, avoir gagné*. These are especially useful in constructions with *après*:

Après avoir pris cette photo, le photographe a été arrêté
After taking/having taken this photo, the photographer was arrested

(See also Section 17.7.)

French infinitives may or may not translate as infinitives in English. Forms ending in *-ing* often provide better translations.

Vendre des meubles ne m'intéresse pas
Selling furniture does not interest me

J'aime beaucoup être allé en Grèce, mais je n'y retournerai plus: il y a trop de touristes
I like having been to Greece but I won't go back again: there are too many tourists

J'aime chiner au marché aux puces
I like to bargain-hunt at the flea-market

(See Section 16.2.2 for negation with infinitives.)

There are FIVE main ways in which infinitives are used in French:

(a) As **complements to other verbs:**

Esmée refuse de **sortir**   *Esmée refuses to come out*

DOI: 10.4324/9781003373926-12

(b) As **complements to adjectives:**

C'est utile à **savoir**   *It's useful to know*

(c) As **complements to nouns:**

Défense de **fumer**   *No smoking*

(d) As subordinate infinitive clauses:

Se détendre le week-end, c'est important pour la santé
To relax at weekends is important for one's health

(e) As **polite commands:**

Ralentir   *Slow down*

Soulever, écarter doucement   *Lift and separate carefully* (instructions for opening a packet of coffee)

12.2 Infinitives as complements to other verbs

Infinitives may immediately follow other verbs:

Marion veut **partir**
Marion wants to leave

or they may follow the direct object or the indirect object of another verb:

Sophie a encouragé Tristan à **démissionner**
(follows the direct object)
Sophie has encouraged Tristan to resign

Pierre a demandé à Miguel de **finir** la structuration du site
(follows the indirect object)
Pierre asked Miguel to complete the design of the site

In such cases it is important to know whether there is a **linking preposition**: ... *a encouragé Tristan à démissionner*, ... *a ordonné à Miguel de finir*, or **no preposition** at all: ... *veut partir*. This is a difficult area for English speakers because in English infinitives are only ever preceded by *to*.

It is not easy to give firm rules because usage is sometimes idiosyncratic. However, rough rules-of-thumb can be given by grouping verbs together into loose meaning classes. Each class tends to select one option or the other – *à*, *de*, or no linking preposition – when followed by an infinitive. The classes are listed in the following sections. Within each section verbs are listed **alphabetically**, and at the end of the chapter there is a comprehensive, alphabetically ordered, quick reference **index** to all the verbs taking infinitive complements listed in this chapter. There are special rules dealing with the agreement of the past participle in verb + infinitive constructions. These are dealt with in Sections 9.3.3 and 9.3.9.

12.3 **Verbs which take infinitive complements without a linking preposition**

12.3.1 **'Movement' verbs without objects**

Movement verbs which do not have objects typically take infinitive complements without a preceding preposition:

aller dîner quelque part	*to go and have dinner somewhere*
s'en aller vivre ailleurs	*to go and live somewhere else*
courir téléphoner à la police	*to run and phone the police*
descendre commander une bière	*to go down and order a beer*
monter chercher ses lunettes	*to go up and look for one's glasses*
partir s'installer à Paris	*to leave to go to live in Paris*
rentrer prendre son maillot de bain	*to go home and get one's swimming costume*
retourner faire des courses	*to go back to do some shopping*
revenir ouvrir les fenêtres	*to come back to open the windows*
sortir acheter un journal	*to go out to buy a newspaper*

The verb *être* in the past tense, with an infinitive complement, is sometimes used to mean 'go': *nous avons été la voir* 'we went to see her'.

12.3.2 **'Movement' verbs with objects**

Movement verbs with objects typically take infinitive complements without a preceding preposition:

amener un copain dîner chez soi	*to bring a friend home for dinner*
emmener ses enfants jouer sur la plage	*to take one's children to play on the beach*
envoyer Marie chercher le docteur	*to send Marie to fetch the doctor*
mener son troupeau paître en haute montagne	*to take one's flock to graze high in the mountains*

12.3.3 **'Modal' verbs**

Verbs of 'obligation', 'necessity', and 'possibility' – modal verbs – take infinitive complements without a preceding preposition (see also Section 11.2):

devoir parler au directeur	*to have to speak to the director*
oser critiquer sa patronne	*to dare to criticize one's boss*
pouvoir persuader son oncle	*to be able to persuade one's uncle*
savoir parler italien	*to be able to speak Italian*
vouloir construire une rocade	*to want to build a ring-road*

12.3.4 **Verbs of 'saying'**

Verbs of saying typically take infinitive complements without a preceding preposition:

affirmer connaître le patron	*to state that one knows the boss*
confirmer avoir reçu le paquet	*to confirm that one received the package*
déclarer comprendre ce livre	*to declare that one understands this book*
dire se méfier des infox	*to say that one worries about fake news*
nier avoir déconnecté la box	*to deny having disconnected the router*
prétendre être heureux	*to claim to be happy*
reconnaître s'être trompé	*to admit that one was wrong*

dire, with an indirect object, can also be used as a verb of **ordering** (see Section 12.5.16). In this case, it takes an infinitive complement preceded by the preposition *de: dire à quelqu'un de fermer la porte* 'to tell somebody to close the door'.

12.3.5 **Verbs of 'thinking' and 'imagining'**

Verbs of thinking and imagining typically take infinitive complements without a preceding preposition:

croire avoir fini	*to believe that one has finished*
estimer pouvoir prendre le train	*to reckon to be able to take the train*
(s')imaginer avoir gagné la partie	*to imagine having won the match*
penser rencontrer un ami	*to think one might meet a friend*
se rappeler avoir visité l'abbaye	*to remember having visited the abbey*

But *se souvenir* 'to remember' takes infinitive complements with the preposition *de: se souvenir d'avoir visité l'abbaye*.

12.3.6 **Verbs expressing 'personal attitude' to something**

Verbs which express 'liking', 'wishing', or 'inclination' typically take infinitive complements without a preceding preposition:

adorer dîner au restaurant	*to love eating out*
aimer travailler le soir	*to like to work in the evenings*
aimer autant rester chez soi	*to just as soon stay at home*
aimer mieux éviter les embouteillages	*to prefer to avoid traffic jams*
compter commencer bientôt	*to count on starting soon*
daigner donner son opinion	*to deign to give one's opinion*
désirer dormir un peu	*to want to sleep a little*
entendre être obéi	*to mean to be obeyed*
espérer partir en vacances	*to hope to go on holiday*
préférer manger seul	*to prefer to eat alone*
souhaiter faire la connaissance de quelqu'un	*to wish to make somebody's acquaintance*

aimer can sometimes be found with an infinitive complement preceded by *à: aimer à travailler le soir*.

12.3.7 **Seem**

sembler 'to seem' and verbs with similar meaning to *sembler* take infinitive complements without a preceding preposition:

s'avérer être efficace	*to turn out to be effective*
paraître dire la vérité	*to appear to be telling the truth*
se révéler avoir des consequences inattendues	*to turn out to have unexpected consequences*
sembler préférer les légumes	*to seem to prefer vegetables*

12.3.8 'Perception' verbs

Verbs expressing the manner in which an event is perceived take infinitive complements without a preceding preposition:

écouter les enfants réciter une poésie	*to listen to the children reciting a poem*
entendre l'horloge sonner trois heures	*to hear the clock strike three o'clock*
regarder un acteur recevoir une récompense	*to watch an actor accepting an award*
sentir ses pieds s'enfoncer dans la boue	*to feel one's feet sink into the mud*
voir Paul partir	*to see Paul leave*

12.3.9 *faire* and *laisser*

The verbs *faire* and *laisser* take infinitive complements without a preceding preposition:

faire travailler Mathieu	*to make Mathieu work*
faire payer l'utilisateur pour accéder aux articles	*to charge users for getting access to the articles*
laisser Mathieu travailler	*to let Mathieu work*
laisser travailler Mathieu	*to let Mathieu work*
laisser tomber le football pour le rugby	*to drop football and take up rugby instead*

(For the placement of object pronouns in these constructions, see Section 3.2.32.)

It is possible, but not necessary, to delete *se* in the verbs *se taire* 'to be quiet' and *s'asseoir* 'to sit down' when they follow *faire* (and sometimes also *laisser*):

Il a fait (se) taire les enfants
He made the children be quiet

Elle a fait (s')asseoir tout le monde
She got everyone to sit down

12.4 Verbs which take infinitive complements preceded by the preposition *à*

12.4.1 Verbs of 'beginning' and 'continuing'

Verbs which signal the beginning or continuation of an action typically take an infinitive complement preceded by *à*:

se mettre à rédiger un rapport	*to start to draft a report*
persister à demander une réponse	*to persist in asking for a reply*

Commencer and *continuer* are verbs which take an infinitive complement preceded interchangeably by *à* or by *de*:

commencer à/d'écrire son journal intime	*to begin to write one's diary*
continuer à/de faire des efforts	*to continue to make an effort*

The following verbs can take infinitive complements preceded by *par*:

commencer par enlever le papier peint	*to begin by removing the wallpaper*
finir par vendre sa maison	*to finish by selling one's house*

These are nearly always rendered in English by a construction involving 'by + verb + ing' and contrast with the use of the same verbs with infinitives preceded by *à* or *de*:

commencer à/d'enlever le papier peint	*to begin to remove the wallpaper*
finir de tondre le gazon	*to finish mowing the lawn*

12.4.2 **Verbs expressing 'manner'**

Verbs which express the manner in which an action is conducted typically take an infinitive complement preceded by *à*:

s'abaisser jusqu'à demander de l'argent à ses proches	*to stoop to asking one's family and friends for money*
s'appliquer à apprendre le russe	*to apply oneself to learning Russian*
s'apprêter à parler	*to get ready to speak*
s'attarder à bavarder dans le restaurant	*to linger chatting in the restaurant*
se borner à considérer les points principaux	*to limit oneself to considering the main points*
concourir à assurer la défaite de l'ennemi	*to combine to defeat the enemy*
condescendre à faire quelque chose	*to condescend to do something*
conspirer à produire une catastrophe	*to conspire to produce a catastrophe*
s'entêter à comprendre pourquoi l'écran a gelé	*to be determined to understand why the screen froze*
se limiter à corriger les plus grosses erreurs	*to limit oneself to correcting the worst errors*
s'obstiner à découvrir la vérité	*to be bent on discovering the truth*
s'oublier à regarder toute une série d'un coup	*to become absorbed in binge-watching a series*
s'en tenir à changer quelques détails	*to stick to changing a few details*
travailler à se faire aimer	*to work to get oneself liked*

12.4.3 **Pronominal verbs expressing an 'emotional reaction'**

Pronominal verbs which express a subject's emotional reaction to an event typically take an infinitive complement preceded by *à*:

s'abêtir à trop travailler	*to become stupid by working too hard*
s'abrutir à trop regarder les écrans	*to become stupefied from spending too much time staring at screens*
s'affoler à imaginer le pire	*to panic imagining the worst*
s'amuser à agacer le chat	*to have fun annoying the cat*
se délecter à visiter Bruges	*to take delight in visiting Bruges*
s'énerver à rattacher constamment ses lacets	*to get annoyed constantly retying one's laces*
s'ennuyer à faire un travail monotone	*to get bored doing a monotonous job*
se plaire à tout critiquer	*to take pleasure in criticizing everything*

Exceptions:

s'étonner d'être si calme	*to be surprised to be so calm*
s'inquiéter de trouver la route bloquée	*to worry about finding the road blocked*
s'irriter d'avoir à expliquer chaque point trois fois	*to be annoyed by having to explain each point three times*
se réjouir de/à écrire des contes pour enfants	*to take real pleasure in writing children's stories*

12.4.4 **Pronominal verbs of 'effort'**

Pronominal verbs which express the effort with which an action is undertaken typically take an infinitive complement preceded by *à*:

s'**acharner à** trouver une solution	*to try desperately to find a solution*
s'**égosiller à** appeler les enfants	*to go hoarse calling the children*
s'**épuiser à** travailler	*to exhaust oneself working*
s'**éreinter à** traîner une valise	*to tire oneself out dragging a suitcase along*
s'**essoufler à** monter la côte	*to get out of breath climbing the hill*
s'**évertuer à** conclure l'affaire	*to do one's utmost to close the deal*
se **fatiguer à** répéter l'avertissement	*to tire oneself out repeating the warning*
se **tuer à** le dire	*to be sick and tired of saying it*
s'**user à** repeindre la maison	*to wear oneself out repainting the house*

12.4.5 **Pronominal verbs expressing 'dedication'**

Pronominal verbs which express the dedication with which an action is undertaken typically take an infinitive complement preceded by *à*:

s'**attacher à** traduire la pensée de l'auteur	*to be careful to convey the author's thoughts*
s'**aventurer à** faire des suggestions	*to be so bold as to make suggestions*
se **décider à** prendre sa retraite	*to persuade oneself to retire*
s'**essayer à** gérer un restaurant	*to try one's hand at running a restaurant*
se **hasarder à** faire une course en montagne	*to venture to go up a mountain*
se **résigner à** tout perdre	*to resign oneself to losing everything*
se **résoudre à** changer d'emploi	*to come to terms with having to change jobs*
se **risquer à** jouer en Bourse	*to take risks by playing the Stock Exchange*

Note the following differences in meaning when some of these verbs are used with *à* and with *de*:

se **décider à** prendre sa retraite	*to persuade oneself to retire*
décider de prendre sa retraite	*to decide to retire*
s'**essayer à** gérer un restaurant	*to try one's hand at running a restaurant*
essayer de gérer un restaurant	*to try to run a restaurant*
se **risquer à** investir à l'étranger	*to take risks by investing abroad*
risquer de tout perdre	*to risk losing everything*
se **résoudre à** changer d'emploi	*to accept having to change jobs*
résoudre de changer d'emploi	*to resolve to change jobs*

Note the difference in meaning and preposition when non-pronominal equivalent verbs are used.

12.4.6 **Verbs expressing 'aspiration' and 'success'**

Verbs which express the aspiration to do something, or success in achieving it, typically take an infinitive complement preceded by *à*:

arriver à obtenir gain de cause	*to manage to get one's way*
aspirer à dominer sa peur	*to aspire to overcome fear*
chercher à revendre sa start-up	*to seek to sell on one's start-up*
être disposé à favoriser qn	*to be inclined to favour sb*
incliner à quitter son emploi	*to be inclined to give up one's job*
parvenir à créer une cagnotte en ligne	*to succeed in setting up group fundraising online*
réussir à gagner la course	*to succeed in winning the race*

tendre à éviter les problèmes	*to have a tendency to avoid problems*
tenir à payer sa part	*to be keen on paying one's share*
viser à remporter la victoire	*to aim to be victorious*

12.4.7 **Verbs expressing 'unwillingness'**

Verbs which express an unwillingness to do something typically take an infinitive complement preceded by *à*:

hésiter à critiquer qn	*to hesitate to criticize sb*
rechigner à vendre ses livres	*to baulk at selling one's books*
renoncer à tout relire	*to give up on the idea of re-reading everything*
répugner à tout faire soi-même	*to be very reluctant to do the work oneself*

12.4.8 **Verbs of 'forcing'**

Verbs which express the pressure put on someone to do something typically take an infinitive complement preceded by *à*:

condamner qn **à** vivre sans ressources	*to condemn sb to live in poverty*
contraindre Julie **à** revenir	*to force Julie to come back*
forcer une entreprise **à** baisser ses prix	*to make a company reduce its prices*
obliger Dorian **à** partir	*to make Dorian leave*

Note that the following verbs, when used in the passive, take an infinitive complement preceded by *de*:

être contraint de démissionner	*to be obliged to resign*
être forcé de rentrer	*to have to go home*
être obligé de travailler à l'étranger	*to be forced to work abroad*

12.4.9 **Verbs of 'inviting'**

Verbs which invite someone to do something typically take an infinitive complement preceded by *à*:

appeler un tiers **à** arbitrer	*to call on a third party to arbitrate*
assigner le témoin **à** comparaître	*to call on the witness to appear*
autoriser les clients **à** s'en servir	*to authorize the clients to make use of it*
inviter Raoul **à** donner son avis	*to invite Raoul to give his opinion*

12.4.10 **Verbs of 'training' and 'teaching'**

Verbs which train or teach someone to do something typically take an infinitive complement preceded by *à*:

accoutumer un malade **à** prendre moins de calmants	*to get a sick person used to taking fewer painkillers*
apprendre à ses élèves **à** parler italien	*to teach one's pupils to speak Italian*
dresser un chien **à** aller chercher le journal	*to train a dog to fetch the newspaper*
enseigner à Jacques **à** jouer au tennis	*to teach Jacques to play tennis*
habituer un citadin **à** travailler en plein air	*to get a town-dweller used to working in the open air*
préparer quelqu'un **à** traverser une période de chômage	*to prepare somebody for a period of unemployment*

Note that *apprendre* and *enseigner* are the only two verbs in French which take both an indirect object preceded by *à* and an infinitive preceded by *à*:

apprendre à quelqu'un **à** faire quelque chose	*to teach somebody to do something*
enseigner à quelqu'un **à** faire quelque chose	*to teach somebody to do something*

Verbs which English speakers often think have indirect objects, but which in fact have direct objects, are:

aider quelqu'un **à** faire quelque chose	*to help somebody to do something*
inviter quelqu'un **à** faire quelque chose	*to invite somebody to do something*
obliger quelqu'un **à** faire quelque chose	*to make somebody do something*

12.4.11 **Verbs of 'encouragement' and 'cajoling'**

Verbs which encourage or cajole someone to do something typically take an infinitive complement preceded by *à*:

amener Olivier **à** reparler de l'accident
to bring Olivier to talk about the accident again

conduire quelqu'un **à** se repentir
to bring somebody to repent

convier son frère **à** réfléchir
to suggest that one's brother should think something over

décider quelqu'un **à** changer de cap
to make somebody decide to change direction

déterminer quelqu'un **à** s'inscrire **à** l'université
to make somebody decide to go to university

encourager son chiot **à** faire ses besoins dehors
to encourage one's puppy to do his business outside

engager quelqu'un **à** repenser un projet
to bring somebody to reconsider a plan

entraîner des adolescents **à** vaper
to encourage youngsters to vape

exhorter quelqu'un **à** mener campagne
to exhort somebody to campaign

inciter le gouvernement **à** agir
to incite the government to act

pousser Noëmie **à** se marier
to push Noëmie into getting married

Note also the following contrasts involving *décider*:

décider quelqu'un **à** partir	*to bring somebody to leave*
décider de partir	*to decide to leave*
se décider à partir	*to decide to leave* (after much thought)

12.4.12 Verbs expressing 'the dedication of time, money to doing something'

consacrer ses loisirs **à** monter des sites	*to spend one's free time setting up websites*
dépenser de l'argent **à** jouer en ligne	*to spend money gambling online*
mettre deux heures **à** ranger ses affaires	*to take two hours to tidy one's things*
occuper son temps **à** lire des romans policiers	*to spend one's time reading crime novels*
passer son temps **à** faire des mots croisés	*to spend one's time doing crosswords*
utiliser ses connaissances **à** former des jeunes	*to use one's knowledge to train young people*

12.4.13 Verbs of 'discovering'

attraper qn **à** télécharger des films illégalement	*to catch sb downloading films illegally*
prendre qn **à** fouiller dans un tiroir	*to catch sb going through a drawer*
surprendre qn **à** voler des bijoux	*to catch sb stealing jewellery*

12.5 Verbs which take an infinitive complement preceded by *de*

There is no real community of meaning in the verbs which take an infinitive complement preceded by *de* but some grouping by meaning is possible.

12.5.1 Verbs of 'advising somebody to do or not to do something'

avertir qn **de** ne pas recommencer
to warn sb not to do it again

conjurer qn **de** laisser les choses comme elles sont
to plead with sb to leave things as they are

conseiller (à qn) **de** ne pas intenter de procès
to advise sb not to bring something to court

convaincre son employeur **de** hausser les salaires
to convince one's employer to raise salaries

décourager son chiot **de** faire ses besoins dans la maison
discourage one's puppy from doing his business in the house

déconseiller (à qn) **de** prendre l'autoroute
to advise sb not to take the motorway

désaccoutumer qn **de** fumer
to encourage sb to lose the habit of smoking

déshabituer qn **de** s'endormir en écoutant des podcasts
to get sb out of the habit of going to sleep whilst listening to podcasts

dissuader qn **de** manifester dans la rue
to persuade sb not to demonstrate in the street

enjoindre (à qn) **de** s'inscrire à un parti politique
to suggest to sb that they join a political party

persuader qn **de** vendre son studio
to persuade sb to sell his/her/their studio

recommander (à qn) **de** ne pas trop insister
to suggest to sb not to insist too much

suggérer (à qn) **d'**envoyer un email d'excuses
to suggest to sb that they send an email to apologise

Note that while *décourager* takes an infinitive complement preceded by *de*, *encourager* takes an infinitive complement preceded by *à*:

encourager son chiot **à** faire ses besoins dehors
to encourage one's puppy to do his business outside

12.5.2 Verbs of 'allowing', 'admitting', and 'agreeing'

accepter de télécharger l'appli de sa banque	*to agree to download one's bank's app*
choisir de suivre son dernier module en ligne	*to choose to do one's last module online*
convenir de retrouver qn à 20h	*to agree to meet up with sb at 8.00 p.m.*
décider d'observer le Ramadan	*to decide to observe Ramadan*
dispenser un étudiant **de** faire un test	*to exempt a student from a test*
entreprendre de réétablir des liens	*to undertake to re-establish links*
jurer à son père **de** lui rendre visite	*to swear to one's father to visit him*
obtenir de pouvoir sortir tôt	*to get permission to go out early*
permettre (à qn) **de** rembourser sans payer les intérêts	*to allow somebody to pay back without interest*
résoudre de ne plus boire de café	*to resolve to drink no more coffee*

12.5.3 Verbs expressing the idea of 'anger'

enrager d'avoir perdu toutes ses données
to be very angry about having lost all of one's data

être furieux d'être exclu du groupe
to be furious at being excluded from the group

s'indigner de se voir refuser l'entrée du club
to be indignant at being refused entry to the club

menacer les grévistes **de** les licencier
to threaten the strikers with being sacked

12.5.4 Verbs of 'asking for' and of 'attempting to'

demander à Valentin **de** surveiller les enfants	*to ask Valentin to keep an eye on the children*
essayer de chanter une chanson	*to try to sing a song*
implorer qn **de** revenir	*to implore sb to come back*
parler de faire le tour du monde	*to speak of doing a world tour*

prier qn **de** bien vouloir partir	*to ask sb to kindly leave*
proposer à une municipalité **de** construire un théâtre	*to put to a town hall the idea of building a theatre*
supplier qn **de** faire attention	*to beg sb to be careful*
tâcher de terminer le travail à temps	*to try to finish the work on time*
tenter de résoudre le problème sans avoir recours à l'extérieur	*to attempt to resolve the problem without asking for outside help*

Note: *demander à qn de faire qc* 'to ask somebody to do something', but *demander à faire qc* 'to ask to do something'.

12.5.5 **Verbs of 'blaming', 'making responsible for'**

accuser qn **d'**avoir collaboré avec l'ennemi
to accuse sb of having collaborated with the enemy

blâmer qn **d'**avoir été négligent
to blame sb for having been careless

charger qn **d'**apporter à manger tous les jours
to make sb responsible for bringing in food every day

gronder son fils **d'**avoir cassé l'écran de la tablette
to tell your son off for having broken the screen of the tablet

reprocher à qn **d'**avoir perdu les clefs
to hold it against sb that they lost the keys

soupçonner qn **d'**avoir dissimulé la vérité
to suspect sb of not having told the truth

12.5.6 **Verbs of '(self-)congratulation'**

s'applaudir d'avoir écrit au président
to be pleased with oneself for having written to the president

féliciter qn **d'**avoir terminé sa thèse
to congratulate sb on finishing their thesis

se flatter d'être le meilleur joueur
to imagine that one is the best player

se glorifier d'avoir monté le projet tout seul
to be very proud of having put together the project unaided

louer qn **d'**avoir gagné une course
to praise sb for having won a race

mériter de gagner
to deserve to win

se vanter d'être le meilleur joueur de l'équipe
to boast of being the best player in the team

12.5.7 **Verbs of 'denial'**

s'abstenir de boire de l'alcool
se disculper d'avoir voulu supplanter qn

refuser de s'abaisser à un compromis

to abstain from drinking alcohol
to exonerate oneself from having wanted to take over from sb
to refuse to stoop to a compromise

Exception: *nier* takes an infinitive complement without a linking preposition:

nier être impliqué dans l'affaire

to deny being implicated in the affair

12.5.8 **Verbs of 'excusing' and 'pardoning'**

excuser qn **d'**être arrivé en retard
to overlook sb's late arrival

pardonner (à qn) **d'**avoir fait souffrir la famille
to pardon sb for having caused the family pain

12.5.9 **Verbs of 'forbidding'**

défendre à un enfant de jouer à la console après 21h
to forbid a child to play video games after 9 p.m.

interdire à qn **de** se faire faire un tatouage
to forbid sb to have a tatoo done

interdire aux trottinettistes de circuler sur le trottoir
to prohibit the use of scooters on the pavement

12.5.10 **Verbs of 'being fearful'**

appréhender de devoir se présenter devant un tribunal
to be fearful of having to appear before a court

avoir peur de conduire
to be afraid to drive

craindre de devoir démissionner
to be afraid of having to resign

frémir de penser à ce qui aurait pu arriver
to shudder to think what might have happened

s'inquiéter d'avoir à rentrer
to worry about having to go home

pâlir de voir son ex en couple
to blanch at seeing one's ex with a new partner

redouter de devoir reconfigurer l'alarme
to fear having to reconfigure the alarm

se soucier de créer une bonne impression
to care about making a good impression

trembler de penser qu'on a failli se faire écraser
to tremble to think that one nearly got run over

12.5.11 Verbs of 'forgetting'

négliger de protéger ses documents
to neglect to protect one's files

omettre de préciser à son hôte qu'on arrivera en retard
to forget to tell one's host that one will be late

oublier de signaler une absence
to forget to report an absence

12.5.12 Verbs of 'hurrying' or 'delaying'

se dépêcher d'aller chez le boulanger avant la fermeture
to hurry to get to the baker's before it shuts

se hâter de mettre en œuvre ses propres idées
to want to quickly put one's own ideas into operation

12.5.13 Verbs of 'delighting' or 'regretting'

avoir regret de ne jamais avoir dit à qn qu'on l'aimait
to regret not ever having told sb that one loved him/her

regretter d'avoir choisi la solution de facilité
to regret having chosen the easy way out

se réjouir d'avoir été élu
to be delighted at having been elected

se repentir d'avoir acheté un portable bas de gamme
to regret having bought a cheap mobile

12.5.14 Verbs of 'pretending'

affecter de ne pas être au courant de ce qui se passe
to pretend not to know what's happening

faire semblant de ne pas avoir entendu
to pretend not to have heard

feindre d'être malade
to pretend to be ill

12.5.15 Verbs of 'pre-planning'

envisager de vivre sur une péniche
to imagine living on a canal boat

méditer de dire ses quatre vérités à son frère
to think about telling one's brother some home truths

préméditer de quitter son travail	*to plan on leaving one's job*
projeter de monter son entreprise	*to give some thought to setting up one's own company*
proposer de partir tout seul dans le Midi	*to propose going to the south of France on one's own*
ruminer d'écrire ses mémoires	*to have it in mind to write one's memoirs*

12.5.16 **Verbs of 'ordering'**

commander à un bataillon **de** se préparer	*to order a batallion to get ready*
dire à Soisic **de** rejoindre le groupe	*to tell Soisic to join the group*
écrire à Manon **d'**aller voir sa mère	*to write to Manon to go and see her mother*
hurler à qn **de** passer le ballon	*to shout to sb to pass the ball*
ordonner à qn **de** quitter les lieux	*to order sb to leave the premises*
prescrire à qn **de** se reposer	*to order sb to rest*
répondre à qn **de** se taire	*to tell sb in response to be quiet*
sommer qn **de** venir aussi vite que possible	*to instruct sb to come as quickly as possible*
téléphoner à sa mère **d'**envoyer de l'argent	*to phone one's mother to send money*

12.5.17 **Verbs of 'finishing' and of 'stopping somebody doing something'**

s'abstenir de fumer pendant trois mois	*to refrain from smoking for three months*
achever de construire sa maison	*to finish building one's house*
arrêter de faire l'idiot en cours	*to stop playing the fool in class*
cesser de participer aux matchs de football	*to stop taking part in football matches*
empêcher qn **de** partir en vacances	*to stop sb going on holiday*
éviter de faire les mêmes erreurs	*to avoid making the same mistakes*
finir de se préparer	*to finish getting ready*

12.5.18 **Verbs of 'thanking'**

remercier qn **de** vous avoir invité à déjeuner
to thank sb for having invited you for lunch

savoir gré à qn **de** bien vouloir répondre rapidement
to be grateful to sb for replying quickly

12.5.19 **Impersonal verbs expressing 'personal reaction' to an event**

Compare some of the impersonal verbs below, which take *de*, with the same verbs used personally, which take *à* (see Section 12.4.3):

Ça m'**agace de** les voir sans occupation	*It annoys me to see them idle*
Ça m'**amuse de** le voir en colère	*It amuses me to see him angry*
Ça l'**attriste d'**apprendre qu'elle est malheureuse	*It saddens him to learn that she is unhappy*
Ça me **consterne de** l'apprendre	*It dismays me to learn that*
Ça me **dégoûte de** voir ce gaspillage	*It appals me to see this waste*
Ça m'**ennuie d'**être suivi par des journalistes	*I find it wearing to be followed by reporters*
Ça la **fâche d'**avoir à se justifer auprès de toi	*It irritates her to have to justify herself to you*
Ça les **fatigue de** faire la navette	*It tires them to go back and forth*

Ça l'**intéresse de** voir le manuscrit   *It interests him to see the manuscript*
Ça l'**intrigue de** savoir ce qu'ils ont dit   *It intrigues him to know what they said*
Ça nous **irrite d'**avoir à refaire le travail   *It irritates us to have to do the work again*

12.5.20 Other verbs with infinitive complements preceded by *de*

s'**affliger d'**avoir causé de la peine à qn
to be sorry to have caused sb pain

ambitionner de paraître dans un film
to have ambitions to appear in a film

avoir le droit de donner son avis
to have the right to give one's opinion

en avoir marre de tout faire à la maison
to be fed up with doing everything in the house

brûler de jouer dans l'équipe du collège
to have a great desire to play in the school team

comploter de renverser le gouvernement
to plot to overthrow the government

consoler qn **d'**avoir perdu un parent
to console sb for having lost a relative

se contenter de vivre à la campagne
to be happy to live in the country

dédaigner d'accorder un entretien à un journaliste
to be snooty about giving an interview to a journalist

défier qn **de** dire la vérité
to challenge sb to tell the truth

dégoûter qn **de** manger des fraises
to put sb off eating strawberries

désespérer de pouvoir sortir de prison
to despair of getting out of prison

douter de pouvoir faire qc
to doubt that one will be able to do sth

s'**efforcer de** devenir influenceur
to do one's best to become an influencer

entreprendre de récupérer l'argent perdu
to undertake to get back the money

envier qn **d'**avoir démissionné
to envy sb for having resigned

être tenu de remplir ses obligations
to be obliged to meet one's obligations

se garder de raconter la vérité
to make sure not to tell the truth

gémir d'avoir à payer ses dettes
to groan at having to pay one's debts

se mêler de monter une affaire
to take it upon oneself to start a business

offrir de dédommager les victimes
to offer to recompense the victims

plaindre qn **de** ne pas avoir d'enfants
to pity sb because they don't have children

presser qn **de** s'acquitter de ses dettes
to put pressure on sb to pay off their debts

prévoir de gagner beaucoup d'argent
to foresee making lots of money

promettre d'emmener toute la famille aux Etats-Unis
to promise to take the whole family to the United States

réclamer de pouvoir s'asseoir où on veut
to demand to be allowed to sit where one wishes

se remettre d'avoir été attaqué dans la rue
to recover from having been attacked in the street

se réserver de déterminer soi-même sa fin de vie
to reserve the right to decide for oneself how one's life will end

rêver de devenir milliardaire
to dream of becoming a millionaire

rougir de devoir parler en public
to blush at having to speak in public

sourire de voir les enfants s'amuser dans le jardin
to smile at seeing the children playing in the garden

12.6 **Omission of objects before infinitives**

The direct or indirect objects of verbs with infinitive complements may be omitted in French when they have a non-specific or indefinite interpretation. English requires an object if an infinitive is used:

Le succès encourage à continuer
*Success encourages **one** to continue*

Ce résultat force à repenser le problème
*This result forces **us** to rethink the problem*

Dans cette région, c'est l'irrigation qui a permis d'améliorer le rendement agricole
*The irrigation of the region has allowed **someone (e.g. farmers)** to improve crop yield*

L'expérience enseigne à être prudent
*Experience teaches **one** to be careful*

Cette déclaration autorise à penser que les dirigeants ont changé d'avis
*This declaration allows **us** to think that the leaders have changed their opinion*

12.7 **Infinitives as complements to adjectives**

Adjectives take infinitive complements preceded either by *à* or *de*, never without a preposition.

12.7.1 **Infinitives following adjectives in impersonal constructions**

Adjectives used in impersonal constructions take an infinitive complement preceded by *de:*

Dans ce quartier il est dangereux **de** sortir le soir
In this part of the town it is dangerous to go out in the evening

Il ne sera pas évident **de** faire parler le disque dur
It won't be easy to get the hard drive to reveal its secrets

Il serait étonnant **de** trouver Jules dans une boîte de nuit
It would be surprising to come across Jules in a night club

Il est nécessaire **de** demander des explications précises
It is necessary to ask for precise explanations

Il est rare **de** voir Corentin jouer au rugby
It is rare to see Corentin play rugby

Il est regrettable **de** ne pas avoir de recours contre la pollution par le bruit
It is unfortunate that there is no redress against noise pollution

Other common adjectives which can be used impersonally in this way are:

agréable **de** faire qc	*pleasant to do sth*
bon **de** faire qc	*good to do sth*
commode **de** faire qc	*convenient to do sth*
difficile **de** faire qc	*difficult to do sth*
facile **de** faire qc	*easy to do sth*
important **de** faire qc	*important to do sth*
(im)possible **de** faire	*(im)possible to do sth*
intéressant **de** faire qc	*interesting to do sth*
inutile **de** faire qc	*useless to do sth*
mauvais **de** faire qc	*bad to do sth*
merveilleux **de** faire qc	*amazing to do sth*
pénible **de** faire qc	*irksome to do sth*
simple **de** faire qc	*simple to do sth*
utile **de** faire qc	*useless to do sth*

12.7.2 **Infinitives following adjectives used personally**

When the adjectives in Section 12.7.1 are used personally (that is to describe a noun or personal pronoun), they take an infinitive complement preceded by *à*. Compare the personal and impersonal constructions in the following:

La pâte à pain est agréable **à** toucher
Dough is nice to handle

Il est agréable **de** toucher de la pâte à pain
It's nice to handle dough

Les feuilles vertes du chou-fleur sont bonnes **à** manger
The green outer leaves of cauliflowers are good to eat

Il est bon **de** manger les feuilles vertes du chou-fleur
It's good to eat the green outer leaves of cauliflowers

C'est difficile **à** faire
That's difficult to do

Il est difficile **de** le faire
It's difficult to do that

L'intelligence artificielle va être difficile **à** canaliser
AI will be difficult to control

Il va être difficile **de** canaliser l'intelligence artificielle
It will be difficult to control AI

Avec tout ce que tu as mis dedans, les poubelles sont difficiles **à** sortir
With all that you've put in them, the dustbins are difficult to put out

Il est difficile **de** sortir les poubelles, avec tout ce que tu as mis dedans
It's difficult to put out the dustbins with all that you have put in them

Ces problèmes sont faciles **à** résoudre
These problems are easy to solve

Il est facile **de** résoudre ces problèmes
It is easy to solve these problems

Cette machine à laver est impossible **à** réparer
This washing machine is impossible to repair

Il est impossible **de** réparer cette machine à laver
It is impossible to repair this washing machine

La défaite est difficile **à** accepter
Defeat is hard to accept

Il est difficile **d'**accepter la défaite
It is hard to accept defeat

Since the pronouns *il* and *ce* can be used both impersonally and personally, this means that alternations like the following can be found:

Au début **il** était difficile **de** comprendre Zaïda
At first it was difficult to understand Zaïda

Au début **elle** (i.e. Zaïda) était difficile **à** comprendre
At first she was difficult to understand

C'est beau **de** voir tous ces enfants jouer ensemble
It's wonderful to see all these children playing together

C'est beau **à** voir
It's wonderful to see

(See also Section 3.1.22 for discussion of this construction.)

12.7.3 **Infinitives following adjectives of 'manner' take *à***

Adjectives which describe the manner in which an action is carried out typically take an infinitive complement preceded by *à*:

Nous ne sommes pas prêts **à** oeuvrer contre le changement climatique
We are not ready to work against climate change

Vu ses qualifications, elle est propre **à** assumer ces fonctions
With her qualifications, she is suitable for the job

Other common adjectives which behave in this way are:

être disposé/enclin/porté **à** faire qc	*to be inclined to do sth*
être habile **à** faire qc	*to be skilful in doing sth*
être prompt **à** faire qc	*to be prompt in doing sth*
être seul **à** faire qc	*to be alone in doing sth*

12.7.4 **Infinitives following adjectives which take *de***

Most other adjectives which take an infinitive complement select the preposition *de*:

Nous sommes très heureux **d'**apprendre votre mariage
We are very happy to hear the news of your wedding

Nous vous sommes reconnaissants **d'**avoir contribué à notre cagnotte en ligne
We are grateful to you for having taken part in our online fundraising

Vous êtes libre **d'**essayer	*You are free to try*
(*but* Libre à vous **d'**essayer	*Up to you to try*)

Other common adjectives which take *de*:

certain/sûr **de** faire qc	*sure to do sth*
content **de** faire qc	*pleased to do sth*
désireux **de** faire qc	*keen to do sth*
désolé **de** faire qc	*sorry to do sth*
étonné **de** faire qc	*astonished to do sth*

fier **de** faire qc	*proud to do sth*
impatient **de** faire qc	*impatient to do sth*
(in)capable **de** faire qc	*(in)capable of doing sth*
susceptible **de** faire qc	*likely to do sth*

12.8 Infinitives as complements to nouns

Nouns take infinitive complements preceded either by *à* or by *de*, never without a preposition.

12.8.1 Infinitives following nouns related to verbs and adjectives

Nouns related to verbs and adjectives which take an infinitive complement preceded by *à* or *de* typically take the same preposition:

inviter qn **à** faire qc	l'invitation **à** faire qc
disposé **à** faire qc	la disposition **à** faire qc
craindre **de** faire qc	la crainte **de** faire qc
défendre à qn **de** fumer	Défense **de** fumer
interdire à qn **de** faire qc	Interdiction **de** pénétrer en ces lieux
menacer qn **de** faire qc	la menace **de** faire qc
ordonner à qn **de** faire qc	l'ordre **de** faire qc
permettre à qn **de** faire qc	la permission **de** faire qc
désireux **de** faire qc	le désir **de** faire qc
impatient **de** faire qc	l'impatience **de** faire qc

12.8.2 Infinitives following nouns involved in the event described by an infinitive take *à*

Nouns which are understood as being involved in the event described by the infinitive (as subject, direct object, indirect object, instrument, or time when the event takes place) typically take an infinitive preceded by *à*:

un appartement **à** rénover
('appartement' is understood as the object of 'rénover')
a flat to renovate

C'était un soir **à** se promener sur la plage
('soir' is understood as the time when walking takes place)
It was an evening for walking on the beach

Other common examples:

un appartement **à** louer	*a flat to rent*
du bois **à** brûler	*firewood*
une chambre **à** coucher	*a bedroom*
un exemple **à** ne pas suivre	*an example not to be followed*
un fer **à** repasser	*an iron*
un homme **à** craindre	*a man to be feared*
une idée **à** examiner	*an idea to explore*
une maison **à** vendre	*a house for sale*
un pays **à** voir l'hiver	*a country to see in winter*
une poêle **à** frire	*a frying pan*

une pomme à cuire	a cooking apple
des repas à emporter	take-away meals
un roman à lire	a novel to read
une salle à manger	a dining room

12.8.3 Some common idioms in which the preposition is *à*

avoir droit à des bénéfices	to be entitled to benefits
avoir intérêt à faire qc	to have a stake in doing sth
avoir du mal à faire qc	to experience some difficulty in doing sth
avoir plaisir à faire qc	to take pleasure in doing sth
être d'âge à faire qc	to be old enough to do sth
Nous sommes cinq à faire qc	there are five of us doing sth
être le dernier à faire qc	to be the last to do sth
être d'humeur à faire qc	to be in a mood for doing sth
être le premier à faire qc	to be the first to do sth
être le seul à faire qc	to be the only one to do sth
prendre plaisir à faire qc	to take pleasure in doing sth

12.8.4 Most other nouns take the preposition *de*

avoir l'air/l'apparence **de** faire qc	to appear to be doing sth
avoir besoin **de** faire qc	to need to do sth
avoir de la chance **de** faire qc	to be lucky to do sth
avoir le droit **de** faire qc	to have the right to do sth
avoir envie **de** faire qc	to want to do sth
avoir hâte **de** faire qc	to be quick to do sth
avoir honte **de** faire qc	to be ashamed to do sth
avoir raison **de** faire qc	to be right to do sth
avoir tort **de** faire qc	to be wrong to do sth
avoir le toupet/le culot **de** faire qc	to have the cheek to do sth
avoir la veine **de** faire qc	to be lucky to do sth
la façon/la manière **de** faire qc	the manner of doing sth
le moment **de** faire qc	the moment to do sth
les moyens **de** faire qc	the means to do sth
l'occasion **de** faire qc	the opportunity to do sth
le temps **de** faire qc	the time to do sth

12.9 Infinitives in subordinate clauses

Infinitives in subordinate clauses may play the role of subjects or objects. The examples we have quoted extensively above where infinitives follow the verb and/or are introduced by *à* and *de* mainly show infinitive clauses playing the role of objects in the sentence. They can also be subjects.

In some cases, they are linked to the main clause by the use of *c'est*; in other cases, they directly precede the main verb. In many cases, both *c'est* and *est* are possible with minimal stylistic difference. *Voici* and *voilà* may also play a linking role:

Partir c'est mourir un peu
To leave is to die a little

Se cacher la vérité, **c'est** remettre le problème à plus tard
Hiding the truth from oneself is putting the problem off until later

Mettre les politiques devant les réalités, **voilà** le problème
Getting politicians to face up to reality, that's where the problem is

S'accorder sur l'essentiel, **voilà** ce qu'on doit faire
What we must do is agree on the basics

Pleurer ne sert à rien
Crying won't get us anywhere

Se fâcher dans cette situation ne fera qu'aggraver les choses
In this situation getting angry will make matters worse

Manger trop gras nuit à la santé
Eating too much fatty food is bad for your health

Appeler les secours était la seule chose à faire
To call the emergency services was the only thing to do

Habiter Paris est très agréable
Living in Paris is very pleasant

Jouer aux jeux vidéo était son seul passetemps
Playing video games was her only hobby

Se détendre le weekend, **c'est** important pour la santé
For health reasons it is important to relax at weekends

12.10 Infinitives as polite commands

In certain cases, instructions are conveyed by means of infinitives rather than the more forceful imperatives. This is particularly the case where the audience is non-specific, as in road-users, consumers, or students taking exams:

Ralentir: Enfants (*or* Attention: Ecole)	*Slow down. School*
Soulever, écarter doucement	*Lift and separate carefully* (instructions for opening a packet of coffee)
Cliquer sur les bonnes réponses	*Click the correct answers*
Ne **répondre** qu'à l'une des questions de la section ci-dessous	*Answer only one question in this section*
Ouvrir doucement	*Be careful when opening*
Ne pas **renverser**	*Don't spill*
Ne pas **révéler** vos infos personnelles	*Don't give away your personal data*
A **manier** avec précaution	*Be careful when handling*
Remettre entre les mains de …	*Only to be given to … personally*
Appuyer sur le bouton	*Press the button*
Agiter avant d'ouvrir	*Shake before opening*

12.11 **Quick-reference index to verbs taking infinitive complements**

s'abaisser à faire qc (Section 12.4.2)	*to stoop to doing sth*
s'abêtir, s'abrutir à faire qc (Section 12.4.3)	*to become stupid from doing sth*
s'abstenir de faire qc (Sections 12.5.7 and 12.5.17)	*to refrain from doing sth*
accepter de faire qc (Section 12.5.2)	*to agree to do sth*
accoutumer qn à faire qc (Section 12.4.10)	*to get sb used to doing sth*
accuser qn d'avoir fait qc (Section 12.5.5)	*to accuse sb of having done sth*
s'acharner à faire qc (Section 12.4.4)	*to be bent on doing sth*
achever de faire qc (Section 12.5.17)	*to finish doing sth*
adorer faire qc (Section 12.3.6)	*to adore doing sth*
affecter d'avoir fait qc (Section 12.5.14)	*to pretend to have done sth*
affirmer avoir fait qc (Section 12.3.4)	*to state that one has done sth*
s'affliger d'avoir fait qc (Section 12.5.20)	*to be sorry to have done sth*
s'affoler à faire qc (Section 12.4.3)	*to panic doing sth*
aider qn à faire qc (Section 12.4.10)	*to help sb do sth*
aimer faire qc (Section 12.3.6)	*to like doing sth*
aimer autant faire qc (Section 12.3.6)	*to just as soon do sth*
aimer mieux faire qc (Section 12.3.6)	*to prefer doing sth*
s'en aller faire qc (Section 12.3.1)	*to go and do sth*
aller faire qc (Section 12.3.1)	*to go and do sth*
ambitionner de faire qc (Section 12.5.20)	*to have ambitions to do sth*
amener qn faire qc (Section 12.3.2)	*to bring sb along to do sth*
amener qn à faire qc (Section 12.4.11)	*to bring sb to the point of doing sth*
s'amuser à faire qc (Section 12.4.3)	*to have fun doing sth*
appeler qn à faire qc (Section 12.4.9)	*to call on sb to do sth*
s'applaudir d'avoir fait qc (Section 12.5.6)	*to congratulate oneself on having done sth*
s'appliquer à faire qc (Section 12.4.2)	*to apply oneself to doing sth*
appréhender de faire qc (Section 12.5.10)	*to be fearful of doing sth*
apprendre à qn à faire qc (Section 12.4.10)	*to teach sb to do sth*
s'apprêter à faire qc (Section 12.4.2)	*to get ready to do sth*
arrêter de faire qc (Section 12.5.17)	*to stop doing sth*
arriver faire qc (Section 12.3.1)	*to come to do sth*
arriver à faire qc (Section 12.4.6)	*to succeed in doing sth*
aspirer à faire qc (Section 12.4.6)	*to aspire to do sth*
assigner qn à faire qc (Section 12.4.9)	*to call on sb to do sth*
s'attacher à faire qc (Section 12.4.5)	*to cling to doing sth*
s'attarder à faire qc (Section 12.4.2)	*to linger doing sth*
attraper qn à faire qc (Section 12.4.13)	*to catch sb doing sth*
s'attrister à faire qc (Section 12.4.3. or 12.4.4)	*to be saddened doing sth*
autoriser qn à faire qc (Section 12.4.9)	*to authorize sb to do sth*
s'aventurer à faire qc (Section 12.4.5)	*to be so bold as to do sth*
s'avérer être qc (Section 12.3.7)	*to turn out to be sth*
avertir qn de faire qc (Section 12.5.1)	*to warn sb to do sth*
avoir le droit de faire qc (Section 12.5.20)	*to have the right to do sth*
en avoir marre de faire qc (Section 12.5.20)	*to be fed up doing sth*
avoir peur de faire qc (Section 12.5.10)	*to be afraid to do sth*
avoir regret d'avoir fait qc (Section 12.5.13)	*to regret having done sth*
blâmer qn d'avoir fait qc (Section 12.5.5)	*to blame sb for having done sth*
se borner à faire qc (Section 12.4.2)	*to limit oneself to doing sth*
brûler de faire qc (Section 12.5.20)	*to have a great desire to do sth*
cesser de faire qc (Section 12.5.17)	*to stop doing sth*

charger qn de faire qc (Section 12.5.5) — *to make sb responsible for doing sth*

chercher à faire qc (Section 12.4.6) — *to seek to do sth*

choisir de faire qc (Section 12.5.2) — *to choose to do sth*

chuchoter à qn de faire qc (Section 12.5.16) — *to whisper to sb to do sth*

commander à qn de faire qc (Section 12.5.16) — *to order sb to do sth*

commencer à/de faire qc (Section 12.4.1) — *to start to do sth*

commencer par faire qc (Section 12.4.1) — *to start by doing sth*

comploter de faire qc (Section 12.5.20) — *to plot to do sth*

compter faire qc (Section 12.3.6) — *to count on doing sth*

concourir à faire qc (Section 12.4.2) — *to combine to do sth*

condamner qn à faire qc (Section 12.4.8) — *to condemn sb to doing sth*

condescendre à faire qc (Section 12.4.2) — *to condescend to do sth*

conduire qn à faire qc (Section 12.4.11) — *to bring sb to do sth*

confirmer avoir fait qc (Section 12.3.4) — *to confirm having done sth*

conjurer qn de faire qc (Section 12.5.1) — *to plead with sb to do sth*

consacrer du temps à faire qc (Section 12.4.12) — *to spend time doing sth*

conseiller à qn de faire qc (Section 12.5.1) — *to advise sb to do sth*

consoler qn d'avoir fait qc (Section 12.5.20) — *to console sb for having done sth*

conspirer à faire qc (Section 12.4.2) — *to conspire to do sth*

se contenter de faire qc (Section 12.5.20) — *to be happy to do sth*

continuer à/de faire qc (Section 12.4.1) — *to continue to do sth*

contraindre qn à faire qc (Section 12.4.8) — *to force sb to do sth*

convaincre qn de faire qc (Section 12.5.1) — *to convince sb to do sth*

convenir de faire qc (Section 12.5.2) — *to agree to do sth*

convier qn à faire qc (Section 12.4.11) — *to invite sb to do sth*

courir faire qc (Section 12.3.1) — *to run to do sth*

craindre de faire qc (Section 12.5.10) — *to fear to do sth*

croire avoir fait qc (Section 12.3.5) — *to believe to have done sth*

daigner faire qc (Section 12.3.6) — *to deign to do sth*

décider de faire qc (Sections 12.4.5, 12.4.11, and 12.5.2) — *to decide to do sth*

décider qn à faire qc (Section 12.4.11) — *to make sb decide to do sth*

se décider à faire qc (Sections 12.4.5 and 12.4.11) — *to make up one's mind to do sth*

déclarer avoir fait qc (Section 12.3.4) — *to declare that one has done sth*

déconseiller à qn de faire qc (Section 12.5.1) — *to advise sb not to do sth*

décourager qn de faire qch — *to discourage sb from doing sth*

dédaigner de faire qc (Section 12.5.20) — *not to lower oneself to do sth*

défier qn de faire qc (Section 12.5.20) — *to challenge sb to do sth*

défendre à qn de faire qc (Section 12.5.9) — *to forbid sb to do sth*

dégoûter qn de faire qc (Section 12.5.20) — *to put sb off doing sth*

se délecter à faire qc (Section 12.4.3) — *to take delight in doing sth*

demander à qn de faire qc (Section 12.5.4) — *to ask sb to do sth*

démentir avoir fait qc (Section 12.3.4) — *to deny having done sth*

se dépêcher de faire qc (Section 12.5.12) — *to hurry to do sth*

dépenser de l'argent à faire qc (Section 12.4.12) — *to spend money doing sth*

désaccoutumer qn de faire qc (Section 12.5.1) — *to wean sb off doing sth*

descendre faire qc (Section 12.3.1) — *to go down and do sth*

désespérer de faire qc (Section 12.5.20) — *to despair of doing sth*

déshabituer qn de faire qc (Section 12.5.1) — *to wean sb off doing sth*

désirer faire qc (Section 12.3.6) — *to want to do sth*

déterminer qn à faire qc (Section 12.4.11) — *to make sb decide to do sth*

devoir faire qc (Section 12.3.3)	*to have to do sth*
dire avoir fait qc (Section 12.3.4)	*to say that one has done sth*
dire à qn de faire qc (Section 12.5.16)	*to tell sb to do sth*
se disculper d'avoir fait qc (Section 12.5.7)	*to exonerate oneself from having done sth*
dispenser qn de faire qc (Section 12.5.2)	*to allow sb not to do sth*
dissuader qn de faire qc (Section 12.5.1)	*to dissuade sb from doing sth*
douter de pouvoir faire qc (Section 12.5.20)	*to doubt that one is able to do sth*
dresser un animal à faire qc (Section 12.4.10)	*to train an animal to do sth*
écouter qn faire qc (Section 12.3.8)	*to listen to sb doing sth*
écrire à qn de faire qc (Section 12.5.16)	*to write to sb to do sth*
s'efforcer de faire qc (Section 12.5.20)	*to force oneself to do sth*
s'égosiller à dire qc (Section 12.4.4)	*to go hoarse saying sth*
emmener qn faire qc (Section 12.3.2)	*to take sb to do sth*
empêcher qn de faire qc (Section 12.5.17)	*to prevent sb from doing sth*
encourager qn à faire qc (Sections 12.4.11 and 12.5.1)	*to encourage sb to do sth*
s'énerver à faire qc (Section 12.4.3)	*to get annoyed doing sth*
engager qn à faire qc (Section 12.4.11)	*to bring sb to do sth*
enjoindre à qn de faire qc (Section 12.5.1)	*to suggest to sb that they do sth*
s'ennuyer à faire qc (Section 12.4.3)	*to get bored doing sth*
enrager d'avoir fait qc (Section 12.5.3)	*to be angry about having done sth*
enseigner à qn à faire qc (Section 12.4.10)	*to teach sb to do sth*
entendre faire qc (Section 12.3.6)	*to intend, mean to do sth*
entendre qn faire qc (Section 12.3.8)	*to hear sb doing sth*
s'entêter à faire qc (Section 12.4.2)	*to be bent on doing sth*
entraîner qn à faire qc (Section 12.4.11)	*to cause sb to do sth*
entreprendre de faire qc (Section 12.5.20)	*to undertake to do sth*
envier qn d'avoir fait qc (Section 12.5.20)	*to envy sb for having done sth*
envisager de faire qc (Section 12.5.15)	*to imagine doing sth*
envoyer qn faire qc (Section 12.3.2)	*to send sb to do sth*
s'épuiser à faire qc (Section 12.4.4)	*to exhaust oneself doing sth*
s'éreinter à faire qc (Section 12.4.4)	*to tire oneself out doing sth*
espérer faire qc (Section 12.3.6)	*to hope to do sth*
s'essayer à faire qc (Section 12.4.5)	*to try one's hand at doing sth*
essayer de faire qc (Sections 12.4.5 and 12.5.4)	*to try to do sth*
s'essouffler à faire qc (Section 12.4.4)	*to get out of breath doing sth*
estimer avoir fait qc (Section 12.3.5)	*to reckon to have done sth*
s'étonner de faire qc (Section 12.4.3)	*to be surprised at doing sth*
être contraint de faire qc (Section 12.4.8)	*to be obliged to do sth*
être disposé à faire qc (Section 12.4.6)	*to be inclined to do sth*
être forcé de faire qc (Section 12.4.8)	*to have to do sth*
être furieux d'avoir fait qc (Section 12.5.3)	*to be furious at having done sth*
être obligé de faire qc (Section 12.4.8)	*to be forced to do sth*
être tenu de faire qc (Section 12.5.20)	*to be obliged to do sth*
s'évertuer à faire qc (Section 12.4.4)	*to do one's utmost to do sth*
éviter de faire qc (Section 12.5.17)	*to avoid doing sth*
excuser qn d'avoir fait qc (Section 12.5.8)	*to excuse sb for having done sth*
exhorter qn à faire qc (Section 12.4.11)	*to exhort sb to do sth*
faire faire qc à qn (Section 12.3.9)	*to make sb do sth*
faire semblant de faire qc (Section 12.5.14)	*to pretend to do sth*
se fatiguer à faire qc (Section 12.4.4)	*to tire oneself out doing sth*
feindre d'avoir fait qc (Section 12.5.14)	*to pretend to have done sth*
féliciter qn d'avoir fait qc (Section 12.5.6)	*to congratulate sb on having done sth*
finir de faire qc (Sections 12.4.1 and 12.5.17)	*to finish doing sth*

finir par faire qc (Section 12.4.1)	*to finish by doing sth*
se flatter de faire qc (Section 12.5.6)	*to imagine oneself doing sth*
forcer qn à faire qc (Section 12.4.8)	*to make sb do sth*
frémir de faire qc (Section 12.5.10)	*to shudder at doing sth*
se garder de faire qc (Section 12.5.20)	*to make sure not to do sth*
gémir de faire qc (Section 12.5.20)	*to groan at doing sth*
se glorifier d'avoir fait qc (Section 12.5.6)	*to be proud of having done sth*
gronder qn d'avoir fait qc (Section 12.5.5)	*to scold sb for having done sth*
habituer qn à faire qc (Section 12.4.10)	*to get sb used to doing sth*
se hasarder à faire qc (Section 12.4.5)	*to venture to do sth*
se hâter de faire qc (Section 12.5.12)	*to hasten to do sth*
hésiter à faire qc (Section 12.4.7)	*to hesitate to do sth*
hurler à qn de faire qc (Section 12.5.16)	*to shout to sb to do sth*
s'imaginer faire qc (Section 12.3.5)	*to imagine doing sth*
implorer qn de faire qc (Section 12.5.4)	*to implore sb to do sth*
inciter qn à faire qc (Section 12.4.11)	*to incite sb to do sth*
incliner à faire qc (Section 12.4.6)	*to be inclined to do sth*
s'indigner d'avoir fait qc (Section 12.5.3)	*to be furious at having done sth*
s'inquiéter de faire qc (Sections 12.4.3 and 12.5.10)	*to worry about doing sth*
interdire à qn de faire qc (Section 12.5.9)	*to forbid sb to do sth*
inviter qn à faire qc (Sections 12.4.9 and 12.4.10)	*to invite sb to do sth*
s'irriter de/à faire qc (Section 12.4.3)	*to become irritated doing sth*
jurer (à qn) de faire qc (Section 12.5.2)	*to swear (to sb)* to do sth
laisser qn faire qc (Section 12.3.9)	*to let sb do sth*
se limiter à faire qc (Section 12.4.2)	*limit oneself to doing sth*
louer qn d'avoir fait qc (Section 12.5.6)	*to praise sb for doing sth*
méditer de faire qc (Section 12.5.15)	*to think about doing sth*
se mêler de faire qc (Section 12.5.20)	*to be mixed up in doing sth*
menacer (qn) de faire qc (Section 12.5.3)	*to threaten to do sth (sb with doing sth)*
mener qn faire qc (Section 12.3.2)	*to take sb to do sth*
mériter de faire qc (Section 12.5.6)	*to deserve to do sth*
mettre x jours à faire qc (Section 12.4.12)	*to take x days to do sth*
se mettre à faire qc (Section 12.4.1)	*to start doing sth*
monter faire qc (Section 12.3.1)	*to go up and do sth*
négliger de faire qc (Section 12.5.11)	*to neglect to do sth*
nier avoir fait qc (Section 12.3.4)	*to deny having done sth*
obliger qn à faire qc (Sections 12.4.8 and 12.4.10)	*to make sb do sth*
s'obstiner à faire qc (Section 12.4.2)	*to be bent on doing sth*
obtenir de qn de faire qc (Section 12.5.2)	*to get permission from sb to do sth*
occuper son temps à faire qc (Section 12.4.12)	*to spend one's time doing sth*
offrir à qn de faire qc (Section 12.5.20)	*to offer sb (the chance of)* doing sth
omettre de faire qc (Section 12.5.11)	*to omit to do sth*
ordonner à qn de faire qc (Section 12.5.16)	*to order sb to do sth*
oser faire qc (Section 12.3.3)	*to dare to do sth*
oublier de faire qc (Section 12.5.11)	*to forget to do sth*
s'oublier à faire qc (Section 12.4.2)	*to become absorbed in doing sth*
pâlir de faire qc (Section 12.5.10)	*to blanch at doing sth*
paraître faire qc (Section 12.3.7)	*to appear to do sth*
pardonner à qn d'avoir fait qc (Section 12.5.8)	*to pardon sb for having done sth*
parler de faire qc (Section 12.5.4)	*to speak of doing sth*
partir faire qc (Section 12.3.1)	*to leave to do sth*

parvenir à faire qc (Section 12.4.6)	*to succeed in doing sth*
passer son temps à faire qc (Section 12.4.12)	*to spend one's time doing sth*
penser faire qc (Section 12.3.5)	*to think one might do sth*
permettre à qn de faire qc (Section 12.5.2)	*to allow sb to do sth*
persister à faire qc (Section 12.4.1)	*to persist in doing sth*
persuader qn de faire qc (Section 12.5.1)	*to persuade sb to do sth*
plaindre qn d'avoir fait qc (Section 12.5.20)	*to pity sb for having done sth*
se plaire à faire qc (Section 12.4.3)	*to take pleasure in doing sth*
pousser qn à faire qc (Section 12.4.11)	*to push sb into doing sth*
pouvoir faire qc (Section 12.3.3)	*to be able to do sth*
préférer faire qc (Section 12.3.6)	*to prefer to do sth*
préméditer de faire qc (Section 12.5.15)	*to think about doing sth beforehand*
prendre qn à faire qc (Section 12.4.13)	*to catch sb doing sth*
préparer qn à faire qc (Section 12.4.10)	*to prepare sb for doing sth*
prescrire à qn de faire qc (Section 12.5.16)	*to order sb to do sth*
presser qn de faire qc (Section 12.5.20)	*to put pressure on sb to do sth*
prétendre avoir fait qc (Section 12.3.4)	*to claim to have done sth*
prévoir de faire qc (Section 12.5.20)	*to foresee doing sth*
prier qn de faire qc (Section 12.5.4)	*to ask sb politely to do sth*
projeter de faire qc (Section 12.5.15)	*to think about doing sth*
promettre à qn de faire qc (Section 12.5.20)	*to promise sb to do sth*
proposer (à qn) de faire qc (Sections 12.5.4 and 12.5.15)	*to propose doing sth (to sb)*
se rappeler avoir fait qc (Section 12.3.5)	*to remember having done sth*
rechigner à faire qc (Section 12.4.7)	*to baulk at doing sth*
réclamer de faire qc (Section 12.5.20)	*to demand to do sth*
recommander à qn de faire qc (Section 12.5.1)	*to recommend sb to do sth*
reconnaître avoir fait qc (Section 12.3.4)	*to admit to having done sth*
redouter de faire qc (Section 12.5.10)	*to fear doing sth*
refuser de faire qc (Section 12.5.7)	*to refuse to do sth*
regarder qn faire qc (Section 12.3.8)	*to watch sb doing sth*
regretter d'avoir fait qc (Section 12.5.13)	*to regret having done sth*
se réjouir de/à faire qc (Sections 12.4.3 and 12.5.13)	*to take pleasure in doing sth*
remercier qn d'avoir fait qc (Section 12.5.18)	*to thank sb for having done sth*
se remettre d'avoir fait qc (Section 12.5.20)	*to recover from having done sth*
renoncer à faire qc (Section 12.4.7)	*to give up doing sth*
rentrer faire qc (Section 12.3.1)	*to go home and do sth*
se repentir d'avoir fait qc (Section 12.5.13)	*to regret having done sth*
répondre à qn de faire qc (Section 12.5.16)	*to tell sb in response to do sth*
reprocher à qn d'avoir fait qc (Section 12.5.5)	*to reproach sb for having done sth*
répugner à faire qc (Section 12.4.7)	*to be reluctant to do sth*
se réserver de faire qc (Section 12.5.20)	*to reserve the right to do sth*
se résigner à faire qc (Section 12.4.5)	*to resign oneself to doing sth*
résoudre de faire qc (Sections 12.4.5 an 12.5.2)	*to resolve to do sth*
se résoudre à faire qc (Section 12.4.5)	*to accept having to do sth*
retourner faire qc (Section 12.3.1)	*to go back and do sth*
réussir à faire qc (Section 12.4.6)	*to succeed in doing sth*
se révéler avoir/être qc (Section 12.3.7)	*to turn out to have/be sth*
revenir faire qc (Section 12.3.1)	*to come back and do sth*
rêver de faire qc (Section 12.5.20)	*to dream of doing sth*
risquer de faire qc (Section 12.4.5)	*to risk doing sth*
se risquer à faire qc (Section 12.4.5)	*to take risks in doing sth*
rougir de faire qc (Section 12.5.20)	*to blush at doing sth*

ruminer de faire qc (Section 12.5.15)	*to think about doing sth*
savoir faire qc (Section 12.3.3)	*to be able to do sth*
savoir gré à qn de faire qc (Section 12.5.18)	*to be grateful to sb for doing sth*
sembler faire qc (Section 12.3.7)	*to seem to do sth*
sentir qn faire qc (Section 12.3.8)	*to feel sb do sth*
sommer qn de faire qc (Section 12.5.16)	*to instruct sb to do sth*
sortir faire qc (Section 12.3.1)	*to go out and do sth*
se soucier de faire qc (Section 12.5.10)	*to care about doing sth*
souhaiter faire qc (Section 12.3.6)	*to wish to do sth*
soupçonner qn d'avoir fait qc (Section 12.5.5)	*to suspect sb of having done sth*
sourire de faire qc (Section 12.5.20)	*to smile at doing sth*
se souvenir d'avoir fait qc (Section 12.3.5)	*to remember having done sth*
suggérer à qn de faire qc (Section 12.5.1)	*to suggest doing sth to sb*
supplier qn de faire qc (Section 12.5.4)	*to beg sb to do sth*
surprendre qn à faire qc (Section 12.4.13)	*to surprise sb doing sth*
tâcher de faire qc (Section 12.5.4)	*to try to do sth*
téléphoner à qn de faire qc (Section 12.5.16)	*to phone sb to do sth*
tendre à faire qc (Section 12.4.6)	*to have a tendency to do sth*
tenir à faire qc (Section 12.4.6)	*to be bent on doing sth*
s'en tenir à faire qc (Section 12.4.2)	*to stick to doing sth*
tenter de faire qc (Section 12.5.4)	*to try to do sth*
travailler à faire qc (Section 12.4.2)	*to work at doing sth*
trembler de faire qc (Section 12.5.10)	*to tremble to do sth*
se tuer à faire qc (Section 12.4.4)	*to be sick and tired of doing sth*
s'user à faire qc (Section 12.4.4)	*to wear oneself out doing sth*
utiliser ses connaissances à faire qc (Section 12.4.12)	*to use one's knowledge in doing sth*
se vanter d'avoir fait qc (Section 12.5.6)	*to boast of having done sth*
viser à faire qc (Section 12.4.6)	*to aim to do sth*
voir qn faire qc (Section 12.3.8)	*to see sb doing sth*
vouloir faire qc (Section 12.3.3)	*to want to do sth*

FREE

**INSTRUCTOR
& STUDENT
RESOURCES**

For more resources to practice your French grammar, including practice activities/quizzes for students, further resource links, and an instructor guide, please visit https://routledgelearning.com/frenchgrammarandusage.

13 Prepositions

13.1 Introduction

Prepositions are forms like *de, à, dans, en, sur, par, pour, avec, au-dessus de, du haut de, à cause de,* etc. For many French prepositions, one can normally find an English counterpart which is used in the same way in a majority of cases. For example:

de ≈ 'of':	une boîte **d'**allumettes ≈ *a box* ***of*** matches
	trois kilos **de** sucre ≈ *three kilos* ***of*** sugar
à ≈ 'at':	**à** trois heures ≈ ***at*** three o'clock
	être **à** l'école ≈ *to be* ***at*** school
dans ≈ 'in':	**dans** sa chambre ≈ ***in*** her room
	dans les années quatre-vingt-dix ≈ ***in*** the nineties

However, there are many cases where there is no direct relation between the prepositions used in each language. For example:

un pichet rempli **de** cidre
*a pitcher filled **with** (NOT *of) cider*

tenir un livre **à** la main
*to hold a book **in** (NOT *at) one's hand*

*It's kind **of** you*
C'est gentil **à** (NOT *de) vous

*She is good **at** languages*
Elle est bonne **en** (NOT *aux) langues

This chapter lists the major French prepositions alphabetically, illustrates their main uses, and gives their English equivalents in Sections 13.2–13.58. English prepositions and their French counterparts are listed in Section 13.59.

13.2 *à*

13.2.1 *à* = 'at'

Referring to place

Le camion ralentissait à chaque virage	*The lorry slowed down at every bend*
Elle est à l'école, au café, au cinéma	*She is at school, at the café, at the cinema*
à l'église, au restaurant, à la pharmacie	*at church, at the restaurant, at the chemists*
Si on se réunissait au café?	*Shall we meet at the café?*
Il était assis au chevet de sa mère	*He was sitting at his mother's bedside*
Mis en bouteille à la source	*Bottled at the spring*
au bord du lac	*at the edge of the lake*
elle est à l'ordinateur	*she is at the computer*

DOI: 10.4324/9781003373926-13

Referring to time

à trois heures, à minuit, à midi	*at three o'clock, at midnight, at midday*
à la nuit tombée, au crépuscule	*at nightfall, at dusk*

BUT *au petit matin* is translated by: '**in** the early morning'.

au petit déjeuner, au dîner	*at breakfast, at dinner*
à la fin, au début	*at the end, at the beginning*
une chose à la fois	*one thing at a time*
à toute vitesse	*at full speed*
Il est mort à 26 ans	*He died at 26*

13.2.2   *à* = 'to'

au nord, au sud, à l'est, à l'ouest	*to the north, to the south, to the east, to the west*

N.B.: l'Afrique du Sud: *South Africa*; au sud de l'Afrique: *to the south of Africa*; l'Afrique australe: *southern Africa*.

Elle va à l'école, au café, au cinéma, à l'église,	*She is going to school, to the café, to the cinema, to*
au restaurant, à la pharmacie	*church, to the restaurant, to the chemists*
monter à sa chambre	*to go up to one's room*
tourner à droite, à gauche	*to turn to the right, to the left*

'**to**' most countries of masculine gender is *à*:

au Japon	*to Japan*
au Danemark	*to Denmark*
au Portugal	*to Portugal*
au Canada	*to Canada*
aux Etats-Unis, aux USA	*to the United States, to the USA*

(For countries of feminine gender, and most countries of masculine gender beginning with a vowel, 'to' is *en*: *en France, en Grèce*, etc., see Section 13.26.1. See also Section 2.2.2. For the gender of countries, see Section 1.2.6.)

'**to**' most small islands, and larger islands which are some distance away, is *à*:

à Malte, à Jersey, à Guernsey, à Chypre, à la Martinique, à la Réunion, à Madagascar, à Tahiti, aux Philippines
to Malta, to Jersey, to Guernsey, to Cyprus, to Martinique, to Reunion, to Madagascar, to Tahiti, to the Philippines

N.B.: 'to' larger islands close to Europe, and very large islands generally is *en*: *en Sicile, en Sardaigne, en Crète, en Nouvelle-Zélande*, etc.

'**to**' towns and cities is *à*:

à Paris, à Londres, à Berlin	*to Paris, to London, to Berlin*

13.2.3   *à* = 'in'

Referring to place

vivre à Paris	*to live in Paris*
à cet endroit (BUT **dans** ce lieu)	*in this place*

au village (BUT **en** ville)	*in the village (in town)*
se reposer au jardin, au parc, au salon	*to rest in the garden, in the park, in the sitting room*

à in these cases is a simple statement of location; *dans* is used when the 'containing' properties of the location are given more emphasis, for example:

se promener au parc
to walk in the park (simple statement of location)

perdre ses clefs dans le parc
to lose one's keys in the park (the park is the area within which the keys were lost)

Compare:

Ils sont partis se promener au parc	*They have gone for a walk in the park*
On se promenait dans le parc quand on a perdu nos clefs	*We were walking in the park when we lost our keys*
vivre à Paris	*to live in Paris (simple statement of location)*
Il est difficile de se garer dans Paris	*It's difficult to park in Paris (i.e. within Paris, as opposed to anywhere else)*
au deuxième rang du parterre	*in the second row of the stalls*
à l'arrière	*in the back*
à l'intérieur	*inside*
tenir quelque chose à la main	*to hold something in one's hand*
porter une fleur au chapeau	*to wear a flower in one's hat*
au paradis (BUT en enfer)	*in heaven (in hell)*

'**in**' most countries of masculine gender is à:

au Japon	*in Japan*
au Danemark	*in Denmark*
au Portugal	*in Portugal*
au Canada	*in Canada*
aux Etats-Unis, aux USA	*in the United States, in the USA*

(For countries of feminine gender, and most countries of masculine gender beginning with a vowel, 'in' is *en: en France, en Iran*, etc. See Sections 13.26.1 and 1.2.6.)

'in' or 'on' most small islands, and larger islands which are some distance away, is *à*:

à Malte, à Jersey, à Guernsey, à Chypre, à la Martinique, à la Réunion, à Madagascar, à Tahiti, aux Philippines
in Malta, in Jersey, in Guernsey, in Cyprus, in Martinique, in Reunion, in Madagascar, in Tahiti, in the Philippines

N.B.: 'in' large islands close to Europe, and very large islands generally, is *en: en Sicile, en Sardaigne, en Crète, en Nouvelle-Zélande*, etc.

'**in**' towns and cities is *à*:

à Paris, à Londres, à Berlin, à Marseille	*in Paris, in London, in Berlin, in Marseilles*

Referring to time

la veille au soir	*in the evening of the day before*
à l'entracte	*in the interval*
vivre au 21e siècle	*to live in the 21st century*
arriver à temps	*to arrive in time*

13.2.4   *à* = 'on'

Je le ramasserai au retour	*I'll pick it up on my way back*
Il est arrivé à pied	*He arrived on foot*
Il l'avait appris au service militaire	*He had learned it when he was on military service*
Elle a essayé de le contacter à plusieurs reprises	*She tried to contact him on several occasions*
à la page 2	*on page 2*
à ski(s)	*on skis*
à la télévision/à la radio	*on (the) television/on (the) radio*
se mettre à genoux	*to get down on one's knees*
avoir une cicatrice à la jambe	*to have a scar on one's leg*
frapper à la porte, à la vitre	*to knock on the door, on the window*
les pommes étaient à terre	*the apples were on the ground*
il est à l'ordi	*he's on the computer*

Modes of transport

à bicyclette/trotinette	*on a bicycle/scooter*
à pied	*on foot*
à cheval	*on horseback*
à dos de chameau	*on a camel*

BUT also: *en vélo, en taxi, en voiture, en ambulance*, etc. (see Section 13.26.5).

13.2.5   *à* = 'by'

s'avancer pas à pas	*to move forward step by step*
partir un à un	*to leave one by one*
travailler à la lumière d'une bougie	*to work by the light of a candle*
fabriquée à la main	*made by hand*
reconnaître quelqu'un à sa voix	*to recognize somebody by his/her voice*

13.2.6 *à* used where English typically uses compound nouns

une tasse à thé	*a tea cup*
un livre à couverture de cuir	*a leather-bound book*
un moulin à vent, à café	*a windmill, coffee mill*
un homme à cheveux gris, aux cheveux gris	*a grey-haired man*
un homme à barbe	*a bearded man*
une fille aux cheveux d'or	*a golden-haired girl*
un billet à 35€	*a 35 euro ticket*
une pompe à chaleur	*a heat pump*
un bateau à roue	*a paddle steamer*
une chambre à air	*an inner tube*
une omelette aux champignons	*a mushroom omelette*

| une sauce au vin | *a wine sauce* |
| de la soupe à l'oignon | *onion soup* |

13.2.7 *à* = no preposition in English

La falaise était à pic	*The cliff was steep*
Les volets étaient à demi fermés	*The shutters were half closed*
avoir mal à la tête	*to have a headache*
Rennes est à 348 kilomètres de Paris	*Rennes is 348 kilometres from Paris*
un restaurant à deux pas d'ici	*a restaurant a stone's throw from here*
Ils se sont arrêtés à mi-chemin	*They stopped halfway*
à l'envers	*back to front, upside down, inside out*
rentrer à la maison	*to go home*

In the case of sports: *au, à la* is used:

jouer au tennis, au football, au rugby, au billard, etc.
to play tennis, football, rugby, billiards, etc.

But in the case of musical instruments: *du, de la* is used:

jouer **du** piano, **du** violon, **de** la flûte, etc.
to play the piano, the violin, the flute, etc.

13.2.8 *à* = other uses

monter/descendre à l'étage	*to go upstairs/to go downstairs*
C'est à vous de décider	*It's up to you to decide*
C'est gentil à vous de m'aider	*It's kind of you to help me*
C'est aimable à lui	*That's nice of him*
un oncle à lui (*also* un de ses oncles)	*an uncle of his*
un album à moi (*also* un de mes albums)	*an album of mine*
boire à la bouteille, à la source	*to drink from the bottle, from the spring*
emprunter de l'argent à la banque	*to borrow money from the bank*
un repas à la française	*a meal in the French style*
des pâtes à l'italienne	*Italian-style pasta*

13.3 *après/d'après*

après la fin du film	*after the end of the film*
après le repas	*after the meal*
après avoir acheté une glace	*after buying an ice cream*
après être arrivé	*after arriving*
Il n'arrête pas de crier après tout le monde	*He shouts at everyone*
demander après quelqu'un (both these uses of *après* are informal)	*to ask after somebody*
d'après les réseaux sociaux	*according to the social networks*
d'après ce qu'on m'a dit	*from what I've been told*
D'après leur tête, ils ont perdu le match	*From the look on their faces, they lost the match*
D'après vous, lequel est le meilleur?	*In your view, which is better?*
un tableau d'après Van Gogh	*a painting in the style of Van Gogh*

13.4 *auprès de*

Auprès de ces héros, nous sommes peu de chose (formal)
Compared with these heroes, we are nothing

se plaindre auprès des autorités
to complain to the authorities

un ambassadeur auprès de la République française
an ambassador to France

13.5 *autour de*

autour de l'aéroport	*around the airport*
tourner autour de la question	*to go around the question*
Nous arriverons autour de huit heures	*We will arrive around eight*

13.6 *avant*

s'arrêter juste avant le tournant	*to stop just before the bend*
avant le mois de juin	*before June*
avant l'entracte	*before the interval*
avant l'aube	*before dawn*
avant le weekend	*before the weekend*
arriver avant qn	*to arrive ahead of sb*
faire passer qn avant les autres	*to let someone go first*

N.B.: 'ahead of' in the sense of 'outstripping' one's rivals is *en avant de: Il est en avant de ses contemporains* 'He is ahead of his contemporaries'.

13.7 *avec*

Il devait venir avec moi au garage	*He was to come with me to the garage*
une voiture avec des banquettes de cuir	*a car with leather seats*
Elle est arrivée avec son père et sa mère	*She arrived with her father and mother*
s'entendre bien avec quelqu'un	*to get on well with somebody*
parler avec quelqu'un	*to speak with somebody*
remplir un verre avec de l'eau	*to fill a glass with water*
mouiller un ragoût avec du vin blanc	*to thin a stew with white wine*
Ce camembert est fait avec le lait de nos vaches	*This camembert is made with milk from our cows*

N.B.: In some of these examples, it is also possible to use *de: remplir un verre d'eau, mouiller un ragoût de vin blanc*:

se raser avec un rasoir électrique	*to shave with an electric razor*
nettoyer le tapis avec un aspirateur sans fil	*to clean the carpet with a cordless vacuum cleaner*
On s'est moqué d'eux, avec Souleyman	*Souleyman and I made fun of them*
On a fini l'article, avec Amandine (informal)	*Amandine and I have finished the article*
aller quelque part avec la voiture	*to go somewhere by car*

(For modes of transport, see also Section 13.26.5.)

13.8 *bout: au bout de*

au bout de mon jardin	*at the bottom of my garden*
au bout de trois heures	*after three hours*

13.9 *cause: à cause de, pour cause de, pour raison de*

A cause de sa maladie, il n'a pas pu venir	*Because of his illness, he couldn't come*
Le restaurant est fermé pour cause de décès	*The restaurant is closed due to a bereavement*
Il a démissionné pour raison de santé	*He resigned for health reasons*

13.10 *chez*

Je suis chez moi samedi	*I am at home on Saturday*
Ils l'ont ramené chez eux	*They brought him back to their house*
Elle est venue chez nous en pleine nuit	*She came to our house in the middle of the night*
Est-il vrai que chez les Britanniques on boit du thé toute la journée?	*Is it true that, among the British, tea is drunk all day long?*
Chez Sam Mendes, le décor est très important	*In Sam Mendes, the setting is very important*

13.11 *contre*

Je n'ai rien contre lui	*I have nothing against him*
protéger ses plantes contre le froid	*to protect one's plants against the cold*
une table posée contre le mur	*a table placed against the wall*
agir contre qn	*to act against sb*
changer des euros contre des dollars	*to change euros for dollars*
livraison contre remboursement	*cash on delivery*

13.12 *côté: à côté de, du côté de*

La boucherie est à côté de la pharmacie	*The butchers is next to the chemist's*
Elle s'est assise à côté de moi	*She sat down next to me*

A côté de ses œuvres précédentes, celle-ci est moins impressionnante
Compared with his earlier works, this one is less impressive

rouler du côté de Brive	*to travel in the direction of Brive*
arriver du côté de Brive	*to arrive from the direction of Brive; to be coming from Brive*
habiter du côté de Brive	*to live around Brive*

N.B.: *Du Côté de chez Swann* (the title of one of the volumes of Proust's *A La Recherche du temps perdu*) literally means 'around where Swann lives' and has been translated by Proust's English translator as *Swann's Way*.

13.13 *cours: au cours de*

au cours de la semaine	*during the week*
au cours de sa carrière	*in the course of his career*

13.14 *dans*

13.14.1 *dans* = 'in'

	J'ai aperçu la ferme dans la vallée	*I saw the farm in the valley*
	Elle était assise dans son fauteuil	*She was sitting in her armchair*
BUT	s'asseoir sur une chaise, sur un banc, sur un siège	*to sit on a chair on a bench on a seat*
	Il y avait de la pluie dans l'air	*There was rain in the air*

Nous l'avons croisé dans la rue, dans l'allée, dans l'avenue
We passed him in the street, in the alley, in the avenue

BUT **sur** la place, **sur** la route, **sur** le chemin, **sur** le boulevard, **sur** la chaussée, **sur** le trottoir
in the square, on the road, on the track, on the boulevard, in the road (as opposed to pavement), on the pavement

N.B.: When streets are named, there is usually no preposition in French for 'in': *Je l'ai rencontré rue de Rivoli* 'I met him in the rue de Rivoli', *Nous l'avons croisé boulevard Montparnasse* 'We passed him in the boulevard Montparnasse', *Il y avait un accident place du Châtelet* 'There was an accident in the place du Châtelet'.

Il est dans sa chambre	*He is in his room*
Elle habite dans un vieil appartement	*She lives in an old apartment*
Je l'ai lu dans un journal, dans un livre	*I read it in a paper, in a book*
dans tous les sens	*in every direction*
dans les années trente	*in the thirties*
Il vit dans la misère	*He lives in poverty*
Cela l'a laissé dans le doute	*That left him in doubt*

dans with the meaning 'in' is used with French *départements*, English counties, and American states:

dans le Calvados	dans le Yorkshire	dans le Massachusetts
dans la Marne	dans l'Essex	dans le Nevada
dans le Finistère	dans le Lancashire	dans l'Arizona
dans la Haute-Garonne		
dans l'Aveyron		
dans l'Isère		

dans is also used with the meaning 'in' with countries and towns modified by adjectives, quantifiers, or other expressions:

dans toute la France	*in all France*
dans la Pologne ravagée	*in war-torn Poland*
dans le sud de l'Espagne	*in southern Spain*
dans le Mexique d'aujourd'hui	*in today's Mexico*
dans le vieux Paris	*in old Paris*

BUT *en France, en Italie, en Espagne, à Paris*, etc. (see Section 13.26.1).

13.14.2 *dans* = 'in(side)'

Le manteau est dans l'armoire	*The coat is in the wardrobe*
Mettez le couteau dans le tiroir	*Put the knife in the drawer*
un message dans une bouteille	*a message in a bottle*

Modes of transport

Nous sommes venus dans (*or* par) le bus, dans (*or* par) le train, dans un taxi, dans une ambulance (Also - nous sommes venu en bus, en train, en taxi, en ambulance)
We came by bus, by train, by taxi, in an ambulance

dans is used when the 'containing' properties of the vehicle are given prominence, e.g.:

Elle a perdu son porte-monnaie dans le bus
She lost her purse on the bus

Il est décédé dans l'ambulance
He died in the ambulance

BUT also

en auto, en voiture	*by car*
en vélo, à bicyclette	*by bike*
à cheval	*on horseback*
en navire	*by ship*
en avion	*by plane*
en hélicoptère	*by helicopter*
en ambulance	*by ambulance*
en taxi	*by taxi*

(See Section 13.26.5.)

13.14.3 *dans* = '(in)to'

Elle est allée dans la cour	*She went into the yard*
emmener quelqu'un dans un restaurant	*to take somebody to a restaurant*

13.14.4 *dans* = 'in' (after a certain period of time has elapsed)

Je reviendrai dans une heure
I'll come back in an hour's time (i.e. after an hour has elapsed)

Il peut le faire dans quinze jours	*He can do it in a fortnight's time*
Je l'attends dans deux jours	*I expect him in two days*

Nous le ferons dans un instant
We'll do it in a moment (i.e. later)

This use of *dans* contrasts with *en* 'in' (within a certain period of time – see Section 13.26.3):

Je l'aurai lu en une heure	*I'll have read it (with)in an hour*
Il peut le faire en quinze jours	*He can do it (with)in a fortnight*
Ça se fait en un instant	*That's done in an instant*

13.14.5 *dans* = 'during'

Je le ferai dans la semaine	*I'll do it during the week*
Elle a fini de repeindre le salon dans la journée	*She finished redecorating the lounge during the day*
Il était tombé malade dans la nuit	*He became ill during the night*
Je l'avais vu dans la semaine	*I had seen him during the week*

13.14.6 *dans* = 'around', 'or so'

Nous avons gagné dans les mille euros	*We won around a thousand euros*
Ça pèse dans les 500 grammes	*That weighs around 500 grams*
Il avait dans les 26 ans	*He was around 26*

13.14.7 *dans* = 'among'

Il a disparu dans les sapins	*He disappeared among the firs*
J'ai cherché dans mes papiers	*I looked among my papers*

parmi is also possible with non-human objects: *Il a disparu parmi les sapins, J'ai cherché parmi mes papiers.* BUT in talking of people, 'among' can only be *parmi* or *entre*:

Il n'était pas parmi les spectateurs
He wasn't among the spectators

Elle se faufilait parmi les manifestants
She threaded her way among the demonstrators

Nous pourrons en discuter entre nous
We will be able to discuss it among ourselves

13.14.8 *dans* = 'on'

Nous l'avons rencontré dans l'escalier	*We met him on the stairs*
Il bricolait dans des fermes	*He did odd jobs on farms*

13.14.9 *dans* = 'from'

Elle a pris le portefeuille dans le tiroir
She took the wallet from the drawer

Il a pris ses clés dans sa poche
He took his keys from his pocket

Ils avaient découpé des photos dans un magazine
They had cut out photos from a magazine

Il boit son café dans un bol
He drinks his coffee from a bowl

J'ai trouvé l'idée dans un livre
I got the idea from a book

BUT *sortir, retirer un portefeuille du tiroir.*

13.15 *de*

13.15.1 *de* = 'of'

une tasse de thé	*a cup of tea*
une boîte d'allumettes	*a box of matches*
un verre de vin	*a glass of wine*
un bol de café	*a bowl of coffee*

N.B.: There is a contrast between *une tasse de thé* 'a cup of tea' and *une tasse à thé* 'a tea-cup'. The first describes a cup which happens to have tea in it, and the second describes a cup designed for drinking tea from. Tea cups can hold substances other than tea, so one can say *une tasse à thé de sucre* 'a tea-cup of sugar' (NOT *une tasse de thé de sucre*). Similarly *une boîte de lettres* 'a box of letters' contrasts with *une boîte aux lettres* 'a letter box' and *un verre de vin* 'a glass of wine' contrasts with *un verre à vin* 'a wine glass' (see Section 13.2.6).

une route pleine de virages	*a road full of bends*
J'entendais le bruit de la fête	*I heard the noise of the party*
le bombardement de Marseille en 1944	*the bombing of Marseilles in 1944*
la moitié des spectateurs	*half of the spectators*
la plupart de la population	*most of the population*
un tiers des concurrents	*a third of the competitors*
trois de mes amis	*three of my friends*
le plus grand joueur de tous	*the greatest player of all*
le plus intelligent de nous tous	*the most intelligent of all of us*

13.15.2 *de* = 'with'

une rue bordée de platanes	*a street lined with plane trees*
un mur couvert d'affiches	*a wall covered with posters*
un vestibule encombré de chaussures	*a hall cluttered with shoes*
un pichet rempli de cidre	*a pitcher filled with cider*
un parcours du combattant semé d'embûches	*an assault course full of obstacles*

par is a less frequently used equivalent of *de* in these cases, with an indefinite article: *une rue bordée par des platanes, un mur couvert par des affiches*, etc.

rougir de honte	*to go red with shame*
tomber de fatigue	*to drop with tiredness*
trembler de peur	*to tremble with fear*
piétiner d'impatience	*to dance with impatience*
crier de colère	*to shout with anger*
sauter de joie	*to jump with joy*

13.15.3 *de* = 'in'

vêtu de noir	*dressed in black*
habillé d'un costume bleu	*dressed in a blue suit*

After a superlative ('best in …', 'biggest in …', etc.) or after *seul, dernier, premier, jamais*:

le jeu vidéo le plus haletant du monde	*the most exciting video game in the world*
le train le plus rapide d'Europe	*the fastest train in Europe*
la seule fois de ma vie	*the only time in my life*
jamais de ma vie je n'ai eu aussi peur	*never in my life have I been so scared*
d'une certaine manière, façon	*in a certain manner, fashion*
trois dimanches de suite	*three Sundays in a row*
boire un café d'un trait	*to drink a coffee in one go*
Il est paralysé des jambes	*he is paralysed in the legs*
large d'épaules	*broad in the shoulders*

13.15.4 *de* = 'from'

regarder quelqu'un d'en haut	*to watch somebody from above*
le train de Paris	*the train from (also for) Paris*
Elle venait de Marseille	*She came from Marseilles*
Il est sorti de derrière la maison	*He came out from behind the house*
regarder les choses d'un même œil	*to see things from the same perspective*
aller de Londres à Paris	*to go from London to Paris*
passer du rouge au vert	*to go from red to green*
citer quelque chose de mémoire	*to cite something from memory*
faire quelque chose de colère	*to do something from anger*

N.B.: *le train de Paris* is ambiguous between 'the train **from** Paris' and 'the train **for** Paris'; *le train en provenance de Paris* is unambiguously 'the train **from** Paris'; and *le train à destination de Paris* is unambiguously 'the train **for** Paris'.

13.15.5 *de* = 'by'

Je le connais de vue, de réputation	*I know him by sight, by reputation*
un film de François Truffaut	*a film by François Truffaut*

de often corresponds to 'by' when a state is being described:

Il est connu de tous, détesté de certains, adoré de beaucoup
He is known by everyone, detested by some, adored by many

Il était accablé de fatigue, de sommeil, de douleur
He was overcome by tiredness, by sleep, worn down by pain

Le logiciel est bourré de virus
The software is overrun by viruses

When 'by' introduces an agent, and an event rather than a state is involved, *par* is usually used (as for example in passives: see Section 8.6):

Il a été effrayé par l'orage	*He was frightened by the storm*
Benjamin a été mordu par mon chien	*Benjamin was bitten by my dog*

But when a passive can be understood as a state, rather than an event, *de* may be used:

Quand il est arrivé au commissariat, il était accompagné de sa femme
When he arrived at the police station, his wife was with him

Les enfants ne sont autorisés que s'ils sont accompagnés d'un adulte
Children are not allowed unless accompanied by an adult

13.15.6 *de* = 's (possessive)

la sœur de sa mère	*his mother's sister*
le vélo de mon oncle	*my uncle's bike*
la maison de mes parents	*my parents' house*
le nom de son chien	*his dog's name*

13.15.7 *de* = 'than' (*plus de, moins de*)

elle gagne plus de 9 000 euros par mois	*she earns more than 9,000 euros a month*
moins d'une dizaine de personnes assistaient au cours	*fewer than ten people were at the lecture*
cela est arrivé il y a plus de trente ans	*that happened more than thirty years ago*
interdit aux moins de 15 ans	*no children under 15*

N.B.: *plus de, moins de* contrast with *plus que, moins que*. Whereas *plus de* and *moins de* are typically followed by a numeral, *plus que* and *moins que* introduce an implied clause:

Elle gagne plus de 9 000 euros	BUT	Elle gagne plus que sa sœur (ne gagne)
		She earns more than her sister (earns)
Il travaille moins de 2 heures par jour		*He works less than 2 hours a day*
Il travaille moins que son frère (ne travaille)		*He works less than his brother (works)*

13.15.8 *de* = no preposition in English

Linking nouns to make them compound nouns

un vieux tronc d'acacia	*an old acacia tree*
un homme d'affaires, une femme d'affaires	*a businessman, a businesswoman*
la boîte de vitesses	*the gear box*
un vélo de course	*a racing bike*

Introducing parts of countries, states, towns, etc., in relation to the points of the compass

l'Afrique du Sud	*South Africa*
le Sud de l'Afrique	*southern Africa*
l'Italie du Sud	*southern Italy*
la France du Nord	*northern France*
les pays de l'ouest	*western countries*
la Gare du Nord	
la Gare de l'Est	

With many quantifiers

la plupart des gens	*most people* (also '*most of the people*')
beaucoup de gens	*many people*
bien des gens	*many people*
la moitié des gens	*half the people* (also '*half of the people*')

For more on these quantifiers, see Section 6.9.

With the following adjectival construction used frequently in informal French

une journée de libre	*a free day*
encore un problème de réglé	*one more problem solved*
il y avait trois passants de blessés	*three passers-by were injured*

Linking indefinite or negative nouns and adjectives

quelqu'un d'important	*someone important*
personne d'intéressant	*nobody interesting*
rien d'autre	*nothing else*
quelque chose de drôle	*something funny*

After *ce que…*

Ce qu'il y a de plus beau dans l'exposition, c'est le tableau de Constable
What's most beautiful in the exhibition is the painting by Constable

Ce qu'il y a de pénible avec la technologie, c'est qu'elle vous fait défaut au moment où l'on en a le plus besoin.
What's annoying with technology is that it lets you down when you most need it.

Ce qu'ils produisent de bon, c'est le fromage de chèvre
What they produce that is good is goat's cheese

Measurements

un mur épais d'un mètre	*a wall one metre thick*
une rivière longue de 200 kilomètres	*a 200-kilometre long river*
une clôture haute de cinq mètres	*a five-metre high fence*
Elle est âgée de 15 ans	*She is 15*
Le train est en retard de 20 minutes	*The train is 20 minutes late*

(For measurements, see also Section 6.5.1.)

13.15.9 *de* = other uses

Je ne me nourris que de légumes bio	*I live on organic vegetables*
être de permanence	*to be on duty, on call*
On n'a plus revu Fanny de l'après-midi	*We didn't see Fanny again for the rest of the afternoon*
traiter quelqu'un de voleur	*to call somebody a thief*
Quoi de neuf?	*What's new?*
Quoi de plus éprouvant?	*What can be more harrowing?*

13.16 *dehors: en dehors de*

une randonnée en dehors de la ville
a hike outside the town

En dehors de ses cousins, elle ne connaît personne
Apart from her cousins, she knows no-one

13.17 *delà: au-delà* de

au-delà de la frontière	*beyond the frontier*

13.18 *dépit: en dépit de*

En dépit de mes conseils, elle s'est mariée	*In spite of my advice, she got married*

13.19 *depuis*

depuis longtemps	*for a long time*
depuis toujours	*from time immemorial*

Elle sait faire défiler des vidéos sur sa tablette depuis l'âge de 4 ans!	*She has known how to play videos on her tablet since she was four.*

Je suis là depuis trois jours	*I have been here for three days*
Je ne l'ai pas vu depuis trois jours	*I haven't seen him for three days*

(For tenses with depuis, see Section 10.4.4.)

depuis … (jusqu'à) can be used as an alternative to *de … à* when distance is being emphasized:

Il a marché depuis le port jusqu'au parc	*He walked right from the harbour to the park*
Elle a crié depuis le jardin	*She shouted from the garden*
Le bruit nous arrivait depuis la terrasse	*The noise reached us from the terrace*
Déroule la page depuis le haut jusqu'en bas	*Scroll down the page from the top to the very bottom*
Je te parle depuis Kuala Lumpur	*I'm speaking to you from Kuala Lumpur*

13.20 *derrière*

une rue derrière la grande place	*a street behind the main square*
derrière chez lui	*behind his house*
Allez vous mettre par-derrière la cloison	*Go and stand behind the partition (par-derrière implies movement)*

N.B.: 'behind' in the sense of 'not keeping up with' is *en retard*: *Il est en retard par rapport aux autres enfants de sa classe* 'He is behind the other children in his class'.

13.21 *dès*

dès la nuit tombée, dès l'aube	*from nightfall, from dawn*
dès son arrivée	*as soon as he arrived*
Dès que je suis entré, j'ai compris que quelque chose ne tournait pas rond	*As soon as I came in, I knew that something was wrong*
dès maintenant	*from now on*
dès lors	*from then on*
dès l'enfance	*from childhood*

13.22 *dessous: au-dessous de/par-dessous*

Au-dessous de la salle à manger il y a une piscine
Below the dining room there is a swimming pool

La température est tombée au-dessous de zéro
The temperature fell below zero

Il a rampé par-dessous la barrière
He crawled under the gate (par-dessous implies movement)

13.23 *dessus: au-dessus de/par-dessus*

J'ai regardé le ciel au-dessus du village	*I looked at the sky above the village*
Au-dessus de la porte d'entrée il y avait un panneau	*Above the entrance there was a sign*
porter un manteau par-dessus sa veste	*to wear a coat over one's jacket*
sauter par-dessus une barrière	*to jump over a gate*

13.24 *devant*

devant l'église	*in front of the church*
devant chez lui	*in front of his house*
mettre un pied devant l'autre	*to put one foot in front of the other*
Je l'ai laissé devant un chemin obscur	*I left him at the beginning of a dark track*
marcher devant qn	*to walk in front of sb*
comparaître devant le tribunal	*to appear before the court*

13.25 *durant*

durant la nuit, durant l'été	*during the night, during the summer*

N.B.: *durant* is an equivalent of *pendant*, but typically restricted to formal French. Unlike *pendant*, it can follow the noun it modifies: *Elle s'est reposée la semaine durant* 'She rested throughout the week'.

13.26 *en*

13.26.1 *en* = 'in'

en, rather than *dans*, is used where there is no definite or indefinite article:

en plein air	*in the open air*
en bonne santé	*in good health*
en terminale	*in year 13 (final year secondary school)*
une région riche en forêts	*a region rich in forests*
une thèse pauvre en idées	*a thesis poor in ideas*
en cas d'urgence	*in an emergency*
avoir confiance en quelqu'un	*to have confidence in somebody*
en format PdF	*in pdf format*

Il est sorti en tenue de soirée, en maillot de bain, en bras de chemise
He went out in evening dress, in his swimming costume, in short sleeves

Elle est en ville, en prison, en province
She is in town, in prison, out of town (i.e. 'in the provinces')

BUT where an article is used, *dans* is usual:

être transporté dans une prison lointaine	*to be taken to a distant prison*

Months

en janvier, en février, en mars, ... en novembre, en décembre
in January, in February, in March, ... in November, in December

Seasons

en automne, en été, en hiver … BUT **au** printemps
in autumn, in summer, in winter … in spring

Years

en 1992, en 1485, etc.
en l'an 1992, en l'an 1485, etc.   *in the year 1992, in the year 1485, etc.*

BUT: **dans** les années 90   *in the 90s*
    au 21e siècle   *in the 21th century*

Languages

en allemand, en anglais, en français, en arabe, en espagnol, en flamand, etc.
in German, in English, in French, in Arabic, in Spanish, in Flemish, etc.

en is used for 'in' or 'to' countries and continents of feminine gender:

en France   en Afrique
en Espagne   en Amérique
en Italie   en Europe
en Allemagne   en Australie
en Grèce   en Asie
en Turquie   en Chine

en is also used for 'in' or 'to' countries of masculine gender which begin with a vowel:

en Afghanistan
en Israël
en Iran

'in' or 'to' masculine countries not beginning with a vowel is usually *au* or *aux*:

au Japon   au Canada
au Portugal   au Danemark

N.B.: *aux Etats-Unis, aux USA*. See Section 13.2.3.

en is used for 'in' or 'to' French regions of feminine gender:

en Normandie
en Bretagne
en Provence
en Touraine

BUT *dans* is normally used with French regions of masculine gender:

dans le Berry
dans le Périgord
dans le Forez

dans is normal for 'in' or 'to' with French départements, British counties, and American states (see Section 13.14.1).

en is used for 'in' or 'to' large islands:

en Sicile	en Crète
en Sardaigne	en Nouvelle-Zélande

See also Section 13.2.3.

13.26.2 *en* = 'in' used with articles in fixed expressions

regarder en l'air	*to look up*
des idées en l'air	*unrealistic ideas*
en la circonstance	*in the circumstances*
en l'occurrence	*as it turns out*
en l'espèce	*in this particular case*
en ce cas	*in this case*
en son for intérieur	*in his heart of hearts*

13.26.3 *en* = 'in' (within a certain period of time)

Il a fait des progrès en deux ans	*He has made progress in two years*
Je l'aurai lu en une heure	*I'll have read it in an hour*
Ça se fait en un instant	*It's done in a second*
le tour du monde en 80 jours	*around the world in 80 days*

This contrasts with *dans* = 'in' (after a certain period of time has elapsed):

Il peut le faire dans quinze jours	*He can do it in two weeks' time*
Je l'attends dans deux jours	*I expect him in two days*
Je le ferai dans un instant	*I'll do it in a minute*

13.26.4 *en* = 'made from'

une statue en bronze	*a bronze statue*
un décor en velours rouge	*a red velvet decor*
une montre en or	*a gold watch*
une robe en soie	*a silk dress*
un pont en ciment	*a concrete bridge*

13.26.5 *en* = modes of transport

The following are common in informal French:

voyager en taxi, en vélo	*to travel by taxi, by bike*
en bicyclette, en moto	*by bicycle, on a motorbike*
en avion, en car	*by plane, on a coach*
en train, en voiture	*by train, by car*
en ambulance	*in an ambulance*
en bateau	*by boat*
en motoneige	*on a skidoo*

13.26.6 *en* = 'on'

en vacances, en congé	*on holiday, on leave*
en vente	*on sale*

en route	*on the way*
en voyage	*on a trip*
en moyenne	*on average*
en feu	*on fire*
en ligne	*online*

13.26.7 *en* = 'with'

une maison en briques	*a house built with bricks*
alimenter un restaurant en fruits et légumes	*to supply a restaurant with fruit and vegetables*
ravitailler des terroristes en armes	*to supply terrorists with weapons*

13.26.8 *en* = 'at'

en fin de semaine	*at the end of the week*
en haut de page	*at the top of the page*
en mer	*at sea*
en plein sommet	*right at the summit*
en même temps	*at the same time*
les deux pays étaient en guerre	*the two countries were at war*
sa vie est en jeu	*her life is at stake*
être fort en langues, en maths	*to be good at languages, Maths*
en vitesse (informal)	*at speed*

13.26.9 *en* = 'from'

aujourd'hui en huit	*a week from today*
lundi en quinze	*two weeks from Monday*

13.26.10 *en* = 'as'

parler en spécialiste	*to speak as an expert*
se déguiser en clown	*to dress up as a clown*
recevoir qc en cadeau	*to receive something as a present*
agir en lâche	*to act as a coward*
en signe de deuil	*as a sign of mourning*

13.26.11 *en* = 'into'

transformer la maison en hôtel	*to transform the house into a hotel*
changer une défaite en victoire	*to change a defeat into victory*
traduire un texte en allemand	*to translate a text into German*

13.26.12 *en* = no preposition

se mettre en colère	*to become angry*
une télévision en couleur	*a colour television*
un film en noir et blanc	*a black and white film*

13.27 *entre/d'entre*

la distance entre deux points	*the distance between two points*
une dispute entre eux	*a dispute between them*
J'ai le rapport entre les mains	*I have the report in my hands*
la frontière entre deux pays	*the border between two countries*
la plupart d'entre eux	*most of them*
beaucoup d'entre mes amis	*many of my friends*
une dizaine d'entre les serveurs	*ten or so of the waiters*
le moins beau d'entre nous	*the least handsome among us*
Lequel d'entre vous le fera?	*Which of you will do it?*
chacun d'entre eux *or* chacun d'eux	*each of them*
personne d'entre les invités	*no-one among the guests*
aucun d'entre les spectateurs *or* aucun des spectateurs	*none of the spectators*

13.28 *envers*

ressentir de la haine envers qn	*to feel hatred towards sb*
être bien disposé envers qn	*to be well disposed towards sb*
ma gratitude envers votre oncle	*my gratitude to your uncle*

13.29 *excepté*

Excepté les grand-parents, tous étaient partis
Apart from the grandparents, everyone had left

N.B.: *hormis* 'with the exception of' is also possible, but rather formal.

13.30 *face: en face de*

Le parc est en face du bureau de poste	*The park is opposite the post office*

13.31 *faute de*

Faute d'argent, l'entreprise a fait faillite
Through lack of money, the company went bankrupt

J'accepterai le poste, faute de mieux
I'll accept the job, for want of anything better

13.32 *force: à force de*

A force de travail, il a réussi	*Through working, he succeeded*

13.33 *grâce à*

Grâce à ton aide, je pourrai l'acheter	*Thanks to your help, I will be able to buy it*
C'est grâce à toi que j'ai pu le faire	*It's thanks to you that I could do it*

N.B.: *grâce à* is always positive, so cannot be used to translate sentences like: 'Thanks to you we lost the contract'. Here *à cause de* is required: *A cause de toi nous avons perdu le contrat.*

13.34 *haut: du haut de*

sauter du haut de la falaise	*to jump from the cliff*
Elle nous toisait du haut de ses 15 ans	*She looked down at us from the height of her 15 years*

N.B.: 'from' tall objects like cliffs, towers, buildings is usually *du haut de*, rather than *de* alone.

13.35 *hors de*

hors de danger	*out of danger*
hors de saison	*out of season*
hors de lui	*beside himself with anger*
hors d'haleine	*out of breath*
sauter hors de son lit	*to jump out of one's bed*
une randonnée hors de la ville	*a hike outside the town*

13.36 *jusqu'à*

jusqu'à demain	*until tomorrow*
jusqu'au bout	*right to the end*
depuis Paris jusqu'à la Manche	*from Paris to the Channel*

N.B.: 'not ... until' is *pas... avant*: *Je ne viendrai pas avant demain* 'I won't come until tomorrow'.

(For the conjunction *jusqu'à ce que*, see Section 17.3.8.)

13.37 *lieu: au lieu de*

au lieu de son frère	*instead of his brother*
au lieu de rester là sans rien faire, appelle les secours!	*don't just stand there doing nothing, call the emergency services!*

13.38 *long: le long de*

rouler le long du quai	*to travel along the river bank* (as in Paris or London)

Tout au long du boulevard il y avait des marchands forains
All along the boulevard there were market traders

13.39 *lors de*

lors de mon séjour en France	*at the time of my stay in France*
lors de leur première rencontre	*when they first met*

13.40 *malgré*

malgré son enthousiasme, ses défauts, le mauvais temps, sa promesse
in spite of his enthusiasm, his faults, the bad weather, his promise

13.41 *par*

13.41.1 *par* = 'through'

regarder par la fenêtre	*to look through the window*
passer par la forêt	*to go through the forest*
aspirer l'air par la bouche	*to breathe through the mouth*
Je l'ai eu par un boulanger de Tours	*I got it through a baker from Tours*

13.41.2 *par* = 'by', 'per'

Le village était coupé par la neige	*The village was cut off by the snow*
Par bonheur, il s'est évadé	*By good fortune, he escaped*
Il tenait son fils par la main	*He held his son by the hand*
prendre qn par surprise	*to catch sb by surprise*
travailler par groupes de quatre	*to work in groups of four*
heure par heure	*hour by hour*
Ils sortaient un par un	*They came out one by one*
La suite coûte 250 € par personne	*The suite is 250 euros per person*
par nuit	*per night*

L'Etranger, par Albert Camus, est l'un des romans français les plus étudiés
'The Outsider', by Albert Camus, is one of the most widely studied French novels

N.B.: *par* is used after a pause, *de* otherwise:

un roman d'Albert Camus	*a novel by Albert Camus*

When 'by' introduces an agent, *par* is usually used:

Il a été effrayé par l'orage	*He was frightened by the storm*
Benjamin a été mordu par mon chien	*Benjamin was bitten by my dog*

But when a passive can be understood as a state, rather than an event, *de* may also be used:

Quand il est arrivé au commissariat, il était accompagné de sa femme
When he arrived at the police station, his wife was with him

(See also Section 13.15.5.)

13.41.3 *par* = 'on'

se rouler par terre	*to roll oneself on the ground*
se jeter par terre	*to throw oneself on the ground*
par une belle journée de printemps	*on a fine day in spring*
commander qqc par Internet	*to order something on the internet*

13.41.4 *par* = 'from', 'out of'

faire qc par crainte	*to do sth out of fear*
par orgueil, par respect de qn	*from pride, from respect for sb*
par amitié, par honte	*out of/from friendship, from shame*
par jalousie, par pudeur	*from jealousy, from modesty*
par ignorance	*out of/from ignorance*

13.41.5 *par* = 'in'

par temps de pluie	*in wet weather*
sortir par beau temps	*to go out in fair weather*
par milliers	*in (their) thousands*
par ordre alphabétique	*in alphabetical order*
par endroits	*in places*
par écrit	*in writing*

13.42 *parmi*

parmi les spectateurs	*among the spectators*
parmi la foule	*among the crowd*

Une rumeur courait parmi les gens de la ville
A rumour was spreading among the townspeople

parmi mes papiers	*among my papers*

(See also Section 13.14.7.)

13.43 *part: de la part de*

parler de la part des étudiants	*to speak on behalf of the students*
C'est de la part de qui?	*Who's calling? Who's it from?*

13.44 *partir: à partir de*

à partir de demain	*from tomorrow*

13.45 *passé*

Passé le pont, on s'est arrêté un instant	*Once passed the bridge, we stopped for a minute*
Passé minuit il n'y a plus de taxis	*After midnight there are no more taxis*

13.46 *pendant*

pendant la guerre	*during the war*
Nous avons dansé pendant une éternité	*We danced for ages*
Je te l'expliquerai par SMS pendant la semaine	*I'll explain it to you by text during the week*

13.47 *pour*

Pour ma part, je suis heureux
For my part, I'm happy

Elle le faisait exprès pour attirer l'attention
She did it on purpose (in order) to attract attention

donner un cadeau à qn pour son anniversaire
to give a present to sb for his/her birthday

Il se prend pour un champion
He considers fancies himself as a champion

s'en aller pour de bon
to go away for good

passer pour intelligent
to be considered intelligent

être bon pour qn, dur pour qn, gentil pour qn, (in)juste pour qn, sévère pour qn
to be good to (or for) sb, hard on sb, kind to sb, (un)just to sb, severe on sb

N.B.: The verb *payer* 'to pay for' is not usually followed by *pour*:

payer la tournée	*to pay for a round (of drinks)*
On ne voulait pas que je paie ma place	*They didn't want me to pay for my seat*

Unless money is involved or a person is being paid for:

payer 600 euros pour un micro-ondes	*to pay 600 euros for a microwave oven*
Je ne paie pas pour toi!	*I'm not paying for you!*

N.B.: Expressions such as 'for two days', 'for three weeks', 'for several years' are usually translated by the time expression alone (i.e. without *pour*) when they refer to events in the past:

Elle est restée deux jours	*She stayed for two days*
Il est resté trois semaines	*He stayed for three weeks*

When the time expression refers to a period in the future in relation to the time of speaking, *pour* is used:

Elle partira pour deux jours	*She'll be away for two days*
Il voulait s'absenter pour trois semaines	*He wanted to be away for three weeks*

When the events that take place during the time period are stressed, *pendant* is the usual form:

Il a été malade pendant la nuit	*He was ill during the night*
Elle va travailler pendant deux jours	*She is going to work for two days*

13.48 *près de*

Il s'est assis près de moi	*He sat down next to me*
Je l'ai aperçu près du pont	*I spied him near the bridge*

13.49 *quant à*

Quant à moi, je suis heureux
For my part, I'm happy

Quant à leur start-up, elle est en train de dévisser en bourse
As for their start-up, it's losing heavily on the stock exchange

13.50 *sans*

sans moi	*without me*
sans sel	*without salt*
sans rien dire	*without saying anything*
sans me regarder	*without looking at me*

13.51 *sauf*

Sauf ma mère, toute la famille était là
With the exception of my mother, all the family was there

13.52 *selon*

selon l'opinion générale	*according to the common view*
selon la loi	*by law, under the law*

13.53 *sous*

sous la table	*under the table*
s'abriter sous un arbre	*to shelter under a tree*
nager sous l'eau	*to swim under the water*
sous l'ancien régime	*under the 'ancien régime'*
sous clef	*under lock and key*
sous les verrous	*under lock and key*
sous le règne de Louis XIV	*in the reign of Louis XIV*

sous la chaleur, sous la pluie, sous le soleil
in the heat, in the rain, in the sun

sous Word, sous Excel
in Word, in Excel

sous format texte
in text format

aliment sous vide
vacuum-packed food

tu veux voir tes notifications sous forme de liste ou sous forme d'icônes?
would you like to view your notifications as a list or as icons?

Sous prétexte de se renseigner pour les trains, elle a discrètement envoyé un SMS à sa copine
On the pretext of finding out about trains, she discreetly texted her friend

promettre sous serment	*to promise on oath*
interdire qc sous peine d'amende	*to prohibit sth on pain of a fine*
vendre qc sous conditions	*to sell sth on condition*
J'ai un dictionnaire sous la main	*I have a dictionary to hand*
passer l'affaire sous silence	*to keep quiet about the matter*
manifester sous les fenêtres de la mairie	*to demonstrate in front of the town hall*

13.54 *suite: par suite de*

par suite d'un accident	*following an accident*

13.55 *suivant*

suivant son habitude	*as was his custom*

13.56 *sur*

J'ai mis ma main sur son épaule	*I put my hand on his shoulder*
Il me regardait, appuyé sur les coudes	*He watched me, leaning on his elbows*
Elle était assise sur un vieux tronc d'arbre	*She was sitting on an old tree trunk*
sur le seuil	*on the threshold, on the doorstep*
Elle attendait sur les marches de la mairie	*She was waiting on the steps of the town hall*
lire qc sur une affiche	*to read sth on a poster*
chercher sur Google, sur You Tube, sur l'Internet	*search on Google, on YouTube, on the internet*
faire des recherches sur l'Internet	*carry out research on the internet*
ces écouteurs ne marchent pas, elle les a eus sur internet	*these earbuds don't work, she got them on the net*
Je l'ai vu sur la place	*I saw him in the square*
sur la route, sur le chemin	*on the road, on the track*
sur le boulevard, sur la chaussée	*on the boulevard, in the road*
sur le trottoir	*on the pavement*
Il a laissé la clef sur la porte	*He left the key in the door*
Les garçons étaient assis sur trois rangées de fauteuils	*The boys were sitting in three rows of seats*
marcher sur les pas de quelqu'un	*to follow in somebody's footsteps*
aller sur le terrain de football	*to go onto the football pitch*
sur la patinoire	*onto the ice rink*
revenir sur ses pas	*to retrace one's steps*
un salon qui donne sur la rivière	*a sitting room which overlooks the river*
Elle va sur ses vingt-six ans	*She is nearly 26*
deux sur trois	*two out of three*
Sur dix, trois étaient partis	*Of ten, three had left*
Sur mon salaire, il ne restait que 50 euros	*Of my salary, only 50 euros remained*
Quatre chats sur cinq le préfèrent	*Four out of five cats prefer it*
Sur la fin, j'étais fatigué	*Towards the end, I was tired*

The use of 'sur' has recently spread to many contexts where other prepositions are traditionally used (in, at etc. or no preposition). The effect is considered to be informal.

J'habite sur Montrouge	*I live in Montrouge*

J'étais à la manifestation sur Denfert-Rochereau — *I was at the demonstration at (square) Denfert-Rochereau*

Ici on est sur du coton tandis que là on est sur de la soie — *This one is cotton whereas that one is silk*

13.57 *travers: à travers/au travers de/en travers de*

Il me parla à travers la porte fermée
He talked to me through the closed door

L'arbre était tombé en travers de la route
The tree had fallen across the road

Elle expose ce scandale des années 90 au travers d'une intrigue littéraire bien menée
She reveals this 90's scandal through a well-written literary plot

13.58 *vers*

se diriger vers la maison	*to head for the house*
vers le haut du col	*towards the top of the pass*
vers 10 heures	*around 10 o'clock*
vers la fin de mars	*towards the end of March*
Il avait vers 26 ans	*He was around 26 years old*

13.59 **French translations for common English prepositions**

Figures refer to the sections where the French prepositions are dealt with.

Across: *de l'autre côté de; en travers de; au-dessus de*

across the room
de l'autre côté de la pièce

The barricade had been erected across the street
La barricade avait été érigée en travers de la rue — Section 13.57

They will have to build a bridge across the motorway
Ils devront construire un pont au-dessus de l'autoroute — Section 13.23

After: *après; derrière*

after the meal	après le repas	Section 13.3
after arriving	après être arrivé	
to ask after sb	demander après qn	

to come after sb (e.g. in a race)	arriver derrière qn	Section 13.20
to clean up after sb	nettoyer derrière qn	

Among: *dans; parmi; entre; d'entre; chez*

to disappear among the firs	disparaître dans les sapins	Section 13.14.7
to search among one's papers	chercher dans/parmi ses papiers	
among the spectators	parmi les spectateurs	Section 13.42
among the crowd	parmi la foule	
among friends	entre amis	
several among you	plusieurs d'entre vous	Section 13.27
among the British	chez les Britanniques	Section 13.10

Around (approximately): *dans; vers; environ, autour de*

He was around 26 years old	il avait vers 26 ans, il avait 26 ans environ	Section 13.58
	Also: Il avait dans les / vers les 26 ans	
	il avait autour de 26 ans	Section 13.14.6
to win around 4,000 euros	gagner dans les 4 000 euros	

As: *en; en tant que; comme*

to speak as an expert	parler en spécialiste
to dress as a clown	s'habiller en clown
to receive sth as a present	recevoir qc en cadeau
to act as the representative of	agir en tant que représentant de
to act as an intermediary	servir comme intermédiaire

At: *à; en; par; chez*

to slow down at every bend	ralentir à chaque virage	Section 13.2.1
to be at school	être à l'école	
at the cinema, at church	au cinéma, à l'église	
at 3 o'clock	à 3 heures	
at the beginning, at the end	au début, à la fin	
one thing at a time	une chose à la fois	
at the same time	en même temps	Section 13.26.8
at odd moments	par instant(s)	
at his house, at my house	chez lui, chez moi	Section 13.10
at the weekend	en fin de semaine	Section 13.26.8
at the top of the page	en haut de page	
at sea	en mer	
right at the summit	en plein sommet	
at war	en guerre	
at stake	en jeu	
at speed	en vitesse	
to be good at languages	être bon en langues	

By: *de; par; à; avant; selon*

to know sb by sight	connaître qn de vue	Section 13.15.5
to be known by everyone	être connu de tous	
a film by François Truffaut	un film de François Truffaut	
to be accompanied by one's wife	être accompagné de sa femme	
to be frightened by the storm	être effrayé par l'orage	
to be bitten by a dog	être mordu par un chien	
to recognize sb by his/her voice	reconnaître qn à sa voix	Section 13.2.5

to move forward step by step	s'avancer pas à pas	
to leave one by one	partir un à un (*or* un par un)	
to work by the light of a candle	travailler à la lumière d'une bougie	
to hold sb by the hand	tenir qn par la main	Section 13.41.2
to work in groups	travailler par groupes	
hour by hour	heure par heure	
by night	par nuit	
cut off by the snow	coupé par la neige	
by the weekend	avant le weekend	Section 13.6
by the rules	selon les règles	
by law	selon la loi	Section 13.52

by taxi, by bicycle, by train, by plane, by car, by ambulance, by boat, by bus:

en taxi (*or* dans un taxi), en vélo (*or* à vélo)	Section 13.26.5
en train (*or* dans le train), en avion (*or* par avion)	
en voiture (*or* avec la voiture), en ambulance (*or* dans une ambulance)	
en bateau (*or* par bateau), en bus (*or* dans le bus)	

During: *dans, pendant, durant, au cours de*

I'll do it during the week	
Je le ferai dans (*or* pendant *or* au cours de) la semaine	Section 13.14.5

From: *de; depuis; du haut de; à; dans; en; d'après; sur*

to watch sb from above	regarder qn d'en haut	Section 13.15.4
to cite sth from memory	citer qc de mémoire	
from afar	de loin	
from close by	de près	
to go from London to Paris	aller de Londres à Paris	
He complained all the way from	Il s'est plaint depuis Londres	
London to Paris	jusqu'à Paris	
to jump from the cliff	sauter du haut de la falaise	Section 13.34
to borrow sth from sb	emprunter qc à qn	Section 13.2.8
to drink from the bottle	boire à la bouteille	
to take a wallet from the drawer	prendre un portefeuille dans le tiroir	Section 13.14.9
to cut photos from the newspaper	découper des photos dans le journal	
a week from today	aujourd'hui en huit	Section 13.26.9
a fortnight from Monday	lundi en quinze	

to do sth from fear, from shame, from ignorance	
faire qc par (*or* de) crainte, par (*or* de) honte, par (*or* d')ignorance	Section 13.41.4

from what I'm told	d'après ce qu'on me dit	Section 13.3
from the look on his face	d'après son expression	
	d'après la tête qu'il faisait	
They selected five from ten	Ils en ont sélectionné cinq sur dix	

364 Prepositions

In: *de; à; en; dans; par; sur; sous; no preposition used in French*

dressed in black	vêtu *or* habillé de noir	Section 13.15.3
to go out in evening dress	sortir en tenue de soirée	Section 13.26.1
in a swimming costume	en maillot de bain	
in shirt sleeves	en bras de chemise	
the first, last, only time in my life	la première, dernière, seule fois de ma vie	Section 13.15.3
the fastest train in Europe	le train le plus rapide d'Europe	
three Sundays in a row	trois dimanches de suite	
paralysed in the arms, legs	paralysé des bras, des jambes	
broad in the shoulders	large d'épaules	
to live in Paris	vivre à Paris	Section 13.2.3
in the shade	à l'ombre	
in the back, in one's hand, in paradise	à l'arrière, à la main, au paradis	
in the garden, in the cinema	au jardin, au cinéma	
in the restaurant, in school	au restaurant, à l'école	
in the village, in the park	au village, au parc	

BUT

in town	en ville	Section 13.26.1
in hell	en enfer	
in Japan, in Denmark, in the United States, in Malta, in Jersey	au Japon, au Danemark, aux Etats-Unis, à Malte, à Jersey	Section 13.2.3
in France, in Spain	en France, en Espagne	Section 13.26.1
in the evening, in the morning	au soir, au matin	Section 13.2.3
in the 21st century	au 21e siècle	
in the interval	à l'entracte	
to glimpse sth in the valley	apercevoir qc dans la vallée	Section 13.14.1
to meet sb in the rue de Rivoli, on the boulevard Montparnasse	rencontrer qn rue de Rivoli, boulevard Montparnasse	
to meet sb in Yorkshire, to meet sb in Nevada, in the Calvados region	rencontrer qn dans le Yorkshire rencontrer qn dans le Nevada, dans le Calvados	
I'll come back after an hour	Je reviendrai dans une heure	Section 13.14.4
I'm expecting him in two days	Je l'attends dans deux jours	
I'll have read it within an hour	Je l'aurai lu en une heure	Section 13.26.3
He can do it in (under) two weeks	Il peut le faire en quinze jours	
in January, in February	en janvier, en février	
in the autumn, in the summer, in the winter	en automne, en été, en hiver	Section 13.26.1
in the spring	au printemps	
in 1992, in the year 1992	en 1992, en l'an 1992	

in the 90s	dans les années 90	
in German, in Spanish	en allemand, en espagnol	
in wet weather	par temps de pluie	Section 13.41.5
in their thousands	par milliers	
in alphabetical order	par ordre alphabétique	
in places	par endroits	
to see sb in the square	voir qn sur la place	
to be sitting in three rows of seats	être assis sur trois rangées de fauteuils	
in the reign of Louis XIV	sous le règne de Louis XIV	Section 13.53
in Word, in Excel	sous Word, sous Excel	

Into: *dans; en; à*

to go into the yard	aller dans la cour	
to turn the house into a hotel	transformer la maison en hotel	
to burst into tears	éclater en larmes	Section 13.26.11
to go into the office	aller au bureau	
to get into bed	se mettre au lit	

Of: *de; à; sur; d'entre*

a cup of tea	une tasse de thé	Section 13.15.1
half of the spectators	la moitié des spectateurs	
It's kind of you, nice of you	C'est gentil à vous, aimable à vous	Section 13.2.8
one of my uncles	un oncle à moi (un de mes oncles)	
Of ten, three had left	Sur dix, trois étaient partis	Section 13.56
most of them	la plupart d'entre eux	Section 13.27
each of them	chacun d'(entre) eux	

On: *de; à; dans; en; par; sur; sous; no preposition*

I live just on organic vegetables	Je ne me nourris que de légumes bio	Section 13.15.9
to be on duty or on call	être de permanence	
to look on the bright side	voir les choses du bon côté	
on several occasions	à plusieurs reprises	Section 13.2.4
on page 2	à la page 2	
on the television/on the radio	à la télévision/à la radio	
to knock on the door	frapper à la porte	
to be on the ground	être à terre	
on one's return	au retour	
on a bicycle, on foot, on horseback	à bicyclette, à pied, à cheval	
on military service	au service militaire	
to meet sb on the stairs	rencontrer qn dans l'escalier	Section 13.14.8
to do odd jobs on farms	bricoler dans des fermes	

on fire	en feu	Section 13.26.6
on holiday	en vacances	
on leave	en congé	
on sale	en vente	
on the way	en route	
on a trip	en voyage	
on average	en moyenne	
to throw things on the ground	jeter des choses par terre	Section 13.41.3
on a fine spring day	par une belle journée de printemps	
order something on line	commander qc par Internet	
to put one's hand on his shoulder	mettre la main sur son épaule	Section 13.56
leaning on one's elbows	appuyé sur les coudes	
to sit on a chair, a bench, a seat	s'asseoir sur une chaise, un banc, un siège	
on the road, on the pavement	sur la route, sur le trottoir	
on social media	sur les réseaux sociaux	
she got them on the net	elle les a eus sur internet	
to promise on oath	promettre sous serment	Section 13.53
to sell sth on condition	vendre qc sous conditions	
on Mondays	le lundi	
The drinks are on me/My round!	C'est ma tournée!	

Out of: *de; en dehors de; hors de; sur*

to pull a rabbit out of a hat	sortir un lapin d'un chapeau	Section 13.15.4
Get out of here!	Sortez d'ici!	
out of the town	en dehors de la ville	Section 13.16
out of the question	hors de question	
five out of ten	cinq sur dix	Section 13.56

Than: *de; que*

She earns more than 5,000 euros a month	Elle gagne plus de 5 000 euros par mois
She earns more than me/than I do	Elle gagne plus que moi (Section 13.15.7)
He works less than 2 hours a day	Il travaille moins de 2 heures par jour

Through: *par; à travers; au travers de; par moyen de*

to look through the window	regarder par la fenêtre	Section 13.41.1
to go through the forest	passer par la forêt	
to breathe through the mouth	aspirer l'air par la bouche	
to go through fields	passer à travers champs	Section 13.57
to go through difficulties	passer au travers des problèmes	
through an advert	par moyen d'une annonce	

To: *à; en; dans; sous; jusqu'à; pour; avec*

to the north, to the south	au nord, au sud	Section 13.2.2
to go to school, to the cinema, to the café	aller à l'école, au cinéma, au café	
to go up to one's room	monter à sa chambre	
to the right, to the left	à droite, à gauche	

to Japan, to Denmark	au Japon, au Danemark	
to Malta, to Jersey	à Malte, à Jersey	
to Paris, to London	à Paris, à Londres	
to Sicily, to New Zealand	en Sicile, en Nouvelle-Zélande	Section 13.26.1
to France, to Spain	en France, en Espagne	
to Europe, to Africa	en Europe, en Afrique	
to Normandy, to Brittany	en Normandie, en Bretagne	
to Essex, to Massachusetts	dans l'Essex, dans le Massachusetts	
to have a dictionary to hand	avoir un dictionnaire sous la main	Section 13.53
to go up to 2,000 euros	aller jusqu'à 2 000 euros	
a purchase to the value of…	un achat de la valeur de …	
to keep something to oneself	garder quelque chose pour soi	
to be kind to sb	être gentil avec qn	

Under: *sous; moins de; inférieur à; selon*

under the table, under the water	sous la table, sous l'eau	Section 13.53
under twenty euros	moins de vingt euros	Section 13.15.7
a price under a thousand euros	un prix inférieur à mille euros	
under the law	selon la loi	Section 13.52

With: *de; à; avec*

a street lined with plane trees	une rue bordée de platanes	Section 13.15.2
to fill with water	remplir d'eau (*or* avec de l'eau)	
to cover with posters	couvrir d'affiches (*or* avec des affiches)	
to go red with shame	rougir de honte	
to tremble with cold	trembler de froid	
a man with a grey beard	un homme à la barbe grise	Section 13.2.6
to water the garden with a	arroser le jardin avec un arrosoir	Section 13.7
watering can		
to speak with sb	parler avec qn	
to arrive with sb	arriver avec qn	

FREE

**INSTRUCTOR
& STUDENT
RESOURCES**

For more resources to practice your French grammar, including practice activities/quizzes for students, further resource links, and an instructor guide, please visit https://routledgelearning.com/frenchgrammarandusage.

14 Question formation

14.1 Introduction

There are two main types of question: yes/no questions, to which it is possible to answer simply 'yes' or 'no':

Aimez-vous la musique techno? Oui	*Do you like techno music? Yes*
Est-ce que tu as fait tes devoirs? Non	*Have you done your homework? No*

and information questions, to which it is impossible to answer simply 'yes' or 'no', but which require a piece of information in response:

Quand partira Damien? Demain	*When will Damien leave? Tomorrow*
Qui a-t-il rencontré? Fabienne	*Who did he meet? Fabienne*

Information questions involve the use of a question word or phrase like *qui, que, quand, comment, où, pourquoi, pour quelle raison, avec quel ami, de quoi*, etc.

14.2 Yes/no questions

There are three ways in which yes/no questions can be asked in French. Each is characteristic of a particular style of French, ranging from the informal to the formal.

14.2.1 Yes/no questions formed with rising intonation

The simplest way to form a yes/no question in French is to add rising intonation to the final syllables of a declarative sentence:

Tu as quelque chose à dire?	*Do you have anything to say?*
Elle va rester ici?	*Is she going to stay here?*
Sylvain est venu?	*Has Sylvain come?*
Je peux t'envoyer mes photos sur ton téléphone?	*Can I send you my photos on your phone?*

This kind of yes/no question is very common in informal French, but less common in more formal spoken French and not normally used in written French (unless direct speech is being recorded, or an informal style is being imitated).

14.2.2 Yes/no questions formed with *est-ce que*

Yes/no questions may also be formed by placing the question formula *est-ce que* at the beginning of a declarative sentence:

Est-ce que tu as quelque chose à dire?	*Do you have anything to say?*
Est-ce qu'elle va rester ici?	*Is she going to stay here?*
Est-ce que Damien est venu?	*Has Damien come?*
Est-ce que je peux t'envoyer mes photos sur ton téléphone?	*Can I send you my photos on your phone?*

DOI: 10.4324/9781003373926-14

Yes/no questions formed with *est-ce que* can be used in all styles of French, informal and formal, spoken and written.

14.2.3 **Yes/no questions formed by inverting the verb and subject**

Yes/no questions may be formed by inverting the subject and the verb which agrees with it. Such inversion takes two forms, depending on whether the subject is an unstressed pronoun or not.

Subject is an unstressed pronoun

If the subject is an unstressed pronoun, it changes places with the verb which agrees with it:

Es-tu content?	*Are you happy?*
Est-ce le livreur?	*Is it the delivery man?*
Avez-vous bien compris?	*Have you really understood?*
Peut-on se changer dans les vestiaires?	*Can you change in the changing rooms?*
Avaient-ils reçu de ses nouvelles?	*Had they had news of him?*
Avait-elle pu réunir les actionnaires?	*Had she been able to assemble the shareholders?*

Such subject–verb inversion is possible with all verbs in French, whereas in English it is only possible with 'auxiliary' verbs like 'have', 'be', 'can', 'will', 'do', etc.:

Aime-t-il le Roquefort?	*Does he like Roquefort?*
Descend-elle en ville?	*Is she going down into town?*
Apprenez-vous le piano depuis longtemps?	*Have you been learning the piano for long?*
Prennent-ils le train?	*Are they taking the train?*

Subject is not an unstressed pronoun

If the subject is anything other than an unstressed pronoun, i.e. a proper noun, noun phrase, or stressed pronoun, then the subject is placed first, followed by the verb and an unstressed subject pronoun agreeing with the subject is inserted to the right of the verb:

Gaspard est-il content?	*Is Gaspard happy?*
Les joueurs peuvent-ils se changer dans les vestiaires?	*Can the players change in the changing rooms?*

Cela est-il vrai?	*Is that true?*
Personne ne veut-il m'accompagner?	*Doesn't anyone want to come with me?*

Les élèves avaient-ils reçu les résultats?	*Had the pupils received the results?*
Julie viendra-t-elle demain?	*Will Julie come tomorrow?*

N.B.: It is impossible to invert a subject which is not an unstressed pronoun with an agreeing verb:

NOT *Viendra Julie demain?
NOT *Est cela vrai?
NOT *Peuvent les joueurs se changer dans les vestiaires?
NOT *Est Gaspard content?

Yes/no questions formed with inversion are typically used in more formal spoken and in written French.

14.2.4 **Insertion of** -t- **between inverted verb and subject**

When the inversion of subject and verb results in two vowels becoming adjacent, the consonant -t- is inserted between them:

A-**t**-il 17 ans?	*Is he 17?*
Aura-**t**-elle faim?	*Will she be hungry?*

This rule also applies where the verb ends in -e, even though in the spoken language the -e is not
pronounced:

Epouse-**t**-il Jamila?	*Is he marrying Jamila?*
Dîne-**t**-elle avec nous ce soir?	*Is she dining with us this evening?*

Where a verb already ends in a -t or a -d in the written language, it is pronounced as 't' in questions:

Est-elle contente?	*Is she happy?*
Impriment-ils tous leurs emails?	*Do they print (out) all their emails?*
Vos amis sont-ils partis?	*Have your friends left?*
Lucas vend-il sa voiture?	*Is Lucas selling his car?*
Le voyage te rend-il malade?	*Is the journey making you feel ill?*

14.2.5 **Inversion of the verb and** *je* **in yes/no questions**

Inversion of the verb with first person *je* to form a yes/no question is characteristic of only the
most formal French. Many speakers and writers these days would avoid it and use *est-ce que*.
Furthermore, there are idiosyncratic restrictions on its use.

In the present tense, inversion between *je* and some very common verbs of one syllable is frequent:

Ai-je le droit? (avoir)	*Am I allowed to?*
Dois-je vous téléphoner? (devoir)	*Should I phone you?*
Puis-je vous déranger? (pouvoir)	*May I disturb you?*
Suis-je heureux? (être)	*Am I happy?*
Vais-je me laisser tromper? (aller)	*Am I going to let myself be deceived?*
Ne **dis-je** pas la vérité? (dire)	*Am I not telling the truth?*

but with most other verbs such inversion is impossible:

NOT *Mens-je?	*Am I lying?*
NOT *Prends-je le bus?	*Am I taking the bus?*

In future and conditional tenses, however, inversion with these same verbs is more acceptable
(but again only in the most formal styles):

Mentirais-je?	*Would I lie?*
Prendrai-je le bus?	*Shall I take the bus?*

Where a verb ends in -e and it is inverted with *je*, the -e becomes -é:

Demandé-je?	*Am I asking?*

This, however, is extremely rare in modern French (although it can occasionally arise as a joke).

14.2.6 *n'est-ce pas?*

n'est-ce pas? is the invariable French equivalent of English 'tag' question forms like 'doesn't he?', 'haven't you?', 'mustn't I?', etc.:

Il habite à Paris, **n'est-ce pas**?	*He lives in Paris, doesn't he?*
Vous avez vendu le terrain, **n'est-ce pas**?	*You've sold the land, haven't you?*
Je dois m'adresser au sous-directeur, **n'est-ce pas**?	*I must speak to the assistant director, mustn't I?*
Elle n'a pas encore signé **n'est-ce pas**?	*She hasn't signed yet, has she?*

In everyday usage, *n'est-ce pa*s is felt to be old-fashioned or quite formal, and it is heard less often than its reputation in the eyes of foreigners as a typical French question tag would suggest. Even in formal spoken contexts, such as the examples above, it tends to be replaced by 'non' if the sentence is in the positive (*Il habite à Paris, non?*) and 'si' if the sentence is in the negative (*Elle n'a pas encore signé, si?*).

14.2.7 Use of *jamais, rien, aucun* in yes/no questions

In questions, *jamais, rien, aucun*, and *personne* may mean 'ever', 'anything' and 'any':

Est-ce que vous avez **jamais** pensé à tout quitter?	*Have you ever thought of leaving it all behind?*
A-t-il **rien** fait de meilleur?	*Has he done anything better?*
A-t-elle eu **aucune** réponse?	*Has she received any reply?*

14.2.8 *oui, si, non*, and *merci* as responses to yes/no questions

non is the normal way of saying 'no' to yes/no questions, both affirmative and negative:

Tu viens?	-Non
Tu ne viens pas?	-Non

oui is used to say 'yes' to affirmative yes/no questions, but *si* is used to say 'yes' to negative questions:

Tu viens?	-Oui
Tu ne viens pas?	-Si

In each case the force of the response may be increased by adding *mais* or *bien sûr que*:

Tu viens?	-Mais oui	-Mais non
	-Bien sûr que oui	-Bien sûr que non
Tu ne viens pas?	-Mais si	-Mais non
	-Bien sûr que si	-Bien sûr que non

merci 'thank you' used alone as a response to a yes/no question is normally treated as a response of 'No, thank you':

Voulez-vous du fromage?	-Merci
Would you like some cheese?	*-No, thank you*

Voulez-vous du fromage?	-Oui, merci
	-Je veux bien
	-S'il vous plaît
	-Volontiers
	-Avec plaisir
Would you like some cheese?	*-Yes, please*

14.3 Information questions

There are four ways of asking information questions in French. Each is appropriate to a particular level of formality of style.

14.3.1 Information questions formed with rising intonation

The simplest way to form an information question is to replace an item in a declarative sentence by a question word or phrase and add rising intonation to the final syllables of the sentence. (For question words and phrases, see Section 14.6.) For example, taking a declarative sentence such as

Thibault achètera une nouvelle imprimante demain
Thibault will buy a new printer tomorrow

information questions can be formed related to *demain, une nouvelle imprimante,* or *Thibault* simply by replacing the relevant words with a question word:

Thibault achètera une nouvelle imprimante **quand**?
When will Thibault buy a new printer?

Thibault achètera **quoi** demain?
What will Thibault buy tomorrow?

Qui achètera une nouvelle imprimante demain?
Who will buy a new printer tomorrow?

This kind of information question is very common in informal French. The last example above involving *qui?* (where the subject is questioned) is also normal in formal styles (see Section 14.3.6). But the other types are less common in formal spoken and in written styles (unless direct speech is being reported, or an informal style is being imitated).

The full range of question words and phrases (see Section 14.6) may be used in this way, except *que?* 'what'. Instead, the stressed form of *que? – quoi? –* is used:

Vous avez vu **quoi**?	*What did you see?*
Elle a dit **quoi**?	*What did she say?*
Farida a écrit **à qui**?	*Who did Farida write to?*
Elle parle de **quoi**?	*What is she talking about?*
Tu recommanderais **quelle série**?	*Which (TV) series would you recommend?*
Ils ont invité **combien de gens**?	*How many people did they invite?*
Vous l'avez vu **où**?	*Where did you see it?*
Adrien reviendra **quand**?	*When will Adrien come back?*

14.3.2 Information questions formed by 'fronting' a question word or phrase

Here is another common way of forming information questions in many informal or very informal contexts. It involves replacing an item in a declarative sentence by a question word or phrase and then moving the question word or phrase to the front of the sentence, without making any other changes:

Qui vous avez vu?	*Who did you see?*
A qui Farida a écrit?	*Who did Farida write to?*
Quel film tu recommanderais?	*Which film would you recommend?*
Combien de gens ils ont invités?	*How many people did they invite?*
De quoi tu voulais me parler?	*What did you want to speak to me about?*
Où vous l'avez vu?	*Where did you see it?*
Pourquoi la police l'a arrêté?	*Why did the police arrest him?*
C'est **quoi**, ce bazar? (informal)	*What on earth is this mess?*
C'est **qui** celui-là? (informal)	*Who the hell is this?*

Nearly all question words can be used in this way except direct object *que?, quoi?* 'what?' Instead, *qu'est-ce que?* is used (see Section 14.3.3):

Qu'est-ce qu'elle a dit?	*What did she say?*
Qu'est-ce que tu faisais dans ma chambre?	*What were you doing in my room?*

14.3.3 Information questions formed with *est-ce que?*

Information questions may be formed by 'fronting' a question word or phrase, as described in Section 14.3.2, and in addition inserting *est-ce que?* between the question word or phrase and the rest of the sentence. Questions of this type may be used in all styles of French, formal and informal. The full range of question words and phrases (see Section 14.6) may be used in this construction except *quoi?* 'what?' – the unstressed variant *que?* is required instead:

Qui est-ce que vous avez vu?	*Who did you see?*
Qu'est-ce qu'elle a dit?	*What did she say?*
Quel film est-ce que tu recommanderais?	*Which film would you recommend?*
A qui est-ce que Farida a écrit?	*To whom did Farida write?*
Combien de gens est-ce qu'ils ont invités?	*How many people did they invite?*
Où est-ce que vous l'avez vu?	*Where did you see it?*
Quand est-ce que Thibault reviendra?	*When will Thibault come back?*
Pourquoi est-ce que la police l'a arrêté?	*Why did the police arrest him?*

14.3.4 *qui est-ce qui?, qui est-ce que?, qu'est-ce qui?,* and *qu'est-ce que?*

qui est-ce qui? is used to form questions dealing with animate subjects:

Qui est-ce qui a pris mon crayon?	*Who took my pencil?*
Qui est-ce qui va avoir le prix?	*Who will get the prize?*

qu'est-ce qui? is used to form questions dealing with non-animate subjects:

Qu'est ce qui a bloqué le lave-vaisselle?	*What blocked the dishwasher?*
Qu'est-ce qui s'est passé?	*What happened?*
Qu'est-ce qui a effrayé les fillettes?	*What frightened the little girls?*
Qu'est-ce qui lui est arrivé, à Paul?	*What happened to Paul?*

qui est-ce que? is used to form questions dealing with animate direct objects:

Qui est-ce que vous avez vu?	*Who did you see?*
Qui est-ce qu'ils ont invité à la fête?	*Who did they invite to the party?*

qu'est-ce que? is used to form questions dealing with non-animate direct objects:

Qu'est-ce que vous avez dit?	*What did you say?*
Qu'est-ce que Reza va acheter?	*What is Reza going to buy?*
Qu'est-ce qu'elle a pris dans la grange?	*What did she take from the barn?*
Qu'est-ce que c'était, ce bruit, dehors?	*What was that noise, outside?*

Compare the following uses of *qu'est-ce?*, *qu'est-ce que?*, and *qu'est-ce que c'est?*:

Qu'est-ce? (very formal)	*What is it?*
Qu'est-ce que c'est?	*What is it?*
Qu'est-ce que c'est que ça?	*What on earth is that?*
Qu'est-ce qu'une 'jonque'?	*What's a 'jonque'?*
Qu'est-ce que c'est qu'une 'jonque'?	*What is a 'jonque'?*
Qu'est-ce que ça veut dire 'jonque'?	*What does 'jonque' mean?*
Qu'est-ce que ça peut bien être une 'jonque'?	*What on earth is a 'jonque'?*

14.3.5 **Information questions formed by the inversion of verb and subject**

Information questions may be formed by 'fronting' a question word or phrase (as described in Section 14.3.2), and in addition inverting the subject and the verb which agrees with the subject. This kind of question is usually found in formal spoken and in written French. It takes two forms depending on whether the subject is an unstressed pronoun or not.

Subject is an unstressed pronoun

If the subject is an unstressed pronoun, it changes places with the verb which agrees with it:

Qui avez-**vous** vu?	*Who did you see?*
Qui est-**ce**?	*Who is it?*
A qui a-t-**elle** écrit?	*To whom did she write?*
Quelle série recommanderais-**tu**?	*Which (TV) series would you recommend?*
Combien de personnes ont-**ils** invitées?	*How many people have they invited?*
Où l'avez-**vous** vu?	*Where did you see it?*
Quand reviendra-t-**il**?	*When will he come back?*
Pourquoi l'ont-**ils** arrêté?	*Why have they arrested him?*

(For inversion with *je*, see Section 14.2.5.)

Subject is not an unstressed pronoun

If the subject is not an unstressed pronoun, i.e. if it is a proper noun, noun phrase, or stressed pronoun, then the subject is placed first after the question word, followed by the verb and an unstressed subject pronoun agreeing with the subject is inserted to the right of the verb:

Qui **Zac** a-t-il rencontré?	*Who did Zac meet?*
A qui **Liane** donnera-t-elle l'argent?	*To whom will Liane give the money?*
Quelles statistiques **la presse** préfère-t-elle, celles des syndicats ou celles de la police?	*Which figures does the press prefer, the unions' or the police's?*
Combien de tutos **ton frère** a-t-il enregistrés?	*How many tutorials did your brother record?*
Où **Renaud** va-t-il faire ses courses?	*Where is Renaud going to do his shopping?*
Quand **le train** arrivera-t-il à Limoges?	*When will the train arrive at Limoges?*

Pourquoi **les examens** ont-ils toujours lieu en juin?
Why do the exams always take place in June?

(For insertion of -*t*-, see Section 14.2.4.)

14.3.6 **Exceptional behaviour of subject *qui?* and subject and object *que?* in information questions**

When the subject is animate and questioned by *qui?* 'who', there is no inversion with the verb:

Qui parle?	*Who is speaking?*
Qui a tourné ce film?	*Who made this film?*

NOT *Qui parle-t-il?
NOT *Qui a-t-il tourné ce film?

que? 'what' can never be used directly as non-animate subject 'what' and nor can its stressed form *quoi?*. Instead, *qu'est-ce qui?* must be used:

Qu'est-ce qui brille dans le ciel?	*What's shining in the sky?*
Qu'est-ce qui a grignoté les gâteaux dans le placard?	*What has eaten the cakes in the cupboard?*
Qu'est-ce qui plairait à Clarisse?	*What would Clarisse like?*
Qu'est-ce qui a été donné à Julien?	*What was given to Julien?*

and

NOT *Que brille dans le ciel?
NOT *Qu'a grignoté les gâteaux?
NOT *Quoi plairait à Clarisse?
NOT *Quoi a été donné à Julien?

When *que?* 'what' is a direct object, it may be used with verb and subject inversion, providing that the subject is a pronoun:

Que dit-il?	*What does he say?*
Que pense-t-elle?	*What does she think?*
Qu'ont-ils décidé?	*What have they decided?*

But it may not be used with inversion when the subject is a proper noun, noun phrase, or stressed pronoun:

NOT *Que le docteur dit-il?	*What does the doctor say?*
NOT *Que Marie pense-t-elle?	*What does Marie think?*
NOT *Que le conseil municipal a-t-il décidé?	*What has the council decided?*

Instead, either *qu'est-ce que?* must be used:

Qu'est-ce que le docteur dit?	*What does the doctor say?*
Qu'est-ce que Marie pense?	*What does Marie think?*
Qu'est-ce que le conseil municipal a décidé?	*What has the council decided?*

Or a different kind of inversion must be used involving the subject and the whole verb group, but without the insertion of an unstressed pronoun:

Que dit le **docteur**?	*What does the doctor say?*
Que pense **Marie**?	*What does Marie think?*
Qu'a décidé **le conseil municipal**?	*What has the council decided?*
Que va faire **Marie**?	*What is Marie going to do?*
Qu'aurait dû déclarer **le ministre**?	*What should the minister have declared?*

This kind of inversion is known by linguists as 'stylistic inversion'.

14.3.7 'Stylistic inversion' in information questions

In formal spoken and in written French, as an alternative to subject–verb inversion of the kind: *Où Blandine est-elle allée?* 'Where did Blandine go?', it is also possible (with many question words and phrases) to invert the subject with the whole verb group, but without insertion of an unstressed pronoun:

Où est allée **Blandine**?

Notice that *Blandine* and *est allée* have inverted, but without insertion of an agreeing unstressed pronoun. Stylistic inversion of this kind is possible with:

Object *que?*

Qu'avait dit le **docteur**?	*What had the doctor said?*
Qu'a décidé **le conseil municipal**?	*What has the council decided?*

Prepositional object *qui (à qui?, de qui?, avec qui?, etc.)*

A qui s'est adressé **Jérôme**?	*To whom did Jérôme go and speak?*
De qui aura parlé **la présentatrice**?	*Who will the presenter have spoken about?*

Prepositional object *quoi (à quoi?, de quoi?, avec quoi?, etc.)*

A quoi aurait dû penser **Marion**?	*What ought Marion to have thought about?*
De quoi dépend **le succès d'un jeu vidéo**?	*What does the success of a video game depend on?*

Object and prepositional object *quel?, quand?, combien?*

quel

Quel plat a commandé **Noah**?	*Which dish did Noah order?*
A quelle heure partira **Thomas**?	*At what time will Thomas leave?*
Par quelle porte sont sortis les clients?	*Which door did the customers come out of?*

quand

> **Quand** est entré **Léontine**? *When did Léontine come in?*
> **Depuis quand** travaille **Sarah**? *How long has Sarah been working?*

combien

> **Combien de kilos** a perdu **Sofiane**? *How many kilos has Sofiane lost?*
> **Combien de cidre** produit **ce verger**? *How much cider does this orchard produce?*

Stylistic inversion is not possible with *pourquoi:*

> NOT *Pourquoi travaille Nicolas? *Why does Nicolas work?*
> NOT *Pourquoi est partie Margot? *Why did Margot leave?*

Stylistic inversion is also quite restricted by the type of verb with which it can be used. It occurs fairly freely with intransitive verbs which do not have complements:

> **Depuis quand** travaille **Nicolas**? *How long has Nicolas been working?*

And when the questioned phrase is itself a direct object:

> **Quel dessert** recommande **le patron**? *Which dessert does the patron recommend?*

But it is not acceptable when an intransitive verb has an adverbial complement:

> NOT *Depuis quand travaille Nicolas sur une chaîne d'informations?
> *How long has Nicolas been working on a news channel ?*

or with transitive verbs when the direct object is present:

> NOT *Depuis quand connaît Vincent *How long has Vincent known Mariella?*
> Mariella?
> NOT *Où va manger Martial des coquilles *Where is Martial going to eat scallops?*
> Saint Jacques?
> NOT *A qui a donné Paul ce livre? *To whom did Paul give this book?*

14.4 **Order of object pronouns in questions involving inversion**

The order of unstressed object pronouns is unaffected by the inversion of the subject and verb in questions:

> Elle **en** a parlé à Charley **En** a-t-elle parlé à Charley?
> *She spoke of it to Charley* *Did she speak of it to Charley?*

> Il **le lui** avait prêté **Le lui** avait-il prêté?
> *He lent it to her* *Did he lend it to her?*

> Jean **te le** dira Jean **te le** dira-t-il?
> *Jean will tell you so* *Will Jean tell you so?*

> Ils **me** l'ont donné Pourquoi **me** l'ont-ils donné?
> *They gave it to me* *Why did they give it to me?*

14.5 **Order of negative particles in questions involving inversion**

The position of negative particles is unaffected by the inversion of the subject and verb in questions:

Tu **n**'as **jamais** loué un vélo en libre-service?	**N**'as-tu **jamais** loué un vélo en libre-service?
You have never rented a bike?	*Have you never rented a bike?*
Vous **n**'avez **pas** vu cet homme	Qui **n**'avez-vous **pas** vu?
You haven't seen this man	*Who haven't you seen?*
Ils **ne** les appellent **plus**	Pourquoi **ne** les appellent-ils **plus**?
They don't call them any more	*Why don't they call them any more?*

14.6 **Use of question words and phrases: *qui?*, *que?*, *quoi?*, *quel?*, *de qui?*, *avec combien de?*, etc.**

14.6.1 *qui?*

qui? typically translates English 'who?', 'whom?' whether subject, direct object, or object of a preposition:

Subject

Qui a pris la télécommande?	*Who took the remote control?*

Direct object

Qui ces types ont-t-ils ciblés sur les réseaux?	*Who have these guys targeted on social media?*

Object of a preposition

A qui la journaliste a-t-elle posé la question?	*Who did the reporter put the question to?*
De qui parlez-vous?	*Who are you talking about?*
Contre qui avait-il joué?	*Who had he played against?*
Sur qui peut-on compter?	*Who can one count on?*

14.6.2 *que?*, *quoi?*

que?, *quoi?* typically translate English 'what?'. *Que?* is used to question direct objects which are moved to the front of the sentence:

Que dit-il?	*What does he say?*
Qu'est-il arrivé?	*What's happened?*
Que sont-ils devenus?	*What's become of them?*
Que boiront les invités?	*What will the guests drink?*

que? cannot be used to question subjects, rather *qu'est-ce qui?* is used (see Section 14.3.6):

Qu'est-ce qui lui est arrivé?	NOT *Que lui est arrivé?
What happened to him?	
Qu'est-ce qui a taché le mur?	NOT *Qu'a taché le mur?
What made that stain on the wall?	

quoi? is used to question direct objects which are not moved to the front of the sentence. It is also used to form questions related to the objects of prepositions; in this use it can be moved to the front of the sentence:

Direct object

Elles cherchent **quoi**?	*What are they looking for?*
Ça ouvre **quoi**, ça?	*What does that thing open?*
Tu seras **quoi** dans un an?	*What will you be a year from now?*

Object of a preposition

A quoi pensent-elles?	*What are they thinking about?*
Avec quoi peut-on sortir cette carte SIM du téléphone?	*With what can one remove this SIM card from the phone?*
On peut miser **sur quoi**?	*What can one bank on?*
Contre quoi est-ce que les gens manifestent?	*What are people demonstrating against?*

De quoi elle a parlé si longtemps?
What did she speak about for such a long time?

que? and *quoi?* can both be used with infinitives to form questions. *Que?* is used at the front of main clauses:

Que faire?	*What is to be done?*
Que faire de ces piles usagées?	*What shall we do with these used batteries?*
Que dire?	*What can I say?*

quoi? is used in subordinate clauses, and in main clauses where the question word is not fronted:

Elle a demandé **quoi** faire de ces piles usagées
She asked what she should do with these used batteries?

Je rentre tout de suite	-Faire **quoi**?
I'm going home immediately	*-To do what?*

N.B.: *Quoi de neuf?* 'What's new?'

14.6.3 *quel?, quelle?, quels?, quelles?*

quel?, *quelle?*, etc are used to form questions based on nouns and noun phrases: *quel livre?*, *quelle page?*, *quels manuscrits?*, *quelles jolies fleurs?* Notice that *quel?* agrees in gender and number with the noun. Question phrases involving *quel?* can be subjects, direct objects, or objects of prepositions:

Subject

Quel enfant n'a pas rêvé d'avoir un chat ou un chien?
What child hasn't dreamt of having a cat or a dog?

Quel bruit a effrayé les oiseaux?
What noise frightened the birds?

N.B.: When a *quel* phrase is a subject, it is not possible to invert subject and verb or use *est-ce que?*:

NOT *Quel enfant n'a-t-il pas rêvé d'avoir un chat ou un chien?
NOT *Quel enfant est-ce qu'il n'a pas rêvé d'avoir un chat ou un chien?

Object

Quel film tu recommanderais?	*Which film would you recommend?*
Quel film est-ce que tu recommanderais?	*Which film would you recommend?*
Quel film recommanderais-tu?	*Which film would you recommend?*
Quelles fleurs Josette a-t-elle cueillies?	*Which flowers did Josette pick?*

Object of a preposition

A quelle heure part Nordine?	*What time does Nordine leave?*
De quelle ville est-ce que vous parlez?	*Which town are you talking about?*
Il a posté sa photo **sur quel réseau**?	*On which network did he post his photo?*

Sous quel arbre vous avez planté/avez-vous planté les jonquilles?
Which tree did you plant the daffodils under?

Par quelle route les cyclistes sont/sont-ils partis?
By which road did the cyclists leave?

In the last two examples, the verb-pronoun inversion adds a degree of formality to the question.

With the verb *être, quel?* is separated from the noun phrase with which it agrees:

Quels sont **les atouts** de votre équipe?	*What are the strengths of your team?*
Quels sont **vos favoris**?	*Which are your favourites?*
Quelle est **la région** que tu préfères?	*Which is the region you prefer?*

N.B.: *Quel est cet homme?* 'Who is this man?', *Quelle est cette femme?* 'Who is this woman?' are alternatives to *Qui est cet homme?*, *Qui est cette femme?*

14.6.4 *lequel?, laquelle?, lesquels?, lesquelles?*

lequel?, laquelle? … etc. ask 'which' noun or noun phrase when there is a choice of more than one. The form used agrees in gender and number with the noun or noun phrase it questions, whether this is present in the same sentence, or is understood from the context:

Laquelle de **ces couleurs** préférez-vous?	*Which of these colours do you prefer?*
Laquelle préférez-vous?	*Which do you prefer?*
Lesquelles des **applis** trouvez-vous les plus pratiques?	*Which of the apps do you find most useful?*
Lesquelles avez-vous déjà inscrites?	*Which have you already registered?*
On a enfin décidé **quelle race de chien** on va prendre	*We have finally decided which breed of dog we will get*
Laquelle? or **Lequel?**	*Which one?*

When the phrase involving *lequel?* is the direct object, and sometimes when it is the subject of an intransitive verb, it is possible to separate *lequel?* from the noun phrase it modifies:

Laquelle préférez-vous de **ces couleurs**?	*Which of these colours do you prefer?*
Lequel a la meilleure caméra de **ces deux portables**?	*Which of these two mobiles has the better camera?*

N.B.: When a *lequel?* phrase is the subject of a sentence, it is not possible to use *est-ce que?* or to invert subject and verb:

NOT *Lequel de ces deux portables est-ce qu'il a la meilleure caméra?
NOT *Lequel de ces deux portables a-t-il la meilleure caméra?

14.6.5 *combien?*

combien? 'how much?', 'how many?' may be used on its own:

Combien est-ce que ça coûte?	*How much does that cost?*
Combien sont déjà arrivés?	*How many have already arrived?*

Or it may be used with a following prepositional phrase:

Combien de pain nous reste-t-il?	*How much bread do we have left?*
Combien de spectateurs assistaient au match?	*How many spectators were there at the match?*

combien (de)? can be used to question subjects, direct objects, and objects of prepositions:

Subject

Combien d'invités sont déjà arrivés?	*How many guests have already arrived?*

Direct object

Combien d'enfants ont-ils?	*How many children do they have?*

Object of a preposition

Avec combien d'argent minimum peut-on ouvrir un compte en ligne?	*What is the minimum amount of money needed to open an online account?*

When *combien?* is used alone and functions as a direct object, the pronoun *en* is required:

Combien **en** as-tu vu?	*How many did you see?*
Combien est-ce qu'ils **en** ont tués?	*How many did they kill?*

N.B.: When *combien?* is the subject of the sentence, it is not possible to use *est-ce que* or invert the subject and the verb:

NOT *Combien de joueurs est-ce qu'ils ont participé au concours?
NOT *Combien de joueurs ont-ils participé au concours?

Although *combien?* translates 'how much', 'how many', it cannot be used to translate English 'how + adjective/adverb' like 'how big?', 'how tall?', 'how often?', etc. (For these, see Section 14.6.8.)

14.6.6 *comment?*

comment? usually translates English 'how?' when it is not followed by an adjective or adverb (i.e. not 'how big?', 'how often?', etc.):

Comment allez-vous?	*How are you?*
Comment va votre mère?	*How is your mother?*

Comment est-ce qu'elle va?	*How is she?*
Comment s'étaient-ils comportés?	*How had they behaved?*
Comment allez-vous ré-initialiser l'ordinateur?	*How are you going to re-initialise the computer?*
Comment cela se prononce-t-il?	*How is this pronounced?*

comment? also translates 'what?' with the verb *appeler*:

Comment tu t'appelles?	*What's your name?*
Comment appelez-vous ce monument?	*What is this monument called?*
or **Comment** ce monument s'appelle-t-il?	

14.6.7 *où?, quand?, pourquoi?*

où? and *quand?* translate English 'where?' and 'when?', respectively, and are used in the same range of information question constructions as the other question words:

Où vous habitez?	*Where do you live?*
Où habitez-vous?	*Where do you live?*
Où est-ce que vous habitez?	*Where do you live?*
Où Irqam habite-t-il?	*Where does Irqam live?*
Quand vous partez?	*When are you leaving?*
Quand partez-vous?	*When are you leaving?*
Quand est-ce que vous partez?	*When are you leaving?*
Quand Maxence partira-t-il?	*When will Maxence leave?*

When the verb is *être*, 'stylistic inversion' of the subject is normal with *où?* and *quand?* (see Section 14.3.7):

Où est **le portefeuille**?	*Where's the wallet?*
Quand est **son anniversaire**?	*When's his birthday?*

pourquoi? 'why?' is used in the same way as the other two question words except that it cannot be used with stylistic inversion:

Pourquoi il a déménagé?	*Why has he moved?*
Pourquoi a-t-il déménagé?	*Why has he moved?*
Pourquoi est-ce qu'il a déménagé?	*Why has he moved?*
Pourquoi Pierre a-t-il déménagé?	*Why has Pierre moved?*

but NOT *Pourquoi a déménagé Pierre?

14.6.8 Translating *'how big?', 'how fast?', 'how often?'*, etc.

Whereas English 'how?' can question adjectives and adverbs directly, in French there is no simple equivalent. For 'How big is the table?' you CANNOT say things like:

*Comment grande est la table?
*Combien grande est la table?

Instead, alternative expressions have to be found:

De quelle taille est la table?	*How big is the table?*
Avec quelle fréquence y allez-vous?	*How often do you go there?*

Est-ce souvent que vous y allez?	*How often do you go there?*
Dans quelle mesure êtes-vous inquiet?	*How worried are you?*
Dans quelle mesure accepteriez-vous de faire cela?	*How happy would you be to do that?*

14.7 Indirect questions

Indirect questions are questions which are reported as having already been asked. They are introduced by verbs like *comprendre, demander, se demander, dire, expliquer, savoir*:

Qui est venu?	(direct question)
Elle a demandé **qui était venu**	(indirect question)
She asked who came	

Quel piège est-ce qu'on lui tend?	(direct question)
Il n'arrive pas à comprendre **quel piège on lui tend**	(indirect question)
He hasn't grasped what kind of trap they are setting for him	

Quand arrivera-t-il?	(direct question)
Dites-moi **quand il arrivera**	(indirect question)
Tell me when he will arrive	

14.7.1 Word order in indirect questions

There is no subject–verb inversion in indirect questions:

Où sont-ils?
Je ne sais pas **où ils sont**
I don't know where they are

NOT *Je ne sais pas où sont-ils

Pourquoi Nadia est-elle revenue?
Dites-moi **pourquoi Nadia est revenue**
Tell me why Nadia came back

NOT *Dites-moi pourquoi Nadia est-elle revenue

14.7.2 *si* in indirect questions

Direct yes/no questions are introduced by *si* 'if, whether' when they become indirect questions:

Est-ce que Julie viendra demain?
Je me demande **si Julie viendra demain**
I wonder if Julie will come tomorrow

A-t-il bien compris?
On ne sait jamais **s'il a bien compris**
One never knows whether he has understood properly

N.B.: This use of *si* should not be confused with *si* used to introduce hypothetical clauses like: *Si elle m'aimait, elle m'écrirait* 'If she loved me, she would write to me'. In hypothetical *si* clauses the verb cannot appear in future or conditional tenses (see Section 10.8). In indirect questions introduced by *si* it may do so.

14.7.3 *ce qui* and *ce que* in indirect questions

qu'est-ce qui? in a direct question becomes *ce qui* in an indirect question; *que?* or *qu'est-ce que?* becomes *ce que* in an indirect question:

Qu'est-ce qui a ravagé les champs des Rodriguez?
On ne sait pas **ce qui** a ravagé les champs des Rodriguez
They don't know what ruined the Rodriguez's fields

Qu'est-ce qui est arrivé?
Elle se demande **ce qui** est arrivé
She wonders what happened

Que dit-il?
Je ne comprends pas **ce qu'**il dit
I don't understand what he's saying

Qu'est-ce qu'Etienne fera?
Il a expliqué **ce qu'Etienne** ferait
He explained what Etienne would do

All other question words remain the same:

Elle lui demande **à qui** il écrivait	*She is asking him who he was writing to*
Je ne sais plus **de quoi** elle parlait	*I no longer know what she was talking about*
Je ne sais pas **laquelle** lui plaît le plus	*I don't know which he likes more*

14.7.4 Tense in indirect questions

The tense of a verb in a direct question may change if it becomes an indirect question (see Section 10.7). This depends on the tense of the verb which introduces the indirect question (i.e. the tense of *comprendre, demander, dire*, etc.). If the introducing verb is in the present, future, or conditional, the tense of the verb in the indirect question remains the same as in the direct question:

Chante-t-il?	*Is he singing?*
Quand a-t-il chanté?	*When did he sing?*
Qui avait chanté?	*Who had sung?*

Elle ne sait pas s'il chante/quand il a chanté/qui avait chanté
She doesn't know if he sings/when he sang/who sang

When the introducing verb is in the past, however, the verb in the indirect question becomes imperfect or pluperfect if in the direct question it is in the present or past:

Elle ne savait pas s'il chantait/quand il avait chanté/qui avait chanté
She didn't know if he sang/when he had sung/who had sung

and it becomes conditional in the indirect question if it is in the future or conditional in the direct question:

Chantera- t- il?	*Will he sing?*
Qui chanterait?	*Who would sing?*
Elle ne savait pas s'il chanterait/qui chanterait	*She didn't know if he would sing/ who would sing*

For more resources to practice your French grammar, including practice activities/quizzes for students, further resource links, and an instructor guide, please visit https://routledgelearning.com/frenchgrammarandusage.

15 Relative clauses

15.1 Introduction

Clauses within a sentence which modify noun phrases or pronouns are known as 'relative clauses'. The noun phrases/pronouns in italics in the following examples are modified by relative clauses in bold:

Il y avait *deux hommes* **qui sortaient une armoire à glace du camion**
Two men were getting a wardrobe out of the lorry

C'est *lui* **qui me l'a donné**
He is the one who gave it to me

Il n'y avait pas assez de place sur *la clé USB* **qu'il a utilisée** pour copier ses photos
There wasn't enough space on the USB key he used in order to back up his photos

C'est *là* **qu'on creusera le trou**
There's where we will dig the hole

Elle a acheté *une vieille boutique* **dont il ne restait plus que les quatre murs**
She bought an old shop of which only the four walls remained

Le matin, c'est *le moment* **où je prends connaissance de tous mes emails**.
Mornings are when I read all my emails

Il y a *plusieurs arbres* **sur lesquels on a cloué des pancartes**
There are several trees on which notices have been nailed

Relative clauses are introduced by relative pronouns such as *qui, que, dont, où, sur lesquels*, etc. To choose the right relative pronoun you need to know the implied grammatical role played by the 'head' noun phrase/pronoun (those in italics above) in the relative clause.

In *Il n'y avait pas assez de place sur la clé USB **qu'il a utilisée** pour copier ses photos* the noun phrase *la clé USB* is understood as the **object** of *utiliser* in the relative clause: *il a utilisé la **clé** USB pour copier ses photos*. This determines the choice of *que* as the linking relative pronoun.

In *C'est lui qui me l'a donné* the pronoun *lui* is understood as the **subject** of *donner* in the relative clause: *il me l'a donné*. This determines the choice of *qui* as the linking relative pronoun.

Noun phrases/pronouns have a range of implied grammatical roles in the relative clause, each requiring a different form of relative pronoun:

Understood as subject

On l'entend ouvrir *la porte d'entrée* **qui se referme en claquant**
(la porte d'entrée se referme)
He can be heard opening the front door which closes behind him with a bang

DOI: 10.4324/9781003373926-15

Understood as direct object

Dans sa chronique radio Mélanie commente les infox **qu'elle a collectées sur les réseaux sociaux**
(elle a collecté les infox)
In her radio segment Mélanie comments on the fake news she has collected from the social networks

Understood as object of a preposition

L'*acteur* **à qui j'ai envoyé un message** ne m'a jamais répondu
(j'ai envoyé un message à l'acteur)
The actor to whom I sent a message has never replied to me

J'ai vérifié le site **auquel il a fait référence**
(il a fait référence au site)
I checked the site he was referring to

Ils habitaient un appartement **derrière lequel il y avait un abattoir**
(il y avait un abattoir derrière l'appartement)
They lived in a flat behind which there was an abattoir

Voici l'hôtel **dans lequel il a passé les dernières années de sa vie**
(il a passé les dernières années de sa vie dans l'hôtel)
This is the hotel where he spent the last years of his life

15.2 **Use of relative** *qui*

qui is the relative pronoun used when the noun phrase or pronoun heading a relative clause is the implied **subject** of that relative clause, whether animate or inanimate:

Il y avait deux hommes **qui** sortaient une armoire à glace du camion
(deux hommes sortaient une armoire …)
Two men were getting a wardrobe out of the lorry

Quand tu vois un plat **qui** te fait envie sur l'appli, il faut cliquer dessus pour connaître les ingrédients
(un plat te fait envie)
When you see a dish that you fancy on the app, you need to click on it to find out what the ingredients are

Je l'ai croisé dans l'escalier **qui** mène à la cave
(l'escalier mène à la cave)
I passed him on the stairs which lead to the cellar

C'est une série **qui** allie histoire, suspense et romantisme
(la série allie histoire, suspense et romantisme)
It's a series which brings together history, suspense, and romance

N.B.: *voilà* and *voici* may also head subject relative clauses:

Voilà/voici qui complique les choses
That's something which complicates matters

15.2.1 *Je l'ai vu qui...*

With perception verbs like *voir, regarder, entendre, apercevoir*, etc., a construction involving relative *qui* can translate an English present participle construction:

Je l'ai vu **qui** sortait
I saw him leaving

Elle l'a entendu **qui** chantait dans son bain
She heard him singing in his bath

15.2.2 Use of relative *qui* for *celui qui, celle qui, ceux qui,* and *celles qui*

Sometimes relative *qui* may be used alone with the same meaning as *celui qui/que, celle qui/ que, ceux qui/que,* and *celles qui/que.* Such constructions are known as 'free' relative clauses (see also Section 15.9):

Tout est possible **à qui** sait ménager son effort
Everything is possible for he who knows how to harness his energies

J'ai invité **qui** vous savez
I invited you know who

15.3 Use of relative *que*

que is the relative pronoun used when the noun phrase or pronoun heading the relative clause is the implied direct **object** of the relative clause, whether animate or inanimate:

L'homme **qu'**on vient d'appeler Rossi se lève
(on appelle l'homme Rossi)
The man who has just been called Rossi gets up

Elle est née dans le village **qu'**on a détruit pour faire le barrage
(on a détruit le village)
She was born in the village which they destroyed to build the dam

Je cherche une coque pour le portable **que** je viens d'acheter
(je viens d'acheter le portable)
I'm looking for a case for the mobile that I have just bought

J'ai toujours souffert du nom **que** je porte
(je porte ce nom)
I have always suffered because of my name

C'est un poste **que** j'aurais aimé avoir
(j'aurais aimé avoir ce poste)
It's a job that I would have liked to have had

Unlike English, the relative pronoun in French may never be omitted:

NOT *C'est un poste j'aurais aimé
NOT *Elle est née dans le village on a détruit pour faire le barrage etc.

N.B.: The past participle agrees with noun phrases or pronouns which head object relative clauses. This is made visible in the case of feminine and plural noun phrases or pronouns, as in:

… **la tarte** que les enfants ont dévor**ée** en rentrant de l'école

This is because *la tarte* is an instance of a preceding direct object, and past participles agree with preceding direct objects (see Section 9.3.4).

15.4 **Preposition plus *qui***

When the noun phrase or pronoun heading a relative clause is the implied object of a preposition in that relative clause and is furthermore animate, the normal relative pronoun to use is *qui* (except when the preposition is *de* – see Section 15.6):

à	Le touriste **à qui** j'ai parlé vient du Québec (j'ai parlé au touriste) *The tourist I spoke to comes from Quebec*
en	C'est un commerçant **en qui** on peut avoir confiance (on peut avoir confiance en ce commerçant) *He's a shopkeeper in whom one can have confidence*
sur	L'intermédiaire **sur qui** on comptait s'est avéré malhonnête (on comptait sur l'intermédiaire) *The go-between we were counting on turned out to be dishonest*
par	Le porte-parole de l'Élysée **par qui** les mauvaises nouvelles sont souvent annoncées, n'a rien dit cette fois-ci (les mauvaises nouvelles sont annoncées par le porte-parole de l'Elysée) *The spokesperson for the Elysée Palace by whom bad news is normally announced said nothing this time.*
avec	Il n'a jamais revu le co-locataire **avec qui** il a passé toute la période du confinement (il a passé toute la période du confinement avec ce co-locataire) *He has never again seen the flatmate with whom he spent the entire lockdown period*
pour	L'institut de sondages **pour qui** beaucoup avaient un grand mépris, a correctement prédit les résultats du vote (beaucoup avaient un grand mépris pour l'institut de sondages) *The pollsters for whom many people had a lot of contempt accurately predicted the results of the vote*
près de	Le jeune homme **près de qui** il est assis le reconnaît (il est assis près du jeune homme) *The young man next to whom he's sitting recognizes him*

N.B.: When objects of the prepositions *parmi* and *entre* are animate, the normal relative pronoun to use is *lesquels* or *lesquelles* (see Section 15.5), and not *qui*:

Un groupe de grimpeurs **parmi lesquels** on compte des Américains
A group of climbers amongst whom there are Americans

Des collègues **entre lesquelles** il y avait une grande solidarité
(Female) colleagues amongst whom there was a lot of solidarity

15.5 **Use of *lequel* in relative clauses**

When the noun phrase or pronoun heading a relative clause is the implied object of a preposition and is inanimate, the normal relative pronoun to use is one of the forms of *lequel* (except in the case of *de*: see Section 15.6).

Lequel has the following forms:

	Singular	Plural
Masculine	lequel	lesquels
Feminine	laquelle	lesquelles

Furthermore, the *le-*, *la-*, etc. components combine with a preceding *à* or *de* to form:

	Singular	Plural	Singular	Plural
Masculine	auquel	auxquels	duquel	desquels
Feminine	à laquelle	auxquelles	de laquelle	desquelles

à	Le site **auquel** elle a fait référence …
	The site she referred to …
	Le webinar **auquel** je vais participer …
	The webinar in which I shall be taking part …
dans	Cela illustre les contradictions **dans lesquelles** s'enferme le Royaume-Uni
	That illustrates the contradictions within which the United Kingdom is locked
autour	Elle habite une maison **autour de laquelle** il y a une haie de lauriers
	She lives in a house around which there is a laurel hedge
durant	Des weekends interminables, **durant lesquels** je ne savais quoi faire
	Interminable weekends during which I didn't know what to do

N.B.: English 'The reason why …' is translated in French by *La raison pour laquelle* … and NOT **La raison pourquoi….*

The prepositions *parmi* and *entre* are followed by *lesquels/lesquelles* whether the implied object is animate or inanimate:

Un groupe de grimpeurs **parmi lesquels** on compte des Américains
A group of climbers amongst whom there are Americans

Des collègues **entre lesquelles** il y avait une grande solidarité
(Female) colleagues amongst whom there was a lot of solidarity

Des papiers **parmi lesquels** j'ai trouvé notre arbre généalogique
Papers among which I found our family tree

Des haies **entre lesquelles** il avait planté des rosiers
Hedges between which he had planted rose bushes

15.5.1 **Use of *lequel* as a subject and object relative pronoun**

The use of *lequel* as a relative pronoun where the head of the relative clause is an implied subject or object is literary and extremely rare (it is also used in French legal texts). It is usually said that *lequel* is used in this way either to avoid ambiguity or to avoid the repetition of *qui*:

Il allait se marier avec la sœur d'un collègue de travail, **laquelle** avait fait ses études en Autriche
He was going to marry the sister of a colleague from work who had studied in Austria

laquelle is used here to make it clear that the person who had studied in Austria is the *sœur* rather than the *collègue* – *laquelle* can only refer to *sœur*, whereas *qui* could refer to either *sœur* or *collègue*.

15.6 **Use of *dont, de qui, duquel/de laquelle/desquels/ desquelles***

15.6.1 *dont*

When the noun phrase or pronoun heading a relative clause is the implied object of *de* in that relative clause, *dont* is the normal relative pronoun to use, whether the object of the preposition is animate or inanimate:

Cela représente un effort **dont** je suis parfaitement capable
(je suis capable **de** l'effort)
That is an effort I am capable of

La maladie **dont** il est mort
(il est mort **de** cette maladie)
The illness from which he died

The *de* phrase which is turned into *dont* may itself be the complement of another noun phrase:

Une copine **dont** le frère a enregistré un CD
(**le frère de** la copine a enregistré un CD)
A friend whose brother recorded a CD

Une maison **dont** les volets étaient fermés
(**les volets de** la maison étaient fermés)
A house whose shutters were closed

When the *de* phrase which turns into *dont* is the complement of an object, *dont* is separated from the object, unlike in English:

Une collegue **dont** j'ai rencontre **le frère** pendant mes vacances
(j'ai rencontre **le frère de** cette collegue . . .)
A colleague whose brother I met on holiday

Une maison **dont** on avait fermé les volets
(on avait fermé **les volets de** cette maison)
A house whose shutters had been closed

N.B.: *dont* can be used to translate English 'including' and 'of which' in sentences like:

Il y a 30 éoliennes dans la région, **dont** 28 endommagées
There are 30 wind turbines in the region, 28 of which are damaged

Trois personnes sont arrivées, **dont** Cyril
Three people arrived, including Cyril

Ils en ont acheté presque une centaine, **dont** plusieurs valaient très cher
They bought almost a hundred of them, some of which were worth a lot of money

J'en ai vu trois hier, **dont** une verte
I saw three of them yesterday, one of which was green

15.6.2 **Cases where *dont* may not be used**

Where a *de* phrase is itself the complement of a prepositional phrase – as in *il s'intéresse à la vie de cet écrivain* – *dont* may not be used. Nor may *dont* be used after a complex preposition which ends in *de* such as *à l'intérieur de, au bout de, auprès de, autour de, à côté de, en face de, en dehors de, au delà de, en dépit de, près de*. Instead either *de qui* (for animates) or *duquel*, etc. (for both animates and inanimates) must be used. Speakers have a strong preference for using *duquel*, etc.:

un écrivain **à** la vie **duquel** (or, possibly, **de qui**) le documentaire est consacré
a writer on whose life the documentary focuses

une voiture **sur** le capot **de laquelle** trônait un ours en peluche
a car on whose bonnet was perched a teddy bear

Il portait un blazer **dans** la poche **duquel** il y avait toujours un carnet de notes
He was wearing a blazer in whose pocket there was always a notebook

C'était une église **à l'intérieur de laquelle** se trouvait une relique de la couronne d'épines
It was a church in which was a relic from the crown of thorns

Le cheval blanc se trouve souvent dans le champ **à côté duquel** nous avons pique-niqué
The white horse is often in the field near which we had a picnic

N.B.: *duquel*, etc. agrees with the head of the relative clause in gender and number: *une voiture* sur le capot **de laquelle** (*de laquelle* agrees with *voiture* and not *capot*) and *un blazer* dans la poche **duquel** (*duquel* agrees with *blazer* and not *poche*).

15.7 **The use of *où* as a relative pronoun**

15.7.1 **To refer to place**

où is used as a relative pronoun where the noun phrase or pronoun heading a relative clause is understood to be a place adverb in that relative clause:

La station balnéaire **où** j'ai passé mes vacances
(j'ai passé mes vacances **dans cette station balnéaire**)
The seaside resort where I spent my holidays

Un ponton **où** des bateaux sont amarrés
(des bateaux sont amarrés **au ponton**)
A pier to which boats are moored

Là **où** j'ai rangé ma trottinette
(j'ai rangé ma trottinette **là**)
The place where I've parked my scooter

Since many prepositional phrases describing a place also function as place adverbs (see Section 5.6.16) relative clauses involving *où* may be interchangeable with relative clauses involving a preposition plus a form of *lequel*:

La station balnéaire **dans laquelle** j'ai passé mes vacances
Un ponton **auquel** des bateaux sont amarrés

However, *où* is by far the more frequent in modern French.

où may itself be preceded by prepositions like *de* and *par*:

Le pays **d'où** il vient
The country he comes from

La porte **par où** elle est entrée
The door she came through

15.7.2 **To refer to time**

où is also used where the noun phrase or pronoun heading a relative clause is an implied time adverbial in that relative clause and is definite. This use is usually translated in English by 'when':

Le matin, c'est le *moment* **où** je prends connaissance de tous mes emails.
Mornings are when I read all my emails

A l'*époque* **où** elle était encore étudiante
At the time when she was still a student

Similar expressions are:

le jour où …	*the day when …*
à l'heure où …	*at the time (of day) when …*
au temps où …	*in the days when …*
à la saison où …	*during the season when …*

This use of *où* with **definite** noun phrases contrasts with the case where the head noun phrase or pronoun is **indefinite**. Here *que* is used:

Un jour **que** je sortais
One day when I was going out

Une fois **qu'**elle rendait visite à sa tante
Once when she was visiting her aunt

In informal French, *que* is often also used where the head is definite (rather than *où*):

A l'heure **qu'**il est, on ne sait toujours pas s'il va se rétablir
At the time of speaking, we still don't know if he is going to recover

N.B.: Although English uses 'when' in constructions like these, *quand* cannot be used in French:

NOT *C'est le moment quand je prends connaissance de tous mes emails
NOT *Un jour quand je sortais

15.8 **Use of relative** *quoi*

quoi is found as a relative pronoun mainly in formal French. Where the head of the relative clause is *rien, quelque chose, ce*, or a clause and is understood as the object of a preposition in the relative clause, *quoi* is used:

> Il n'y a **rien sur quoi** on puisse se baser
> (on ne peut se baser sur rien)
> *There is nothing on which one can rely*

> C'est **quelque chose à quoi** on peut s'intéresser
> (s'intéresser à quelque chose)
> *It's something you can get interested in*

> **Ce à quoi** tu fais référence
> (tu fais référence à quelque chose)
> *The thing you are referring to*

> Finissez votre travail, **après quoi** on peut dîner
> (on peut dîner après que vous avez fini votre travail)
> *Finish your work, after which we can have dinner*

de quoi followed by an infinitive means 'something':

> Il me faudrait **de quoi** archiver tous mes fichiers
> *I need something on which to archive all my files*

15.9 **Free relative clauses and the use of** *ce qui, ce que, ce dont, ce à quoi, ce sur quoi*, **etc.**

Ordinary relative clauses are headed by noun phrases or pronouns present in the main clause:

> Elle a filmé **les congressistes** (head) *qui assistaient à la réunion* (relative clause)
> *She filmed the delegates who were present at the meeting*

In 'free' relative clauses, the head is non-specific:

> Elle a vu **ceux qui** assistaient à la réunion
> *She saw who was present at the meeting*

> Ils avaient remarqué **celui que** Jo préférait
> *They had noticed who Jo preferred*

When the non-specific head is understood to be animate, *celui qui/que, celle qui/que*, etc., are the appropriate relative pronouns, as in the above examples. When the non-specific head is understood to be inanimate, *ce qui* and *ce que* are used: *ce qui* where the non-specific head is understood as the subject of the relative clause; *ce que* where the non-specific head is understood as the object:

Subject

> On a réparé **ce qui** était cassé
> (quelque chose était cassé)
> *They repaired what was broken*

Je ferai **ce qui** me plaira
(quelque chose me plaira)
I'll do what I please

Direct object

Je crois **ce qu'**il dit
(il dit quelque chose)
I believe what he says

On a vu **ce que** cela a produit
(cela a produit quelque chose)
We saw what that produced

Both *ce qui* and *ce que* may be preceded by *tout* 'all':

Les modérateurs ont supprimé **tout ce qui** avait trait à l'élection
The moderators deleted everything that related to the election

On a vu **tout ce que** cela a produit
We saw all that that produced

N.B.: *ce* is obligatory in these cases: NOT *… *tout qu' était à sa portée;* NOT *… *tout que cela a produit.*

Where the non-specific head is inanimate and is understood as the object of a preposition in the relative clause, *ce* + preposition + *quoi* is used:

Dis-moi **ce à quoi** tu penses
Tell me what you are thinking

Ne jette pas **ce sur quoi** j'écrivais
Don't throw out what I was writing on

Je vais te dire **ce en quoi** j'ai confiance
I'll tell you what I have confidence in

When 'what' or 'which' are understood as the object of *de, ce dont* is used:

Elle a envoyé **ce dont** on avait besoin
She sent what we needed

15.9.1 Use of *ce qui, ce que, ce dont, ce à quoi*, etc., to refer to events

Compare the following:

On a volé les deux ordinateurs **qui** étaient dans l'amphithéâtre
Someone has stolen the two computers which were in the lecture hall

On a volé **ce qui** était dans l'amphithéâtre
Someone has stolen what was in the lecture hall

On a volé les deux ordinateurs, **ce qui** va interrompre les cours
Someone has stolen the two computers, which will disrupt classes

In the first sentence the relative clause *qui étaient dans l'amphithéâtre* modifies the noun phrase *les deux ordinateurs*. In the second sentence there is a 'free relative' where the head is non-specific.

In the third sentence the relative clause modifies the whole preceding clause: *on a volé les deux ordinateurs*.

ce qui, ce que, ce dont, ce à quoi, etc. are used not only to introduce free relatives but also to introduce relative clauses which modify preceding clauses:

> Il a raté le train, **ce qui** l'a mis en colère
> *He missed the train, which made him angry*
> (the missing of the train made him angry, not the train itself)

> Ils avaient annoncé la fin du ticket de caisse papier, **ce qui** avait causé des protestations
> *They'd announced the end of paper till receipts, which had caused protests*

> Elle a réussi à le persuader, **ce que** je n'aurais jamais cru possible
> *She succeeded in persuading him, which I would never have thought possible*

N.B.: Where a relative clause modifies an event, *qui* and *que* alone cannot be used:

> NOT *Il a raté le train, qui l'a mis en colère
> NOT *Elle a réussi à le persuader, que je n'aurais jamais cru possible

Where the verb is indirectly transitive and ends in *de*, two constructions may be possible: one using *ce dont* and one using *de ce que*. *ce dont* is used when the head word is present and *de ce que* is used when there is no head word. *ce dont* is normally rendered into English in these constructions by 'which'; *de ce que* is normally rendered by 'what' or 'that'. This concerns verbs such as *féliciter qn de qc, excuser qn de qc, s'inquiéter de qc, s'irriter de qc, profiter de qc, souffrir de qc* and adjectival constructions such as *être reconnaissant de qc, être stupéfait de qc*.

> Vous avez réalisé votre projet. Je vous félicite (de qc).
> *You have succeeded in your project. I congratulate you (on something)*

> Vous avez réalisé votre projet, **ce dont** je vous félicite
> *You have succeeded in your project, on which I congratulate you*

> Je vous félicite **de ce que** vous avez réalisé
> *I congratulate you on what you have achieved*

> Ils ont fait des bêtises. Ils devront s'excuser (de qc)
> *They did some silly things. They will have to apologize (for sth)*

> Ils ont fait des bêtises, **ce dont** ils devront s'excuser
> *They did some silly things, for which they will have to apologize*

> Ils devront s'excuser **de ce qu'**ils ont fait
> *They will have to apologize for what they did*

> Vous avez fait énormément de choses pour nous. Je suis très reconnaissant (de qc)
> *You have done a great deal for us. I am very grateful (for sth)*

> Vous avez fait énormément de choses pour nous, **ce dont** je suis très reconnaissant
> *You have done a great deal for us, for which I am very grateful*

> Je suis très reconnaissant **de ce que** vous avez fait pour nous
> *I am very grateful for what you have done for us*

Vous êtes venu. Je suis stupéfait (de qc)
You came. I am astonished (about sth)

Vous êtes venu, **ce dont** je suis stupéfait
You came, which astonishes me

Je suis stupéfait **de ce que** vous soyez venu
I am astonished that you should have come

15.10 Translating 'whoever', 'whatever', 'wherever', 'whenever', and 'however' (see Section 15.11 for the use of the subjunctive)

'whoever'

'whoever', understood as the subject of a relative clause, is *quiconque*, and the verb in the relative clause is in the indicative:

Ils acceptent **quiconque** peut donner trois heures par semaine à la collecte de plastique sur la plage
They welcome whoever can give three hours a week of their time to clearing up plastic on the beach

'whoever', understood as the direct object of a relative clause, is *qui que*, and the verb in the relative clause is in the subjunctive:

Qui que vous **nommiez**, les réseaux lui mèneront la vie dure
Whoever you appoint, the social media will make his/her life a misery

N.B.: *quel que* may also mean 'whoever' when used with *être*:

Quel qu'il **soit/Quelle qu'**elle **soit**, je l'accueillerai chaleureusement
Whoever he/she is, I'll give him/her a warm welcome

'whatever'

'whatever', understood as the subject of a relative clause, is *quoi qui*. When it is understood as the object it is *quoi que*. In both cases, the verb in the relative clause is in the subjunctive:

Quoi qui puisse arriver
Whatever may happen

Quoi qu'il fasse
Whatever he does

N.B.: *quoi que*, meaning 'whatever', should be distinguished from the conjunction *quoique* 'although', which is written as a single word.

'whatever X' understood as the subject of a relative clause is translated as in the following examples:

Quel que soit **le prix**, je l'achèterai	*Whatever the price may be, I'll buy it*
Quelles que soient **ses intentions** déclarées, méfie-toi	*Whatever he says he is going to do, don't trust him*

Note that *quel* and *que* are separate words, and that *quel* agrees with the noun which is the subject of the relative clause.

'whatever X', 'whichever X' understood as the object of a relative clause is *quelque(s)*, and the verb in the relative clause is in the subjunctive:

Quelque voiture que vous **choisissiez**, vous bénéficierez d'un rabais
(vous allez choisir une voiture)
Whatever/whichever car you choose, we'll give you a discount

Quelques efforts que vous **fassiez**, on ne vous en accordera aucun crédit
(vous allez faire des efforts)
Whatever efforts you make won't be recognized

One way of distinguishing between the '*quelque* + noun' construction and the '*quel que* + *être* + noun' construction is to see if the verb in the relative clause can be omitted in English. If it can, use *quel que*, if it cannot use *quelque(s)*:

Quel que soit le prix, je l'achèterai	*Whatever the price (may be)*, I'll buy it
Quelque voiture que vous choisissiez, vous bénéficierez d'un rabais	*Whatever/Whichever car you choose*'('*choose*' *cannot be omitted*), *we will give you a discount*

N.B.: *être* can never be omitted from the *quel que* constructions in French, even though 'be' can be omitted in English.

'wherever'

'wherever' is *où que*, with the verb in the relative clause in the subjunctive:

Où qu'il aille, nous le suivrons
Wherever he goes, we'll follow him

'whenever'

'whenever' is *toutes les fois que*, *à chaque fois que*, or simply *quand*, with the verb in the indicative:

Toutes les fois qu'elle a un moment de libre, elle révise son vocabulaire
Whenever she has a free moment she looks over her vocabulary

'however'

'however' + an adjective heading a relative clause can be translated in five ways:

quelque		
si	+ adjective	+ verb in the subjunctive
aussi		
pour		
tout	+ adjective	+ verb in the indicative

However, demanding they may be, we still have to respect our customers' needs

Quelque (*invariable*) **exigeants** qu'ils **soient**, nous avons à coeur de satisfaire nos clients
Si exigeants qu'ils **soient**, nous avons à coeur de satisfaire nos clients
Aussi exigeants qu'ils **soient**, nous avons à coeur de satisfaire nos clients

Pour exigeants qu'ils **soient**, nous avons à coeur de satisfaire nos clients
Tout (*invariable*) **exigeants** qu'ils **sont**, nous avons à coeur de satisfaire nos clients

N.B.: The verb and subject may be inverted after *si* and *aussi* as an alternative to the *que* construction, providing that the subject is a pronoun:

Si exigeants soient-ils, …
Aussi exigeants soient-ils, …

15.11 Indicative and subjunctive in relative clauses

The verb in relative clauses usually takes the indicative form, but there are some kinds of relative clause where the verb is in the subjunctive.

15.11.1 *qui que, quoi que, quel que*, etc.

qui que, quoi qui, quoi que, quel que, quelque, où que, and *si/aussi/pour* are followed by a verb in the subjunctive (see Sections 15.10 and 11.1.12):

Qui que vous **nommiez**	*Whoever you appoint*
Quoi qui **puisse** arriver	*Whatever may happen*
Quoi qu'il **fasse**	*Whatever he does*
Quelque veste que vous **choisissiez**	*Whichever jacket you choose*
Quelle que **soit** la réponse	*Whatever the response*
Quelque Si Aussi Pour } grand qu'il soit	*However big he is*

N.B.: *quiconque* 'whoever' is followed by verbs in the indicative:

Quiconque **touche** à mon ordi aura affaire à moi
Whoever touches my computer will have me to answer to.

15.11.2 Relative clauses expressing hypothetical states of affairs

Relative clauses which modify indefinite noun phrases and express a hypothetical, rather than real, state of affairs, usually have a verb in the subjunctive (see Section 11.1.12):

Elle veut acheter **une maison** qui **ait** une piscine
She wants to buy a house which has a swimming pool

The subjunctive here suggests that she has no particular house in mind – her hypothetically ideal house would be one with a swimming pool. By contrast, a sentence like:

Elle veut acheter **une maison** qui **a** une piscine
She wants to buy a house which has a swimming pool

suggests that she knows of a particular house with a swimming pool which she would like to buy.

15.11.3 **Relative clauses modifying** *le premier, le dernier, le seul,* **and superlatives**

Where a relative clause modifies noun phrases involving *le premier, le dernier, le seul* or a superlative, which can be interpreted as 'the first ever', 'the last one ever', 'the only one ever', etc., then the verb in the relative clause is in the subjunctive (see Section 11.1.8):

C'était **le premier film** qui **ait** traité de ce sujet
It was the first (ever) film that dealt with the topic

Le dernier roman qu'il **ait** écrit avant de mourir
The last (ever) novel he wrote before he died

Le seul portrait que j'**aie** vu d'elle
The only (ever) portrait I saw of her

La femme la plus riche que nous **ayons** photographiée
The richest (ever) woman whom we have photographed

Where the verb in the relative clause is in the indicative, however, the modified noun phrase is interpreted as just one of a set ('the first (of a set)', 'the last (of a set)', 'the biggest (of a set)', etc.):

C'est **le premier film** que j'**ai** vu, et il restera à jamais dans ma mémoire
It's the first film (of the set of those I've seen) that I saw, and it will stay in my memory for ever

C'est **le plus grand** qui a fait le meilleur tir au panier
It's the tallest of (the set of) them who had the best shot at the basket

15.11.4 **Relative clauses in** *si* **clauses, questions, after negation and in other subjunctive clauses**

When relative clauses modify indefinite noun phrases or pronouns in *si* clauses or in questions, or modify noun phrases in negative clauses or clauses which themselves have subjunctive verbs, the verb in the relative clause is usually in the subjunctive:

S'il connaissait **un endroit** qui **convienne** il le dirait
If he knew of a place which would be suitable he would say so

Connaissez-vous un endroit qui **convienne**?
Do you know of a place which would be suitable?

Je ne connais **personne** qui **puisse** m'aider
I know no-one who can help me

Quelles que **soient les circonstances** qui **puissent** expliquer son erreur, je ne peux pas la lui pardonner
Whatever the circumstances which might explain his mistake, I can't forgive him

TABLE 15.A Summary of major relative clause types

Head of clause	Function in clause	Pronoun	Example	Section no.
l'homme/la femme	subject (±animate)	qui	l'homme/la femme qui conduit	Section 15.2
l'autobus	direct object (±animate)	que	l'autobus que je conduis	Section 15.3
une maladie	object of *de* (±animate)	dont	une maladie dont il est mort	Section 15.6.1
une maison	same	dont	une maison dont la porte est fermée	Section 15.6.1
une maison	same	dont	une maison dont on ferme la porte	Section 15.6.1
le touriste	object (+animate) of a preposition	à qui	le touriste à qui j'ai parlé	Section 15.4
le film	object (−animate) of a preposition	auquel	le film auquel il fait référence	Section 15.5
un écrivain	object (+animate) of a preposition in a prepositional phrase	à la vie duquel	un écrivain à la vie duquel il s'intéresse	Section 15.6.2
un sweat-shirt	object (−animate) of a preposition in a prepositional phrase	dans la poche duquel	un sweat-shirt dans la poche duquel il y une clé	Section 15.6.2
la ville	place adverb	où	la ville où je vis	Section 15.7.1
le jour	time adverb (definite)	où	le jour où elle est partie	Section 15.7.2
un jour	time adverb (indefinite)	que	un jour que je sortais	Section 15.7.2
rien, ce, quelque chose, clause	object of a preposition	sur quoi	rien, ce, quelque chose sur quoi on peut compter	Section 15.8
non-specific head	subject or object (+animate)	celui qui/que	j'ai vu celui qui est sorti	Section 15.9
non-specific head	subject (−animate)	ce qui	je ferai ce qui me plaît	Section 15.9
non-specific head	object (−animate)	ce que	je crois ce qu'elle dit	Section 15.9
non-specific head	object of a preposition	ce preposition quoi	il se moque de ce en quoi j'ai confiance	Section 15.9

For more resources to practice your French grammar, including practice activities/quizzes for students, further resource links, and an instructor guide, please visit https://routledgelearning.com/frenchgrammarandusage.

16 Negation

16.1 Introduction

French sentences can be negated by using one of the following expressions:

ne ... aucun	*not any, none*
ne ... guère	*hardly*
ne ... jamais	*not ever, never*
ne ... ni ... ni	*neither ... nor*
ne ... nul	*not any, none*
ne ... pas	*not*
ne ... personne	*not anyone, no-one, nobody*
ne ... plus	*not any more, no longer*
ne ... que	*only*
ne ... rien	*not anything, nothing*

Although *ne ... guère* and *ne ... que* are not strictly negators – they are adverbs – they have similar distributional properties to the other negators, and so we include them in this chapter.

N.B.: The expression *ne ... point* 'not' is no longer used productively in modern French. It is used only in written French by writers who want to create an archaic or regional tone.

Individual words and phrases can be negated by placing the particles *pas, aucun, jamais, rien,* and *personne* (without *ne*) in front of them. For example: *un après-midi pas comme les autres* 'an afternoon unlike others'; *jamais de ma vie* 'never in my life'; *rien d'intéressant* 'nothing interesting'; and so on.

16.2 Location of sentence negators

16.2.1 With verbs marked for tense

In all cases where sentences are negated, the element *ne* (if it is present: see Section 16.4) comes before the verb which is marked for tense in that sentence and before any unstressed object pronouns which are in front of the verb:

Je **ne** dors pas chez moi ce soir	*I'm not sleeping at my place tonight*
Je **n'**ai pas dormi chez moi hier soir	*I didn't sleep at my place last night*
Je **ne** l'entendais pas	*I didn't hear him*
Il **ne** le lui a jamais envoyé	*He didn't ever send it to her*
Elle **n'**a rien voulu me raconter	*She didn't want to tell me anything*

The location of the second element – *pas, jamais, rien, personne,* etc. – varies, however. While all these negative particles immediately follow a main verb when no auxiliary is present:

Il ne me regardait **pas**	*He wasn't watching me*
La boîte ne contenait **que** des bonbons	*There were only sweets in the box*
Ça ne donne **aucun** plaisir	*That's not at all enjoyable*
Il ne mangeait **jamais** le soir	*He never used to eat in the evenings*

DOI: 10.4324/9781003373926-16

In compound tenses (i.e. when the auxiliary *avoir* or *être* is present), *guère, jamais, pas, plus*, and *rien* immediately follow the auxiliary verb:

Il n'en a **pas** voulu	*He didn't want any of it*
Je n'ai **jamais** vu la mer	*I have never seen the sea*
Elle n'a **plus** voulu continuer	*She didn't want to continue*
Je ne l'ai **guère** connue	*I hardly knew her*
On ne m'a **rien** pris	*They didn't take anything from me*

By contrast, *personne* behaves just like an object, an indirect object, or the object of a preposition:

Je n'ai vu **personne**	*I didn't see anyone*
Il n'a parlé à **personne**	*He didn't speak to anyone*
Elle n'est sortie avec **personne**	*She didn't go out with anyone*

and *aucun* precedes an object, an indirect object, or the object of a preposition:

Ils n'ont vendu **aucun** tableau	*They didn't sell a single picture*
Je ne le vendrais à **aucun** prix	*I wouldn't sell it at any price*
Il n'a confiance en **aucun** autre que lui-même	*He doesn't trust anyone else but himself*

nul is mainly used in formal French, but sometimes in informal French with humorous intent or in set phrases (see also Section 16.8):

On ne connaît **nul** programme qui puisse complètement garantir la sécurité de vos transactions en ligne
No known programme can fully guarantee the security of your online transactions

Ces pensées ne lui laissaient **nul** repos
These thoughts allowed him no rest

The location of *que* and *ni* varies depending on the intended meaning:

Je ne me permets un café **qu'**après avoir fini mon travail
I only allow myself a coffee after I have finished my work

Je ne me permets **qu'**un café après avoir fini mon travail
I only allow myself one coffee after I have finished my work

Elle ne m'a **ni** vu **ni** entendu
She neither saw me nor heard me

Elle n'a vu **ni** lui **ni** sa femme
She saw neither him nor his wife

Je n'ai envoyé de SMS **ni** à sa mère **ni** à son notaire
I sent a text neither to her mother nor to her solicitor

N.B.: *Je ne fais que, tu ne fais que, il ne fait que*, etc. mean 'I do nothing but, you do nothing but, he does nothing but' etc.: *Il ne fait que mentir/travailler/se plaindre*, etc. 'He does nothing but lie/ work/complain', etc.

16.2.2 **With infinitives**

Where the verb in a negated sentence is an infinitive, *ne* and *guère, jamais, pas, plus*, and *rien* normally both precede the infinitive:

J'ai dormi au bureau, de manière à **ne pas** perdre de temps
I slept at the office so as not to waste any time

J'étais le seul à **ne jamais** boire d'alcool
I was the only one never to drink alcohol

Il pense **ne plus** croire en Dieu
He thinks he doesn't believe in God any more

Elle donnait l'impression de **ne guère** s'intéresser à mes activités
She gave the impression of hardly being interested in my activities

Il a envie de **ne rien** faire de la journée
He feels like doing nothing all day

Both elements of the negation also usually precede an infinitive auxiliary verb (*avoir* or *être*):

J'étais certain de **ne pas** avoir laissé mon mot de passe en visibilité
I was certain I hadn't left my password visible

J'espère **ne rien** avoir oublié
I hope I haven't forgotten anything

For some speakers, however, the second element of the negation in these cases can optionally follow the auxiliary, without any change in the meaning:

J'étais certain de **n'**avoir **pas** laissé mon mot de passe…
J'espère **n'**avoir **rien** oublié

In the case of *ne … aucun, ne … nul, ne … personne*, the second component follows the verbal elements:

Je voudrais **ne** voir **personne**
I would like to see no-one

Elle me reprochait de **n'**avoir écrit à **personne**
She blamed me for not having written to anyone

Ils ont déclaré **n'**avoir eu **aucune/nulle** intention de le faire
They declared that they had no intention of doing it

Il s'étonnait de **n'**avoir ressenti **aucun/nul** désir de le faire
He was surprised not to have felt any desire to do it

que and *ni … ni* also follow the verb in infinitives, but their location varies depending on the intended meaning:

Je voudrais **ne** voir **que** Cédric deux fois par semaine et vous voir en couple trois fois
I would like to see only Cédric twice a week and both of you as a couple three times

Je voudrais **ne** voir Cédric **que** deux ou trois fois par semaine
I would like to see Cédric only two or three times a week

Elle espère **ne** rencontrer **ni** lui **ni** sa sœur
She hopes to meet neither him nor his sister

Elle espère **ne** rencontrer son voisin **ni** au marché **ni** au café
She hopes to meet her neighbour neither at the market nor in the café

N.B.: Verbs in clauses dependent on negated clauses take the subjunctive:

Ce n'est pas que je **sois** particulièrement timide
It's not that I'm particularly shy

Je ne connais personne qui **mette** autant d'acharnement à réussir
I don't know anyone (else) who puts so much energy into succeeding

(See Section 11.1.8.)

16.3 **Order of negators in multiple negation**

Two or more of *guère, jamais, pas, personne, plus, rien*, and so on, may be combined quite acceptably in French to produce a multiple negation. The normal ordering of these elements is as indicated in the following tables:

ne…	pas	past participle or infinitive	que

Il n'y a **pas que** des héros dans l'armée — *There aren't only heroes in the army*
Il n'a **pas** écrit **que** des contes de fees — *He didn't only write fairy stories*

ne…	jamais guère	plus	rien	past participle or infinitive	personne	que

On **ne** le verra **jamais plus** — *We'll never see him again*
On n'en verra **jamais rien** — *We'll never see anything of it*
On n'en verra **plus rien** — *We won't see anything more of it*
On n'en verra **jamais plus rien** — *We won't see anything more of it ever again*

Elle n'a **jamais plus** écrit — *She never wrote again*
Elle n'a jamais **rien** écrit — *She never wrote anything*
Elle n'a **plus rien** écrit — *She wrote nothing again*
Elle n'a **jamais plus rien** écrit — *She never wrote anything again*

Elle n'a **jamais plus rien** écrit — *She never wrote anything again*
qu'une brochure de publicité — *except an advertising brochure*

Ça n'impressionnera **jamais personne** — *That will never impress anyone*
Ça n'impressionnera **plus personne** — *That won't impress anyone any more*
Ça n'impressionnera **jamais plus personne** — *That will never impress anyone again*

Il n'a **jamais** critiqué **personne** — *He never criticized anyone*
Il n'a **plus** critiqué **personne** — *He didn't criticize anyone again*
Il n'a **jamais plus** critiqué **personne** — *He didn't ever criticize anyone again*

Elle n'a **guère plus** écrit après son deuil — *She hardly ever wrote again after her bereavement*

N.B.: The order … *plus jamais* … is also quite common: *On ne le verra plus jamais* 'We'll never see him again', *Plus jamais ça!* 'Never again!'

16.4 **Omission of *ne* in sentence negation**

It is very common in modern spoken French for speakers to omit the *ne* of *ne … pas*, and to a lesser extent the *ne* of other negative expressions, except in the most formal of styles:

C'est pas vrai	*It's not true*
J'ai pas eu le temps de le faire	*I didn't have time to do it*
Je sais pas	*I don't know*
Elle l'avait pas lu	*She hadn't read it*

16.5 **Order of negative elements in questions and imperatives**

The location and ordering of negative elements in questions and imperatives are the same as in declaratives:

Tu ne dors pas chez toi ce soir	
Ne dors-tu pas chez toi ce soir? (formal)	*Aren't you sleeping at your house tonight?*
Il n'a jamais vu la mer	
N'a-t-il jamais vu la mer? (formal)	*Hasn't he ever seen the sea?*
On ne lui avait rien appris	
Ne lui avait-on rien appris? (formal)	*Had they taught him nothing?*
Elle n'avait vu personne	
N'avait-elle vu personne? (formal)	*Had she seen no-one?*
Taquine-le!	
Ne le taquine pas!	*Don't tease him!*
Fais ça!	
Ne fais jamais ça!	*Never do that!*
Touchez quelque chose!	
Ne touchez rien!	*Don't touch anything!*
Présentez-lui quelqu'un!	
Ne lui présentez personne!	*Don't introduce anyone to him!*

(For the ordering of pronouns in affirmative and negative imperatives, see Section 3.2.31.)

16.6 *ne … pas*

16.6.1 **Negating sentences**

ne … pas translates English 'not' (for the omission of *ne*, see Section 16.4):

Ce **n'est pas** vrai	*It's not true*
Je **ne** me rappelle **pas** les circonstances	*I don't remember the circumstances*
Je **n'ai pas** eu le temps de comprendre	*I didn't have time to understand*
Ça fait/Voilà longtemps qu'on **ne** s'est **pas** vu	*It's been a long time since we saw each other*

N.B.: *ne … point* 'not' is an archaic form which is still found in some regional varieties of French as an equivalent of *ne… pas*. Some writers use it to give a regional or archaic flavour to their writing.

After *ne … pas*, any indefinite article (i.e. one of *un(e)*, *du*, *de la*, *des*) preceding a direct object becomes *de*:

Elle a rempli **un** formulaire en ligne
She filled in an online form

Elle n'a pas rempli **de** formulaire en ligne
She didn't fill in an online form

On lui a fait **du** mal
They did him harm

On ne lui a pas fait **de** mal
They didn't do him any harm

Il crée **des** sites
He creates sites

Il ne crée pas **de** sites
He doesn't create sites

However, *un(e)* can appear before a direct object after *ne … pas* but then it means 'not one', rather than 'not a':

On n'entendait pas **un** bruit dehors   *We couldn't hear a single noise outside*

(See Section 2.5.)

pas un(e) followed by a noun can function as the subject of a negative sentence. Note the presence of *ne*:

Pas un brin d'herbe **ne** bougeait dans la prairie
Not one blade of grass stirred on the plain

Where *du*, *de la*, and *des* appear before a direct object after *ne … pas*, they are instances of *de* + definite article (and not indefinite articles):

Elle n'a pas parlé **du** mal qu'on lui a fait
*She didn't speak of **the** harm they did her*
(versus: *On ne lui a pas fait de mal* 'They didn't do her any harm)

Il ne s'occupe pas **des** sites cette année
*He isn't busy with **the** sites this year*
(versus *Il ne crée pas de sites cette année* 'He's not creating sites this year')

(See Section 2.5.)

When adverbs are located sentence-internally in sentences negated by *ne … pas*, they usually appear immediately before *pas*:

Il ne savait **visiblement pas** que faire de son grand corps
You could see that he didn't know what to do with his big frame

Je ne l'entendais **même pas**
I didn't even hear him

Je ne l'ai **toujours pas** compris
I still don't understand him

N.B.: *davantage* 'more' used in conjunction with *ne … pas* has a similar meaning to *ne … plus*:

J'ai fait un effort pour **ne pas** dépenser **davantage**
I made an effort not to spend any more

16.6.2 **Omission of *pas***

In formal French, the *pas* of *ne … pas* may be omitted with a small number of verbs.

With *cesser de* + infinitive

Elle **ne** cessait de répéter que c'était de sa faute
She went on repeating that it was her fault

With *savoir* followed by a question word like *quoi, comment*

Je **ne** sais comment ils se débrouillent
I don't know how they manage

Il y avait un je **ne** sais quoi de douceur dans l'air
There was a hint of mildness in the air

N.B.: *ne* + *savoir* in the conditional means 'wouldn't know how to', 'couldn't': *On ne saurait trop vous remercier* 'We wouldn't know how to thank you', *Il ne saurait vous expliquer pourquoi* 'He couldn't explain why to you'.

With *oser* + infinitive

Il **n'**osa refuser de le faire
He didn't dare refuse to do it

Elle **n'**osa demander un second rendez-vous
She dared not ask for a second appointment

With *pouvoir* + infinitive

Elle **ne** pouvait se l'expliquer
She couldn't explain it to herself

Je **ne** puis accepter cette décision
I can't accept this decision

pas is sometimes also omitted after interrogative *qui, que, quel*, after hypothetical *si*, after some sentence initial adverbs, and in the expressions *n'importe qui, n'importe quoi*:

Qui **ne** serait ému dans ces circonstances?	*Who wouldn't be moved in these circumstances?*
Que **ne** donnerait-il pour une bonne douche?	*What wouldn't he give for a nice shower?*
Quel homme **n'**en serait fier?	*What man wouldn't be proud of it?*
C'est Séverine, si je **ne** me trompe	*It's Séverine, unless I'm mistaken*
N'importe qui pourrait le faire	*Anyone could do it*
J'inventerai **n'**importe quoi pour faire plus vrai	*I'll make up anything to make it sound more realistic*

16.6.3 **Negating words and phrases**

pas alone is used to negate words or phrases which do not contain verbs.

Nouns

Je ne garde rien d'elle. Même **pas** une mèche de cheveux
I keep nothing of hers. Not even a lock of hair

Il lui posa une question. **Pas** de réponse
He asked her a question. No reply

Je le ferai. **Pas** de problème
I'll do it. No problem

Adjectives

Les autres la considéraient comme une fille **pas** bavarde
The others considered her to be a quiet girl

Il avait une intonation chantante **pas** déplaisante
He spoke in a singsong voice, not unpleasant

Adverbs

J'habite **pas** loin de la mer
I live not far from the sea

C'était un bel après-midi. Un après-midi **pas** tout à fait comme les autres
It was a fine afternoon. An afternoon not entirely like the others

Conjunctions

Il me regardait; **pas** comme un frère, plutôt comme un juge
He looked at me; not as a brother, more as a judge

16.6.4 Use of *non* and *non pas* to negate words and phrases

non can be an equivalent for *pas* for negating adjectives, adverbs, and conjunctions in formal French (although *pas* is more often used even in formal styles):

un supplément **non** compris	*something extra which is not included*
habiter **non** loin de la mer	*to live not far from the sea*
non comme un frère	*not as a brother*

N.B.: *non* or *pas* are equally likely in formal French in expressions like: *Prêt ou non, je pars/Prêt ou pas, je pars*, 'Ready or not, I'm leaving'. But if the negated item is repeated, *pas* is more usual: *Prêt ou pas prêt, je pars*.

non is often used when it is combined with *mais* in the expression *non X… mais (aussi)*:

Je l'ai fait **non (pas)** pour arranger quelqu'un d'autre **mais** pour ma propre convenance
I did it not to suit someone else, but to suit myself

Il faut que tu changes **non seulement** l'écran **mais aussi** le disque dur.
You need to change not only the screen but also the hard drive.

On entendait **non plus** la mer, **mais** le chuchotement du vent dans les arbres
One no longer heard the sea, but the wind rustling in the trees

non or *non pas* may negate an infinitive which is contrasted with an affirmative infinitive:

Il faut travailler pour vivre, et **non (pas)** vivre pour travailler
One has to work to live and not live to work

non (pas) que is a conjunction which introduces subordinate clauses in which the verb is in the subjunctive:

Il a parlé de Besançon; non (pas) qu'il veuille y aller
He spoke about Besançon; not that he wants to go there

(See also Section 17.3.8.)

non, pas, and *non pas* are interchangeable in formal French when a contrast is drawn between a positive and negative statement:

| Il est gallois et | non
pas
non pas | anglais |

16.7 *ne ... que*

ne ... que translates English 'only' (for the omission of *ne*, see Section 16.4):

Ce **n'**est **qu'**après qu'il l'a remarqué
He only noticed it afterwards

Je **ne** le vois **qu'**une fois par semaine
I only see him once a week

Il **n'**y avait **qu'**une explication
There was only one explanation

Les dons **ne sont arrivés que** lorsque la télévision a fait une soirée spéciale cancer
Donations only started coming in when a cancer special evening was organised on TV

In combination with other negators like *pas, jamais, plus, personne, ne ... que* can take on various meanings:

Il **n'**y a **pas que** des héros dans l'armée
There aren't just heroes in the army

Elle n'avait **jamais** parlé à un agent de police **que** pour demander son chemin
She had never spoken to a policeman except to ask for directions

Il ne me reste **plus que** trois traites à payer
I've only got three more instalments to pay

16.8 *ne ... aucun(e), ne ... nul(le)*

ne ... aucun(e), ne... nul(le) translate English 'no', 'none' (for the omission of *ne*, see Section 16.4):

Il **n'**a eu **aucune (nulle)** hésitation à proposer son aide
He had no hesitation in offering to help

Except for set phrases, some of which are given at the end of this section, *ne... nulle part* 'nowhere', *ne... nulle* is mainly used in formal French (see also Section 16.2.1).

Ne... aucun(e) is found in both written and spoken French, but tends to be replaced by *pas* in informal spoken French:

Il **n'a pas** eu d'hésitation à proposer son aide

Only *aucun(e)* and not *nul(le)* may be followed by a prepositional complement:

Je **ne** connais **aucune** de ses amies	*I know none of her friends*
Je **n'**en connais **aucune**	*I don't know any of them*

(NOT *Je ne connais nulle de ses amies/Je n'en connais nulle)

Both *aucun(e)* and *nul(e)* are rare in the plural. Instead one would use *pas de* or *sans*:

Il **n'a pas d'**amis/Il est **sans** amis — *He has no friends*

aucun(e) can negate direct objects, indirect objects, objects of prepositions, and subjects:

Ça **n'**avait **aucun** sens	*That made no sense*
Il **n'**a parlé à **aucun** des trois	*He didn't speak to any of the three*
Aucune voiture américaine **n'**était signalée dans les environs	*No American car had been reported in the area*
Aucun de nous **n'**est entré là-bas	*None of us entered there*
Aucun n'est entré	*None went in*

aucun(e) may be used alone as a response to a question:

Combien reste-t-il d'oranges sanguines? **Aucune**
How many blood oranges are left? None

The adverbs *aucunement* and *nullement* are formal equivalents of the expression common in spoken French: *pas du tout* 'not at all':

Elle n'en est aucunement/nullement/pas du tout fière
She is not at all proud of it

N.B.: *nul(le)* is also an adjective with the meaning 'zero' or 'nil'. In this use, it is found in all styles of French:

Les risques sont **nuls**	*The risks are nil*
Nulle part	*Nowhere*
Sans **nul** doute	*Without the shadow of a doubt*
Elle est **nulle** en orthographe	*She is useless at spelling*
C'était un **nul**, ce plombier!	*That plumber was useless!*
Non, ne fais pas ça, c'est **nul**! (informal)	*No, don't do that, it's wrong/stupid /pointless*
Match **nul**	*A draw*
Bulletin **nul**	*Spoiled ballot*
Nul et non avenu	*Null and void*

Nul is also used in set phrases and in formal, legal texts, etc.:

Nul n'est censé ignorer la loi
Ignorance of the law is no excuse

A l'impossible **nul n'**est tenu
Nobody is expected to achieve the impossible

16.9 *ne … jamais*

ne … jamais translates English 'not ever','never' (for the omission of *ne*, see Section 16.4):

Il **ne** mangeait **jamais** le soir   *He never ate in the evenings*
Je **n'**ai **jamais** vu la mer   *I have never seen the sea*

Like English 'never', *jamais* may sometimes be located at the beginning of the sentence, but without the subject–verb inversion of English:

Jamais je **n'**ai vu autant d'algues
Never have I seen so much seaweed

Jamais plus elle **ne** serait tout à fait elle-même
Never again would she be quite herself

After *ne … jamais* any indefinite article (i.e. one of *un(e), du, de la,* and *des*) preceding a direct object becomes *de*

J'ai **de la** petite monnaie   Je n'ai jamais **de** petite monnaie
I have change   *I never have change*

Elle porte **un** casque   Elle ne porte jamais **de** casque
She wears a helmet   *She never wears a helmet*

(See Section 2.5.)

jamais can be used without *ne* with the meaning 'never':

C'est maintenant ou **jamais**   *It's now or never*
Es-tu allé à Rennes? **Jamais**   *Have you been to Rennes? Never*

In formal French it can also be interpreted as 'ever' in questions, hypothetical sentences, or comparisons:

As-tu **jamais** envisagé de changer de formation?
Have you ever thought moving to a different course?

Si une malle s'était **jamais** trouvée dans le grenier, elle n'y était plus
If there had ever been a trunk in the attic, it was no longer there

Elle chante mieux que **jamais**
She is singing better than ever

When adverbs are located sentence-internally in sentences negated by *ne … jamais*, they usually appear immediately before *jamais*:

Je n'ai **d'ailleurs** jamais parlé à personne
What's more, I've never spoken to anyone

Je ne la vois **pratiquement** jamais
I hardly ever see her

16.10 *ne … plus*

ne … plus translates English 'no longer', 'not any more' (for the omission of *ne*, see Section 16.4):

Elle **ne** savait **plus** pourquoi elle était sur cette route
She no longer knew why she was on this road

Soudain, je **n'**en peux **plus**
Suddenly, I can't take any more

Elle **n'**a **plus** travaillé après la naissance de sa fille
She didn't work again after the birth of her daughter

N.B.: *ne ... pas plus* is NOT the French for 'not any more'. *ne ... pas plus* means 'not more than'. Compare:

Elle **ne** semblait **pas** avoir **plus** de vingt ans
She didn't appear to be more than 20
Elle **ne** semblait **plus** avoir vingt ans
She didn't seem to be 20 any more

After *ne... plus*, any indefinite article (i.e. one of *un(e)*, *du*, *de la*, and *des*) preceding a direct object becomes *de*:

J'ai **un** crayon   Je n'ai plus **de** crayon
I have a pencil   *I don't have a pencil any more*

Elle vend **du** lait   Elle ne vend plus **de** lait
She sells milk   *She doesn't sell milk any more*

When adverbs are located sentence-internally in sentences negated by *ne ... plus*, they usually appear immediately before *plus*:

Je ne me rappelle **même** plus ce qu'il racontait
I don't even remember what he was saying

plus de + noun can mean 'no more':

plus de pain, merci   *no more bread, thanks*
plus de place!   *no (more) room*

Je me suis retournée: **plus de** valise   *I turned round: my suitcase had disappeared*

non plus is typically used in conjunction with one of the other negators to translate English 'either', 'neither', or 'nor':

Il **ne** mangeait jamais le soir, **ni** sa femme **non plus**
He never ate in the evenings, and neither did his wife

Ce **n'**est **pas non plus** que je sois particulièrement timide
It's not that I'm particularly shy either

Il **ne** pouvait **pas non plus** reporter son rendez-vous avec ce client-là
Nor could he postpone his meeting with that particular customer

Il **n'**avait **jamais non plus** levé la main sur qui que ce soit
Neither had he ever raised his hand to anyone

Elle fouilla dans la boîte à gants. **Rien non plus**
She rummaged in the glove compartment. Nothing there either

Pour son fils **non plus**, ça **n'**allait **pas** fort
Things weren't going well for his son either

16.11 *ne ... guère*

ne ... guère translates English 'hardly' and is an equivalent of the adverb *à peine*, which is used without a preceding *ne:*

On **ne** parlait **guère**
On parlait **à peine**
We hardly spoke

Cette histoire **n'**avait **guère** semblé croyable
Cette histoire avait **à peine** semblé croyable
This story had hardly seemed credible

After *ne... guère* any indefinite article (i.e. one of *un(e)*, *du*, *de la*, *des*) preceding a direct object becomes *de:*

Il y a **des** visiteurs   Il n'y a guère **de** visiteurs
There are visitors   *There are hardly any visitors*

N.B.: *à peine* cannot be followed by a plural noun phrase: NOT *il y a à peine des visiteurs.*

guère may stand alone as a response to a question:

Combien en avez-vous acheté?   **Guère** (à peine quelques-uns)
How many did you buy?   *Hardly any*

16.12 *ne ... rien*

ne ... rien translates English 'nothing', 'not anything' (for the omission of *ne*, see Section 16.4). *rien* itself may be a direct object, the object of a preposition, or the subject of the sentence. When it is a direct object it is located immediately after the verb marked for tense:

On **ne** m'a **rien** pris   *Nothing was taken from me*
Je **ne** sais **rien** prévoir   *I am incapable of planning anything*

When it is the object of a preposition it is located in the normal position for prepositional phrases:

Cela **n'**a abouti à **rien**
That led to nothing

Je **n'**avais besoin de **rien**
I needed nothing

Je **n'**aurais abandonné le vélo pour **rien** au monde
I wouldn't have given up cycling for anything

When it is a subject, it appears in subject position:

Rien ne lui faisait mal
Nothing did him any harm

Rien ne différenciait ce jour des autres
Nothing distinguished that day from the others

Rien ne m'avait échappé
Nothing had escaped me

N.B.: *Je n'en sais rien* means 'I haven't a clue'.

Expressions such as 'nothing interesting' and 'nothing else' are rendered in French by *rien* + de + adjective:

Il n'y a là **rien d'important**   *It's nothing important*

When *rien* + *de* + adjective functions as a direct object with a verb in a compound tense, *rien* follows the verb marked for tense:

Il ne dit **rien d'intéressant**   *He doesn't say anything interesting*
Je n'ai **rien** trouvé **d'intéressant**   *I found nothing interesting*
Il ne m'a **rien** dit **de surprenant**   *He said nothing surprising to me*

However, when the *rien* + *de* + adjective functions as anything other than a direct object, it is not split in this way:

Je n'ai pensé à **rien d'intéressant** à faire   *I didn't think of anything interesting to do*
Rien d'autre n'est arrivé   *Nothing else happened*

N.B.: The adjective remains invariably masculine in these constructions.

When adverbs are located sentence-internally in sentences negated by *ne ... rien*, and where *rien* is the direct object, they usually appear immediately in front of *rien*:

Il n'y aura **probablement** rien pour moi à la maison
There would probably be nothing for me at home

rien can stand alone (without *ne*) with the meaning 'nothing':

Qu'est-ce que vous voyez? **Rien**   *What do you see? Nothing*
C'est mieux que **rien**   *It's better than nothing*
C'est un **rien**   *It's nothing*

In formal French, it can also be interpreted as 'anything' in questions or hypothetical sentences:

N'avez-vous **rien** vu?   *Didn't you see anything?*
Elle est partie avant que j'aie **rien** dit   *She left before I said anything*

16.13 *ne ... personne*

ne ... personne translates English 'no one', 'not anybody' (for omission of *ne*, see Section 16.4). Like *rien*, *personne* can function as a direct object, the object of a preposition, or the subject of the sentence. Unlike *rien*, when it is a direct object it appears in the normal position for direct objects:

Ne montrez votre mot de passe à **personne**
Do not let anyone see your password

Je n'ai vu **personne**
I saw no one

Ça, vous **ne** pourrez le faire croire à **personne**
As far as that goes, you won't be able to make anyone believe it

Ils **ne** l'ont fait avec **personne**
They didn't do it with anyone

Personne n'était dupe de cette photo trafiquée
Nobody was fooled by this fake photo

personne may take an adjective complement preceded by *de:*

Je n'ai vu personne **de** louche
I saw nobody suspicious

Personne **d'**étranger ne s'était présenté à la réception
Nobody foreign had come to reception

N.B.: The adjective is invariably masculine in these constructions.

personne can stand alone (without *ne*) with the meaning 'no one', 'nobody':

Qui a frappé?	**Personne**
Who knocked?	*Nobody*

In formal French, it can also be interpreted as 'anyone' in questions, hypothetical sentences, or comparisons:

As-tu rencontré **personne**?
Did you meet anyone?

Je le sais mieux que **personne**
I know it better than anyone

16.14 *ne ... ni... ni*

ne ... ni... ni translates English 'neither ... nor'. The *ni... ni* elements can range over subjects:

Ni la prof **ni** ses élèves **n'**étaient au courant
Neither the teacher nor her students knew about it

over direct objects:

Elle **n'**a apporté **ni** bloc-notes **ni** stylo
She brought neither note pad nor pen

over prepositional phrases:

Il **n'**avait posé de question **ni** à son père **ni** à sa mère
He had asked neither his mother nor his father a question

Elle **n'**a répondu **ni** d'un mot **ni** d'un signe
She replied neither verbally nor with a gesture

over participles and adjectives:

Je **n'**ai **ni** vu **ni** entendu la querelle
I neither saw nor heard the argument

Elle **n'**est **ni** heureuse **ni** malheureuse
She is neither happy nor unhappy

Where two verbs marked for tense are involved, the phrase *ne … ni ne…* is used:

Je **ne** comprends **ni n'**accepte un tel comportement
I neither understand nor accept such behaviour

Where, in English, a negation is followed by 'or', or 'nor', or 'and', *ni* is used in French:

Ils **ne** voulaient accepter **ni** chèque, **ni** carte, **ni** liquide, uniquement un virement bancaire
They wouldn't take a cheque, a credit card or cash, just a bank transfer

Il **ne** mangeait jamais le soir, **ni** sa femme
He never ate in the evenings, nor did his wife

Rien **ni** personne **n'**avait réussi à déchiffrer le code
Nothing and no one had yet managed to crack the code

ni is similarly used with the meaning 'or' or 'nor' after *sans*:

Le voyage aurait été impossible **sans** GPS **ni** boussole
The journey would have been impossible without a SatNav or a compass

Je fais ce qu'elle faisait mais **sans** son talent, **ni** sa chance
I do what she did but without her talent or her good luck

16.15 *sans* used with other negators

Negators like *aucun(e)*, *jamais*, *plus*, *rien*, *personne* take on the meanings 'any', 'ever', 'again', 'anything', and 'anyone' when used in conjunction with *sans*:

sans aucune hésitation	*without any hesitation*
sans jamais reculer	*without ever retreating*
sans plus se mettre en colère	*without getting angry again*
sans rien dire	*without saying anything*
sans déranger personne	*without disturbing anyone*

16.16 *ne* used alone

There are a number of contexts in which *ne* can be used alone. All of them are found in only the most formal of written styles. In less formal styles, the *ne* is simply absent:

In fixed expressions

à Dieu **ne** plaise! (can also be used humorously)	*God forbid!*
Il **n'**a eu garde de se montrer	*He carefully refrained from showing his face*

In clauses dependent on comparatives

Il se porte moins bien que je **(ne)** pensais
His health is less good than I thought

Il est tout autre qu'on **(ne)** croit
He is quite different from what one imagines

La vie est plus chère qu'elle **(ne)** l'était il y a un an
The cost of living is higher than it was a year ago

In clauses dependent on verbs which express fear such as *craindre, avoir peur que, redouter que, appréhender que*

Je crains qu'il **(ne)** vienne
I'm afraid that he will come

N.B.: When the verb of fearing is itself negated, *ne* is possible in the dependent clause only if the main clause is a question: *Je ne crains pas qu'il vienne* 'I'm not afraid that he'll come'; *Ne craignez-vous pas qu'il (ne) vienne?* 'Aren't you afraid that he will come?'

In clauses dependent on verbs which express some kind of prevention such as *empêcher que, éviter que, prendre garde que*

Mets ton ordi à l'ombre pour éviter qu'il **(ne)** surchauffe
Put your laptop in the shade to stop it overheating

After the conjunctions *à moins que, avant que,* **and** *sans que*

Sans qu'ils **(ne)** sachent
Without them knowing

In clauses dependent on some verbs expressing doubt or denial which are themselves negated or questioned, such as *douter que, ignorer que, nier que*

Je ne doute pas qu'il **(ne)** soit intelligent
I don't doubt that he's intelligent

Personne n'ignore qu'elle **(n')**ait été la cause de ses malheurs
Nobody is unaware that she has been the cause of her own misfortunes

Niera-t-on qu'il **(n')**ait commis une faute?
Will it be denied that he has made a mistake?

In clauses dependent on the expressions *il s'en faut que* **and** *peu s'en faut que*

Il s'en faut de beaucoup qu'il **(n')**ait réussi
He is far from having succeeded

FREE

INSTRUCTOR & STUDENT RESOURCES

For more resources to practice your French grammar, including practice activities/quizzes for students, further resource links, and an instructor guide, please visit https://routledgelearning.com/frenchgrammarandusage.

17 Conjunctions and other linking constructions

17.1 Introduction

All languages have devices for linking words, phrases, and clauses into more complex structures. This chapter deals with the linking function of conjunctions, past participles, present participles, and gerunds.

17.2 Coordinating conjunctions

TABLE 17.A ...

Conjunction	Translation	Comments
et	*and*	Where coordinating conjunctions link two clauses, the verb in the second clause is always in the indicative, e.g. *il y avait des virus,* **mais** *je ne* **pouvais** *pas les supprimer* 'There were viruses, but I wasn't able to get rid of them'.
et ... et	*both... and*	
mais	*but*	
ou	*or*	
ou ... ou soit ... soit	*either... or*	
puis	*then*	means '(first) X then Y'
car	*for (because)*	mainly used in formal French
or	*now (however)*	A logical connector mainly used in more formal French (see Section 17.2.1)

Coordinating conjunctions link words, phrases, or clauses into more complex structures:

Le concours est ouvert aux Français **et** aux étrangers
The competition is open to French citizens and to foreigners

J'inviterai **et** lui **et** sa sœur
I'll invite both him and his sister

Il y avait trois librairies, **mais** aucune n'était ouverte
There were three bookshops, but none of them was open

Dis-moi la vérité **ou** je confisque ton portable
Tell me the truth or I'll take your phone away

Il arrivera **soit** demain **soit** après-demain
He will arrive either tomorrow or the day after

J'ai ramassé mon sac, **puis** je suis descendu à l'étage du dessous
I picked up my bag, then went down to the floor below

DOI: 10.4324/9781003373926-17

Je ne comprenais pas sa question, **car** cela ne correspondait guère à sa personnalité
I did not understand his question, for it was hardly in keeping with his character

Coordinating conjunctions differ from subordinating conjunctions (see Section 17.3) in that they, and the word, phrase, or clause they introduce, normally cannot be placed at the front of the sentence, whereas subordinating conjunctions usually can. Compare *car* 'for' (a coordinating conjunction) with *parce que* 'because' (a subordinating conjunction close in meaning):

Il comparaîtra demain, **car** nul n'est au-dessus de la loi	NOT	***Car** nul n'est au-dessus de la loi, il comparaîtra demain
He will appear in court tomorrow, for nobody is above the law		**For nobody is above the law, he will appear in court tomorrow*

Il comparaîtra demain, **parce que** nul n'est au-dessus de la loi
He will appear in court tomorrow because nobody is above the law

Parce que nul n'est au-dessus de la loi, il comparaîtra demain
Because nobody is above the law, he will appear in court tomorrow

Coordinating conjunctions never introduce clauses in which the verb is in the subjunctive, whereas a number of subordinating conjunctions do (see Sections 17.3.8 and 17.5).

17.2.1 *or*

or 'now', 'however' is a conjunction which marks the next step in a narrative or a logical argument:

'*or*' used for contrasting ideas and for logical concatenation of ideas

Le but était de vacciner toute la population. **Or** certains s'opposaient au vaccin par principe.
The aim was to vaccinate the entire population. However some were opposed to vaccination on principle

Tous les humains sont mortels; **or**, le Roi est un humain; donc le Roi est mortel
All humans are mortal; (now,) the King is a human; therefore the King is mortal

'*or*' used in a sequential narrative:

Or, Cyril était déjà marié lorsqu'il a rencontré Aurélie
Now, Cyril was already married when he met Aurélie

'now' in English can function as a coordinating conjunction (as above), a subordinating conjunction of time, and a time adverb. The subordinating conjunction of time function is fulfilled in French by *maintenant que* (see Section 17.3.1). The time adverb function is translated in French by *maintenant* or *alors* if 'now' refers to an event in the past:

Cyril est **maintenant** marié
Cyril is now married

Cyril était **alors** marié
Cyril was now (= then) married

17.3 **Subordinating conjunctions**

Subordinating conjunctions introduce an item (usually a clause) which is dependent on another clause (for the use of subordinating conjunctions with infinitives; see Section 17.6):

Il comparaîtra demain, **parce que** nul n'est au-dessus de la loi
He will appear in court tomorrow because nobody is above the law

Je continue à dire 'chez nous', **bien que** l'appartement ne nous appartienne plus
I continue to say 'at our flat', although the flat no longer belongs to us

Comme il n'arrête pas de se plaindre, je l'évite le plus possible
As he does nothing but complain, I avoid him as much as possible

Some introduce clauses in which the verb is in the indicative (as *parce que* and *comme* above). Others introduce verbs in the subjunctive (like *bien que*).

17.3.1 **Subordinating conjunctions of time followed by the indicative**

TABLE 17.B ...

Conjunction	Translation	Comments
après que	*after*	*après que* may sometimes be heard followed by a verb in the subjunctive, by analogy with *avant que* (see Section 17.3.8)
aussitôt que, dès que, sitôt que, dès lors que	*as soon as*	
aussi longtemps que	*as long as*	Substitute another adverb for *longtemps* to create similar conjunctions: *aussi vite que, aussi peu que*
chaque fois que, toutes les fois que	*every time*	
depuis que	*since*	Understood as 'from the time when'
maintenant que	*now*	
pendant que	*while, as*	Understood as 'during the time when'
quand, lorsque	*when*	
tant que	*while, as*	Understood as 'the whole time while'
une fois que	*Once*	

Après que sa femme **est** morte, il a déménagé
After his wife died, he moved house

Sitôt que je **serai** rentré, je t'appellerai
As soon as I get home, I will call you

On jouera aussi longtemps que tu **veux**
We'll play as long as you wish

Toutes les fois que nous **passons** chez elle, elle est sortie
Every time we stop by her place, she's out

Depuis qu'il **est** chez nous, il semble de plus en plus épanoui
Since he has been at our house, he seems more and more fulfilled

Maintenant que je **suis** connecté, je peux t'appeler en visio
Now I am connected I can call you on a video call

On a eu le temps de prendre un café pendant que les autres **se préparaient**
We had time for a coffee while the others were getting ready

Elle était déjà malade quand je l'**ai** connue
She was already ill when I first knew her

Tant qu'on n'**aura** pas convaincu les climato-sceptiques, la planète sera en danger
For as long as we haven't convinced the climate-deniers, the planet will be in danger

Une fois qu'il **a eu** fait ses valises, il est descendu au bar commander un sandwich
Once he had finished packing his bags, he went down to the bar to order a sandwich

17.3.2 Future and conditional tenses in clauses introduced by *quand, lorsque, aussitôt que, dès que, sitôt que, dès lors que, tant que, and après que*

When subordinate clauses introduced by *quand, lorsque, aussitôt que, dès que, sitôt que, dès lors que, tant que*, or *après que* are linked to main clauses in which the verb is in a future or conditional tense, the verb in the *quand, lorsque*, etc. clause is also in the future or conditional. This is different from English where the verb in a 'when', 'as soon as', etc. clause is usually in the present or past:

Est-ce que tu m'**enverras** un SMS quand il **arrivera**?
*Will you text me when he **arrives**?*

Dès qu'elle **reviendra**, j'**allumerai** le feu
*As soon as she **comes** back, I will light the fire*

Si on partait à midi, il **ferait** encore jour quand on **arriverait**
*If we left at midday, it would still be daylight when we **arrived***

Where the event in the *quand, lorsque*, etc. clause would be translated by the perfect or pluperfect tense in English, French has the compound future or compound conditional:

Il **arrivera** quand je **serai parti**
*He will arrive when I **have left***

S'il ne prenait pas l'avion avant mardi, il **arriverait** après que je **serais parti**
*If he didn't catch the plane until Tuesday, he would arrive after I **had left***

Je **remplirai** le formulaire, aussitôt que je l'**aurai** reçu
*I will fill in the form as soon as I **have received it***

J'**aurais rempli** le formulaire aussitôt que je l'**aurais** reçu
*I would have filled in the form as soon as I **had received it***

More generally, when an event described in a *quand, lorsque*, etc. clause has not yet taken place, the verb is in a future or conditional tense:

Dès qu'il **aura** dit 'oui', faites-le signer
As soon as he says 'yes', get him to sign

17.3.3 **Double compound past and compound pluperfect tenses in clauses introduced by** *quand, lorsque, aussitôt que, dès que, sitôt que, dès lors que, tant que,* **and** *après que*

When clauses introduced by *quand, lorsque,* etc. describe an event which takes place prior to an event described by a past tense verb in the main clause, French can use the double compound past or the compound pluperfect in the *quand, lorsque,* etc. clause (although it is not obligatory to do so – see Section 10.5.3):

avoir eu + past participle
avoir été + past participle

Aussitôt que j'**ai eu fini** de visionner le débat, j'ai commencé à rédiger le rapport
As soon as I finished watching the debate I began to draft the report
(My watching the debate took place prior to my writing the report)

Quand elle **a été revenue**, il lui a présenté ses excuses
When she came back, he offered her his apologies

When the verb in the main clause is in the compound past tense, the verb in the *quand, lorsque,* etc. clause is in the double compound past tense (as in the above examples); when the verb in the main clause is in the pluperfect, the verb in the *quand, lorsque,* etc. clause is in the compound pluperfect:

Aussitôt que j'**avais eu fini** de visionner le débat, j'avais commencé à rédiger le rapport
As soon as I had finished watching the debate I began to draft the report

Alternatively, one can simply use the ordinary compound past and pluperfect tenses in the *quand, lorsque,* etc. clause: *Aussitôt que j'avais fini de visionner le débat, j'ai commencé …, Quand elle est revenue, il lui a présenté…*

N.B.: The double compound past can also be used in main clauses when adverbs expressing urgency or speed accompany a past event:

J'**ai eu vite fini** de visionner le débat
I quickly finished watching the debate

Il **a eu bientôt fait** de lui dire ce qu'il pensait d'elle
He had soon told her what he thought of her

The use of the double compound tense emphasizes the idea that the event is over and done with.

In formal styles of written French where the dominant tense is the simple past (see Section 10.5.2), a form of the verb called the 'past anterior' is used in the contexts described above. The past anterior consists of the simple past forms of *avoir* or *être* and the past participle:

Aussitôt que j'**eus fini** de visionner le débat, je commençai à rédiger le rapport
As soon as I had finished watching the debate I began to draft the report

Après qu'elle **fut sortie**, il emballa son cadeau d'anniversaire
After she went out, he wrapped her birthday present

J'**eus vite fini** de visionner le débat
I had quickly finished watching the debate

17.3.4 **Tenses with *depuis que, voilà/voici... que, il y a ... que***

When *depuis que* 'since', 'for' introduces a clause describing an event whose consequences are ongoing at the time it is being reported, the tense of the verb in that clause differs systematically from English as follows:

English perfect: French present
English pluperfect: French imperfect

Depuis que nous **vivons** ensemble, je la vois travailler tard le soir
*Ever since we **have been living** together, I have seen her working late into the evening*
(We are still living together at the time I am reporting that she works late into the evening)

Depuis que nous **vivions** ensemble, je la voyais travailler tard le soir
*Ever since we **had been living** together, I saw her working late into the evening*
(We were still living together at the time I was reporting that she worked late into the evening)

But when *depuis que* introduces a clause describing an event which has been completed by the time it is reported, without ongoing consequences, the tenses are the same as in English:

Depuis qu'il **a fini** ses études, je le vois beaucoup plus
*Since he **has finished** his studies, I see a lot more of him*
(His studies are over at the time I am reporting seeing a lot more of him)

Depuis qu'il **avait fini** ses études, je le voyais beaucoup plus
*Since he **had finished** his studies, I saw a lot more of him*
(His studies were over at the time I was reporting that I was seeing a lot more of him)

voilà/voici... que and *il y a ... que* which also mean 'since', 'for' when used with time expressions – *voilà plusieurs années que ...* 'it's been several years since ...', *il y a/avait un mois que ...* 'it has/had been a month since ...' – behave just like *depuis que*. When the clause introduced by these expressions describes an event whose consequences are ongoing at the time it is being reported, either the present tense or the imperfect tense is used in French where English uses, respectively, the perfect and the pluperfect:

Voilà/voici plusieurs années qu'elle **travaille** tard le soir
*For several years now she **has been working** late into the evening*

Il y avait un mois que je la **connaissais**
*I **had known** her for a month*

But when the clause describes an event which has been completed at the time it is reported, the compound past tense or the pluperfect is used:

Voilà/voici deux ans qu'elle **a arrêté** de fumer
It's been two years since she stopped smoking

Il y avait un mois qu'il **avait disparu**
It was a month since he had disappeared

For tenses with *depuis* as a preposition, see Section 10.4.4.

17.3.5 **Non-time subordinating conjunctions normally followed by the indicative**

TABLE 17.C ...

Conjunction	Translation	Comments
ainsi, de même que	*just as*	
(au fur et) à mesure que, à proportion que	*as*	with the meaning: 'all the while'
attendu que, vu que, étant donné que, dès lors que	*seeing that, given that, since*	*dès lors que* also has a time meaning: *Dès lors qu'elle a su la vérité, elle a cessé de lui faire confiance* 'As soon as she knew the truth, she lost confidence in him'
(pour) autant que	*as far as*	Is sometimes followed by the subjunctive to express uncertainty
plutôt que	*rather than, more than*	*ne* can be optionally inserted in front of the subordinate verb

Je regardais la lune **de même qu'**elle devait la regarder/**ainsi** qu'elle devait la regarder
I looked at the moon just as she must have been looking at it

A mesure qu'il parlait, il s'animait
As he spoke he became more animated

Vu qu'il est déjà midi, je propose qu'on reprenne après le déjeuner
Seeing that it is already midday, I propose that we restart after lunch

Je délègue **autant que** je peux
I delegate as much as I can

Pour autant que je **sache**, ils sont partis lundi
As far as I know, they left on Monday
(My knowledge is uncertain, and so a subjunctive is used)

Il sommeille **plutôt qu'**il ne dort
He is dozing rather than sleeping

TABLE 17.C *(Continued)*

Conjunction	Translation	Comments
comme	*as, like*	also has a time meaning: *Il arrivait comme midi sonnait* 'He arrived as midday was chiming'
comme si	*as if*	
puisque	*since*	Not to be confused with *depuis que* – see Section 17.4.1
excepté que, sinon que, outre que, sauf que	*except that*	
parce que	*because*	

Comme le navigateur me bombarde de publicités, j'évite le plus possible de l'utiliser
As the browser swamps me with adverts, I avoid using it as much as possible

On a eu un été **comme** on n'en a jamais vu
We had a summer like we have never seen before

Elle a baissé la tête **comme si** elle avait honte
She lowered her head as if she was ashamed of something

Elle parle arabe **puisque** sa mère est marocaine
She speaks Arabic since her mother is Moroccan

Elle n'avait rien à dire, **sinon qu'**elle était prête à voter pour l'amendement
She had nothing to say except that she was ready to vote in favour of the amendment

Il est resté ici **parce qu'**il n'avait pas de quoi payer le billet
He stayed here because he couldn't afford the ticket

TABLE 17.C *(Continued)*

Conjunction	Translation	Comments
selon que, suivant que	*depending on whether*	
si, même si, quand même	*if, even if*	for tenses with *si*, see Section 17.3.6
tandis que, alors que	*while, whereas*	*alors que* also has a time meaning: *Alors qu'il se promenait dans le parc, il a rencontré un vieil ami* 'While he was walking in the park, he met an old friend'

Je prends le bus ou j'y vais en vélo, **selon qu'**il pleut ou qu'il fait beau
I take the bus or go on my bike, depending on whether it is raining or is fine

Si on le branche là-dessus, on peut tenir jusqu'à demain matin
If you get him going on that subject, we'll be here until tomorrow morning

Même s'il était arrivé, je n'aurais pas pu lui parler
Even if he had arrived, I couldn't have spoken to him

Quand même il m'aurait dit le contraire, ça n'aurait rien changé
Even if he had said the exact opposite, it wouldn't have changed anything

Il est blond, **alors que** nous deux, nous sommes bruns
He is blond, while the two of us are dark-haired

17.3.6 *si* and the tense to use in *si* clauses (see also Section 10.8)

There are two *si*'s in French which function like conjunctions. One introduces indirect questions and can always be translated by 'whether':

Etait-elle venue?   Je ne savais pas **si** elle était venue
Had she come?   *I didn't know if/whether she had come*

Indirect questions are introduced by verbs such as *comprendre, demander, se demander, dire, expliquer, savoir* – see Section 14.7. In this usage the verb in the *si* clause can appear in all the tenses including future and conditional tenses:

Je ne sais pas **si** elle **viendra**
I don't know if/whether she will come

On se demande **si** elle l'**achèterait**
We wonder if/whether she would buy it

The other *si* introduces hypothetical clauses:

Je n'aurais pas envoyé de SMS **si** j'avais pu la joindre à son portable
I wouldn't have sent a text if I had been able to reach her on her mobile

Here *si* cannot be translated by 'whether' and describes what might have happened but didn't.

The verb in hypothetical *si* clauses can never appear in future or conditional tenses. Typical sequences of tenses are illustrated in Table 17.D:

TABLE 17.D Sequence of tenses in *si* clauses

Main clause		*si* clause	
Present, future, conditional		**Present, imperfect**	
Je le fais	*I do it*	si je peux	*if I can*
Je le ferai	*I'll do it*	si je peux	*if I am able*
Je le ferais	*I would do it*	si je pouvais	*if I was able*
Imperfect, compound conditional		**Imperfect, pluperfect**	
Je le faisais	*I used to do it*	si je pouvais	*if I was able*
Je l'aurais fait	*I would have done it*	si je pouvais	*if I was able*
		si j'avais pu	*if I had been able*

17.3.7 **Alternatives to (*même*) *si* in written French for constructing hypothetical clauses**

One alternative to hypothetical *si* clauses in very formal French (literature, speeches, etc.) is a verb in the conditional tense or in the past subjunctive tense inverted with the subject:

Devrait-il y passer la nuit, il mettrait /il allait mettre la touche finale à son dernier chapître
Dût-il y passer la nuit, il mettrait/il allait mettre la touche finale à son dernier chapître

Both mean: *Even if he had to be up all night, he would finish writing the last chapter (of his book).*

Another is to use *quand* (*même*) followed by a verb in the conditional:

Quand (même) il me le **jurerait** sur l'honneur, je ne le croirais pas
(Even) if he were to swear to me on his honour that it was so, I wouldn't believe him

or a conditional clause followed by *que*:

Il me le **jurerait sur l'honneur** que je ne le croirais pas
(Same meaning as the sentence above)

This construction can also be found in informal contexts:

C'est trop tard, il me **donnerait** son accord demain que je l'enverrais bouler
It's too late, (even) if he gave me his agreement tomorrow, I'd send him packing

17.3.8 Subordinating conjunctions normally followed by the subjunctive

TABLE 17.E Time conjunctions

Conjunction	Translation	Comments
avant que	before	ne can be optionally inserted in front of the subordinate verb
en attendant que	waiting for	
jusqu'à ce que	until	

Avant que personne (n')ait pu lui demander d'explication, il a dit 'C'est moi le coupable'
Before anyone could ask him to explain himself, he said 'I am the guilty one'

En attendant que le beau temps revienne, on passait les soirées à lire au coin du feu
Waiting for the fine weather to return, we spent the evenings reading by the fireside

Attendez pour prendre la photo **jusqu'à ce que** le soleil soit plus bas dans le ciel
Wait to take the photo until the sun is lower in the sky

N.B.: 'not until', where it means 'not before', is translated by *pas avant que*:

Je ne signerai **pas avant que** vous (ne) m'ayiez donné des explications convaincantes
I won't sign until you've given me some believable explanations

TABLE 17.F Non-time conjunctions

Conjunction	Translation	Comments
bien que quoique encore que malgré que	although	encore que is found only in formal French malgré que is found in informal spoken French but is very much frowned upon. (The correct options are either bien que, or malgré + noun.)
afin que pour que	in order that, so that	

Je continue à dire 'chez moi', **bien que** l'appartement ne nous appartienne plus
I continue to say 'at home' although the flat no longer belongs to us

Il promenait la poussette le long du lac, **pour que** le bébé prenne l'air
He was pushing the buggy along beside the lake for the baby to get some fresh air

Qu'est-ce qu'elle t'a dit **pour que** tu sois si malheureux?
What did she say to you to make you so unhappy?

TABLE 17.F (*Continued*)

Conjunction	Translation	Comments
de façon que de manière que de sorte que si bien que	*so that*	Followed by the indicative these describe something which has happened Followed by the subjunctive they express a wish that something might happen
tel que	*such as*	*tel* in *tel que* agrees with the noun it refers to

Elle riait **de telle façon qu'**on **comprenait** parfaitement son embarras
She laughed in such a way that her embarrassment was obvious
(Her embarrassment was obvious, so the verb introduced by *de telle façon que* is in the indicative)

Il y aura des subventions **de façon que** les propriétaires **puissent** installer des panneaux photo-voltaïques
There will be government help so that house-owners can put in solar panels

Telle que vous l'**avez** décrite, la statue sera trop grande pour la galerie du rez-de-chaussée
Such as you have described it, the statue will be too big for the ground floor gallery

S'il avait créé un scandale **tel que** les médias s'en soient mêlés, ton témoignage aurait été primordial
If he had created such a scandal that the media had got involved, your testimony would have been invaluable

TABLE 17.F (*Continued*)

Conjunction	Translation	Comments
(soit/ou) que … (soit/ou) que	*whether… or*	
à moins que	*unless*	*ne* can be optionally inserted in front of the subordinate verb – it is most likely in formal French
pour peu que; si peu que	*however little*	
pourvu que; à condition que	*providing that*	Conditional and future are possible in informal spoken French

Qu'il soit vacciné **ou qu'**il ait récemment eu le Covid, pour l'instant il est protégé
Whether he is vaccinated or whether he recently had Covid, at the moment he is protected

A moins qu'elle ne vende la maison de son vivant, en principe c'est nous qui héritons
Unless she sells the house in her lifetime, in principle we will inherit

Pour peu qu'on habite dans une zone où la réception est bonne, on peut télécharger des films
You just have to live in an area where the reception is good and you can download films

Pourvu que tout le monde soit d'accord, je commence tout de suite
Providing that everyone agrees, I'll start straight away

TABLE 17.F *(Continued)*

Conjunction	Translation	Comments
à supposer que, supposé que, en supposant que, en admettant que	*supposing that*	
non que	*not that*	
sans que	*without*	*ne* can be optionally inserted in front of the subordinate verb in formal French
de peur que, de crainte que	*for fear that*	*ne* can be optionally inserted in front of the subordinate verb in formal French

A supposer que l'ADN vous désigne comme le père, qu'est-ce que vous allez faire?
Supposing that the DNA shows you are the father, what will you do?

Je leur ai demandé de reprendre la scène; **non qu'**ils l'aient mal jouée, mais il y a eu un bruit extérieur au mauvais moment
I asked them to redo the scene; it's not that they messed it up, but there was a noise outside at the wrong moment

Elle aurait bien pu quitter le village **sans que** je m'en aperçoive
She could easily have left the village without me noticing

Elle s'enfermait le soir **de crainte qu'**on (ne) vienne l'attaquer
She locked herself in at night for fear that someone would come and attack her

17.4 **Conjunctions sometimes confused by English speakers**

Some conjunctions have several functions which only partially overlap between English and French.

17.4.1 *'since'*

(a) meaning 'from the time when' = *depuis que*

Depuis qu'elle n'habite plus la même rue que moi, on ne se voit presque plus
Since she no longer lives in the same street as me, we hardly see each other any more

(b) meaning 'given that' = puisque, comme, vu que, étant donné que

Puisque j'ai du réseau ici, je vais pouvoir lui envoyer notre localisation
Since I can get the internet here, I'll be able to send her our location

Comme mes frères l'énervent, elle les évite le plus possible
Since my brothers annoy her, she avoids them as much as possible

17.4.2 *'while'*

(a) meaning 'during the time that' = *pendant que*

J'ai travaillé sur le scénario tous les jours **pendant que** le bébé dormait
I worked on the script every day while the baby was sleeping

(b) meaning 'for as long as' = *tant que*

Tant qu'elle faisait tout ce qu'il voulait, son frère était satisfait
While she did everything he wanted, her brother was satisfied

(c) meaning 'whereas', 'while' = *alors que, tandis que*

Il est blond **alors que** nous deux, nous sommes bruns
He is blond whereas/while the two of us are brown-haired

Elle s'occupe du bébé **tandis que**, moi, je fais tout le travail
She looks after the baby while I do all the work

There are two possible types of comparison with *tandis que*: One is simultaneity-based and the other contrast-based.

Elle change le bébé **tandis que** je range les jouets
but
Elle ne pense qu'au bébé **tandis que**, moi, je m'inquiète pour mon travail

N.B.: *alors que* can sometimes mean 'while' in the sense of 'during the time that': *Alors qu'il se promenait dans le parc, il a rencontré un vieil ami* 'While he was walking in the park, he met an old friend'.

17.4.3 'as'

(a) meaning 'all the while' = *à mesure que*

A mesure que l'intelligence artificielle se développe, on accumule les arguments qui lui sont hostiles
As AI develops, more and more hostile arguments are being made against it

(b) meaning 'at the same time as' = *comme*

Il arrivait **comme** midi sonnait
He arrived as midday was striking

(c) meaning 'in the manner of' = *comme*

Les footballeurs juniors s'embrassaient **comme** ils l'avaient vu faire à la télévision
The young footballers hugged each other as they had seen it done on the television

17.4.4 'when'

(a) meaning 'at the time when' = *quand, lorsque*

Quand sa femme est revenue, il lui a promis de faire une thérapie
When his wife came back, he promised her he'd see a therapist

(b) meaning 'whereas' = *alors que*

Je me demandais pourquoi il venait chez nous, **alors qu'**il habitait de l'autre côté de la frontière
I wondered why he was coming our way when he lived on the other side of the border

17.5 **Repeated subordinating conjunctions**

When clauses introduced by subordinating conjunctions are themselves linked together, *que* replaces the first conjunction (and is obligatory in French, while the repeated conjunction in English is often omitted):

Quand je suis pressé et **que** je sors la voiture du parking, j'ai du mal à éviter le pilier
When I'm in a hurry and (when) I get the car out of the car park, I have trouble avoiding the pillar

The form of the verb in the clause introduced by *que* is in most cases the same as that of the verb in the first clause (indicative or subjunctive):

Même quand j'étais gosse, et **que** je vivais à la campagne, je ne jouais pas dehors
Even when I was a child, and (when) I lived in the country, I didn't play outside

Bien qu'il plaisante et **qu'**il feigne l'indifférence, en réalité il est très touché
Although he is joking and pretending it doesn't matter, in fact he is really moved

However, when *si* is repeated by *que*, the verb in the clause introduced by *que* is in the subjunctive:

S'il fait beau demain, et **que** nous **ayons** le temps, nous pourrions aller à la plage
If it is fine tomorrow, and (if) we have time, we could go to the beach

(See also Section 11.1.10.)

17.6 **Subordinating conjunctions used with infinitive clauses**

TABLE 17.G Subordinating conjunctions without *que*

Followed by *de*	
afin de (finir le premier)	*in order to (finish first)*
avant de (monter à l'étage)	*before (going upstairs)*
de crainte de/de peur de (déranger les voisins)	*for fear of (disturbing the neighbours)*
à condition de (faire des bénéfices)	*subject to (making a profit)*
à moins d'(avoir une augmentation)	*unless (I/you/we etc. get a pay rise)*
Followed by *à*	
(aller) jusqu'à (déclarer le contraire)	*(to go) as far as (stating the opposite)*
de manière à/de façon à/de sorte à (assurer la victoire)	*so as to (be certain of victory)*
Not followed by another preposition	
pour (finir le premier)	*in order to (finish first)*
sans (faire du bruit)	*without (making a noise)*

A number of the conjunctions which introduce clauses with finite verbs can also be used without *que* to link infinitive clauses to a main clause as shown in Table 17.G.

Je m'étais arrêté **afin de/pour** redémarrer le GPS
I had stopped to reboot the satnav

Avant de payer j'ai passé l'addition au peigne fin
Before paying I scrutinized the bill

Il ne peut pas rencontrer un copain **sans** lui parler de ses problèmes sentimentaux
He can't say hallo to a friend without talking about his emotional problems

N.B.: *plutôt que* 'rather than', 'more than' exceptionally keeps the *que*, but also adds *de* when it introduces an infinitive: *Plutôt que de chercher partout, on devrait commencer par les tiroirs du bureau* 'Rather than searching everywhere, we should start with the desk drawers'.

Where the subject of a main clause is the same as the subject of a subordinate clause linked to it, it is more natural in French to use an infinitive than a finite clause:

Il a sorti le paquet de café **avant de** brancher la bouilloire
He took out his packet of coffee before he plugged in the kettle
(*il* is the subject both of *a sorti* and *brancher*)

rather than: *Il a sorti le paquet de café avant qu'il (n')ait branché la bouilloire.*

Je n'irai pas **à moins d'**être certain d'avoir une place assise
I won't go unless I'm certain of getting a seat
(*je* is the subject both of *irai* and *être certain*)

rather than: *Je n'irai pas à moins que je (ne) sois certain d'avoir une place assise.*

A number of other conjunctions which are not capable of introducing finite clauses in modern French can introduce infinitive clauses:

faute d'(avoir assez d'argent)
through lack of (having enough money)

à force de (s'entraîner)
by dint of (training)

au lieu de (dormir)
instead of (sleeping)

loin de (chercher à vous tromper)
far from (seeking to cheat you)

près de (renoncer)
close to (giving up)

quant à (proposer de vous accompagner)
as for (proposing to go with you)

17.7 *après avoir/être* + past participle linking an infinitive clause to a main clause

A frequently used construction translating English 'having V-ed', 'after V-ing' is *après* + the infinitive form of *avoir* or *être* and a past participle:

Après avoir mangé sa glace à la fraise, elle s'est essuyé la bouche sur sa manche
Having eaten/after eating her strawberry ice-cream, she wiped her mouth on her sleeve

Après avoir expliqué à son père comment sauvegarder toutes ses photos, elle a promis de lui montrer plus tard comment les recadrer
After having explained to her father how to save all his photos, she promised she'd show him later how to crop them

Après être allée chez le kiné, elle a constaté qu'elle avait moins mal
Having gone/after going to see the physio, she found that it didn't hurt so much

17.8 Past participle phrases used as linkers

The past participles of verbs which are conjugated with *être* in compound tenses (see Section 8.2.2) can be used without *après* to link subordinate clauses to main clauses, where English usually uses 'having V-ed':

Arrivé à la gare, il a acheté un sandwich
Having arrived at the station he bought a sandwich

Couché de bonne heure, j'ai lu
Having gone to bed early, I read

Partie pour de bon, elle n'a plus l'intention de revenir
Having left for good, she no longer intends to return

The past participles of verbs referring to bodily posture are used where English uses 'V-ing': *assis* 'sitting', *appuyé* 'leaning', *agenouillé* 'kneeling', *couché* 'lying', etc.:

Je suis resté debout toute la séance, **appuyé** contre le mur
I remained standing throughout the showing, leaning against the wall

Assis sur un banc, on a parlé longtemps
Sitting there on a bench, we talked for a long time

Assises sur un banc, on a parlé longtemps toutes les deux
Sitting there on a bench, we talked for a long time

17.9 Present participles and gerunds

This section concerns French verb forms ending in *-ant*. They are formed from the stem of the first-person plural (*nous*) of the present tense by deleting *-ons* and replacing it with *-ant*: *donnons/donnant*, *finissons/finissant*, and *dormons/dormant*. They can also have a compound form composed of the *-ant* form of the auxiliary and the past participle of the verb: *ayant donné, ayant fini, ayant dormi*, and *étant devenu*.

-ant forms have three main roles: they can function as **adjectives**, in which case they agree with the noun to which they refer, they can function as **present participles**, in which case they do not agree with any noun, and they can function as **gerunds** with the added form *en* (*en donnant, en finissant*, and *en dormant*).

17.9.1 *ant* forms as adjectives

Like all adjectives, *-ant* forms can occur close to a noun or be linked to it by a verb such as *être*, *devenir*, and *paraître* (see Section 4.1.1). In both cases they agree with the noun.

une histoire passionnante	a fascinating story

une histoire passionnante — a fascinating story
Cette histoire est passionnante — This story is fascinating
une publicité séduisante — a seductive advert
Cette publicité est séduisante — This advert is seductive
une femme plaisante — an agreeable woman
Cette femme est plaisante — This woman is agreeable
une chaise roulante/un fauteuil roulant — a wheelchair
une ferme avoisinante — a neighbouring farm
une injustice criante — a flagrant injustice

17.9.2 *-ant* forms as present participles

-ant forms can be used to form subordinate clauses. When they do so, they are called present participles. Used in this way, they are invariable (i.e. they do not agree with any noun):

Les circonstances **aidant**, ils ont terminé le projet à la date prévue
Given the favourable conditions, they finished the project on the agreed date

Voyant arriver sa sœur, elle s'est éloignée
Seeing her sister arrive, she left

Sachant qu'ils allaient perdre leur étoile au Michelin, ils ont préféré s'expatrier
Knowing they were going to lose their Michelin star, they chose to move abroad

Il était heureux d'y aller, **reconnaissant** ce qu'il devait à son ancien collège
He was pleased to go there recognizing what he owed to his old school

Attirant un public international, l'exposition a atteint un million de visiteurs
Attracting an international audience, the exhibition reached a million visitors

Cette grange, **avoisinant** les bâtiments principaux, pourrait être transformée en maison d'habitation
This barn, adjoining the main buildings, could be converted into living accommodation

Les histoires de Roald Dahl, **passionnant** les enfants de toutes les nations, ont été traduites en plusieurs langues
Roald Dahl's stories, fascinating the children of every nation, have been translated into several languages

Roulant à soixante-dix à l'heure, le conducteur n'a pas pu éviter un piéton
Driving at seventy kilometres an hour, the driver was unable to avoid a pedestrian

In some cases, where the present participle follows a noun, it may be difficult to decide whether it is an adjective or a present participle. In the following examples, the *-ant* forms are all present participles, and hence invariable:

un blog **ridiculisant** le gouvernement
a blog poking fun at the government

une voiture **roulant** lentement avait été aperçue la veille
a car driving slowly had been noticed the previous day

des manifestants **hurlant** des slogans passaient sous ses fenêtres
demonstrators shouting slogans passed below his windows

la belle au bois **dormant**
Sleeping Beauty

Je les ai surpris dans la clairière, **dormant** profondément
I came across them in the clearing, fast asleep

You can usually tell if an *-ant* form is an adjective (and hence must agree with a noun) if you can replace it by an ordinary adjective and still have a grammatical phrase. Compare:

un blog passionnant	*a fascinating blog*
un blog ennuyeux	*a boring blog (OK – adjective)*
une chaise roulante	*a wheelchair*
une chaise haute	*a highchair (OK – adjective)*
un blog ridiculisant le gouvernement	**un blog ennuyeux le gouvernement (not OK – present participle)*
une voiture roulant lentement	**une voiture haute lentement (not OK – present participle)*
des manifestants hurlant des slogans	**des manifestants délicats des slogans (not OK – present participle)*

The decision depends on whether the action described by the *-ant* form is seen mainly as a state (=adjective) or as an action (=verb).

N.B.: Where English has a simple *-ing* form, French may require a compound present participle:

Etant partis à l'aube, nous sommes arrivés avant la nuit
Having left at dawn, we arrived before nightfall

Ayant ramassé ses vêtements en hâte, il s'enfuit par la fenêtre
Having picked up his clothes in a hurry, he fled through the window

Ayant repéré deux gendarmes plus loin dans la rue, elle leur a demandé de l'aide
Spotting two police officers further up the street, she asked them for help

17.9.3 **Set expressions with invariable present participles**

argent comptant	*in cash*
Ils veulent être payés en argent comptant	*They want to be paid in cash*
ne pas avoir un sou vaillant	*not to have a red cent*
J'admets que je n'ai pas un sou vaillant	*I admit I am totally broke*
ce disant	*in so saying*
Ce disant il a fait un geste maladroit et a renversé un verre	*In so saying he made a clumsy gesture and knocked over a glass*
chemin faisant	*on the way*
Chemin faisant on a chanté des chansons	*We sang songs on the way*
donnant donnant	*a fair exchange, swop*
Nous sommes d'accord si c'est donnant donnant	*We agree as long as it's a fair exchange*
strictement parlant	*strictly speaking*
Strictement parlant je ne devrais pas vous le répéter	*Strictly speaking I should not say this to you*

tambour battant
La droite a mené la campagne tambour battant d'un bout à l'autre

in an energetic manner
The right led a thoroughly energetic campaign
from the beginning to the end

17.9.4 *-ant* forms used as gerunds with *en*

Where present participles are preceded by *en* they are known as 'gerunds'. By using *en*, a speaker or a writer may be emphasizing the fact that the event described in the main clause and the event described in the gerundive clause take place simultaneously. This is often translated into English by 'while' or 'as':

En attendant Mathias, je me suis installé au café d'en face
While waiting for Mathias, I sat down in the café opposite

Je l'avais vue pendant la semaine, **en rentrant** de l'école
I had seen her during the week, as I came back from school

J'ai transféré la photo à ma soeur **en faisant** une capture d'écran
I sent the photo to my sister by capturing a screenshot

Comment est-ce que tu arrives à tant bavarder **en conduisant**?
How do you manage to talk so much while you are driving?

Alternatively, the use of *en* with a gerund may emphasize a link of cause and effect between the gerundive clause and the main clause; this is translated by 'in' or 'by' in English:

En déclarant que vous étiez sur place vous vous êtes incriminé
In admitting that you were there you have incriminated yourself

En gérant une boutique comme si c'était un supermarché, on s'expose à l'échec
In managing a small shop as if it were a supermarket, you are running the risk of failure

Fanny a indiqué qu'elle ne voulait plus sortir avec lui **en refusant** son invitation
Fanny showed that she no longer wanted to go out with him by refusing his invitation

En augmentant le prix de vente vous risquez de voir chuter le nombre d'acheteurs
By increasing the retail price you run the risk of reducing the number of buyers

On a décoré la pièce **en mettant** des fleurs partout
We fixed up the room by putting flowers everywhere

When a gerund is preceded by *tout en*, it suggests that the event described in the gerundive clause is going on all the while the event described in the main clause takes place:

Tout en me parlant, il nettoyait les vitres
All the while she was speaking, he was cleaning the windows

Tout en discutant de la pluie et du beau temps, il regardait discrètement dans le rétroviseur
Whilst chatting about this and that, he was keeping a discreet eye on the rear-view mirror

J'ai supprimé l'application du bureau **tout en sachant** que je ne pouvais pas la désinstaller du disque dur
I deleted the app from the desktop while knowing full well that I could not remove it from the hard disk

When present participles are used without *en*, they can refer to any of the participants in the main clause: subject, direct object, and object of a preposition:

Je l'avais vue pendant la semaine, **rentrant** de l'école
*I had seen her during the week as **I** (or **she**) came back from school*

When *en* is present, however, the gerund can only refer to the subject of the main clause:

Je l'avais vue pendant la semaine, **en rentrant** de l'école
*I had seen her during the week as **I** (NOT *she) came back from school*

N.B.: Gerunds may also be formed from compound present participles. These are frequently translated into English by a simple '-ing' form:

En ayant refusé de poursuivre des études supérieures, elle s'est privée de bien des possibilités
By refusing to undertake higher education, she cut herself off from a number of possibilities

En ayant contesté nos méthodes, il s'est exclu de notre groupe
By questioning our methods, he has excluded himself from our group

FREE

**INSTRUCTOR
& STUDENT
RESOURCES**

For more resources to practice your French grammar, including practice activities/quizzes for students, further resource links, and an instructor guide, please visit https://routledgelearning.com/frenchgrammarandusage.

Appendix 1
Orthographic Conventions

Capital letters, lower-case letters and representing speech in written French

We note here briefly some of the differences between written English and written French in the conventions relating to the use of capital and lower-case letters, and in representing direct speech.

Small letters for days of the week, months and seasons

English uses capital letters, where French uses lower-case letters:

Il arrive lundi (mardi, mercredi, …)
He arrives on Monday (Tuesday, Wednesday, …)

Nous partirons en janvier (en février, en mars, …)
We shall leave in January (February, March, …)

English can optionally use capital or lower-case letters with seasons, while French always uses lower-case letters:

Elle travaille dix-huit heures par jour en été (au printemps, …)
She works eighteen hours a day in Summer (in Spring, …)

Small letters for streets, roads, avenues, etc.

English uses capitals, where French uses lower-case letters:

11, place de la République
11 Russell Square

Je l'ai vue rue de Rivoli
I saw her in Regent Street

Small letters for titles

English uses capitals, where French uses lower-case letters:

Le professeur Bouvier
Professor Bouvier

Le docteur Picot
Doctor Picot

Small letters for adjectives indicating origin, but capital letters for nouns

English always uses capital letters to introduce adjectives and nouns describing the origin or religious affiliation of a person or entity. French uses lower-case letters to introduce adjectives describing origin, lower-case letters to introduce adjectives and nouns describing religious affiliation, but capital letters to introduce nouns describing origin:

un touriste français (adj)	un Français de ma connaissance (noun)
a French tourist	*a Frenchman I know*
un livre américain (adj)	un Américain célèbre (noun)
an American book	*a famous American*
un prêtre catholique (adj)	un catholique célèbre (noun)
a Catholic priest	*a famous Catholic*

Small letters for languages

English always uses capital letters to introduce adjectives and nouns describing languages, whereFrench always uses lower-case letters:

la langue française (adj)
the French language

Elle parle bien le français (noun)
She speaks French well

Capitals and lower-case letters in citing book titles

Although there are different conventions for the use of capitals and lower-case letters in citing book titles, one common convention in French is to capitalize every word up to and including the first noun:

L'Etranger
L'Art de vivre
Le Grand Meaulnes
Les Petits Enfants du siècle

In English, common conventions are to capitalize the first letter of every word, or to capitalize the first word and the 'content' words (and not the function words) or to treat the title like an ordinary sentence:

The Decline And Fall Of The Roman Empire
The Decline and Fall of the Roman Empire
The decline and fall of the Roman empire

Representing direct speech

Direct speech can be opened and closed by *guillemets*. Unlike English, where speech marks enclose only the speech itself, in French guillemets enclose dialogues, and are only closed when the whole dialogue is at an end:

«Et voilà, dit le père, filant sur la route. En voilà encore une de tirée.
-Eh, oui», répliqua la mère.
(From Christiane Rochefort, *Les Petits Enfants du siècle*)

'Well,' said our father, belting along the road. 'That's another one [holiday] over with.'
'Yes,' our mother replied.

Alternatively, speech can be introduced by dashes ('*tirets*') in both languages:

    - Etes-vous prêt?
    - Pas encore.

    - *Are you ready?*
    - *Not yet.*

Verbs reporting who said what are always inverted with the subject in French:

    «C'est plus fort en goût», **précise Vincent**
    «C'est plus fort en goût», **précise-t-il**
    'It has a stronger taste,' Vincent adds/he adds

    «Le moulin, clef de l'économie», **annonce un panneau**
    'Mills are the key to economic success,' a sign announces

    «Ce n'est pas vrai», **répondirent les autres tranquillement**
    'It's not true,' the others replied calmly

Spaces in French where none exist in English

In French, texts published in France you will find spaces before and after the symbols below:

; : ! ? % and mathematical symbols

French style quotation marks, such as "un mot" and << un mot >> also have a space before and after the written words.

Example: Je lui ai demandé: " Tu me crois ? "

Opening and closing brackets also have a space.

Appendix 2 Nouvelle Orthographe

Summary of *Nouvelle Orthographe* proposals

Introduction

In 1990, the *Conseil Supérieur de la Langue Française* produced a report on the orders of the Prime Minister which recommended a certain number of changes to the spelling of the French language. Little by little these have been making their way into usage in metropolitan France and in the rest of the Francophone world. All school and reference books, i.e. dictionaries, grammar books, and other language 'authorities', including spellcheckers, will now cite these forms as correct usage, alongside or in preference to the 'Traditional' ones. The *Académie française* has made it clear, however, that '*Aucune des deux graphies ne peut être tenue pour fautive*' and therefore both the 'Proposed' forms and the more 'Traditional' forms will coexist for a number of years. The new forms are slowly making progress in newspapers, magazines, and broadcast forms, and some books have been written using only the Proposed new forms. It will take time for them to be widely accepted (see the References).

Numbers

Complex numbers can all have a hyphen regardless of whether they are more or less than a hundred (see Section 6.1.2):

Traditional	Proposed
Vingt-deux	Vingt-deux
Cent deux	Cent-deux
Mille cent dix-huit	Mille-cent-dix-huit
Cinq mille deux cent dix-neuf	Cinq-mille-deux-cent-dix-neuf

N.B.: Under the new system there is a difference between *quarante et un tiers* = forty plus one third and *quarante-et-un tiers* = forty-one thirds (41 thirds).

Nouns

It is proposed that many words traditionally written with a hyphen can now be written as one word (see Sections 1.2 and 1.4):

Words where the first element is contr(e)-, entr(e)-, extra-, and ultra-.

Traditional	Proposed
Un contre-appel	Un contreappel
Extra-terrestre	Extraterrestre
Un porte-monnaie	Un portemonnaie

Scientific words whose first part ends in ends in -o, e.g. auto-, hydro-, and socio-.

Traditional	Proposed
Une auto-école	Une autoécole
Socio-culturel(le)	Socioculturel(le)

Onomatopoeic words:

Traditional	Proposed
Un boui-boui	Un bouiboui
Un bla-bla	Un blabla

Foreign words:

Traditional	Proposed
Un a priori	Un apriori
Un week-end	Un weekend

Compound nouns (see Section 1.4)

Made from a verb plus a noun

Made from a verb and 'tout'

Made with 'basse-, mille-, or haute-'

Others:

Traditional	Proposed
Un tire-bouchon	Un tirebouchon
Un passe-partout	Un passepartout
Un fourre-tout	Un fourretout
Une basse-cour	Une bassecour
Un mille-patte	Un millepatte
Un croque-monsieur	Un croquemonsieur

Plurals

Once these words become single words all the issues of how to make them plural (see Section 1.3.9) disappear: they are all made plural by adding an '-s'.

Borrowings into French from other languages such as English or Latin can be made plural also by adding an '-s', regardless of whether the form borrowed represents a singular or a plural in the original language:

Traditional	Proposed
Un minimum; des minima	Un minimum; des minimums
Un gentleman; des gentlemen	Un gentleman; des gentlemans

Where compound nouns made up of a verb and a noun, or a preposition and a noun still retain a hyphen, the singular form can be written only with a singular noun which becomes plural by adding an '-s'.

Traditional	Proposed
Un essuie-mains	Un essuie-main; des essuie-mains
Un cure-dents	Un cure-dent; des cure-dents
Un garde-meuble	Un garde-meuble; des garde-meubles
Un après-midi	Un après midi; des après-midis

Grave accent

The future and the conditional forms of verbs like *céder* can have a grave accent (see Sections 7.4 and 7.6.9).

Traditional	Proposed
Je céderai	je cèderai
Je célébrerai	je célèbrerai

In verbs ending in *-eler* and *-eter*, the syllable before the unstressed syllable can have a grave accent and the consonants will not be doubled. Nouns which are derived from these verbs will also have a grave accent.

Il nivellera	il nivèlera
Il renouvellera	il renouvèlera

Nouns

Nivellement	nivèlement
Morcellement	morcèlement
Renvouvellement	renouvèlement

N.B.: This does not apply to *appeler* or *jeter* or to verbs derived from them.

In a number of words where the pronunciation has changed over the years, a grave accent can replace an acute accent.

Traditional	Proposed
Le céleri	Le cèleri
Un événement	Un évènement
Réglementaire	Règlementaire
Une sécheresse	Une sècheresse

Circumflex

The circumflex found on 'i' and 'u' can be removed:

Traditional	Proposed
Apparaître	Apparaitre
Maître	Maitre
Brûlure	Brulure

Except in the following cases:

a) In the simple past conjugation: *nous vîmes*
b) In the imperfect subjunctive: *qu'il fût, qu'il reçût*
c) In the pluperfect subjunctive: *qu'il eût pris*
d) In those words where the presence of the circumflex indicates a difference in meaning, e.g. *dû, mûr, sûr* vs *du, mur, sur* as without the circumflex the words would be confused. Similarly, the circumflex must be kept on the forms of the verb *croître* so as not to confuse them with the verb *croire*.

N.B.: This does not apply to proper nouns, e.g. Benoît.

Past participle

The past participle of *laisser* followed by an infinitive can be invariable (see Sections 9.3.3, 9.4, 9.3.6, and 9.3.9).

Traditional	Proposed
Elle s'est laissée séduire	Elle s'est laissé séduire
Les cadeaux que nous lui avons laissés offrir	Les cadeaux que nous lui avons
	laissé offrir

Dieresis

The dieresis can be placed on the vowel which has to be pronounced.

Traditional	Proposed
Aiguë	Aigüe
Arguer	Argüer
Une gageure	Une gageüre

Anomalies

A number of specific words which are considered anomalous can be modified. Thus, *-illier* can become *-iller*, and two *'ll'*s can become one.

Traditional	Proposed
Quincaillier	Quincailler
Serpillière	Serpillère

(but not for trees and vegetables: e.g. Groseillier)

Vantail	Ventail
Nénuphar	Nénufar
Douceâtre	Douçâtre
Oignon	Ognon
Shampooing	Shampoing

References

Grand vadémécum de l'orthographe moderne recommandée Chantal Contant Publisher De Champlain S.F livres@dechamplain.ca

Journal Officiel de la République française 1990 No 1006.12.1990

Nouvelleorthographe.info.echelle.pdf

Renouvo (Réseau pour la nouvelle orthographe du français): renouvo.org

(This site contains information about the proposals, e.g. a list of the words concerned and also the extent to which they have been implemented in different countries.)

Further reading

Grammar

Le Bon Usage Maurice Grévisse/André Goose, 16th edition, 2016, Paris/Louvain: De Boeck supérieur.

This is the source book for most scholars writing about French grammar. It was first published in 1936 and has since been updated regularly. It contains many references from authors illustrating the grammatical points made. It explains the points of grammar in great detail and with considerable subtlety and it is nowhere judgemental about usage.

Le Grévisse de l'Enseignant: Grammaire de Référence, 2ème edition, Jean Christophe Pellat and Stéphanie Fonvielle, 2022, Paris: Magnard.

This is a different take on the information in Grévisse presented in a way which is useful for teachers and students alike. It is based on modern French linguistics and offers a detailed description of French grammar from that perspective. There is also an accompanying set of exercises in a companion volume.

The Foundations of French Syntax Michael Allan Jones, 1996, Cambridge: Cambridge University Press.

This detailed analysis of the principal areas of French grammar combines the insights of modern (generative) linguistics with those of more traditional grammarians. As such, it offers theoretical analyses which suggest that there are relationships between areas of syntax which traditional grammars see as separate but modern linguistic theory can show to be linked to one another.

The Structure of Modern French Maj-Britt Mosegaard Hansen, 2016, Oxford: Oxford University Press.

This work takes a more structural approach to French grammar and provides a detailed account of French grammar with many cross-references to English.

Le Bescherelle: La Conjugaison Collectif, 2019, Paris: Hatier.

This is the standard French reference book for everyone who needs to check that they have the right form of conjugation of French verbs.

Originally published in 1843, this "bible" of French verb conjugation is now accompanied by other Bescherelle works on many aspects of the French language, both on paper and online, via apps and a podcast. To keep track of these developments, consult https://www.bescherelle.com/qui-sommes-nous.

French language

Le Grand Livre de la Langue française M. Yaguello (ed.), 2003, Paris: Seuil.

This edited volume contains an account of many aspects of the French language from several French language scholars: Claire Blanche Benveniste, Jean-Paul Colin, Françoise Gadet, Émile Genouvrier, Chritiane Marchello-Nizia, Jean Pruvost, Bernard Tranel and Marina Yaguello.

The French Language Today: A Linguistic Introduction A. Battye, A-M Hintze, P.A. Rowlett: 2nd edition, 2000, London: Routledge.

This book, written by British scholars, covers the external history of the French language, the standardisation of French and its distribution in the world today, the sound system of French, French word structure, the sentence structure of French and varieties of French.

Le français dans tous les sens Henriette Walter, 1998, Paris: Fixot.

This well-regarded volume is an entertaining history of many aspects of French vocabulary.

La Grammaire française dans tous ses états M. Yaguello, 2021, Paris: Points.

This is a very entertaining account of aspects of the French language by a very experienced French linguist drawing on native intuitions and observations.

Le français va très bien merci Les linguistes attérrés, 2023, Paris: Tracts Gallimard.

This is a reaction from a set of linguists who reject notions that French is in some way in decline. They see changes in the language as part of a natural evolution and would like others to see it in the same way. However, their position is the subject of debate with more traditional linguists.

Always of interest is the website of *L'Académie française* – www.académie-française.fr – which provides a wealth of information about the French language, especially the sections *Questions de langue* and *Dire et Ne Pas Dire.* The Academy published the report *La Féminisation des Noms de métiers et de fonctions* in 2019 as a significant contribution to the debate around the new terminology for the roles of women.

Nouvelle Orthographe

Les Rectifications de l'Orthographe 1990 Conseil Supérieure de la Langue Française, Journal officiel de la République française, Edition de Documents Administratifs, No 100 Directions des Journaux Officiels.

This is the original official document which recommended the changes to modern orthography.

Les rectifications orthographiques de 1990 Cahiers de l'Observatoire des pratiques linguistiques No1, Délégation générale à la langue française et aux langues de France, Liselotte Biedermann-Pasques and Fabrice Jejcic, 2006, Orléans: Presses Universitaires.

This is an update on where the proposed changes had got to in 2006.

www.renouvo.org (Réseau pour la nouvelle orthographe du français).

This is the website which seeks to keep track of what is happening with these changes, how widespread they are and who is changing what and where. It includes a list of the words implicated in the changes as well as a bibliography and links to sites in other Francophone areas. It also tells you how to get hold of the *Vadémécum de l'orthographe recommandée.*

Inclusive writing

In this area we are dealing with material which is under discussion at the highest levels of French administration and politics: it was discussed in the *Sénat* and the *Assemblée nationale* in the autumn of 2023. Most documents are online: some of these may change or disappear at any time and many new ones will appear. Below are some of the references available at the time of writing

Canadian sources are more accepting and / or more developed in their approach than many metropolitan French documents, some of which entirely reject 'écriture inclusive'.

Visibles/Lisibles Guide d'écriture inclusive ÉTS École de Technologie Supérieure, 2022, Université du Québec.

This guide is made available to students of the ETS in Quebec and sets out the policy which the school wishes to observe in the documents which circulate within the institution.

Inclusivement vôtres! Guide de rédaction inclusive: lnrs.ca>l'inrs>guide-de-rédaction inclusive.

This originates with the Institut national de la recherche scientifique in Quebec and sets out to do a similar job to the ETS document above.

Règles de grammaire neutre et inclusive Divergenres, 2021, Québec.

This short Canadian document is written to set out what a 'neutral and inclusive' grammar would look like from an LBGTQ+ perspective and it therefore includes many proposed forms and uses which are not widely accepted.

Guide pratique pour une communication publique sans stéréotype de sexe Haut Conseil à l'égalité entre les femmes et les hommes, le 29 septembre 2022.
Guide Égalité-femmes-hommes- Mon entreprise s'engage www.égalité-femmes-hommes.gouv.fr, le 15 avril 2022.
Usage d'un langage neutre du point de vue du genre www.europarl.europa.eu European Parliament 2018.

Manuel d'écriture inclusive Raphaël Haddal, 2016, and 2019, Mots Clés.net.
This document originates in France and puts forward the arguments for fairly radical changes with illustrations of how inclusive writing can be used.

L'écriture inclusive non-sexiste - Par où commencer? Michel Lessard, 7 février 2022, Espaces Idées: Canada.
Grammaire non-sexiste de la langue française Michel Lessard et Suzanne Zaccour 2017 M Editeur: Canada.
Grammaire pour un français inclusif Alexendra Dupuy, Michel Lessard, Suzanne Zaccour, Somme toute, 2nd edition, 2023.
Guide de Grammaire Neutre et Inclusive, Divergenres, divergenres.org.
Relire et Corriger www.relire et corriger.net (6 outils d'écriture inclusive sans point médian).

This is a website run by Sophie Maziane who presents herself as a professional in the world of communication and the purpose of the website is to provide professional advice to those who wish to write well and inclusively.

Déclaration de l'Académie française sur l'écriture dite "inclusive" 26 octobre 2017.

The first sentence of this document makes clear the point of view adopted: "Prenant acte de la diffusion d'une <écriture inclusive> qui prétend s'imposer comme norme, l'académie française élève à l'unanimité une solennelle mise en garde."

Pourquoi je suis contre l'écriture inclusive Sabina Matrullo Contrepoints le 31 octobre 2021.

Index

References are made to sections.

For Product Safety Concerns and Information please contact our EU
representative GPSR@taylorandfrancis.com Taylor & Francis Verlag GmbH,
Kaufingerstraße 24, 80331 München, Germany

Printed and bound by CPI Group (UK) Ltd, Croydon, CR0 4YY
07/05/2025
01862901-0001